GUIDE TO

U.S. FOREIGN POLICY

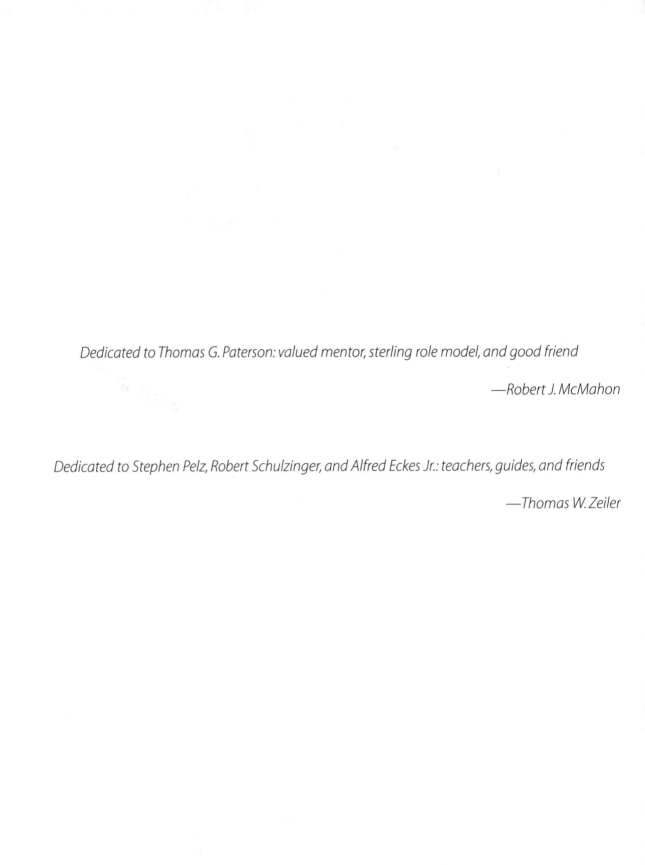

Dedicated to Thomas G. Paterson: valued mentor, sterling role model, and good friend

—Robert J. McMahon

Dedicated to Stephen Pelz, Robert Schulzinger, and Alfred Eckes Jr.: teachers, guides, and friends

—Thomas W. Zeiler

CQ PRESS GUIDE TO

U.S. Foreign Policy

A DIPLOMATIC HISTORY

VOLUME II

EDITED BY

ROBERT J. McMAHON
OHIO STATE UNIVERSITY

THOMAS W. ZEILER
UNIVERSITY OF COLORADO

$SAGE reference | CQPRESS

Los Angeles | London | New Delhi
Singapore | Washington DC

Los Angeles | London | New Delhi
Singapore | Washington DC

FOR INFORMATION:

CQ Press

An Imprint of SAGE Publications, Inc.

2455 Teller Road

Thousand Oaks, California 91320

E-mail: order@sagepub.com

SAGE Publications Ltd.

1 Oliver's Yard

55 City Road

London EC1Y 1SP

United Kingdom

SAGE Publications India Pvt. Ltd.

B 1/I 1 Mohan Cooperative Industrial Area

Mathura Road, New Delhi 110 044

India

SAGE Publications Asia-Pacific Pte. Ltd.

3 Church Street

#10-04 Samsung Hub

Singapore 049483

Acquisitions Editor: Doug Goldenberg-Hart

Production Editor: Tracy Buyan

Copy Editor: DWJ BOOKS LLC

Typesetter: C&M Digitals (P) Ltd.

Proofreaders: Lawrence Baker,
                        Stefanie Storholt

Indexer: Scott Smiley

Cover Designer: Malcolm McGaughy,
                              McGaughy Design

Marketing Manager: Kristi Ward

Printed in the United States of America.

Library of Congress Cataloging-in-Publication Data

Guide to U.S. foreign policy : a diplomatic history / editors, Robert J. McMahon, Thomas W. Zeiler.

p. cm.
Includes bibliographical references and index.

ISBN 978-1-60871-910-5 (cloth)

1. United States—Foreign relations. I. McMahon, Robert J., 1949— II. Zeiler, Thomas W.

E183.7.G83 2012
327.73—dc23   2012003068

12 13 14 15 16 10 9 8 7 6 5 4 3 2 1

★ SUMMARY TABLE OF CONTENTS

★ TABLE OF CONTENTS

Volume I

Volume I

Volume II

Volume II

★ LIST OF ILLUSTRATIONS

Volume I

Volume I

PART IV

DIPLOMACY STRETCHED TO ITS LIMITS: THE EARLY COLD WAR ERA

Volume II

PART V

THE END OF THE COLD WAR

Volume II

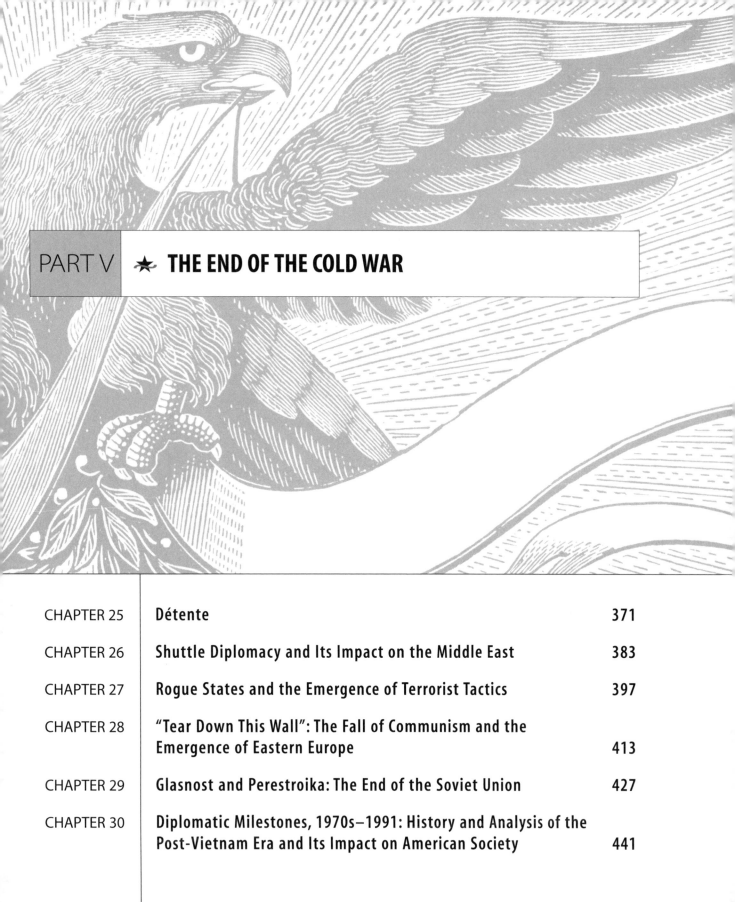

PART V ★ **THE END OF THE COLD WAR**

chapter 25

Détente

by Jussi M. Hanhimäki

"**W**E HAVE ENTERED an era of negotiations," announced President Richard M. Nixon (1969–1974) in his inaugural address in January 1969. He was correct. By contrast with the tension, sometimes quite acute, that characterized Soviet-American relations since soon after the end of World War II (1939–1945), during the 1970s, the United States and the Soviet Union engaged in arms control agreements and summitry that represented a marked shift toward a new level of civility, if not amicability, between the two superpowers.

AN ERA OF NEGOTIATIONS

As the United States simultaneously broke from its earlier non-recognition policy vis-à-vis the People's Republic of China (PRC), while the Soviets and the Chinese exchanged blows along their border in 1969, the view of the Cold War as a bipolar confrontation had become, it seemed, a thing of the past. In Europe, the question of a divided Germany moved toward stabilization with the advent of inter-German relations, a four-power agreement on the status of Berlin, and a series of bilateral treaties between the Federal Republic of Germany on the one hand, and the USSR, Poland, and other Soviet bloc countries on the other. In the early 1970s, moreover, the talks that eventually led to the Conference on Security and Cooperation in Europe (CSCE), culminating in the signing of the Helsinki Final Act in August 1975, finally got under way. A new era in East-West relations appeared to be emerging, not least due to changes in the American approach to the Soviet Union. Some even talked about the Cold War as history. Détente, a French word that means "an easing of tension," had taken its place.

By the late 1970s, however, Soviet-American détente was all but dead. Already, in the mid-1970s, the policies of reducing military tension through negotiations and agreements came under increasing pressure in international affairs and among the superpowers themselves. Although the Jimmy Carter (1977–1981) administration negotiated a Strategic Arms Limitation Treaty (SALT II), the Soviet invasion of Afghanistan in late 1979 caused Carter to stop the ratification process then under way in Washington. In fact, already earlier in the year, Carter had signaled a "hardened" approach by approving the deployment of new missiles systems in Europe (Pershing and cruise missiles) as a response to the Soviet deployment of its new medium-range missiles (SS-20) two years earlier. The Iranian Revolution of 1979 and the subsequent hostage crisis that overshadowed the last year of Carter's presidency served to increase the demands inside the United States for a more robust American foreign policy. The election in 1980 of Ronald Reagan (1981–1989), who openly called for a more belligerent American foreign policy, signaled the final end of the era of negotiations that Nixon had announced a decade earlier. In short, within a few years, the optimistic climate of the early part of the decade had given way to what some scholars see as a second Cold War in the early 1980s.

What explains the rise and fall of détente? Did it represent a radical break with the past (a move, perhaps, from idealism to realism), or was it simply an attempt to prolong an unnatural bipolarity within the international system? What were its main achievements and shortcomings? What caused its demise? Did it leave a lasting legacy? There are no easy answers to these questions. Ultimately, détente transformed the international system in unexpected ways without bringing about an end to the Cold War.

ROOTS OF DÉTENTE: CRISES, CHALLENGES, AND THE QUEST FOR STABILITY

The building of the Berlin Wall in 1961 and the Cuban Missile Crisis of 1962 represented a heightening of Cold War

KEY CONCEPTS

Détente. Much like "the Cold War," *détente* is a term that defies easy definition or periodization. There was no official declaration of détente, and no clear-cut end. In general terms, however, one can define détente as an era in which subsequent American administrations attempted to redefine their relationship with the Soviet Union in order to increase predictability and reduce the potential of direct military confrontation. Its origins lay in the 1960s, but détente's heyday, if measured by specific policy achievements, was the early 1970s, when the Nixon and Ford administrations concluded various agreements with the Soviet Union and commenced an era of superpower summitry.

Sometimes called *peaceful coexistence* (a term the Soviets tended to favor), the era of détente stretches from the early 1960s to the late 1970s, incorporating a transformation in the interstate relationship between the two superpowers, the end to the Peoples Republic of China's virtual isolation from international affairs, and the transformation of East-West relations in Europe.

Détente ultimately fell out of favor in the late 1970s due to a combination of domestic and international pressures. In the United States, critics, including Ronald Reagan and Jimmy Carter, argued that détente was both immoral as well as a policy born out of weakness. Externally, détente evolved against the backdrop of violent conflicts in the developing world that gave zest to the ongoing confrontation between the United States and the Soviet Union, between East and West, between capitalism and socialism. The Soviet invasion of Afghanistan in December 1979 is usually seen as the final trigger toward renewed Soviet-American confrontation that signaled the end of a period of limited cooperation.

SALT II. Negotiated from 1977 to 1979, between the United States and the Soviet Union, SALT II was the first arms control agreement that was aimed at cutting back, rather than merely limiting the growth of, strategic nuclear weapons possessed by the United States and the USSR. Signed in Vienna on June 18, 1979, SALT II limited each side's strategic forces to 2,250 of all categories of delivery vehicles. Although the treaty was never ratified by the U.S. Senate, because of the Soviet invasion of Afghanistan in December 1979, both sides honored the terms of the agreement until 1986, when the Reagan administration accused the Soviets of violating SALT II and formally withdrew from the pact.

dangers. At the same time, those two events, which produced no outright military engagement between the United States and the Soviet Union, introduced some elements of stability into international relations.

In particular, the twin crises in Europe and the Caribbean brought home two salient facts. First, neither the Soviets nor the Americans were willing to risk bloodshed to change the status quo of a divided Germany and a divided Berlin. Second, leaders in Moscow and Washington recognized the need for improved communications between the two capitals to avoid the possibility of an accidental nuclear war; hence, in 1963, a "hot line" was installed, creating a direct telephone connection between the White House and the Kremlin. Perhaps paradoxically, the heightened tensions of the early 1960s drove the United States and the Soviet Union gradually toward détente.

The World of MAD

Indications of this pending "normalization" of the Soviet-American relationship were particularly evident in the field of nuclear armaments. In August 1963, together with Great Britain, the United States and the Soviet Union signed the Partial Nuclear Test Ban Treaty (NTBT), which barred nuclear weapons tests in the atmosphere, in outer space, and underwater. Although the treaty had serious shortcomings—for example, underground tests were still allowed, and neither China nor France signed it—the 1963 agreement represented a watershed in the long road toward further efforts at regulating the nuclear arms race. Five years later, the Nuclear Non-Proliferation Treaty (NPT) incorporated a far broader agenda of non-proliferation, disarmament, and the peaceful use of nuclear energy. Unlike the 1963 treaty, the 1968 NPT was endorsed by the PRC and France, which, in the meantime, had both successfully tested their nuclear weapons.

However, the treaties of the 1960s did not end the nuclear arms race. In fact, the 1960s witnessed both proliferation as well as escalation in numbers and development of additional capabilities. The French, who had conducted their first test in 1960, developed their independent nuclear weapons capability (the so-called force de frappe). The PRC successfully tested a nuclear weapon in 1964 and moved to build their arsenal. Both countries argued that an independent nuclear capability added to their security as a means of deterrence, as a way of dissuading countries that already possessed nuclear weapons from attacking them. In truth, acquiring nuclear weapons may have been more important for reasons of international prestige as well as military strategy, because, ultimately, the French and Chinese, as well as the British, nuclear forces remained miniscule in comparison to those possessed by the two superpowers.

If measured by numbers of nuclear weapons or the advances in technology, the United States enjoyed a significant edge in nuclear arms throughout the 1960s. For example, in 1960, the Americans had a stockpile of roughly eighteen thousand nuclear warheads, compared to the Soviets' twenty-five hundred (*i.e.,* an advantage of roughly 8:1). By 1968, after a massive Soviet buildup, the equivalent figures were approximately thirty thousand to eleven thousand (a 3:1 numerical advantage). The United States also stayed ahead technologically by developing, for example, the Multiple Independently-Targeted Re-Entry Vehicle (MIRV) ahead of the Soviets. Moscow responded by pushing ahead with the development of an anti-ballistic missile system (ABM) that was to neutralize a potential American nuclear strike. In 1967, Americans followed suit. Indeed, the arms race, despite the treaties signed, continued virtually unabated in the 1960s.

However, the proliferation of American and Soviet nuclear stockpiles had produced a new constellation of strategic perceptions. In simple terms, it was impossible for either the Soviets or the Americans to destroy the other side's nuclear arsenal with a first strike. That a retaliation, or a second strike, would cause immense damage was a certainty; enjoying a numerical edge thus lost its strategic significance. Washington and Moscow therefore lived in a strategic environment known as Mutually Assured Destruction (and appropriately abbreviated MAD): a nuclear confrontation, no matter what the cause or which side initiated it, would result in an apocalyptic chain reaction, with large parts of the United States and the Soviet Union destroyed. Indeed, many were beginning to share the conviction of George Kennan, expressed as early as 1958, "that the weapon of mass destruction is a sterile and hopeless weapon which may for a time serve . . . as an uncertain sort of shield against utter cataclysm, but which cannot in any way serve the purposes of a constructive and hopeful foreign policy."[1] While no key policymakers, either in the United States or the Soviet Union, advocated outright nuclear disarmament, there was a growing sense of futility about the continuous buildup and development of weapons systems that no sane person would contemplate using. Indeed, as nuclear weapons systems continued to command a large proportion of national defense budgets with little practical benefit, the rational choice was to seek ways of limiting a further escalation. In this regard, the world of MAD pushed the Americans and the Soviets toward the negotiating table to find ways of avoiding a nuclear holocaust. By 1968, a tentative agreement had been reached for the commencement of the negotiations that, in 1969–1972, would lead to the first Strategic Arms Limitations Treaty (SALT I).

Trouble with Vietnam

Many other factors contributed to the desire for improved East-West relations in the 1960s. From the American perspective, the debacle in Vietnam (1945–1975), by the late 1960s, had proven costly in terms of lives lost and the expenditures incurred. The full deployment of U.S. ground troops had brought a half million American soldiers to South Vietnam by 1968, while a sustained bombing campaign had wreaked havoc throughout the region. The Johnson administration (1963–1969), however, had little to show for all its efforts. The January 1968 Tet Offensive indicated that the enemy's resistance was far from broken. The war did serious damage to U.S. prestige around the globe, prompting widespread criticism among allied nations. At home, Vietnam not only produced a widespread antiwar movement that questioned the basic assumptions of the country's policy in Vietnam, but also a rethinking of the validity of America's Cold War policies. Indeed, in 1968, the United States witnessed widespread political unrest that contributed to Lyndon Johnson's decision to bow out of the presidential race. The assassination of the civil rights leader Dr. Martin Luther King, Jr., and Robert Kennedy, the popular antiwar Democratic presidential candidate, contributed to an image of a divided country, unsure of its future direction at home and abroad.

Difficulties with Allies

To these developments one must add the growth of dissenting voices within the key Cold War alliances. Within the North Atlantic Treaty Organization (NATO), French President Charles de Gaulle (in office 1959–1969) advocated a more independent European policy (led by France) and, in 1966, withdrew France from the alliance's military structure. He was a vocal critic of America's role in Vietnam. Perhaps most worryingly for U.S. policymakers, de Gaulle also made independent initiatives toward the Soviet Union, visiting Moscow in 1966 and talking about a "Europe from the Atlantic to the Urals," a Europe that included the Soviet Union but not the United States. Whereas de Gaulle would resign in 1969 with his hopes of a more independent Europe largely unfulfilled, the 1960s also saw the emergence of a new West German foreign policy. Disillusioned by the apparent failure of the non-compromising policies toward the Soviet Union and East Germany to bring the prospect of a united Germany any closer to reality, the West German Social Democrats offered an alternative route with their *Ostpolitik*. First as foreign minister and, as of 1969, as the chancellor, Willy Brandt (in office 1969–1974) would launch a series of initiatives aimed at opening bridges to the Soviet bloc.

Throughout the 1960s, the United States—in part willingly, in part by necessity—gradually aligned its policies with those of the more détente-minded Western Europeans. In part as a response to de Gaulle's search for a more independent "third way," NATO adopted, in 1967, the Harmel Report, a policy document that emphasized the need to achieve détente with the Warsaw Pact. NATO was, therefore, no longer just a security organization committed to defending Western Europe against a potential military attack from the East, but also a political organization seeking to reduce the threat of such an attack through negotiations with the would-be aggressors. The Johnson administration also launched a series of bridge-building initiatives toward the Soviet bloc in the 1960s, trying to open up new avenues for trade and other exchanges. When it came down to Germany's *Ostpolitik*, though, the Americans found it increasingly difficult to balance their interest in "normalizing" the existing division with the West Germans' continued interest in searching for ways to move toward unification. This dilemma, much like the Gaullist challenge, was in large part ameliorated by events in the Soviet bloc that, in the fall of 1968, served as a reminder of the rationale behind Europe's East-West division.

Dissent in the Soviet Bloc

In the Soviet bloc, dissatisfaction over Moscow's dominance had become evident already in the early 1960s, when the Sino-Soviet split gradually emerged into public view. To a lesser degree than in Western Europe, the Soviet bloc experienced its own centrifugal tendencies in the 1960s that underlined the different nature of the Warsaw Pact as opposed to NATO. No one was allowed to contemplate exiting the Soviet-led military alliance; the Hungarians had experienced the practical consequences of such an attempt in 1956. Yet repression ultimately underlined the fragility of the alliance and served as a practical example of the fact that the American "empire" in Western Europe was one built upon a multilateral invitation by the founding members of NATO; the Soviet empire was based upon a unilateral imposition of Moscow's hegemony.

In the 1960s, some Eastern European leaders did find room for independence. As early as 1960, Enver Hoxha (in power 1941–1985), the Stalinist dictator of Albania, openly criticized the Soviet Union. As a result, his country was subjected to Soviet economic pressure but turned to China for economic assistance instead. Although Albania remained nominally a member of the Warsaw Pact until 1968, its "defection" was symbolic of the admittedly minor cracks in the Soviet hold on Eastern Europe. Potentially more disconcerting than Albania's move to the Chinese camp was Romania's independent course. Romanian leaders George Gheorghiu-Dej (in power 1948–1954, 1955–1965) and, after 1965, Nicolae Ceausescu (in power 1965–1989) were ruthless authoritarians who combined repression at home with an independent foreign policy. The latter, at least partly geared toward increasing their domestic popularity, resulted in Romania's consistent resistance to any kind of economic integration in the Soviet bloc. In 1967, Ceausescu ventured toward risky territory by recognizing the Federal Republic of Germany, and thus breaking Soviet bloc unity on this issue (the USSR had, though, recognized the FRG earlier). Yet while refusing to participate in the 1968 Warsaw Pact invasion of Czechoslovakia, Romania remained a member of the alliance. It was no wonder that Ceausescu often was described as the eastern version of de Gaulle: someone willing to issue a challenge to the superpower in the name of national pride, but unwilling to risk a complete breakdown in relations.

Not even the August 1968 Warsaw Pact crackdown on Czechoslovakia could change the momentum toward détente which had been built over the preceding years. Of course, the ruthless intervention that destroyed the internal Czech efforts to build "socialism with a human face," the Prague Spring, was a brutal reminder about the limits of internal reform within the Soviet zone. The public justification, the Brezhnev Doctrine, made it clear that any threat to the socialist system was not to be tolerated. As Anatoly Dobrynin, at the time the Soviet ambassador (served 1962–1986) to Washington, puts it in his memoirs, the Prague invasion was "a true reflection of the sentiments of those who ran the Soviet Union" at the time; that is, "[a] determination never to permit a socialist country to slip back into the orbit of the West."[2]

Yet the crackdown on Czechoslovakia, together with the armed clashes along the Sino-Soviet border in March 1969, provided evidence of the growing tensions among the Communist countries. If the United States was suffering from a crisis of international legitimacy due to its misguided intervention in Vietnam, the Soviet Union was no longer the unchallenged standard-bearer of international socialism it had been in the past. In particular, the Soviet leadership suffered from a crisis of legitimacy that could, some thought, be redressed if the Soviet Union's status as the world's other superpower was more formally recognized by the West.

The roots of détente thus lay in a complex web of developments that were as much a result of the follies of military intervention, the impractical, if not self-defeating, nature of the nuclear arms race, and pressures from allies. The pressure from American domestic political actors to rethink and reshape foreign policy, if only to end the war in

Vietnam, was immense. Indeed, the overall sense in the United States was that the certainties of the early Cold War and America's unquestioned leadership position in the free world were in jeopardy. While the Johnson administration had attempted to open a dialogue with the Soviet Union and find a way out of Vietnam, it had been singularly unsuccessful. A clear shift in policy was imperative.

THE ARCHITECTS OF DÉTENTE

The "Realpolitik" approach, diplomacy based on power and practical considerations, advocated by the new Nixon administration seemed to offer a more viable (and less costly) alternative for safeguarding American interests. At its basis lay the notion that the adversaries of the United States, most specifically the Soviet Union and China, acted more out of national interest than ideological convictions. Given the military clashes between the two Communist powers, the United States appeared to have a particularly tempting opportunity to play the Chinese and Soviets off each other through a careful application of rewards and pressures. Triangular diplomacy, as the policy was dubbed, essentially meant that Washington aimed at having better relations with Moscow and Beijing than the latter two had with each other. Among other benefits, the Nixon administration hoped to use the Soviet Union and the PRC, the two major external supporters of North Vietnam, to help bring about an "acceptable" end to the Vietnam War. In simplified terms, U.S. policymakers assumed that the Soviets would be willing to exert pressure on Hanoi in return for better relations with the Americans; the Chinese could, according to this equation, be induced to do the same if they were offered full diplomatic recognition by the United States.

Nixon and Kissinger's Structure of Peace

In broad terms, Richard M. Nixon offered to build a new "structure of peace." In speeches and articles during, before, and after the November presidential 1968 elections, Nixon outlined a relatively straightforward, if rather vague, new grand design for American foreign policy. He summarized it in his inaugural address on January 20, 1969, by emphasizing the new administration's interest in talking to anyone—the Soviets, the Chinese, the Vietnamese apparently included—who wished to do so. As Nixon put it: "Where peace is unknown, make it welcome; where peace is fragile, make it strong; where peace is temporary, make it permanent... After a period of confrontation, we are entering an era of negotiation. Let all nations know that during this administration our lines of communication will be open.... We cannot expect to make everyone our friend, but we can try to make no one our enemy."[3]

Crucially, Nixon and his national security adviser, Henry Kissinger (served 1969–1975), who would emerge as a virtual foreign policy czar by the end of the first Nixon administration, considered the world as a whole, as a structure in which different pieces were interrelated. In 1969, Kissinger publicly ruminated how "the crises which form the headlines of the day are symptoms of deep-seated structural problems ... The current international environment is in turmoil because its essential elements are all in flux simultaneously."[4]

The trouble, as both Nixon and Kissinger recognized, was that the real world rarely fit a conceptual model. A structure of peace was a wonderful rhetorical device and a commendable goal. Yet like all grand designs before and after, it was, almost if by some natural law, hostage to fortune and contingency. The world was, after all, always in turmoil. Friends and adversaries would act differently than expected; domestic constraints would prove difficult to contain and control. During his years in power, even as he achieved many of the goals of 1969, Nixon would experience the unexpected on numerous occasions, both on the foreign policy and domestic front. Yet he and Kissinger would remain relatively consistent on one specific theme: without abandoning its Cold War goal of containing the Soviet Union, the United States needed to adopt new foreign policy methods. If the Nixon administration was to sustain America's global power and influence, it had to do this without the overt use of military force. Thus, if only for political purposes, Nixon billed himself as the antithesis of his predecessor. Lyndon Johnson had made war and intervened (in Vietnam, in the Dominican Republic); Nixon was going to make peace.

Non-American Architects

However, while Nixon and Kissinger are often credited for détente, it is important to note that in the late 1960s, there were a number of other leaders around the globe who recognized the need to move beyond the climate of the early Cold War. European leaders—France's de Gaulle and, particularly during the Nixon administration, West Germany's Brandt—were key figures in putting further pressure on the United States to improve relations with the Soviet bloc. In the Soviet Union, Leonid Brezhnev (in power 1964–1982) and others were keen on gaining recognition of the Soviet Union as an equal to the United States, if only to enable them to cut down on the wasteful spending on the nuclear arms race and in order to gain access to superior Western technology through increased East-West trade. Also, in the late 1960s, the fact that the PRC's Chairman Mao Zedong (in power 1943–1976) was more concerned with the Soviet, rather than the American, threat made possible the eventual process of Sino-American rapprochement.

PUBLIC PORTRAIT: *LEONID BREZHNEV (1906–1982)*

Leonid Ilyich Brezhnev was the general secretary of the Communist Party of the Soviet Union (CPSU) between 1964 and 1982 (only Josef Stalin served in that post for a longer period). Of Ukrainian origin, Brezhnev was educated as an engineer, working in a metallurgical factory in the 1920s and 1930s. During World War II, Brezhnev, by then a member of the Communist Party, worked as a political commissar in the front lines. After the war, he was elected to the Supreme Soviet with the support of Nikita Khrushchev, a fellow Ukrainian who established a dominant position in the party hierarchy following Stalin's death in March 1953. That year, Brezhnev was appointed to the Central Committee and, in 1957, to the Politburo. Three years later, he became the president of the Presidium of the Supreme Soviet and, in effect, Khrushchev's deputy.

Brezhnev's subsequent career was closely tied to the evolution of détente. The Cuban Missile Crisis was seen as an embarrassment to Moscow and led to the downfall of Khruschev. In October 1964, Brezhnev replaced Khrushchev as the first secretary of the Soviet Communist Party, ultimately becoming the most influential leader in the Soviet Union. Under his leadership, the Soviet Union gradually became more receptive to the possibilities of a limited rapprochement with the United States, particularly as the cost of the nuclear arms buildup created severe difficulties to the Soviet state. At the same time, however, Brezhnev was no moderate: he supported the antagonistic policy toward China, approved of the Warsaw Pact invasion of Czechoslovakia in 1968, and was intolerant toward domestic dissent.

In the early 1970s, Brezhnev developed a relatively good working relationship with his American counterpart, President Richard Nixon. The two men met during the Soviet-American summits of 1972, 1973, and 1974, and took joint credit for the agreements that highlighted the onset of détente. Because Nixon's resignation due to the Watergate scandal in August 1974 took Brezhnev by surprise, he was unable to develop a comparable rapport with subsequent American presidents (Gerald Ford, Jimmy Carter, and Ronald Reagan). Simultaneously, the aging general secretary began supporting a more adventurous Soviet foreign policy in Africa and, in December 1979, approved the Soviet invasion of Afghanistan.

Leonid Brezhnev died in November 1982 as superpower tensions were again escalating because of Afghanistan and the uncompromising policies and rhetoric of the Reagan administration. His life and career had spanned almost the entire history of the Soviet state, and Brezhnev had led the Soviet Union during the administrations of five American presidents. While he was hardly solely responsible for the various foreign policy shifts that took place during his leadership, Brezhnev deserves significant responsibility for both the rise as well as the fall of détente.

Importantly, the leadership in the United States and the Soviet Union at this time did not conceive their policies as amounting to a revolution; if anything, their policy goals were conservative in nature. Both wanted to spend less, not more, on their respective military budgets. Neither wished to intervene directly but preferred to promote strong regional allies and proxies. Both Nixon and Brezhnev saw themselves as the leaders of superpowers, countries with global influence and, perhaps, a certain responsibility for the maintenance of global stability. Indeed, with the possible exception of Willy Brandt, leaders in the East and the West were searching for stability rather than radical change; all of them, with the possible exception of China's leaders, regarded World War II as their formative experience. The architects of détente, on both sides of the Iron Curtain, ultimately valued stability as much as, if not more than, moral principles or ideological beliefs. It was this shared quest for stability that, to a large extent, made the subsequent flowering of Soviet-American détente possible.

THE HIGHPOINTS OF SOVIET-AMERICAN DÉTENTE

The early 1970s were the highpoint of détente as, after a few years of often secretive diplomacy, Nixon's "era of negotiations" finally came to full bloom. Most spectacularly, after more than two decades of U.S. policy refusing to recognize the People's Republic of China, the United States finally opened a relationship with the PRC in 1971 and 1972.

Kissinger first visited Beijing secretly in July 1971, and Nixon later arrived in the Chinese capital for a series of high-level meetings with Mao Zedong and Premier Zhou Enlai (in power 1949–1976) in February 1972. At the conclusion of the visit, the two countries signed the Shanghai communiqué, a document that extolled a new era of peaceful coexistence between Washington and Beijing. Although neither side conceded anything significant, the visit opened the road toward full Sino-American normalization by the end of the 1970s.

Limits of Triangular Diplomacy

While Nixon dubbed his week-long visit a "journey of peace," the new Sino-American relationship did not translate into a major diplomatic tool; there was less to triangular diplomacy than met the eye. After 1971, there were very few instances when the Soviet Union practiced restraint that could be directly attributed to its concern over what they must have considered an axis of evil of sorts, the new "strategic partnership" between Washington and Beijing.

Although the China factor was not inconsequential in determining American policy (usually in favor of the Chinese), it seems to have given little incentive for the Soviets to act according to American desires. In some ways, it was almost the diplomatic equivalent of America's short-lived nuclear monopoly in the aftermath of World War II: the fact that the opening had taken place was important, but its practical application to other contexts was extremely difficult. While the opening to China cemented Nixon's reputation as a foreign policy president, the global impact of the journey of peace to Beijing would only be felt in the long term.

Soviet-American Agreements

The central point of the Nixon administration's foreign policy in the early 1970s was the developing relationship with the Soviet Union. After years of public and secret negotiations, the Soviet-American détente was truly launched in 1972. During the first Nixon-Brezhnev summit in May 1972, the two countries signed the SALT I (the first series of Strategic Arms Limitation Talks, 1969–1972) and Anti-Ballistic Missile (ABM) agreements.

The treaties did not bring an end to the nuclear arms race but represented a significant first: Americans and Soviets agreed to limit their respective missile arsenals and continue further negotiations. Although criticized at home by hawks for giving the Soviets too much and by doves for not going far enough, the SALT and ABM agreements symbolized the long road that the United States and the Soviet Union had traveled during the decade following the Cuban Missile Crisis of 1962. While the signing of the SALT I agreements was a key milepost of Nixon-era détente, it did not herald a sudden transformation toward a world of nuclear disarmament. In fact, there would be no SALT II (the subsequent 1972–1979 Strategic Arms Limitation Talks) until the Carter administration was in power, and even then no ratification would take place.

Soviet-American détente did continue, though, well beyond the 1972 Moscow summit. In fact, at the summit the two sides had signed a declaration called the Basic Principles of Soviet-American relations that, while not a formal treaty, publicly emphasized both sides' commitment to minimizing

After signing the Agreement on the Prevention of Nuclear War at the White House on June 22, 1973, President Richard Nixon and Soviet Communist Party Chief Leonid Brezhnev exchange pens used in signing the agreement.

SOURCE: UPI Photo/Frank Cancellare.

international tensions and refraining from unilateral actions that might provoke the other power. In 1973, Leonid Brezhnev visited the United States to sign, among other agreements, the Prevention of Nuclear War (PNW) agreement. In the summer of the following year, Nixon returned to the Soviet Union for further talks on nuclear weapons, European security, the Middle East crisis, and other issues. A few months after Nixon's resignation in August 1974, his successor, Gerald Ford, flew to Vladivostok, Russia, to hammer out a working outline of a future SALT II agreement.

IN THEIR OWN WORDS: *PRESIDENT RICHARD NIXON'S ADDRESS TO THE NATION, JULY 3, 1974*

After his last summit as president, Richard Nixon returned to the United States and delivered a brief speech at Loring Air Force Base in Maine. Emphasizing the continued improvement in Soviet-American relations, particularly on nuclear arms agreements and negotiations, Nixon heralded the onset of a new era in superpower relations and international affairs:

> At this year's summit, we advanced further the relationship that we began two years ago in Moscow and that we continued at last year's summit in the United States. In the communiqué we issued earlier today in Moscow, both sides committed themselves to this goal, the imperative necessity of making the process of improving United States-Soviet relations irreversible.
>
> We are prepared, we in the United States, to reduce our military strength but only through a process in which that reduction is mutual and one that does not diminish the security of the United States of America. It is to that end that we have been working.

> Two years ago in my report to the Congress on returning from the first of the United States-Soviet summits, I expressed the hope that historians of some future age will write of the year 1972, not that this was the year America went up to the summit and then down to the depths of the valley again, but that this was the year when America helped to lead the world up out of the lowlands of war and on to the high plateau of lasting peace.
>
> And now, two years, two summits later, the realization of that hope has been brought closer. The process of peace is going steadily forward. It is strengthened by the new and expanding patterns of cooperation between the United States and the Soviet Union.

SOURCE: Richard Nixon, "Address to the Nation on Returning from the Soviet Union," July 3, 1974, in *Public Papers of the Presidents, Richard Nixon, 1974* (Washington, DC: U.S. Government Printing Office, 1975), 579–80.

Limits of Détente

Notwithstanding numerous high-level meetings, Soviet-American relations were far from harmonious. In October 1973, for example, the outbreak of the Yom Kippur War between Israel and surrounding Arab states produced a potentially dangerous proxy confrontation between the United States (which supported Israel) and the Soviet Union (which armed Egypt and Syria), causing the president to order American nuclear forces on high alert. Ultimately, though, the crisis was solved via Kissinger's hectic Shuttle Diplomacy. In Southeast Asia, despite the Paris Agreements of January 1973, the war in Vietnam continued until eventual unification in 1975. By early 1974, Soviet-American summitry may well have become a semi-permanent feature of the international system. Yet in most regions of the world, Soviet-American competition continued to affect and often fuel military conflict. Despite détente, confrontation had hardly given way to cooperation.

From the perspective of Soviet-American relations, therefore, the achievements of the early 1970s were relative. Global peace did not break out; détente did not replace competition; there was hardly a durable structure of peace. Nixon and Kissinger had initiated an era of regular high-level superpower meetings that would continue throughout the remainder of the Cold War. In subsequent years, despite the chilling of the superpower relationship, presidents Jimmy Carter and Ronald Reagan would meet with their Soviet counterparts as well. Indeed, the historian John Lewis Gaddis aptly describes détente as "institutionalized negotiations as a form of Cold War competition."[5]

In the end, Soviet-American détente may have brought some degree of stability, but its overall impact on international relations was limited. No revolution ensued in part because détente did little to curtail the Soviets or the Americans from seeking to maximize their power in developing and non-aligned nations. Moreover, in the U.S. détente was among the casualties of one of the most severe internal political crises the country had ever experienced.

EUROPEAN DÉTENTE

Détente was not limited to bilateral Soviet-American relations. In particular, the easing of East-West relations extended to Europe, where the contribution of West German Chancellor Willy Brandt was particularly important. By 1972, Brandt's *Ostpolitik* had resulted in the partial normalization of the division of Germany through agreements over Berlin and an opening of relations between West Germany and a number of Eastern European governments (including East Germany and Poland). While American policymakers appreciated the stability that resulted from such agreements, however, Washington's views were also influenced by the potentially disruptive effect that independent West German efforts might have on transatlantic unity. In the mid-1970s, this concern was highlighted in such notions as Finlandization, the worry that West Germany might be willing to distance itself from NATO in order to improve relations with the Soviet Union and consequently raise the possibilities of a German-German rapprochement, even unification, much as Finland had accommodated the Soviet Union to avoid conflict.

Helsinki Accords

Détente did not bring about German reunification. Yet in Europe, another significant outcome of the détente process was the Conference on Security and Cooperation in Europe (CSCE) and the signing of the Helsinki Final Act by thirty-five nations in August 1975. Almost four decades later, the CSCE still exists, although it was named the Organization for Security and Cooperation in Europe in the 1990s. It remains, arguably, the most significant organizational outcome of the era of détente.

The original proposal for a pan-European security conference was made by Soviet Foreign Minister Vyacheslav Molotov (served 1953–1956) in 1954, mainly as a way of undermining the growing role and potential enlargement of NATO. Because the United States and Canada were not invited, the proposal was turned down by NATO countries; instead, the years of 1954 and 1955 saw the creation of the Warsaw Pact, and the Federal Republic of Germany joining NATO. The idea lived on until, on March 17, 1969, the Warsaw Pact issued the Budapest appeal, an open call for a conference on security and cooperation in Europe. Two months later, the Finnish president, Urho Kekkonen (in office 1956–1982), at the Soviet Union's urging, acted as a neutral go-between, offering Helsinki as the site for such a conference. Most significantly, the latter invitation was directed to all European countries as well as the United States and Canada. It took several years before the talks could get on track. Only in November 1972 did the initial Multilateral Preparatory Talks begin at the Dipoli Conference Center, outside of Helsinki.

Stage I of the CSCE talks lasted through summer 1973, concluding with a foreign ministers' meeting in Helsinki in early July. In late August of that year, the talks moved to Geneva for Stage II, a series of "real" negotiations (Stage I had been charged with agreeing on the agenda and terms of reference of the CSCE) during which a large number of committees and subcommittees worked on the various aspects (or Baskets) on the agenda. Stage II was the crucial stage in which the final shape of the Helsinki Accords took form. It was also a long and arduous affair, as representatives of thirty-five nations engaged in seemingly endless disputes over the various provisions to be included in the Final Act.

It lasted until July 1975. Like Stage I, the Geneva Stage II concluded with a foreign ministers' meeting and was then followed by the high-level three-day summit in Helsinki (Stage III) that opened on July 30. Attended by the heads of state of the participant countries, the Helsinki summit was a largely ceremonial affair, but one that, to many in Europe, represented a significant turning point in East-West relations and the codification of European détente.

SHIFTS IN FOREIGN POLICY: *THE AFTERMATH OF THE HELSINKI ACCORDS*

Historians have for some time debated the impact that détente had on subsequent developments in international relations. They have paid particularly close attention to the role, or lack thereof, that the 1975 Helsinki Accords had on the subsequent demise of the Cold War in Europe. While no consensus exists, a strong body of opinion holds that the content of this document played an instrumental role in unleashing the internal forces that brought about the collapse of totalitarian order in Eastern Europe. Yet there is a similarly widespread understanding that the signatories present at the Conference on Cooperation in Europe in late July and early August 1975 did not view such an outcome as particularly likely. If Helsinki helped transform Europe, it was largely as an unintended consequence rather than as a conscious effort.

The Helsinki Accords were a remarkable document. The four so-called "Baskets" dealt with virtually every aspect of pan-European security. While Basket I, for example, dealt with such traditional security issues as the inviolability of borders; Baskets II and III dealt with economic issues and, perhaps most controversially, human rights. Basket IV, rarely mentioned, was perhaps the most important of all: it identified the follow-up of the CSCE process, thus making it clear that the issues identified in other parts of the document would not become a dead letter. In other words, the signing ceremony at Helsinki's Finlandia Hall on August 1, 1975, was as much the beginning of a process as it was a closure of the multilateral negotiation marathon that had stretched far beyond the time limits anticipated in 1972.

THE FINAL DOCUMENT

Remarkable, and perhaps somewhat overrated, though the CSCE's final document was, it was also inherently contradictory, producing diametrically opposite interpretations. It was widely criticized in the United States as basically recognizing Soviet control over Eastern Europe. At issue was Basket I, which spelled out the inviolability of Europe's postwar borders and guaranteed non-interference in the internal affairs of the signatories. While the Soviets cherished this as a guarantee against the potential spread of Western propaganda in their sphere, prominent Republican politicians like Strom Thurmond and Jesse Helms charged that this amounted to a formal acknowledgement of the legitimacy of the Soviet sphere of influence. During the 1976 Republican primaries, Ronald Reagan used this "sellout" argument to attack Gerald Ford's foreign policy record. Détente, he charged, was inherently immoral.

Although Reagan eventually lost the Republican nomination to Ford, the Democratic candidate, former Georgia governor Jimmy Carter, returned repeatedly to the theme of immorality. And the charge stuck. In the United States, the Helsinki Accords were seen mainly as an international agreement that recognized the Soviet Union's control of Eastern Europe as legitimate and as further proof of the lack of idealism in the conduct of détente. Given that the central theme of the Nixon and Ford administrations' foreign policies had indeed been to emphasize the need for negotiations with America's main totalitarian foe, it was no surprise that such criticism struck a chord with the American public, already weary of the Watergate scandal, which had exposed the unsavory character of Ford's predecessor.

ANOTHER VIEW

There was, though, another side to the Helsinki Accords. Basket III explicitly called for the signatories to respect human rights, including the freedom of thought, conscience, religion, or belief. Although such provisions were initially ignored by Soviet bloc governments as a necessary concession for the recognition of postwar borders, the CSCE did signal the emergence of human security as an important and recognized aspect of international relations. Most importantly, the CSCE was publicized, and studied, throughout the Soviet bloc.

The practical impact of Basket III was almost immediate. In spring 1976, a group of Soviet intellectuals, including such prominent scientists and dissidents as the 1975 Nobel Peace Prize laureate Andrei Sakharov, created the Moscow Helsinki Watch Group to monitor the Soviet Union's compliance with the CSCE's human rights provisions. Although the group was repressed, its actions inspired similar groups throughout the Soviet bloc (such as the Charter 77 in Czechoslovakia, which included the future president Vaclav Havel). In 1982, these groups formed the International Helsinki Federation for Human Rights. By then, the Helsinki Accords had become a kind of a manifesto that united the various groups opposing totalitarian regimes throughout Soviet-dominated Europe.

Another important provision was included in the CSCE: while renouncing violence and military force, it did recognize the possibility that borders might be changed through "peaceful means." This was important for those Germans who still held up unification as a realistic goal.

LEGACY OF THE HELSINKI ACCORDS

In the end, the CSCE did launch and mark a certain rebirth of Europe. After all, for the first time since the end of World War II, the CSCE negotiations provided a forum in which all-European negotiations could take place. In Helsinki and Geneva, under the umbrella of the CSCE, East-West contacts were fostered in a way that could hardly have been possible a decade earlier. Western Europeans, in particular, found in the CSCE a forum for putting the recommendations of the 1970 Davignon Report, the first effort to launch what today is called European Common Foreign and Security Policy, into practice for the first time. In fact, Western Europeans tended to dominate much of the negotiation process, because the Americans showed but minimal interest, and the Soviets (and selected Eastern European governments) tried to keep the agenda, and the results, as limited as possible.

Herein lay the key to the long-term significance of the CSCE and of European détente. Unlike superpower détente, it did not focus on nuclear weapons or what could be considered traditional security issues. What the CSCE, one of the key products of European détente, brought clearly to the international arena was a focus on human security—on people rather than states.

Although the final meeting was unprecedented in the scope of its participants and the comprehensiveness of its substance, the CSCE was not, at the time, uniformly popular. The Helsinki Final Act was a vast document that dealt with such a wide range of issues as human rights, recognition and sanctity of the borders drawn after World War II, free movement of people and information, and economic relations between East and West. At the time of its signing, however, much of the Final Act went unnoticed, particularly in the United States, although some of its specifics did come under close scrutiny. For example, the CSCE was criticized in the United States for effectively recognizing Soviet control over Eastern Europe. In the Soviet bloc, Communist leaders largely ignored the provisions regarding human rights. Nevertheless, the CSCE had a major long-term significance: it signaled the emergence of human security as an important and recognized aspect of international relations, and it would later be used as a manifesto by numerous dissident and human rights groups inside the Soviet Union and its satellites.

DÉTENTE HALTED

The August 1975 signing of the Helsinki Final Act was, in effect, the last superpower summit of the era of "high détente." In fact, growing domestic criticism of détente in the United States along with a series of regional crises that pitted Moscow against Washington were already helping destroy the legitimacy of the "era of negotiations."

Much of the domestic American criticism came to the fore during the 1976 presidential elections. In the Republican primaries, Ronald Reagan, the former governor of California, criticized détente alternatively as an immoral abandonment of Eastern Europe and hence a betrayal of American principles, or as a self-imposed denial of the United States' strategic superiority over the Soviet Union. While Reagan did not capture the Republican nomination in 1976, Georgia's Democratic governor, Jimmy Carter, eventually defeated the incumbent president, Gerald R. Ford, by using many of the same arguments. Indeed, détente had become a dirty word in American politics, symbolized by Ford's decision to ban the use of the term in his campaign.

External Troubles

While under siege from domestic critics in the United States, détente was also in trouble because neither the Soviet Union nor the United States was willing to abandon the search for unilateral advantage in the Third World. After the 1973 Middle East war, American diplomats worked studiously, and successfully, to deny the Soviets a significant role in the subsequent peace process. In 1974 and 1975, the Soviets, as well as the Chinese, continued to provide substantial military aid to North Vietnam, thereby undermining the remote possibility that the 1973 Paris Agreements could have prevented an eventual takeover of all of Vietnam by Hanoi, as happened in late April 1975.

To take one further example, in 1975 and 1976, the Soviets and the Americans were involved on opposite sides in the Angolan conflict, which erupted soon after the independence of this African nation from Portugal. By late 1975, the United States was backing two of the three Angolan factions fighting over control of the newly independent nation. Nonetheless, the Popular Movement for the Liberation of Angola (MPLA), supported by Soviet material aid and by the presence of thousands of Cuban troops, emerged victorious in early 1976.

JIMMY CARTER AND THE COLLAPSE OF DÉTENTE

When Jimmy Carter entered the White House in January 1977, détente had already suffered a number of blows at home and abroad. Yet Carter did not abandon the idea of negotiations with the Soviet Union. Between 1977 and 1979, Moscow and Washington negotiated the SALT II agreement. This was in some ways even more remarkable given the unilateral introduction by the Soviet Union, at the start of Carter's presidency, of new medium-range nuclear missiles (SS 20) in Europe.

While the Carter administration may have been willing to negotiate over nuclear weapons, it also trumpeted moral issues. Carter's insistence on supporting human rights activists in Eastern Europe and the Soviet Union drew Moscow's ire and was seen by Brezhnev as an attempt at subverting Communist rule from within. Added to these tensions were the numerous crises of the Arc of Crisis, the geographic area extending from Northeastern Africa to Pakistan.

Conflict in the Horn of Africa

In the late 1970s, the wrangling over various regional conflicts further eroded the basis of détente. Remarkably, seen from today's perspective, the 1977–1978 war between Ethiopia and Somalia over the Ogaden Desert was viewed, both in Washington and Moscow, as a key conflict in Cold War terms. Jimmy Carter's national security adviser, Zbigniew Brzezinski (served 1977–1981), won support within the administration for viewing Soviet bloc aid to Ethiopia as a direct challenge to the United States.

On the Soviet side, some leaders believed that through receiving Soviet advisers and Cuban troops, the leftist military regime in Ethiopia could become a star example of how socialism might triumph in Africa. Although no borders changed as a result of the Ethiopian victory in the war, many in Washington came to see the conflict in the Horn of Africa as an end-point for superpower détente. The final nails in the coffin of U.S.-Soviet cooperation came with the unfolding of events in Iran and Afghanistan.

Iran and the Death of Détente

Substantively, the Iranian revolution of 1978 and 1979 was the first manifestation in a series of collisions between political Islam and the West. Yet this crisis further accelerated the death of détente. The fall of the Shah of Iran (in power 1941–1979) and the success of the deeply anti-American Islamic revolution came at a time when doubts about the course of American foreign policy had already been expressed due to the events in Angola in the mid-1970s and, more recently, in the Horn of Africa. While the role of the Soviet Union in Iran was virtually non-existent, the loss of a strong regional ally, a cornerstone of U.S. policy in the Persian Gulf region, was an unexpected blow to the Carter administration's foreign policy and, ultimately, to the president's political future. Indeed, visiting Tehran in late 1977, Carter had made a fateful toast: "Iran, because of the great leadership of the Shah, is an island of stability in one of the more troubled areas of the world," he told the audience gathered for a state dinner in Tehran on December 31, 1977.

Soon after, events unfolded in a manner that transformed U.S. foreign policy in the Middle East for decades to come. Only weeks after Carter's visit, anti-shah riots broke out in Tehran. From Paris, the exiled conservative Shi'a Muslim cleric Ayatollah Ruhollah Khomeini used his access to media outlets to criticize the brutal methods by which the shah's police and army attacked the demonstrators. Suddenly an international celebrity, Khomeini openly called for the abdication of the shah. In November 1978, the Iranian leader declared martial law. Yet with millions of people joining the demonstrations throughout Iran, it was too late to stop the tide of revolution. In January 1979, the shah fled the country, having first appointed a member of the opposition, Shapour Bakhtiar (in office 1979), as the prime minister. Bakhtiar, however, found his career short-lived. Upon his return to Tehran on February 1, 1979, Khomeini appointed his own prime minister, Mehdi Bazargan (in office 1979). Over the next few years, under Supreme Leader of Iran Ruhollah Khomeini (in power 1979–1989), the Islamic Republic of Iran—a unique mixture of Islamic theocracy and populist democracy—replaced Pahlavi Iran.

The fall of the shah was a severe setback to the Carter administration's foreign policy in the region and, ultimately, on a global scale. His national security adviser, Zbigniew Brzezinski, considered the loss of Iran as an ally the biggest American foreign policy setback of the Cold War, even more significant than the Vietnam War. Iran's transformation from ally to enemy translated into the loss of significant military and intelligence facilities. Iran's oil was an important energy resource for the West, particularly to America's NATO allies. Moreover, the turmoil in Iran seemed to offer the Soviet Union an opportunity to reverse the setbacks it had suffered in the Middle East since the late 1960s. Indeed, in spring 1979, the Iranian crisis caused a thorough reassessment of U.S. policy, which would lead to the Carter Doctrine.

Intervention in Afghanistan

While the Carter administration contemplated the unwelcome turn of events in Iran, the Soviet Union faced its own debacle in the region. In April 1978, as the shah's regime began to crack under waves of protest, the Afghan Communist Party (the People's Democratic Party of Afghanistan [PDPA]) launched a successful coup d'etat against the government of President Mohammed Daoud (in office 1973–1978). Although the coup was apparently planned without the direct participation of the Soviet Union, Moscow found itself closely tied to the fortunes of the new People's Democratic Republic of Afghanistan, a regime that was ridden with internal rivalries and increasingly threatened by a growing Islamist movement supported by Pakistan. Throughout most of 1978 and 1979, the Soviets increased military, economic, and advisory assistance, but, despite appeals, refused to send in combat troops to shore up the Communist government of Hafizullah Amin (in office 1979). After a series of internal purges in October 1978, however, the relationship between Kabul and Moscow deteriorated rapidly. The Soviets began to seriously consider a full-scale military intervention. By November 1979, as chaos reigned and Amin made approaches to the United States and sought a cease-fire with the Islamists, the Soviets finally decided in favor of intervention to oust the troublesome Amin and replace him with a more reliable leader. On December 12, the Politburo gave its approval. What Brezhnev, for one, believed would be "a limited operation over in a few weeks time" commenced on Christmas Day 1979. When he died in November 1982, no end was in sight; the initial Soviet invasion force of eighty thousand had swelled up to 130,000.

While the Soviet action was intended mainly to shore up the flagging Communist regime in Kabul, the Carter administration, already besieged by the unfolding of events in Iran, interpreted it as another step in a global Communist challenge. The United States cut trade links with the Soviet Union, boycotted the 1980 Moscow Olympics, and intensified a renewed military buildup, which had begun the year before. The SALT II treaty, signed in June 1979, limited each nation to 2,250 nuclear missiles, with no more than 1,320 MIRVs, and many U.S. senators balked at the treaty. The Carter administration withdrew it from consideration, and SALT II was never ratified. In this sense, it was the Afghan invasion that killed détente, although many experts would argue that even before the events of December 1979, it was unlikely that the Senate would have passed a new comprehensive arms control agreement with the

Soviet Union. The senators who opposed the treaty saw it as a symbol of perceived American weakness. For example, the Senate Armed Services voted to recommend against the ratification two weeks prior to the Soviet invasion of Afghanistan. Indeed, the new direction in international affairs, so well under way in the early 1970s, had come to a decisive halt by the end of that decade. In his January 1980 State of the Union Address, President Carter unveiled the Carter Doctrine, pledging that the United States would use military force if necessary to defend its national interests in the Persian Gulf region.

Détente's demise coincided with an American presidential election. Besieged abroad and facing an economic malaise in the United States, Jimmy Carter was soundly defeated by Ronald Reagan in November 1980. While the new president is credited by many as having restored American purpose and power, his election and subsequent policies meant that the "era of negotiations" would not resume until Mikhail Gorbachev (in office 1985–1991) came to power in Moscow in spring 1985.

THE LEGACIES OF DÉTENTE

Even with the seeming disappearance of détente by the early 1980s, and the emergence of what is sometimes referred to as the "New Cold War," the "era of negotiations" had left a fundamental imprint on the Cold War international system. To be sure, détente represented an essentially conservative turn in international affairs. Its architects aimed to stabilize

a situation that, by the early 1960s, had threatened to escalate into a nuclear exchange. For the United States, détente also represented a welcome opportunity to scale back certain excessive and costly external commitments (most specifically the five hundred thousand troops stationed in Vietnam).

Equally, it seems that détente's immediate results, while spectacular (opening relations with China, SALT agreement with the Soviets), lacked domestic American support and international respect, or even, in the view of many, relevance. As a result, détente did not provide a lasting "structure of peace," as Nixon, in some of his hyperbolic speeches, had called for.

Yet while détente as conceived in the early 1970s did not last, it did introduce numerous elements (such as the notion of human security) into the international system that ultimately, at times unintentionally, worked to undermine the validity of the Cold War itself. In the late 1970s and the 1980s, for example, numerous dissident groups inside the Soviet bloc used the Helsinki Final Act's human rights provisions as a tool for undermining totalitarian controls, and calling for political freedoms, within their countries. In the long run, détente, ironically, discredited the international system it was meant to stabilize.

See also: **Chapter 26: Shuttle Diplomacy and Its Impact on the Middle East; Chapter 28: "Tear Down This Wall"; Chapter 29: Glasnost and Perestroika; Chapter 30: Diplomatic Milestones, 1970s–1991.**

ENDNOTES

1. George Kennan, "A Sterile and Hopeless Weapon," in Kennan, *The Nuclear Delusion: Soviet-American Relations in the Atomic Age* (New York: Pantheon, 1976), 7.

2. Anatoly Dobrynin, *In Confidence: Moscow's Ambassador to Six Cold War Presidents* (New York: Times Books, 1995), 183.

3. Cited in Jussi Hanhimäki, "Conservative Goals, Revolutionary Outcomes: The Paradox of Détente," in *Cold War History* 8: 4 (November 2008), 506–07.

4. Henry Kissinger, *American Foreign Policy* (New York: Norton, 1969), 52.

5. John L. Gaddis, "Why Did the Cold War Last as Long as It Did?" in Odd Arne Westad, ed., *The Fall of Détente* (Oslo: Scandinavian University Press, 1997), 155.

FURTHER READING

Bundy, William. *A Tangled Web: The Making of Foreign Policy in the Nixon Presidency.* New York: Hill & Wang, 1998.

Burr, William, ed. *The Kissinger Transcripts: The Top Secret Talks with Beijing and Moscow.* New York: The New Press, 1999.

Garthoff, Raymond. *Détente and Confrontation: American Soviet Relations from Nixon to Reagan.* 2nd ed. Washington, DC: Brookings Institution, 1994.

Hanhimäki, Jussi M. *The Flawed Architect: Henry Kissinger and American Foreign Policy.* New York: Oxford University Press, 2004.

———. *The Rise and Fall of Détente: American Foreign Policy and the Transformation of the Cold War.* Washington, DC: Potomac Books, 2012.

Herring, George C. *From Colony to Superpower: U.S. Foreign Relations since 1776.* New York: Oxford University Press, 2008.

Kissinger, Henry. *White House Years.* New York: Little, Brown, 1979.

———. *Years of Upheaval.* New York: Little, Brown, 1982.

Ouimet, Matthew J. *The Rise and Fall of the Brezhnev Doctrine in Soviet Foreign Policy.* Chapel Hill: University of North Carolina Press, 2003.

Suri, Jeremi. *Power and Protest: Global Revolution and the Rise of Détente.* Cambridge, MA: Harvard University Press, 2003.

Thomas, Daniel C. *The Helsinki Effect: International Norms, Human Rights, and the Demise of Communism.* Princeton, NJ: Princeton University Press, 2001.

chapter 26

Shuttle Diplomacy and Its Impact on the Middle East

by Paul Thomas Chamberlin

THE YEARS BETWEEN the 1967 Arab-Israeli war and the 1979 Egypt-Israel Peace Treaty witnessed both the dramatic transformation of the Arab-Israeli conflict and the ascendency of the United States as the most influential superpower in the Middle East. No American figure loomed larger over this period than Henry Kissinger, who entered the picture in 1969 as Richard Nixon's national security adviser. Kissinger would play a pivotal role in guiding the diplomacy of the Nixon (1969–1974) and Gerald Ford (1974–1977) administrations, and, toward the Arab-Israeli conflict, establishing an approach that came to be known as shuttle diplomacy.

THE ROOTS OF SHUTTLE DIPLOMACY

The June 1967 Arab-Israeli war was a watershed in the history of the Arab-Israeli conflict, the peace process, and Middle Eastern politics. Although the origins of the war trace back to 1947, the precipitating crisis began in spring 1967. In those months, Israel had stepped up its military efforts to curtail guerrilla operations along its borders with Syria and Jordan. Two dramatic events—the November 1966 raid on the village of Samu in the Jordanian-controlled West Bank, and an air battle between Israeli and Syrian jets in April 1967—signaled rising tensions between Israel and its Arab neighbors and increased pressure on Egyptian President Gamal Abdel Nasser (in office 1956–1970) to take a more forceful stand vis-à-vis Israel.

The Drift toward War

The momentum toward war escalated in May 1967, when the Soviet Union passed false information to the Egyptian government that Israel was planning an attack on Syria. Facing declining support at home, the result of a stagnant political and economic system and a bloody foreign intervention in Yemen, Nasser, then president of the United Arab Republic, was now forced to make some gesture in support of Syria or risk losing a degree of his influence in the region. In response, Nasser issued a request that the United Nations

Emergency Force (UNEF), consisting of UN peacekeepers stationed in the Sinai to separate Egyptian and Israeli forces since 1956, be removed. As the peacekeepers pulled out, Nasser began moving military units into the Sinai. Because this first move was greeted with enthusiasm throughout the Arab world, Nasser upped the ante by closing the Straits of Tiran to Israeli shipping. The Israeli government had made it known that it would look on the closure of the straits, which would cut off Israel's access to the Red Sea and Indian Ocean, as an act of war.

It is doubtful, however, that Nasser intended the showdown with Israel to escalate to a full-scale armed conflict. Indeed, a substantial portion of the Egyptian military was stationed in Yemen. Rather, the more likely explanation is that Nasser hoped to bolster his domestic and regional standing through a display of diplomatic brinkmanship and expected the United States, Soviet Union, or United Nations to defuse the brewing crisis. Nevertheless, the drift toward war continued through the spring of 1967. Israel pressed both the United States and Great Britain to force the opening of the straits, to no avail, while members of the Israeli cabinet debated whether or not to launch an attack on Egypt.

A War That No One Wanted

In the Arab world, Egypt's actions created a rising tide of support for Nasser's challenge to Israel (although twelve years later, Egypt would become the first Arab nation to recognize the Jewish state's right to exist). Swept up in this movement, Jordan's King Hussein (reigned 1953–1999) signed a mutual defense treaty with Egypt, on May 30, thus consolidating an alliance among Syria, Egypt, and Jordan, three of Israel's four neighbors. News of Jordanian involvement substantially increased the perception of a national security threat in Israel: while an Egyptian assault would come through the sparsely populated Negev Desert, and a Syrian attack would have to cross the rugged Golan Heights, a Jordanian assault would move through the West Bank directly into the heart of Israel.

KEY CONCEPTS

Shuttle diplomacy. Beginning in the 1970s, Secretary of State Henry Kissinger was perhaps the most prominent figure on the U.S. diplomatic scene. Shuttle diplomacy was Kissinger's approach to the Arab-Israeli peace process following the 1973 war. In contrast to other schemes that called for a comprehensive settlement to the conflict, shuttle diplomacy was built on a step-by-step approach to bilateral agreements between Israel and its neighbors. Moreover, unlike the comprehensive approaches, shuttle diplomacy allotted no role to the Soviet Union. Although it eventually proved effective in generating a peace treaty between Israel and Egypt, Kissinger's shuttle diplomacy would fail to achieve resolutions between Israel and Syria, the Palestinians, and Iraq.

Resolution 242. On November 22, 1967, Resolution 242 was passed unanimously by the UN Security Council, in response to the new regions established by the 1967 Arab-Israeli war. Intended to provide a framework for resolving the conflict, Resolution 242 was built around a land-for-peace formula, in which Israel would exchange Arab territory—the West Bank, Gaza Strip, Sinai, and the Golan Heights—for peace agreements with its Arab neighbors. Although it was intended as a general statement regarding a plan for the comprehensive settlement to the Arab-Israeli dispute, UN 242 quickly won detractors, because of its exclusion of the Palestinians (referred to as Arab refugees rather than as a nation) from its proposed framework for peace. However, all of the major players in the conflict would at some point work to undermine UN 242 in favor of their own visions for a regional settlement.

While fears of an imminent attack reached a fever pitch among the Israeli public, Israeli leaders and U.S. intelligence officers remained skeptical about the likelihood of an Egyptian-Syrian-Jordanian attack. Analysts deemed that Egyptian troop movements were not large enough to suggest preparations for a full assault on Israel and noted that Israeli military capabilities, particularly the Israeli air force, outmatched those of its Arab neighbors. A matter of greater concern, however, was the strain that a full-scale mobilization of Israel's armed forces for a prolonged length of time would place on Israel's economy and society. Israel's civilian leadership also faced heavy pressure from military leaders pushing for confrontation. U.S. President Lyndon Johnson (1963–1969) warned the Israelis that American analysts had seen no indication that Egypt was planning to attack and, even if they did, Israel would "whip the hell out of them." He added: "Israel will not be alone unless it decides to go it alone." Thus, Washington sent a series of mixed signals to the Israelis, leading to a debate among historians over whether the Johnson administration gave Israel a green or a yellow light to go to war. Believing that the United States would stand by Israel in the event of a conflict, the Israeli cabinet made the fateful decision to attack Egypt and Syria on June 4, 1967, launching a war that none of the participants wanted.[1]

A Short but Far-Reaching Conflict

The war began the following day on June 5, when Israeli jets attacked Egyptian airfields, destroying the majority of Egypt's air force as it sat on the ground, and then turning to strike the Syrian and Jordanian air forces. By the end of the day, the Israel Defense Forces (IDF) had decimated the surrounding Arab air forces and guaranteed air superiority for the remainder of the war. IDF ground units invaded the Sinai, achieving swift victories against disorganized Egyptian forces and taking possession of the peninsula by the end of June 8. As fighting continued in the Sinai, the IDF attacked Jordanian forces in the West Bank, seizing Jerusalem on June 7. On the morning of June 9, Israel invaded Syria, despite the latter's acceptance of a cease-fire four hours earlier, attacking fortified positions in the Golan Heights. On June 10, after heavy fighting, the IDF gained control of the Golan, effectively bringing the war to an end.

While the war itself had been surprisingly short, the aftereffects would last for generations. Although territorial conquest had not been one of Israel's stated war aims (which had been to reopen the Straits of Tiran, force Egyptian units out of the Sinai, and "restore the deterrent power of the IDF"), the spectacular and largely unexpected gains made by the IDF resulted in an ad hoc expansion of its goals.[2] The victory left Israel in control of vast tracts of land comprising the Sinai Peninsula, the Golan Heights, the West Bank, and the Gaza Strip. It also placed approximately one million Arabs under Israeli occupation.

THE JOHNSON ADMINISTRATION

In both the run-up to the 1967 Six-Day War and its aftermath, the Johnson administration was, for the most part, distracted by the ongoing conflict in Vietnam. Wary of being pulled into another conflict in the Middle East at the same time that the United States was waging war in Southeast Asia, officials in the Johnson White House sought to limit the scale of U.S. involvement in the Arab-Israeli dispute. This wariness helps to explain some of Johnson's mixed signals to the Israelis in spring 1967. Officials in the Johnson administration concluded that they would rather have Israel deal with the matter of Straits of Tiran itself, for instance, than risk a direct confrontation with Egypt. Compounding matters, Washington was also reluctant to ratchet up tensions in the region for fear of raising tensions with Moscow and turning the Middle East into a flashpoint for nuclear war.[3]

Despite their desire to maintain a distance from the conflict, U.S. military personnel would become embroiled in the 1967 war in what became known as the *Liberty* Incident. On June 8, 1967, the fourth day of the war, the naval intelligence vessel USS *Liberty* was in position thirteen miles off the coast of the Sinai to monitor fighting between Israel and Egypt. After watching the *Liberty* for several hours, Israeli warplanes attacked the ship with rockets, napalm, and torpedoes. The attack left thirty-four American sailors dead and another 171 wounded. Afraid that the ship was being attacked by Soviet or Arab jets, the captain of the nearby aircraft carrier *America* launched U.S. planes armed with nuclear weapons to defend the *Liberty*. The nuclear-armed planes were called back, but the specter of a nuclear confrontation remained. The government of Israel offered an apology for the attack, claiming to have mistaken the *Liberty* for a hostile vessel. A number of top-level U.S. officials, including Secretary of State Dean Rusk, were not persuaded by Israel's explanations. "I didn't believe them then, and I don't believe them to this day," Rusk remembered. "The attack was outrageous." The incident remains highly controversial among historians.[4]

A Lack of U.S. Strategy

While it managed to move past the fallout from the *Liberty* attack, the Johnson administration failed to develop a working strategy for dealing with the Middle East in the wake of the 1967 war. The war fundamentally altered regional politics and created the necessary components for what might have been a comprehensive peace to the Arab-Israeli conflict. Prior to 1967, the Arab states had little incentive to negotiate with Israel. Certainly, the plight of the Palestinians and the poor performance of the Arab militaries in the 1948 war gave Cairo, Damascus, and Amman cause for embarrassment, but they had little reason to move toward any sort of peace with Israel during this period. Israel's spectacular gains in 1967 changed all this, however. IDF control of the Sinai, the West Bank, and the Golan Heights gave Israel what it considered to be more defensible borders, as well as a good deal of leverage over the surrounding Arab states. This basic formula, "land for peace," represented the most promising prospect for a negotiated settlement to the Arab-Israeli conflict since the creation of the Jewish state in 1948, a fact that was apparent to Israel, the United States, and the United Nations.

With this in mind, the Johnson administration pushed for the mutual recognition of all states in the region, a respect for the territorial integrity of those states, and some equitable solution for the "Arab refugees." The international community's support for a solution along these lines was confirmed on November 22, 1967, when the UN Security Council voted unanimously in favor of UN Resolution 242, which called for the evacuation of Israeli forces from all Arab territories occupied since the June war, in exchange for the Arab states' recognition of Israel and the termination of all claims of belligerency. The United Nations appointed Swedish diplomat Gunnar Jarring as special envoy charged with implementing UN 242. These efforts, which would last until 1973, became known as the Jarring Mission.

Obstacles to the Jarring Mission

The land-for-peace formula ran into an obstacle in September 1967, however, when the Arab League issued the Khartoum Resolution. The resolution, which became famous for its "Three Noes," rejected the prospect of peace, recognition, and negotiations with Israel, and pledged Arab solidarity against the Jewish state. The resolution represented the Arab states' refusal to enter into diplomatic negotiations with Israel in an effort to regain territory that, in their eyes, had been wrongfully taken from them. A second obstacle materialized in late 1967 and in the early months of 1968 with the rise of an energized Palestinian guerrilla movement in the West Bank, Gaza, Jordan, and Lebanon. The Israeli military presence in the West Bank and Gaza combined with the sharp decline in Nasser's influence helped generate growing support for Palestinian fighters. In March 1968, Yasser Arafat's (chairman of the Executive Committee of the PLO, 1969–2004) Fatah, despite a significant military defeat, achieved a major political victory when Palestinian guerrillas inflicted unexpected casualties against the IDF during a large Israeli raid against the Jordanian village of al-Karama. In the coming months, as Fatah (the Movement for the Liberation of Palestine) and several other guerrilla groups gained a controlling influence over the Palestine Liberation Organization (PLO), they emerged as an even more vocal opponent of a political settlement with Israel. The PLO's calls for the creation of a secular, democratic state in the region, which began to appear after 1968, were understood correctly by the Israeli government as tantamount to the dissolution of the Jewish state.

Another obstacle to the Jarring Mission was the Israeli government and its position concerning the occupied territories. While Damascus, Cairo, and Amman were generally supportive of Jarring's efforts, the Israeli government worked to stall the ambassador's progress.[5] Although the prospect of

IN THEIR OWN WORDS: *UNITED NATIONS SECURITY COUNCIL 242, 22 NOVEMBER 1967*

Resolution 242, sponsored by British Ambassador Lord Caradon, was adopted unanimously by the UN Security Council on November 22, 1967, in the aftermath of the 1967 war. It was adopted under Chapter VI of the United Nations Charter. The UN's plan for guiding the Middle East peace process, the resolution deals with five key principles: withdrawal of Israeli forces, "peace within secure and recognized boundaries," freedom of navigation, a just settlement of the refugee problem, and security measures including demilitarized zones.

The Security Council,

Expressing its continuing concern with the grave situation in the Middle East,

Emphasizing the inadmissibility of the acquisition of territory by war and the need to work for a just and lasting peace in which every State in the area can live in security,

Emphasizing further that all Member States in their acceptance of the Charter of the United Nations have undertaken a commitment to act in accordance with Article 2 of the Charter,

1. *Affirms* that the fulfillment of Charter principles requires the establishment of a just and lasting peace in the Middle East which should include the application of both the following principles:

(i) Withdrawal of Israel armed forces from territories occupied in the recent conflict;

(ii) Termination of all claims or states of belligerency and respect for and acknowledgment of the sovereignty, territorial integrity and political independence of every State in the area and their right to live in peace within secure and recognized boundaries free from threats or acts of force;

2. *Affirms further* the necessity

(a) For guaranteeing freedom of navigation through international waterways in the area;

(b) For achieving a just settlement of the refugee problem;

(c) For guaranteeing the territorial inviolability and political independence of every State in the area, through measures including the establishment of demilitarized zones;

3. *Requests* the Secretary-General to designate a Special Representative to proceed to the Middle East to establish and maintain contacts with the States concerned in order to promote agreement and assist efforts to achieve a peaceful and accepted settlement in accordance with the provisions and principles in this resolution;

4. *Requests* the Secretary-General to report to the Security Council on the progress of the efforts of the Special Representative as soon as possible.

SOURCE: Security Council Resolutions – 1967, http://www.un.org/documents/sc/res/1967/scres67.htm.

exchanging land for peace appealed to large segments of the Israeli leadership, there were powerful arguments in favor of keeping the Israeli-controlled territories. The first of these concerned the tremendous boost to Israel's security provided by the West Bank, Sinai, and Golan Heights. The IDF's control of these territories vastly increased Israel's strategic depth, making the relatively small state much easier to defend and assuring that any future war with its Arab neighbors likely would be fought on these territories rather than in Israeli population centers. The totality of Israel's victory also left little incentive for the Israeli government to enter into negotiations with the surrounding states, especially in light of bellicose rhetoric flowing out of Damascus and Cairo. Indeed, in the years following the war, the IDF appeared to be a virtually invincible military force in the region. Vocal segments of Israeli society, which became increasingly powerful constituencies in Israeli politics, also called for the annexation of the Arab lands, particularly the holy city of Jerusalem and large parts of the West Bank. In June 1967, and in the years following the 1967 war, state-supported Israeli groups (with tacit U.S. support), sometimes violently, began settlement activity on lands won in that conflict.

No Signs of Peace

The immediate aftermath of the 1967 war was thus a highly promising yet paradoxical opportunity for peace. The necessary elements for a peace settlement seemed to have been created by the war—namely, the land-for-peace formula, dramatic proof of Israel's ability to defend itself, and the sustained attention of the superpowers and the United Nations. However, none of the major players was yet ready to enter into serious peace negotiations. The scope of Israel's victory had the effect of reducing Israel's willingness to negotiate and forcing the humiliated governments in Cairo and Damascus to search for a means to regain a measure of prestige before they could engage in the peace process. Israeli control of the West Bank, and to a lesser degree of Gaza, helped generate a powerful new force of opposition in the PLO (which refused to recognize Israel), and calls within Israel itself for the annexation of Arab territory. Finally, the Johnson administration remained distracted by the unfolding crisis in Southeast Asia while the Soviet Union rushed to rearm its allies in the Arab world. By the time Johnson left the White House in early 1969, it was clear that the next president would have to deal with the conflict in the Middle East.

As the momentum toward a settlement stalled, fighting between Egypt and Israel was renewed in a series of clashes that came to be known as the War of Attrition. Hoping to whip up superpower interest in the region and jumpstart the diplomatic process, Egypt began launching sporadic artillery barrages against Israeli units in the Sinai, which elicited reprisals from the IDF. These armed attacks escalated in March 1969, as Cairo sought to weaken Israeli defensive positions on the east side of the Suez Canal. Moreover, renewed hostilities led both sides to seek additional arms from their respective superpower patrons, the United States and Soviet Union.[6]

NIXON, KISSINGER, AND THE ROGERS PLAN

Although they were interested in making progress in the Arab-Israeli peace process, Richard M. Nixon and his national security adviser, Henry Kissinger, did not place the Middle East at the top of their list of foreign policy priorities. The incoming administration was instead focused on finding some way to end the war in Vietnam that fell short of a full-scale U.S. defeat and, as time would show, transforming Washington's relationship with Moscow and Beijing. For this reason, the president delegated authority for the region to Secretary of State William Rogers, who would oversee the Middle East, while Nixon and Kissinger concentrated on Vietnam, China, and the Soviet Union. Thus, Rogers would take the lead in Middle Eastern affairs during Nixon's first years in office.

The Rogers Plan

In December 1969, Secretary Rogers and the U.S. State Department presented a scheme to implement peace negotiations in the Arab-Israeli conflict using UN Resolution 242 as its basic blueprint. The Rogers Plan was a reflection of the Nixon administration's stated goal of taking a more balanced approach to the Arab-Israeli conflict. This scheme would entail placing pressure both on the Arab states and Israel to accept the land for peace formula and added efforts to persuade Israel to arrive at a just settlement of the question of Palestinian refugees. The Rogers Plan's end result would be a return, for the most part, to pre-1967 borders, the likely repatriation of substantial numbers of Palestinian refugees, and the potential for the creation of a Palestinian state on the West Bank.

Golda Meir's Position

When visiting Washington, Israel's new prime minister, Golda Meir (1969–1974), had insisted that her government would never accept a land-for-peace formula that might result in the creation of a Palestinian state, which she and

In late 1973, U.S. Secretary of State Henry Kissinger met with Israeli Prime Minister Golda Meir (center), shortly after the Yom Kippur War. Kissinger's shuttle diplomacy during the mid-1970s led to several bilateral agreements between Israel and its Arab neighbors, which culminated in the 1979 peace treaty between Egypt and Israel. Nonetheless, many problems in the region remain unresolved, particularly the status of the Palestinians.

SOURCE: Israel Sun Ltd.

others argued would threaten Israeli security. After reading the Rogers Plan, she announced defiantly, "Nobody in the world can make us accept it. . . . We didn't survive three wars in order to commit suicide." Israel's supporters in the United States also mobilized to oppose Rogers's efforts. By February 1970, as historian Douglas Little notes, 70 senators and 280 members of the House of Representatives had come out against the plan and in favor of increasing arms sales to Israel.[7]

Torpedoing the Rogers Plan

As congressional opposition mounted, tensions within the Nixon administration dealt the final blow to the Rogers Plan. While Rogers concentrated on moving Israel and its neighbors toward UN 242, Nixon and Kissinger remained focused on Washington's global priorities, particularly the conflict in Vietnam and its relationship with the Soviet Union. Both men were prone to exaggerate Soviet influence in the developing world and thus came to believe that the road toward peace in the Middle East, and Southeast Asia, ran through Moscow. By linking progress in regions of the developing world to shifting relationships between the Great Powers, Kissinger and Nixon hoped to achieve diplomatic victories on multiple fronts. This approach clashed with the Rogers Plan and the Jarring Mission, which concentrated on regional, rather than global, dynamics.

Kissinger also rejected the land-for-peace formula, arguing instead in favor of standstill diplomacy. In his eyes, Washington had no reason to pressure Israel to enter into negotiations with its Arab neighbors. Rather, the United States should work to strengthen its ally, thereby reinforcing Israel's negotiating position. Because Israel held all the cards, Kissinger argued, it had the ability to dictate its terms to the surrounding Arab states. Given enough time, he insisted, Syria and Egypt would realize that their patron, the Soviet Union, could do nothing to bring Israel to the negotiating table. As they came to recognize their predicament, the Arab powers would conclude that the only means of regaining their lost territory lay in cooperation with the United States, which in turn could exert some pressure on the Jewish state. In this way, Kissinger argued, standstill diplomacy could undermine Soviet influence in the Arab world. Thus it was in Washington's best interest to undermine progress toward the realization of UN 242.[8]

The Rogers-Kissinger Split

These policy differences contributed to the growing rivalry that had broken out between Rogers and Kissinger. Although Nixon had delegated authority over Middle Eastern affairs to Rogers and the State Department, Kissinger moved to exert influence over the region as well. The combination of policy differences, Kissinger's large ego, and his desire to control all aspects of the administration's foreign policy led him to undermine Rogers's efforts. The Rogers-Kissinger split was apparent to the Israeli government as well, further undercutting the muscle of the Rogers Plan. In September 1969, Nixon established a "special channel between Kissinger and [Israeli Ambassador Yitzhak Rabin] to sidestep the State Department." Three months later, as Rogers prepared to announce his plan for peace, Nixon passed a message to Rabin, explaining that the United States did not plan to enforce the provisions of the plan, giving Israel no particular reason to deal with Rogers. Nixon and Kissinger had effectively torpedoed the Rogers Plan.[9]

Stalemate and the Road to 1973

Nixon's and Kissinger's destruction of the Rogers Plan and the failure of the Jarring Mission to make substantial progress toward the implementation of UN 242 ensured that an uneasy stalemate would remain for the foreseeable future. As their desperation mounted, various Arab figures struggled for some change to the status quo. Egypt's War of Attrition had failed to achieve significant military or diplomatic gains. Meanwhile, various guerrilla groups in the PLO continued their attacks against Israel from bases in Jordan and Lebanon. The PLO was fast gaining support on the world stage and, in the next several years, would gain the endorsement of the UN General Assembly, the Organization of African Unity, and the Non-Aligned Movement, in addition to continued backing from many socialist states. While a majority of governments in the international community supported the Palestinians, Israel and the United States (and many of its allies) labeled the PLO a "terrorist" organization, citing its violent attacks against civilians, and refused to

recognize the group. This debate over whether the PLO and other militants were "freedom fighters" or "terrorists" remained a contentious one well into the next century. Historically who represents a "terrorist" and who represents a "liberation fighter" has been more a question of individuals' and governments' perspectives rather than a technical definition. In this case, all major combatants in the Arab-Israeli conflict have called their opponents "terrorists" and have been labeled as "terrorists" by those same opponents.

As they gained influence, however, Palestinian fighters became increasingly dangerous threats to their host governments. At the same time, damaging Israeli reprisals embarrassed the regimes in Beirut and Amman and led to calls for these governments to reassert their authority. Under these pressures, Jordan's King Hussein launched a large-scale crackdown on PLO guerrillas in September 1970. The battle between Jordanian security forces and Palestinian guerrillas threatened to erupt into another regional war when Syrian units crossed into Jordan before being withdrawn in response to threats of Israeli intervention. While King Hussein remained in power, the crisis in Jordan would have repercussions throughout the region. Perhaps the most notable casualty of the war in Jordan was Egypt's President Nasser, who died from a heart attack in the wake of his efforts to bring an end to the conflict. He would be succeeded by Anwar Sadat. The crisis in Jordan also helped Syria's Hafiz al-Assad (in power 1971–2000) maneuver to gain control over the regime in Damascus. Although its forces were crushed by King Hussein's army, the PLO regrouped in Lebanon and began launching external guerrilla operations, which would turn Western Europe into a battleground between Palestinian fighters and Israeli intelligence in the coming years.

The most notorious incident occurred in September 1972, when a splinter group named Black September launched an attack on the Israeli team at the Munich Olympic Games. This resulted in the violent deaths of eleven Israeli athletes, one West German police officer, and five Palestinian gunmen. The reaction in the White House was one of shock and anger. A furious Richard Nixon told Henry Kissinger that the attackers "want to make it appear that they've stopped the games." Like the United States, many voices in the world community insisted that the massacre confirmed accusations that the PLO was nothing more than a terrorist organization; however, the incident also drew global attention to the plight of the Palestinians. Moreover, Israeli reprisals against Palestinian refugee camps, which killed dozens of civilians, generated a resolution condemning Israeli actions in the UN Security Council. Angry that the resolution made no mention of the Munich massacre, the United States exercised a lone veto for the first time in its history. The divide between the supporters of Palestinian "freedom fighters" and the opponents of Palestinian "terrorists" could not have been more clear.

PUBLIC PORTRAIT: *ANWAR SADAT (1918–1981)*

Anwar Sadat was born in a small village in the Nile Delta, one of thirteen siblings in a poor family. He attended the Royal Military Academy in Cairo and enlisted in the army, where he met Gamal Abdel Nasser and joined the clandestine Free Officers Movement. The movement was composed of a number of junior military officers who were upset by the incompetence and corruption of their superiors and King Farouk (reigned 1936–1952) in Egypt. On July 23, 1952, the Free Officers staged a coup, in which they overthrew the monarchy and established a revolutionary republic. It was here that Sadat first gained prominence as the voice of the Free Officers on Egypt's radio networks.

Under Nasser's presidency, Sadat occupied a number of senior positions. He was vice president when Nasser died unexpectedly in 1970, leaving Sadat as the immediate successor to the executive office. Few observers expected Sadat to remain in power for long. The new president, who had not been one of Nasser's more prominent subordinates, faced powerful challengers, particularly from the left. Sadat surprised his critics, however, when he managed to consolidate his regime by launching a purge of Nasserists in the Egyptian government and announcing a corrective revolution.

As part of this move to establish his new regime, Sadat initiated a new push for peace in the Arab-Israeli conflict. He was desperate to regain control of the Sinai, which had been lost in the 1967 war, both to secure the peninsula's oil wells and to erase the humiliation of defeat from the war. Sadat's diplomatic overtures made little headway with Israel and the United States, however, and he concluded that more drastic measures would be necessary. In June 1972, Sadat made the shocking move of expelling some twenty thousand Soviet military advisers stationed in Egypt, Moscow's largest foreign military mission. This expulsion appears to have served several purposes: a message to the Soviets that Cairo was dissatisfied with limited arms shipments, a tactical maneuver to clear the way for another war in the region, and a diplomatic overture to the

United States and Israel. In this last respect, Sadat's move failed, as neither the United States nor Israel seized this opportunity to renew serious diplomatic efforts with Egypt.

Thus, Sadat concluded that the only way to break the diplomatic deadlock that had set in over the Arab-Israeli conflict was to start another war. On October 6, 1973—Yom Kippur, the holiest day in Judaism—Egypt and Syria launched a coordinated attack on Israeli positions across the Suez Canal and the Golan Heights, respectively. Although Israel would ultimately prevail on the battlefield, the war proved to be a diplomatic success for Sadat. In the wake of the 1973 war, a new round began in the peace process, which culminated in the Sinai II Agreement, the Camp David Accords, and, ultimately, the Egypt-Israel Peace Treaty. Sadat was instrumental in the process, which also had the effect of pulling Egypt away from the Soviet sphere of influence and bringing the largest nation in the Arab world into alignment with the United States.

At the same time that Sadat was engineering this revolution in Egypt's foreign policy, he was transforming the political and economic system at home. Sadat's *Infitah* reversed many of the goals of Nasser's Arab Socialism, opening the Egyptian economy to massive private investment from both domestic and foreign parties. This introduction of capitalist mechanisms into the economy proved highly controversial, however, especially among the millions of Egypt's poor. Indeed, under Sadat's new economic system, the already substantial rift between the wealthy elite and impoverished Egyptians would grow much wider. This combination of economic dislocation, anger over Sadat's decision to make peace with Israel, and long-suppressed religious strife burst forth on October 6, 1981. As he presided over a parade commemorating the 1973 war, Sadat was assassinated by a small group of Islamic radicals with distant ties to the Muslim Brotherhood. His successor, Hosni Mubarak, would rule Egypt until being ousted by massive popular protests in 2011.

While the Palestinian attacks grabbed U.S. and international headlines, the new leaders in Egypt and Syria laid plans to liquidate the after-effects of the 1967 war. In Cairo, Anwar Sadat faced an urgent need to consolidate his power and establish his legitimacy over a state in the midst of economic and political turmoil. In particular, Sadat was desperate to find some means of regaining the Sinai and its oil reserves and reopening the Suez Canal. He first attempted to achieve these goals through diplomacy, accepting UN 242. The Israeli government rebuffed his approaches, however, and Sadat turned to military means to address what had become a diplomatic stalemate. A central component of this military approach entailed a massive transfer of weapons from the Soviet Union. The Soviet-Egyptian relationship was deteriorating, however, and Sadat tried one even more dramatic diplomatic gambit. In July 1972, Sadat expelled approximately twenty thousand Soviet military advisers from Egypt in a desperate effort to curry favor with the United States. Nixon and Kissinger failed to reciprocate,

however, instead concluding that Kissinger's standstill diplomacy was working.[10]

Roots of the 1973 War

With this stalemate firmly in place, the necessary elements for a new war in the Middle East had been established. Sadat and Syrian President Hafiz al-Assad had already begun preparations for a surprise attack on Israeli positions in the Sinai and the Golan Heights. Sadat's goal was not to destroy Israel, nor was it to regain territory lost during the 1967 war. Rather, he intended to use the war to restart the peace process. Though they were aware of Egyptian and Syrian military maneuvers, U.S. and Israeli officials dismissed the warning signs, rejecting the notion that Sadat and Assad would attack a militarily preponderant Israel.

Thus, on October 6, 1973, when Egyptian units staged a dramatic crossing of the Suez Canal and Syrian forces attacked Israeli positions in the Golan Heights, Israel and the United States were caught off guard. The timing of the attack on Yom Kippur, the holy Jewish Day of Atonement, added to the surprise. Egyptian and Syrian forces achieved initial success. In the Sinai, Egyptian troops used bridging equipment and water cannons to breach IDF defenses along the canal, the vaunted Bar-Lev line, and break through to the eastern bank. Once across, Egyptian units attacked Israeli tanks with shoulder-launched missiles while remaining under the protective umbrella of surface-to-air missiles, which held off Israeli airstrikes. Meanwhile, in the north, Syrian units strained IDF defensive lines on the Golan and began pushing Israeli forces back. While Assad was intent on reclaiming the Golan Heights, Sadat adopted a defensive position along the canal. He had achieved his diplomatic goal of destroying the myth of Israeli invincibility and elected to keep his forces under the protection of Egyptian anti-aircraft missiles and refrain from engaging in the type of mobile warfare in the Sinai that would benefit Israel.[11]

The IDF launched its counteroffensive on October 8 and quickly managed to reverse the tide of the war. Nonetheless, Egyptian and Syrian forces put up a considerably stronger resistance than in previous wars. Both the United States and the Soviet Union were concerned about the prospect of the war escalating into a superpower confrontation and agreed, in principle, to work toward a cease-fire. Each superpower hoped that its clients would gain the upper hand, however. Moscow sought to establish a cease-fire on October 9, assuming that this date would mark the high point of the Arab offensive before Israel would have a chance to push back. Washington, in contrast, sought a later cease-fire that would allow the IDF to regain some of the ground lost in the initial phase of the war.

The Tide of War Turns

Nevertheless, Henry Kissinger was reluctant to provide too much support to Israel for fear of recreating the prewar status quo, whereby the Jewish state would feel little pressure to negotiate with its Arab neighbors. Thus, he stalled on Israeli requests for arms shipments to replace those lost in the initial Arab assault. As David Lesch explains, Kissinger hoped that the war's outcome would be a "partial victory for both sides that would bring about more symmetry in the bargaining situation." Israeli threats to deploy its nuclear arsenal, however, led Washington to institute a massive arms airlift to its ally on October 14. The Soviet Union, meanwhile, channeled a moderate flow of weapons to Damascus with the goal of supporting Syria's efforts to maintain its position in the Golan.[12]

After repeated pleas from Damascus, Sadat renewed his offensive into the Sinai on October 14, leaving behind the protection of Egyptian missile defenses in an attempt to relieve pressure on Syria. This decision would prove disastrous, as the IDF escalated its assault on Egyptian forces on October 15. Over the coming days, the Israelis regained much of the ground lost during the first days of the war and managed to establish a position on the west bank of the canal, cutting off Egyptian troops on the opposite side of the waterway. As the tides of the war turned, Moscow began pushing at the United Nations for a cease-fire in order to prevent the IDF from erasing the Arab gains during the war. The UN Security Council passed Resolution 338, which called for an immediate cease-fire, on October 22. However, Israeli forces, determined to destroy all of Sadat's gains, continued fighting. Desperate to save its most important ally in the region, Moscow threatened to intervene directly if the IDF was not stopped. Henry Kissinger responded by placing U.S. nuclear forces on alert, the highest state of readiness since the 1962 Cuban Missile Crisis, in a condition known as DEFCON 3, thereby generating fears about the war in the Middle East escalating into World War III. Israel finally stopped its offensive on October 25, bringing the war to an end.[13]

Consequences of the War

One of the most far-reaching, and generally unforeseen, consequences of the war came with the mobilization of an oil boycott by the Arab members of the Organization of Petroleum Exporting Companies (OPEC) on October 19, 1973. The move was significant for a number of reasons. Most immediately, it signaled the solidarity of conservative Arab states such as Saudi Arabia with Egypt and Syria, and served as retribution for Washington's perceived one-sided support for Israel, especially in the wake of the Nixon administration's decision to send Israel $2.3 billion in military aid.

More broadly, however, the oil boycott represented the climax in a decades-long story of the Arab states' quest to wrest control over their own natural resources from Western interests. Likewise, it served as a further warning over the West's increasing dependence on Middle Eastern oil and the continuing importance of petroleum as a strategic commodity in global affairs. The embargo would last until March 1974, producing a spike in oil prices around the world and leading to shortages and long lines at gasoline stations. In the longer term, the embargo and OPEC's rising power sparked economic decline during the rest of the decade and into the 1980s, triggered in part by a steady increase in global oil prices.

Meanwhile, the October 1973 war transformed the diplomatic landscape of the Arab-Israeli conflict. Although they had been pushed back by the Israeli counteroffensive, the Arab combatants had fought surprisingly well during the course of the war. The initial Egyptian-Syrian offensive demonstrated not only that Arab regimes could fight but also that they could coordinate their activities against Israel. The war had given both sides, Arab and Israeli, new impetus to enter into serious peace negotiations. For Egypt and Syria, the war restored a measure of the honor lost during the 1967 war. For Israel, the latest conflict demonstrated that Egypt and Syria could once again challenge the Israeli military. Sadat's strategy had been successful. Both sides could claim a measure of victory.

POSTWAR PEACE PROCESS AND SHUTTLE DIPLOMACY

The 1973 war created the diplomatic situation necessary for the land for peace formula to be implemented, but the question of how that formula would be put into place remained unresolved. The situation in Washington remained volatile as the Watergate scandal developed. The struggle between William Rogers and Henry Kissinger had finally come to an end in 1973, when Nixon appointed Kissinger as his secretary of state. That year also witnessed the end of the U.S. war in Vietnam, thus allowing Kissinger to focus on other areas. With the crisis of the October war, Kissinger turned his attention to the Middle East and the Arab-Israeli peace process.

In the wake of the conflict, the United States had moved into an even more central position in the peace process. As a series of UN resolutions critical of Israel in the late 1960s and 1970s suggested, Israel's international isolation had increased, leaving the Jewish state even more dependent on Washington. Likewise, the Arab states had come to recognize what Kissinger had been arguing for some time: the United States, and not the Soviet Union, held the key to breaking the diplomatic deadlock in the Arab-Israeli conflict.

Kissinger recognized that the greater part of international pressure fell on Israel. Already backed by the Soviet Union, Egypt and Syria had won the support of much of Europe, Japan, the developing world, and the United Nations. He was determined to insulate Israel and the negotiating process from this pressure. In doing so, Kissinger would also cut the Soviet Union out, enhancing Washington's position in the Middle East, and work to strengthen the positions of "moderate" regimes in the Arab world that were friendly to the United States, while at the same time weakening those Arab elements that he deemed "radical." Kissinger's end goal would be to give himself a free hand in the negotiating process. In this, William Quandt has observed, "he was remarkably successful."[14]

Alternative Routes to Peace

Another basic question concerned the mechanics of peace negotiations between the Arab states and Israel. On this point, two basic tracks emerged. International opinion favored a large, UN-sponsored peace conference that would include all the major belligerents, along with the two superpowers and the United Nations. This conference would be held in Geneva and aimed at hammering out a comprehensive settlement to the Arab-Israeli conflict. Kissinger favored a different track, however, which focused on bilateral negotiations and agreements between the various belligerents. In his view, the Geneva Conference was likely to be too volatile a forum in which disagreements between any of the many figures could stall or even sink the larger endeavor. In contrast, bilateral negotiations would simplify matters. Moreover, the bilateral approach fed into Kissinger's goals of keeping Moscow out of the negotiations, isolating radical elements in the Arab world, and making Washington the sole power broker in the peace process. Kissinger was prepared to tolerate the proceedings at Geneva, however, because they would give the larger peace process an air of legitimacy in the international community and help to placate the Soviet Union. However, according to Kissinger's plan, the substantive agreements would take place in his bilateral forums. Although Washington would consider the possibility of seeking a comprehensive settlement a number of times in the coming months and years, this bilateral, step-by-step approach would win out.[15]

First Tentative Steps toward Peace

The initial steps in these agreements concerned transforming the cease-fire into the disengagement of Israeli and Arab military forces. Of particular concern was the issue of relieving the Egyptian Third Army, which had been cut off on the eastern bank of the Suez Canal by an Israeli offensive in the final days of the war. Likewise, early negotiations focused on the return of Arab and Israeli POWs. At the same time, Kissinger was working to push the belligerents toward participation at the Geneva Conference, scheduled to begin December 18, 1973. The single most contentious issue in the run-up to Geneva concerned the question of Palestinian participation. Egypt took the lead, supported by much though not the entire Arab world, in pushing for the PLO to be included at the Geneva Conference, pointing out that the Palestinian question lay at the heart of the Arab-Israeli conflict. Indeed, the prospect of a comprehensive peace that did not include the most powerful political force among the Palestinians seemed untenable. Israel made it clear, however, that it would not participate if the PLO were seated. As Nixon and Kissinger pushed Israel to agree to attend, Syria also voiced its reservations about Geneva and the conference was pushed back to December 21. Eventually, the conference did meet for opening remarks with Israel in attendance but without delegations from Syria or the PLO. "A symbol now existed," Quandt explains, "a useful fiction perhaps, and a forum" where further discussions might take place.[16]

Shuttle Diplomacy at Work

The Geneva Conference having convened, Kissinger next set to work on constructing his bilateral framework between

Egypt and Israel. As part of these exchanges, Kissinger undertook his first foray into "shuttle diplomacy," traveling back and forth between Israel and Egypt in January 1974. On January 18, the Egyptians and Israelis met at Kilometer 101 to sign the final disengagement accords, put together by Kissinger, with each side pulling its military forces back from the cease-fire lines. This included Israeli withdrawal from the west bank of the Suez Canal and Egypt's agreeing to reopen the canal so that nonmilitary vessels would be able to bring supplies to Israel.

Kissinger next turned his attention toward disengagement agreements between Syria and Israel. At the end of February, he departed for Damascus, where he met with Syrian President Hafiz al-Assad. The two men established a working relationship, but the negotiations achieved little progress. Assad was driving a harder bargain than Sadat, and he was less inclined to compromise on substantive issues. Furthermore, Kissinger was ultimately less interested in achieving progress on the Syrian front than on the Egyptian, because the latter represented the linchpin of his designs for the region. As negotiations with Syria continued, and after a fair amount of pressure, Washington received the good news that the Arab oil producers would be lifting the embargo against the United States.

Kissinger now adopted a strategy designed to isolate Syria from the rest of the Arab world. If Assad remained obstinate, Kissinger would proceed with bilateral arrangements between Israel and other Arab states, leaving Syria alone in its defiance. In late March, Kissinger flew to the Soviet Union for a meeting with Premier Leonid Brezhnev (in power 1964–1982) in which the secretary of state came under fire for trying to lock Moscow out of the peace process. Soviet leaders argued that the negotiations must be returned to Geneva and that Moscow be included in any further exchanges between Washington and Damascus. Kissinger's shuttle diplomacy continued through the spring of 1974 until the end of May, when he finally managed to establish disengagement agreements between Israel and Syria. Israel would remain in control of much of the Golan Heights, although it would return the provincial capital of Quneitra to Syria, after the controversial decision to destroy most of the city, and allow UN peacekeeping troops into the region to serve as a buffer.[17]

Ford and Sinai II

While Kissinger was busy with his shuttle diplomacy in the Middle East, the Watergate affair was wreaking havoc on the Nixon administration. Richard Nixon resigned in disgrace on August 9, 1974, rather than face impeachment for his role in the scandal. His successor, Gerald R. Ford (1974–1977), would be the only U.S. president to serve without winning election as either a presidential or vice presidential candidate. The new president tended to defer to Kissinger

in matters of foreign policy, and thus the step-by-step process of bilateral negotiations instituted under Nixon, rather than the more ambitious comprehensive settlement envisioned by the Geneva process, continued. Kissinger's goals of insulating Israeli from international pressure, keeping the United States at the center of the peace process, sidelining the Soviet Union, and isolating Syria and the PLO remained in place.

Kissinger's next efforts turned toward the Jordanian-Israeli front. While Jordan and Israel enjoyed relatively good relations compared to those between Israel and its other neighbors, both sides were subject to pressures that dampened prospects for peace. King Hussein was wary of alienating the wider Arab world by appearing too conciliatory toward Israel. Domestic forces inside Israel, particularly those elements that were intent on holding on to the West Bank, pulled the Jewish state away from cooperation with Jordan. Compounding the situation was the matter of the PLO and the West Bank. Prior to 1967, Jordan had controlled the area, and King Hussein maintained his designs on it. The emergence of the PLO, however, presented a challenge both to these claims and the king's authority over the substantial population of Palestinians inside Jordan. Bitter relations between the PLO and Amman since the 1970 crackdown in Jordan made the matter especially sensitive to both groups.

Kissinger and the PLO

Kissinger was loath to grant any sort of recognition to the PLO (the organization threatened both Israel and Jordan and was opposed to UN 242) and reluctant to integrate the Palestinians into an already complicated peace process. As he would explain to his staff, it was "absolutely not in the American interests to surface the Palestinian issue." Instead, he hoped to use King Hussein as the spokesman for the Palestinians in the current peace negotiations with Israel. This was a tall order: King Hussein and the PLO were clearly enemies, the organization was gaining support in the occupied territories and in parts of the international community, and the Palestinian issue had emerged as perhaps the core issue of the Arab-Israeli dispute. Sidelining the PLO would not be as easy as Kissinger hoped. At its meeting in Rabat, Morocco, in late October 1974, the Arab League moved unanimously to name the PLO as the sole legitimate representative of the Palestinian people, rejecting the prospect of having King Hussein or any other non-Palestinian leader speak on behalf of Palestinians. This endorsement was followed in November by a similar move in the UN General Assembly, which culminated in a climactic speech by the PLO's chairman, Yasser Arafat (in power 1969–2004). This diplomatic victory for the PLO dashed Kissinger's hopes of keeping the Palestinian issue out of the post-1973 peace negotiations.[18]

SHIFTS IN FOREIGN POLICY: *TRANSFORMATION IN THE MIDDLE EAST*

The years between the 1967 war and the 1978 Camp David Accords witnessed a transformation in the U.S. position in the Middle East. Following the 1967 war, the United States consummated an already close relationship with Israel, which, according to Douglas Little, in *American Orientalism* (2002), transformed the Jewish state from a diplomatic liability into a strategic asset. In the wake of the 1967 war, Israel emerged as a preponderant military force in the Middle East closely aligned with U.S. Cold War interests in the region. Although it would have remained a powerful player regardless, U.S. aid to Israel—in the form of massive arms shipments and financial packages—helped preserve Israel's position as a regional hegemon. While this support helped to assure that Israel's purported nuclear weapons remained unused, it also decreased the pressure on the Jewish state to resolve its longstanding disputes with Syria, Lebanon, and the Palestinians. Moreover, Washington's support helped to shield Israel from the international outcry over the continued occupation of Arab territories, the ongoing construction of settlements inside them, and the 1982 invasion of Lebanon. Ultimately, the special relationship between the United States and Israel, which caused diplomatic tensions with some of America's allies, and the Palestinian cause in the years following 1967 have been identified by many as a root cause of the perceived "anti-Americanism" in the Middle East.

U.S. INFLUENCE IN THE MIDDLE EAST

These years were also pivotal in the larger history of the Cold War, as they marked the ascendency of U.S. power in the Middle East. A complex set of factors, not the least of which was Henry Kissinger's grand strategy for the region, enabled the United States to supplant the Soviet Union as the most influential superpower in the Arab world. Kissinger's shuttle diplomacy must receive a substantial share of the credit for this transition, as his stated goal was always to increase U.S. influence in the region at the expense of the Soviet position. This victory included a substantial cost, however. Washington's Great Power ascendency in the Middle East would not usher in a period of regional peace, nor would it make the region substantially safer for U.S. interests. To the contrary, Kissinger's success in ratcheting down Soviet influence in the Middle East had the effect of increasing Washington's responsibility for the region's troubles, at least in the eyes of many in the wider world. Whether through its support for authoritarian regimes in places such as Iran and Saudi Arabia, its backing of Israel, or its ongoing opposition to the PLO, the United States government appeared to many as the principal foreign culprit for the region's troubles.

Although Kissinger's diplomacy represented a victory in the U.S.-Soviet rivalry, its impact in the Middle East was more problematic. Kissinger's decision to push bilateral negotiations while undermining Rogers's and Jarring's efforts to reach a comprehensive settlement to the Arab-Israeli conflict grew out of Cold War priorities. If the United States could position itself as sole arbiter of the dispute, it could weaken Soviet influence in the Arab world. In this regard, Kissinger's tactics were effective. However, Kissinger's diplomacy ultimately subordinated the effort to achieve a broad regional peace, a Geneva-type settlement, to Washington's Cold War strategies. The struggle to establish a regional peace that would include all the major players in the conflict took a backseat to Kissinger's attempts to undermine Moscow's standing in the Arab

world. Likewise, the secretary's conviction that bilateral agreements between Israel and its Arab neighbors would be less difficult to achieve than a comprehensive agreement was almost certainly correct. However, bilateral, step-by-step diplomacy decreased the long-run prospects of a comprehensive peace in favor of short-term gains. The ultimate effect of U.S. diplomacy in the Arab-Israeli conflict in the years between 1973 and 1979 was to freeze further progress toward a Geneva-type settlement. Once the bilateral framework for negotiations was established, it proved impossible for Kissinger's successors to dismantle. The removal of Egypt as a belligerent in the Arab conflict with Israel helped to prevent another regional war, but it also lessened the pressure on Israel to come to terms with Syria, Lebanon, and the Palestinians. Rather than executing the land-for-peace formula envisioned in the wake of the 1967 war, Kissinger's shuttle diplomacy split the Arab bloc and undermined the Arab states' bargaining positions with Israel. Perhaps the greatest shortcoming of this diplomacy concerned its failure to address probably the most central issue of the conflict: the fate of the Palestinians. By torpedoing the prospects of a Geneva-style settlement, shuttle diplomacy all but guaranteed that the Palestinian question would be left to be solved by later generations.

A PEACE TREATY BUT NO REGIONAL PEACE

Finally, although another regional war would not take place in the twentieth century, shuttle diplomacy did not usher in a period of peace in the Middle East. In spring 1975, amid Kissinger's efforts to seek an Egyptian-Israeli peace agreement, a civil war erupted in Lebanon. The conflict in Lebanon soon became a battleground in the larger Arab-Israeli conflict, as Syrian, Palestinian, Israeli, and Lebanese forces all joined in the fighting. Israel's invasion of Lebanon and 68-day siege of Beirut in 1982 marked the peak of the violence, which would continue until 1990. The presence of Israeli troops in southern Lebanon would ultimately politicize the Shi'a population of Lebanon, giving rise to the Hezbollah movement. Likewise, only days after the signing of the 1979 Egypt-Israel Peace Treaty in Washington, a national referendum held in Iran turned the once-bulwark of U.S. policy in the Middle East into an Islamic republic, which became one of Washington's most hostile opponents in the region. Two years later, Islamic militants gunned down Anwar Sadat, Egypt's architect of peace with Israel, as he presided over a parade commemorating of the 1973 war. Sadat was succeeded by Hosni Mubarak, who set up an autocratic regime that lasted three decades in the largest state in the Arab world.

Meanwhile, Israel's occupation of the West Bank and Gaza continued into the twenty-first century. While the Israeli government continued to insist on the need for what it considered to be defensible borders, Palestinian anger over the occupation and continued construction of settlements sparked the First and Second Intifadas in 1987 and 2002. The Intifadas amounted to low-level conflicts between heavily armed Israeli soldiers and Palestinian protesters, many of whom pelted Israeli security forces with stones. These tensions ultimately would undermine support for secular organizations like the PLO and aid in the rise of Hamas, which launched a wave of suicide attacks against Israeli population centers. As of 2012, the prospect of a comprehensive peace envisioned in the 1970s still appeared very far away.

New Overtures to Egypt

With his efforts to broker an agreement between Israel and Jordan stalled, Kissinger turned back to the Egyptian front. Sadat was still anxious to regain the Sinai, and he was pressing for further Israeli withdrawals. The Israeli government recognized the value of cementing a more durable pledge against further belligerency with Cairo in hopes of driving a wedge between the Arab states. If Egypt could be taken out of the equation as a potential combatant, Syria would be isolated, and Israel would be assured of not having to fight a war against the combined forces of its two largest and most powerful Arab neighbors in the future. This strategy, endorsed by both Israel and Kissinger, drew harsh criticism from Syria and the Soviet Union. Moscow was still insisting on a return to Geneva and a push for a comprehensive settlement to the Arab-Israeli conflict. Nevertheless, Kissinger's bilateral efforts between Israel and Egypt continued into 1975, now slowed by political groups inside Israel and the United States who opposed a settlement that would require surrendering more territory, a situation that left Kissinger exasperated.[19]

Significant progress in negotiations between Egypt and Israel would not come again until summer 1975, when Yitzhak Rabin's (in office 1974–1977 and 1992–1995) government in Israel began to show signs of wanting to make further concessions contingent on security guarantees from the United States, including an American presence in the Sinai as a buffer and increased arms sales. In return, Israel would pull its forces further back and return Sinai oil fields to Egyptian control. The result of this round of negotiations was the Sinai Interim Agreement, signed in Geneva in early September 1975. Although it received little fanfare at the time, Sinai II, as the agreement came to be known, would transform the Arab-Israeli conflict. At its root, the agreement was a pledge by Egypt and Israel to resolve any future disputes by peaceful means. The agreement established a deepening relationship between Washington and Cairo, which pulled Egypt into alignment with the United States (and away from the Soviet Union), thereby linking the Egyptian state with Israel. Sinai II laid the groundwork for Egypt to join Israel as one of Washington's most important allies in the region, radically changing the face of the region in the larger Cold War rivalry. At the same time, the construction of the U.S.-Egyptian-Israeli partnership left Syria and the PLO isolated. By the time Kissinger's term as secretary of state came to an end, when Ford's loss in the 1976 election to Jimmy Carter (1977–1981) brought the Democrats back into the White House, the basic outlines of the peace process had been drawn.

CARTER AND THE ROAD TO CAMP DAVID

Carter entered office with the intention of carrying on the work of his predecessors in resolving the Arab-Israeli conflict. His two key advisers, Secretary of State Cyrus Vance (in office 1977–1980) and National Security Adviser Zbigniew Brzezinski (1977–1981), pushed for action in 1977. Unlike Kissinger, Vance and Brzezinski both sought to find some means of integrating the Palestinians and the PLO into a comprehensive regional settlement. The obstacle to the inclusion of the PLO remained Israel's refusal to deal with the organization as long as it refused to recognize the Jewish state's right to exist. PLO leaders argued that this recognition represented the best negotiating card they possessed and were thus unwilling to concede it as a precondition for negotiations. Carter and his advisers were convinced, however, that Israel must find some means of dealing with the Palestinians and the PLO. Carter went so far as to call for the creation of a Palestinian "homeland" in March 1977. In another departure, Carter abandoned the obsessive secrecy that had characterized the Kissinger era in an effort to make the peace process more transparent.[20]

The situation in Israel changed dramatically in 1977, however, with the victory of the right-wing Likud Party and the election of Prime Minister Menachem Begin (in office 1977–1983), former leader of the Zionist paramilitary group, the Irgun. This ended the Israeli left's nearly three-decades-long control of the government. In addition to taking a more hawkish stance on national security issues, including a pledge never to deal with the PLO, Begin and Likud spoke out in favor of the construction of settlements on lands conquered in 1967, particularly in the West Bank, which he vowed never to give up. The Israeli government's insistence on such controversial issues complicated Carter's efforts to seek a comprehensive peace.[21]

Sadat Travels to Jerusalem

Meanwhile, in Cairo, President Sadat was still eager to reach some sort of settlement with Israel that would allow his government to focus instead on Egypt's domestic challenges. On November 9, 1977, Sadat shocked observers by declaring his willingness to travel to Jerusalem in search of peace. He made good on this promise on November 19 when he arrived in Jerusalem to meet with Prime Minister Begin and deliver a speech before the Knesset, the Israeli parliament. Despite this dramatic display, Begin and Sadat remained at odds over the issue of the Palestinians and the West Bank. Whereas Begin insisted on retaining control of the area and refused to consider the creation of a Palestinian state, Sadat pushed Israel to admit the Palestinians' right to self-determination. These exchanges soon reached an impasse, however, and momentum toward a comprehensive approach to the peace process stalled. Carter concluded that the only option was to abandon the comprehensive track and shift his focus toward bilateral negotiations between Egypt and Israel. The legacy of Kissinger's diplomacy in the region had won out over

Carter's efforts to seek a comprehensive resolution to the Arab-Israeli conflict.

Negotiations at Camp David

In 1978, Carter convened talks between Sadat and Begin at Camp David in Maryland, which lasted from September 5 through September 17. For nearly two weeks, Sadat and Begin argued over the details of a potential settlement between their two countries and the possibility of a wider peace agreement in the region. The talks came close to collapsing a number of times, as Begin, who arrived with the strongest negotiating position, remained steadfast in the face of Carter's and Sadat's proposals. In the end, Sadat was forced to make the majority of the concessions. The end result was two agreements, the first bilateral, the second comprehensive. The bilateral agreement provided for a phased Israeli withdrawal from the rest of the Sinai, in exchange for the normalization of diplomatic and economic relations between Israel and Egypt. The second agreement outlined a plan for the implementation of a comprehensive settlement to the Arab-Israeli conflict along the lines set out by UN 242. In March 1979, Sadat and Begin signed the Egyptian-Israeli Peace Treaty in accordance with the terms set out in the Camp David Accords, making Egypt the first Arab state to arrive at an official peace with Israel.[22]

Peace between Israel and Egypt

The signing of the peace treaty between Egypt and Israel marked the most dramatic achievement of the peace process of the 1970s. Once the principal Arab belligerent in the conflict, Egypt was now the first of Israel's neighbors to accept peace with the Jewish state. Once Moscow's most important ally in the Middle East, Cairo was now locked into a security partnership with the United States—and, by extension, Israel.

As part of the peace agreements, the United States agreed to aid packages of nearly $3 billion and $2 billion annually to Israel and Egypt, respectively, making the two states the largest and second-largest recipients of U.S. foreign aid. Sadat regained the Sinai, but at a tremendous price. He was now viewed by many in the region as a traitor to the Arab cause in general and the Palestinian people in particular. The bilateral approach to the peace process engineered by Kissinger had separated the largest and most powerful Arab state from the wider Arab world. Once in place, this bilateral approach precluded the efforts of regional players and U.S. leaders to redirect the peace process back toward comprehensive efforts to resolve the regional conflict. With the Egyptian front silent, Israeli forces secured their control of the West Bank, Gaza, and the Golan Heights, where the construction of settlements continued; the Palestinian question remained unresolved; and Syria remained in an official state of war with Israel.

In the coming decade, Israel would launch an invasion of Lebanon, a battle that did not bring the benefits Israel had hoped for; Sadat would be assassinated by Islamic militants; and Iran would emerge as a new force of radical leadership in the Middle East. Kissinger's shuttle diplomacy had achieved its goals of pulling Egypt out of the Arab-Israeli conflict and away from the Soviet Union, but it had not brought peace to the region.

See also: **Chapter 18: Middle East Diplomacy; Chapter 25: Détente; Chapter 38: U.S.-Israeli Relations and the Quest for Peace in the Middle East.**

ENDNOTES

1. Avi Shlaim, *The Iron Wall* (New York: W. W. Norton, 2001), 236, 239–41.
2. Ibid, 242.
3. Douglas Little, *American Orientalism* (Chapel Hill: University of North Carolina Press, 2002), 240.
4. Ibid, 240–41.
5. Ibid, 283–84.
6. Charles Smith, *Palestine and the Arab-Israeli Conflict* (Boston: Bedford St. Martin's, 2001), 309–10.
7. Little, 286.
8. Salim Yaqub, "The Weight of Conquest: Henry Kissinger and the Arab-Israeli Conflict," in *Nixon in the World,* Fredrik Logevall and Andrew Preston, eds. (New York: Oxford University Press, 2008), 227–48.
9. Smith, 312.
10. David Lesch, *The Arab-Israeli Conflict* (New York: Oxford University Press, 2007), 240–41.
11. Smith, 320–21.
12. Lesch, 247–49.
13. Ibid, 249–51.
14. William Quandt, *Peace Process* (Washington, DC: Brookings Institution, 2005), 132.
15. Ibid, 135.
16. Ibid, 138–41.
17. Ibid, 147, 151.
18. Ibid, 157–59.
19. Ibid, 159–64.
20. Ibid, 179–83.
21. Smith, 350.
22. Lesch, 262–64.

FURTHER READING

Golan, Matti. *The Secret Conversations of Henry Kissinger: Step-by-Step Diplomacy in the Middle East.* New York: Quadrangle, 1976.

Hahn, Peter L. *Caught in the Middle East: U.S. Policy toward the Arab-Israeli Conflict, 1945–61.* Chapel Hill: University of North Carolina Press, 2004.

Heikal, Mohamed. *Secret Channels: The Inside Story of Arab-Israeli Peace Negotiations.* New York: HarperCollins, 1996.

Herring, George C. *From Colony to Superpower: U.S. Foreign Relations since 1776.* New York: Oxford University Press, 2008.

Lesch, David. *The Arab-Israeli Conflict: A History.* New York: Oxford University Press, 2007.

Little, Douglas. *American Orientalism: The United States and the Middle East since 1945.* Chapel Hill: University of North Carolina Press, 2002.

Kissinger, Henry. *White House Years.* New York: Little, Brown, 1979.
———. *Years of Upheaval.* New York: Little, Brown, 1982.
———. *Years of Renewal.* New York: Simon & Schuster, 1999.

Quandt, William B. *Peace Process.* Washington, DC: Brookings Institution, 2005.

Shlaim, Avi. *The Iron Wall.* New York: W. W. Norton, 2000.

Smith, Charles D. *Palestine and the Arab-Israeli Conflict.* Boston: Bedford St. Martin's, 2001.

Stein, Kenneth W. *Heroic Diplomacy: Sadat, Kissinger, Carter, Begin and the Quest for Arab-Israeli Peace.* New York: Routledge, 1999.

Stivers, William. *America's Confrontation with Revolutionary Change in the Middle East.* New York: St. Martin's Press, 1986.

United Nations Security Council Resolution 242. Accessed February 8, 2012.http://www.un.org/documents/sc/res/1967/scres67.htm

Yaqub, Salim. "The Weight of Conquest: Henry Kissinger and the Arab Israeli Conflict," in *Nixon and the World,* Frederik Logevall and Andrew Preston, eds. New York: Oxford University Press, 2008.

chapter 27

Rogue States and the Emergence of Terrorist Tactics

by Carol K. Winkler and Andrew D. Barnes

URING THE COLD WAR (1945–1991), U.S. leaders faced challenges to international law and world peace from rogue global actors who, in pursuit of their own ends, engaged in terrorism or supported terrorist groups. Alliances with foreign states served as force multipliers for extremist groups, based on terrorists' needs for funding, weaponry, travel restrictions, training and intelligence. Conversely, states willing to sponsor terrorism gained a low-budget means of extending their influence both at home and abroad, while simultaneously raising the stakes for the United States to pursue its objectives in foreign spheres of influence. At times, rogue states worked together to accomplish their ends, usually through short-lived, variable relationships. Such formal and informal alliances further complicated U.S. decision-making by constraining the available range of options for responding to terrorism.

The Cold War years yield important insights into how U.S. diplomatic history has developed regarding rogue actors. From the end of World War II (1939–1945) to the end of the 1980s, the Soviet Union and, to a lesser extent, China competed with the United States for influence over developing countries for access to resources and expanded regional influence. Less developed countries, and even some groups that had not yet achieved state status, recognized the benefits of terrorist tactics for furthering their own agendas.

ASPIRATIONAL ROGUE STATES

Until the early 1970s, the United States lacked any publicly articulated, overarching policy governing diplomacy with non-state rogue actors who aspired to statehood. Instead, the nation's leaders handled such acts of violence on a case-by-case basis, with limited or no public comment by the chief executive. In instances where the U.S. government decided to comply with, rather than ignore or refuse, terrorists' demands, the United States typically negotiated and made concessions through third parties, such as businesses, U.S. allies, or foreign

governments. Common strategies employed to meet terrorists' demands included ransom payments, safe passage, prisoner releases, and allowances for prosecutions in nations sympathetic to the perpetrators or their cause, with the full arsenal of diplomatic, legal, economic, and military options also available to motivate a change in a rogue actor's behavior. At times, U.S. leaders tilted toward efforts at rapprochement; at others, they inclined toward methods characteristic of the rogue elements themselves.

Status of the PLO

One aspirational rogue state of particular interest to the United States after World War II was the Palestine Liberation Organization (PLO) and its related Muslim splinter groups. The stated goals of the PLO were the liquidation of Israel and the creation of a Palestinian state. Between 1964 and 1967, the PLO established branch offices in "the UAR, Syria, Lebanon, Iraq, Kuwait, Qatar, Libya, Algeria, Morocco, Sudan and Aden."[1] It affiliated with the Popular Front for the Liberation of Palestine, an organization repeatedly active in political airline hijackings and linked with the infamous assassin Carlos the Jackal. The PLO was also involved with the Irish Republican Army (IRA), the Baader-Meinhof gang in West Germany, the Red Brigades in Italy, the Marxist Popular Democratic Front for the Liberation of Palestine, and the Black September Organization in the Middle East, among others.[2] After a splintered collection of fedayeen groups suffered humiliating defeat at the hands of Jordan in 1970, many of the more established groups fighting for the Palestinian cause coalesced under the new leadership of Yasser Arafat (in power 1964–2004) and the PLO. With subsequent funding and military assistance from Iraq, Libya, and the Soviet Union, the new PLO grew into an organized consortium of militant non-state actors in opposition to U.S. strategic goals around the globe.[3]

Under Arafat's chairmanship, the PLO sought to improve its diplomatic standing within the international

KEY CONCEPTS

Rogue states and terrorist tactics. At moments throughout U.S. history, the nation's leaders have labeled nations that repeatedly reject international law and threaten world peace as "rogue nations." Such nations typically rely on established patterns of terrorist behavior, such as skyjackings, hostage taking, bombings, assassinations, kidnappings, and torture, to accomplish their political objectives. However, no consensus exists on what behaviors qualify as "rogue" or "terrorist." Both terms have flexible meanings that have expanded and contracted over time in the service of U.S. foreign policy goals. During the years of the Cold War, the nation's leaders increasingly recognized and relied upon the terms' adaptable applications to warrant the use of their powers as commanders in chief in the face of an American public reluctance to use military force. Further, the interpretation of who qualifies as a rogue nation is context-dependent, as nations that U.S. leaders consider to be clearly meeting the definition simply do not qualify from the perspective of other international actors.

State sponsors of terror. After the United States experienced the lengthy embarrassment of having its embassy personnel held in Tehran during the Iranian hostage crisis (1979–1981), the U.S. Congress passed a law empowering the secretary of state to maintain a list of "state sponsors of terror." The legislation's goal was to facilitate and standardize the economic and diplomatic response options available for use against rogue states. Foreign state actions qualifying as state sponsorship of terror included, but were not limited to, "logistical aid, provision of weapons and/or training, granting of safe-havens, use of diplomatic pouches and/or documentation, and—in some cases—actual targeting (sic) and/or provision of information about the selected target."

community. One of its primary strategies for accomplishing that goal was to dissociate itself publicly from militant splinter groups using violence to further the Palestinian cause. On March 1, 1973, for example, eight members of the Black September Organization kidnapped U.S. Ambassador to Sudan Cleo Allen Noel Jr., U.S. Charge d'Affaires George Curtis Moore, Belgian Charge d'Affaires Guy Eid, and several others during a farewell reception honoring Moore at the Saudi Arabian Embassy in Khartoum. The kidnappers demanded America's release of Robert F. Kennedy assassin Sirhan Sirhan, Jordan's release of Black September Organization leader Abu Daoud and his sixteen other imprisoned colleagues, and Germany's release of members of the Baader-Meinhof gang.[4] After President Richard M. Nixon (1969–1974) announced that the United States would not "pay blackmail"[5] to obtain the hostages' release, the perpetrators received the code word to kill via radio broadcast and executed Noel, Moore, and Eid.[6]

Despite Yasser Arafat's insistence that the PLO was not involved in the events at Khartoum, U.S. intelligence concluded, "The Khartoum operation was planned and carried out with the full knowledge and personal approval of Yasser Arafat, Chairman of the Palestine Liberation Organization (PLO), and the head of the Fatah. Fatah representatives based in Khartoum participated in the attack, using a Fatah vehicle to transport the terrorists to the Saudi Arabian Embassy."[7] The linkages to Fatah further implicated Arafat, as he was one of the two original co-founders of that group in the late 1950s.

The response of the Nixon administration to the Khartoum kidnappings signaled a substantial shift in U.S. policy toward rogue actors using terrorist tactics. Borrowing from the Israeli government's response to the Black September Organization's earlier kidnapping and murdering of nine Israeli athletes at the 1972 Munich Olympic Games, Nixon adopted a general policy of no negotiation/no concessions with terrorists. Nixon publicly announced his new approach, known to only a select few members of his executive branch beforehand, at a ceremony honoring the memories of Noel and Moore. He defended his actions as a necessary step to stop future terrorists from becoming emboldened by the success of their predecessors.[8] Future U.S. presidents publicly adopted Nixon's approach and reaffirmed the nation's commitment to no negotiations with or concessions to terrorists.[9]

Despite U.S. findings of Arafat's culpability in the Khartoum kidnappings, the PLO chairman's campaign to normalize relations with the international community flourished. In 1976, the PLO opened its first office in Moscow. In 1979, Arafat conducted official visits to Spain and Turkey. By 1980, India, France, Britain, and Italy had all accepted formal relations with the PLO, and Arafat addressed the UNESCO General Conference in Belgrade. With its new international standing, the PLO was positioned to conduct operations throughout much of the world without formal impediments common to rogue organizations. Throughout the 1970s and into the 1980s, the PLO provided training, supplies, and military armaments to revolutionary causes worldwide. Operating as a force projection for the Soviet Union, and at times in collaboration with Cuba, the PLO's rogue activities went beyond the Middle East to El Salvador, Guatemala, and Nicaragua.[10]

SHIFTS IN FOREIGN POLICY: *RESPONDING TO ROGUE STATES*

The emergence of modern-day rogue states' use of terrorist tactics dates back in many ways to 1947, when the British signaled their intent to end their mandate over Palestine, established with U.S. consent in the 1924 Balfour Declaration. Left to decide Palestine's fate, the United Nations decided to divide the area into an Arab and a Jewish state, prompting the Arab delegation to walk out of the General Assembly in protest. With only one day remaining before the British mandate expired, the Jews declared the existence of the independent state of Israel on May 14, 1948. Within minutes, President Harry S. Truman declared *de facto* recognition of the new state. America's ongoing support for Israel's continued existence would motivate Arab states and groups alike to engage in terrorist tactics in the coming decades.

The Truman Doctrine, outlined to the U.S. Congress in 1947 and followed by the Marshall Plan signed into law a year later, obligated the United States to help free states around the globe respond to rogue states or groups using terrorist methods. In an effort to contain the Soviet Union and foster "economic stability and orderly political processes" of weakened states in the aftermath of World War II, Truman first implemented the doctrine by asking Congress for economic and financial aid to Greece and Turkey. He explained, "I believe that it must be the policy of the United States to support free people who are resisting attempted subjugation by armed minorities or by outside pressures." The Marshall Plan specifically offered economic aid to European countries and was designed "[t]o promote world peace and the general welfare, national interest, and foreign policy of the United States through economic, financial, and other measures necessary to the maintenance of conditions abroad in which free institutions may survive and consistent with the maintenance of the strength and the stability of the United States." (From the Department of State Briefing Paper: Central America. February 1, 1983. "Briefing Book, Ambassador Kirkpatrick Visit to Central and South America, February 3–12, 1983." Box 90500, Files of Jacqueline Tillman. Ronald Reagan Library.)

Over the course of the next three decades, the U.S. passed legislation that leveraged export and commerce controls in an effort to minimize the terrorist activities of rogue states. The Export Administration Act of 1949 initially imposed strict controls on the export of goods and dual-use technologies that had military applications. The act, however, was amended from 1969 through the mid-1980s to loosen export restrictions that fostered America's trade interests. The Antihijacking Act of 1974 empowered the U.S. secretaries of transportation and state to alter bilateral air transportation agreements with nations that failed to appropriately respond to U.S. notifications of inadequate security conditions. The Foreign Assistance Act of 1961, as amended in 1976, required the president to terminate foreign aid assistance for one year to governments that committed acts of international terrorism, except in cases where national security interests dictated otherwise. The International Security Assistance Act of 1977 required the president to terminate arms sales to foreign countries engaged with terrorists, again with the national security exception. Despite the apparent force of these policies, U.S. presidents routinely invoked their discretion to avoid implementing the law's requirements.

Recognizing the need to correct the rift between the legislative intent to create successful counterterrorism policy and executive authority, Congress passed the Fenwick Amendment to the 1979 Export Administration Act. The act empowered the U.S. secretary of state to create a list of state sponsors of terrorism that had established patterns of assisting terrorists. It also required the executive branch to report back to Congress any sale of goods or technology over $7 million that would contribute to the other nation's military logistics or capability to help facilitate acts of international terrorism. The 1979 act provided latitude to the executive branch to choose whether to impose export controls based on assessments of whether the resulting controls would achieve the administration's intended foreign policy goals, would adversely impact America's economic standing, would likely be offset by the actions of other nations, or would be counterbalanced by negative results.

During the 1980s, both international and national legal frameworks placed increasing pressure on states that sponsored terrorism. In 1983, the UN passed the International Convention Against the Taking of Hostages, which expanded state powers to secure their citizens' release, created information exchanges to prevent terrorism, established foreign state jurisdiction over hostage situations, and instituted broader extradition powers. Soon thereafter, Congress passed the 1985 Terrorist Protection Act, which elevated terrorism to a federal crime and codified joint jurisdiction over terrorist crimes, previously the sole province of the foreign state's sovereignty. The new legal context removed national boundaries as a major obstacle to the apprehension and prosecution of those engaged in terrorist tactics.

When Ronald Reagan signed NSDD 138 on April 3, 1984, he expanded U.S. policy from a focus on prosecution of terrorist actors to one designed to prevent terrorist acts aided by state sponsors. Supplied with a significant expansion of funding to implement the new initiative, National Security Adviser Robert McFarlane notified Attorney General Edwin Meese (in office 1985–1988) that NSDD 138's "[b]asic purpose in view of increasingly heavy involvement of states in terrorism is to shift policy focus from passive to active defense measures. . . ." Reagan's directive authorized preemptive raids, assassinations of lower-level state officials and suspected guerrillas, and sabotage particularly in North Korea, Iran, Syria, Libya, Cuba, Nicaragua, and the Soviet Union. While the CIA and Defense Department carried out the preemptive raids, Reagan's directive instructed the Department of State "to intensify efforts to achieve cooperation of other governments," "to develop the full range of overt options to deal with terrorism," and "to accelerate defensive measures for personnel and facilities overseas including those of alerts, training, etc." The State Department, with the assistance of the Justice Department, was also "to present any legislation needed." After the first year of the directive's implementation, Vice President George Bush claimed success in a letter to President Reagan. He noted that American deaths from terrorism had dropped from thirty-eight to twelve, and that "working unilaterally or with other friendly nations, the United States had taken preemptive action in several hundred instances to stop possible terrorist acts against Americans and American interests."

DIPLOMATIC STRATEGIES OF ROGUE STATES

During the years of the Cold War, the United States considered North Korea, Iran, Iraq, Libya, Syria, and Cuba to be rogue states based on their usage and/or sponsorship of terrorist tactics. U.S. responses varied based on geopolitical considerations, available resources, allies' reactions, and outcome evaluations of how foreign leaders reacted to previous diplomatic strategies.

North Korea

The United States and Soviet Union divided the Korean peninsula along the 38th parallel at the end of World War II. The split resulted in competing alliances between the Republic of Korea (ROK) (with the United States), and the Democratic People's Republic of Korea (DPRK) (with the Soviet Union). These alliances continued after the Korean War (1950–1953), because although the two Korean governments reached an armistice agreement, they had not signed a formal peace treaty. Mounting tensions, continued hostile acts, the geopolitical significance in a bipolar world, and the operations of the Soviet navy prompted the United States to seek out more information about the Soviet Union's and North Korea's intentions. The United States ordered the USS *Pueblo* to set sail from Yokosuka, Japan, on January 9, 1968. It was tasked to travel along the North Korean coast gathering intelligence on Soviet naval movements and to detect submarine activity.[11]

North Korean naval forces seized the *Pueblo* and its eighty-three crew members during patrols on January 23, 1968. The North Koreans towed the ship to Wonsan and moved the crew to secure facilities, where they were subjected to severe torture and inhumane treatment during their captivity.[12] The crew's seizure was baffling to U.S. military and intelligence officials, who considered the *Pueblo*'s mission both legal and routine. As Admiral Moorer testified before the House Committee on Armed Services, "It so happens that this was the first mission for the *Pueblo*, but it was not the first mission of this type. As I have stated, the *Banner* had already performed 16 missions of this type."[13] President Lyndon B. Johnson (1963–1969) appointed Major General Gilbert Woodward to lead the U.S. team in the negotiations with DPRK Major General Chung Kuk Pak. The talks began on January 24, 1968.

Claiming the *Pueblo* was operating in territorial rather than international waters, Pak laid out three demands. Known over time as the "three A's," Pak insisted (1) the United States must admit that the USS *Pueblo* had violated national sovereignty by traveling inside North Korea's territorial waters, (2) the United States must apologize for acts of aggression against the peaceful nation of North Korea, and (3) the United States must offer assurances that it would not again engage in militarily aggressive tactics.[14] The United States did not admit guilt and publicly denied violating the DPRK's territorial waters, although in private some reservations persisted about the location of the *Pueblo* prior to the seizure.[15]

While the hostages remained in captivity, the United States considered military retaliation. The *Pueblo* seizure, however, took place within the broader context of the Vietnam War (1945–1975), where North Korea was supplying the Communist north. With limited forces in place in Vietnam, the Johnson administration considered activating reserves so that it could divert troops to Korea.[16] The Central Intelligence Agency (CIA) calculated that the goal of the Kim Il Sung (in power 1948–1994) regime was "to maintain pressure on the United States during the current Communist offensive in South Vietnam."[17] The perceived futility of military options to achieve the hostages' release, rather than concerns about diversion, proved the motivating factor for the U.S. decision to engage the North Koreans diplomatically.[18] For almost a year, diplomacy faltered despite U.S. proposals for compromise.[19] Nevertheless, a memo from Under Secretary of State Nicholas Katzenbach laid out the negotiating posture that eventually broke the stalemate. It stated, "We can . . . sign their document, prefacing our signature with an explanatory statement and repudiating the document as soon as the crew are free."[20] This message was presented to Pak, and he agreed to the release if Woodward signed the document. Any declaration prior to or after the release was of no consequence to him.[21] On December 23, 1968, Woodward stood before television cameras and stated, "The position of the United States Government . . . has been that the ship was not engaged in illegal activity, that there is no convincing evidence that the ship at any time intruded into the territorial waters claimed by North Korea, and that we could not apologize for actions which we did not believe took place . . . I will sign the document to free the crew and only to free the crew."[22]

Less than five months after the *Pueblo* crew's return, the North Korean regime took issue with another United States intelligence mission. An EC-121 was on a routine intelligence mission that maneuvered within eleven miles of the coast of North Korea.[23] Ninety nautical miles off the coast, the United States lost contact with the plane, which had been shot down after North Korea scrambled two MIG fighter jets.[24] Like the Johnson administration earlier, the Nixon administration considered Vietnam its primary interest in the region. Again, the United States could not afford to divert troops or risk becoming engaged in a second war.[25] A proportional military response was not readily available.[26] Secret negotiations to end the Vietnam War hampered diplomatic solutions.[27] U.S. National Security Adviser Henry Kissinger (in office 1969–1975) advocated filing a complaint at the UN while taking no other action.[28] Nixon agreed, announcing, "I have today ordered that these flights be continued. They will be protected. This is not a threat; it is simply a statement of fact."[29]

Iran

After World War II, the United States considered Iran, with its direct access to Middle Eastern oil, a necessary ally to help sustain the economies of Western Europe and the United States. To help ensure that the United States enjoyed favorable relations with Iran, a CIA coup in August 1953 replaced the democratically elected leader of Iran, Dr. Mohammad Mosaddeq (in office 1951–1953), with Shah Muhammad Reza Pahlavi (in power 1941–1979) as the Iranian president.[30] Having underestimated Iran's domestic political turmoil and the salience of anti-American messages inside Iran, the U.S. government was surprised when a revolution succeeded in toppling the shah and installing Ayatollah Ruhollah Khomeini (in office 1979–1989) as supreme leader.[31] The failure to foresee the Iranian transition in leadership resulted from the abundant confidence the United States had in both its ability to influence internal politics in Iran and the shah's ability to maintain control of the Iranian population.[32]

On November 4, 1979, a revolutionary student group laid siege to the U.S. embassy in Tehran, after the Carter administration had allowed the shah into the United States for medical treatment, a move perceived by many Iranians as a precursor to the shah's return to power. Inspired when Ahmed Khomeini, the ayatollah's son, scaled the compound wall to join them in their success, the students assumed control of the embassy property and held its staff hostage. The Jimmy Carter administration (1977–1981) was initially reassured by the Iranian government that the seizure was nothing more than a brief university sit-in. The release of the embassy personnel actually occurred four hundred and forty-four days after the hostage crisis began, just hours after the inauguration of Ronald Reagan (1981–1989) as president.

When the Iranians' early refusal to release the hostages became clear, the Carter team implemented unilateral measures designed to bring quick pressure on the regime in Tehran. The administration froze all Iranian assets in U.S. financial institutions and encouraged European banks to follow America's lead. It also deported Iranian students studying in American universities.

At the same time, the United States began to pursue bilateral negotiations through intermediaries. By mid-November of 1979, the PLO secured the release of thirteen female and black hostages. On November 10, the head of the Roman Catholic Church, Pope John Paul II (reigned 1978–2005), sent an emissary to pressure Khomeini for the release of the hostages.[33] Algeria worked as a key third-party mediator in the early stages of the crisis.[34] Reported through the Algerian mediator, the Carter administration accepted a list of demands presented by Iranian negotiator Abol Hassan Bani-Sadr in a speech on November 12. His demands

included that the United States unfreeze Iranian assets, return assets of the shah, and offer a security assurance that the United States would not intervene in Iran's affairs.[35] The two sides came tantalizingly close to a deal when the United States accepted each of the demands on the condition that the Iranians were willing to frame the demands in more dignified terms for the United States. A telegram sent to the Swiss ambassador declared that the United States was willing to unfreeze state assets held in U.S. and European banks, to provide a legal framework whereby Iranian citizens could petition U.S. courts for assets of the shah, to rescind U.S. economic sanctions on Iran, and to consider a possible renewal of arms sales.[36]

Just as the negotiating teams were set to conclude their task, the Iranians replaced chief negotiator Bani-Sadr with Sadeq Gotzbedah. Neither the Khomeini regime nor the Iranian Revolutionary Council offered an explanation for the switch. Gotzbedah took a much harder line than his predecessor, claiming, "There's no room for negotiation at present."[37] Frustrated with the lack of results, the Carter administration increased international pressure on Khomeini to release the hostages in December 1979. The Carter team pushed through a UN resolution denouncing the detention of U.S. diplomatic personnel and sought a legal claim against Iran in the International Court of Justice. Neither approach produced tangible results. By April 1980, Carter escalated the unilateral measures by declaring an embargo on any goods, including oil, coming from Iran, and by making exports of U.S. goods to Iran illegal.

The Soviet invasion of Afghanistan in December 1979 created new challenges for the United States as it coped with the hostage crisis. A March 1980 assessment presented to the National Security Council, titled "Building Up Our Deterrent Capabilities," described why the United States had to prevent Soviet expansion into Iran: "The effect of Soviet control of those [Persian Gulf] resources, either through overt military action or by internal subversion or political intimidation, would destroy the free-market economies and dissolve our alliances in Europe and in East Asia."[38] Another internal assessment, "Foreign Policy: Coherence in the Sense of Direction," concluded, "The stakes are so great . . . that it is strategically imperative the U.S. orchestrate a credible response with our Allies and to the extent feasible the nations of the region" to reject the Soviet advances.[39] The same memo concluded that Iran played a central role in the regional stability necessary to check the Soviet Union and provide European allies with the oil necessary to sustain their economies.

The strategic context presented by Iran in light of the Soviet invasion of Afghanistan caused the Carter administration to recalibrate. In February 1980, White House Chief of Staff Hamilton Jordan (in office 1979–1980) noted in a memo to President Carter, "Our objective continues to be to get the hostages out safely at the earliest possible date without having to take risks that are unacceptable. If anything,

In the early morning of October 23, 1983, the Eighth Marines Headquarters building in Beirut, Lebanon, was destroyed by a terrorist-driven truck laden with explosives. The resulting explosion and the collapse of the building killed 241 American troops, many still asleep in their bunks. The Americans had been sent to Lebanon at the request of the Lebanese government in summer 1982 to establish a peacekeeping force in the conflict between warring Muslim and Christian factions.

SOURCE: Philippe Bouchon/AFP/Getty Images.

our objective has been modified since the Afghanistan invasion to include, 'and in a way that does not jeopardize the possibility of a reconciliation of U.S.-Iranian relations.'"[40] The Hamilton memo concluded that a rescue mission had the best chance of demonstrating resolve to the Soviets yet not threatening enough as a military action to destabilize relations with the Iranian government.[41] Carter followed Jordan's advice and rejected military options in favor of a rescue mission and continued diplomacy. Ultimately, Carter aborted the rescue mission after the five helicopters reached their target but fell below the minimum needed to successfully complete the mission. As those helicopters then left to return home, eight U.S. servicemen died in a midair collision between a fixed wing C-130 and a RH-53D helicopter.[42]

In the mid-1980s, the United States and Iran became involved in another set of high-profile negotiations during the Iran-Contra affair. The scandal broke on November 3, 1986, when the Lebanese newspaper *Al Shiraa* reported that U.S. National Security Adviser Robert McFarlane (in office 1983–1985) had attended a secret meeting in Tehran to negotiate an arms sale to Iran. The Reagan administration had sold TOW and Hawk missile parts to Iran through Israel from August 1985 to November 1986 in an effort to obtain the release of more than a dozen U.S. hostages held in Lebanon's Becca Valley. Members of Hezbollah had previously taken the hostages to deter a U.S. military counterstrike for the 1983 suicide bombing of the U.S. Marine

barracks in Lebanon. Independent Counsel Lawrence Walsh concluded that the Reagan administration had violated U.S. arms embargoes and diverted profits from Iranian arms sales to help support the Contras, who were fighting the socialist Sandinistas for control of Nicaragua. [43]

Initially, the Reagan administration negotiated the arms sales with Iranian arms merchant Manucher Ghorbanifar, but shifted to former Iranian President Hashemi Rafsanjani's nephew as a second channel. [44] While Reagan admitted by early December that "mistakes were made" in his policies' implementation, he insisted he had not intended "to do business with Khomeini, to trade weapons for hostages, nor to undercut our policy of antiterrorism."[45] However, as Walsh explained in *Iran Contra: The Final Report,* "On December 5, 1985, President Reagan signed the finding requested by the CIA that: (1) stated the CIA's activities were part of an authorized effort to secure the release of American hostages in exchange for shipments of weapons, (2) directed the Congress not be notified, and (3) retroactively sought to approve the CIA activities already completed."[46] During the months of the Iran-Contra affair, three American hostages were released, three others were captured, and two were killed.

Iraq

With the ascendancy of the Ba'ath Party after both the 1958 and 1968 coups, Iraq fortified relations with the Soviet Union to counterbalance U.S. influence in the Middle

East.[47] An early sign of Iraq's shift away from the United States occurred in 1959, when it withdrew from the Baghdad Pact, a joint defense agreement between Turkey, Pakistan, Iran, and Great Britain. In 1955, Secretary of State John Foster Dulles (in office 1953–1959) had helped create the Pact to complement the North Atlantic Treaty Organization (NATO) and the Southeast Asia Treaty Organization (SEATO) in the Middle East.[48] Further strains with the United States became evident in 1972, when Iraq and the Soviet Union signed a Treaty of Friendship and Cooperation permitting Iraq to purchase arms and technical assistance.

In 1979, Ba'ath Party member Saddam Hussein (in office 1979–2003) became Iraq's president. That same year, Iraq officially appeared on the U.S. list of state sponsors of terrorists. The rationale for including Iraq involved its pattern of association with Hamas and the Palestinian Islamic Jihad, two terrorist groups that planned attacks targeting the Arab world, the United States, and Israel during the 1970s. Another major factor for Iraq's inclusion stemmed from its involvement with the Abu Nidal group, a radical, violent Palestinian guerrilla organization led by PLO's representative in Baghdad, Sabri al-Banna. Iraq provided safe haven and funding to the Abu Nidal group, which, in turn, served as a front organization for Iraq.[49]

Having lost its key regional ally as the Iranian hostage situation persisted, the United States had moved to strengthen relations with Iraq in the late 1970s and early 1980s. The State Department under Carter in 1977 and Reagan in 1981 sent diplomatic envoys to Iraq. Saddam Hussein's subsequent demand that Abu Nidal leave his country, his public disavowal of terrorism, and Secretary of State Alexander Haig's (in office 1981–1982) assurance that Iraq had shown "a greater sense of concern about the behavior of Soviet imperialism in the Middle East area" convinced the Reagan administration to remove Iraq from its list of state sponsors of terror.[50] The removal occurred despite the administration's knowledge that Abu Nidal's group remained in Iraq and was continuing its terrorist operations. The Reagan administration concluded that the goal of moderating the Iraqi regime superseded the potential benefits from imposing sanctions from the Export Administration Act.[51] By 1984, the United States granted Iraq full diplomatic privileges.

With the removal of export controls and expanded bilateral contacts, economic relations between the United States and Iraq flourished during the 1980s. The GSM-102/103 programs, administered by the Commodity Credit Corporation of the U.S. Department of Agriculture, approved approximately $4.6 billion in credit guarantees to cover U.S. commodity sales to Iraq.[52] By the late 1980s, the United States imported one-fourth of Iraq's oil, supplied 30 percent of Iraq's agricultural needs, and provided billions of dollars of contracts bolstering U.S.-Iraq

trade relations.[53] After illegal lending practices between BNL and Iraq surfaced, the administration of George H. W. Bush (1989–1993) terminated the bank's participation but continued to authorize $500 million in new credit guarantees in 1990.[54]

Stronger ties between the United States and Iraq also emerged in relation to Iraq's military program during the Iran-Iraq War (1980–1988). With the Soviet Union arming both sides of the conflict, the United States initially adopted a neutral stance. Over time, however, the posture of the United States tilted in favor of Iraq to win the war. To facilitate that end, the CIA provided intelligence on Iranian troop positions to the Iraqis, the State Department permitted lax enforcement of U.S. bans of third-party weapon sales to Iraq, and the Commerce Department sold Iraq helicopters, dual-use technologies, and biological and viral agents.[55]

At various points throughout the 1980s, events threatened but did not break the newly formed bilateral U.S.-Iraqi relations. When Israel bombed Iraq's nuclear reactor in 1981, Vice President George Bush publicly condemned the act as "not in keeping with international standards."[56] After an Iraqi missile struck the USS *Stark* and killed thirty-seven American servicemen protecting oil tankers in the gulf in 1987, the United States accepted Iraq's apology and offer of compensation.[57] When the U.S. Congress responded to Iraq's use of mustard gas and nerve toxins to kill more than five thousand Kurds by considering a bill to impose economic sanctions, the White House intervened to dilute the bill's strong language. Instead, the United States responded by substantially expanding licenses to sell dual-use technology to Iraq.[58] In October 1989, President George H. W. Bush signed NSD 26, which continued the policy of cooperative engagement, authorized U.S. firms to participate in the rebuilding of Iraq after the Iran-Iraq War, and allowed sales of non-lethal military assistance. The rationale for the policy was: "Normal relations between the United States and Iraq would serve longer-term interests and promote stability in both the Gulf and the Middle East."[59]

Iraq's August 2, 1990, military attack upon and continuing occupation of Kuwait fundamentally altered the diplomatic relations between the two countries. Assured in the months preceding the incursion by both a U.S. congressional delegation and U.S. Ambassador April Glaspie (in office 1988–1990) of America's intention to continue building stronger relations with Iraq, Saddam Hussein miscalculated the U.S. reaction to his move on Kuwait. The Bush administration led the effort to have the UN pass twelve resolutions that called for Iraq's withdrawal from Kuwait, rebuked Iraqi actions, and outlined the response measures open to the international community. The Bush team rejected extensions of economic sanctions amid concerns that time aided Iraq and could break the international coalition to remove Iraq from Kuwait.[60] The administration publicly spurned a proposal by the Soviet Union to grant concessions to Iraq in exchange for an agreement to leave Kuwait prior to the onset of military operations. In a final effort to convince the Iraqi regime that coalition forces would not tolerate continued occupation, Secretary of State James Baker (in office 1989–1992) met with Iraqi Foreign Minister Tariq Aziz (in office 1983–1991) on January 9, 1991. Invoking the earlier U.S. policy of no negotiation/no concessions with terrorists, President Bush narrowly framed Baker's actions at that meeting in Geneva as "not to negotiate, but to communicate."[61] Military operations against Iraq began January 16, 1991.

Libya

With the acquiescence of the Allied forces in the aftermath of World War II, King Idris al-Sanusi (reigned 1951–1969) declared that Libya was an independent nation in 1951. During the years of the Sanusi monarchy (1951–1969), Libya was a close U.S. ally based on the nations' mutual needs. The United States wanted to locate Wheelus Airbase in Libya to facilitate its Cold War operations against the Soviet Union, and to have U.S. oil companies gain access to Libyan territory for oil exploration and development. Libya needed the base lease payments to undergird its new economy and wanted the technical expertise of U.S. oil companies to help discover and develop its oil reserves. A bilateral agreement gave the U.S. rights to the base until 1970, in exchange for military, technical, and economic assistance. The two nations' mutual strategic relationship resulted in the United States investing $100 million in Libya by 1959, making the new nation the largest recipient of U.S. foreign aid.[62]

Muammar el-Qaddafi's rise to power after the 1969 bloodless coup against King Idris prompted important changes in U.S.-Libyan relations in the early 1970s. Qaddafi chose to capitalize on Libya's 1955 Petroleum Law, which was written to favor local interests through short leases and land restrictions. The United States accepted the repeated price hikes and turned Libya into its second-highest Arab exporter of oil.[63] The United States even passively accepted Qaddafi's early support of revolutionary groups, by

PUBLIC PORTRAIT: *MUAMMAR EL-QADDAFI (1942–2011)*

Born in Surt to Bedouin parents who, along with sixty other family members, herded livestock in the Libyan deserts, Muammar el-Qaddafi rose to power after the September 1, 1969, military coup in Libya. Denied the former regime's requisite certificate for a university education, Qaddafi entered the Military Academy, rose to the level of captain, and became chairman of the Revolutionary Command Council within one week after the bloodless revolution transferred power away from the Sanusi monarchy. Four months after Qaddafi took power, nine other military officers raised in middle class families from less prestigious tribes than those of the former monarchy joined the Revolutionary Command Council.

Driven by the humiliating defeat of the joint Arab military to the Israelis in the 1967 Six-Day War, Qaddafi embraced a populist philosophy built on the principles of freedom, socialism, and unity. In general line with the views of Egyptian President Gamal Abdel Nasser (in office 1956–1970), he sought to liberate individuals from ignorance, poverty, and injustice, to free Libya from external imperialistic forces, and to revive and strengthen the Arab world. He viewed religion and nationalism, rather than economic factors, as the foundational elements of his nation's future. Consequently, he condemned both Soviet communism's embrace of atheism and what he considered to be the United States' imperialist tendencies. In his *Green Book*, Qaddafi described his alternative philosophy to Marxism and capitalism, which he called the Third Universal Theory. The book outlined governing guidelines designed to facilitate citizen empowerment free from interference by political parties or other intermediaries.

After assuming power, Qaddafi moved quickly to realize national independence for the Libyan people. He negotiated with Great Britain and the United States to remove their respective military bases from Libya, an outcome he accomplished less than a year after the revolution. He increased revenue by increasing oil prices and nationalizing Libyan oil companies. He announced a Libyan stance of neutrality between the Soviet Union and the United States, as he worked to gain advantage with both nations.

For Qaddafi, the unresolved Palestinian situation was a core concern, both because it served as a key cause of the Arab world's decline and as a critical impetus to bind disparate Arab factions together toward pan-Arabism. In an attempt to expel Israel from Palestine, Qaddafi provided financial and other material support to the non-Marxist Al Fatah segment of the Palestine Liberation Organization and tied Libya's "bilateral relations with other states to their position on the Palestinian issue...." In an effort to counterbalance the stronger Israeli military force, he helped train and arm the Palestinian Revolutionary Movement, before eventually breaking away and joining forces with Egypt and Syria to form the United Arab Republic.

Libya's oil reserves provided Qaddafi with substantial revenues (estimated at $24 billion in 2000) to accomplish his objectives. As Libya's oil-related income increased in the 1970s and 1980s, Qaddafi increased his support for revolutionary movements around the globe, including in the Middle East, sub-Saharan Africa, Latin America, the Caribbean, and South and Southeast Asia, with resistance from the Reagan administration in the 1980s. In 2011, protesters confronted Qaddafi and called for his overthrow, which resulted in a civil war. The United States and NATO supported the rebels, bombing Tripoli and other Qaddafi strongholds. Qaddafi, who refused to resign, went into hiding, but he was captured and killed by rebel forces on October 20, 2011.

interceding to block Israeli plans to counterstrike and abandoning U.S. proposals to provide assistance to standing regimes.[64] In short, concern for the several thousand Americans living in Libya and protection of the flow of Libyan oil prompted the United States to initially adopt a conciliatory posture.

Further strains occurred in the mid to late 1970s. By 1973, Qaddafi had nationalized 51 percent of its American oil companies and was repeatedly urging Arab producers to use oil as a weapon against the United States. He opposed many U.S. plans for Arab-Israeli settlements, leading up to his public disavowal of the 1978 Camp David Accords.[65] After the United States blocked a 1973 delivery of C-130 transport planes, Qaddafi responded by purchasing approximately $12 billion of tanks and other modern military weapons from the Soviet Union.[66] The size of the purchases raised fears that Qaddafi was either currently or would soon begin arming revolutionary groups around the globe. The United States responded by prohibiting the sale of all military equipment to Qaddafi's regime and including Libya on the U.S. 1979 list of state sponsors of terrorism. When two thousand Libyans protested and burned the U.S. embassy in response to Khomeini's call for Muslim solidarity after the 1979 Iranian embassy seizure, the Libyan government did little to protect American diplomats.

By the 1980s, diplomatic relations between the two countries worsened to the point of virtually severing altogether. In May 1980, the United States closed its embassy in Tripoli after Libya had detained two U.S. nationals in response to attacks on the French embassy.[67] Based on reports that Libya was employing "assassination squads" to eliminate Libyan dissidents both in and outside of the United States, the Reagan administration ordered Libya's Washington embassy closed and its diplomats expelled.[68]

In 1982, the United States placed licensing requirements on exports of American goods shipped to Libya, with the exception of food, medicine, and medical supplies. The United States placed an embargo on Libyan oil and asked its NATO allies to disallow Qaddafi's state visits.[69] Publicly, administration spokespersons subsequently engaged in a campaign to label Qaddafi a terrorist. Reagan referred to Qaddafi as "the mad dog of the Middle East,"[70] and claimed to have evidence that Libya was planning thirty-five future attacks against U.S. citizens.[71] A State Department white paper noted, "The main targets of Libyan terrorist activities have been expatriate Libyan dissidents and leading officials of moderate Arab and African governments."[72] The same white paper accused Libya of links to Middle East radicals such as "the Popular Front for the Liberation of Palestine-General Command, the Fatah dissidents, and the Abu Nidal Group," reported on "a Libyan plot to blow up the American Embassy Club in Khartoum," and catalogued Libya's alleged involvement in political violence in the Arab world, Sub-Saharan Africa, Latin America, the Caribbean, and South and Southeast Asia. The paper concluded with fifty-seven entries catalogued under the heading "Chronology of Libyan Support for Terrorism 1980–85."[73]

After an April 5, 1986, explosion in a West Berlin discotheque left one American serviceman dead and another fifty wounded, administration officials maintained they had decisive proof that Qaddafi had directed the attack. Armed with intercepts between the bombers and the Libyan government both the day before and the day after the attack,[74] U.S. officials pressed European foreign ministers to impose economic sanctions on Libya, to no avail.[75] The following day, the United States conducted a bombing raid on Libya that resulted in the alleged death of Qaddafi's daughter.

On December 21, 1988, Libya responded to the U.S. bombing campaign by exploding a bomb on Pan Am Flight 103 over Lockerbie, Scotland, which killed 259 passengers and crew and eleven 11 bystanders on the ground. Tracing coat fibers from the suitcase bomb back to Libyan security guard Abdel Basset Al-Megrahi, prosecutors obtained a guilty verdict and life sentence from a Scottish court, as well as confirmation of Libyan involvement. U.S. leaders also suspected Syrian and Iranian involvement based on particular aspects of the bomb used in the attack and subsequent confirmation by Iranian defectors.[76] In August 2008, the Libyan government agreed to pay $2.7 billion in restitution to the victims' families in three installments. In exchange, the United States and the UN dropped economic sanctions against Libya and removed Libya from its list of state sponsors of terrorism.

Syria

Immediately after World War II, the Syrian government lacked the internal stability to function as a key diplomatic partner of the United States in the Middle East. In 1949, Syria underwent three military coups and was controlled by six different governments. By 1951, the Truman administration (1945–1953) decided not to sell military equipment to any Arab country bordering Israel (including Syria), based on fears that the potential for a regional arms race would violate its Tripartite Declaration of 1950.[77]

During the administration of Dwight D. Eisenhower (1953–1961), the Syrians gradually shifted to a closer alliance with the Soviet Union. Initially, Syria embraced a policy of neutralism, refusing to participate in a joint Iraq-Turkey military alliance to forestall Communist or Soviet expansion in the region. The 1954 overthrow of the military dictator Adib al-Shiskakli led to civilian elections that instilled a Syrian government that strengthened Soviet-Syrian relations. The Soviets sold Syria arms in October 1956 valued at more than $7 million.[78] On

On December 21, 1988, Pan Am Flight 103 exploded over Lockerbie, Scotland, killing all 259 people on board and eleven on the ground. One hundred seventy-nine of the passengers were Americans. The bombing, the responsibility for which was eventually traced to Libya, shattered America's sense of safety and security, bringing the threat of terrorism from distant rogue states to the forefront.

SOURCE: AP Photo/File.

January 5, 1957, the divide between Syria and the United States widened as President Eisenhower announced "the Eisenhower Doctrine" before the U.S. Congress. Insisting the Soviets had a "desire to dominate the Middle East" and that "The free nations of the Mid East need, and for the most part want, added strength to assure their continued independence," Eisenhower asked legislators to grant him powers to assist Middle Eastern nations with economic development, military assistance, and use of U.S. armed forces to respond to "overt armed aggression from any nation controlled by International Communism."[79] In October 1957, Salah al-Din Al-Bitar complained to the UN about a foiled CIA plot to overthrow the Syrian government.[80] Syria subsequently expelled U.S. Ambassador James S. Moore, and Syrian Ambassador Faris Zain Al-Din went back to Syria.

Another key source of strain between the United States and Syria in the 1960s and 1970s was Syria's relations with Israel. At the conclusion of the 1967 Arab-Israeli war, Israel secured and continued to hold the Golan Heights, a 450-square-mile land tract previously belonging to Syria. When Israel refused Syrian demands for the unconditional, full return of the Golan Heights, Syria unsuccessfully attempted to militarily reclaim it in the 1973 war between Egypt and Israel. By 1974, Syrian President Hafiz al-Asad (in office 1971–2000) abandoned the strategy of using his state's military force against Israel, publicly accepted UN Security Council resolutions 242 and 338, and agreed to a peace process whereby Israel returned the Golan Heights in exchange for a guaranteed peace. Syrian meetings with Henry Kissinger, Cyrus Vance, Zbigniew Brzezinski, and Jimmy Carter resulted in the relaxation of U.S. trade restrictions on Syria. As a recent Congressional Research Service Issue Brief reported, "Since 1950, the United States has provided a total of $627.5 million in aid to Syria: $34 million in development assistance, $438 million in economic support, $155.4 million in food assistance, and $61 thousand in military training assistance. Most of this aid was provided during a brief warming trend in bilateral relations between 1974 and 1979."[81]

Syria's relations with neighboring Lebanon also functioned to test U.S.-Syrian bilateral relations. In 1976, Syria sent between thirty-five thousand and forty thousand military forces into Lebanon as part of an Arab League peacekeeping force in response to the Lebanese civil war. The Ta'if agreement, approved by the Lebanese parliament on November 4, 1989, called for the "[d]isbanding of all Lebanese and non-Lebanese militias" and called on Syria to "not permit any act that poses a threat to Lebanon's security, independence and sovereignty."[82] The Syrian mobilization, however, continued at somewhat reduced levels for three decades and leveraged heightened Syrian influence over Lebanese domestic affairs and regional policies.[83] Articulating U.S. views of Syrian-Lebanese relations after the 1983 suicide bombing of the marine barracks in Lebanon, Assistant to the President Edward Hickey Jr. wrote to White House Chief of Staff James Baker (in office 1981–1985), Deputy Chief of Staff Michael Deaver (in office 1981–1985), and National Security Adviser Robert McFarlane, "Lebanon is key to the balance in the Mideast. It is the buffer between Israel and Syria. If it falls to Syrian/Soviet influence, other Arab states will not take the risks necessary to achieve a settlement with Israel. The Mideast is key to the economic life of NATO—and if that key falls to anti-Western powers, it becomes a key to the politics—as well as the economics—of the West."[84]

Beginning in 1979, the United States placed Syria on its list of state sponsors of terrorism. Robert McFarlane described the rationale for Syrian's inclusion: "Syria and Iran played significant roles in encouraging Middle Eastern terrorism such as the bombing of the [U.S.] Embassy in Beirut carried out by Iranian-supported Lebanese Shi'ite radicals operating from Syrian-controlled territory . . . Damascus has become the home for one of the most dangerous Palestinian terrorist groups, Black June headed by Abu Nidal, who has targeted US, Israeli, Jordanian and UK interests."[85] The United States sharply curtailed access to American exports, but still permitted the foreign nation to buy civilian aircraft.[86] A December 1986 State Department report accused Syria of "support for and direct involvement in international terrorism," based on trial court evidence showing that Syrian intelligence services had provided passports, money, a bomb, and training for how to use the bomb in the aborted April 1986 attack on El Al, the national airline of Israel.[87]

The next key shift in U.S.-Syrian relations took place after Saddam Hussein's 1990 incursion into Kuwait. As the George H. W. Bush administration attempted to persuade Syria to join coalition forces in response to the Iraqi occupation, the U.S. State Department released a public fact sheet denouncing its earlier assumptions of Syrian involvement in the bombing of Pan Am Flight 103. The State Department concluded, "We lack information indicating direct collaboration among Iran, Syria, and Libya, either in sponsoring the PFLP-GC's planned bombings of aircraft or in Libya's bombing of Pan Am 103."[88] Syria subsequently joined the multinational coalition force that ejected Iraq from Kuwait.

Cuba

In the years leading up to President Fulgencio Batista's (in office 1940–1944, 1952–1959) 1959 overthrow by Fidel Castro's 26th of July Movement, Cuba depended on the United States as its primary trading partner.[89] As the Cuban rebellion intensified in early 1958, the Eisenhower administration responded in four ways: it arrested Batista's enemies operating from U.S. ports, embargoed arms shipments to Batista in an effort to remain neutral in the civil war, permitted continued U.S. military presence to advise the Cuban Air Force attacking the rebels, and refueled a Cuban government transport plane tasked to correct a mistaken shipment of small rockets. The combined effect was to "[weaken] the Batista regime while incurring the wrath of the rebels."[90] In a move threatening to Cuba's future leader, former ambassador William Pawley traveled to Cuba on December 9, 1958, to persuade Batista to resign in favor of a military junta unsympathetic to either the Batista or Castro.[91] After

Batista fled and Fidel Castro (in power 1959–2008) assumed power, the United States quickly recognized the Castro government on January 7, 1959.

In hopes of protecting Marxist revolutionary regimes throughout the region, Castro quickly became involved in armed guerrilla violence throughout Latin America. As a U.S. State Department Special Report recalled, "In 1959, Castro aided armed expeditions against Panama, the Dominican Republic, and Haiti. Later, during the early and mid-1960s, Guatemala, Colombia, Venezuela, Peru, and Bolivia all faced serious Cuban-backed attempts to develop guerrilla forces."[92] Cuba's reliance on armed violence rather than the Soviet's preferred doctrine of "peaceful coexistence" placed early strains on Soviet-Cuban bilateral relations.[93]

As Castro began employing anti-U.S. rhetoric and effectuating the resignations of anti-Communist government ministers in late 1959, the United States increased its quotas for Cuban sugar imports in one last effort to strengthen bilateral relations. Cuba's willingness to aid armed expeditions into Panama, the Dominican Republic, and Haiti, growing concerns about Castro's moves to annex holdings of American property owners, his refusal to resolve problems of U.S. firms' expropriations, and his potential impact on "communist nationalist elements elsewhere in Latin America" resulted in the United States assuming "a more openly critical and challenging posture vis-à-vis Cuba. . . ."[94] As the Eisenhower administration implemented each step toward eventual elimination of its sugar quotas, Castro responded by annexing all private land holdings, nationalizing Cuba's petroleum refineries, and signing a five-year pact on February 13, 1960, for loans and sugar quotas with the Soviet Union. The United States instituted partial and full trade embargoes, trained the Cuban exiles in Guatemala who were defeated at the Bay of Pigs in March 1960, and activated assassination plots against Castro.[95]

The Soviets countered by providing Cuba more than $8 million a day in assistance (equivalent to about one-fourth of its gross national product), guaranteeing oil supplies at one-third of the world market price, and making payments for Cuban sugar four to five times higher than the world price.[96] They sent Soviet troops, surface-to-air missiles, and other military equipment to Cuba. After the administration of John F. Kennedy (1961–1963) imposed a naval blockade during the 1962 Cuban Missile Crisis, the Soviet Union agreed to verifiable removal and a future ban on its strategic weapons in Cuba. Castro balked at the Soviet acceptance of U.S. verification and at not being involved in crafting the conflict's resolution, but the Soviets still removed the missiles and the United States did not send its armed forces to overthrow the Castro regime.

By the late 1960s, U.S.-Cuban relations appeared to be improving. National Security Adviser Henry Kissinger informed President Nixon that the Cuban government was willing to help end airline hijackings. Castro agreed to receive some Cubans from the United States and permit hijacked U.S. citizens to return from Cuba, even though the United States had previously rejected a 1961 Cuban request essentially asking for a similar accommodation.[97] Behind the scenes, however, tensions remained as the United States discovered that the Soviets had built the Cienfuegos submarine facility from August 15 to September 15, 1970.[98] In October, the United States and Soviets clarified their 1962 understanding and banned ballistic missiles on submarines operating from Cuban facilities.[99]

In the early years of the Carter administration, the United States attempted a conciliatory foreign policy toward the Cuban government in hopes of normalizing relations between the two countries. In 1977, the United States signed a bilateral fishing agreement, revoked travel restrictions to Cuba for two weeks as a show of good faith, and legalized the purchase of Cuban goods by U.S. citizens. In June 1977, Cuba and the United States agreed to the creation of interest sections, whereby the two countries could establish delegations in the other's country under the auspices of third-country partners. The Carter administration conditioned normalization of relations on "a substantial commitment to the non-interference in the internal affairs of the Western Hemisphere nations, a decrease in its military involvement in Africa, and [a demonstration of Cuba's] commitment to human rights by releasing political prisoners."[100]

The Carter administration's efforts at rapprochement, however, failed to moderate the Cuban regime's support for revolutionary activity around the globe. The Reagan State Department publicly recounted how Castro was using his substantial funding stream from the Soviet Union to unite radical groups, provide training, supply weapons, encourage terrorism and provide military advisers in Nicaragua, El Salvador, Guatemala, Costa Rica, Honduras, Jamaica, Guyana, Grenada, Dominican Republic, Colombia, Chile, Argentina, Uruguay, Angola, and Ethiopia.[101]

Reversing the Carter administration's policies, Reagan reestablished the travel ban and prohibition on American's spending in Cuba. He also failed to renew the bilateral fishing agreement. He responded militarily to the influential Cuban presence in Grenada on October 25, 1983, by overcoming the opposition and installing a provisional government. To help bolster allied nations fighting Cuban troops throughout Central America, the Reagan administration adopted a strategy that included promotion of economic revitalization, democratization, and security support.[102] By 1985, the United States banned all travel by Cuban officials to the United States. The Reagan administration bolstered funding for its Nicaraguan operations through proceeds of its arms sales to Iran, while Cuba secured an agreement with the Soviet Union for $3 billion of continued funding over the next five years.

IN THEIR OWN WORDS: *AMERICAN LEADERS ON ROGUE STATES AND TERRORISM*

I believe that it must be the policy of the United States to support free peoples who are resisting attempted subjugation by armed minorities or by outside pressures.

Harry S. Truman, March 12, 1947

Experience shows that indirect aggression rarely succeeds where there is reasonable security against direct aggression where the government disposes of loyal security forces, and where economic conditions are such as not to make Communism seem an attractive alternative.

Dwight D. Eisenhower, January 5, 1957

... [O]nce the individual, the terrorist, or the others, has a demand that is made, that is satisfied, he then is encouraged to try it again. And that is why the position of your Government has to be one in the interest of preserving life, of not submitting to international blackmail or extortion anyplace in the world.

Richard Nixon, March 6, 1973

If you ask me why these two contradictory statements proved to be the key to effect the release of our men, the North Koreans would have to explain it.... The simple fact is that the men are free and our position on the facts of the case is unchanged.

Secretary of State Dean Rusk, December 23, 1968

Just as the Barbary powers were held responsible for their piratical actions as well as the actions of independent pirates who exploited the permissive environment, the US could bring pressure to bear on state actors to "police" their spheres of influence.

National Security Assistants Don Gregg and Doug Menarchik, September 24, 1985

SOURCES: Available at The American Presidency Project, *Dwight D. Eisenhower, Richard Nixon, and Harry S. Truman* (http://www.presidency.ucsb.edu); the Bush Presidential Library, *Memorandum for the Vice President,* Gregg and Menarchik; *The New York Times,* article on Secretary of State Dean Rusk.

ONGOING CONCERNS

From 1945 to the late 1980s, rogue states relied on terrorist tactics to restore a Palestinian homeland, eliminate Israel, support the revolutionary overthrow of foreign monarchies, protect their own revolutionary regimes, and gain strategic influence through international alliances. The United States responded based on its own interests of containing Soviet influence, securing access to Middle Eastern oil resources, protecting Israel's security, and safeguarding U.S. citizens and property abroad. The use of terrorist tactics by rogue states will remain an ongoing phenomenon that defies any lasting, effective remedy. For some states, the benefits to be gained by terrorist violence outweigh any attendant risks. With political and economic risks of its own, the United States will need to refine and improve its diplomatic approaches to rogue states around the globe.

See also: **Chapter 18: Middle East Diplomacy; Chapter 35: The Global War on Terrorism.**

ENDNOTES

1. Roberta Goren (Jillian Becker, ed.), *The Soviet Union and Terrorism* (London: George Allen and Unwin, 1984), 107.

2. Ibid., 142–83.

3. Ibid., 116, 122.

4. Korn, 104, 128–29.

5. Richard Nixon, "The President's News Conference of March 2, 1973," Public Papers, Document 63, John T. Woolley and Gerhard Peters, *The American Presidency Project* [online], Santa Barbara, CA, accessed on June 9, 2011, at: www.presidency.ucsb.edu/ws/index.php?pid=4123axzz1PH7sRFJv.

6. Korn, 168.

7. The Seizure of the Saudi Arabian Embassy in Khartoum, Intelligence Memorandum, Washington, June 1973, in *Foreign Relations of the United States, 1969–1976, Volume E-6, Documents on Africa, 1973–1976,* Document 217.

8. Richard Nixon, "Remarks at a Ceremony Honoring Slain Foreign Service Officers," March 6, 1973, John T. Woolley and Gerhard Peters, *The American Presidency Project* [online], Santa Barbara, CA, accessed on June 5, 2011, at: http://www.presidency.ucsb.edu/ws/index.php?pid=4132.

9. See: Jimmy Carter, "American Federation of Labor and Congress of Industrial Organizations Remarks at the 13th Constitutional Convention, November 15, 1979"; Ronald Reagan, "Remarks Announcing the Release of the Hostages From Trans World Airlines Hijacking Incident, June 30, 1985," John T. Woolley and Gerhard Peters, *The American Presidency Project* [online], Santa Barbara, CA, accessed on June 9, 2011, at: www.presidency.ucsb.edu/ws/index.php?pid=31691axzz1PH7sRFJv and www.presidency.ucsb.edu/ws/index.php?pid=38841axzz1PH7sRFJv.

10. Goren, 116–17, 175–76.

11. Record of the Pueblo's Orders received by Captain Bucher, in *Inquiry into the U.S.S. Pueblo and EC-121 Plane Incidents,* Report of the Special Subcommittee on the U.S.S. Pueblo, *Committee on Armed Services,* House of Representatives, July 28, 1969, 639–40.

11. The treatment of prisoners is well documented. See: Trevor Armbrister, *A Matter of Accountability: The True Story of the Pueblo Affair* (Guilford, CT: Lyon's Press, 2004); Mitchell Lerner, *The Pueblo Incident: A Spy Ship and the Failure of American Foreign Policy* (Lawrence: University of Kansas Press, 2002).

12. *Committee on Armed Services,* 710.

13. Telegram #103961 from American Embassy Seoul to State Department, January 25, 1968, JL, NSF, country file: Korea, Box 255, Korea cables and memos, vol. 5, tab 9/67–3/68, as cited by Lerner.

14. National Security Archives and Records Administration, RG 59, Central Files 1967–69, POL 33–6 KOR N-US. Secret; Nodis. Drafted by Brown on December 2. See: Person, J (2010). *New Evidence on North Korea,* North Korea International Documentation Project, accessed on June 1, 2011, at: http://www.wilsoncenter.org/topics/pubs/New-Evidence-North-Korea-Reader.pdf (on the location of the Pueblo at the time of seizure, see: *Notes of the President's Lunch Meeting with Senior American Advisors,* 2–3).

15. *Notes of the President's Lunch Meeting with Senior American Advisors,* Special Files Collection, folder, "Tom Johnson's Notes of Meetings. Box 2. January 9, 1968, 1–2, accessed from the Digital National Security Archive, Document Code HN01566.

16. *North Korea Remains Unyielding in Pueblo Crisis,* in Central Intelligence Bulletin, Central Intelligence Agency Electronic Freedom of Information Act Reading Room, February 2, 1968, 1, accessed at the Digital National Security Archives, Document Code HN01584.

17. See *Notes of the President's Lunch Meeting with Senior American Advisors,* 4–5.

18. Instructions for the Twenty-Sixth Meeting, Telegram from the Department of State to the Embassy in Korea, Central Files 1967–69, POL 33–6 KOR N-US, National Archives, Foreign Relations of the United States, Vol. XXIX, accessed on September 27, 2011, at: http://www.state.gov/www/about_state/history/vol_xxix/zh.html.

19. Ibid. Also, James F. Leonard had been working with U.S. negotiators behind the scenes. Flummoxed one night, his wife suggested to him that she saw no harm in signing a document that was clearly understood by the rest of the world to be false. This became known as the "Leonard Proposal." See: Ambrister, *Matter of Accountability;* and Christian F. Ostermann and James F. Person, *Crisis and Confrontation on the Korean Peninsula, 1968-1969: A Critical Oral History,* Woodrow Wilson International Center for Scholars, 50–1, accessed on June 1, 2011 at: www.wilsoncenter.org/topics/pubs/NKIDP_Critical_OralHist_textL.pdf.

20. Summary of the 26 Closed Meeting at Panmunjom, telegram from the Embassy in Korea to the Department of State, Central Files 1967–69, POL 33–6 KOR N-US, National Archives, *Foreign Relations of the United States, Vol. XXIX,* accessed on September 27, 2011, at: http://www.state.gov/www/about_state/history/vol_xxix/zh.html.

21. *Statement Signed at Panmunjom, Rusk's Explanation and McCloskey's Remarks,* in *The New York Times,* December 23, 1968.

22. *NSC Meeting on North Korean Downing of U.S. EC-121 Reconnaissance Aircraft,* National Security Council Institutional

Files, Folder "NSC Minutes Originals 1969," Box 109, National Archives: Richard Nixon Presidential Library and Museum, accessed at the Digital National Security Archives, Document Code KT00018.

23. Kissinger Telephone Conversation Transcripts (Telcons), Chronological Files, Folder "April 15–22, 1969," Box 1, National Archives: Richard Nixon Presidential Library and Museum, accessed at the Digital National Security Archives, Document Code KA00524.

24. *Conversation with Joseph Alsop,* Kissinger Telephone Conversation Transcripts (Telcons), Chronological Files, Folder "April 15–22, 1969," Box 1, National Archives: Richard Nixon Presidential Library and Museum, accessed at the Digital National Security Archives, Document Code KA00525.

25. See NSC Meeting, 1969.

26. *Conversation with Ambassador Yost,* Kissinger Telephone Conversation Transcripts (Telcons), Chronological Files, Folder "April 15–22, 1969," Box 1, National Archives: Richard Nixon Presidential Library and Museum, accessed at the Digital National Security Archives, Document Code KA00522.

27. *Conversation with President Nixon,* Kissinger Telephone Conversation Transcripts (Telcons), Chronological Files, Folder "April 15–22, 1969," Box 1, National Archives: Richard Nixon Presidential Library and Museum, accessed at the Digital National Security Archives, Document Code KA00529.

28. Richard Nixon, "*The President's News Conference, April, 18, 1969,*" Public Papers, Document 156, John T. Woolley and Gerhard Peters, *The American Presidency Project* [online], Santa Barbara, CA, accessed on June 9, 2011, at: http://www.presidency.ucsb.edu/ws/index.php?pid=2004axzz1PH7sRFJv.

29. James Goode, *The United States and Iran, 1946–51: The Diplomacy of Neglect* (New York: St. Martin's Press, 1989), 109.

30. Gary Sick, *All Fall Down: America's Tragic Encounter with Iran,* 1st ed. (New York: Random House, 1985), 3–4. See Russell Moses, *Freeing the Hostages: Reexamining U.S.-Iranian Negotiations and Soviet Policy, 1979–1981* (Pittsburgh, PA: University of Pittsburgh Press, 1966), 5.

31. Sick, 3–4.

32. Ibid., 224.

33. Moses, 297–99.

34. Ibid., 48.

35. Telegram to Ambassador Lang, February 1980, Folder "Iran 2/80," Box 34, Office Files of Hamilton Jordan, Jimmy Carter Presidential Library.

36. Ibid., 52.

37. *Building Up Our Deterrent Capabilities,* Files, Brzezinski collection, Folder "Meetings NSC 293: 325–80," Box 32, Jimmy Carter Presidential Library.

38. *Foreign Policy: Coherence in Sense of Direction,* Files, Brzezinski collection, Folder "Meetings SSC 293: 325–80," Box 32, Jimmy Carter Presidential Library.

39. Hamilton Jordan, *Memo to President Carter* [n.d.], Folder "11/79," Box 34, Office Files of Hamilton Jordan Collection, Jimmy Carter Presidential Library.

40. Ibid.

41. Sick, 297.

42. Lawrence E. Walsh, *Iran-Contra: The Final Report* (New York: Times Books, 1993), xiii–xv.

43. Walsh, 10–24.

44. Ronald Reagan, Radio Address to the Nation on the Iran Arms and Contra Aid Controversy, Dec 6, 1986, *Public Papers of the Presidents,* accessed at: http://www.reagan.utexas.edu/archives/speeches/1986/120686a.htm.

45. Lawrence E. Walsh, *Iran-Contra: The Final Report* (New York: Times Books, 1993), 16.

46. Steven Metz, *Iraq and the Evolution of American Strategy* (Washington, D.C.: Potomac Books, 2008), 3–4.

47. Jones, 306.

48. For a listing of the terrorist acts and those planned for U.S. targets associated with Iraq, and further description of the Abu Nidal group, see Philip Jenkins, *Images of Terror: What We Can and Can't Know About Terrorism* (New York: Aldine de Gruyter, 2003), 169–171.

49. As cited in Barry Rubin, "The United States and Iraq: From Appeasement to War," in *Iraq's Road to War,* Amatzia Baram and Barry Rubin, eds. (New York: St. Martin's Press, 1993), 257.

50. Nancy Berg Dyke, Memo through Admiral Murphy to Vice President, March 25, 1982, Folder "Narco-Terrorism [3 of 5]," OA/ID 19850, Bush Vice Presidential Records, National Security Affairs, George Bush Presidential Library.

51. Banca Nazionale Del Lavoro (BNL), Folder "USDAGSM 102–3 Credits to Iraq," OA/ID 06375, Files of Clair Sechler, Cabinet Affairs, Bush Presidential Records, George Bush Presidential Library.

52. Nafeez Mosaddeq Ahmed, *Behind the War on Terror: Western Secret Strategy and the Struggle for Iraq* (Gabriola Island, BC, Canada: New Society Publishers, 2003), 57.

53. Key Facts on "Iraq gate," Folder "Iraq [1], OA/ID CFO1992," Files of John Schmitz, Counsels Office, Bush Presidential Records, George Bush Presidential Library.

54. Ahmed, 50–56.

55. As quoted in Rubin, 257.

56. Statement by Assistant to the President for Press Relations [Marlin] Fitzwater on the Attack Against the U.S.S. Stark, May 19, 1987, John T. Woolley and Gerhard Peters, *The American Presidency Project* [online], Santa Barbara, CA, available at: http://www.presidency.ucsb.edu/ws/?pid=34294.

57. Ahmed, 55–56.

58. George Herbert Walker Bush, Memo of National Security Directive 26 to the Vice President, the Secretary of State, the Secretary of the Treasury, The Secretary of Defense, the Attorney General, the Secretary of Energy, the Director of the OMB, the Assistant to the President for National Security Affairs, the Director of Central Intelligence, the Chairman of the Joint Chiefs of Staff, The Director of the United States Arms Control and Disarmament Agency, and the Director of the USIA, October 2, 1989, Folder "Working Files-Iraq Pre-8/2/90," OA/ID CF01043 [1 of 6], Richard Haass, Subject File, National Security Council, Bush Presidential Records, George Bush Presidential Library.

59. American Embassy in Riyadh, Telegram to Secretary of State, Examining Our Military Options, October 29, 1990, Folder "Working Files-Iraq, 10/90," OA/ID CF1478 [2 of 6], Richard Haass, Subject File, National Security Council, Bush Presidential Records, George Bush Presidential Library.

60. George H. W. Bush, "The President's News Conference on the Persian Gulf Crisis, January 9, 1991," John T. Woolley and Gerhard Peters, *The American Presidency Project* [online], Santa Barbara, CA, accessed on June 9, 2011, at: http://www.presidency.ucsb.edu/ws/index.php?pid=19202#axzz1PH7sRFJv.

61. Vandewalle, 43–45.

62. Henry Kissinger, *Years of Upheaval* (Boston: Little, Brown, 1982), 860.

63. El Warfully, 65.

64. El Warfully, 89.

65. St. John, 80–81.

66. Salah El Saadany, 148.

67. Terrorist Attacks and U.S.-Libyan Relations [n.d.], Folder "Libya Sensitive 1986, 1 of 7," Box 91668, Files of Howard Teicher, Ronald Reagan Library.

68. Ibid.

69. St. John, 82.

70. Ronald Reagan, "President's News Conference, April, 9, 1986," John T. Woolley and Gerhard Peters, *The American Presidency Project* [online], Santa Barbara, CA, accessed on June 9, 2011, at: http://www.presidency.ucsb.edu/ws/index.php?pid=37105axzz 1PH7sRFJv.

71. Ronald Reagan, "Interview with Foreign Journalists," April 22, 1986, John T. Woolley and Gerhard Peters, *The American Presidency Project* [online], Santa Barbara, CA, accessed on June 9, 2011, at: http://www.presidency.ucsb.edu/ws/index.php?pid=37173 &st=&st1=#axzz1mZAKqFy7.

72. Libya Under Qaddafi: A Pattern of Aggression [n.d.], Folder "Libya Sensitive 1986, 7 of 7," Box 91668, Files of Howard Teicher, Ronald Reagan Library.

73. Ibid.

74. Stanton H. Burnett, Memo to the Director and Deputy Director, April 15, 1986, Folder "Libya: USIA," Box 30, Oliver L. North Files, Ronald Reagan Library.

75. Edward R. Drachman and Alan Shank, *Presidents and Foreign Policy: Countdown to 10 Controversial Decisions* (Albany: State University of New York Press, 1997).

76. For a discussion of Syria and Iran's motives and potential means of involvement, see Jenkins, 11–14.

77. Rami Ginat, *Syria and the Doctrine of Arab Nationalism: From Independence to Dependence* (Brighton, UK: Sussex Academic Press, 2005), 71.

78. Ginat, 166.

79. Dwight D. Eisenhower, "Special Message to the Congress on the Situation in the Middle East, January 5, 1957," John T. Woolley and Gerhard Peters, *The American Presidency Project* [online], Santa Barbara, CA, accessed on June 9, 2011, at: www.presidency .ucsb.edu/ws/index.php?pid=11007#axzz1P0DZeIhR.

80. Salah Bitar, Letter to Secretary-General of the United Nations (Hammarskjold), October 15, 1957, Doc no. 187, in *The Arab States and the Arab League: A Documentary Record, Vol. II: International Affairs*, edited by Muhammad Khalil (Beirut: Khayats, 1962), 342–43.

81. Alfred B. Prados, "Syria: U.S. Relations and Bilateral Issues," in *CRS Issue Brief for Congress*, IB92075, July 27, 2006, 11.

82. The Ta'if Accord, available online at http://www.al-bab .com/arab/docs/lebanon/taif.htm.

83. Alfred B. Prados, "Syria: U.S. Relations and Bilateral Issues," *CRS Issue Brief for Congress*, IB92075, March 13, 2006, 1–3.

84. Edward V. Hickey Jr., Memo to the White House for Baker, Deaver, and McFarlane, October 23, 1983, Folder "Lebanon Bombing/ Airport October 23, 1983," Box 91353, Executive Secretariat, National Security Council: Records: Country File, Ronald Reagan Library.

85. McFarlane, August 15, 1984.

86. Dyke, March 1982.

87. Department of State, Syrian Support for International Terrorism: 1983–86, Special Report No. 157, December 1986, 1.

88. Department of State, The Iranians and the PFLP-GC: Early Suspects in the Pan Am 103 Bombing, November 15, 1990, Folder "Pan Am 103," CF 00703, Press Office/Foreign Affairs, Bush Presidential Records, George Bush Presidential Library.

89. David C. Jordan, *Revolutionary Cuba and the End of the Cold War* (Lanham, MD: University Press of America, 1993), 65–66.

90. Jorge I. Dominguez, *To Make a World Safe for Revolution: Cuba's Foreign Policy* (Cambridge, MA: Harvard University Press, 1989), 11–12.

91. Ibid., 13.

92. Department of State, Cuba's Renewed Support for Violence in Latin America, Special Report No. 90, December 14, 1981, 2.

93. Ibid., 3.

94. Memorandum From the Assistant Secretary of State for Inter-American Affairs (Rubottom) to the Under Secretary of State (Dillion), December 29, 1959, in *Foreign Relations of the United States, 1958–1960, Volume VI, Cuba, Document 414,* available at http://history.state.gov/historicaldocuments/frus1958-60v06/d414.

95. Dominguez, 24–25.

96. Department of State, "Cuba's Renewed Support for Violence in Latin America," Special Report No. 90, December 14, 1981, 2–3.

97. Memorandum from the President's Assistant for National Security Affairs (Kissinger) to President Nixon, Washington, February 7, 1969, in *Foreign Relations of the United States, 1969–1976, Volume E-10, Documents on American Republics, 1969–1972, Document 196.*

98. Minutes of a Meeting of the National Security Council, Washington, September 23, 1970, in *Foreign Relations of the United States, 1969–1976, Volume E-10, Documents on American Republics, 1969–1972, Document 226.*

99. Dominguez, 50.

100. David C. Jordan, *Revolutionary Cuba and the End of the Cold War* (Lanham, MD, University Press of America, 1993), 116.

101. Department of State, "Cuba's Renewed Support for Violence in Latin America," Special Report 90, December 14, 1981.

102. Department of State Briefing Paper: Central America, February 1, 1983, Folder "Briefing Book, Ambassador Kirkpatrick Visit to Central and South America, February 3–12, 1983 [1 of 3]," Box 90500, Files of Jacqueline Tillman, Ronald Reagan Library [9988].

FURTHER READING

Armbrister, Trevor. *A Matter of Accountability: The True Story of the Pueblo Affair.* Guilford, CT: Lyon's Press, 2004.

Dominguez, Jorge I. *To Make a World Safe for Revolution: Cuba's Foreign Policy.* Cambridge, MA: Harvard University Press, 1989.

Goren, Roberta. *The Soviet Union and Terrorism.* Jillian Becker, ed. London: George Allen & Unwin, 1984.

Jenkins, Philip. *Images of Terror: What We Can and Can't Know about Terrorism.* Edison, NJ: Transaction Publishers, 2003.

Korn, David A. *Assassination in Khartoum.* Bloomington: Indiana University Press, 1993.

Lerner, Mitchell B. *The Pueblo Incident: A Spy Ship and the Failure of American Foreign Policy.* Lawrence: University of Kansas Press, 2002.

Metz, Steven. *Iraq and the Evolution of American Strategy.* Washington, DC: Potomac Books, 2008.

Moses, Russell Leigh. *Freeing the Hostages: Reexamining U.S.-Iranian Negotiations and Soviet Policy, 1979–1981.* Pittsburgh, PA: University of Pittsburgh Press, 1966.

El Saadany, Salah. *Egypt and Libya From Inside, 1969–1976: The Qaddafi Revolution and the Eventual Break in Relations, by the Former Egyptian Ambassador to Libya.* Mohamed M. El-Behairy, translator. Jefferson, NC: McFarland & Company, 1994.

Sick, Gary. *All Fall Down: America's Tragic Encounter with Iran.* 1st ed. New York: Random House, 1985.

Vandewalle, Dirk J. *A History of Modern Libya,* Cambridge, UK: Cambridge University Press, 2006.

Walsh, Lawrence E. *Iran-Contra: The Final Report.* New York: Times Books, 1993.

Winkler, Carol K. *In the Name of Terrorism: Presidents on Political Violence in the Post-World War II Era.* Albany: State University of New York Press, 2006.

chapter 28

"Tear Down This Wall"

The Fall of Communism and the Emergence of Eastern Europe

by Gregory Domber

OUTSIDE OF FLASHPOINT moments during the Cold War, such as the Berlin uprising in 1953, the Polish and Hungarian revolutions in 1956, and the Soviet invasion of Czechoslovakia in 1968, interactions with the Communist states of Eastern Europe tended to be seen as a subset of relations with the Soviet Union. Interests driven by superpower competition generally trumped any bilateral concerns for Poland, Hungary, Czechoslovakia, East Germany, Bulgaria, Romania, Albania, and Yugoslavia. With détente's focus on East-West relations in the late 1960s and 1970s, Eastern Europe moved into slightly greater prominence, but the general pattern held: President Jimmy Carter (1977–1981) and President Ronald Reagan (1981–1989) both gave Eastern Europe their full attention during the Polish Crisis of 1980–1982, but Reagan's policy was colored by broader desires to undermine Soviet power around the world. The revolutions of 1989–1990 shattered this context for U.S.–Eastern European relations, with one Communist regime after another failing due to a combination of internal decay, indigenous political opposition, and outside pressure. Following the revolutions of 1989, the administrations of George H. W. Bush (1989–1993) and then Bill Clinton (1993–2001) promoted policies to fully reintegrate the former Communist states into Europe, utilizing multilateral global forums like the International Monetary Fund (IMF), supporting the expansion of the European Union, and, most importantly, reshaping and enlarging the North Atlantic Treaty Organization (NATO) to encompass these emerged states.

The reemergence of Eastern Europe, which reached a symbolic crescendo with the 1989 fall of the Berlin Wall, cannot and should not be seen as a product of American policy. Rather, the Eastern Europeans themselves caused the collapse of communism and the creation of new, vital states in a reintegrated Europe. The United States was not the driving force behind these movements for self-liberation and recreation. Nonetheless, American policies did shape political decisions in Eastern Europe by promoting human rights and political opposition prior to 1989. As the only remaining superpower after 1991, U.S. influence increased, significantly helping expand the architecture of Western institutions eastward to create a stable, prosperous Europe.

DIFFERENTIATION: U.S. FOREIGN POLICY AND EASTERN EUROPE

American policy toward Eastern Europe during the majority of the Cold War was dominated by a policy that came to be known as differentiation. Differentiation emerged after the 1956 Hungarian revolution and went through a number of variations, but it basically called for Washington to reward individual Eastern European nations for demonstrating independence from the Kremlin. This independence was more often exhibited in foreign affairs, by breaking with the Soviets on matters of Warsaw Pact policy (Romania and Yugoslavia had been much more supportive of the reform movement in Czechoslovakia in 1968 than other bloc members), or on reactions to international events (Romania and Yugoslavia remained close with China despite the Sino-Soviet split). Differentiation was meant to create tension within the Soviet bloc and foster a process to move the regimes out from under Soviet dominance. As President Richard M. Nixon (1969–1974) put it, "... we could needle our Moscow friends by arranging more visits to the Eastern Europe countries to remind Moscow that we had options."[1]

The Eastern Europeans focused on the potential economic benefits of closer relations with the United States. Significant growth in heavy industries after World War II (1939–1945) created much more urban and modern states, but consumer goods, the service sector, and housing had been neglected. At times, even food was scarce, and in all cases, the governments heavily subsidized basic needs to keep prices artificially low. To remedy these imbalances during détente, Communist governments found success by turning to Western Europe and then the United States for expanded trade opportunities and imports of American technology and food. Most-favored-nation (MFN) status,

KEY CONCEPTS

Differentiation. The term *differentiation* is often used to describe American foreign policy toward Eastern Europe from the mid-1950s to the fall of the Communist governments in those nations. The policy of differentiation sought to create tension between the Soviet Union and members of the Eastern bloc by rewarding those nations that strayed from the official Soviet line.

which Poland and Yugoslavia already enjoyed, was extended to Romania in 1975 and Hungary in 1978. As a single example of this dynamic period, the Polish regime received new credits for American foodstuffs; created the United States-Poland Trade Commission; signed agreements for cooperative scientific and technological projects, including cooperative research on coal extraction; saw an increase in tourism in both directions; and welcomed new offices in Warsaw for companies such as International Harvester, U.S. Steel, and Westinghouse. In addition, a Holiday Inn was constructed in Krakow, and the regime successfully opened several joint ventures, including, for example, a copper-rolling mill constructed under American supervision. The economic ministries for each bloc country planned to pay for the influx of capital by increased exports to the West, but most countries were not able to balance their trade and came to rely on the Export-Import Bank and loan guarantees to make up the difference. Between 1971 and 1979, Eastern European debt to the United States exploded from $9.3 billion to $68.7 billion, of which Poland owed approximately $20 billion.[2]

Impact of the Helsinki Accords

Another essential focus of détente for Eastern Europeans was the Conference on Security and Cooperation in Europe (CSCE), which culminated in the signing of the Helsinki Final Act on August 1, 1975. In the months after the signing of the Final Act, rights activists in both East and West sprang into action, empowered and provoked by the new public commitments to human rights. Following the publication of the text in the Soviet Union, eleven prominent Soviet dissidents, including Jewish refusenik Anatoly Shcharansky and scientist Yuri Orlov, created the Moscow Helsinki Group to report to the West on Soviet human rights abuses. Similarly, Vaclav Havel and dissidents in Czechoslovakia signed an open letter on January 1, 1977, that catalogued human rights abuses in their country and proclaimed the creation of Charter 77, a grassroots effort to publicize the inconsistencies between Czechoslovak law, its international obligations, and the actual human rights situation. In Poland, longtime members of the opposition created the Workers' Defense Committee (*Komitet Obrony Robotników*, KOR) to provide social services to the families of workers who had lost their jobs following a strike outside Warsaw in 1976. KOR eventually morphed into the Social Self-Defense Committee KOR (KSS-KOR) and took on the larger task of promoting workers' rights generally. KSS-KOR was joined by the Movement for the Defense of Human and Civil Rights, as well as a Polish Helsinki Committee, all of which worked to report human rights abuses.

On Capitol Hill, Congresswoman Millicent Fenwick (R-NJ; in office 1975–1983) founded the Commission on Security and Cooperation in Europe, later chaired by Representative Dante Fascell (D-FL; in office 1955–1993). Members of the Helsinki Commission traveled to Western Europe to meet with other Helsinki signatories to survey reporting. The Americans also took unofficial trips to Eastern Europe and the Soviet Union to meet with well-known dissidents. In Washington, the commission compiled and translated various Eastern European and Soviet *samizdat* publications (censored dissident publications from across the Soviet bloc, which individuals reproduced by hand, or were published in secret locations in small numbers, and then were passed from one reader to another) on human rights abuses to keep the American public aware of what was occurring in the Soviet bloc and to keep political pressure on American politicians to push for change. In the two years after the signing of the final act, as each of these organizations became aware of the existence of the others, a transnational network of Helsinki Watch groups came together, with the American Helsinki Commission a key lynchpin for publicizing the reporting work of dissidents in the East. This transnational network gained traction for their cause at the first CSCE follow-up meeting in Belgrade. The American delegate to the meeting broke diplomatic precedent by naming names, referring to specific human rights abusers and individuals abused, showing that the Carter administration's commitment to human rights was not just rhetorical.[3]

Solidarność in Poland

In August 1980, two concurrent trends in Eastern Europe, faltering economic performance and an increasingly organized opposition, converged to provoke an acute political crisis in Poland, centered initially along the Baltic Coast in the Lenin Shipyards in Gdańsk. As with earlier Polish strikes and crises in 1956, 1970, and 1976, workers initially protested against food price increases meant to rationalize the price system and better reflect the actual costs to the government. Unlike previous strikes, this time the workers included expressly political as well as economic demands in their strike announcement. They also elected Lech Wałęsa (president of Poland, 1990–1995), an electrician who had been fired for political activity, as their head negotiator. Joining with other strikers along the Baltic Coast in an Inter-Factory Strike Committee, the Gdańsk workers laid out a list of twenty-one demands to end their occupation strike, addressing social, economic, and political concerns. Deciding against the use of force, the Polish Communist Party sent negotiators. With a cast of advisers by his side drawn from KSS-KOR and other dissident groups, Wałęsa successfully negotiated and signed the Gdańsk Agreements on August 31, 1980, allowing unprecedented political concessions, including: independent trade unions, the right to strike without reprisals, the right to freedom of expression, pay increases, improved working conditions, Saturdays off, and Sunday Masses broadcast over loudspeakers. The Inter-Factory Strike Committee quickly expanded into a national movement, the Independent Self-Governing Trade Union NSZZ "Solidarność" (referred to as Solidarność, or the English equivalent, Solidarity). The trade union grew to include nearly 9.5 million members, or more than one in four Poles, including members of the Communist Party.

From August 1980 to December 1981, Solidarność focused on consolidating the concessions agreed to in Gdańsk. The process of officially registering the union alone lasted until mid-November 1980. Once officially registered, the union began to push for the economic reforms that had been agreed upon, including work-free Saturdays. Overall, this sixteen-month period involved a precarious tug-of-war between the people and the party to determine Poland's future. Solidarność's main demands remained relatively consistent and included calls to cease attacks on the union, pass a law legalizing independent trade unions, hold elections to national councils, establish an independent council made of government and union

officials to guide economic reforms, and provide Solidarność with media access.[4]

Across the Atlantic, the crisis spanned the final year of the Carter administration and Reagan's first year in office, during which both presidents kept a watchful eye on events. The primary American concern throughout the crisis was a Soviet-led invasion, as had occurred in Hungary in 1956 and Czechoslovakia in 1968 under the auspices of the Brezhnev Doctrine. Therefore, Washington focused most of its public efforts on keeping the events in Poland an internal process without "external interference." Washington closely watched Soviet troop movements and build-ups with spy satellites, looking for any signs of an invasion. When American analysts and politicians feared that an invasion was imminent in both December 1980 and March 1981, they used a full array of diplomatic tools to make sure the Soviets understood the detrimental consequences of invading Poland, including public and private pronouncements in bilateral and multilateral forums explaining the punitive steps the United States would take if the Soviets intervened.

As a secondary policy focus, the Carter and Reagan administrations offered economic "carrots" to the Polish regime if it allowed political liberalization to continue. By the end of 1980, Polish debt to the West, which had risen to about $23 billion, was beginning to come due, weighing down an already weak economy that was experiencing major shortages. The cost of living rose 15 percent in the first six months of 1981, and in July, a 20-percent cut in meat rations was announced. These weaknesses were only exacerbated by the strain of strikes and political instability. The Carter and then Reagan administrations understood that the "fate of Poland's challenge to Soviet hegemony and Communist orthodoxy depended largely on economic forces," so the Reagan White House worked with Congress to stabilize the internal economic conditions by providing concessionary sales of $60 million in grain.[5] In August 1981, the Reagan administration also signed an agreement to delay payment of 90 percent of Poland's debt to the United States for eight years. As late as December 8, the NSC was considering sending a new $740 million aid package, made up mostly of credits for purchasing American grain and food. As explained by a high-level CIA official, American "national security interests are well served by gambling $740 million (or other sums) in credits in the hope that it will allow the Polish experiment to continue and in the knowledge that the experiment's very survival will contribute to the long-term unraveling of the Soviet position in Eastern Europe."[6]

Return of Communist Domination in Poland

The Polish crisis came to an end on the night of December 12, 1981, not with a Soviet invasion but with the head of the Polish United Workers' Party (PZPR), General Wojciech Jaruzelski, solving the problem internally and declaring martial law. Within hours of giving the orders, thousands of Solidarność activists had been rounded up and interned. Within a few days, the entire country had been pacified by the Polish military with minimal bloodshed, and the acute period of political instability ended. The Reagan administration was both shocked and surprised by these events in Warsaw, despite the fact that the United States had been receiving intelligence from a Polish officer who was on the committee charged with planning for martial law. The Reagan administration reacted angrily to the declaration of martial law and condemned the blatant disregard for human rights, invoking Poland's commitments under the Helsinki Final Act.

On December 23, as workers, Polish émigrés, and sympathetic citizens protested around the world, Reagan announced a series of sanctions against the Polish government: halting the renewal of Export-Import Bank insurance credits, suspending all LOT (the Polish national airline) flights to and from the United States, suspending Poland's rights to fish in American waters, and working with NATO to increase restrictions on technology trade with Poland. Lower-level sanctions that were not announced included blocking meetings of the U.S.-Poland Trade Commission and forums to promote scientific and technical cooperation. After Solidarność was officially de-legalized by the courts later in the year, the administration also revoked Poland's MFN status. Each of these sanctions was designed to be reversible if the Polish government met three conditions: end martial law, release all political prisoners, and restart negotiations between the government and representatives of the people (generally understood to include Solidarność and the Catholic Church). Unfortunately, in the first months of 1982, it became increasingly clear that the sanctions would not be immediately successful; Jaruzelski's regime was going to stay the course and turned toward the Soviet bloc for greater economic and political support.

PUBLIC PORTRAIT: *RONALD REAGAN (1911–2004)*

Ronald Reagan's public career consistently centered on advocating a fight against communism. Reagan won the 1980 Republican nomination and the presidency in part by criticizing the policy of détente as a "one-way street that the Soviet Union has used to pursue its own aims," and calling for more resolute relationship with the Soviets that he characterized as "Peace through Strength." In his first term, Reagan expanded the arms buildup begun by Jimmy Carter, increasing defense spending from $1.1 trillion to $1.5 trillion, revitalizing American nuclear forces with Pershing missiles in Europe, completing the B-2 bomber program, and updating American conventional forces to create a more mobile force capable of responding to regional conflicts. He also added a new category to the arms race by proposing the creation of the Strategic Defense Initiative (SDI), a space-based weapon that would serve as a defensive shield able to destroy Soviet ICBMs. Reagan buttressed these spending priorities with a bellicose rhetorical campaign in 1982 and 1983 seemingly rejecting the possibilities of superpower cooperation, going as far as labeling the Soviet Union an "evil empire" and calling on the West to take the offensive to promote democracy.

Reagan's second term, however, struck a very different tone. Aware that his statements had provoked a Soviet war scare in 1983, Reagan toned down his speeches for the 1984 campaign, providing folksy metaphors about the possibilities for constructive superpower dialogue. When Mikhail Gorbachev became Soviet general secretary in 1985, Reagan pursued an active summit agenda with meetings over the next four years in Geneva, Reykjavik, Washington, Moscow, and Governor's Island in New York. Because of a series of candid conversations during these summits, and Reagan's growing trust for Gorbachev, the two were able to move beyond strong disagreements about SDI to eliminate intermediate nuclear forces and create a foundation for later agreements to reduce long-range strategic arms. These agreements were made despite resistance from Congress and within the White House. Most importantly, Reagan left office with superpower cooperation and the normalization of relations at a new high point.

Coming to terms with this redirection in Reagan's policies necessitates moving beyond Reagan's public rhetoric and persona. At his core, Reagan was a nuclear abolitionist, who criticized the immorality of standing nuclear doctrine (MAD) and latched on to the defensive possibilities of SDI because they offered a path, no matter how long, to making nuclear weapons obsolete. In part because of this view, he quietly pursued superpower dialogue through personalized letters sent to each of the Soviet leaders in office during his watch. His intentions only became public when he found a suitable negotiating partner. Finally, like all presidents, Reagan was a product of the advice he was given. As more neo-conservative voices (Secretary of Defense Caspar Weinberger and Director of Central Intelligence William Casey, for example) left the administration, advocates of a more pragmatic approach toward the Soviets (Secretary of State George P. Shultz, Vice President George H. W. Bush) gained sway. Over his two terms, Reagan did not reverse his perspective on communism or the Soviet Union; he redefined his policies to successfully pursue core priorities. Ultimately, Reagan's policies shaped the international environment at the end of the 1980s, which allowed Eastern European leaders to move toward reform and provoke the collapse of the Communist systems in Eastern Europe and the Soviet Union.

THE REAGAN ADMINISTRATION RESPONDS

Throughout his public career as a spokesman for General Electric, governor of California, and then candidate for the presidency, Reagan distinguished himself as a staunch anticommunist and a critic of détente, which he thought had given too many concessions to the Soviets without seeing a corresponding change in their actions. For Reagan, the declaration of martial law presented a chance to intensify a battle against communism in general. As Reagan noted in his diary, "This may be the last chance in our lifetime to see a change in the Soviet empire's colonial policy re Eastern Europe."[7] Reagan saw Solidarność as an organization that could undermine Communist power in Eastern Europe, and he was not going to abandon those hopes now that Solidarność was under attack. Even more grandly, Reagan believed that he had been handed a historical opportunity to turn back communism, akin to Franklin D. Roosevelt's (1933–1945) decision to lead America into World War II to defeat fascism.[8]

In the days following the announcement of sanctions against Poland, Reagan began to privately and publicly make the case for Soviet complicity in the declaration of martial law. He sent letters to key NATO allies and even to Soviet General Secretary Leonid Brezhnev, utilizing intelligence information from the American spy Col. Ryszard Kuklinski to make the case that the Soviets had been intimately involved in Polish events, having pressured the Poles to stabilize the situation by threatening invasion for months. On December 29, Reagan explained to the American public that the "Soviet Union [bore] a heavy and direct responsibility for the repression in Poland" and announced another list of sanctions aimed at them, including: suspending Aeroflot service, closing the Soviet purchasing commission, suspending new and renewed export licenses for high-technology equipment and materials, postponing negotiations on long-term grain agreements, suspending U.S.-Soviet maritime agreement negotiations, calling for a review of all U.S.-Soviet exchange agreements, and expanding the list of oil and gas equipment that needed licenses for export to the USSR.[9]

Controversy among the Allies

Within the greater Atlantic community, Reagan's sanctions were highly controversial. Western European governments, most notably the West Germans, led by Chancellor Helmut Schmidt (in office 1974–1982), were sympathetic to Jaruzelski's plight and expressed relief that the crisis had been resolved without a Soviet invasion. Several frantic missions by mid-level diplomats in December 1981 fostered points of agreement with the British, French, and Italians, but in the face of continued West German resistance, a special meeting of the North Atlantic Council of NATO in January 1982 was not able to reach agreement on a coordinated sanctions regime against Poland, only an agreement not to undermine each other's individual sanctions. The issue of coordinating sanctions against the Soviet Union was not pursued, because it clearly would have been blocked by Schmidt. Showing a sensitivity to West European concerns, the Reagan administration held back on one of its strongest weapons against the Polish regime by paying for overdue loans, keeping Poland from being declared in default, an outcome that would have harmed European and West German banks, in particular, which had loaned much larger sums than the United States. When a CSCE follow-up meeting then occurring in Madrid reconvened in February 1982, the NATO allies finally acted together to condemn martial law as a violation of human rights, but the United States remained nearly alone in pursuing economic sanctions.

This moment of unity was soon overshadowed by vocal West European opposition to American sanctions against the Soviet Union. Since 1979, the Europeans had been negotiating with the Soviets to build a three thousand-mile natural gas pipeline to run from Siberia through the Soviet Union and Czechoslovakia to West Germany. Because American technology was essential to the project, President Reagan's announcement that Washington would suspend export licenses on an expanded list of oil and gas equipment deeply concerned the Europeans. Throughout the winter and spring of 1982, American emissaries, including George P. Shultz (then president of Bechtel Corporation), traveled repeatedly to Europe to explain Washington's reasoning and to fight for coordinated sanctions against the Soviets. The Americans found no success. When President Reagan made an extended trip to Europe in June 1982 for a meeting of the G-7, he too attempted to inspire allied consensus but was rebuffed. When he returned home, Reagan decided to unilaterally declare sanctions on pipeline technology and make them retroactive and extraterritorial, meaning that existing contracts to supply turbines designed to move natural gas through the pipeline, made with French subsidiaries of American companies, would be blocked. The Western Europeans erupted in a chorus of anger. The French government elevated the crisis to a breaking point by forcing French companies to fulfill their agreements with Moscow.

In the midst of the intra-alliance fight, Secretary of State Alexander Haig (in office 1981–1982) tendered his letter of resignation, which the president accepted. Haig was quickly replaced by George P. Shultz (in office 1982–1989), who again tried to repair relations with the Europeans. Ultimately, the Reagan administration compromised and let the existing gas pipeline project move forward, but got the Europeans to agree to "security-minded principles" to determine economic exchanges with the Soviet bloc, specifically: to refrain from any new natural gas agreements with the Soviet Union, to enhance restrictions on technology exports through COCOM, and to harmonize export credit policies.

Beyond the purview of the NATO framework, the Reagan administration came to work closely on Poland-related issues with the Vatican. A native Pole, Pope John Paul II (reigned 1978-2005), the former bishop Karol Wotyła from Krakow, was wildly popular in his home country, with many people pointing toward his triumphant papal visit in 1979 as a moment of national unity and an important precursor to the events of August 1980. For the Reagan administration, the pope's well-documented anti-Communist beliefs and the Catholic Church's institutional saturation around Poland made the Vatican a useful source of intelligence and analysis. Throughout the Polish Crisis (and afterward), Director of Central Intelligence William Casey met with the pope to exchange information, and in the aftermath of the declaration of martial law, the United States coordinated closely with the pope to keep public pressure on Jaruzelski and the Soviets to release prisoners and respect human rights. As time went on, Reagan continued to brief the Vatican regularly on American strategy vis-à-vis Poland, with the pope acting as a kind of public voice for the Polish people and private confidant of the Reagan administration, who influenced the timing and direction of American policy.

George P. Shultz as Secretary of State

George P. Shultz's replacement of Alexander Haig also had broader ramifications for Eastern European policy. The Reagan administration was divided into two basic camps regarding economic policy toward the Soviet bloc: the pragmatists and the ideological "Cold Warriors." The idealist group included strong neo-conservative voices that consistently advocated using economic warfare to strain the Soviet system and undermine Soviet power, and to cut Eastern Europeans off from Western economic opportunities, forcing them to divert resources from the Warsaw Pact, and weakening the appeal of communism by causing quality of life to deteriorate, and by necessitating harsher police regimes. Both sides rejected the goals of détente, but the pragmatists in the cabinet "wanted to control trade but also to use it by linkage as a carrot to gain Soviet concessions," keeping economic agreements as a tool to influence Eastern European decision making.[10]

With Shultz heading the diplomatic corps, the pragmatists had an eloquent advocate who (unlike Haig) had the president's trust. Therefore, while the hard-liners in the cabinet successfully pushed for Reagan to sign NSDD-75, which codified a neo-conservative approach to the Soviet Union, Shultz was able to get Reagan to continue differentiation in Eastern Europe. NSDD 54, "United States Policy toward Eastern Europe," signed by Reagan in September 1982, sought "to encourage diversity through political and economic policies tailored to individual countries," to support liberalizing trends, to further human and civil rights, to reenforce the pro-Western orientation of their peoples, to lessen economic and political dependence on the Soviet Union, and to encourage private markets and free trade unions. Finally, differentiation was calibrated to discriminate between countries in terms of their "relative independence from the Soviet Union in the conduct of foreign policy" and "greater internal liberalization as manifested in a willingness to observe internationally recognized human rights and to pursue a degree of pluralism and decentralization, including a more market-oriented economy."[11] In the case of Poland, differentiation led to a step-by-step negotiating process in which the United States took a graduated approach to lifting sanctions, that is, trading small reforms (lifting martial law or releasing a majority of political prisoners) for individual sanctions (allowing charter flights by LOT or granting fishing rights).

Promoting Democracy

In 1982, President Reagan also put his own mark on American human rights policy by emphasizing democracy promotion. During his June 1982 trip to Europe, Reagan spoke to the British Parliament, referencing the situation in Poland and calling on the West to "take action to assist the campaign for democracy." Specifically, Reagan called on his allies "to foster the infrastructure of democracy—the system of a free press, unions, political parties, universities—which allows people to choose their own way, to develop their own culture, to reconcile their own differences through peaceful means. . . . For the sake of peace and justice, let us move toward a world in which all people are at last free to determine their own destiny."[12] Working to institutionalize Reagan's call to action, a non-governmental organization called the American Political Foundation (which had a board of directors of influential policymakers like Dante Fascell, the vice president of the U.S. Chamber of Commerce, the heads of the Republican and Democratic national committees, and AFL-CIO President Lane Kirkland), succeeded in getting Capitol Hill to fund the creation of the National Endowment for Democracy.

SHIFTS IN FOREIGN POLICY: *PROMOTING DEMOCRACY*

The National Endowment for Democracy (NED) was designed as a quasi-non-governmental organization (NGO); it receives funds from Congress but operates independently from the U.S. government. Shortly after its founding, NED soon included four sister organizations that received the lion's share of funding: the National Democratic Institute for International Affairs (run by the Democratic Party), the International Republican Institute (run by the Republican Party), the U.S. Chamber of Commerce's Center for International Private Enterprise, and the AFL-CIO's Free Trade Union Institute (FTUI). These organizations either administer programs themselves (election monitoring, training in passive resistance or organizing techniques, and the like) or grant money to specific projects or individual groups working to promote democracy around the world. Rather than funding new operations housed in the Department of State, Congress and President Ronald Reagan specifically supported NED, because as an NGO it would not be constrained by official government policy priorities. NED could promote democratic institution building and opposition activities in the Soviet bloc, consistent with broader goals in the region. It could also work in countries like South Africa, South Korea, and the Philippines, where the White House had closer ties with the existing governments. NED's NGO status also created a certain amount of plausible deniability for democracy activists, because they were not accepting money directly from the American government, a common charge used to smear the reputations of the groups working in the host country.

NED FUNDS

In the 1980s, the majority of money destined for causes in Eastern Europe was appropriated to FTUI, because the AFL-CIO already had well-developed contacts with the political opposition, specifically in Poland. Over the course of 1982, Solidarność had reconstituted itself as an underground organization with a strong transnational network of supporters and smugglers. With the express blessing of Lech Wałęsa, the union even founded an official Solidarity Coordinating Office Abroad in Brussels. The coordinating office had a small staff, an operating budget, and was designed to represent Solidarność's interests by raising money, publicizing union pronouncements and human rights abuses, and smuggling money and material to the union structures operating in the underground. The office received about $300,000 per year through NED programs (roughly two-thirds of their operating budget) from 1984 to 1989, augmented by a few special grants of $1 million in 1988 and 1989. This money was used to smuggle printing equipment, communications equipment, and money to support union functions like paying striking workers and their families. Overall, from 1984 to 1989, NED provided about $10 million in congressional money to the Polish opposition, most of it to Solidarność-affiliated groups.

In addition to money sent through FTUI, NED money also gave block grants to the Polish-American Congress. The Polish-American Congress then administered smaller grants to groups working in Western Europe, like the Committee in Support of Solidarity, the Institute for Democracy in Eastern Europe, and OKNO (the Polish acronym for Education, Culture, Science which spells the word "window"), and ran smuggling operations to get money and material to groups inside

Poland. Most organizations had members who had been active in or linked to the Helsinki monitoring network. Once in Poland, NED funds reached a wide variety of opposition causes. American money supported émigré groups in Western Europe like the Paris-based publication *Kultura*; funded underground publishing houses, like NOWA, producing samizdat in Poland; paid for humanitarian aid destined for persecuted writers and opposition members; promoted "independent culture" activities like lectures on politically taboo subjects hosted in private homes (the so-called Flying University); sponsored art shows in Warsaw apartments; bankrolled performances of plays by banned authors, held in churches; paid legal bills for dissidents on trial; and even supported scientific and academic research that the Polish government deemed inappropriate or politically suspect.

Once the money left the United States, it was handled exclusively by Poles. Polish émigrés took the risks of smuggling the money and material, and Poles working in their own country decided how best to utilize the support once it reached its destination. Although the United States acted as a financier for dissidence, given the realities of working with an underground organization, NED accepted that its clients could not send detailed reports on how the money was being used. The U.S. government was not in any kind of position to direct the Polish opposition on how to transform its own country. More importantly, Congress, the White House, and the president himself trusted the members of the Polish opposition to be able to act for themselves. As Reagan said, "We did not envision ourselves as moving into a country and overthrowing the government on behalf of the people. No, this thing had to be internal people themselves. . . . We could just try to be helpful." Ultimately, direct American influence was limited, but congressional money was essential in supporting and empowering a robust culture of political and cultural opposition in Poland throughout the 1980s, helping nurture and sustain Solidarność.

THE SPREADING INFLUENCE OF NED

As Communist power weakened in Eastern Europe, NED moved its operations farther east, increasing its work in the Soviet Union, the Baltic Republics, and Ukraine. Once new governments formed in Eastern Europe, NED transitioned from supporting opposition groups to fostering institution building. More recently, NED money supported the *Otpor!* movement in Serbia in 2000, which successfully unseated Slobodan Milošević (in office 1997–2000). In Ukraine, NED-funded projects were also instrumental in organizing the grassroots movement that led to new elections after the 2004 presidential election, which was rigged in favor of Victor Yanukovych. New elections, held on December 2004 and deemed free and fair by international observers, resulted in opposition candidate Victor Yushchenko's victory (in office 2005–2010). This series of political events in Ukraine, from November 2004 through January 2005, is known as the Orange Revolution. A number of the dissidents and organizations prominent during the 2011 Arab Spring in Egypt also had received direct and indirect support from the endowment. NED continues to work around the globe today.

To understand the genesis of political change in Eastern Europe in the 1980s, however, it is necessary to move beyond a discussion of American policy. In the mid-1980s, differentiation was making small gains to get Eastern European countries to liberalize, and democracy promotion was keeping the political opposition alive, but significant changes in Eastern European governments did not occur until after Mikhail Gorbachev (in office 1985–1991) became Soviet general secretary in March 1985. Gorbachev understood that the Soviet system was stagnating and needed to be revitalized to better compete with the United States and the West. Gorbachev was particularly driven by a desire to increase the average Soviet citizen's standard of living, so he sought ways to make the Soviet economy function more efficiently.

In terms of foreign policy, Gorbachev focused on "new thinking." In its most basic formulation, "new thinking" recognized that the energy and economic subsidies that the Soviet Union paid to maintain its empire in Eastern Europe, not to mention the enormous costs of sustaining its Warsaw Pact forces, were bankrupting the Soviet system. In a sort of grand bargain, Gorbachev made clear to the Soviet client states in Eastern Europe that the Soviet Union would no longer economically prop up Eastern European governments. In return, these regimes would receive greater political leeway to reform their domestic systems, both political and economic, as they saw fit.

Burgeoning Reformers

The more progressive leaders in Eastern Europe forged close relationships with Mikhail Gorbachev and took new initiatives to restructure. In September 1986, Jaruzelski oversaw a final amnesty for political prisoners, establishing a *modus vivendi* with the political opposition that it could pursue its

underground activities with little fear of being jailed for long periods of time. The Polish government also inaugurated a second stage of economic reforms meant to rationalize price structures and to decentralize decision making in the export market by allowing individual industries greater freedom to act independently. Hungary removed the longtime head of the party, Janos Kadar (in office 1956–1988), in May 1988. Reform-minded communists then pushed for legislative changes to its law on associations, allowing more independent organizations including a trade union, several democratic groups, and a non-Communist youth movement. In Poland, following a series of unsettling strikes in May and August 1988, Jaruzelski opened secret negotiations with Wałęsa and the broader political opposition to try to find some kind of power-sharing agreement, in which the opposition would trade its social capital to support painful economic changes in return for nominal power in reformed political structures.

THE GEORGE H. W. BUSH ADMINISTRATION

When George H. W. Bush took office in January 1989, he faced an Eastern European landscape in flux. The Bush

---

IN THEIR OWN WORDS: *PRESIDENT RONALD REAGAN AT THE BRANDENBURG GATE, JUNE 12, 1987*

In a speech at the Brandenburg Gate near the Berlin Wall, on June 12, 1987, President Ronald Reagan challenged Soviet leader Mikhail Gorbachev to "Tear down this wall!" and destroy the symbol of Communist oppression that had been built in 1961. Finally, in November 1989, as the peoples of Eastern Europe threw off their repressive Communist governments, citizens of East and West Germany began chipping away at the wall. Reagan's speech is remembered as an important moment in Cold War history.

> In the 1950's, Khrushchev predicted: "We will bury you." But in the West today, we see a free world that has achieved a level of prosperity and well-being unprecedented in all human history. In the Communist world, we see failure, technological backwardness, declining standards of health, even want of the most basic kind—too little food. Even today, the Soviet Union still cannot feed itself. After these four decades, then, there stands before the entire world one great and inescapable conclusion: Freedom leads to prosperity. Freedom replaces the ancient hatreds among the nations with comity and peace. Freedom is the victor.
>
> And now the Soviets themselves may, in a limited way, be coming to understand the importance of freedom. We hear much from Moscow about a new policy of reform and openness. Some

political prisoners have been released. Certain foreign news broadcasts are no longer being jammed. Some economic enterprises have been permitted to operate with greater freedom from state control. Are these the beginnings of profound changes in the Soviet state? Or are they token gestures, intended to raise false hopes in the West, or to strengthen the Soviet system without changing it? We welcome change and openness; for we believe that freedom and security go together, that the advance of human liberty can only strengthen the cause of world peace.

> There is one sign the Soviets can make that would be unmistakable, that would advance dramatically the cause of freedom and peace. General Secretary Gorbachev, if you seek peace, if you seek prosperity for the Soviet Union and Eastern Europe, if you seek liberalization: Come here to this gate! Mr. Gorbachev, open this gate! Mr. Gorbachev, tear down this wall!

SOURCE: Ronald Reagan: "Remarks on East-West Relations at the Brandenburg Gate in West Berlin," June 12, 1987, Gerhard Peters and John T. Woolley, *The American Presidency Project* [online], accessed October 1, 2011, at http://www.presidency.ucsb.edu/ws/?pid=34390.

administration's first step was to take stock of current policy, so the president ordered a series of policy review processes that lasted into spring 1989. Events in Europe continued to progress. In January, the Hungarian parliament passed legislation authorizing the creation of political parties. In Poland, the government and opposition opened a series of official round table negotiations that ran from February to April, focusing on restructuring the country's social, economic, and political institutions. These agreements also formalized a plan to hold semi-free elections in June, in which non-Communist candidates would be allowed to compete for 35 percent of seats in the existing Sejm (parliament) and for 100 percent of a newly created Senat. A new, powerful office of president, elected by a joint vote of the Sejm and Senat, was also created. In summer 1989, similar negotiations took place in Hungary, with an agreement passed in October that called for a free presidential election at the end of November, with parliamentary elections shortly thereafter.

In spring 1989, when the policy review process had ended, President Bush gave a series of high-profile speeches outlining his administration's vision for the future. At a speech in Hamtramck, Michigan, Bush made clear that economic benefits would come to countries that liberalized—a continuation of differentiation. He spoke specifically of lower tariffs, possibilities for new loans through OPIC, support for projects through the IMF, help in rescheduling loans with the United States and in multilateral forums, and providing new money in the form of a private enterprise fund. Bush predicated America's whole position regarding reform on stability and evolutionary change, expressing the belief that allowing self-determination and liberalizing markets to improve Eastern Europeans' economic situation would promote stability in East-West relations by decreasing tensions between the two blocs: "With prudence, realism, and patience, we seek to promote the evolution of freedom. . . . Let us support the peaceful evolution of democracy in Poland."[13] In terms of his grand vision, Bush hoped for "a growing community of democracies anchoring international peace and stability."[14] At its core, America's foreign policy was meant to improve stability in the international system by promoting gradual and stable transformation.

Supporting Reform in Eastern Europe

In July, President Bush visited Hungary and Poland to reward the reformers and meet with the opposition. His public and private actions left a clear impression that both sides of the equation were necessary for transition to move forward. As the PZPR interpreted his visit, "Bush repeatedly, and also publicly, expressed esteem for the initiators of change, of which he considered the front of the line to be

General Jaruzelski as well as the present political management."[15] When Bush continued his trip in Hungary, he followed a similar playbook, publicly supporting members of the Communist government. He even told a group of Communist reformers, ". . . we are not going to complicate things for you."[16]

For their part, Eastern European citizens pushed the pace of change in the region well beyond the comfort zones of political leaders. In Hungary, more than two hundred thousand people witnessed the reburial of Imre Nagy and other heroes from 1956, prompting the government to move quickly toward elections. Poles resolutely rejected Communist politicians by voting for ninety-nine out of one hundred Solidarity delegates to the Senate (the other candidate was an independent) and filling the complete 35 percent of the parliament open to them with Solidarność candidates. By rejecting a special category of Communist leaders who ran unopposed on a "national list," Polish voters also threw the power-sharing agreement into a series of political crises. Through savvy backroom negotiations capitalizing on dissention within the Communist coalition, Solidarność was able to gain a majority of votes in the combined parliament and form its own government. When Gorbachev was contacted, he famously remained committed to his policy of "new thinking" and acquiesced to a Solidarność-led government.

Fall of the Berlin Wall

During summer 1989, the hard-line government of East Germany, led by Erich Honecker (in office 1971–1989), found itself in a major refugee crisis. After the Hungarian government opened its border with Austria in May, tens of thousands of East Germans, mainly young, educated workers and their families, began to use their vacation in Hungary as a way to escape to the West. When the East German government stopped issuing visas to Hungary, East Germans began to travel to Czechoslovakia instead, with thousands seeking refuge and asking for asylum on the grounds of the West German embassy in Prague. A deal was eventually brokered with the help of the United States to transfer these people on a train through East Germany into the West.

Simultaneously, what had been a very small dissident movement within East Germany also was gaining momentum. Regular meetings of dissidents for a peace vigil that had been occurring weekly since the mid-1980s at the St. Nicholas Church in Leipzig ballooned in September from a handful of participants to several thousand, with many chanting "We're staying" to illustrate their desire to reform the GDR rather than flee to the West. On October 9, the crowd in Leipzig reached one hundred thousand, and despite Honecker's preparations and vague orders to crack

West Berliners gather in front of the Berlin Wall on November 11, 1989, as they watch people demolishing a section of the wall to open a new crossing point between East and West Berlin. During summer 1989, tens of thousands of East Germans fled their oppressive Communist regime to a new life of freedom in the West.

SOURCE: Getty/Gerard Malie.

down violently, the demonstration remained peaceful. A few days later, Honecker was forced out of office and replaced by a new generation. These reformers sought ways to decrease pressure on the East German state— nearly one million East Berliners rallied on November 4 to demand an end to the Communist Party's monopoly on power—and agreed to allow citizens new rights to get visas to travel freely to the West. The announcement of this decision, however, was botched by the government spokesman, who mistakenly announced in a news conference attended by West German reporters that the policy change was to take effect immediately. East Berliners who saw reports about the surprising announcement on West German television began to mass at the border crossings. Despite standing orders to shoot anyone crossing the boundary, and no guidance on what to do from their superiors, East German border guards independently decided to let the people cross into West Berlin. In elation and celebration, West Berliners also made their way to the border, famously popping champagne on the Berlin Wall and greeting the visitors from the East.

The Collapse of Communism Spreads

With Communist authority collapsing symbolically and in actuality, people living under still-brutal regimes mobilized as well. Todor Zhivkov (in office 1954–1989), the leader of Bulgaria, was forced out of power in 1989 in a bloodless palace coup the day after the Berlin Wall fell. In Czechoslovakia, the leaders of Charter 77 and a number of youth groups became more outspoken over the

course of 1989 as other Eastern European governments democratized. New political parties were formed and, in November, a series of marches brought hundreds of thousands of people into the streets of Prague to call for the end of the regime. Following a nationwide general strike, the Communist government fell apart, a coalition government was quickly formed, and, by January 1, 1990, a reconstituted national assembly had made Vaclav Havel (in office 1989–2003) president. In Romania, a dispute over removing a popular and controversial minister from his church in Timisoara led to large-scale demonstrations in downtown Bucharest calling for the end of Nicolae Ceausescu's (in office 1965–1989) regime. When these demonstrations turned violent (the identity of the shooters remains disputed), members of the regime turned against their former leader. After a brief trial, Ceausescu and his wife were executed, with a presidential election held in 1990.

President George H. W. Bush has repeatedly said that the worst thing he could have done in November 1989 was "dance on the Berlin Wall." He has also categorized the American role in the revolutions of 1989 as that of a "responsible catalyst."[17] For the first eleven months of 1989, however, Bush and his administration played a reactive role, responding to events on the ground, not catalyzing them. The accelerating pace of change in Eastern Europe and the rapid fall of Communist power throughout the region were barely conceivable at the beginning of the year. The Bush administration and the president's own worldview reflected assumptions about the permanence of the Cold War and its structures. Quite simply, Bush "enjoyed and embraced" the Cold War world he had inhabited his whole career.[18] The accelerating pace of change driven by Eastern Europeans themselves was unsettling. With the violent crackdown against Chinese protesters in Tiananmen Square in June 1989 as an example, the Bush administration was unsure of the limits of conservative and reactionary forces in the Soviet bloc. The administration worried about a violent backlash either centered in Moscow or within the individual Eastern European governments, with hard-line communists reasserting their power. Bush and his administration undoubtedly wanted to see democracy expand its foothold in Eastern Europe, but the policies they pursued called for promoting evolutionary change rather than ringing in revolutionary transformations.

German Reunification

At the end of 1989 and into early 1990, Bush shifted his policies to get ahead of the wave of revolution sweeping the region. Shortly after the fall of the Berlin Wall, West German Chancellor Helmut Kohl (in office 1982–1988) referenced the possibility of German reunification. Thinking back to World War II, British Prime Minister Margaret Thatcher (in office 1979–1990), French President François Mitterrand (in office 1981–1985), and Gorbachev all were worried that unification might lead to the reemergence of an old-style, unified Germany. For his part, Bush became an early supporter of unification, meeting with Kohl on December 3, 1989, to hear his plans. At a NATO meeting the following day, Bush announced that it was time to provide the "architecture for continued change."[19]

From then on, Bush worked closely with Kohl to smooth the way to unification. Mitterrand got on board after he received assurances that a new Germany would remain part of the European Community and would help accelerate the implementation of a unified currency and central European bank, policies that were an essential part of creating the more advanced European Union (EU). Under American pressure, Thatcher remained privately skeptical but put her hopes in Gorbachev to block German aspirations. Eastern European politicians' protests against reunification subsided after Kohl made clear that the new Germany would accept its existing border at the Oder-Neisse line. Gorbachev, who was facing an increasingly difficult domestic situation as the Soviet Union began to crumble, became the main stumbling point. However, consistent with his ideals, Gorbachev told Kohl in February that he viewed unification as an internal German matter, to be decided by the German people themselves.

Kohl and Bush then sought the fastest model for reunification, choosing to utilize existing institutions rather than take the time to create new European or German ones.

They found a handy mechanism in the West German Basic Law from 1949, which included an article explaining that former parts of Germany could opt to become part of the West German state. By approaching unification this way, the new Germany would be bound by all of its existing international obligations and automatically be part of organizations to which West Germany had been a member, including the European Community and NATO. After his political party, the Christian Democrats, won significant gains in East German elections in March, it was clear that Kohl had the popular support to pursue monetary, political, and territorial union.

Germany and NATO

The final point of contention was German membership in NATO. Bush wanted to keep a unified Germany in NATO; both he and Kohl had made ambiguous statements about their intentions and then backtracked on informal statements to not allow NATO to move east. Gorbachev continued to push his own vision of Germany remaining in both NATO and the Warsaw Pact to help create the kind of "common European home" that he envisioned. The Soviet Union, however, also needed money to pay for the removal and resettlement of Soviet troops leaving East Germany and to help gain new credits from Western banks, which had stopped lending as the internal situation in the Soviet Union destabilized.

To make Germany's continued inclusion in NATO more palatable to Gorbachev's domestic critics, Bush worked to rebrand the alliance, crafting statements emphasizing NATO's defensive nature and its role as a forum for political coordination. In September 1990, Gorbachev acquiesced to American and German desires to see NATO expand eastward by accepting economic aid to ease the decision— DM12 billion to pay for resettling troops and a DM3 billion interest-free credit line.

NATO Expands Further East

With that precedent, both the Bush and Clinton administrations pursued continued NATO expansion eastward. In 1990, the Bush administration proposed to create a regular process for the six members of the Warsaw Pact (including the Soviets) and the members of NATO to meet once a year at the ministerial level to promote diplomatic exchanges. Clinton expanded this framework with the Partnership for Peace, which initiated military-to-military exchanges as well. Early in 1993, Clinton also found himself pressured by the Eastern Europeans to expand. Havel, now president of the Czech Republic after it had separated from Slovakia, and Wałęsa, now president of Poland, wanted to be part of NATO to ensure that Soviet troops never returned, as well as to assist with the continued integration of Europe. Clinton was moved by these appeals, and within a year he was committed to expansion, not as a question of whether, but when.[20] Despite strong resistance because of concerns that expansion would further alienate Russia from the West or make the alliance irrelevant, Clinton pushed for a quick process. He believed expansion would reward and bolster ongoing economic and political reforms in Eastern Europe, improve his political position with Americans of Eastern European descent, demonstrate his Wilsonian ideals of spreading democracy, and provide an example of American leadership when parts of the world were questioning the future of the United States and NATO because of inaction following ethnic conflict in the Balkans. Because of American leadership, NATO signed the NATO-Russia Founding Act and officially invited Poland, Hungary, and the Czech Republic to join in 1997.

Integrating Eastern Europe into the Global Economy

In addition to favoring multilateral organizations to create a new security environment, Bush and then Clinton also favored multilateral organizations to restructure Eastern European economies. At a regional level, Bush encouraged EC/EU economic programs for Eastern Europe. The United States also had significant influence over essential international economic organizations, including the World Bank, IMF, the Paris Club of governmental lenders, and the London Club of private lenders. By 1989, the region owed approximately $110 billion to Western lenders, with debt servicing costing between 40 and 75 percent of hard currency export income. Economic growth had slowed to a standstill, and each of these countries was saddled with corruption, the inefficiencies of state socialism, and rampant inflation. For solutions on how to move forward, the Eastern Europeans turned toward the apparent victor in the Cold War. As one scholar has summarized, "Indeed the transformation of the world economy ignited a neoliberal policy offensive in the West to parallel the Western human rights offensive."[21]

In 1990, economic theory on how to transform economies was dominated by the "Washington Consensus," which had been drawn from experiences in reworking economies in Latin America in the 1980s. The United States, the IMF, and the World Bank insisted that the Eastern European countries follow this path by adopting a radical and comprehensive reform program focused on creating macroeconomic stabilization, market liberalization, and privatization of the economy. In Poland, Finance Minister Leszek Balcerowicz adopted a policy called "shock therapy," which took a rapid approach to reform, a system also followed by the Czechoslovaks. To gain control over inflation, currencies were nominally pegged to other currencies, wage controls were implemented, and the IMF

stepped in with stabilization funds, ultimately lending $27 billion to the region by 1997. To liberalize markets, price controls were ended overnight; tariff and trade barriers were quickly decreased, with some goods like computers and telecommunications becoming duty free; and currencies were made fully convertible. Government-sponsored monopolies were broken up, and state property was privatized, with the sale of industries as joint-stock companies to private entities or through a voucher system, in which workers were given stock in their companies. In addition, it became clear that each country needed to create the infrastructure for markets to work: new tax systems, central banks out of state banks, new private banks, stock exchanges, and massive amounts of new legislation and regulatory bodies. The process of accession to the EU was particularly helpful in providing guidance on building this market infrastructure.

Debates over the proper route to prosperity did not question the assumptions of the Washington Consensus but rather the proper pace of changes. Rapid changes in Poland and Czechoslovakia led to deep cuts in social services and sharply declining incomes. The pain tended to be intense but quick. Countries that took a slower approach, modeled on Chinese transformation, did not see the same sharp declines, but slow privatization often led to rent-seeking, in which industry managers, entrepreneurs, and then oligarchs manipulated the sale and regulation of private property for personal enrichment. Rent-seeking was a more persistent problem in Hungary and the post-Soviet states. Overall, in Eastern Europe, GDP growth dropped precipitously in 1990 and 1991, but reached 0 percent at the end of 1992, and then remained between 3 percent and 5 percent through 2005.[22]

Legacy: Eastern Europe in Today's World

In the decade after the revolutions of 1989, the United States promoted its own vision for Eastern Europe's economic transformation and integration in regional and global economic and security structures, remodeling Cold War institutions to make them vital and central in a more globalized world. Both George H. W. Bush and Bill Clinton also worked to ensure that the United States remained central to these revised and revived multilateral organizations, securing a continued role in Europe for the only remaining superpower. By maintaining significant continuity with the Cold War era, however, Washington kept open the possibility that old rivalries and outdated animosities could resurface with Russia. On the other hand, as new threats to American security surfaced in the twenty-first century, this revitalized NATO structure proved essential to American war planning in the conflicts in Afghanistan and Libya and provided new allies for prosecuting those involved in the war on terror, whether it was through support for rendition activities or by providing significant numbers to the coalition of the willing. Finally, by supporting European Union policies for greater political and economic integration across the continent, the United States helped foster a new European era, with both the strength to be the third-largest economy in the world but an overstretched infrastructure for coordination that may prove unable to respond to the challenges of the new century.

See also: **Chapter 19: Korea and Anti-Communist Policies in East Asia; Chapter 25: Détente; Chapter 29: Glasnost and Perestroika; Chapter 30: Diplomatic Milestones, 1970s–1991.**

ENDNOTES

1. Henry Kissinger, *White House Years* (New York: Little, Brown, 1979), 144.

2. Raymond Garthoff, *Détente and Confrontation: American-Soviet Relations from Nixon to Reagan,* rev. ed. (Washington, DC: Brookings Institution, 1994), 553. Debts to Western European banks and governments were even greater.

3. On the creation of the CSCE monitoring process and, particularly, the American role in it, see Sarah Snyder, *Human Rights Activism and the End of the Cold War: A Transnational History of the Helsinki Network* (New York: Cambridge University Press, 2011), esp. chs. 1–3.

4. Andrzej Paczkowski, *Spring Will Be Ours: Poland and the Poles from Occupation to Freedom,* Jane Cave, translator (University Park: Pennsylvania State University Press, 2003), 442.

5. NSC Briefing Memorandum, "Economic Aid to Poland," dated July 6, 1981, Ronald Reagan Presidential Library, Executive Secretariat NSPG, Box 1, NSPG 0019, July 14, 1981.

6. Memorandum from Robert M. Gates to the Director of Central Intelligence, "Assistance to Poland: Tuesday's NSC Meeting," dated December 4, 1981, National Security Archive, Soviet Flashpoints Originals, Box 1.

7. As quoted in Peter Schweizer, *Reagan's War: The Epic Story of His Forty-Year Struggle and Final Triumph over Communism* (New York: Doubleday, 2002), 166. For the full entry, dated December 21, see: Reagan, *The Reagan Diaries,* Douglas Brinkley, ed. (New York: HarperCollins, 2007), 57.

8. Richard Pipes, *Vixi: Memoirs of a Non-Belonger* (New Haven, CT: Yale University Press, 2003), 171.

9. "Statement on U.S. Measures Taken against the Soviet Union Concerning Its Involvement in Poland, December 29, 1981," in *Public Papers of the President* (1981), available on the Ronald Reagan Presidential Library's website: http://www.reagan.utexas.edu.

10. Raymond Garthoff, *The Great Transition: American-Soviet Relations and the End of the Cold War* (Washington, DC: Brookings Institution, 1994), 45.

11. A copy of NSDD 54, dated September 2, 1982, is located in the Ronald Reagan Presidential Library, National Security Decision Directives, Box 1.

12. "Address to Members of the British Parliament, June 8, 1982," in *Public Papers of the President* (1982), available on the Ronald Reagan Presidential Library website: http://www.reagan.utexas.edu.

13. "Remarks to Citizens in Hamtramck, Michigan," April 17, 1989, in *Public Papers of the President* (1989), available at the George Bush Presidential Library's website: http://bushlibrary.tamu.edu.

14. "Remarks at the United States Coast Guard Academy Commencement Ceremony in New London, Connecticut," May 24, 1989, and "Remarks at the Texas A&M University Commencement Ceremony in College Station," May 12, 1989, in *Public Papers of the President* (1989), available at the George Bush Presidential Library's website: http://bushlibrary.tamu.edu.

15. Notatka Informacyjna dot. wizyty oficjalnej prezydenta Stanów Zjednoczonych Ameryki George H. Bush (9–11 lipca 1989 r.) [Background note re President of the United States of America George H. Bush official visit (July 9–11, 1989)], July 18, 1989, in Henryk Szlajfer, ed., *Ku wielkiej zmianie: Korespondencja między Ambasadą PRL w Waszyngtonie a Ministerstwem Spraw Zagranicznych, styczeń-październik 1989* [Towards great change: Correspondence between Communist Embassy in Washington and the Ministry of Foreign Affairs, January to October 1989] (Warsaw: Instytut Studiów Politycznych PAN, 2008), 177–97.

16. Robert Hutchings, *American Diplomacy and the End of the Cold War* (Washington, DC: Woodrow Wilson Center Press, 1997), 66.

17. George Bush and Brent Scowcroft, *A World Transformed* (New York: Alfred A. Knopf, 1998), 117.

18. "Response by Jeffrey A. Engel, Texas A&M University," in *H-Diplo Roundtable Review,* Vol. 11, No. 25 (May 2010), p. 20, available at http://www.h-net.org/~diplo/roundtables/PDF/Roundtable-XI-25.pdf.

19. As quoted in Mary Sarotte, *1989: The Struggle to Create Post-Cold War Europe* (Princeton, NJ: Princeton University Press, 2009), 79.

20. See James M. Goldgeier, "NATO Expansion: Anatomy of a Decision," in *The Washington Quarterly* 21, no. 1 (Winter 1998), 85–102.

21. Ivan T. Berend, *From the Soviet Bloc to the European Union: The Economic and Social Transformation of Central and Eastern Europe since 1973* (New York: Cambridge University Press, 2009), 43. The statistics come from page 33.

22. Anders Aslund, *How Capitalism Was Built: The Transformation of Central and Eastern Europe, Russia, and Central Asia* (New York: Cambridge University Press, 2007), 59.

FURTHER READING

Garthoff, Raymond. *The Great Transition: American-Soviet Relations and the End of the Cold War.* Washington, DC: Brookings Institution, 1994.

Herring, George C. *From Colony to Superpower: U.S. Foreign Relations since 1776.* New York: Oxford University Press, 2008.

Kotkin, Stephen. *Uncivil Society: 1989 and the Implosion of the Communist Establishment.* New York: Modern Library, 2009.

Mann, James. *The Rebellion of Ronald Reagan: A History of the End of the Cold War.* New York: Viking, 2009.

Sarotte, Mary. *1989: The Struggle to Create Post-Cold War Europe.* Princeton, NJ: Princeton University Press, 2009.

chapter 29

Glasnost and Perestroika

The End of the Soviet Union

by Christopher Tudda

THE ELEVATION OF Mkhail Gorbachev (in office 1985–1991) to general secretary of the Soviet Union in 1985 marked a crucial step in the end of the Cold War between the East and the West. Combined with the shift in the foreign policy approach of Ronald Reagan (1981–1989) and his support for Gorbachev's reforms, as well as George H. W. Bush's (1989–1993) and Gorbachev's management of the Eastern European revolution, the reunification of Germany, and the international coalition that demanded the Iraqi withdrawal from Kuwait, the Cold War ended with the collapse of the Soviet Union in December 1991.

Few scholars or contemporaries expected this transformation when Ronald Reagan became president of the United States in 1980. Reagan had not only been a longtime anti-communist, he also had strongly criticized his own party's policy of détente with the Soviet Union. He had taken the unusual step of challenging the incumbent Republican president, Gerald Ford (1974–1977), in 1976, because he believed that Ford and his secretary of state, Henry Kissinger (in office 1973–1977), had appeased the Soviet Union. During the 1980 presidential campaign, Reagan said that President Jimmy Carter (1977–1981) had allowed the Soviets to invade Afghanistan, the Sandinistas to take power in Nicaragua, and the U.S. military to atrophy.

After his election, Reagan increased defense spending on both strategic (nuclear) and conventional forces, including rebuilding the U.S. Navy. He also ramped up America's covert activities. He authorized a massive increase in covert aid to the *mujahideen* in Afghanistan and the *contras* in Nicaragua, and he used the power of the bully pulpit to challenge the Soviet Union and its allies through public speeches.

REAGAN: A STRONG STANCE AND THEN MODERATION

Evidence has emerged from both U.S. and Soviet archives, however, that Reagan's public and secret attempts to challenge the Soviet Union backfired and instead led to a deep freeze in the Cold War that nearly led to a hot war. A month after the "evil empire" speech, Reagan proposed the Strategic Defense Initiative (SDI), which he envisioned as a defense shield that would ultimately make nuclear weapons obsolete. The Soviets, however, interpreted SDI as a means for the development of a nuclear first-strike capability that would prevent them from responding in kind. On September 1, 1983, Soviet fighters shot down an unarmed passenger plane, Korean Air Lines Flight 007, killing all 269 passengers, including a U.S. congressman. The plane had accidentally strayed into Soviet airspace, and the Soviet air defense command mistook it for a U.S. spy plane. Despite an international uproar, Secretary General Yuri Andropov (in office 1982–1984), the former head of the KGB (secret police), angrily accused the United States of concealing a spy flight behind the passenger plane and called the flight a deliberate U.S. provocation.

Two months later, U.S. and North Atlantic Treaty Organization (NATO) forces conducted a ten-day war games exercise code-named "Able Archer." During the exercise, NATO forces used a new communications system to simulate a higher level of nuclear alert. Soviet intelligence officials incorrectly feared that the exercise was the precursor to a preemptive nuclear attack on Soviet forces, and in turn put Soviet nuclear facilities in East Germany and Poland on high alert. U.S. intelligence began to receive signals that the Soviets expected a U.S. or NATO attack. Only two weeks later, on November 23, 1983, the United States began to deploy Pershing II intermediate-range nuclear missiles in Western Europe. The Soviets responded by walking out of the Strategic Arms Reductions Talks (START) in Geneva.

Reagan Pulls Back

Reagan seems to have been sobered by the Soviet reaction to Able Archer, and increasingly the evidence indicates

KEY CONCEPTS

Glasnost. In this atmosphere of international tension and a leadership upheaval, the 54-year-old Mikhail Gorbachev became general secretary of the Soviet Communist Party. Gorbachev called for "New Thinking" in Soviet domestic and foreign policies. He introduced *perestroika,* or restructuring, as well as *glasnost,* or openness, in order to reform and revitalize the Soviet system.

These domestic reforms accompanied Gorbachev's new diplomatic initiatives. In order to restore the socialist command economy, he believed that the Soviet Union must cut its defense budget and reduce its overseas commitments. He began to call for cuts in nuclear armaments, in particular his 1986 proposal to eliminate intermediate-range nuclear weapons from Europe. Reagan reversed course and supported Gorbachev's liberalization programs. President George H. W. Bush continued to support Gorbachev and helped manage the end of the Cold War and the peaceful dissolution of the Soviet Union. While he began to implement a new economic agenda, Gorbachev also argued that the Soviet system could not be fixed without a revolution in everyday life. Glasnost would necessarily complement perestroika. The rigid and dogmatic Stalinist system that had perverted the Soviet Communist experiment required change. Gorbachev recognized that the pervasive fear that was epitomized by the forced collectivization of the 1930s, the gulags, and the omnipresence of the KGB needed to be eased. Political reforms such as liberalization of basic freedoms such as speech, assembly, religion, and the press would help perestroika succeed. In order to achieve these goals, he began to surround himself with a group of like-minded individuals who had come of age under Khrushchev's reign and called themselves "the children of the Twentieth Party Congress" (the venue in which Khrushchev gave his "de-Stalinization" speech). Frustrated for almost twenty years by Brezhnev's return to Stalinism, the group had also been particularly disillusioned by his quashing of the Czechoslovakian reform movement in 1968.

Perestroika. By the 1980s, the Cold War had entered a new and a more dangerous phase. After the Soviet Union invaded Afghanistan and the United States Senate refused to ratify the second Strategic Arms Limitation Treaty (SALT II) in 1979, the Carter administration initiated a military buildup and began to aid covertly the *mujahidin* guerillas who were fighting the Soviets in Afghanistan. During his presidential campaign, Ronald Reagan rejected détente, or a relaxation of relations with the Soviets, a policy that had been adopted by his three predecessors, and challenged the Soviet Union around the world. The term literally means "restructuring" and represented the political and economic components of what Gorbachev called "New Thinking." Perestroika required that the Soviet Union eliminate corruption; set new work goals; fight rampant alcoholism, which reflected an overall societal stultification and resentment of the Communist system; increase industrial and agricultural production; and introduce technological, administrative, and bureaucratic innovations. Achieving these lofty and radical goals would require patience, consensus-building, and the removal of many of the Brezhnev acolytes who dominated not only the Politburo but also much of the state leadership in Moscow and in the Republics.

that he began to have second thoughts about his confrontational policies. On November 18, he noted in his diary that he and Secretary of State George Shultz (in office 1982–1989) had talked about "setting up a little in house group of experts on the Soviet U. to help us in setting up some channels. I feel the Soviets are so defense minded, so paranoid about being attacked that without in any way being soft on them we ought to tell them no one here has any intention of doing anything like that."[1] Shultz, the National Security Council's Soviet expert Jack Matlock, and others who favored better relations with Moscow supported Reagan's change in approach. On January 16, 1984, for the first time, Reagan publicly called for accommodation with the Soviet Union and stated that "we have common interests and the foremost among them is to avoid war and reduce the level of arms."[2]

Reagan's more conciliatory approach fell on deaf ears in Moscow for a year. Soviet General Secretary Konstantin Chernenko (in office 1984–1985), who had taken office after

Andropov's death in February 1984, also was sickly, and his hold on power was tenuous at best. After Chernenko's death in March 1985, Andropov's protégé, Mikhail Gorbachev, became the new secretary general; he was a largely inexperienced but ambitious Politburo member who wanted to pick up where Nikita Khrushchev (in office 1953–1964) had left off without making the mistakes the fiery and controversial Khrushchev had made.

The Gorbachev Challenge

Gorbachev wanted to strengthen and revive the Soviet system, not turn it into a democratic, capitalistic society. Therefore, he called for *perestroika* (restructuring) of the entire system from the top down.

Gorbachev Gains Internal Support

Gorbachev and his most trusted advisers, such as Anatoly Chernyaev, Andrei Grachev, and Eduard Shevardnadze, argued that none of these domestic reforms could possibly

PUBLIC PORTRAIT: *MIKHAIL GORBACHEV (1931–)*

Mikhail Gorbachev was born in 1931 in Stavropol, in southern Russia, to a peasant farmer and his wife. Shortly thereafter, his grandfather and other farmers who resisted then-Premier Josef Stalin's (in power 1922–1953) forced collectivization of agriculture were sent to the Siberian gulag. This incident became seared in Gorbachev's memory and demonstrated the flaws in the Soviet system. Gorbachev graduated from Moscow State University in 1955 with a law degree, but, most importantly, he joined the Konsomol (the Young Communist League) to advance within the system. Although Gorbachev believed in both communism and the Soviet system, he wanted to create a "new society" based on true equality. When Stalin's successor, Nikita Khrushchev, exposed Stalin's crimes, in particular the famines that cost millions of farmers' lives after the forced collectivization, in the famous February 1956 "de-Stalinization" speech, Gorbachev and other reformers believed that the system would be reformed. Khrushchev's ouster in 1964 and the return of a more Stalinist system, however, tempered Gorbachev's enthusiasm.

The 1968 "Prague Spring," the subsequent Soviet/Warsaw Pact invasion, and the promulgation of the "Brezhnev Doctrine," which gave the Soviet Union the right to interfere in the internal affairs of Warsaw Pact and other Communist bloc nations, also fundamentally influenced Gorbachev. Once

again, another Soviet leader had perverted socialism's ideals. Gorbachev, however, kept his beliefs to himself and began to gradually climb the ladder of the city of Stavropol's Communist Party and political apparatus. He came to the attention of the authorities in Moscow and in 1979 was elected to the Soviet Politburo.

A protégé of Yuri Andropov, Gorbachev began to challenge for the leadership of the party shortly after Andropov's death in February 1984. In December, he visited the United Kingdom and immediately made an impression. His youth, his Western mannerisms, his sense of humor, his vivacious and stylish wife, Raisa, his telegenic personality, and his willingness to improve relations with the West contrasted sharply with his predecessors, all of whom had been in their 80s and represented the rigid, confrontational past. In a television interview, British Prime Minister Margaret Thatcher famously remarked, "I like Mr. Gorbachev. We can do business together," in spite of his deep belief in his own political system (In *The Reagan Diaries,* Douglas Brinkley, ed. [New York: HarperPerennial, 2007, 198–99]). Four months later, after Konstantin Chernenko's death, Gorbachev became general secretary. Gorbachev's calls for restructuring and openness resonated in the West, and he developed strong personal relationships with Thatcher, West German Chancellor Helmut Kohl, and, ultimately, Reagan and Bush.

succeed without revolutionizing Soviet foreign policy. Perestroika would fail if the Soviet Union continued to spend upward of 40 percent of its Gross Domestic Product (GDP) on the military. The decades-long quest for nuclear parity with, or even superiority over, the United States had bankrupted the economy and prevented true communism from being realized.

Some of Gorbachev's advisers had also been horrified by the invasion of Afghanistan; not only had it been costly in terms of blood and treasure, it also had taken on the appearance of a colonial occupation, which true communism rejected. The invasion, coupled with expensive expansion into other developing areas like Africa, they argued, had needlessly provoked the United States and generated a reaction that threatened to destroy the Soviet Union. The Soviet Union must repudiate the mistrust, suspicion, and fear of the late Brezhnev years and readopt true détente. This required ideological adjustment, and Gorbachev began to push for an end to the old ideas of class divisions and an inevitable confrontation between capitalism and communism. The two sides, they contended, not only could coexist but also had become increasingly interconnected by the late twentieth century.

Gorbachev's Diplomacy

Mikhail Gorbachev undertook his first important diplomatic foray only a few short months before he became general secretary. In December 1984, he traveled to the United Kingdom and met with its conservative prime minister, Margaret Thatcher (in office 1979–1990). Gorbachev told Thatcher that he wanted to reduce the dangers of armed confrontation between East and West, and he argued that it made little sense to continue an arms race that could destroy both sides, and the world, many times over. He also shared with Thatcher his reform plans, as well as his nation's need to increase its overseas trade.

Secretary of State George Shultz recalled that Reagan had noticed Gorbachev's public statement in London that he wanted not only to reduce but also to eliminate nuclear arms stockpiles, as long as the United States abandoned SDI. Shultz said that "the Soviets now were leaning toward us, moving toward *our* agenda."[4] This is an important point: Reagan may have toned down his confrontational rhetoric, but his policy of firmness toward the Soviet Union had not fundamentally changed. After her public comment that she could do business with Gorbachev, Thatcher quickly flew to the United States and told the president that

Gorbachev "was an unusual Russian in that he was much less constrained, more charming, more open to discussion and debate," and, more importantly, "was an advocate of economic reform and was willing to slacken Soviet control over its economy." Gorbachev, she emphasized, said, "it is in our common interest—indeed it is our duty—to avoid a conflict."[5]

When he learned that Chernenko had died, Reagan sent Shultz and Vice President George H. W. Bush (in office 1981–1989) to represent him at the funeral in Moscow. At Shultz's recommendation, Reagan wrote a letter to Gorbachev asking for a meeting between the two leaders and inviting Gorbachev to visit the United States. After the funeral, Gorbachev told the two Americans that he wanted to reestablish détente but also move beyond it. The Soviet Union, he said, had "no expansionist ambitions," did not want to fight the United States, and promised to renew the Geneva START negotiations. Impressed, Shultz told Bush, "In Gorbachev we have an entirely different kind of leader in the Soviet Union than we have experienced before." Gorbachev followed up the meeting with a letter of his own to Reagan that reiterated his comments to Bush and Shultz and called for talks that would improve relations between the two nations. He also thanked Reagan for his invitation but for the moment deferred any meeting between the two leaders.[6]

Moving Closer Together

Over the next seven months, the two leaders exchanged a dozen letters and finally agreed to meet in Geneva in November. In a demonstration of his "new thinking," Gorbachev unilaterally announced a moratorium on nuclear tests in August. After the United Nations General Assembly meeting, Soviet Foreign Minister Eduard Shevardnadze (in office 1985–1990) visited the White House. Reagan said he wanted Gorbachev to know that "I really meant 'arms reductions' & I wasn't interested in any détente nonsense." Reagan also noted that "[f]or the first time they talked of real verification procedures."[7]

Reagan, meanwhile, concluded that the Soviets needed arms control, as new CIA reports demonstrated that the Soviet Union had become "an economic basket case," and Gorbachev could not "face the cost of competing with us." Accordingly, he continued to prioritize SDI in order to force the Soviets to make the necessary changes in their own arms control posture.[8] Gorbachev resolved to press Reagan to abandon SDI but at the same time stress that the Geneva summit represented "only the beginning of a greater and regular dialogue and in general 'we need to know how to live together,' we are different, but we must learn to respect this difference."[9]

Summit Meeting Issues

A cursory review of the memoir literature and some of the available primary sources from the fall of 1985 demonstrates that both sides worried about the atmospherics of the Geneva summit. The hawks in the Reagan administration believed that the younger, dynamic Gorbachev would be able to bully the older president and force him into concessions, in particular the abandonment of SDI, by making the summit a test of propaganda. Gorbachev's advisers, meanwhile, worried that a summit just for the sake of a meeting between the leaders would damage Gorbachev's reform plans at home, because their hawks also wanted to increase defense spending and would torpedo perestroika. Ironically, the hawks in both countries also feared that if the two developed a cordial personal relationship, they might arrive at significant arms reductions agreements.

On the surface, during these first meetings, the hawks on both sides could take comfort in knowing that little in practical terms had changed. Both men stuck to their guns on arms control. Gorbachev told Reagan that SDI would lead to an arms race in space; Reagan replied that SDI would lead to the eradication of nuclear weapons. They also argued about human rights, intervention in regional issues, East-West trade, and the spread of each other's ideological systems to other nations, and made little concrete progress.

However, ample evidence also demonstrates that Gorbachev's call for a new "beginning" in U.S.-Soviet relations had resonated with Reagan, and that the hawks would in actuality find little to like. Both men agreed that neither side trusted the other, and that this mistrust could lead to a nuclear war that neither side could win. Indeed, during their first meeting, Reagan remarked, "Countries do not mistrust each other because of arms, but rather countries build up their arms because of the mistrust between them." Both nations, he stressed, needed to live together; they did not have to like each other's government, and "each could follow its own way, but with peaceful competition." Gorbachev agreed and emphasized that "this meeting is important in itself" and expressed his willingness to hold more private meetings. He also stressed that despite "squalls in the bilateral relationship" between the two superpowers, "I can definitely state that in the USSR there is no enmity toward the United States or its people."[10] Both agreed on the desirability of a 50-percent cut in each side's intercontinental ballistic missile stockpiles.

A Turning Point

Gorbachev's adviser Anatoly Chernyaev wrote in his diary that in spite of the logjam over arms control, "a turning point in international relations is taking shape. We are coming closer to acknowledging that no one will start a war; to understanding that we cannot keep provoking it either in the name of communism, or in the name of capitalism."[11] The two nations issued a joint statement noting that subsequent summits would be held in Moscow and Washington, and more importantly affirmed that "nuclear war cannot be won and must never be fought." Gorbachev's interpreter Pavel Palazchenko called this point "revolutionary" considering Reagan's first-term rhetoric about challenging the Soviet Union with nuclear diplomacy.[12]

Unwilling to lose any momentum, Gorbachev jumpstarted the new relationship only two months later when he announced, on January 15, 1986, that the Soviets would unilaterally give up all their nuclear weapons by 2000 and proposed that the two nations remove all their intermediate-range missiles from Europe. This was an important concession, because for the first time a Soviet leader had not included British and French missiles in the U.S. stockpile. He also extended his nuclear test ban moratorium by three months and offered the United States the chance to conduct on-site inspection of stockpile elimination, a concession that his predecessors had rejected, and a demonstration of his willingness to allow a form of glasnost into diplomacy.

Of course, Reagan would have to scrap SDI in return. In his diary, Reagan called the proposal "a h—l of a propaganda move. We'd be hard put to explain how we'd turn it down." Still, he refused to give up SDI, but he resolved to press forward with arms reductions negotiations. On February 3, he dismissed some of his advisers' contentions that the proposal was "a publicity stunt." He said that if SDI actually worked, "we'll work out how it can be used to protect the whole world, not just us."[13]

In his diary, Chernyaev praised Gorbachev's "bold" move and stressed that Gorbachev had made the announcement because in order to "revive the country and set it on a steady track, it is necessary to free it from the burden of the arms race, which is depleting more than just economics." Andrei Grachev also emphasizes the domestic component of Gorbachev's announcement and contends that Gorbachev "trapped" his opponents in the military into having to accept at least a 50-percent cut in Soviet strategic forces, because they had conceded such a cut would not harm national security.[14] Gorbachev's concrete proposal served notice to his allies and adversaries in the Soviet system not only that he was serious about perestroika but also that a symbiotic relationship existed between his foreign policy aims and his domestic reforms, and that radical proposals were needed to fix the mess before it imploded.

Reagan followed up on Gorbachev's proposal and in February sent two letters to Moscow, the first insisting that he would go ahead with SDI and the second explaining that he took Gorbachev's proposal seriously. Gorbachev did not reply until early April and essentially ignored Reagan's letters, instead asking for another one-on-one meeting in Europe. Reagan hedged about agreeing to such a meeting, preferring to leave the START talks to lower levels.

The Impact of the Chernobyl Disaster

However, before anything constructive could be worked out, disaster struck: on April 26, 1986, an explosion at the Chernobyl nuclear power plant in Ukraine released an enormous cloud of radiation that drifted into the western Soviet Union and into Western Europe, the worst nuclear accident in history. Chernobyl not only exposed the need for perestroika but also exposed the limits of glasnost: it showed the decrepitude of the Soviet nuclear program, the military's control over the program, and the bureaucracy's inability to evacuate locals and inform them about the severity of the disaster. Not until alarms went off at a Swedish nuclear power plant did the Soviets admit to the world what had happened.

Evidence demonstrates that the Chernobyl disaster convinced Gorbachev to move even further into arms reduction talks, push perestroika, and also implement glasnost. Embarrassed by the public relations disaster, Gorbachev told the Soviet Foreign Ministry that his government would "do anything in its capabilities to loosen the vice of defense expenditures," and urged his diplomats to ditch the old Brezhnev style of "senseless stubbornness." The Soviet Union would instead further engage the United States in arms reduction talks. Chernobyl also highlighted the catastrophe that would occur if the Soviets and the United States launched a nuclear war. Indeed, in a July 3 Politburo meeting, he said that Chernobyl "is an extraordinary event bordering on the use of a nuclear weapon."[15]

Reykjavik Summit

After diplomatic back-and-forth, Gorbachev and Reagan finally met six times over two days in Reykjavik, Iceland, in October 1986. These meetings, initially described as a failure, ultimately hastened the end of the Cold War. At first, both leaders agreed for the first time to remove INF forces from Europe and eliminate all nuclear weapons by 1996, a more ambitious goal than Gorbachev's original goal of the year 2000. However, once again, Gorbachev demanded that Reagan drop SDI and repeated his assertion that the system would give the United States first-strike capability and move the arms race into space. For his part, Reagan insisted that SDI would eliminate all nuclear weapons, his ultimate goal, and again promised to share the technology with the Soviet Union.

Although the international press reported that the summit had ended in disaster, and although both Gorbachev and Reagan were at first disappointed that they had failed to resolve their outstanding issues—Reagan wrote in his diary, "I was mad," after Gorbachev said arms control talks would end if Reagan did not kill SDI—both leaders publicly called Reykjavik another step in arms reductions talks. Both men explained that each understood and respected the other's position and decided to concentrate on where they agreed rather than harp on SDI.[16]

This relative optimism proved to be well-founded, especially on Reagan's part, because on February 28, 1987, Gorbachev announced that he would agree to reduce INF forces in Europe regardless of whether or not Reagan continued to develop SDI. This was a huge victory for Reagan, because it validated his posture of sticking with SDI whether or not it led to an agreement and reinforced his belief that the Soviet Union could not afford to compete with the United States.

Gorbachev's Crises and Successes

Gorbachev had to make this concession because perestroika had failed to make even a small dent in reforming the Soviet economy. Industrial production had decreased by 6 percent, while Moscow's foreign debt had increased. An audit discovered that the government had an 80 billion ruble deficit. At least 40 percent of the government's entire expenditures went to the military; the government sent approximately 40 billion rubles in annual aid to Vietnam, 25 billion to Cuba, and had never been paid for all the military equipment it had furnished to Iraq, Libya, and Syria since the 1950s. The occupation of Afghanistan was also bleeding dry the Soviet treasury and, increasingly, the Soviet army, as casualties mounted.

Meanwhile, the investment of some 200 billion rubles into modern industrial equipment had not borne any fruit, and it was simply too early to tell if all the money would result in tangible change in the economy. In addition, an unexpected plunge in the world price of oil and the fall in sales from Gorbachev's anti-alcohol campaign led to a massive revenue shortage. Subsidies to keep the price of food low cost another 100 billion rubles. Despite all his talk, Gorbachev had not implemented any of the even modest or temporary capitalist reforms he had called for when he began to implement perestroika. Wages remained frozen, and the economy seemed teetering on chaos.[17]

Success of the Washington Summit

Gorbachev simply had no choice but to press for significant arms reductions even if it meant conceding SDI to Reagan. Reagan, in the midst of his own domestic problems thanks to the Iran-Contra scandal and a steep drop on the New York Stock Exchange, also needed a foreign policy breakthrough. Both leaders once again exchanged letters while arms control talks continued in Geneva. Finally, Reagan invited Gorbachev to visit Washington for three days of meetings.

On December 8, 1987, they signed the INF Treaty at the White House, the first time that the two powers had reduced rather than simply limited nuclear weapons.

The Washington summit proved to be not only a substantive success for arms reduction but another enormous victory for Gorbachev's reform programs. He quickly capitalized on this propaganda coup and, exactly two months after the INF Treaty signing, announced to the Soviet people that he would begin withdrawing troops from Afghanistan. He remarked, "We already lost 13,000 killed and 43,000 wounded. Over one million people have lived through a nightmare. Not to mention the economy: we spent 5 billion a year. We should get out of that country from any point of view, human or economic." It is also important to note that this coincided with the Reagan's announcement that he would continue to fund the mujahedeen resistance, even after a Soviet withdrawal, unless Gorbachev cut off all aid to the Afghanistan government. Reagan's decision to raise the costs of the Soviet intervention in Afghanistan, just like his emphasis on SDI, seemed to have caused Gorbachev to change his policy. On April 14, the Soviets officially agreed to begin withdrawals on May 15, when they signed the Geneva Accords.[18]

Fixing COMECON

Shortly after taking care of Afghanistan, Gorbachev tried to fix another drain on the Soviet economy: the Council for Economic Assistance (COMECON), an economic organization consisting mainly of Moscow's Eastern European allies, needed to be reformed. In particular, Gorbachev wanted to end Moscow's guarantee of low prices for raw materials (especially oil and gas) while serving as the market for Eastern Europe's finished products. He essentially wanted COMECON to adopt true market principles, or at least a socialist version of market principles, and make the Eastern bloc interdependent.

The Eastern Europeans were not happy about this, because they had essentially been living off Moscow's largesse since the 1940s and had failed to develop their own industries or a middle class, and they knew little about capitalist theory and business practices. Gorbachev also wanted his allies to adopt his domestic program of technological and industrial innovation and modernization. Neither Moscow nor its allies, however, could afford the high cost of such investment.

Ideological Concessions

Gorbachev's economic program also included political reforms that mirrored his major push for glasnost at home that he had initiated in 1987. First, Gorbachev said every nation had the right to pursue its own "path of social development," be it capitalism or socialism, without being dictated to by the Soviet Union (or the United States). Based largely on the ideas of the 1968 Prague Spring, this ideological concession mirrored his call for "freedom of choice" within the Soviet Union and ultimately had profound implications for the end of the Cold War.[19]

Gorbachev began to ease restrictions on press and speech, allowed underground *samizdat* (Soviet dissident) writers, actors, screenwriters, television and movie directors, playwrights, and other members of the dissident intelligentsia to produce without harassment by the secret police; he also began releasing political prisoners. Most importantly, he allowed them to openly criticize Lenin, Stalin, Brezhnev, and his own policies. Gorbachev then put his money where his mouth was and invited Reagan not only to visit Moscow but also to walk through Red Square, the heart of the Kremlin, and meet ordinary Soviet citizens. For the most famous and consistent American anti-communist, the man who had condemned détente, to visit the Soviet Union indicated that Reagan had also fully changed his opinion about the necessity to improve relations. During their stroll, a Western reporter asked him whether he still considered the Soviet Union an "evil empire." Reagan replied, "No, I was talking about a different time and a different era."[20]

Reagan Addresses Moscow State University

Gorbachev, in a move none of his predecessors would have even considered, allowed the president to speak directly to Soviet students at his alma mater, Moscow State University, on May 31, 1988. Reagan told the audience that the technological and informational revolution that had begun sweeping the world depended on "freedom of thought, freedom of information, freedom of communication," not to mention free markets. He criticized centralized planning, denounced creeping bureaucratization, and praised political pluralism, religious and political freedom, and "the right to question and change the established way of doing things."

Reagan had not only relayed the fundamental tenets of American conservative ideology (or nineteenth-century liberalism) but also had explicitly endorsed glasnost. He quoted the famous Russian novelist Boris Pasternak, who had written that "what has for centuries raised man above the beast is not the cudgel, but an inward music—the irresistible power of unarmed truth," and praised Gorbachev's attempts to change Soviet society. Human rights, he said, were universal, and the sooner the Soviet Union respected them, the easier it could change.

The Momentum of Glasnost

Reagan's endorsement helped Gorbachev further push glasnost. Only a month later, Gorbachev instituted political reforms by calling for a new legislature, the Congress of People's Deputies, which would be elected by Soviet citizens.

President Ronald Reagan delivered a historic address to students at Moscow State University on May 31, 1988, the first U.S. president to do so. About the speech, The New York Times *editorialized, "When people someday look back to the milestones of the cold war, they are likely to remember the day Ronald Reagan extolled freedom, while Lenin looked on."*

SOURCE: Courtesy Ronald Reagan Library.

He also called for a new executive system to be installed that would create the position of president as head of state. Gorbachev also began the process of devolving more power from the central government to the Republics.

He also extended this call for openness to relations with the Soviet bloc. In a memorable December 7, 1988, speech to the United Nations General Assembly in New York (he became the first Soviet leader to address the international body since Khrushchev in 1960), he told the world that "radical and revolutionary changes are taking place and will continue to take place within individual countries and social structures . . . our times are making corrections here, too. . . . Internal transformational processes such as *perestroika* and *glasnost* cannot achieve their national objectives merely by taking 'course parallel' with others without using the achievements of the surrounding world and the possibilities of equitable cooperation." He then renounced "interference in those internal processes with the aim of altering them according to someone else's prescription"; doing so "would be all the more destructive for the emergence of a peaceful order." Essentially, Gorbachev had renounced not only the Brezhnev Doctrine, which had governed intra-Eastern bloc relations for two decades, but also the use of force in any part of the world in order to spread socialism.

He went further, however, and said, "Freedom of choice is a universal principle to which there should be no exceptions," a stunning rejection of the fundamental tenets of Marxism-Leninism. However, it is important to emphasize that, once again, Gorbachev argued that to do this would *strengthen* socialism: "We are not giving up our convictions, philosophy, or traditions . . . in order to involve society in implementing plans for restructuring it had to be made more truly democratic . . . restructuring has now encompassed politics, the economy, spiritual life, and ideology . . . this means a profound reorganization of production relations and the realization of the immense potential of socialist property." Finally, Gorbachev announced that he would unilaterally begin to withdraw a half million Soviet troops and six tank divisions from

Eastern Europe in 1989 and convert defense industry plants into civilian production facilities.[21]

That afternoon, Gorbachev officially met for a half hour with Reagan for the last time, as well as with the newly elected president, George H. W. Bush, at Governor's Island in New York Harbor. Gorbachev and the president reminisced about how their personal relationship had deepened since their first meeting, and the Soviet leader remarked "that in a rather difficult time they had been able to begin movement toward a better world." Reagan said that while he was "proud of what they had accomplished together," more needed to be done.

Bush said he wanted "to build on what President Reagan had done," because "what had been accomplished could not be reversed." Bush also said, however, that he needed "a little time to review the issues" and would be "putting together a new team" of foreign policy advisers. Gorbachev told the incoming president that he saw "good prospects" for further cooperation with the new administration" and emphasized that his "country had become a different one. It would never go back to what it had been three years before regardless of whether he or someone else were leading it." In his diary, Reagan called the meeting "a tremendous success" and said Gorbachev had displayed a "better attitude than at

SHIFTS IN FOREIGN POLICY: *THE SOVIETS AND AMERICANS FORM A PARTNERSHIP*

Gorbachev's assumption of power eventually led to the end of the Cold War, because both perestroika and glasnost had diplomatic implications. He designed both of these governing philosophies, it must be emphasized, to reform and strengthen communism, not to replace it. Just as Vladimir Lenin had temporarily allowed capitalism under his New Economic Program in the 1920s, Gorbachev said that the Soviet Union could borrow from democratic capitalism in the short term in order to fix the mistakes and the deep, structural inadequacies of its Communist system. Communism, in the long run, would prevail. Perestroika and glasnost could therefore be ideologically justified, and Gorbachev, at least for a few years, successfully prevented the Old Guard, who did not want to mend the system, from retaking power.

CHANGES IN SOVIET POLICY

For these domestic reforms to succeed, Gorbachev had to fundamentally change Soviet foreign policy. Years of providing military aid around the world, particularly in Africa and Latin America, propping up the economies of the Communist bloc, and the costs of an enormous standing army at home (the Soviet Union comprised the largest land mass in the world and required that troops be stationed in the Arctic, on the borders of Europe and China, and in the Pacific) and in Eastern Europe had taken their toll. Enormous discrepancies in its balance-of-payments structure had begun to strain the Soviet treasury to the point of near bankruptcy. Gorbachev calculated that if he did not cut defense spending, his

domestic reforms could not succeed. Over the next few years, he publicly proposed massive reductions in nuclear arms and troop levels in Europe, actions that would have been unthinkable under his predecessors.

Gorbachev's changes to Soviet foreign policy paralleled those of Ronald Reagan. After his inauguration in 1981, Reagan had followed through on his campaign promises and began a confrontational policy against the Soviet Union. He began a massive conventional and nuclear military buildup that dwarfed Carter's; called the Soviet Union an "evil empire"; proposed that the United States build a satellite-based weapons system, the Strategic Defense Initiative (SDI), to defend against a nuclear attack; backed "freedom fighters" in Afghanistan, Nicaragua, Poland, Africa, and Asia; and re-emphasized the importance of propaganda through such mechanisms as Radio Free Europe and the Voice of America. Reagan believed that all of these proposals would force the Soviets to either spend money they did not have in order to keep up with the West, or give up in the face of the free world's overwhelming power.

REAGAN RESCINDS HIS CONFRONTATIONAL APPROACH

By late 1983, Reagan began to change his approach after the downing of Korean Air Liner 007 and Able Archer. Reagan seemed to believe that he had acted too belligerently, and that Moscow, then in the throes of a leadership crisis because of Brezhnev's death, Andropov's ill health, and the question of his successor, had refused to be intimidated by Reagan's pressure tactics.

any of our previous meetings. He sounded as if he saw us as partners making a better world."[22]

GEORGE H. W. BUSH AND GORBACHEV

Although he had served as Reagan's vice president for the past eight years, in reality, Bush and his new team, which included Secretary of State James Baker (in office 1989–1992) and National Security Adviser Brent Scowcroft (in office 1989–1993), wanted to reassess U.S.-Soviet relations. In a February 15, 1989, memorandum called National Security Review-3, the president noted that while "[i]t would be unwise thoughtlessly to abandon policies that have brought us this far," he worried that regardless of the "remarkable changes" that had occurred within the Soviet Union, it remained "an adversary with awesome military power whose interests conflict in important ways with ours . . . [m]y own sense is that the Soviet challenge may be even greater than before because it is more varied." Bush therefore tasked his national security team with determining the Soviet Union's domestic and foreign policy objectives, assessing the internal situation in the Soviet Union, and determining what short- and long-term policies toward Moscow would be most effective.[23]

Baker called what the various agencies recommended to Bush on March 14 "mush," more suited to an academic presentation than to a policy discussion. None of the agencies, Baker recalled, seemed willing to act outside their own comfort zones and come up with an "activist" approach to deal with the Soviet Union.[24] Could Gorbachev succeed with his democratic reforms? If he succeeded, should the United States help him? What if he failed? Frustrated, Scowcroft ordered an NSC group headed by Soviet expert Condoleezza Rice to draft a shorter "think piece" about Gorbachev rather than a piece of grand strategy. Rice argued that the United States needed to move "beyond containment" by accelerating Eastern Europe's movement away from the Soviet bloc and convincing Gorbachev to move further toward the West. Scowcroft, Baker, and Bush accepted Rice's argument.[25]

Observers, in particular Gorbachev and the NATO allies, noticed the so-called pause brought about by the Review and began to get impatient, especially given that all Soviet troops had left Afghanistan in February, Gorbachev announced in April that he would cease production of weapons-grade uranium, and the Polish government had officially recognized Solidarity and created a new senate subject to popular elections.

At the same time, Reagan rejected another round of SALT; he wanted a *reduction* of arms, not simply their *limitation*. Accordingly, the Strategic Arms Reduction Talks (START) began in 1983. He also genuinely believed that SDI could eradicate the threat of nuclear war and said of the traditional doctrine of Mutually Assured Destruction (MAD), "I don't think there's any morality in that at all." The Soviet leadership crisis also affected his calculations; he famously remarked, "They keep dying on me," which made the type of superpower summits that had become famous during the 1970s seemingly impossible. To Reagan, Gorbachev seemed to be the leader for whom he had been waiting his entire first term.

In November 1986, Gorbachev and Reagan met in Reykjavík, Iceland, in what became the most important U.S.-Soviet summit meeting of the Cold War. While the two leaders essentially agreed to remove intermediate-range weapons from Europe, Gorbachev demanded that Reagan cease production of SDI as his price for a treaty. The meeting ended on a discordant note, and observers initially considered the summit a failure. In retrospect, however, Reykjavík signified an important first step, for Gorbachev abandoned his demands on SDI, and in November 1987, the two sides signed the INF Treaty in Geneva, which eliminated all intermediate force missiles. In 1988, Gorbachev began to withdraw Soviet troops from Afghanistan, allowed Reagan to visit Moscow and speak publicly about freedom and human rights, renounced the Brezhnev Doctrine, and announced that he would withdraw a half million Soviet troops from Eastern Europe.

BUSH AND GORBACHEV CONTINUE THE MOMENTUM

George H. W. Bush, Reagan's vice president, succeeded Reagan and continued to support Gorbachev. In 1989, Gorbachev allowed the "Velvet Revolution" to proceed in Eastern and Central Europe, and every Eastern European state, with the exception of Romania, peacefully replaced communism with democracy. The Berlin Wall fell in November 1989, and, a month later, he and Bush met in Malta. In fall 1990, Bush convinced Gorbachev to join the diplomatic alliance that demanded that Saddam Hussein withdraw his troops from Kuwait, and in July 1991, they signed the START Treaty, completing the process that had begun under Reagan and Andropov.

Meanwhile, it had become increasingly clear that far from strengthening the system, both perestroika and glasnost hastened the end of the Soviet Union. Once the Soviet people enjoyed a taste of freedom and Gorbachev's reforms, they wanted more. The Baltic Republics and other restive minorities in the southern, mainly Muslim, republics began to agitate for autonomy. Meanwhile, the hard-line Stalinists who had always opposed Gorbachev's reforms staged a brief coup in August 1991, which Gorbachev barely survived. In fact, one of his political opponents, Boris Yeltsin, actually rallied the anti-coup forces who forced the hard-liners out of power.

The writing was on the wall, and only four months later, Gorbachev resigned after the Commonwealth of Independent States replaced the Soviet Union. The Cold War ended soon thereafter with the dissolution of the Soviet Union.

Soviet General Secretary Mikhail Gorbachev, President Ronald Reagan, and President-elect George H. W. Bush met on Governor's Island, New York, on December 7, 1988. The three leaders were instrumental in bringing about the end of the Cold War.

SOURCE: Courtesy Ronald Reagan Library.

Bush realized that he needed to announce his new policy, and on April 17, he told an audience in Hamtramck, Michigan, a city with a large Polish-American population, that "liberty is an idea whose time has come in Eastern Europe," and said that "the true source of tension" in the Cold War "is the imposed and unnatural division of Europe." He finally said that the United States supported Gorbachev's change within the Soviet Union, and called the new agreement in Poland "a watershed in the postwar history of Eastern Europe." Poland, he said, would soon be given tariff preferences, and he called for it and other Eastern bloc nations to adopt free market economies.

On May 12, in a commencement speech at Texas A&M University, the president said, "We are approaching the conclusion of an historic postwar struggle between two visions: one of tyranny and conflict and one of democracy and freedom." He also publicly proclaimed that he would move U.S. policy toward Rice's "beyond containment" idea of actively promoting "the integration of the Soviet Union into the existing international system," as long as it continued to move "toward greater openness and democratization."[26]

Cracks in the Soviet Monolith

Events in the Soviet Union began to demonstrate that perestroika and glasnost had begun to take on lives of their own, and not always with positive results. On March 26, the Soviets held the first contested elections for the Congress of People's Deputies.

Candidates debated on television, and the proceedings were not censored by the government. Even though most of the newly elected deputies were Communist Party members and the election was a far cry from Western standards, the fact that people with different views of socialism could air their differences showed that the Soviet system had begun to take the baby steps necessary to move toward democratization.

The economy continued to struggle, however, and unrest began to stir in the republics. On April 9, 1989, the first of what Grachev called the "nationalities bombs" exploded in Tbilisi, Georgia, while Gorbachev visited London. Tens of thousands of Georgians rallied and called for Georgian independence. Soviet troops called in by the leader of the republic used batons, spades, and gas against the demonstrators, who refused to vacate the streets. The resulting stampede caused by the fleeing demonstrators killed nineteen demonstrators, seventeen of them women. The central government, as well as Gorbachev, initially blamed the deaths on the demonstrators, but as Chernyaev confidentially noted in his diary: "In general, wherever you look . . . the country is in torment. The country is unwell. And *glasnost* is like a sick person's feverish delirium. As of yet, there are no signs of improvement."[27]

Eventually, Gorbachev declared a ban on the use of force against demonstrators, but his popularity at home started to decline, while nationalist sentiment continued to grow, especially after the three Baltic Republics—Estonia, Latvia, and Lithuania—began to make demands that ultimately led to calls for independence. The genie had started to leave the bottle. Bush responded with National Security Directive 23 on September 22, 1989, which called for the "demilitarization of Soviet foreign policy," the "renunciation of the principle of class conflict," and "self-determination for the countries of East-Central Europe."[28]

Liberalization in Eastern Europe

While Gorbachev tried to keep a lid on things at home, he backed the latest moves taken by the Eastern Europeans toward liberalization, and by the end of 1989, every single member of the Soviet bloc had renounced communism. He quickly faced two important diplomatic challenges. First, he had to decide whether or not to use force to restore his nation's security zone. Ultimately, his inaction in the face of the fall of the Berlin Wall and the Velvet Revolution demonstrated that his determination not to use force to quell revolution in the wake of the Tbilisi massacre dictated that he would allow Eastern Europe to discard communism.

His second dilemma went to the heart of the Cold War. On November 28, West German Chancellor Helmut Kohl (in office 1982–1998) announced a plan for the reunification of Germany. For four decades, the Soviet government had considered the division of Germany crucial to its national security, because it believed that a reunified Germany would be inherently expansionist. Before he could decide on a plan of action, Gorbachev met with Bush in Malta in December. For the first time, Gorbachev said he did not consider the United States an enemy and endorsed a NATO presence in Europe, believing the organization's troops could maintain continental stability. Because the issue of Germany was so contentious, the two leaders decided to hold off on substantive discussions and instead discussed the global ramifications of the revolutions that had just occurred in Europe.

German Reunification

Over the next seven months, however, Bush, Gorbachev, and Kohl haggled over German unification. Kohl initially said that Germans alone should decide their future and refused to agree to reunification with neutralization. Gorbachev, on the other hand, wanted to internationalize the issue and have the Four Powers— the United States, the Soviet Union, the United Kingdom, and France—settle Germany as they had done since the end of World War II (1939–1945). Bush suggested a compromise, what he called the "Two Plus Four" plan, that would let the two Germanys decide internal issues of reunification, such as citizenship, currency, and the like, while the other nations would handle the external issues, such as diplomatic relations.

Gorbachev agreed to the formula but continued to resist a formal reunification plan until the end of May, when, in a meeting with Bush in Washington, he acknowledged the fact that only Germans could determine their own future. A true revolution in international diplomacy, and almost all of it with little to no bloodshed, had just occurred, as Gorbachev conceded that he could not prevent German reunification. In the final "Two Plus Four" agreement, signed in Moscow in September 1990, the four powers renounced their rights in Germany, including Berlin.

The reunified Germany consented to uphold West Germany's signature of the 1967 Non-Proliferation Treaty, agreed that the former East Germany and Berlin would become a permanent nuclear-free zone, and reaffirmed the new nation's 1945 border with Poland. Reunification occurred on October 3, 1990, and the new, reunified Germany became a sovereign state on March 15, 1991.

The International Coalition against Iraq

This revolution continued when, on August 3, 1990, a day after Iraq invaded Kuwait, Secretary of State James Baker and Soviet Foreign Minister Eduard Shevardnadze announced that the United States and the Soviet Union publicly condemned the invasion. In his memoirs, Baker called this "the day the cold war ended."[29] Iraq, which had been a Soviet client state for decades, ultimately faced the largest international coalition in world history. Bush and Baker successfully convinced Gorbachev to approve a UN resolution calling for the creation of a U.S.-led international army to force Saddam Hussein (in power 1979–2003) to withdraw from Kuwait. The U.S.-led coalition forced Hussein to withdraw after only four days of conflict in March 1991, and Bush honored the terms of the resolution by not sending U.S. troops to Baghdad to overthrow Hussein.

Bush and Gorbachev believed that they had created a partnership that would govern international relations for the foreseeable future. Bush, who had been initially cautious about supporting Gorbachev when he assumed office, subsequently did his best to preserve Gorbachev's power, because he worried that reactionary Stalinists could seize power and reverse the course of perestroika and glasnost.

Gorbachev's Final Year

Despite his best efforts, Gorbachev failed to create a stable, new system. In January 1991, Soviet troops fired on unarmed demonstrators in Vilnius, Lithuania, killing fourteen, despite the fact that Lithuania had declared its independence a year earlier. Meanwhile, the Soviet economy continued to falter. Although Baker had convinced Saudi Arabia to extend a $4 billion line of credit to the Soviet Union in the fall of 1990 to move the economy further toward market reforms, the effort failed miserably. While wages and government spending increased, production declined, which led to inflation, which further destabilized the economy.

THE END OF THE SOVIET UNION

By the spring, conditions had worsened to the point that many of Gorbachev's biggest supporters began to turn to Boris Yeltsin, the former first secretary of the Moscow City Communist Party Committee, whom they believed represented true reform. On June 12, Yeltsin (in office 1991–1999) defeated Gorbachev's candidate and became the first president of the Russian Soviet Republic. On July 23, delegates from the republics began to draft a Union Treaty that would replace the Soviet Union with a confederation that devolved more power to the individual republics.

Bush continued to support Gorbachev and visited Moscow in late July 1991, where the two men signed the START treaty, another landmark arms control achievement that reduced the number of intercontinental ballistic missiles. Furthermore, in an August 1 speech to the Ukrainian parliament, Bush warned against "suicidal nationalism" and stressed that revolution in the republics should remain peaceful. While his critics believed that this indicated Bush's lack of support for legitimate nationalist aspirations (one critic dubbed it the "chicken Kiev" speech), Bush believed that a headlong rush into independence would lead to a violent reaction by those opposed to what they believed would lead to the break-up of the Soviet Union. Bush clearly wanted Gorbachev to preside over an orderly transition to some type of confederation, as did Gorbachev, but what neither leader realized was that the forces that Gorbachev had unleashed, either pro- or anti-glasnost and -perestroika, could not be restrained.

Apparently the draft Union Treaty was the last straw for Gorbachev's opponents. On August 18, 1991, two days before the treaty's scheduled signing, a self-described "State Committee for the State of Emergency," led by Vice President Gennady Yanayev (in office 1990–1991), took advantage of the vacationing Gorbachev and staged a brief three-day coup. Television images of Soviet tanks surrounding the Kremlin were beamed around the world. Unfortunately for Gorbachev, who had been detained, ordinary Soviet citizens saw his rival Yeltsin rally the anti-coup forces and the hundreds of thousands of demonstrators who turned out and removed the backers of the coup. Although he could not communicate with Yeltsin, Bush nevertheless demanded that the Gorbachev government be restored.

While Gorbachev did return to power, it was only a matter of months before he was sent packing by democratic means. Bush recognized that the situation in Moscow had fundamentally changed, and although he remained as loyal to Gorbachev as possible, every time he publicly referred to the Soviet Union, he made sure to mention both Gorbachev and Yeltsin. Shortly after the abortive coup, Gorbachev resigned as general secretary of the Communist Party. Bush recognized the independence of the three Baltic States on September 2, and by the end of October, all the republics officially declared their independence.

IN THEIR OWN WORDS: *MIKHAIL GORBACHEV'S FAREWELL ADDRESS, DECEMBER 26, 1991*

December 1991 proved to be perhaps the most difficult month of Mikhail Gorbachev's brief but pivotal term as secretary general of the Soviet Union. Despite his best efforts to fix the Communist system in which he so deeply believed, perestroika and glasnost had succeeded only in hastening the system's demise. After resigning his post as president, Gorbachev appeared on Soviet television on December 26, 1991, "and faced reality."

Thanks to the formation of the Commonwealth of Independent States, he reflected on the previous six years:

> . . . I find it necessary to inform you of what I think of the road that has been trodden by us since 1985. . . . Destiny so ruled that when I found myself at the helm of this state it already was clear that something was wrong in this country.

Despite an abundance of natural and human resources, Gorbachev said:

> . . . we were living much worse than people in the industrialized countries were living and we were increasingly lagging behind them. The reason was obvious even then. This country was suffocating in the shackles of the bureaucratic command system. Doomed to cater to ideology, and suffer and carry the onerous burden of the arms race, it found itself at the breaking point. . . .

Perestroika and glasnost, he contended, had been necessary to save the Soviet experiment from itself. Furthermore, he argued that:

> All the half-hearted reforms—and there have been a lot of them—fell through, one after another. This country was going nowhere and we couldn't possibly live the way we did. We had to change everything radically.

Gorbachev could not admit, however, that the system that had been so broken could not be fixed by his own "half-hearted reforms," and once he chose to try to reform the system, it collapsed under its own inherent contradictions.

SOURCE: Available at http://www.nytimes.com/1991/12/26/world/end-of-the-soviet-union-text-of-gorbachev-s-farewell-address.html.

Seeing the inevitability of the central government's breakup, Gorbachev tried to hang on and proposed an updated version of the Union Treaty, but Yeltsin wanted an arrangement more like the British Commonwealth, where all the states in the arrangement kept their independence. Yeltsin won the argument in December, when he secretly met with the leaders of Ukraine and Belarus, who decided to dissolve the Soviet Union and create the Commonwealth of Independent States. The three leaders informed Bush, who said he would recognize the new arrangement. On December 21, every republic with the exception of Georgia signed the declaration. Gorbachev resigned five days later, and on December 25, 1991, the Soviet Union dissolved with a whimper.

Ironically, the Cold War ended thanks to a combination of diplomatic firmness and rhetorical restraint on the part of Ronald Reagan, and Mikhail Gorbachev's desire to create true communism in the Soviet Union. Reagan's determination to increase defense spending, most notably through the Strategic Defense Initiative, and Gorbachev's corresponding desire to implement perestroika and glasnost had profound ramifications for international relations, because Gorbachev's more idealistic version of socialism required a pragmatic weakening of his nation's massive military might. Reagan correctly understood the underlying weakness of the Soviet system and exploited this through his defense measures. At the same time, Reagan recognized that the Soviet Union was finally enjoying a leader who was willing to make deeply significant concessions that acknowledged this reality.

George H. W. Bush, meanwhile, deserves some credit for helping manage the end of the Cold War. Bush believed that he had to walk a tightrope between urging too much reform and helping to cause a violent reaction that could restore the hard-liners in Moscow. In a final irony, neither Bush nor Gorbachev recognized that perestroika and glasnost actually hastened the demise of the Soviet Union, and neither expected Yeltsin to rally the pro-democracy (Russian-style, to be sure) forces to reject the August 1991 coup. Nevertheless, both leaders could take comfort in knowing that Gorbachev's reforms, as well as the Reagan and Bush administrations' support for them, likely helped ensure that the dissolution of the Soviet empire occurred relatively peacefully in comparison to the fall of other twentieth-century empires.

See also: **Chapter 28: "Tear Down This Wall"; Chapter 30: Diplomatic Milestones, 1970s–1991.**

ENDNOTES

1. Ronald Reagan, "Address to the Nation and Other Countries on United States-Soviet Relations," January 16, 1984, in *The Public Papers of the Presidents, Ronald Reagan, 1984,* The American Presidency Project [online], available at: http://www.presidency.ucsb.edu/ws/index.php?pid=39806&st=&st1=#axzz1MAYmizuY.

2. Quoted in Vladislav M. Zubok, *A Failed Empire: The Soviet Union in the Cold War from Stalin to Gorbachev* (Chapel Hill: University of North Carolina Press, 2007), 282.

3. George Shultz, *Turmoil and Triumph: My Years as Secretary of State* (New York: Charles Scribner and Sons, 1993), 507–08.

4. "Memorandum of Conversation between Thatcher and Reagan," December 28, 1985, The Margaret Thatcher Foundation website, http://www.margaretthatcher.org/document/109185.

5. Shultz, *Turmoil and Triumph,* 528–34.

6. "Diary Entry," September 27, 1985, in Ronald Reagan, *The Reagan Diaries* (New York: Harper, 2007), 356.

7. Reagan, "Diary Entry," November 13, 1985" and "Memorandum," November 1985" quoted in Martin Anderson and Annelise Anderson, *Reagan's Secret War: The Untold Story of His Fight to Save the World from Nuclear Disaster* (New York: Crown, 2009), 223–25.

8. "Diary Entry," November 12, 1985, in *The Diary of Anatoly Chernyaev 1985,* The National Security Archive, http://www.gwu.edu/~nsarchiv/NSAEBB/NSAEBB192/Chernyaev_Diary_translation_1985.pdf.

9. "Memorandum of Conversation between Reagan and Gorbachev," November 19, 1985, in Anderson and Anderson, *Reagan's Secret War,* 232–36.

10. "Diary Entry," November 24, 1985, in *The Diary of Anatoly Chernyaev, 1985,* The National Security Archive, available at: http://www.gwu.edu/~nsarchiv/NSAEBB/NSAEBB192/Chernyaev_Diary_translation_1985.pdf.

11. Pavel Palazchenko, *My Years with Gorbachev and Shevardnadze: The Memoirs of a Soviet Interpreter* (University Park: Pennsylvania State University Press, 1997), 45.

12. "Diary Entry," January 15, 1986, and "Diary Entry," February 3, 1986, in *The Reagan Diaries,* 383, 388.

13. Andrei Grachev, *Gorbachev's Gamble: Soviet Foreign Policy and the End of the Cold War* (Cambridge, UK: Polity Press, 2008), p. 69.

14. The first quote is from Zubok, *A Failed Empire,* 289; the second is from Grachev, *Gorbachev's Gamble,* 81.

15. U.S. and Russian transcripts of the four meetings are available on The National Security Archive website at http://www.gwu.edu/~nsarchiv/NSAEBB/NSAEBB203/index.htm; see also "Diary Entry," October 12, 1986, in *The Reagan Diaries,* 444–45.

16. Numbers are from Zubok, *A Failed Empire,* 298–99.

17. Quoted in Grachev, *Gorbachev's Gamble,* 109–10, and Shultz, *Turmoil and Triumph,* 1088–91.

18. Quoted in *Gorbachev's Gamble,* 120–21.

19. Quoted in James Mann, *The Rebellion of Ronald Reagan: A History of the End of the Cold War* (New York: Penguin, 2009), 304–05.

20. Ronald Reagan, "Remarks and a Question-and-Answer Session with the Students and Faculty at Moscow State University," May 31, 1988, in *The Public Papers of the Presidents, Ronald Reagan, 1988,* The American Presidency Project [online], available at: http://www.presidency.ucsb.edu/ws/index.php?pid=35897&st=&st1=#axzz1MjC5f47Z.

21. "Excerpts from Address by Mikhail Gorbachev, 43rd U.N. General Assembly Session," December 7, 1988, available at http://isc.temple.edu/hist249/course/Documents/gorbachev_speech_to_UN.htm.

FURTHER READING

Chernyaev, Anatoly et al. *My Six Years with Gorbachev.* University Park: Penn State University Press, 2000.

Engel, Jeffrey. *The Fall of the Berlin Wall: The Revolutionary Legacy of 1989.* New York: Oxford University Press, 2009.

Gates, Robert M. *From the Shadows: The Ultimate Insider's Story of Five Presidents and How They Won the Cold War.* New York: Simon & Schuster, 1996.

Gorbachev, Mikhail. *At the Summit: How the Two Superpowers Set the World on a Course for Peace.* New York: Richardson, Steirman & Black, 1988.

Herring, George C. *From Colony to Superpower: U.S. Foreign Relations since 1776.* New York: Oxford University Press, 2008.

Leffler, Melvyn. *For the Soul of Mankind: The United States, the Soviet Union, and the Cold War.* New York: Hill & Wang, 2008.

Maynard, Christopher. *Out of the Shadow: George H. W. Bush and the End of the Cold War.* College Station: Texas A&M University Press, 2008.

Ouimet, Matthew J. *The Rise and Fall of the Brezhnev Doctrine in Soviet Foreign Policy.* Chapel Hill: University of North Carolina Press, 2003.

Sarotte, Mary Elise. *1989: The Struggle to Create Post-Cold War Europe.* Princeton, NJ: Princeton University Press, 2009.

chapter 30

Diplomatic Milestones, 1970s–1991

History and Analysis of the Post-Vietnam Era and Its Impact on American Society

by Daniel Sargent

In November 1968, Richard M. Nixon (1969–1974) won his second campaign for the presidency. Back in 1960, when he ran against John F. Kennedy (1961–1963), Vietnam was an unknown land for most Americans. Since then, it had become distressingly familiar. Some thirty-six thousand Americans had died there, fighting to defend South Vietnam against a Communist insurrection supported by North Vietnam and, indirectly, the Soviet Union and China. Within the United States, Vietnam became more divisive as the war progressed. While some Americans remained committed to the war, others argued that it was futile. For President Nixon, Vietnam presented agonizing choices. Should American forces stay, or should they come home? Could the war be won? If not, could Washington negotiate a peace settlement that would preserve South Vietnam's independence—the goal for which the United States had gone to war in the first place?

THE NIXON ADMINISTRATION AND VIETNAM

Political circumstances both at home and in the world defined Nixon's choices in Vietnam. While he believed that a "silent majority" of Americans still supported the war, he also recognized that enthusiasm was waning as the military campaign deteriorated into stalemate. Restoring domestic political tranquility, he believed, depended upon the war's timely resolution. At the same time, Nixon feared that abandoning South Vietnam would tarnish the reputation of the United States throughout the world. Would small countries trust American commitments, Nixon asked, if Washington abandoned Saigon to an uncertain fate? As president, Nixon thus had to grapple with domestic and international imperatives that pushed in different directions.

Believing that America's commitment to the global containment of communism would not permit a simple liquidation of the war effort, Nixon struggled instead to mitigate the war's burdens.

The Nixon administration started multiple new initiatives. The key innovation was "Vietnamization," which aimed to bolster South Vietnam's military capacities, thereby enabling both the drawdown of American forces and the termination of the military draft. At the same time, Nixon sought a peace settlement that would permit the extrication of U.S. troops from Vietnam. Even as it sought peace, however, the Nixon administration escalated the war's violence, bombing North Vietnam and expanding the fighting into Cambodia. Brutal force, Nixon and his National Security Adviser Henry Kissinger (in office 1969–1975) hoped, might intimidate the north and reassure the south, such that both would agree to a political settlement.

Ending the War

After three years, the Vietnam War took a turn toward resolution, but at this point Nixon was more the captive of events than the shaper of them. The U.S. Congress, frustrated with the administration's progress toward peace, threatened to cut appropriations for the war in Indochina. Backed into a corner, the Nixon administration hastily negotiated the Paris Peace of January 1973. Under its terms, the United States withdrew its remaining forces from South Vietnam. Within about two years, hostilities between the two Vietnams would resume, ending only in April 1975 with a decisive North Vietnamese victory and the country's reunification. So far as Nixon and Kissinger were concerned, the outcome of the war in the winter of 1972–1973 revealed the capacity of domestic politics to thwart America's global

KEY CONCEPTS

New World Order. At the Cold War's end, President George H. W. Bush talked about the advent of a "new world order." Much discussed at the time and since, the phrase marked the transition from the Cold War into a new historical phase, one that would be harder to define than the era of Soviet-American confrontation had been. What did Bush mean when he talked about a "new world order"? Quoting Winston Churchill, he described a world in which "the principles of justice and fair play . . . protect the weak against the strong." International law, multilateral institutions, and human rights were central aspects of the new world order concept as President Bush used it. Although Bush put the accent on the "new," there was much that was old about the concept. Woodrow Wilson, after all, had based his concept of a new international order upon similar commitments—the rule of law and multilateral institutions. Bush himself acknowledged that the "new world order" concept was not so much a new departure as a rehabilitation of older ideas when he stated that the United Nations, now "freed from Cold War stalemate," would for the first time be able "to fulfill the historic vision of its founders." In other words, Bush hoped that with the passing of the long-standing Soviet-American estrangement in 1991, the international institutions that emerged out of World War II, specifically the United Nations, would at last be able to serve effectively as the guardians of international peace and security.

Bush's vision of a new world order was in many ways more cautious than it was transformative. That did not prevent the phrase from becoming controversial within the United States. Critics on the political fringe, such as the conservative presidential candidate Pat Buchanan, pounced upon the phrase as proof that Bush, and other internationalists, proposed to make American sovereignty subordinate to international institutions. The phrase, as it was debated in the early 1990s, revealed not only a continuity in the enthusiasm of American internationalists, from Wilson to Bush, for international law and institutions, but also the deep suspicion and hostility that such schemes have stirred in other Americans.

Superpower rivalries. At the end of the 1960s, there was much to fear in the Cold War world. Both superpowers had the capacity to destroy each other in a fusillade of nuclear missiles, which had not been the case in the fearful late 1940s. Yet Americans at the end of the 1960s appeared to be rather less afraid of the Soviet Union than an earlier generation had been. Vietnam was a more urgent foreign policy crisis, while domestic politics still preoccupied many in the aftermath of the civil rights movement's heroic phase.

Gesturing, as it did, toward a resolution of Cold War rivalries, Nixon's détente with the Soviet Union was nonetheless popular with the American people in the early 1970s. That support for it began to wane from the mid-1970s, however, revealed how complacent Americans had become about the Cold War. Though the nuclear arsenals were larger than ever, the Cold War had become so customary that actual conflict between the superpowers seemed highly unlikely. Confident that the superpowers would not come to blows, some Americans began to argue that détente neglected human rights in the Soviet Union. Another critique of détente argued, however, that Nixon's pursuit of stability was consigning the United States to second place in the Cold War, giving the Soviet Union the opportunity to get ahead.

In the late 1970s, these alternative perspectives began to coalesce. Carter and Reagan both emphasized human rights in the USSR, even as they worked to rebuild America's military advantages. The era of détente, looking back, appeared an unusual interlude during which the United States had sought peace as a means to stability but in which Americans had been insufficiently fearful of instability to accept the compromises, both moral and strategic, that détente came to entail.

commitments. As he led the country out of Vietnam, Nixon lamented what he took for the resurgence of isolationist sentiment in the United States.

A New Isolationism?

President Nixon was not the only American to worry about a new isolationism in the early 1970s. Events support the perception, widely shared, that Americans wanted to disengage from the world. In spring 1971, Senator Mike Mansfield (D-MT; in office 1953–1977) introduced an amendment to the Selective Service Bill, which would have slashed U.S. troop commitments to NATO. Only determined lobbying by the Nixon administration defeated it. The following summer, Senator George McGovern (D-SD; in office 1963–1981) received his party's presidential nomination. Addressing the Democratic National Convention, he called upon his countrymen to "come home" from costly foreign wars and overseas commitments. For committed internationalists, such

talk revealed the dangers of a resurgent isolationism. Would Americans, weary of Vietnam's burdens, back away from the international commitments that they had sustained since the late 1940s? If so, what would be the consequences for the United States and for the larger international community?

Committed to American leadership in the world, Richard Nixon sought to adjust the burdens of American responsibility in order to sustain those very burdens. He thus acknowledged that American power had in some respects entered an era of limits. The economic power and political consensus that sustained American international commitments in the 1940s had dwindled over a generation. As president, Nixon sought to accommodate these shifts in circumstances. To this end, he produced a foreign policy doctrine bearing his name, the "Nixon Doctrine." It avowed that the United States would henceforth require allies such as South Vietnam to provide the manpower necessary for defending themselves against internal enemies. In another pragmatic thrust, Nixon reduced the defense budget, calculating that a prudent reduction in spending would protect military expenditures against the more savage cuts that Congress would otherwise inflict. The overall logic was one of cautious retrenchment; by moderating the burdens of superpower responsibility, Nixon sought to protect America's basic commitments to Cold War internationalism against the domestic critics and cutters.

Nixon's Initiatives with the Soviet Union and China

At the same time as Nixon worked to scale back American military spending, he also cultivated relations with the Soviet Union and the People's Republic of China. With the Soviet Union, Nixon pursued a strategy that became known as "détente." It aimed to stabilize superpower relations in ways that would preserve American advantages in the Cold War. Toward China, Nixon embarked upon an "opening," which sought not only to improve relations with the People's Republic but also to convert Beijing, now estranged from Moscow, into a tacit American ally. Nixon thus tried to make himself the central player in a triangle of superpower relations, from which position he would manipulate Sino-Soviet tensions to the advantage of the United States. This diplomatic concept revealed how concerns about limits shaped Nixon's foreign policy, from its tactics to its grand strategy. Détente, Nixon intended, would stabilize Cold War commitments, reducing the costs of the superpower rivalry, much as the Nixon Doctrine was moderating the burdens of American military commitments overseas.

So far as the Soviet Union was concerned, Nixon feared that the Cold War balance of power had slipped eastward during the 1960s. Here, the nuclear arms race provided special cause for concern. During the 1950s, the United States had led the way in the development and deployment of nuclear weapons. That changed during the 1960s. After the 1962 Cuban Missile Crisis, the Soviet Union expanded its nuclear forces. The United States, meanwhile, stabilized its own strategic forces, confident that it possessed enough nuclear warheads to deter any Soviet attack upon itself or its allies. By the turn of the 1970s, the balance of nuclear firepower was shifting in favor of the Soviet Union, which now possessed more intercontinental ballistic missiles (ICBMs) than did the United States. The question of how to stall this relative decline preoccupied the Nixon administration. The solution that Nixon devised involved reciprocal incentives; the United States would offer concessions to Moscow in return for Soviet concessions on issues important to the United States. This approach soon produced the first bilateral agreement to control the nuclear arms race. The Strategic Arms Limitation Treaty (SALT I), signed in summer 1972, committed both sides to not expanding their fleets of intercontinental missiles. For the United States, this stabilization prevented the balance of military power from slipping further toward the Soviet Union.

While Soviet-American détente resembled a holding action, the China "opening" was among Nixon's most creative initiatives. Since the Communist Party's 1949 triumph in China's long civil war, there had been no official relations between the United States and the People's Republic. That Nixon, an anti-communist of long-standing, would be the president who opened relations was stunning, if not entirely illogical. For one thing, Nixon did not have to fear a right-wing backlash at home, as a Democrat might have. For another, the China opening was part of a coherent strategy to rebalance Cold War politics. Never an isolated venture, the China opening served a larger strategic purpose. The Sino-American relationship quickly developed into a tacit anti-Soviet alliance, in which the fear and antipathy that Washington and Beijing both felt toward Moscow became the adhesive of their own relationship.

The China relationship also provided the Nixon administration with some advantages in its dealings with the Soviet Union; after visiting Beijing, Nixon found the Soviets to be more pliable than they had been before. Nixon's triangular diplomacy thus helped to supplement America's waning resources of material power; if the Soviet-American competition had devolved into a military stalemate, adept diplomacy, Nixon hoped, might provide new influence. As innovative a concept as triangular diplomacy was, however, it did not bring any fundamental rethinking of America's world role. Rather, it accepted the permanence of Cold War divisions and worked to manipulate the balance of power to the advantage of the United States. Ultimately, it was a strategy for the promotion of international stability rather than change.

SHOCKS AND CRISES

Within the Cold War's Western bloc, change was afoot, whether Nixon sought it or not. At the end of World War II (1939–1945), the United States had been the West's dominant power, especially in terms of its economic power. Abject and ruined, Western Europe and Japan depended upon American imports and American assistance. A generation later, much had changed. West European and Japanese industries had rebounded, and American importers were feeling the competition. Foreign cars became a common sight on American roads, marking the relative decline of the Detroit automobile industry. The waning of American economic primacy within the West destabilized the international economic institutions, known as the "Bretton Woods" institution, which the United States had set up at the war's end. The dollar became a source of instability for the world economy; when a major dollar crisis broke in summer 1971, Nixon was forced to suspend its convertibility into gold. Soon, the system of fixed exchange rates that had existed under Bretton Woods was swept away, in part by changes in the underlying value of currencies but also because of the globalization of financial markets, which made fixed exchange rates difficult to maintain.

Richard Nixon and Henry Kissinger worried, meanwhile, that the consolidation of the European Economic Community would strain the unity of the West, which had been the focus of American internationalist commitments for a generation. With the purpose of bolstering the West's unity and purpose, Kissinger, now secretary of state (in office 1973–1977), declared 1973 the "Year of Europe." The initiative was poorly received. With Europe now capable of standing on its own feet, some European leaders favored a more independent role in the world. For example, West Germany had since 1969 been pursuing *Ostpolitik*, an independent policy toward the Communist world. This "eastern policy" sought to liberalize relations across the Iron Curtain with the purpose of promoting long-term change in the Communist bloc. Ostpolitik nonetheless alienated American leaders, who feared that it might weaken the unity of the West. At the same time, Western European leaders harbored their own suspicions of Soviet-American détente, which seemed to raise the possibility of a Soviet-American understanding in which the voices of even allies, such as West Germany, would be marginalized.

Crisis in the Middle East

The grumbling that afflicted the West during 1973 exploded into crisis at the year's end. The source lay not within the Western Alliance but in the Middle East. In October 1973, Egypt and Syria attacked Israel, starting the Yom Kippur War. The war began badly for Israeli forces, who found themselves surprised by the assault. For the United States and other Western countries, the war presented difficult dilemmas. Preoccupied with the Cold War balance of power, Henry Kissinger was unwilling to see Egypt, a nominal client of the Soviet Union, defeat Israel, an ally of the United States. Egypt, however, enjoyed strong support among its Arab neighbors, who supplied much of the oil that the West now imported. The economic and the security interests of the West, it seemed, were divided.

When Washington intervened to support Israel with an airlift of military hardware, Saudi Arabia and other oil-producing nations retaliated with an oil boycott. While directed against the United States, the boycott slashed oil deliveries to the world market, producing energy shortages and price spikes throughout the West. American motorists found themselves waiting in long lines to purchase gasoline.

The Oil Crisis

The oil crisis had global repercussions. Most obviously, it represented a psychological shock for the West. The crisis strained the West's unity; while the United States sought to develop a "consumer cartel" that would bargain with the oil producers on equal terms, several of its European allies preferred to seek special deals with the Arab governments. The economic consequences were no less profound. Cheap energy had nurtured the West's remarkable postwar growth from the late 1940s to the late 1960s. With the oil crisis, the era of cheap energy came to an end. The oil shock was not the only (nor necessarily the primary) cause of the inflation that gripped the West in the 1970s, but a fourfold increase in the price of energy over 1973 and 1974 exacerbated an economic crisis in which Western governments struggled to deal with inflation and sluggish growth. For the United States, in particular, the oil crisis marked the shock of interdependence. With Texas and California unable to match the nation's appetite for hydrocarbons, Americans became dependent on foreign exporters to keep their engines running. No wonder that President Gerald R. Ford (1974–1977), Nixon's successor, remarked in 1975 that "the world economy has become interdependent."[1]

One interpretation took the oil crisis for an inversion of power. After centuries of imperialism, was the West getting its comeuppance at the hands of the Global South or Third World, the nations of the Southern Hemisphere that were colonized and exploited by Europe and the United States? The reality was more complicated. The oil crisis benefited oil producers at the expense of consumers, but these categories cut across the North-South divide. Western countries with substantial oil reserves, such as Canada and Great Britain, enjoyed windfalls of their own. Developing countries that lacked oil reserves suffered acute balance-of-payments crises, as they struggled to pay for their oil imports. What soon transpired was an informal system of "petrodollar recycling," in which private banks took in money from oil exporters like Saudi Arabia and lent it to oil-importing countries. The oil crisis thus spurred the ongoing development of financial globalization, one of the key historical legacies of the 1970s, while many developing countries found themselves impoverished and indebted. Some developing countries formed a caucus at the United Nations, the Group of 77 (G-77), to press for reform of the world economic order, including the creation of cartel agreements for agricultural products. It came to little. For now, the South still lacked the unity and the strength to reshape a world economy in which the Western countries remained the dominant, if bruised, force.

The End of Imperialism

The 1970s nonetheless marked one triumph for the Global South. With the collapse of the Portuguese empire in 1974 and 1975, the long era of European imperialism at last passed into history. The twilight of colonialism did not bring democracy's dawn, however. In fact, the prospects for democracy in the developing world deteriorated from the mid-1960s. Major developing countries such as Indonesia, the Philippines, and Brazil suffered coups; other states, such as Nigeria and Pakistan, experienced bloody civil wars. Even India, the world's largest democracy, went through a period of "emergency," during which constitutional protections were suspended. While democracy's travails in the Global South were mainly a consequence of local conditions, the Cold War did not help. The United States frequently aligned itself with authoritarian regimes, finding them a useful ally against communism. American support for Third World dictators peaked under Richard Nixon, who took a cynical attitude when it came to democracy's prospects in the Global South.

Notoriously, Nixon and Kissinger encouraged the Chilean military to overthrow that country's Marxist president, Salvador Allende, which it did in 1973. After the coup, the military began a campaign of violent repression against the Chilean left. For the United States, the strategic logic was little different from that which had animated involvement in the overthrow of Iran's prime minister, Mohammad Mosaddeq, in 1953, and Guatemala's president, Jacobo Arbenz, in 1954. Yet evolving circumstances in the 1970s, including rising awareness of human rights, made the Chilean coup more controversial in the United States than earlier acts of Cold War expedience had been.

NEW CHALLENGES, NEW APPROACHES

Until the early 1970s, the idea of human rights was substantially absent from the vocabulary of statecraft. After a quarter of a century, the Universal Declaration of Human Rights (1948) still had little bearing on the foreign policy of the United States, or most other countries. During the Nixon years, however, Americans became increasingly attentive to the human dimension of international relations. Some Americans reflected on the human consequences of the Vietnam War. Others fixated upon civil wars in Nigeria and Pakistan, which claimed heavy human casualties and produced accusations of genocide. In 1973, the House of Representatives convened a series of hearings on human rights in U.S. foreign policy, the first official inquiry to be devoted to that topic. It concluded that the United States had badly neglected human rights during the Cold War and called upon the White House to be more attentive to them in the future. Over the next few years, Congress worked to force the executive branch's hand on this issue, passing laws that limited the provision of military and developmental assistance to countries that violated the human rights of their citizens. New laws required the State Department to produce annual reports analyzing human rights conditions in

countries receiving American assistance, a category that included much of the non-Communist developing world.

Congressional activism on human rights suggested how the domestic environment in which U.S. foreign policy had to be made was changing in the early 1970s. Richard M. Nixon fell into political disgrace during 1974, after White House involvement in a 1972 burglary at the Democratic National Committee was publicly revealed. Watergate, as the scandal became known, weakened the executive branch. The 1974 congressional elections produced a swing toward the Democratic Party. Emboldened by Nixon's disgrace, some members of Congress questioned core assumptions of his Cold War policy and promoted alternatives. Besides promoting human rights, so-called "new internationalists" held hearings on CIA misadventures in the developing world, known as the Church and Pike Committee hearings, and passed statutes curtailing the activity of the intelligence agencies on American soil.

Determined to prevent future Vietnams, Congress also acted to inhibit the use of military force overseas. The War Powers Act of 1973 required the president to seek congressional approval before committing U.S. forces to war, while the Case-Church Amendment prohibited further military action in Southeast Asia. At the beginning of 1976, Congress acted to restrict the provision of military assistance to anti-Communist factions in Angola, fearful that involvement in that country's civil war might escalate. Henry Kissinger, who continued to serve as secretary of state under President Gerald R. Ford, warned that Congress was making the pursuit of an effective Cold War foreign policy impossible.

While Kissinger blamed his critics for making foreign policy unmanageable, others discerned a deeper, more structural crisis of "governability" in the United States. In 1974, political scientist Samuel Huntingdon argued that democratic politics had become so fractious and so plural as to inhibit the making of effective national policy.[2] The argument contained some insight. Until the late 1960s, Cold War internationalism had commanded a broad spectrum of support, despite periodic dissents on the left and right. After Vietnam, the spectrum of debate broadened.

Détente and Interdependence

Some Americans, like Kissinger, believed that the imperatives of anti-Soviet containment remained urgent. Others disagreed. The de-escalation of Cold War rivalries in an era of détente, some argued, and the advent of new international dilemmas mandated new approaches to foreign policy. Prominent among the new challenges that the 1970s posed were dilemmas associated with what we know today as globalization, but which people at the time called interdependence. While international society remained, on the face of things, dominated by nation-states, the rapid growth of transnational economic, social, and cultural exchange, especially within the West, was beginning to entwine the fates of nations in new and complex ways. Interdependence became a popular theme among political scientists who studied international relations in the 1970s. Some economists even argued that interdependence made national economic policy impossible. Here, the oil crisis of 1973–1974 demonstrated the point, revealing the inability of national governments to protect their economies against external shocks.

Concerned that new economic interdependence required coordination of governance, in 1973, business leader David Rockefeller created the Trilateral Commission as a forum to promote cooperation between North American, Western European, and Japanese academics and business leaders. The Trilateral Commission produced a series of studies that advocated inter-governmental cooperation on problems of common interest, from the management of international finance to energy conservation. While the Trilateral Commission advocated intense cooperation among governments, Western leaders began, more cautiously, to explore new approaches to policy coordination during the 1970s. Here, the short-lived Ford administration had an important role to play. Ford participated in head-of-state summits at Rambouillet, France, in 1975 and Puerto Rico in 1976, which created the

G-7 group of advanced industrialized countries. These summits provided leaders with an opportunity to share perspectives and even to devise ways of cooperating to meet common challenges. In the last decades of the twentieth century, they became a prominent feature of the international landscape.

The Carter Administration and Human Rights

Jimmy Carter's (1977–1981) election as president brought an end to eight years of Republican leadership. A southern Democrat and former Georgia governor, Carter was a minor figure on the national stage before the election. He brought not only a fresh face to the White House but also a new orientation toward foreign policy. Carter strove to break free of the Cold War assumptions and outlook that had dominated U.S. foreign policy since the Truman administration. He did not always succeed, but he focused attention on problems that Nixon and Kissinger had neglected. These included the management of interdependence among the Western countries, the accommodation of the Global South's demands for a more equitable world order, and the promotion of human rights on the international stage.

SHIFTS IN FOREIGN POLICY: *HUMAN RIGHTS AND THE CARTER ADMINISTRATION*

In 1977, the Universal Declaration of Human Rights, which the United Nations approved in 1948, was almost thirty years old. For the first two decades after 1948, however, human rights had remained a marginal theme in international relations. Neither the United States nor the Soviet Union had made their promotion a foreign policy goal, while most countries in the world still regarded external surveillance of their domestic affairs as a violation of their sovereignty. Much changed in the declaration's third decade. Non-governmental organizations (NGOs) such as Amnesty International worked with some success to raise the profile of human rights. Serious violations of human rights occurred in contexts as far apart as Latin America's Southern Cone, where the "disappearance" of political radicals was pervasive, and the Soviet Union, which clamped down harshly on political dissenters and attracted widespread attention.

Reflecting the issue's urgency, the U.S. Congress in the mid-1970s passed laws that limited the provision of military and development assistance to countries that violated the rights of their citizens. While these laws were riddled with loopholes, it was significant that Congress had for the first time made the promotion of international human rights a commitment under law. By the time of Jimmy Carter's inauguration, then, human rights was an idea whose time had come.

THE ROOTS OF HUMAN RIGHTS

Jimmy Carter made much of human rights. He talked about it on the campaign trail. He highlighted it as a theme in his inaugural address, declaring that "because we are free we can never be indifferent to the fate of freedom elsewhere" [Available at http://www.presidency.ucsb.edu/ws/index.php?pid=657

5&st=&st1=#axzz1NhfYD053]. In a 1978 address marking the Universal Declaration's thirtieth anniversary, Carter went further still. "Human rights is the soul of our foreign policy," he proclaimed, "because human rights is the soul of our sense of nationhood" [Available at http://www.presidency.ucsb.edu/ws/index.php?pid=30264&st=&st1=#axzz1NhfYD053]. For Carter, human rights was an ancient creed. Thomas Jefferson's Declaration of Independence had, after all, invoked natural rights as a basis for the American War for Independence (1775–1783). Because all men were endowed with certain inalienable rights, Jefferson argued, the colonists were entitled to rebel against Great Britain when it violated their rights. Once independent, however, the United States had not always made the worldwide promotion of human rights a central objective of its foreign policy. Jefferson's rival Alexander Hamilton, after all, argued that diplomacy ought to be based on a clear-sighted calculation of interests, rather than devotion to abstract ideals.

HUMAN RIGHTS IN THE COLD WAR ERA

For much of the Cold War, Alexander Hamilton's logic prevailed. The United States often supported dictators in the developing world, viewing them as a bulwark against Communist subversion. Ironically, American diplomats also refrained, for the most part, from pushing the cause of human rights with the Soviet Union itself, calculating that stability outweighed other goals. This tendency was especially pronounced under President Richard Nixon, who disdained human rights in his pursuit of détente. By 1977, however, many Americans despaired of the ethical compromises and moral equivocations that their foreign policy makers had long performed. Carter channeled the public's desire for a more moralistic, more

Carter's own education in foreign policy came largely from the Trilateral Commission, of which he had been a member. Not part of the Cold War elite that had embroiled the United States in Vietnam, Carter worked to devise alternatives, even to lay the foundations for a post–Cold War foreign policy for the United States.

The Carter administration built upon earlier congressional efforts to reorient U.S. foreign policy toward the promotion of human rights. Carter emphasized human rights in relation to both American allies and adversaries, especially in Latin America and the Soviet Union. As a doctrine that appealed to critics of Communist regimes as well as to critics of authoritarian governments, human rights enjoyed broad support in the United States. Still, the issue received less attention in some cases, such as China and Iran, than it did in others, such as Argentina and the Soviet Union.

The Search for Equity and Peace

Even as it promoted human rights, the Carter administration worked to improve relations with governments in the developing world. Here, the Panama Canal Treaty, which provided for the eventual return of the Canal Zone to Panamanian sovereignty, was an important accomplishment. Though popular with governments throughout Latin America, the Canal Treaty was divisive among the American public and politically costly for the administration.

President Carter's most important accomplishment when it came to the developing world, however, was his negotiation of a peace settlement between Israel and Egypt in 1978. The Camp David Accords, which built on foundations Kissinger laid, ended the long conflict between Israel and Egypt. A secondary effect was to bring Egypt into Washington's system of Cold War alliances, ending Cairo's relationship with the Soviet Union. Though the Camp David Accords did not end the conflict between Israel and Palestinian nationalism, the agreement transformed the politics of the Middle East.

THE COLD WAR RESURGES

For the United States, the Middle East became a focus for engagement during the 1970s. The decade began with

---

idealistic, more American foreign policy, and human rights was the language that defined his new approach.

CARTER'S VIEW OF HUMAN RIGHTS

What did human rights mean for the Carter administration? At their most basic, human rights are specific rights that individual human beings are deemed to hold by the mere virtue of being human. They apply to all people regardless of their citizenship or place of residence. Human rights can be diffuse; the Universal Declaration articulates dozens and dozens of them, from the right to security to the right to education. The Carter administration grouped human rights into three broad categories: liberty rights, political and civil rights, and social, economic, and cultural rights (available at http://www.jimmycarterlibrary.gov/documents/pddirectives/pd30.pdf). It placed most emphasis on the first category, which encompasses the rights of human beings to be free from arbitrary arrest, torture, and death, and the second, which has to do with political participation and expression. Less emphasis was placed on the category of social, economic, and cultural rights. One key distinction is that the first two categories of human rights propose to limit the authority of states over individuals, whereas social and economic rights depend, necessarily, upon government for their realization. This makes them rather trickier to pursue in the international arena.

As president, Carter worked to promote human rights in a number of different ways. He punished some governments that abused the rights of their citizens by curtailing military and development assistance. Notorious violators such as Argentina, Uruguay, and Uganda all found themselves blacklisted. In other cases, Carter refrained from bilateral action, concluding that existing regimes, unpleasant as they were, served useful strategic purposes. The Middle East and East Asia received less scrutiny on human rights grounds from the Carter administration than did Latin America. Besides emphasizing human rights in some bilateral relationships, the Carter administration also worked to promote the theme at the multilateral level. The administration was an enthusiastic supporter of the inter-American human rights apparatus and involved itself in reforming the United Nations Commission for Human Rights, a recently moribund institution that became more effective in the late 1970s.

Human rights was most contentious where it intersected directly with Cold War politics. Here, Carter's record was one of oscillation between zeal and caution. He initially embraced Soviet human rights activists such as Andrei Sakharov and Vladimir Bukovsky. As he became more anxious to conclude a strategic arms limitation treaty (SALT II) with the Soviet Union, however, Carter's human rights emphasis began to lapse. It would be more complicated, Carter learned, to promote universal human rights in complex relationships with powerful foreign states than it was to embrace it in the abstract. The emphasis that Carter accorded to human rights tended to diminish as his presidency progressed. Nonetheless, Carter made the language and ideals of human rights a central concern of presidential diplomacy for the first time. Since 1981, all of Carter's successors have, to greater and lesser extents, defined the promotion of human rights as a central priority. That the issue retains such an important profile in U.S. foreign policy is the ultimate measure of Jimmy Carter's accomplishment.

President Jimmy Carter's (center) efforts to bring peace to the Middle East reflected the growing importance of the region to the United States. Carter personally conducted the tense negotiations between Israeli Prime Minister Menachem Begin (left) and Egyptian President Anwar Sadat at Camp David, the presidential retreat in Maryland. On September 17, 1978, after twelve days of secret meetings, the Camp David Accords were signed at the White House.

SOURCE: Karl Schumacher/AFP/Getty Images.

Nixon and Kissinger worried about the intrusion of Soviet power into the region, though new problems, such as oil, soon jostled for prominence. To bolster regional security, Washington cultivated Iran and Saudi Arabia as regional allies and stabilizers. Before long, however, this strategy of regional alliances ran afoul of change within the region, especially in Iran, where the rapid influx of oil wealth destabilized Shah Reza Pahlavi's (reigned 1941–1979) regime. From the mid-1970s, Pahlavi, a longtime American ally, faced intensifying demands for political and economic reform. While a minority of pro-Western reformers embraced the language of human rights, a larger portion of dissatisfied Iranians turned to religious vocabularies of dissent and rallied behind the Ayatollah Ruhollah Khomenei (in office 1979–1989), leader of Iran's anti-shah Islamist movement.

Impact of the Iranian Revolution

During 1978, massive street protests crippled Pahlavi's regime; with the Carter administration discouraging him from using force against demonstrators, the shah fled the country at the year's end. During 1979, the Iranian Revolution took a sharply anti-American turn. The United States had lost one of its most reliable allies in the region, but worse humiliation awaited.

The Iranian revolution sparked a second energy crisis, which drove up the price of gasoline and exacerbated the sensation of malaise in the United States. In July 1979, Jimmy Carter directly addressed America's "crisis of confidence." Blurring the distinctions between foreign and domestic policy, the president noted that Americans had lost their way, that they had become the captives of events rather than the shapers of them. Renewal, Carter suggested, would hinge upon the revival of national discipline and civic purpose, beginning with a serious effort to reverse American dependence on foreign oil. Although Carter spoke of the need for national revival in a speech that became known as the "malaise speech," his own fortunes only deteriorated. That November 1979, radical Iranian students stormed the U.S. Embassy in Tehran, seizing sixty-six American captives. The plight of these hostages shadowed Carter's last year in office. In spring 1980, the Carter administration launched a rescue attempt using military forces. It failed when an American helicopter crashed in the Iranian desert. The failure of the rescue mission symbolized what appeared, for some, to be a broader crisis of American power and purpose in the world.

Soviet Invasion of Afghanistan

The radicalization of Islamic politics propelled the Iranian revolution, but the reach of Islamism was not restricted to Iran. Though dominated by Sunni Islam, rather than the Shi'ite strand that predominates in Iran, Afghanistan in the late 1970s was torn between socialist and Islamist political projects. Afghanistan's government had been loosely aligned with the Soviet Union, its northern neighbor, since the late 1950s, but the regime in Kabul struggled to control the country's vast and mountainous hinterlands. When the Soviet Union's favorite Afghan client died at the hands of a rival, Soviet leaders feared that Afghanistan might succumb to Islamist pressure, even that it might shift toward the United States.

Fearful of instability, in December 1979, Soviet leaders authorized an invasion, and the Red Army's tanks rolled over the border between the countries. From a certain point of view, Soviet power was sucked into a vortex. From another perspective, Afghanistan was the first Soviet invasion of a country outside the Warsaw Pact since World War II. From Washington, it appeared that an offensive thrust toward the Persian Gulf was in the offing. With Iran's having fallen to the Islamic revolution, America's position in the region appeared vulnerable. Apart from Israel, Saudi Arabia—a vast and wealthy but sparsely populated monarchy—was America's only firm ally in the Middle East. A deeply conservative society in which the Islamic clergy wielded great influence, Saudi Arabia was not itself immune from the currents of radicalization that were transforming the region.

The Carter Doctrine

The Carter administration found itself transfixed by the simultaneous but unrelated threats of Islamic radicalism and Soviet power. Determined to shore up the Middle East, in 1980, Carter propounded a foreign policy doctrine that would bear his name. According to the Carter Doctrine, the United States would resist, by armed force if necessary, attempts by any outside power to gain control over the Persian Gulf. A restatement of traditional Cold War priorities, the Carter Doctrine nonetheless revealed how central the Persian Gulf had become to the United States and its allies in an era of energy interdependence. In the Middle East, at the end of the 1970s, then, dilemmas associated with globalization collided with longstanding Cold War preoccupations to entwine the United States, more surely than ever before ever, in the affairs of the Middle East.

The return of Cold War hostilities at the end of the 1970s was the result of events; namely, the crisis in Afghanistan. However, Soviet-American relations had been deteriorating for several years. Whereas Nixon and Kissinger had refrained from pressuring the Soviet Union over its poor human rights record, Carter took a firmer line. He corresponded with prominent Soviet dissidents and made representations to Soviet leaders concerning human rights within their country. Over time, Carter's emphasis on human rights had a corrosive effect on détente, straining relations with the Soviet leadership. Still, Carter was no less devoted to international peace than to human rights, and he worked hard to negotiate a new arms control agreement with the Soviet Union. SALT II went further than Nixon's SALT agreement had done; rather than simply limit the Cold War arms race at current levels, it committed both sides to reduce their nuclear arsenals. Yet it proved tricky to negotiate, and its reductions were less than what Carter had hoped to achieve. Ultimately, SALT II was never ratified; fearing a tough Senate fight, Carter stalled the ratification process.

IN THEIR OWN WORDS: *FROM PRESIDENTIAL DECISION DIRECTIVE 63, JANUARY 15, 1981*

Shortly before leaving office, President Jimmy Carter issued Presidential Decision Directive 63, which further defined the nation's foreign policy in relation to the Middle East. Combined with his 1980 State of the Union Address, this directive laid the basis of what became known as the Carter Doctrine.

In my State of the Union Address to the Congress in January 1980, I called special attention to our interests in the Southwest Asia and Persian Gulf region. Furthermore, in light of the Soviet invasion of Afghanistan, I declared that:

"An attempt by any outside force to gain control of the Persian Gulf region will be regarded as an assault on the vital interests of the United States. It will be repelled by the use of any means necessary, including military force."

Subsequently, I have directed action to protect the Strait of Hormuz and strengthen our key friends in the region in the face of risks stemming from the Iran/Iraq war. It is U.S. strategy to meet these commitments and to defend our vital interests in the region as a whole by:

—building up our own capabilities to project force into the region while maintaining a credible presence there;

—developing a broad range of military and related response options in and outside the region against the Soviet Union, including U.S. force projection into the region, to compensate for the current Soviet regional advantage in conventional forces;

—making the Soviet Union aware that it will also face a wide range of economic and diplomatic sanctions on a worldwide basis if it intervenes in the region;

—assisting countries in the region: to deter and diminish internal and external threats to stability; and to contribute to deterring and resisting Soviet penetration—political, economic, or military;

—diminishing radical influences in the region and enhancing US security by working for progress toward a comprehensive Arab-Israeli peace settlement....

SOURCE: Available online at http://www.jimmycarterlibrary.gov/documents/pddirectives/pd63.pdf.

After Moscow's invasion of Afghanistan, he withdrew the treaty from Senate consideration in early 1980.

The End of Détente

Détente was over, but the situation in Afghanistan is by no means a sufficient explanation for its end. Political circumstances within the United States powerfully conditioned its demise. Even before Jimmy Carter became president, critics argued that détente was immoral (because it treated the Soviet Union as a legitimate state) and that it left the United States strategically exposed and militarily vulnerable. Some critics argued that U.S. intelligence had dangerously underestimated the Soviet Union's military strength. Responding to their critics, the CIA in 1976 conducted an exercise—known as the Team B exercise—to produce an alternative evaluation of Soviet capacities. It concluded that American analysts had indeed underrepresented Soviet military strength. Though historians now side with the CIA's original estimates and not with the Team B revisions, the exercise powerfully shaped the Cold War's domestic politics.

The Committee on the Present Danger, a bipartisan lobby organization, pushed for larger defense budgets and tougher anti-Soviet policies. Though Republicans were prominent among the Cold War hawks in the 1970s, some Democrats joined their ranks, arguing that the party's mainstream had abandoned the tough-minded anti-communism that was the legacy of Democratic presidents such as Harry S. Truman (1945–1953) and John F. Kennedy. For some of the Democratic hawks, however, Carter's conversion to tough Cold War policies came too late, and they opposed him in the election of 1980, preferring instead to support his rival, former California governor Ronald Reagan.

REAGAN AND THE COLD WAR

When he entered the Oval Office in 1981, Ronald Reagan (1981–1989) wore the reputation of a "Cold Warrior." A sharp critic of détente in the 1970s, Reagan saw the Cold War first and foremost as a struggle between political ideologies and social systems. This set him apart from the foreign policy realists who held that conflict was an inherent feature of a bipolar international system. For Reagan, the problem of the Cold War was the problem of communism, and he confronted it with vigor. Reagan sharpened the Cold War's rhetoric, escalated its military competition, and intensified the struggle for the developing world. Unlike Nixon and Ford, his Republican predecessors, Reagan did not emphasize coexistence and stability as the purposes of his foreign policy. Inverting Marxist theory, Reagan insisted that history was on America's side; the West's eventual triumph over communism, he insisted,

was inevitable. His confidence invigorated the public mood. At the same time, Reagan benefitted from favorable circumstances.

While the long recession of the 1970s lingered into the early 1980s, Jimmy Carter had already initiated the difficult steps that were necessary to tame the inflationary spiral that afflicted the American economy in the 1970s. Stimulated by tax cuts and spending increases, the U.S. economy began to tick upward toward the end of Reagan's first term. That oil prices declined during the 1980s further benefitted the American economy and Reagan's presidency. By the mid-1980s, the pessimism of the 1970s was largely vanquished.

Reagan Heats Up the Cold War

As he restored American self-confidence, Reagan intensified the Cold War. The Carter administration had wrestled with the dilemma of whether or not to install nuclear-tipped cruise missiles in Western Europe to counter an impressive new Soviet weapons system, the SS-20 missile. Reagan answered the question in the affirmative and dispatched cruise missiles to Western Europe, provoking an anguished reaction on the European left. He also announced, quite publicly, his intention to deploy an anti-ballistic missile system, dubbed "Star Wars," capable of intercepting and destroying Soviet missiles bound for the United States. Though defensive in nature, an effective anti-missile shield would have destabilized the Cold War's balance of terror by permitting the United States to use nuclear weapons without fear of Soviet retaliation. For this reason, critics denounced Reagan's missile defense concept as a dangerous departure. Others focused on the technical hurdles that missile defense would have to overcome and emphasized the practical difficulties of building a weapons platform capable of shooting down incoming ballistic missiles.

More direct than missile defense were the efforts that the Reagan administration took to confront communism in Central America. The 1979 fall of Nicaragua's pro-American dictatorship to revolutionaries who called themselves the Sandinistas had destabilized the region. The new president proclaimed a Reagan Doctrine, according to which the United States would assist anti-Communist "freedom fighters" throughout the world in an effort to roll back Soviet influence. Though Reagan provided non-military assistance to the opponents of communism in Eastern Europe and elsewhere, Nicaragua became the epicenter of the Reagan Doctrine's implementation. Setting his administration against the Sandinistas, Reagan dispatched aid and arms to the anti-Communist guerillas, known as the Contras. The consequences for Nicaragua were not good. American involvement fanned the flames of political violence in an impoverished region that prior

PUBLIC PORTRAIT: *MARGARET THATCHER (1925–)*

On the face of things, Margaret Thatcher (in office 1979–1990) was an unlikely candidate to lead Britain's Conservative Party. A woman in a political world dominated by men, Thatcher was in some ways a social, intellectual, and political outsider within her own party. Influenced by critics of socialism such as Friedrich Hayek, Thatcher was committed to reducing state control over the British economy; that is, to reversing a defining pattern of the postwar era. By the 1970s, sectors of Britain's economy, such as mining and telecommunications, were owned by the government, and private enterprise was burdened by extensive government regulation. Ordinary Britons enjoyed extensive welfare provisions and public healthcare, but they did so at the price of inflation, unemployment, and stagnation. In 1979, Thatcher led the Conservative Party to an election victory that made her prime minister, from which position she would implement an ambitious agenda. Focusing on the domestic economy, Thatcher privatized state-owned industries, worked to curtail the political influence of organized labor, and favored the financial sector with extensive deregulation. She cut taxes and raised interest rates to combat inflation. Her tough-minded policies exacerbated a sharp recession in the early 1980s but transformed Great Britain. At the beginning of the Thatcher era, the British economy had been among the most regulated and socialized in Western Europe; by the end of her prime ministership in 1990, Britain was one of Europe's most entrepreneurial and market-oriented economies.

In foreign policy, Thatcher defined herself as a sharp foe of communism and a staunch ally of the United States. She enjoyed a famous rapport with Ronald Reagan and aligned herself closely with his efforts to expand NATO's military capacities in Western Europe. She willingly accepted the installation of American cruise missiles on the British Isles, despite protests from the anti-nuclear left. In 1982, Thatcher ended up taking her country into an unexpected war when Argentina's military government invaded the Falkland Islands, a British territory off the Argentine coast. She decided to repulse the invasion by force and did so at the cost of several hundred British lives. The war nonetheless boosted Thatcher's popularity and helped to ensure her reelection in 1983. In the Cold War, by contrast, Thatcher played a role as peacemaker. One of the first Western leaders to meet with Mikhail Gorbachev, she helped catalyze his relationship with Ronald Reagan. Like Reagan, Thatcher embraced Gorbachev as an authentic reformer, lending him the international support and legitimacy that encouraged his pursuit of political and economic change within the Soviet Union. Later in her career, she opposed Germany's reunification, fearing that it would destabilize the Western European balance of power. Though she eventually diverged from Washington over the German question, Thatcher proved herself the closest and most determined supporter of the United States in the 1980s. In addition to closely aligning Great Britain with the United States in world affairs, her domestic reforms followed the patterns of deregulation and liberalization that defined Reagan's domestic legacy. Whether the cause was her own middle class background, her pro-American instincts, or her ideological approach to politics, Thatcher's own party never embraced her so enthusiastically as British voters did. Despite her leading the Conservatives to three successive election victories, Thatcher's parliamentary colleagues turned against her in 1990, forcing her out of office and into retirement. Her legacy as a transformative leader, however, was secure.

Cold War interventions had already traumatized. Reagan's commitment to the Contras was contentious in the United States, not least because the Contras, like the Sandinistas, were guilty of serious human rights violations. The Nicaraguan operation became scandalous, however, when the public learned that the Reagan White House had created a private corporation to channel arms to the Contras, circumventing a law that limited the delivery of direct American assistance. This covert operation even sold weapons to Iran to finance the delivery of aid to the Contras. When news of it broke in 1986, the Iran-Contra scandal threatened to engulf Reagan's presidency.

Fortunately for President Reagan, the Cold War's transformation in the second half of the 1980s created new avenues for engaging the Soviet Union. Reagan's embrace of the historical opportunities that he encountered secured him a new reputation as a Cold War peacemaker and contributed to the Cold War's peaceful resolution. To understand why the Cold War ended in the 1980s, however, it is necessary to know something about the dilemmas that faced the Soviet Union and Mikhail Gorbachev, the man who in 1985 became its leader.

By the mid-1980s, the Soviet economy had stalled. Though it had performed the tasks of heavy industrialization, the Soviet command economy proved ill-adapted to the challenges of technological innovation. As the West entered an era of post-industrial growth in the 1970s, the Soviet Union fell behind. Lacking centers of creative innovation such as Silicon Valley or Hollywood, the Soviet Union remained a giant rustbelt. A major producer and exporter of oil, it had benefitted in the 1970s from high energy prices. When oil prices fell in the 1980s, however, the Soviet economy slumped further into crisis. Social malaise paralleled the economic collapse. Alcoholism was endemic, and life expectancy for Soviet men declined from the mid-1970s.

Gorbachev's Reforms

To reform the Soviet Union, Gorbachev reached outward. Reinvigorating the Soviet economy, he believed, depended on building bridges to the world, even upon engaging the global economy from which the nation had withdrawn in the 1920s. Yet Gorbachev gambled upon more than trade; the success of his reform program would depend upon major changes in Soviet foreign policy, including resolution of the Afghanistan war and diminution of the military competition with the United States. Ending the Cold War would permit the Soviet Union to reduce military spending and to commit more resources to technological innovation and consumer production.

Despite focusing initially on economic rather than political reform, Gorbachev soon concluded that renewal of the Soviet economy depended upon political liberalization as well, and he embraced thoroughgoing reform. Within a conservative-minded Soviet leadership, however, Gorbachev was an outlier in his enthusiasm for change. By consequence, he and his advisers depended for encouragement and legitimation on foreign governments, including Britain's Margaret Thatcher (in office 1979–1990), West Germany's Helmut Kohl (in office 1982–1998), and, most importantly, Ronald Reagan. Having always identified Communism as the Cold War's fundamental problem, Reagan was quick to encourage and support Gorbachev when it appeared that the Soviet Union might be rethinking its own relationship to Communism.

Reagan had in fact reached out to the Soviet Union as early as 1981. Following an assassination attempt that left him badly wounded, Reagan wrote a personal letter to his Soviet counterpart, Leonid Brezhnev (in office 1964–1982). Could they, Reagan asked, not explore new ways to relieve the tension and hostility that had accumulated between their countries over the past thirty years? Brezhnev was not forthcoming, and Reagan concluded that no useful business could be done with him. Reagan made similar approaches following Brezhnev's death in 1982 and the deaths of his short-lived successors, Yuri Andropov (in office 1982–1984) in 1984 and Constantin Chernenko (in office 1984–1985) in 1985. Gorbachev's arrival expanded the opportunities for East-West dialogue. British Prime Minister and close Reagan ally Margaret Thatcher had hosted Gorbachev shortly before he became leader of the Soviet Union and concluded that he was a man with whom the West could do business.

Personal Diplomacy

An early summit meeting between Reagan and Gorbachev produced little in terms of substantive outcomes, but the two leaders developed a personal rapport. A summit at Reykjavik, Iceland, in 1986 brought them to the cusp of a stunning achievement: the abolition of nuclear weapons. Reagan's Strategic Defense Initiative (SDI) proved the sticking point. Though he offered to share SDI technology with the Soviet Union, Reagan was not prepared to abandon his missile defense system, which thwarted the possibility of a deal on offensive weapons. Reykjavik nonetheless confirmed that both Gorbachev and Reagan were committed to moving beyond the Cold War.

After the summit, the bilateral relationship flourished. Eager to support Gorbachev, Reagan dispatched George Shultz (in office 1982–1989), his secretary of state and a trained economist, to Moscow to help Gorbachev navigate the transition to market economics. In 1987, Gorbachev and Reagan concluded the Intermediate Nuclear Forces (INF) Treaty, which committed both sides to the removal of intermediate-range nuclear forces from Europe, including the cruise missiles that Reagan had installed at the beginning of his term. At this point, some Cold Warriors in the United States began to question whether Reagan had conceded too much. Henry Kissinger and Richard Nixon coauthored an editorial in which they criticized Reagan for lowering the West's military defenses. The backlash marked the distance between Reagan and his Republican predecessors. Nixon and Kissinger had downgraded ideology and waged the Cold War as a balance of power competition; for Reagan, by contrast, the Cold War was an ideological competition.

Once he convinced himself that Gorbachev was rethinking old ideas, however, Reagan was able to transform his own attitudes toward the Soviet Union, far more quickly, in fact, than the foreign-policy realists like Nixon and Kissinger. In February 1988, Gorbachev withdrew Soviet troops from Afghanistan, ending the conflict that catalyzed the Cold War's escalation at the end of 1979. That summer, the last of his presidency, President Reagan paid a triumphal visit to Moscow. While he was there, a reporter asked him whether he still considered the Soviet Union to be an "evil empire," a phrase that he used in 1983. "No," Reagan replied; that had been "another time, another place."[3] Both Ronald Reagan and the Cold War, as it turned out, had traveled far in just five years.

BUILDING A POST–COLD WAR WORLD

For all that had changed between 1983 and 1988, the next three years would make these look like prelude. Addressing the United Nations at the end of 1988, Gorbachev repudiated a doctrine associated with his predecessor, Leonid Brezhnev. The Soviet Union would no longer intervene in Eastern Europe to prevent defections from the East bloc. One foreign ministry spokesperson put a famous spin on Gorbachev's position. If the Soviet Union under the "Brezhnev Doctrine" had claimed the right to intervene at will, what now reigned was the "Sinatra Doctrine": the Eastern Europeans were free to do it their way, a reference

On December 8, 1987, President Ronald Reagan and General Secretary Mikhail Gorbachev signed the Intermediate Nuclear Forces (INF) Treaty at the White House. A major foreign policy milestone of the Cold War, the agreement required the destruction of all U.S. and Soviet ground-launched ballistic and cruise missiles with ranges between 311 miles (500 kilometers) and 3,418 miles (5,500 kilometers).

SOURCE: Courtesy of The Ronald Reagan Museum at Eureka College.

to singer Frank Sinatra's 1969 hit "My Way." The shift proved catalytic. Gorbachev's example encouraged Eastern European reformers and dismayed Communist hard-liners, who could no longer depend on the Red Army to defend them against their own people.

A New World Order Emerges

Some reformist regimes, as in Hungary, began to relax controls, including border controls. In Poland and Czechoslovakia, massive public demonstrations cracked open opportunities for reform and democracy. Faced with similar protests, East Germany's leaders were at first tough-minded. Some cited the example of China's Communist leaders, who, in summer 1989, had turned tanks upon the people in Tiananmen Square. Gorbachev warned against violence, however, and the East German Politburo decided against repression. With crowds baying at the Berlin Wall that separated them from West Berlin, one flustered official declared the border open. On the night of November 11, 1989, East Germans breached, scaled, and assaulted the wall that had for a generation symbolized Europe's division and the East's captivity.

George H. W. Bush (1989–1993), who succeeded Reagan in January 1989, was at first more cautious than Reagan when it came to Gorbachev. Whereas Reagan had embraced the Soviet reformer, the Bush foreign policy team worried that Reagan had been too quick and too credulous. A chill set in during the first months of 1989, as Bush took stock of a turbulent European situation. Gorbachev's reaction to the events of 1989 convinced Bush that Reagan had been right: Gorbachev was a different

kind of leader, and the world was changing. With Eastern Europe in the throes of a post-Communist transition, the Bush administration began to play an active role in the reshaping of European politics. The future of Germany was the central dilemma.

Changes in Europe and the Soviet Union

Germany's division was both a legacy of World War II and, by 1989, a fact of European politics. Britain, France, and the Soviet Union were united in their commitment to the status quo. West Germany, however, remained committed to reunification. While Chancellor Kohl was the architect of reunification, Bush played a crucial role, backing Kohl and reassuring Gorbachev that Germany would never again be able to threaten the Soviet Union. Germany's reunification in 1990 marked the end of the Cold War in Europe and the continent's effective reintegration. Further dramatic change awaited within the Soviet Union itself, however. As Gorbachev's reforms progressed, the Soviet leader found himself caught between conservatives within the Communist Party and the forces of nationalism within the vast multinational state that was the Soviet Union. An abortive coup by Communist hard-liners in August 1991 precipitated the Soviet Union's collapse. Following the coup, the parliament of Russia, the largest Soviet republic, dissolved the Soviet Union and declared the Communist Party illegal. At the year's end, the red flag came down from the Kremlin, and Gorbachev found himself out of a job. "The greatest thing in our lifetimes is this," George H. W. Bush declared. "By the grace of God, America won the Cold War."[4]

The Soviet Union's dissolution left hard questions unanswered. For almost a half century, the Cold War had defined international life, legitimating and structuring the exercise of American influence in the world. What role now awaited the American superpower? What purpose would Cold War institutions such as NATO serve now that the Cold War was over? Would the grand design that Franklin D. Roosevelt (1933–1945) had sketched in 1944–1945—for a world undivided, ruled by law, and ordered by the United Nations—be realized, now that the superpower conflict was over? George Bush in 1990 used the phrase "new world order," and it became a catchword for the future that awaited the Cold War's dissolution. Yet Bush was vague in his elaboration of the term, and his intentions could be only partially inferred from the choices that he made.

The Persian Gulf War

Beyond managing the Cold War's endgame, Bush's most serious foreign policy challenge unfolded in the Persian Gulf, where Iraq invaded Kuwait in August 1990. Iraq's leader, Saddam Hussein (in office 1979–2003), did not expect to provoke a war with the United States. Kuwait was a small and unsympathetic principality, hardly more democratic than Iraq itself. What was at stake from Bush's perspective, however, was the rule of international law. What kind of order would the new world order be, Bush asked, if its foundational act was the devouring of a small and weak country by its better-armed neighbor? To defend the rule of law and to reverse the invasion of Kuwait, Bush constructed a vast international coalition. He liaised with Gorbachev, determined that superpower cooperation, rather than competition, would define the security order of the post–Cold War world.

In early 1991, Bush's coalition went to war. It secured an easy military victory over Saddam's forces but stopped its advance almost as soon as it had turned Iraqi forces out of Kuwait and back into southern Iraq. Bush easily could have taken Baghdad, Iraq's capital, but chose not to do so. Who, Bush asked, would replace Saddam if the United States and its allies toppled him? The Persian Gulf War was a limited war fought with the sanction of the UN Security Council for limited and specific objectives: the defense of international law and the rule of sovereignty. Before long, however, events would reveal just how limited the solutions of 1945 could be when it came to international crises and controversies that occurred not between nation-states but within them.

Aftermath of the War

Like many of its neighbors, Iraq was a state without a deep-rooted sense of nationhood. The modern Iraqi nation dates only to World War I (1914–1918), when the League of Nations carved it out of the territory of the defeated

Soviet leader Mikhail Gorbachev announces his resignation on December 25, 1991, saying, "Due to the situation which has evolved as a result of the formation of the Commonwealth of Independent states I hereby discontinue my activities at the post of president of the Union of Soviet Socialist Republics." He went on, noting, "Free elections have become a reality. Free press, freedom of worship, representative legislatures and a multi-party system have all become a reality."

SOURCE: AP Photo/Liu Leung Shing.

Ottoman Empire. The new country contained sectarian and ethnic schisms between its Sunni Muslim majority and Shi'ite minority and between its Arab population and a Kurdish minority clustered in northern Iraq. During the Gulf War, the United States encouraged the Kurds to revolt against Saddam Hussein's oppressive regime. With the war's abrupt conclusion, however, the Kurdish rebellion ceased to serve a tactical purpose for the West. Saddam, though defeated in Kuwait, was free to turn his forces against the Kurds. Their plight, persecuted and abandoned, tugged at the world's conscience in the months that followed the war's end. Yet there was no obvious solution. The United States and Great Britain tried to enforce a "no-fly zone" that would prevent Saddam from using airpower against the Kurds, but they could not easily prevent Saddam from brutalizing his own people without doing what they had not done and overthrowing his regime. With this messy conclusion, the Gulf War left more questions than it answered.

New Challenges

In going to war against Iraq, the United States had made clear its willingness to play the role of global police officer. This was the role that Franklin D. Roosevelt had claimed during World War II. Much had changed since 1945, however, and new dilemmas had come to the fore. What of the challenges that globalization presented to even the most powerful nation-states, as it chipped away at their autonomy and left them unable to define their economic destinies on their own terms? What of security threats that began not with the armies and navies of nation-states but with individuals, such as the terrorists who turned the infrastructure of globalization against the West when they blew up an intercontinental airliner over Scotland in 1988? And what of crises that unfolded within states, when

dictators like Saddam Hussein terrorized their own people, or when multiethnic societies began to crack apart?

While the Cold War had created fear and mutual insecurity, it had at least structured international relations according to a predictable pattern. In its wake, a more diffuse array of challenges would predominate. As the plight of the Kurds suggested, the strategic vocabularies and concepts of postwar international relations could not necessarily accommodate the dilemmas of human rights, ethnic sectarianism, and state failure. For almost fifty years, the United States had worked to build order and predictability within a divided world of nation-states. How American leaders would respond to challenges that transcended familiar habits and concepts still remained to be determined.

See also: **Chapter 26: Shuttle Diplomacy and Its Impact on the Middle East; Chapter 27: Rogue States and the Emergence of Terrorist Tactics; Chapter 28: "Tear Down This Wall"; Chapter 29: Glasnost and Perestroika.**

ENDNOTES

1. Address at Tulane University, April 23, 1975, American Presidency Project [APP], available at: http://www.presidency.ucsb.edu.

2. Huntington, Samuel, Michel Crozier, and Joji Watanuki, *The Crisis of Democracy: A Report on the Governability of Democracies to the Trilateral Commission* (New York: New York University Press, 1975).

3. Available at: http://www.presidency.ucsb.edu/ws/index.php?pid=35903&st=evil+empire&st1=#axzz1NhfYD.

4. Available at: http://www.presidency.ucsb.edu/ws/index.php?pid=20544&st=grace+of+god&st1=#axzz1NhfY.

FURTHER READING

Dallek, Robert. *Nixon and Kissinger: Partners in Power.* New York: HarperCollins, 2007.

Garthoff, Raymond L. *Détente and Confrontation: American-Soviet Relations from Nixon to Reagan.* Washington, DC: Brookings Institution, 1994.

Herring, George C. *From Colony to Superpower: U.S. Foreign Relations since 1776.* New York: Oxford University Press, 2008.

Kissinger, Henry. *White House Years.* New York: Little, Brown, 1979.

Mann, James. *The Rebellion of Ronald Reagan: A History of the End of the Cold War.* New York: Viking, 2009.

Smith, Gaddis. *Morality, Reason and Power: American Diplomacy in the Carter Years.* New York: Hill & Wang, 1986.

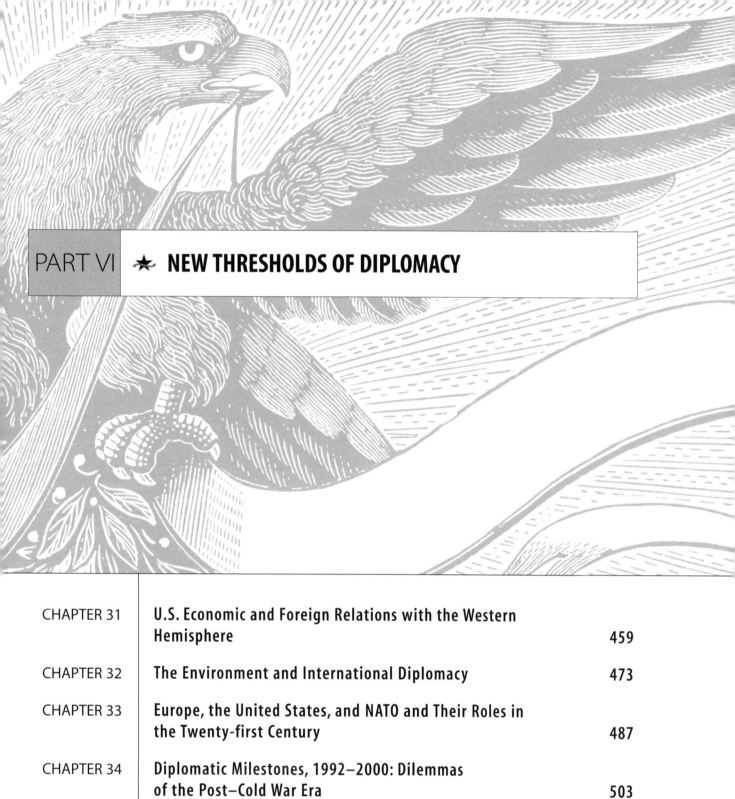

PART VI ★ NEW THRESHOLDS OF DIPLOMACY

chapter 31

U.S. Economic and Foreign Relations with the Western Hemisphere

by James Lutz

THE WESTERN HEMISPHERE became a less important region for U.S. foreign policy in the latter part of the twentieth century. Problems in other regions of the world received increasing attention because of conflicts, resources, or opportunities. The Cold War between the United States and the Soviet Union dominated U.S. foreign policy until the early 1990s. Some situations in the Western Hemisphere reflected Cold War issues, such as the continuing isolation of Cuba and the tension between the United States and Nicaragua, but with the end of the Cold War, such political and diplomatic issues in the region declined somewhat in importance, as economic concerns became relatively more significant. As a consequence, Latin America has become less central to overall U.S. foreign policy in terms of diplomacy but has remained important for economic matters. The shift in importance has also meant that to some extent the United States has relied more on economic politics to influence Latin American governments and less on traditional diplomacy.

The creation of the North American Free Trade Agreement (NAFTA), of course, has been one of the most important economic events of this period. The impetus for NAFTA began with President George H. W. Bush (1989–1993) but was implemented while President William J. Clinton (1993–2001) was in office after he pacified environmental groups and labor unions that feared the adverse consequences of the free trade area. Like other economic activities, NAFTA has been influenced by political events and has had political consequences.

CHANGING CIRCUMSTANCES AT THE END OF THE COLD WAR

A number of significant political events occurred in this period. During the Cold War, the United States was particularly concerned about Soviet allies and outposts in Latin America. Cuba continued to be a Soviet ally under Fidel Castro. A new danger appeared with the ouster of Anastasio Somoza and the creation of the Sandinista

regime in Nicaragua. The United States eventually withdrew support from Somoza because of the brutal tactics that his forces used to deal with popular unrest and because of his manifest unpopularity. The new Sandinista regime marginalized other dissidents who had opposed Somoza. The new regime also became increasingly Marxist-Leninist and developed close ties with Cuba and the Soviet Union. The United States, in return, began to support the Contras, counterrevolutionaries who opposed the new regime. The Contras failed in their violent attempt to overthrow the government, but the attacks did weaken the Sandinistas. Nicaragua, in turn, provided support to leftist revolutionaries elsewhere in the region, especially in El Salvador. The support for the insurgents here was a challenge to the dominant U.S. political and diplomatic positions in Central America.

Until the end of the Cold War, the United States continued its policy of supporting virtually any staunchly anti-Communist government in the Western Hemisphere, whether the regimes were democratic or not. Generally, the United States tended to ignore repressive activities that were directed against local leftist groups and organizations—or against local political groups that Latin American leaders could depict as communist. In other cases, the United States took more direct action. Support for the Contras, for example, was intended to overthrow a pro-Soviet regime. The 1983 invasion of Grenada was another reflection of these types of Cold War concerns. The presence of an obvious Marxist-Leninist regime on this small island would not have constituted a major strategic threat to the United States or its position in the Western Hemisphere. After the creation of the Sandinista regime in Nicaragua, however, another Cuban and Soviet ally in the region would have presented a negative example (from the U.S. perspective) for leftist political groups in other countries. The successful invasion and replacement of the government of Grenada, on the other hand, provided a demonstration of U.S. resolve

KEY CONCEPTS

U.S.-Canada relations. U.S. relations with Canada generally have been different than those with other countries in the Western Hemisphere. The United States and Canada have had positive linkages in the political sphere for more than a century. The two countries have long been political and diplomatic allies. The common border between the two countries has long been an open one, although there have been some new restrictions since the 9/11 attacks on the United States. Canada, on the other hand, has often been cautious in economic dealings with the United States, and there has been a fear that Canada could be swallowed economically and culturally. Even so, economic relations between the two countries have been close. Both Canada and the United States are industrialized countries that follow broadly similar free market practices.

NAFTA. Agreements in the auto industry led to a free trade area in 1989 that later evolved into the North American Free Trade Agreement (NAFTA) in 1993. The Canadian economy needed guaranteed access to the United States. NAFTA also included Mexico, in order to strengthen its economy and encourage its democratic development. The integration of the European Union and its increasingly regional nature of trade in Western Europe have meant a potential loss of markets for Canadian goods and services.

Latin American suspicions. Other countries in the Western Hemisphere, however, have been more concerned with the political and economic power of the "Colossus of the North." Dependency theory reflected the national concerns about global capitalism and the economic domination and exploitation of the region by the United States. Latin America was being turned into a cheap source of food and raw materials. Even Latin Americans who were not concerned about a global system dominated by capitalism have been concerned about penetration of local economies by large businesses headquartered in the United States. As a consequence, there have been periods in which diplomatic and economic relations between the United States and individual countries have been strained due to the disparities in power. Other countries that were not facing problems with the United States still remained wary of U.S. domination. The perception of the United States in Latin America has improved over time, but in many cases ruling or dissident political elites and general populations have remained suspicious not only of the motives of U.S. businesses but of the U.S. government and its political and economic policies. The ability of President Hugo Chavez in to mobilize public opinion in Venezuela and elsewhere in Latin America based on concern about U.S. economic exploitation is simply one of the latest examples of the underlying suspicion that still remains in the region.

and a warning to those leaders or groups that would consider developing close ties with the Soviet Union or Cuba.

Declining Diplomatic Importance

The end of communism and the collapse of the Soviet Union led to major changes in the context of diplomatic relations in the Western Hemisphere. Further, the Sandinistas in Nicaragua had been weakened and faced higher levels of domestic opposition. The political system was eventually transformed. Cuba, as the remaining Marxist-Leninist system, was now isolated. As a consequence, Latin America became less important in a political and diplomatic sense for the United States, because there was no longer a danger of a foreign superpower gaining strategic outposts to threaten the position of the United States. While the United States continued its policy of isolating Cuba, there was now less concern about new leftist regimes. When Hugo Chavez (in power 1999–), with his leftist populist ideology, came into power in Venezuela, he was an irritant rather than a threat to the United States, even when he developed closer ties with Cuba. The George W. Bush (2001–2009) administration clearly would have liked to see Chavez removed from office; his continued presence in power, however, was not really a threat. Even his acquisition of "allies" with new leaders—Rafael Correa in Ecuador and Evo Morales in Bolivia—did not generate the major concerns in the United States that such events would have in the past. Interestingly enough, the end of the Cold War

also meant that governments in Latin America were less responsive to the United States in terms of political agreements or diplomatic support.[1] The governments no longer feared being undermined by local groups supported by the Soviet Union or its local allies.

The end of the Cold War led to other modifications in U.S. foreign policy. Military aid generally declined, since the threat of leftist insurgencies, especially ones linked to a foreign superpower, was less dangerous to U.S. interests. Leftist groups, of course, lost some of their ideological inspiration with the fall of communism and revelation of these economic and social pressures that contributed to the end of the systems. General political concern and military efforts were directed toward specific problems such as the efforts to create a working political system for Haiti. The United States now started to put greater emphasis on supporting democratization in Latin America.[2] Repressive leaders could no longer rely on being steadfastly anti-communist in order to gain U.S. diplomatic and financial support. Involvement in Haiti under the William J. Clinton (1993–2001) administration reflected concerns about creating not only a working political system but a democratic one. Although the United States began to provide more support for democratization in the Western Hemisphere, the spread of democracy in the region was also more broadly a phenomenon with its own momentum. U.S. support for new democracies was, of course,

SHIFTS IN FOREIGN POLICY: *DRUG WARS IN MEXICO*

The problems with drugs in Mexico have raised additional issues about the U.S. relationship with Mexico and have created complications for the diplomatic relations between the two countries. Mexico has been beset by conflict among different drug cartels that are seeking to control the routes by which drugs are transported to consumers in the United States and Canada. The conflicts and associated death tolls have intensified in the first decade of the twenty-first century. The attempts to control the production and transport of drugs have involved serious battles between the cartels. There also has been widespread violence against government officials, including the police and judiciary, and corruption of other members of the government or police. The activities of the criminal groups also have placed pressures on domestic and international businesses. The overall consequences for U.S. foreign policy have not been positive ones.

The negotiation of NAFTA has made the situation in Mexico more important for the United States. This intensifying drug violence has threatened to destabilize the Mexican government, which would be contrary to U.S. interests, as one of the unstated goals for the creation of NAFTA was strengthening the Mexican democratic system. The drug wars threaten that progress and give U.S. opponents of the increasing economic linkages involved in NAFTA ammunition for their efforts to stop the integration or even to reverse it. The drug wars undermine the progress toward integration in other ways. When police, judges, and politicians are intimidated or corrupt, there will be less confidence in any agreements that are reached. The effects of massive drug activity in corrupting a democratic system can be seen in what has happened in Colombia. The drug money has been used to corrupt government officials and hinder activities of the police and military. Because the drug trade is so profitable, the leftist guerrillas at times seem more interested in preserving control of cacao fields than in gaining political objectives. Even private militias supporting the government became more interested in drug profits than peace and stability. A similar situation could occur in Mexico, and there are many indications that such a process has already begun.

ADVANCING THE CAUSE OF DISSIDENTS?

Further, it is possible that the unrest associated with the drug battles could provide opportunities for dissident political groups in Mexico, most likely representing ideologies on the left, to challenge the existing system. The political system also could be challenged by the right, by suggestions that the government must reduce civil liberties and impose more stringent security and control measures in order to combat the drug cartels and eventually to defeat them. While such limitations could eventually defeat and destroy the cartels, they also could greatly weaken the democratic system, which would challenge one of the basic foreign policy goals of the United States.

The drug conflicts present additional problems because of the existence of NAFTA. Since the free trade area came into being, border controls have been reduced. This situation makes it easier for drugs to travel north. It is also somewhat easier for the drug cartels to transfer funds and to launder money, at least for the moment. Criminal gangs have been physically smuggling money back into Mexico to avoid electronic monitoring that is possible in the United States. In the future, the opportunities may be more limited, as U.S. enforcement agencies have greater access to financial flows originating in Mexico if economic integration continues. If border controls are increased to reduce the movement of the drugs or money, the restrictions could negate the advantages of having a free trade area to begin with. Such restrictions could actually reduce total trade flows, since effective border controls to check for drugs would slow down the movement of goods.

IMPORTANCE OF FOREIGN INVESTMENTS

Foreign investment has also been a significant economic type of interaction. Mexico is a vital host country for U.S. investors. Continued violence undoubtedly will limit inflows from the United States. It could even lead to increased outflows of domestic Mexican capital to safer environments, including the United States and Canada, a process made even easier within the structure of NAFTA. The battles between the competing gangs have increased costs for foreign operations and could very well limit future investments. In addition, there have been suspicions that companies have been paying protection money to the gangs in order to avoid problems for themselves and their employees. These payments help to subsidize the gangs and to increase their power. U.S. citizens have been killed in violence associated with drug battles. It is not clear whether the U.S. citizens were targeted as individuals or whether they are the proverbial innocent bystanders. It could be possible that U.S. citizens at random have become victims in order to discourage increased U.S. anti-drug operations in Mexico. High-ranking members of the cartels have been extradited to the United States for trial, avoiding the potential corruption of Mexican courts. The attacks on U.S. citizens might be intended to suggest to the Mexican government that the cartels can threaten the investment climate and the vitality of the tourist sector.

The flow of drugs to the United States can create foreign policy difficulties. There have been continuous disagreements as to whether the solution to drug use lies in stopping the supply or limiting the demand. From the perspective of the Mexican government, the problem is the high demand for drugs in the United States. The domestic violence in Mexico is thus a consequence of the high usage in the United States; therefore, the solution to the violence would be to limit demand. Mexico also has blamed the lack of gun control in the United States for the severity of the problems, since the cartels arm themselves from American sources. Mexico, as a consequence, is paying some of the costs associated with the high level of drug use that exists in the United States, and the failure of the United States to control that usage. If the problem is defined as one of supply, however, then the solution lies in countries where the drugs originate or through which they are transported. (Mexico falls into both categories, depending on whether the drugs in question are produced in Mexico.) With the focus on the demand side then much of the blame for the cost of the violence in Mexico lies with that country, and it has spread to the United States with the failure of the Mexican authorities to deal with the drug cartels involved with the production and movement of drugs in their country. Given these circumstances, the potential exists for diplomatic conflict between the two countries. Of course, both the supply and demand views of the drug problem have validity, which permits politicians in both countries to blame the other government for actions and inactions that contribute to U.S. or Mexican domestic problems. More recently politicians in the United States have suggested that U.S. military intervention in Mexico may be necessary. Even voicing such suggestions creates diplomatic issues for the United States.

quite helpful to creating more democratic regimes, but not essential in all cases.

The issue of illegal drugs also became more important in this period, as greater volumes of drugs were moving from Latin America to the United States. Thus, the United States became more involved in efforts to control the production and movement of drugs. The drug cartels in Colombia were especially active in this regard, even developing ties with producers in countries such as Bolivia and Peru. The cartels allied themselves with leftist guerrilla groups, since they both would benefit from a weak central government. Even with the end of the Cold War, financial, military, and other assistance to the Colombian government increased as part of the efforts to interdict the drugs at the source. The United States even reached an agreement with the government of Colombia so that drug kingpins could be extradited to the United States for trial for criminal activities. This arrangement was later negated when Colombia adopted a new constitution, but it did reflect the importance that drug trafficking held for the United States. The fate of Manuel Noriega (in power 1983–1989) in Panama symbolized these changing priorities that drugs had with the end of the Cold War. His position as dictator was tolerated when he was firmly anti-communist, as U.S. officials looked the other way on issues such as human rights and involvement in drug transportation. With the end of the Cold War, his repressive regime and involvement in drug trafficking led to U.S. military intervention and his ouster from power in 1989. More recently, Mexico has been the scene of drug violence related to the flow of drugs into the United States that has threatened to destabilize that country and to harm political and economic relations between the United States and Mexico. Since 2006, between thirty thousand and forty thousand people have died in the drug wars in Mexico, complicating relations between the two countries along the common border.

ECONOMIC LINKAGES

The United States had strong economic links with other countries in the Western Hemisphere in the past and has maintained and even expanded those links. NAFTA was an especially important agreement for the three member countries, the United States, Canada, and Mexico. For other countries in the region, trade, investment, and aid issues have been important, as have been questions of regional economic cooperation among countries. The United States in this period has managed to alleviate some, but definitely not all, of the concerns of other countries in the Western Hemisphere about economic domination by the United States from earlier times, in which the U.S. government supported American businesses or intervened in support of U.S. economic interests.

Dependency theory is a view that argued that developed countries used trade, investment, and other economic mechanisms as a means of dominating and exploiting the economies of countries in the developing world. Dependency theory developed a strong following in Latin America, and, in fact, many of the most prominent early theorists who developed this view were Latin

PUBLIC PORTRAIT: *WILLIAM "BILL" CLINTON (1946–)*

President William (Bill) Clinton became president in 1993 after serving as governor of Arkansas. He was focused on domestic issues, including the economy, during most of his time in office. He inherited a situation in which many major foreign policy issues had been resolved. The Cold War had ended and the Soviet Union was in the process of dissolving. President George H. W. Bush, his predecessor, had liberated Kuwait and put issues in the Middle East to rest for the moment. Clinton supported efforts to implement the Oslo Accords negotiated between Israel and the Palestinians. Opposition to U.S. policy resurfaced with attacks on the U.S. embassies in East Africa by al Qaeda.

President Clinton successfully moved the North American Free Trade Association treaty through Congress. There was some opposition from elements of both the Democratic and Republican parties that had different concerns about the arrangement. Some Democrats were concerned about labor and environmental standards. Republicans were concerned about negative impacts from increased competition from imports. The successful implementation of NAFTA was an important success, had a major impact on the future of Mexico, and sent a message to other countries about the U.S. commitment to greater economic integration in the Western Hemisphere.

Clinton's presidency was marred by issues in his personal life. His involvement with a legislative intern, Monica Lewinsky, and the subsequent impeachment proceedings in the House of Representatives and his hearing before the Senate, diverted attention from both domestic and foreign issues and weakened his bargaining power with foreign countries. Members of Congress were less amenable to persuasion from his office and could even increase their popularity with voters by confronting him. Foreign leaders would be less likely to negotiate with him, since his ability to push legislation through Congress was compromised by his difficulties. Nonetheless, he left office with a successful economic record of having issued a balanced budget and with maintaining respect for America abroad.

America economists and academics. Although many elements of dependency theory have not been proven (or been disproved), in the 1970s, many members of the political elite subscribed to at least some portions of the theory. As a consequence, it really did not matter in some respects whether dependency theory or its neo-Marxist variations were accurate descriptions of reality; what mattered is that political leaders acted as if they were. The theory influenced decisions by governments and created political tensions between Latin American countries and the United States. With the passage of time, however, dependency theory has progressively lost some of its appeal and has become less central to the views of many Latin American political leaders.

The changing views of the global economy resulted from a number of factors. Global economic integration was proceeding, and a number of countries were obviously benefiting from the changes. It was clear that attempts to industrialize with import substitution that had been the norm in many Latin American countries had not led to the rapid economic growth that was expected. It is possible that the import substitution policies drew some of their impetus from elements of dependency theory, which has suggested that economic development was more likely when countries limited their economic linkages with industrialized, capitalist countries. The import substitution policies practiced in Latin America have been much less successful than the export-led growth of East and South Asian countries that had accepted greater integration into the global economy.[3] One consequence of such export-led growth had been increased economic interactions with markets in the industrialized countries, including the United States. Even when Latin American countries largely abandoned import substitution policies and moved toward reliance on exports, they have not been as well integrated into the global system.[4] Probably the most obvious indication of changing views on links with the United States occurred with the election of Fernando Henrique Cardoso (in office 1995–2003) as president of Brazil. Cardoso was one of the early dependency theorists.[5] While he was president of Brazil, however, he displayed no major policy decisions or patterns that indicated he was still a firm believer in dependency theory in its many parts.

Trade

Geography has always suggested that trade in both goods and services between the United States and other Western Hemisphere countries would be significant. Canada and the United States have been economically connected for generations, a natural consequence of proximity, an open border, and closely connected commercial heartlands. The Canada–United States Free Trade Agreement simply officially ratified the obvious economic links. Interestingly enough, this free trade agreement was suggested by Canada after earlier U.S. suggestions for such an arrangement had been rejected because Canada wanted to maintain its economic independence.[6] The United States has long been the most important trade partner for Mexico as well. Foreign investment, joint industrial enterprises, and service activities have reinforced the economic ties between the two. The creation of NAFTA was logical, given the pre-existing levels of trade between the two countries, since it removed some significant obstacles to trade and other kinds of economic exchanges. The United States became an even larger market for Canadian and Mexican exports, although Canadian and Mexican purchases of U.S. goods decreased somewhat (see Tables 31.1 and 31.2). NAFTA was designed not only to increase trade but to create additional investment opportunities, to enhance service and financial linkages, and to protect intellectual property rights. Additionally, bringing Mexico into a free trade area with the United States and Canada provided another foreign policy benefit, in the form of positive reinforcement for the democratic system in that country. The United States supported the solidification of democracy in Mexico, and the customs union has always had an unwritten expectation that Mexico would continue to have a democratic system in place.

The United States has also been the primary trade partner for most of the other countries in Latin America, although the relative importance of trade with the United States has varied among countries in the region (see Tables 31.1 and 31.2). U.S. firms have found the region to be an important area for investment. The United States has continued to strengthen trade and service ties with many of the countries in the region. The United States even pursued the idea of a Free Trade Area of the Americas, which was intended to promote greater trade and integration throughout the hemisphere. This free trade area was going to be a comprehensive one. It had provisions dealing with agriculture, government procurement policies, investments, market access, antidumping and countervailing duties, subsidies, services, intellectual property rights, competition policies, and dispute settlement processes.[7] This effort faltered, however, in part because of general mistrust by some countries of the United States and its large economy. In addition, there were criticisms of the social costs to Latin American countries that would come with freer markets.[8] There was also increasing domestic concern in the United States that such free trade agreements hurt the U.S. economy.[9] Given the resistance to a hemisphere-wide free trade area, the United States pursued free trade arrangements with individual countries (Chile, Panama) or with smaller regional groups in Central America and the Caribbean.[10]

IN THEIR OWN WORDS: *PRESIDENT WILLIAM CLINTON, "NAFTA: EMBRACING CHANGE," SEPTEMBER 13, 1993*

President William Clinton successfully steered NAFTA through Congress. As he prepared to sign the bill into law, he described how the NAFTA agreement displayed the potential gains that would come with freer trade. His comments also reflected the need to counterbalance the efforts of competitors in Europe and Asia to secure markets and trading advantages.

Businesses do not choose to locate based solely on wages. If they did, Haiti and Bangladesh would have the largest number of manufacturing jobs in the world. Businesses do choose to locate based on the skills and productivity of the work force, the attitude of the government, the roads and railroads to deliver products, the availability of a market close enough to make the transportation costs meaningful, and the communications networks necessary to support the enterprise. That is our strength, and it will continue to be our strength.

As it becomes Mexico's strength and as they generate more jobs, they will have higher incomes, and they will buy more American products. We can win this. This is not a time for defeatism. It is a time to look at an opportunity that is enormous....

This agreement will create jobs, thanks to trade with our neighbors. That's reason enough to support it. But I must close with a couple of other points. NAFTA is essential to our long-term ability to compete with Asia and Europe. Across the globe our competitors are consolidating, creating huge trading blocks. This pact will create a free trade zone stretching from the Arctic to the tropics, the largest in the world....

SOURCE: Available at http://history.msu.edu/hst203/files/2011/02/Clinton-NAFTA.pdf.

Many leaders and others in the Latin American countries have been cautious about entering into free trade areas with the United States due to a continuing fear of economic domination by their large neighbor or by businesses located in the United States.

Many countries in Latin America sought to create free trade areas that excluded the United States and Canada. Such free trade arrangements provided opportunities for local companies to benefit rather than multinationals from outside the free trade area. The conventional wisdom has been that such integration schemes would increase economic development and growth by permitting industries inside the member countries to both specialize for the free trade area and to take advantage of economies of scale, since the free trade area provided a much larger market than any one national market. The Latin American Free Trade Area (LAFTA), the Andean Pact, and Mescosur (Southern Common Market) all were created with such objectives. LAFTA, which was the largest of the attempted groups, never performed up to expectations, but the Andean Pact and Mescosur have shown more promise in recent years. Although these free trade areas were designed, to some extent, to limit U.S. economic influence, the United States also has generally supported these integration efforts. More prosperous countries in South America would result in more stable political systems, which would be in keeping with broad U.S. foreign policy objectives. The more prosperous national economies also would provide increased market opportunities for American firms, a goal of increasing economic importance as the United States faced greater deficits in its balance of trade.

Central America and the Caribbean also have logically fallen into the U.S. trade sphere. The small size of these countries has meant that export levels also would be small, and the small size of the possible shipments would not make major shipments to distant destinations very likely. The United States, however, has provided a nearby large, developed country as a market, and it is much more accessible than Canada. The United States has encouraged economic linkages with and among these countries, looking favorably, for example, upon the Central American Free Trade Agreement (CAFTA) as a development tool for much the same reasons that it supported economic integration in South America. The Ronald Reagan administration (1981–1989) supported the Caribbean Basin Initiative (CBI), which was created to provide some additional trade advantages to the smaller countries and territories in the region. Although the CBI had major limitations, one of its objectives was to give the smaller territories advantages in access to the U.S. market when competing with other developing countries.

Foreign Investment

Of the different kinds of economic activities that involve the United States with other countries in the Western Hemisphere, foreign investment has been one of the most contentious. There have been significant disputes between the host country and foreign investors, and frequently the home country of the foreign investor has become involved in the disputes. The concerns about foreign investment activities include local fears of exploitation and domination, particularly by companies from the United States,

TABLE 31.1 **Latin American Imports from the United States**

Country	Percentage and U.S. Rank as Source of Goods				
	1985	1990	1995	2000	2005
NAFTA					
Canada	70.5 (1)	64.6 (1)	66.8 (1)	64.1 (1)	56.5 (1)
Mexico	69.6 (1)	67.1 (1)	74.5 (1)	73.1 (1)	53.6 (1)
Central America					
Belize	49.7 (1)	57.8 (1)	54.1 (1)	50.2 (1)	40.3 (1)
Costa Rica	34.6 (1)	47.3 (1)	45.3 (1)	51.3 (1)	41.0 (1)
El Salvador	29.4 (1)	37.9 (1)	44.2 (1)	34.8 (1)	36.9 (1)
Guatemala	31.2 (1)	40.3 (1)	44.9 (1)	39.7 (1)	33.9 (1)
Honduras	32.9 (1)	43.3 (1)	46.6 (1)	47.8 (1)	36.8 (1)
Nicaragua	6.7 (5)	12.2 (1)	30.2 (1)	24.3 (1)	20.7 (1)
Panama	31.7 (1)	34.9 (1)	40.2 (1)	33.1 (1)	27.1 (1)
Caribbean					
Bahamas	27.9 (2)	36.2 (1)	81.1 (1)	87.9 (1)	85.9 (1)
Barbados	42.0 (1)	33.8 (1)	40.7 (1)	42.1 (1)	35.9 (1)
Dominica	27.2 (1)	33.3 (1)	33.2 (1)	37.4 (1)	36.6 (1)
Dominican Rep	--	--	--	--	37.7 (1)
Jamaica	42.3 (1)	49.1 (1)	50.7 (1)	45.5 (1)	41.6 (1)
Neth. Antilles*	41.5 (1)	59.2 (1)	54.9 (1)	10.8 (2)	38.4 (1)
St Kitts	47.0 (1)	43.6 (1)	55.2 (1)	73.0 (1)	57.9 (1)
St Lucia	28.9 (1)	37.1 (1)	38.1 (1)	41.3 (1)	14.0 (3)
St Vincent	36.3 (1)	36.4 (1)	37.7 (1)	38.2 (1)	33.2 (1)
Trinidad & Tobago	39.3 (1)	40.5 (1)	50.6 (1)	35.4 (1)	29.2 (1)
Latin America					
Argentina	18.2 (1)	20.1 (1)	20.9 (2)	19.1 (2)	15.8 (2)
Bolivia	20.4 (1)	22.2 (1)	22.4 (1)	24.0 (1)	13.8 (3)
Brazil	19.7 (1)	20.1 (1)	23.7 (1)	23.2 (1)	17.4 (1)
Chile	23.9 (1)	19.5 (1)	25.5 (1)	20.0 (1)	15.7 (1)
Colombia	35.3 (1)	35.4 (1)	33.8 (1)	34.0 (1)	28.4 (1)
Ecuador	34.2 (1)	32.6 (1)	30.7 (1)	25.6 (1)	19.2 (1)
Guyana	--	--	--	--	31.1 (2)
Paraguay	7.9 (4)	12.7 (4)	12.5 (3)	7.3 (4)	5.6 (5)
Peru	28.8 (1)	28.2 (1)	25.2 (1)	23.4 (1)	17.8 (1)
Surinam	--	41.3 (1)	42.4 (1)	26.6 (1)	18.9 (2)
Uruguay	7.6 (4)	9.9 (3)	9.9 (3)	9.8 (3)	6.7 (5)
Venezuela	46.3 (1)	46.7 (1)	42.6 (1)	37.8 (1)	31.5 (1)

SOURCE: *Yearbook of International Trade Statistics*, various years.

-- Data not available.

* The Netherland Antilles is no longer a reporting area.

TABLE 31.2 **Latin American Exports to the United States**

Country	Percentage and U.S. Rank as Market for Goods				
	1985	1990	1995	2000	2005
NAFTA					
Canada	77.8 (1)	75.0 (1)	79.5 (1)	87.2 (1)	83.8 (1)
Mexico	65.1 (1)	70.2 (1)	83.4 (1)	88.6 (1)	85.8 (1)
Central America					
Belize	46.4 (1)	45.6 (1)	36.6 (1)	54.7 (1)	53.9 (1)
Costa Rica	40.1 (1)	45.1 (1)	40.1 (1)	52.0 (1)	42.8 (1)
El Salvador	35.5 (1)	24.1 (1)	34.1 (1)	17.5 (2)	53.5 (1)
Guatemala	35.9 (1)	39.8 (1)	31.3 (1)	36.1 (1)	50.1 (1)
Honduras	48.9 (1)	51.6 (1)	42.7 (1)	55.7 (1)	41.6 (1)
Nicaragua	10.1 (3)	6.6 (1)	42.1 (1)	39.3 (1)	20.7 (1)
Panama	64.1 (1)	45.1 (1)	44.6 (1)	45.9 (1)	44.6 (1)
Caribbean					
Bahamas	87.8 (1)	93.8 (1)	81.1 (1)	78.2 (1)	60.9 (1)
Barbados[1]	57.0 (1)	13.2 (1)	16.0 (2)	13.2 (2)	18.2 (2)
Dominica	4.4 (3)	11.2 (3)	8.1 (3)	7.5 (4)	4.5 (8)
Dominican Rep.	--	66.8 (1)	76.3 (1)	--	--
Jamaica	33.7 (1)	29.8 (1)	36.9 (1)	39.2 (1)	25.6 (1)
Neth. Antilles[2]	54.4 (1)	33.4 (1)	13.9 (1)	4.9 (6)	74.1 (1)
St Kitts	39.4 (1)	50.9 (1)	40.5 (1)	63.3 (1)	91.8 (1)
St Lucia	13.5 (2)	21.5 (2)	26.0 (1)	18.7 (2)	43.9 (1)
St Vincent	9.7 (3)	10.5 (4)	9.4 (4)	2.6 (11)	9.3 (5)
Trinidad & Tobago	61.9 (1)	56.9 (1)	42.9 (1)	46.6 (1)	58.6 (1)
Latin America					
Argentina	12.2 (2)	13.8 (1)	8.6 (2)	11.9 (2)	15.7 (2)
Bolivia	14.1 (2)	20.0 (2)	28.1 (1)	22.0 (1)	14.6 (2)
Brazil	27.1 (1)	24.6 (1)	18.9 (1)	24.5 (1)	19.2 (1)
Chile	20.7 (1)	16.8 (1)	17.9 (1)	16.1 (1)	16.2 (1)
Colombia	32.8 (1)	44.5 (1)	35.6 (1)	50.6 (1)	38.9 (1)
Ecuador	57.1 (1)	53.0 (1)	42.5 (1)	37.9 (1)	50.1 (1)
Guyana	--	--	--	--	15.5 (3)
Paraguay	1.3 (9)	32.6 (1)	44.7 (1)	3.9 (6)	3.3 (9)
Peru	35.4 (1)	23.1 (1)	17.2 (1)	28.0 (1)	14.6 (2)
Surinam	--	11.4 (3)	22.0 (3)	20.1 (2)	--
Uruguay	15.2 (2)	9.4 (2)	6.0 (3)	8.4 (3)	23.2 (5)
Venezuela	45.1 (1)	51.6 (1)	51.0 (1)	59.6 (1)	52.5 (1)

SOURCE: *Yearbook of International Trade Statistics*, various years.

[1] Excludes materials supplied to ships in port.

[2] The Netherland Antilles is no longer a reporting area.

-- Data not available.

since it is often the source of the foreign investment in the other countries. The local issues and concerns about the potential negative effects of foreign investment are different for leaders and populations in Latin America and Canada.

In Latin America, a continuing fear has been that foreign investors would exploit local resources and take advantage of the local populations. Whether or not foreign investment is good or bad for developing countries has been widely researched. There are a number of potential advantages that can come with foreign investment. These advantages

include access to new technologies, contributing to the local economy when local industries are created to serve the foreign investment, employment that would not otherwise be present, training local people who then take their new skills into local industries, increasing productivity and competitiveness, local production that replaces imports, creation of export opportunities that will earn foreign exchange, and provision of the necessary capital that might not otherwise be available.

With foreign investment, however, there is an offsetting set of possible disadvantages. The foreign investors may drive local firms out of business since they cannot compete, use out-of-date technology rather than high-level products, overcharge local branches for use of patents or technology, restrict research and development to the home country at the expense of the country where the investment occurs, cause environmental damage, attract local capital that would otherwise go to local firms, and make economic decisions that are contrary to the economic policies of host governments. Foreign investors can take advantage of low tax liability in one country to limit payments in another country by accounting techniques that maximize profits in countries with the lowest tax rates. There also have been concerns that foreign investors ultimately not only recover their initial investment but also take more money out of the host country than they put in. From the view of some in the United States, an additional disadvantage of foreign investment is the outsourcing of jobs from domestic workers to workers in other countries, including those in Latin America.

Investment in Latin America

There is no consensus as to whether the advantages of foreign investment are greater than the disadvantages. Private firms can exploit natural resources on a timetable that is in keeping with the company's plans rather than what could be in the long-term interest of a Latin American country. A gradual exploitation of mineral resources might serve the national interests better than a more rapid use. As a consequence, the potential for conflict between the foreign investor and the government is present. There is no doubt that in some cases foreign investment has been positive and others in which the result has been negative. There have been examples where foreign investment has not served the interests of host countries, as when United Fruit manipulated economies and political systems and Central America, or when ITT was involved in the overthrow of Salvador Allende in Chile. It has been suggested that foreign investors often prefer authoritarian governments rather than democratic ones, since authoritarian governments are more likely to control labor unions and otherwise protect foreign investments. Foreign investors have not always favored democratic governments, but their biggest concern has usually been with stability, regardless of the level of democracy. A recent survey of chief executive officers of companies that invest in Latin America indicated that they placed the greatest emphasis on the rule of law, protection of property rights, and an effective court system, not on the level of democracy present in a country.[11] The concerns of these CEOs reflect the importance of stability that can facilitate business decisions. There also have been examples

in which foreign investment has fueled growth. The United States, for example, relied on significant amounts of foreign investment to fuel its own development in the nineteenth century, and there have been positive examples from foreign investment in at least some cases in Latin America.

Of course, in the final analysis, many countries in Latin America (and elsewhere in the world) lack sufficient domestic investment funds to stimulate growth—either because there are not enough funds locally, or because domestic investors prefer to invest in the United States or Europe because of greater safety or more consistent returns. Given the shortage of domestic investors, there is a need for foreign sources of capital from foreign aid or private investors. Latin American governments of all types (left or right, democratic or not) have accepted the need for foreign investment.[12] The United States has been a major source of investment funds for most countries in Latin America. Statistics indicate that the United States has provided important investment funds for countries in the Western Hemisphere (see Table 31.3). While foreign investment clearly can create difficulties for host countries, the absence of sufficient funds for investment can be an even worse problem. Issues of shortages could be especially relevant for some of the smaller states in the Caribbean area, since they often lack sufficient domestic sources of capital and their markets are too small to attract foreign investment in most areas. Tourism is an exception, because many Caribbean islands have been able to attract foreign investors to build resort facilities.

TABLE 31.3   **U.S. Share of Foreign Investment Stock in Selected Countries in Western Hemisphere**

Country	U.S. Percentage of Stock of Foreign Investment	
	1995	2000
Argentina	37.1	30.7
Brazil	26.0	23.8
Canada	67.1	60.7
Chile	51.0	25.2
Colombia	51.3	27.0
El Salvador	--	35.7*
Honduras	60.4	22.8
Paraguay	29.9	37.7
Peru	17.2	19.1
Venezuela	43.6	28.3

SOURCE: http://www.unctad.org/Templates/Page.asp?intItemID=3198&lang=1.

*2001.

-- Data not available.

Investment Fears and Concerns

The concerns about foreign capitalists using investment to exploit host countries were an integral part of dependency theory. Those who believe major elements of dependency theory have argued that reliance on integration among the countries in Latin America and local industrialization would limit the entry of foreign investors and thus minimize the exploitation. Dependency theorists have further suggested that foreign investment would provide disproportionate advantages to the foreign capitalists at the expense of the host country.

It is worth noting that the fear of exploitation became greater after World War II (1939–1945), when the foreign investors increasingly have shifted to sources in the United States rather than other countries since the Colossus of the North was so well positioned to use political and military power to supplement economic situations. The United States has generally been regarded as following an imperialistic policy. Dependency theory has been rather flexible in its arguments about the dangers that investment from the United States represents. For example, U.S. multinationals that controlled the copper mines in Chile and Peru were seen as exploiting the minerals to amass profits, while providing few benefits for the host countries. NAFTA (North American Free Trade Agreement) required that Mexico reduce or eliminate domestic content legislation or eliminate export requirements for the final products in sectors where U.S. multinationals saw opportunities for profit through investment.[13] Whatever the United States does, or does not do, is seen as evidence of such policies that are intended to exploit the countries in the Western Hemisphere.[14] Latin American fears of the United States include the argument that the United States has tried to use free trade agreements to support U.S. multinationals seeking to invest and trade in the countries. The multinationals have worked closely with government officials in the United States and in Latin America to further their interests.[15]

Politics and Investment

The political aspects of foreign investment increased when corporate business interests were able to get the U.S. Congress to pass the Hickenlooper Amendment, which prevented the government from providing foreign aid or other assistance to governments that expropriated the holdings of American investors. The Hickenlooper Amendment was followed by other laws that removed insurance for foreign investment, removed trade benefits, and made multilateral loans more difficult.[16] The initial purpose of the law, in 1962, was to punish Castro's Cuba for nationalizing U.S. investments, but it complicated relationships with other countries. When U.S. investments were nationalized with compensation, American investors could claim that the amount of compensation that was paid was insufficient given the value of the investment, and thus constituted expropriation. The

nationalization of the International Petroleum Company by the government of Peru later in the 1960s involved disputes about the value of the company's property. The dispute also created tensions between the United States and Peru because of the Hickenlooper Amendment and the other laws that limited assistance. U.S. presidents have actually tried to avoid applying the laws to Latin American countries other than Cuba or Nicaragua in order to avoid complicating diplomatic relations.[17] Even so, the laws themselves suggested to Latin Americans that the U.S. government will be willing to use its political power to support its investors regardless of the merit of the actions of the host government. Such laws have made U.S. investors appear to be more dangerous to national sovereignty and local political freedom of action than investors from other countries.

Investment in Canada

Canada has not had the same fear of foreign investment as many in Latin American countries have. Like the United States, Canada grew and developed due to foreign sources of investment, including investment in the important natural resource sector. Much of the early investment in Canada came from European sources, especially Great Britain, but with the passage of time, U.S. sources became increasingly important. Many companies developed integrated operations that included plants on both sides of the border. Over time, however, Canadian politicians and citizens have become increasingly concerned about these U.S. investment activities for a number of reasons. There has been some concern about Canada being too directly linked to the larger economy to the south, and the consequent loss of local control over the national economy. There has also been a fear that the U.S. companies would make decisions that would give higher priority to the U.S. economy at the expense of the Canadian economy. These issues help to explain some of the earlier opposition to the creation of a free trade area with the United States that would have more directly tied the Canadian economy to the U.S. economy. Probably the biggest issue, however, has been cultural. Canada has sought to protect its national identity and to avoid being considered just an extension of or part of U.S. culture (a fear that France also has shared). The concern is especially significant in Quebec, where supporters of a separate Quebec nation are already worried about being culturally overwhelmed by English-speaking Canada. Also, Quebec is blessed with major mineral resources that would provide economic viability for a country outside of NAFTA, and even Canada itself. As a consequence of these kinds of fears, Canada sought to protect the information and publishing industries from foreign ownership, especially from investors in the United States. The intent was to prevent what was seen as a distinctly Canadian culture from being absorbed and homogenized by the media of its much larger neighbor. The government and its citizens wanted television, radio, and books to reflect Canadian themes rather those from the United States. With the free trade agreement between the two countries, investments from the United States largely avoided the review process for entry into these sectors, as well as others.[18] Of course, the disparity in size between Canada and the United States has meant that U.S. influences on Canadian culture have been hard to avoid. The rise of the Internet has increased the dominance of U.S. cultural influences in the world at large, including Canada.

A significant level of fear of foreign investment occurs throughout the Western Hemisphere, especially when it originates in the United States, although the fears are somewhat different for different countries. The need for funding for extraction, production, and service activities, however, will lead to its persistence and even to competition among nations to host such investment. Openness to investment, in fact, has been one of the focuses of the World Trade Organization (WTO), with rules on trade-related investment mechanisms that are designed to encourage investment. In fact, the United States, as part of its broader foreign policy, has been one of the countries supporting this focus within the WTO as a means of fostering foreign investment opportunities and increasing global trade. The fact that the new international trade organization has incorporated many of the U.S. views on issues indicates that the United States has been successful in achieving at least some of its policy goals on investment, notwithstanding the concerns of other countries in the Western Hemisphere. The United States also spent significant effort in the negotiations leading up to the WTO to get protection for intellectual property rights included in the rules of the organization. While the United States was more interested in piracy of such intellectual rights in Asian countries, the rules provided protection for copyrights and patents, and royalty payments, for U.S. businesses in Latin America. Protection for such intellectual materials indirectly supported investment as intended.[19] Since the WTO has provided advantages in terms of access to the U.S. market through most-favored-nation status, the other countries in the region have had little choice but to go along with these other rules that come with the WTO.

Other Issues

Foreign aid questions were more important in the past for Latin American countries, especially when the 1961 Alliance for Progress was seen as a Marshall Plan for Latin America. The failure of the Alliance for Progress to match the success of the Marshall Plan, however, led to disillusionment in both the United States and Latin America and less support for continuing aid programs. U.S. foreign aid budgets, which have usually been less than generous, shifted toward supporting allies and even neutral countries in the Middle East. In addition, the end of the Cold War also led to reductions in foreign aid for Latin America, because the United States had less need to use aid and other strategies of economic support designed to minimize the threat of leftists that might have allied their countries with Cuba or the Soviet Union. Although foreign aid has been of declining importance, it is still important for parts of Central America and the Caribbean, where the poorest countries in the hemisphere are located.[20] Foreign aid also has remained important for emergency situations that occur because of natural disasters or crises resulting from political or economic events. Such transfers have become somewhat more important recently, since Hugo Chavez has used economic aid as a means of competing with the United States for influence with other countries.[21] While Venezuela cannot compete on the same level that the old Soviet Union did, it has given foreign aid policies greater salience for U.S. policymakers.

Currency Concerns

Currency issues have at times been a major concern for some nations in the Western Hemisphere for domestic reasons. Links with the dollar, however, usually have not been contentious, because most countries had no alternative to developing links with the U.S. currency, especially after World War II. The dollar has continued to be the most important foreign currency for the region, even more so than it was for the rest of the world. The dollar is important given the existing levels of trade and investment that originated in the United States. A few countries (Panama for a long time, and Ecuador more recently) simply adopted the dollar as their national currency. Other countries have pegged their national currencies directly to the dollar. While this direct link has meant that their currencies fluctuate as the dollar does, it has made sense, since exports, imports, services, investments, and other economic exchanges are linked to the U.S. economy, and global fluctuations in the value of the dollar have less effect. On other occasions, when individual countries have struggled with currency problems, as occurred with the austral in Argentina after the fall of the military regime, the dollar became the de facto currency for a period. While ultra-nationalists may resent the dominant role of any foreign currency, especially the dollar, the link has often provided an element of economic stability for countries experiencing currency problems or hyperinflation. Further, the United States as a conscious policy choice has usually supported countries in the Western Hemisphere that have faced difficulties with their currencies. Argentina demonstrates the advantages and disadvantages that can come with a link to the dollar. Under President Carlos Menem (1989–1999), the peso was pegged to the dollar. Initially, the link helped stabilize the Argentine economy, since the dollar was falling. When the dollar was in recovery, it combined with other economic events to create major difficulties for the Argentine economy. The United States also has helped to maintain the value of the Mexican peso at times. This support, of course, has been self-interested, since the countries have been trade partners and investment sites. Wildly fluctuating currencies create economic problems that can result in decreased growth or even stagnation, and they can also create circumstances in which political unrest can occur. Such unrest could destabilize friendly regimes, including relatively new democratic systems that are seeking to establish themselves. Economic problems could bring to power groups that would be suspicious of, or even hostile to, U.S. economic activities. The election of Hugo Chavez in Venezuela, for example, was due in significant measure to economic problems that the country was facing.

Impact of the 1980s Debt Crisis

The debt crisis of the 1980s involved many Latin American countries that were suddenly facing difficulties in keeping current with repayment schedules. Even though the debt crisis ultimately helped undermine the Communist systems in Eastern Europe, it also negatively affected countries that were friendly to the United States, including those in Latin America. The debt crisis threatened the economic and the political stability of many countries. Default on debt payments would have made the situations even worse. Default also presented problems for the banks in the United States since many of them held a considerable portion of the debt of individual countries in Latin America. The United States, therefore, made considerable efforts to avoid such defaults for both domestic policy and foreign policy reasons. Economic destabilization would negatively affect U.S. trade and investment. As a consequence, the United States was active in providing support to countries in danger of defaulting on their loans. The Clinton administration made important efforts to prop up the Mexican peso in late 1994 and early 1995. Further, there was help for other countries facing debt problems by aid in re-negotiating payment schedules or in reducing interest rates, arranging for debt reductions with U.S. banks holding the notes, working with international banking institutions that provided relief, rescheduling debt, and arranging for a variety of mechanisms for debt swaps, including the sale or transfer of debts at deep discounts to environmental organizations that purchased areas of rain forest or otherwise provided support for the "greening" of Latin America. The various economic stabilization schemes that were supported during the debt crisis focused on liberal markets access and less state involvement in economic issues.[22] These kinds of policies, of course, were the ones favored by the U.S. government as general support for more open market economies. The support for countries in Latin America and elsewhere facing debt issues also

In Laredo, Texas, a U.S. Department of Transportation (DOT) border inspector evaluates the safety of a truck from Mexico as it enters the United States. Under the terms of the 1994 North American Free Trade Agreement (NAFTA), Mexican trucks are permitted to haul goods throughout the United States and are regularly checked by the DOT.

SOURCE: Joe Raedle/Getty Images.

avoided major problems for U.S. banks. Defaults threatened major U.S. banks and, as the crises in the banking industry in the twenty-first century have indicated, could have had major negative economic consequences for the domestic economy in the United States, and by extension other countries in the Western Hemisphere.

Importance of Tourism

Another area of economic activity important in parts of the region is tourism. Many Caribbean islands and parts of Mexico and Costa Rica have developed important tourist industries that provide important source of foreign currencies for purchasing goods and service abroad. For some of the islands, tourism has become an essential economic sector, providing jobs as well as foreign currency. While these locations attract many European and other visitors, Americans (and Canadians to a lesser extent) provide a critical volume of visitors who help to contribute to the prosperity of this sector. Tourists from the Americas (Western Hemisphere) provide the bulk of the tourists for many places in Central America and the Caribbean (see Table 31.4). While individual countries are not listed as the source for these tourists, it is a reasonable assumption that many of the tourists from the Americas come from the United States. Prior to the 9/11 attacks, entry for U.S. visitors was relatively easy; frequently, passports were not necessary, nor were visas, as the countries in question sought to encourage vacation

TABLE 31.4   **Tourism in Latin America, 2005**

Country	Tourist Expenditures (millions)	Tourist Visitors (000)	Percentage of Visitors from Americas
Bahamas	$ 1,603	3,914	92.3
Barbados	905	548	56.9
Belize	204	237	74.1
Costa Rica	1,810	1,679	84.1
Curacao (Netherlands Antilles)*	284	222	55.5
Dominica	56	79	86.0
Dominican Rep.	3,518	3,691	46.4
El Salvador	838	969	96.3
Guatemala	883	1,316	87.3
Haiti	80	112	92.2
Honduras	466	673	90.6
Jamaica	1,783	1,479	83.4
Mexico	12,801	21,915	86.9
Nicaragua	210	712	86.9
Panama	1,108	702	88.0
St. Kitts	115	128	87.8
St. Lucia	356	318	67.5
St. Vincent	104	96	77.7
Trinidad & Tobago	593	463	78.8

SOURCE: *International Statistical Yearbook 2007.*

*The Netherland Antilles is no longer a reporting area.

visitors. Travel to and from these locations became more difficult after 9/11, but tourism has remained important for generating revenue. Tourist facilities also attract investment funds, some of which originate in the United States. Investment in tourist facilities, in fact, has been an area where foreign investors have often supplied capital that was lacking locally.

One final area of economic activity that has had foreign policy implications has been the migration of citizens from many Latin American countries to the United States. The migration is often seen by economists as a response to differences in development levels, standards of living, and opportunities between countries. Just as capital flows to countries in the form of investment, labor moves to areas where labor is scarcer, as suggested by the payment of higher wages. These higher wages are available in the United States, attracting both legal and illegal immigrants. Even when employers pay less than minimum wages in cases where they take advantage of the illegal migrants, the wages are still high enough to attract workers. The impetus for the migration comes from conditions both in the United States and the countries of origin. The migrants are pulled by the opportunities in the United States and pushed to leave their own countries by the lack of employment opportunities. The conclusion of NAFTA encouraged additional immigration from Mexico by more closely linking the U.S. and Mexican markets. Further, the more open border for trade has meant greater opportunities for individuals to cross the border, even if illegally. Remittances from workers from countries in the Caribbean and Central America can account for a significant portion of the total gross domestic product—as much as one-third in some cases.[23]

The high levels of migration have created domestic policy problems in the United States. A variety of groups have opposed both legal and illegal migration from Latin America. Some groups argue that illegal migrants have damaged the U.S. economy, leading to job losses; illegal immigrants' placing additional costs on the education, medical, and welfare systems; and posing cultural threats. Arguments that illegal immigrants generate high costs for citizens continue, even though most analyses do not support this view. In other cases, the negative feelings toward immigrants included legal migrants as well. Some domestic groups appeared to be concerned about changing cultural and social values, which usually result from new residents, whether they are legal or illegal. Efforts by a number of presidents to deal with immigration issues have faltered in the face of domestic opposition that has shown up in Congress. Some presidents, and others, have suggested amnesties for some illegals who have resided in the United States for longer periods of time; however, negative domestic opinion has undercut such proposals. Instead, the United States has increased security measures along its borders with Mexico to interdict the illegal flow of workers.

Domestic concerns and opposition to the presence of the migrants also have had foreign policy implications. The fact that illegal migrants, and even legal migrants, are portrayed very negatively by the domestic groups in the United States, with the resulting publicity, generates negative perceptions in the countries from which the migrants originate. Citizens of countries in Latin America cannot help but notice that their fellow countrypersons are not valued and considered less-than-ideal residents of the United States. The recent Arizona law, passed in 2010, permitting police to request identification of anyone who might be illegal is one such example. Persons who are stopped by the police will be forced to demonstrate that they are citizens or legal residents. The law has alienated Hispanic citizens, with its implications of second-class status. Not surprisingly, this state law also has had negative repercussions with populations in Mexico and elsewhere. As a consequence, when government officials deal with immigration issues, they have to do so very carefully, given the possibility that it could complicate other policy interactions between the United States and other countries in the region. It is perhaps not surprising that it has been American presidents who have proposed immigration reforms. Presidents had to deal with the negative perceptions in Latin America, which have been created by immigration debates. These negative impressions can interfere with other foreign policy objectives of an administration, including better relationships with Latin American countries.

Into the Twenty-first Century

There is little doubt that political and economic relationships between the United States and the rest of the Western Hemisphere will remain strong in the immediate future. Geography alone suggests that the United States will remain an important actor in the diplomatic, political, and economic situations of the countries in the region. The United States will have to be concerned about unfriendly leaders coming to power, although the threat of countries linked to a competing superpower is no longer an issue. Hugo Chavez has demonstrated the problems that an unfriendly leader can create. Geography and the size of the U.S. market make significant trade in goods and services a natural outcome and facilitate higher levels of U.S. investment in the Western Hemisphere. The dollar continues to be a major global currency and will be important as the key hard currency for most of the Americas. NAFTA has provided for greater economic integration for the members. For example, a Congressional Budget Office study found that the first eight years of NAFTA led to increased trade and investment. It also had a slight positive effect on U.S. gross domestic product and did not have a negative effect on U.S. trade balances. The free trade agreement had greater positive effects on the Mexican economy.[24] A variety of other trade arrangements between the United States and individual countries in the region have furthered economic integration. U.S. support for countries facing negative circumstances in the past, such as the debt crisis or other difficulties, has been essential to economic and political stability in the region. Such support is likely to be present in future crises. While the relative role of the United States could decrease (or increase) in the years to come, it will remain large in an absolute sense for the other countries in the Western Hemisphere.

There clearly will be a number of continuing problem areas in U.S. relations with the countries in the region. Drug production in a number of countries, such as Colombia and Mexico, that is destined for American consumers is one such concern. The increasingly violent battles among the drug cartels in Mexico have clearly demonstrated the negative consequences of the drug trade, which have gotten so bad that U.S. diplomatic personnel cannot go out at night. Conflicts over the control of production and the transportation of the drugs into the United States undoubtedly will continue as long as the demand is high. Corruption in the Mexican political system is likely to continue to be a problem in the future.[25] There always will be potential tensions between U.S. leaders and other political leaders in countries in the region, since such conflicts are unavoidable; Chavez in Venezuela is the most obvious. It would be unrealistic, however, to expect political leaders in Latin America to stop blaming the United States for problems or using it as a target for political charges of interference or exploitation, especially given the past history of U.S. involvement in the region, which has been heavy-handed in many cases. The assumptions and suspicions that underlay dependency theory will continue to be believed by some and thus to affect political relationships. Persistent domestic concerns in the United States about legal and illegal migration will continue to have negative effects for U.S. foreign policy, since these concerns implicitly suggest that individuals from Latin American countries are not valued as potential citizens of the country. Thus, while economic factors suggest that the relationships between the United States and other countries in the Western Hemisphere will remain close, there also will be significant tensions and disagreements. Foreign policy makers in the United States, just as in any other state, will always have to deal with such disagreements and problem areas as part of their jobs.

See also: **Chapter 7: The Big Stick and Dollar Diplomacy; Chapter 17: The Cold War; Chapter 22: Relations with Latin America and the Caribbean, 1945–1970.**

ENDNOTES

1. Dinorah Azpuru and Carolyn M. Shaw, "The United States and the Promotion of Democracy in Latin America: Then, Now, and Tomorrow," in *Orbis* 54, no. 2 (2010), 266.

2. Azpuru and Shaw, "The United States and the Promotion of Democracy in Latin America," 252.

3. Atul Kohli, "Nationalist versus Dependent Capitalist Development: Alternate Pathways of Asia and Latin America in a Globalized World," in *Studies in Comparative International Development* 44, no. 1 (2009), 386–410.

4. Javier Reyes, Stefano Schiavo, and Giorgio Fagiolo, "Assessing the Evolution of International Economic Integration using Random Walk Betweenness Centrality: The Cases of East Asia and Latin America," in *Advances in Complex Systems* 11, no. 5 (2008), 685–702.

5. Cf. Fernando Henrique Cardoso, "Development under Fire," in Harry Makler, Alberto Martinelli, and Neil Smelser, eds., *The New International Economy*, Sage Studies in International Sociology (Beverly Hills, CA: Sage, 1982), 141–65.

6. John Ravenhill, "Regional Trade Agreements," in John Ravenhill, ed., *Global Political Economy*, 3rd ed. (Oxford, UK: Oxford University Press, 2011), 192.

7. Joan E. Spero and Jeffrey A. Hart, *The Politics of International Economic Relations*, 6th ed. (Belmont, CA: Thomson Wadsworth, 2003), 256.

8. Jean Grugel, Pia Riggirozzi, and Ben Thirkell-White, "Beyond the Washington Consensus? Asia and Latin America in

Search of More Autonomous Development," in *International Affairs* 84, no. 3 (2008), 499–517.

9. Alfred E. Eckes, Jr., *The Contemporary Global Economy: A History since 1980* (Chichester, UK: Wiley-Blackwell, 2011), 129.

10. Azpuru and Shaw, "The United States and the Promotion of Democracy in Latin America," 257.

11. Glen Biglaiser and Joseph L. Staats, "Do Political Institutions Affect Foreign Direct Investment? A Survey of U.S. Corporations in Latin America," in *Political Research Quarterly* 63, no. 3 (2010), 508–22.

12. Grugel, et al., "Beyond the Washington Consensus?" 517.

13. Ronald W. Cox, "Transnational Capital, the US State and Latin American Trade Agreements," in *Third World Quarterly* 29, no. 8 (2008), 1533.

14. Jerome Slater, "The United States and Latin America: The New Radical Orthodoxy," in *Economic Development and Cultural Change* 25, no. 4 (1977), 759.

15. Cox, "Transnational Capital."

16. Joan E. Spero and Jeffrey A. Hart, *The Politics of International Economic Relations*, 6th ed. (Belmont, CA: Thomson Wadsworth, 2003), 278.

17. Moran, Theodore, *Multinational Corporations and the Politics of Dependence* (Princeton, NJ: Princeton University Press, 1974), 215.

18. Spero and Hart, *The Politics of International Economic Relations*, 147.

19. Gilbert R. Winham, "The Evolution of the Global Trade Regime," in John Ravenhill, ed., *Global Political Economy*, 3rd ed. (Oxford, UK: Oxford University Press, 2011), 154.

20. Leonardo Martinez-Diaz, "Latin America: Coming of Age," in *World Policy* 25, no. 3 (2008), 224.

21. Grugel, et al., "Beyond the Washington Consensus?" 509–10.

22. Grugel, et al., "Beyond the Washington Consensus?" 505.

23. Martinez-Diaz, "Latin America," 224.

24. Congressional Budget Office, *The Effects of NAFTA on U.S.-Mexican Trade and GDP* (Washington, DC: U.S. Government Publications Office, May 2003), 19–20.

25. Colleen W. Cook, *Mexico's Drug Cartels* (Washington, DC: Congressional Research Service, October 16, 2007), 3–4.

FURTHER READING

Crandall, Russell. *The United States and Latin America after the Cold War*. New York: Cambridge University Press, 2008.

Domingue, Jorge I., and Rafael Fernandez de Castro, eds. *Contemporary U.S.-Latin American Relations: Cooperation or Conflict in the 21st Century?* London: Routledge, 2010.

Grow, Michael. *U.S. Presidents and Latin American Interventions: Pursuing Regime Change in the Cold War*. Lawrence: University of Kansas Press, 2008.

Wiarda, Howard. *An Introduction to Latin American Politics and Development*. 7th ed. Boulder, CO: Westview Press, 2011.

chapter 32

The Environment and International Diplomacy

by Thomas Robertson

THE MOST OBVIOUS environmental dimensions of recent U.S. foreign relations have been not only the numerous international conferences and treaties on the environment, in which the U.S. government has taken part since the early 1970s, but also the overseas conservation efforts of both governmental and non-governmental agents. Also, any full assessment of the environmental components of American foreign relations must include the environmental consequences of U.S. military actions and preparations for war, the nation's increasingly global economic reach, and American economic development programs. All of these elements of American policy had significant implications for land, water, and air overseas and at home, as well as for awareness of the scarcity and fragility of the planet's ecosystems. "The twentieth-century American empire," environmental historian Richard Tucker has noted, "has surpassed all others in its grasp of nature's global resources and thus in its worldwide ecological impacts."[1]

WORLD WAR II AND THE ENVIRONMENT

Although accentuating patterns trace back far in American history, World War II (1939–1945) marked a shift in the magnitude and character of the environmental side of American foreign relations. The war was global and total in a way no previous war had been. It saw a new and sustained U.S. engagement with lands across the oceans, at a moment when warfare and the world's economy were themselves shifting because of technological advances in aviation, communications, and weaponry.

Environmentally, the consequences were dramatic. Not only did fighting devastate ecosystems, from the Battle of the Bulge to Iwo Jima, but it also influenced the environment indirectly, through the American military's dependence upon an industrial system itself dependent upon ecosystems scattered around the world. "Obviously the areas where war is actually being fought are violently injured," conservationist Fairfield Osborn wrote in 1948. "Yet the injury is not local but leaves its mark even in

continents far removed from the conflict because of the compelling demand that war creates for forest and agricultural products. These are in truth poured into the furnace of war."[2] To be the "arsenal of democracy," and itself field a military force of roughly fifteen million men and thousands of tanks, trucks, ships, and airplanes, the U.S. military required prodigious amounts of iron, coal, oil, rubber, electricity, aluminum, and wood. Aluminum came from places like British Guiana and uranium from the Belgian Congo. In an era of total, global geopolitical competition, the "furnace of war" drained resources and rearranged landscapes around the planet.

The war's environmental effect can be measured in other ways as well. Preparations for war required a network of military bases and proving grounds around the nation, many on or near relatively untouched natural areas. New technologies also emerged that would have important environmental consequences in the years to come. Nuclear weaponry is the best-known example. The pesticide DDT, which would become the center of Rachel Carson's hugely influential book *Silent Spring* (1962), was first widely used for disease prevention for the U.S. military. Many herbicides were also developed during the war. The need to quickly build housing for millions of troops led to the development of assembly-line techniques for home-building, techniques that, after the war, developer Abraham Levitt combined with the bulldozer, another World War II technology, to create a new and environmentally destructive kind of suburb in places like Levittown, New York. The war also saw the development of a plastics industry that often used toxic substances in production and created objects that were difficult to dispose of responsibly.

However, the war did not always have a negative influence on nature. In places, fighting discouraged human exploitation of resources. In the North Atlantic, for instance, the war allowed fish stocks to rebound after years of depletion. The war also led to the creation of new knowledge that often aided in the protection of nature in future years. Environmental sciences such as geography and

KEY CONCEPTS

"Total" War and the "Total" Environment. Total war is a war in which combatants marshal all available resources and population. During World War II—the quintessential total, global conflagration—the belligerent nations, especially the United States, mobilized unprecedented quantities of resources from around the country and around the world, often, thanks to modern chemistry and physics, with a new intensity and toxicity. Although it never turned hot, the Cold War continued this pattern of total mobilization.

These total wars reshaped nearly all aspects of American life, including relations with nature. "War and nature coevolved," historian Edmund Russell has pointed out. "The control of nature expanded the scale of war, and war expanded the scale on which people controlled nature."

In response, the tool conservationists and environmentalists such as William Vogt, author of *Road to Survival* (1948), and Rachel Carson, author of *Silent Spring* (1962), turned to most frequently to fight back, also had a comprehensive, all-encompassing logic: the science of ecology. Ecology is the branch of biology that examines the interconnections that link together all plants, animals, and nonliving matter on earth. To Vogt and Carson, to think ecologically meant to consider all the far-reaching and long-term consequences for nature of each and every human activity. Too many Americans, Vogt warned in *Road to Survival,* an environmental interpretation of World War II, think "in compartments," and therefore miss the "dynamic, ever-changing relationships between the actions of man and his total environment."

SOURCE: William Vogt, "Let's Examine Our Santa Claus Complex," in *The Saturday Evening Post,* July 23, 1949.

---

oceanography found greater funding. The war also encouraged what geographer Mike Davis has called "homefront ecology," through scrap drives and victory gardens. Moreover, because of the war, conservationists such as Aldo Leopold and Fairfield Osborn grew newly aware of the fragility of nature and the devastating power of human society, developing ideas that would become crucial during the environmental movement of the 1960s. The horrors of nuclear weapons ignited a reexamination of the costs of modern technology.

POSTWAR AMERICAN ABUNDANCE AND RESOURCE USE

American military concerns continued to reshape environments after World War II, but so did the civilian economy. After the war, the United States fashioned an economy of superabundance that, continuing and expanding patterns of frontier resource use from the first days of European settlement in North America, drew resources on an unprecedented scale from around the world. The mass consumption of the prosperous postwar decades—characterized by sprawling suburbs, overstuffed supermarkets, meat-based diets, big cars, recreational travel, and jet planes—required materials that the fields and mines of the United States alone could not provide. American companies found these resources in countries around the planet.

As Richard Tucker has documented, American investment, skills, and managerial energies refashioned landscapes around the world to bring Americans the products they so enjoyed. American sugar companies worked with landed elites in Cuba so that American consumers could enjoy candy bars and ice cream. American fruit companies such as United Fruit reconfigured landscapes in Central America, as did coffee companies in Brazil and, later, Colombia. After the war, Goodyear and U.S. Rubber reestablished plantations in Indonesia. America's growing fondness for beef, which skyrocketed in the 1950s and 1960s especially as fast-food chains proliferated, led cattle ranchers to expand into the savannas of Uruguay and Argentina and the rain forests of Costa Rica. Serving the U.S. domestic market, American investors, loggers, and forest managers working for Georgia-Pacific, Boise-Cascade, International Paper, Weyerhaeuser, and allied local businessmen devastated the hardwood forests of the Philippines. "For all our own material might," President Eisenhower warned during his 1953 inaugural address, ". . . we need for . . . [our] farms and factories vital materials and products of distant lands."[3]

Although all of these commodities had foreign policy consequences, the most consequential commodity of all was oil. Before 1950, enough oil flowed from American wells to meet the country's demand. Afterward, though, U.S. production began to level off, just as U.S. oil consumption increased dramatically, to the point where, in the early twenty-first century, the U.S. imports more than twelve million barrels each day. Most of this comes from Canada, Mexico, Saudi Arabia, Venezuela, and Nigeria, usually at prices low enough to subsidize America's car-, truck-, and airplane-based way of life. Hoping to guarantee this way of life, the United States has for decades routinely used its substantial diplomatic and military power to secure the oil supplies, both for itself and for its major economic and diplomatic allies in Western Europe and Japan. Driven in large part by geopolitical concerns about oil, for example, the United States struck deals with King Abdul Aziz Ibn Saud (reigned 1932–1953) of Saudi Arabia in 1945 and maneuvered to keep the Soviet Union out of Iran in the late 1940s and early 1950s. No clearer statement of oil's central importance to the United States exists than the Carter Doctrine, announced by President Jimmy Carter (1977–1980) in January 1980, not long after the Soviet invasion of Afghanistan: "An attempt by any outside force to gain control of the Persian Gulf region will be regarded as an assault on the vital interests of the United States of America, and such an assault will be repelled by any means necessary, including military force."

Oil is the example par excellence of a commodity crucial for America's civilian economy but also indispensible for the nation's Cold War struggle against communism.

COLD WAR ENVIRONMENTS

The Cold War competition dramatically altered the physical world, as well as human attitudes about that world. The Cold War developed and accelerated military and economic policies that reshaped ecosystems, gobbled up prodigious amounts of resources, and deposited enormous quantities of toxic wastes around the planet. In places such as Vietnam, Laos, and Afghanistan, this damage resulted directly from warfare, but in large parts of the world, including across the United States, environmental damage resulted from preparations for war. Ironically, through these environmental manipulations, the superpowers usually brought their own territories more damage than that of their enemies.

Coordinating science and industry in new and powerful ways, often in secrecy and with little accountability, the United States during the Cold War mobilized material and human resources, both within and across borders, on a previously unimaginable scale; they also created weapons more powerful, far-reaching, and toxic than any previously known. The best example is nuclear weaponry. From World War II until the 1990s, the United States produced tens of thousands of nuclear warheads at a network of more than three thousand industrial sites. Few places were more notorious than the Hanford facility in southeastern Washington State. Between 1944 and 1947, Hanford intentionally released into the air eight thousand curies of iodine-131, a cancer-causing agent. Over the next forty years, it poured billions of gallons of radioactive wastes into the Columbia River, which the public learned only after decades of operations. Above-ground nuclear bomb tests, which the United States conducted in the western Pacific Ocean and at the Nevada Test Site until the Nuclear Test Ban Treaty of 1963,

also caused environmental problems. The March 1954 "Bravo" test on Bikini Atoll, for example, exceeded expectations in its strength and caused radiation sickness and death among unsuspecting fishers and Marshall Island residents. For subsequent tests, people from the Eniwetok Atoll were removed from their home islands for more than two decades. Fallout from all of these tests spread around the world. During the late 1950s, U.S. scientists discovered in milk the carcinogen Strontium-90, a by-product of nuclear tests, and charted the spread of radiation by studying baby teeth. Nuclear waste presented a particularly tricky problem. The United States has tens of millions of cubic meters of waste (including that produced by non-military energy generation); the cleanup will take seventy-five years and cost as much as $1 trillion. The former Soviet Union, it should be noted, has even worse problems. Because of accidents and poor management, their processing plant for nuclear fuel, the Mayak complex in the upper Ob River basin in western Siberia, is now the most radioactive place on earth, and a later storage facility at Lake Karachay has contaminated an area larger than Belgium with radioactivity three thousand times stronger than the Hiroshima bomb.

Nuclear weapons are only one example. Continuous military mobilization over four decades demanded enormous quantities of raw materials. The U.S. military has a gargantuan appetite for oil and other fossil fuels. When historians do the final tally for the causes of global warming during the second half of the twentieth century, they will ascribe a substantial amount of blame to Cold War militaries and Cold War industries. In addition, the military required many other resources. In 1952, a high-level study of U.S. material policy prompted by Korean War scarcities, known as the Paley Commission, identified more than fifty raw materials that the United States needed to keep its military working, many of which were in short supply within the nation's borders. Tracing these materials from mine to factory, and from factory to military base, suggests the enormity of the Cold War's environmental footprint. Jet airplanes, for example, required aluminum, cobalt, and tungsten, which came from mines in Africa and Southeast Asia. Extracting these materials from the earth and transporting them to production sites polluted waterways and the atmosphere.

The perceived need to protect these resources also often drove American policy and spurred interventions in developing regions such as the Middle East, Southeast Asia, and central and southern Africa. Explaining increased U.S. support for the French in Vietnam in 1953, for instance, President Dwight D. Eisenhower (1953–1961) remarked, "If Indochina goes [communist], several things happen right away. The Malayan peninsula, the last little bit of the end hanging on down there, would be scarcely defensible—and tin and tungsten that we so greatly value from that area would cease coming."[4]

Tin, tungsten, and many other materials from around the world fueled America's unparalleled military infrastructure. In the 1950s, the United States maintained nearly four hundred bases around the fifty states, and many more around the world. Many of these bases occupied great swatches of natural habitat. U.S. Army bases alone are home to more than one hundred seventy of the eighteen hundred threatened or endangered species on about one hundred different facilities. Minnesota's Camp Riley provides habitat to the gray wolf, Camp San Luis Obispo to the California red-legged frog, and Fort Bragg to the red cockaded woodpecker. Marine Corps Base Camp Lejeune in North Carolina is home to eight federally listed endangered species. In addition, many of the military's advanced weapons required heavy metals and specialized chemicals that are not easily disposed. Because oversight was often lacking, military bases are now among the most toxic sites in the United States. By the early twenty-first century, one in ten of the Environmental Protection Agency's Superfund sites, the nation's most polluted areas, were Department of Defense (DOD) facilities. American military forces had an even freer hand at overseas locations, where local environmental laws were often weak or nonexistent.

America's "military-industrial complex" also must be included in any tally of the Cold War's environmental impact. Driven largely by the Cold War, military spending became a prominent and persistent sector of the U.S. economy, creating a network of defense-related heavy industries around the United States. Powered by fossil fuels, marshaling scores of dangerous substances, and subject to few regulations, these industries created thousands of environmental problems all over the nation. Furthermore, the Cold War also shaped other aspects of the U.S. infrastructure, often with significant environmental consequences. The Interstate Highway Act of 1956, which facilitated suburban growth and the nation's obsession with automobile travel, was devised during the Eisenhower administration in part for easy evacuation of cities in case of nuclear attack. Dams throughout the American West were seen as part of the industrial system thought of as crucial to winning the Cold War. American leaders knew that military strength required industrial power.

American consumer goods also became an important propaganda tool in the Cold War. U.S. policymakers saw the nation's growing prosperity, especially the rising standard of living of its working class, as a way to prove the superiority of the American way of life. During the 1959 "kitchen debate" with Soviet premier Nikita Khrushchev (in office 1953–1964), for instance, U.S. Vice President Richard M. Nixon used American consumer goods such as refrigerators and washing machines to show "what freedom means." Nixon and other American strategists believed that a desire for consumer goods would attract people around the world to side with the United States.

Although most of the environmental damage of the Cold War came from military preparations, Cold War proxy wars also left behind scarred and poisoned landscapes. Fighting on the Korean Peninsula between 1950 and 1953 decimated forests, contaminated soil, and sullied groundwater. Destroying infrastructure and undermining basic sanitation, the war also fostered diseases such as typhus. During roughly a decade of engagement in Vietnam, American bombers gouged some twenty million craters and dropped approximately one hundred million pounds of Agent Orange and other herbicides, destroying entire forests and leaving more than five thousand square miles of land, an area half the size of Massachusetts, unusable. Hundreds of accidents each year caused by unexploded ordnance remaining from the war continue to injure and kill Vietnamese. Other sites of proxy fighting—Laos, Angola, and Afghanistan—also bear the environmental scars of the Cold War.

AMERICAN ECONOMIC DEVELOPMENT PROGRAMS AND THE ENVIRONMENT

After World War II, the United States also shaped the world's environment through economic development programs. The first large program was the European Recovery Program (ERP), more commonly known as the "Marshall Plan," which aimed to rebuild war-torn Europe after the war. Fearing that economic collapse might render Western Europe vulnerable to communism, between 1948 and 1952, the United States provided more than $13 billion, mostly in grants, to participating nations in an effort to spur production and trade. "An all out production drive here and in the rest of the world," Secretary of the Interior Julius Krug (in office 1946–1949) told Congress in January 1948, "is needed at this time."[5] By 1950, production in Europe was up 25 percent from prewar levels; by 1960, Western Europe had reemerged as the most important production and trade center outside of the United States. During these years, with many of the same economic and geopolitical goals in mind, the United States also oversaw the equally successful reindustrialization of Japan. In subsequent years, concern for supplying Japan and Western Europe with the resources they needed, especially oil, became an important factor driving American foreign policy in the resource-rich developing world.

President Harry S. Truman's (1945–1953) Point Four program to spread economic prosperity to "underdeveloped" areas around the globe, an outgrowth of both humanitarian and Cold War imperatives, also spread environmentally harmful programs. "We must embark on a bold new program," Truman announced in his 1949 inaugural address announcing the program, "for making the benefits of our scientific advances and industrial progress available for the improvement and growth of underdeveloped areas." At the heart of the program was the sharing of America's "imponderable resources in technical knowledge" and also "the better use of the world's human and natural resources." The Point Four program also stressed growth: "Greater production," Truman emphasized, "is the key to prosperity and peace."[6]

Perhaps nothing brought as much environmental change as dams. Starting in the 1940s and accelerating in the early decades of the Cold War, the U.S. Department of State, Bureau of Reclamation, and Army Corps of Engineers, working in tandem with American engineering and consulting firms such as Morrison-Knudsen and Bechtel, assisted developing nations around the globe with scores of massive dam projects. The model for these programs was the Tennessee Valley Authority (TVA), the network of dams and economic planning that remade the American South, and the Boulder Dam on the Colorado River. The TVA's former director, David Lilienthal, became one of the key boosters for U.S. support of dam projects around the world. Lilienthal saw dams as a way to spread both material prosperity and democracy. He was fond of saying, "The United States has no better ambassador-at-large in Asia than the one which bears the initials T.V.A."[7] Lilienthal also saw dams as a key tool in the Cold War competition. Not coincidentally, many of the largest dams were located in countries on or near the southern border of the Soviet Union, from Egypt to the Philippines. Americans helped plan dams along the Nile River in Egypt, the Dez River in Iran, the Helmand River in Afghanistan, the Indus River in India and Pakistan, and the Mekong River in Southeast Asia, although the latter project was never constructed. As historian Richard Tucker has pointed out, these projects brought huge environmental and social costs. Creating artificial reservoirs, extensive irrigation networks, new croplands, electric power grids, and industrial complexes, these projects often stripped mountain forests and denuded fertile valleys. Whole populations were often resettled. Also, dam projects often figured into Cold War faceoffs, such as occurred with the Aswan Dam during the Suez Crisis of 1956.

Cold War programs to increase agricultural efficiency also created environmental problems. The "Green Revolution," one of the most widespread of all the American development programs, developed and dispersed high-yield varieties of wheat, rice, and other staple crops in countries from Indonesia to India to Brazil. Norman Borlaug directed the initial research in Mexico beginning in 1944, with funding from the Rockefeller Foundation. In later decades, the U.S. government funded further research at the Los Banos experimental station in the Philippines. The new varieties yielded much higher amounts of grain per unit of land, but required huge amounts of fertilizers and pesticides such as DDT. Many scientists also believe that the high-yield varieties create monocultures highly susceptible to disease. The high yields came with high costs.

Other examples abound. The United States poured nearly $500 million of technical assistance into Thailand between 1950 and 1965, and even more in subsequent years, mostly to counter Communist advances in the region. Many of these dollars went toward infrastructure development to modernize Bangkok and connect it to its resource hinterland and to markets around the world. The United States upgraded Thailand's rail system, paved a network of heavy-duty all-season roads, dredged a deepwater harbor, and designed a modern air-transport system. Roads were especially important. Subcontracting to U.S. engineering firms and training legions of Thais, the U.S. Agency for International Development (USAID) built thousands of miles of roads radiating from Bangkok around the country. The United States also helped Bangkok redesign major urban arteries, develop a modern telecommunications system, and find water sources for electric generation. These changes were part of what one policy analyst described in 1964 as the "transport revolution" sweeping through Asia and the developing world.[8]

Even health projects brought environmental change. For example, between 1952 and 1972, the United States joined forces with the World Health Organization (WHO) and the government of Nepal in a campaign against malaria in this small Himalayan nation, especially in the fertile flatlands along the Indian border. Both WHO and the United States provided technical expertise for the programs, which centered on DDT spraying, and the United States provided most of the funding. American actors were motivated not only by humanitarian concerns but also by Cold War worries about expanded Chinese influence in the Asian subcontinent. Although the program opened vast areas of Nepal to cultivation, it also badly degraded much of the nation's famous grasslands, which some naturalists had called the Asian Serengeti because of its high density of rare Bengal tigers, Asian elephants, and rhinoceros. The malaria programs also upended the lives of the indigenous peoples of the area, whose limited immunity to malaria had offered a relative degree of autonomy prior to the arrival of the DDT sprayers. The United States and the WHO ran similar programs in scores of nations around the world, but the long-term environmental effects have never been scrutinized.

Underlying all of these programs was a great faith that the United States could spread abundance through the world, especially through advanced technology. Whereas some scholars in the late 1940s and early 1950s believed that the worldwide economic depression of the 1930s had signaled the end of global prosperity, others thought that

America's special mission in the world was to create prosperity through the spread of technology. No one crystallized this optimistic view better than Yale historian David Potter, who argued in his hugely influential 1954 book *People of Plenty* that "an advancing technology," not abundant resources, had created American abundance. Potter believed that America's "mission" in the world was to spread these technologies to new frontiers, and thereby promote prosperity and democracy. "The most effective means by which we could have promoted humanitarian and democratic principles abroad," he wrote, is "not by applauding revolutions conducted in the name of such principles but by imparting to other parts of the world the means that we have developed for raising the standard of living."[9] That meant passing along advanced technology. This idea became the pillar of the dominant approach to economic development of the 1950s and 1960s, the "modernization" school of economic development, which stressed that an infusion of advanced technology at just the right moment could lead to economic "take-off." Poor nations were poor, the most influential of the modernizers, Kennedy administration (1961–1963) adviser Walt Rostow, wrote in 1960, because "the potentialities which flow from modern science and technology were either not available or not regularly and systematically applied."[10] Modernization programs stressed free-market capitalism, rapid growth, and advanced technology, often in nations without the regulatory framework or democratic tradition to prevent the worst environmental problems.

THE COLD WAR AND AMERICAN ENVIRONMENTALISM

In several paradoxical ways, America's growing commercial and military involvement around the world from World War II onward added to mounting concern among Americans about environmental degradation. Perhaps nothing convinced Americans of the drawbacks of modern technology and the fragility of the planet as much as nuclear weaponry. "The age of ecology opened," historian Donald Worster has written, "on the New Mexican Desert, near the town of Alamogordo, on July 16, 1945, with a dazzling fireball of light and a swelling mushroom cloud of radioactive gases."[11] Anxieties about nuclear weapons, radiation and fallout, and waste run throughout the postwar era. Indeed, the movement to ban above-ground nuclear testing that culminated with the Test Ban Treaty of 1963 can be seen as the opening act of the environmental movement that would grow so dramatically during the 1960s.

Nuclear technology advanced the age of ecology in less obvious ways as well. Before World War II, scientists had mostly only theorized the interconnections of animate and inanimate natural systems, the subject matter of the science of ecology. After the war, largely because of radioactive isotopes, they were better able to physically trace these interconnections. A key figure here was Eugene Odum, an ecologist who received funding directly from the U.S. government for his research. In 1951, the United States commissioned Odum to conduct baseline environmental studies at a site in South Carolina, where it planned to build an atomic weapon facility. This grant enabled Odum to launch a program of long-term ecological research on three hundred square miles that would eventually become the University of Georgia's Savannah River Ecology laboratory. In 1954, the Atomic Energy Commission commissioned Odum and his ecologist brother H. T. Odum to examine the effects of nuclear fallout in the Eniwetok Atoll of the South Pacific, where the U.S. government had been testing atomic weapons. The Odum brothers worked many of their findings into *The Fundamentals of Ecology* (1953), the most important American textbook on ecology for a generation. The U.S. Office of Naval Research also conducted a great deal of ecological research.[12]

American involvement in international war, even more broadly than with nuclear weapons, contributed to a growing sense of technology's shortcomings. Even before the nuclear explosions over the Japanese cities of Hiroshima and Nagasaki, World War II had pushed Americans to rethink modern technology. Before the war, most natural history museums, zoos, and films had stressed the violence of nature and the benevolence of humankind, but during the early 1940s, Fairfield Osborn, director of the Bronx Zoo and a leading conservationist, began to contrast the brutality of humans with the orderliness and peacefulness of nature. "Nature knows nothing comparable to war's destruction," Osborn wrote in 1942. "Her ways are more balanced. They provide no injustices so sudden or so bitter. Combat among other living things is, with rare exceptions, neither so general nor so ruthless as that in which man engages."[13] A similar concern motivated David Brower, a World War II veteran and the widely influential executive director of the Sierra Club during the 1950s and 1960s. "Man can undo himself with no other force than his own brutality," Brower wrote in 1968, at the height of concern about the Vietnam War and the formative years of the environmental movement. "The hand that hefted the axe against the ice, the tiger, and the bear now fondles the machine gun as lovingly."[14] Environmental activists also criticized the environmental costs of America's growing military-industrial complex.

The spread of American productive technologies and consumer habits around the world, especially through U.S. development programs, also deeply worried American conservationists and environmentalists. In a 1948 public debate with Paul Hoffman, the coordinator of the Marshall Plan, the massive U.S. aid program to rebuild Europe after World

War II, Fairfield Osborn argued that American foreign policy reflected too much faith in "the dazzling triumphs of materialism and industrialization." The idea of a constantly growing standard of living, he stressed, was an "illusion" peddled by office-seekers.[15] Conservationists such as ornithologist William Vogt warned about the "destructive exploitation" that might accompany Point Four programs, President Truman's aid programs for the developing world: "If Point IV results in speeding up soil erosion, raiding forests and land fertility, destroying watersheds, forcing down water tables, filling reservoirs . . . and wiping out wildlife and other natural beauties, we shall be known not as beneficent collaborators, but as technological Vandals."[16] Later environmentalists would call attention to the environmental problems caused by dams, roads, "Green Revolution" hybrid-seed programs, and other aspects of American overseas development programs. U.S. officials pointed to the important gains that these programs brought and downplayed their long-term environmental effects.

One of the best places to see the complicated overlap of America's growing international role and growing concern about nature is with the population limitation movement of the 1950s and 1960s, a newly emergent, diverse, and increasingly well-organized and well-funded campaign focused on global population growth. The movement was led by American philanthropists, demographers, and birth control activists, as well as naturalists, biologists, and conservationists. At first they operated through organizations such as Planned Parenthood, the International Federation of Planned Parenthood, the Conservation Foundation, and the Population Council, but eventually they also operated through U.S. government policy and United Nations programs.

Some within the movement saw population programs as a way to reduce poverty overseas and prevent environmental degradation. Others stressed the national security implications for the United States. Growing in influence as the "Third World" became a site of Cold War competition and conventional international development programs stumbled, the latter group believed that the imbalance of people and resources around the world threatened American national security. According to this view, environmental mismanagement in even far-flung nations could spark political conflicts that would draw in the United States or spill over onto its doorstep.

The biggest changes in U.S. population policy came during the Lyndon Johnson administration (1963–1969). In 1965, Johnson allowed the U.S. Agency for International Development (USAID) to begin providing advice and technical assistance on population issues. In 1967, Johnson agreed to Title X of the Foreign Assistance Act, which earmarked $35 million for USAID family-planning programs. From 1965 to 1969, U.S. government annual funding for programs in the developing world increased from $2.1 million to $131.7 million. Birth

control became the core of the "basic needs" approach, which dominated American economic aid policy in the late 1960s and 1970s. Johnson administration policies gave a boost to the fledgling environmental movement, not only by calling attention to population matters and resource scarcity but also by fueling discontent among those activists who felt U.S. measures did not go nearly far enough. As Stanford biologist Paul Ehrlich attests in his wildly successful *The Population Bomb* (1968), concern about global overpopulation formed an important strand of the environmental movement of the 1960s and 1970s.

At its best, the population movement helped create the technologies, legal rights, and government funding for families around the world in desperate need; at its worst, it overlooked more influential causes of global poverty and encouraged coercive government-sponsored programs of fertility control targeting poor and nonwhite men and women. As historian Matthew Connelly has shown, Americans played no small role in bringing about India's program of forced sterilization during Prime Minister Indira Gandhi's (in office 1966–1977, 1980–1984) "emergency" rule in the 1970s.

In some cases, even before the environmental movement in the United States in the late 1960s, Americans launched programs overseas with an explicit environmental objective. As development spread around the world in the 1950s and 1960s and left resource depletion and pollution in its wake, a movement to protect wildlife and habitat around the world emerged. At the center of this movement was the establishment of national parks, often with jet-setting international tourists in mind. Yellowstone, established by President Ulysses S. Grant (1869–1877) in 1872, was the world's first national park. Now more than one hundred thousand officially protected conservation areas dot the world map, covering an area roughly the size of South America. Especially after World War II, many Americans helped spread the idea and skills for parks overseas. Americans such as Harold Coolidge, with the International Union for the Conservation of Nature (IUCN), and Russell Train, with the African Wildlife Leadership Foundation and World Wildlife Fund, played key roles. (Train later became the head of the Environmental Protection Agency in 1973.) In 1961, the IUCN joined forces with the U.S. National Park Service to host the First World Congress on National Parks in Seattle, Washington. One hundred forty-five delegates from sixty-three countries attended. Later that decade, the U.S. Park Service began offering training sessions for officials from other nations. The 1960s saw a wave of new parks established around the world, especially in Asia, Africa, and Latin America. While these parks have preserved some of the most important cultural and biological sites in the world, they have sometimes pushed aside the interests of local people, often historically disempowered ethnic and indigenous groups.

TREATIES AND GLOBAL CONVENTIONS

From the 1970s onward, the United States found itself involved in numerous multilateral discussions about environmental issues, often through UN-organized conferences. Sometimes the United States took the lead in pushing environmental programs, but it increasingly found itself isolated and even the target of attacks for Cold War policies or programs that seemed geared to protect American economic autonomy.

The first of the world environmental conferences took place in Stockholm, Sweden, in 1972, where delegates from more than one hundred ten countries and more than four hundred non-governmental organizations (NGOs) came together for the United Nations Conference on the Human Environment. The conference marked the arrival of the environment as an international issue of the first priority, but it was not without discord. After the United States and its Western allies arranged that East Germany not be invited, the Soviet Union led a boycott of Communist bloc nations. Serious divides also emerged between industrialized nations and developing nations. They differed over what exactly to blame for environmental problems, the high population of the developing world or the faulty technologies and high consumption that characterized Western capitalism. Nonetheless, many nations did agree about the problems that came from flawed international development programs. The Stockholm Conference made one hundred nine recommendations for action and established the United Nations Environment Programme (UNEP). The 1970s also saw international agreements on endangered species, migratory species, and world heritage sites.

A burst of diplomacy surrounded concerns about depletion of the ozone layer during the mid-1980s. Ozone is a combination of oxygen atoms that prevents the sun's ultraviolet radiation from harming life on earth. During the 1970s, scientists had theorized that chlorofluorocarbons (CFCs) commonly used in Styrofoam, aerosol cans, and refrigerators would split apart ozone, thereby thinning the earth's shield against solar radiation. Even though more theorized than proven, President Ronald Reagan's administration (1981–1989) supported new international efforts to control chlorofluorocarbons. This was in part because the issue had won the support of the American public, faced no great opposition from American industry, and because the president himself had suffered from skin cancer. With the Montreal Protocol on Substances that Deplete the Ozone Layer, UN member nations agreed to cut production of CFCs in half by 1999. No allowance was made for developing nations. More research subsequently confirmed the theory, and all CFC production was banned by 2000. The Montreal Protocol is often looked to by environmentalists as a model for international cooperation on environmental problems.

Representatives from one hundred seventy-two nations, including one hundred eight heads of state, as well as more than twenty-four hundred NGOs came together in June 1992 in Rio de Janeiro, Brazil, for the United National Conference on Environment and Development, informally known as the "Earth Summit." The conference offered delegates a chance to assess the progress made since the Stockholm Conference twenty years earlier and identify new problems. Key issues included toxic substances used in production processes, water scarcity, public transportation, climate change, and alternative energy. The guiding philosophy was sustainable development, an attempt to bring together economic growth to end poverty with environmental concern. The conference produced a massive and wide-ranging document called Agenda 21, an updating of the 109 recommendations from Stockholm, and many delegates left enthusiastic about the future. This optimism mostly led to disappointment. The Earth Summit showed that the United States had become increasingly nervous about international environmental agreements. President George H. W. Bush (1989–1993) signaled this with uncertainty about whether and how long to visit Rio. In the end, he made only a brief appearance.

One of the most controversial elements of the Earth Summit was the Convention on Biological Diversity (CBD), which the United Nations had been developing for four years. Scientists and environmentalists had for years called attention to species extinctions. The agreement called for stronger measures by member nations within their borders, as well as financial support for international biodiversity programs. Although U.S. delegates agreed with parts of the convention, they particularly frowned upon its provisions regarding biotechnology and intellectual property, which they saw as unnecessary infringements on economic development. In the end, President Bush refused to sign the CBD, but President Bill Clinton (1993–2001), the winner of the Election of 1992, did. The U.S. Congress, however, did not ratify the agreement. Many of the measures of Rio's Earth Summit, including Agenda 21, were followed up on at a subsequent UN conference, the World Summit on Sustainable Development, held in Johannesburg, South Africa, in late August 2002.

Since the late 1980s, the most important international environmental issue has been global warming. In the 1950s, scientists noticed that increased levels of carbon dioxide, caused primarily by human use of fossil fuels and deforestation, had led to a measurable increase in global temperatures because of the release of "greenhouse" gases such as carbon dioxide and methane, which trap solar radiation within the atmosphere. Subsequent research has revealed that levels of carbon dioxide in the atmosphere have increased 30 percent since preindustrial times. Of that, fossil fuel emissions from oil, coal, and natural gas constitute 80 percent of the total.

The problem of climate change is a classic global common issue. It touches all nations and requires substantial international cooperation to resolve. Negotiations, which have been under way for more than two decades now, have been complicated by several factors: the multiple sources of greenhouse gases, scientific uncertainties about some of the issues involved, and reliance on global climate modeling, which is still an unperfected science. The key issue is energy use, which drives the economy of every nation, especially industrialized nations. Even to stabilize carbon dioxide levels would require cutting current emissions by roughly 50 percent. Who will bear the costs of making such a dramatic change?

The industrial world is split on the issue. Those nations with few local sources of fuel and a relatively high degree of energy efficiency, such as Japan and most countries in Western Europe, have tended to push for much more aggressive actions to address climate change. However, countries such as the United States, with large

supplies of inexpensive energy resources and a tradition of highly inefficient resource use, have generally resisted. The largest of the world's developing nations—China, India, and Brazil—also contain large and cheap supplies of resources and have resisted limitations on their use. These nations also argue that, historically, the developed nations are much more responsible for the buildup of greenhouse gases in the world's atmosphere. In the early twenty-first century, the top twenty emitters accounted for about 76 percent of the world's emissions, led by China with 20 percent and the United States with 19 percent.

In 1985, the World Meteorological Organization (WMO) and United Nations Environment Programme (UNEP) helped put the issue on the world's agenda with a conference in Villach, Austria, which yielded a new scientific consensus that global warming was a real and present threat. In 1986, the WMO and the National Aeronautics and Space Administration (NASA) produced a three-volume study arguing that climate change was not a phenomenon of the distant future but was already rapidly transforming ecosystems around the Earth. The hot, dry summer of 1988 and

PUBLIC PORTRAIT: *AL GORE (1948–)*

Albert Gore, Jr. has been one of the leaders of the environmental movement since the 1970s, first as Democratic U.S. congressman and senator from Tennessee, then as the vice president of the United States under President Bill Clinton, and most recently as a champion of awareness about global warming. He is known for moderate views emphasizing appropriate technologies and social justice within a democratic capitalist system.

Gore was born in Washington, D.C., in 1948. He father, Albert Gore Sr., was a longtime Democratic congressman from Tennessee and would later serve as senator until 1971. Gore Jr. graduated from Harvard in 1969, then served in the Vietnam War (1950–1975) as a military journalist. Gore was elected to the U.S. House of Representatives in 1976 and to the U.S. Senate in 1986. While in Congress, he called attention to numerous environmental issues, especially toxic waste and climate change.

Gore's 1992 book, *Earth in the Balance: Ecology and the Human Spirit,* became a *New York Times* bestseller. Seeing the environment as "a global problem that can only be solved on a global basis," Gore called for a "Global Marshall Plan" with six goals: stabilizing world population, developing appropriate technologies, establishing economic accounting methods that incorporate ecological costs, promoting new international agreements, launching an educational campaign about the environment, and promoting social and political reform aimed at sustainability, especially in the developing world.

Elected U.S. vice president in 1992, Gore took a leading role in crafting environmental policy during Bill Clinton's eight years in office. Gore helped place his former staffer Carol Browner (in office 1993–2001) as director of the

Environmental Protection Agency (EPA) and Bruce Babbitt (in office 1993–2001) as secretary of the interior. Environmental groups generally rated the Clinton administration's record as mixed; they generally had good access to the White House but had to contend with a Republican majority in the House and Senate after 1994. In 1997, Gore's personal intervention helped get the Kyoto treaty on climate change back on track. Gore did not make the environment a central issue in the 2000 presidential campaign, despite sharp differences with George W. Bush.

Gore's 2006 film about climate change, *An Inconvenient Truth,* won popular and critical approval, although it failed to sway George Bush and the Republican leaders of the U.S. Senate toward support of legislation. Building from a slide show that Gore had been giving as an educator and speaker for years, the documentary explains in clear and straightforward language the science behind the causes and consequences of global warming. The film won the 2006 Academy Award for Best Documentary Film. Gore shared the 2007 Nobel Prize with the Intergovernmental Panel on Climate Change (IPCC) for "their efforts to build up and disseminate greater knowledge about man-made climate change, and to lay the foundations for the measures that are needed to counteract such change." The film ignited a storm of protest from conservatives, focusing mostly on minor inaccuracies and *ad hominem* attacks of Gore. Some environmental critics faulted Gore for not identifying remedial actions for individuals and for not further challenging consumption.

SOURCE: Al Gore, *Earth in the Balance: Ecology and the Human Spirit* (New York: Houghton Mifflin, 1992).

subsequent testimony in Congress by scientific officials brought the issue a great deal of attention in the United States. In 1988, the WMO and UNEP established the Intergovernmental Panel on Climate Change, the chief source of scientific information about the problem. Its First Assessment Report showed scientific consensus that global warming was a large and imminent threat.

In February 1991, formal negotiations begin within the Intergovernmental Negotiating Committee for a Framework Convention on Climate Change, created by the UN General Assembly. A split quickly emerged between the U.S. team, assembled by the George H. W. Bush administration, and representatives of the industrialized countries of the European community, who pushed for a goal of returning to 1990 emissions levels by 2000. In April 1992, President Bush announced that he would not come to the Earth Summit in Rio if Germany and other European nations did not drop their calls for a commitment to stabilization. At Rio, delegates passed the UN Framework Convention on Climate Change (UNFCCC), agreeing that industrialized nations should reduce their emissions to "earlier levels" by 2000. The United States refused stronger language. Elected in November 1992, President Bill Clinton reversed the Bush policy once in office.

IN THEIR OWN WORDS: *THE KYOTO PROTOCOL*

The Kyoto Protocol was agreed on in 1997 and took effect in 2005, after fifty-five countries, accounting for 55 percent of greenhouse gas emissions, had ratified the treaty. The United States, part of the "Annex I" countries referred to in the protocol, signed on to the treaty when first formulated but never ratified it because of opposition within the U.S. Senate. One of the most important components of the treaty, establishing a system of emissions trading, is described in Article 6 below.

KYOTO PROTOCOL TO THE UNITED NATIONS FRAMEWORK CONVENTION ON CLIMATE CHANGE

Article 3

1. The Parties included in Annex I shall, individually or jointly, ensure that their aggregate anthropogenic carbon dioxide equivalent emissions of the greenhouse gases listed in Annex A do not exceed their assigned amounts, calculated pursuant to their quantified emission limitation and reduction commitments inscribed in Annex B and in accordance with the provisions of this Article, with a view to reducing their overall emissions of such gases by at least 5 per cent below 1990 levels in the commitment period 2008 to 2012....

Article 6

1. For the purpose of meeting its commitments under Article 3, any Party included in Annex I may transfer to, or acquire from, any other such Party emission reduction units resulting from projects aimed at reducing anthropogenic emissions by sources or enhancing anthropogenic removals by sinks of greenhouse gases in any sector of the economy ...

ANNEX A

Greenhouse gases
Carbon dioxide (CO_2)
Methane (CH_4)
Nitrous oxide (N_2O)
Hydrofluorocarbons (HFCs)
Perfluorocarbons (PFCs)
Sulphur hexafluoride (SF_6)

Sectors/source categories
Energy
    Fuel combustion
        Energy industries
        Manufacturing industries and construction
        Transport
        Other sectors
        Other
    Fugitive emissions from fuels
        Solid fuels
        Oil and natural gas
        Other
Industrial processes
    Mineral products
    Chemical industry
    Metal production
    Other production
    Production of halocarbons and sulphur hexafluoride
    Consumption of halocarbons and sulphur hexafluoride
    Other
Solvent and other product use
Agriculture
    Enteric fermentation
    Manure management
    Rice cultivation
    Agricultural soils
    Prescribed burning of savannas
    Field burning of agricultural residues
    Other
Waste
    Solid waste disposal on land
    Wastewater handling
    Waste incineration
    Other

SOURCE: http://unfccc.int/resource/docs/convkp/kpeng.html.

The next important round of negotiations occurred in Kyoto, Japan. The United States proposed emissions trading, in which nations who had reached their limits could purchase credits from nations below their limits. Many nations saw this as a watering down of the limits but agreed to increase the chance of U.S. involvement. The United States also called for a commitment by developing nations such as China and India to control and lower their emissions. In the agreement hammered out, the Kyoto Protocols of 1997, developed nations agreed to targets of reducing emissions of the six main greenhouse gases by an average of 5.2 percent below 1990 levels by 2012. Different goals were established for each nation. The United States was expected to reduce emissions to 7 percent below 1990 levels. The agreement included emissions trading, as well as a "Clean Development Mechanism," credits for nations that invest in or finance green projects in developing countries. The proposal for a commitment by developing nations to control their own emissions was dropped after objections from China and India. Developing nations had also rejected language allowing them to optionally join with nations reducing their emissions. It was agreed that the treaty would take effect once 55 nations, accounting for more than 55 percent of the total amount of greenhouse gases, ratified the agreement.

The United States signed the Kyoto agreement, but the U.S. Senate never ratified it. Opponents in the United States were upset that nations such as China and India were not required to reduce emissions. China and India countered that the United States, Japan, and the developed economies of Europe had created the problem, and that developing nations should be allowed a chance to pursue economic growth. In 2000, diplomats meeting in The Hague almost worked out an agreement by offering credits for forests that take in vast amounts of carbon, such as those in the United States, but European environmentalists nixed the idea. Not long after the election of 2000, aides to President George W. Bush (2001–2009) declared the Kyoto framework "dead." In March 2001, Bush stated, "I oppose the Kyoto Protocol because it exempts 80 percent of the world, including major population centers such

SHIFTS IN FOREIGN POLICY: *CAP AND TRADE*

As part of the climate trade negotiations in Kyoto, Japan, in 1997, the U.S. bargaining team sent by President Bill Clinton's administration proposed a system of emission trading to create more flexibility within the proposed framework for regulating greenhouse gases such as carbon dioxide. Under a system of emissions trading, with a limit or cap on total emissions, nations that had exceeded their limits could trade for credits with nations who undershot their limits. The resulting market would create more flexibility by allowing nations to pay to pollute if it should meet their needs, yet still penalize them, all while guaranteeing that the overall emissions would decline. Despite reservations from environmentalists, "cap and trade" became part of the Kyoto Protocols that eventually went into effect in 2005 after fifty-five nations, accounting for more than 55 percent of the total amount of emissions, ratified the agreement. The United States, the initial proposer of emissions trading, was not one of them.

Emissions trading got its start under the first Bush administration in the late 1980s as a method for addressing sulfur dioxide pollution, otherwise known as "acid rain," from coal-burning power plants in the U.S. Northeast. Emissions were capped, yet utility companies were allowed to trade for permits to meet the limits. Today, sulfur dioxide trading is widely seen as successful.

PRESIDENT CLINTON AND CAP AND TRADE

Embracing emissions trading was quintessential, according to Bill Clinton. In a 1992 speech commemorating Earth Day, President Clinton called for Americans to reject "the false choice" that protecting the environment meant hamstringing the economy. In Clinton's view, it was possible "to bring powerful market forces to bear on America's pollution problems." Clinton was a brand of "new" Democrat hoping to rethink traditional command and control regulation. "I believe it is time for a new era in environmental protection," he said, "which uses the market to help us get our environment back on track—to recognize that Adam Smith's invisible hand can have a green thumb."

The idea of market-based solutions to environmental problems seemed paradoxical to many more militant environmentalists. Wasn't capitalist commodification of nature the cause of many, if not most, environmental problems? Yet, market-based approaches have received support from many more moderate environmentalists. "Markets are powerful," writes well-known environmentalist Bill McKibben in a 2008 essay, "The Greenback Effect: Greed Has Helped Destroy the Planet—Maybe Now It Can Help Save It." Properly managed, markets can tackle global warming and other problems. To those who call for a more fundamental reconfiguration of economic structures, McKibben counters that we simply don't have time. "Markets are quick," he writes. "Given some direction, they'll help." Al Gore, an environmental leader and Clinton's vice president, and another "new" Democrat, also has supported cap-and-trade methods.

A FUTURE FOR CAP AND TRADE?

In recent years, cap and trade has lost a great deal of support, especially among conservatives. In March 2010, *The New York Times* reported that it was "in wide disrepute." Some had begun to rename it "cap and tax," and many Tea Partiers, the wave of small-government conservatives who gained influence during the 2010 election, say it represents the corruption derailing Washington. The weak economy, newly motivated industry opposition, and its own complexity caused its downfall. Critics also pointed to all the concessions and exemptions handed out to large industries in order to win support. Introducing his own climate change bill in 2009, which included provisions for emissions trading, Senator John Kerry (D-MA; in office 1985–) distanced himself from the concept, saying, "I don't know what 'cap and trade' means."

A modified version has been proposed by a bipartisan team of senators, Maria Cantwell (D-WA; in office 2001–) and Susan Collins (R-ME; in office 1997–). Under a system they call "cap and dividend," permits for pollution would be auctioned to producers and wholesalers of fossil fuels, with 75 percent of the money sent to consumers in monthly checks to offset higher bills.

A massive underwater earthquake caused a twenty-three-foot tsunami, devastating Japan on Friday, March 11, 2011. Cooling systems at the Fukushima Daiichi Nuclear Power Station failed shortly after the earthquake, and on Saturday, March 12, there was an explosion at nuclear reactor No. 1. The cooling systems at Fukushima Daini, another plant, also had failed. Ultimately, more than two hundred thousand residents were evacuated from areas surrounding both facilities. The long-term impact of these nuclear meltdowns remains to be seen.

SOURCE: Kyodo/Landov.

as China and India, from compliance, and would cause serious harm to the U.S. economy." Bush also referred to "the incomplete state of scientific knowledge of the causes of, and solutions to, global climate change." Nonetheless, the Kyoto Protocols went into effect in February 2005, not long after Russia ratified the agreement.

In opposing action on the climate change problem despite scientific consensus, President Bush was drawing upon several anti-environmental strands of conservative ideology. Although Republicans had a long history of supporting conservation, going back to Theodore Roosevelt (1901–1909) and even Richard Nixon (1969–1974), anti-environmentalism had become a defining feature of the "new right" conservativism embodied by President Ronald Reagan. While economic conservatives opposed environmental regulations as an unnecessary burden on industry, social conservatives, wary of evolutionary biology, disapproved of what they saw as the secular bias of environmental science. On top of this opposition was a longstanding distrust among conservatives of the United Nations and international treaties. In addition, several industries that faced tighter regulations regarding carbon emissions, such as auto and oil companies, mounted a successful disinformation campaign to sow doubt about climate science when in fact scientific consensus existed. Not all large corporations, and not all Republicans, however, rejected concern about global warming.

Barack Obama (2009–), elected president of the United States in November 2008, campaigned on making climate change a priority for his administration, yet he has not been able to overcome resistance within the U.S. Senate. Also, the economic recession that began in 2008 has made passage of the agreements even more difficult. As of 2012, the United States remains the only industrialized nation that

has not ratified the Kyoto agreements. The countries of the world met again in Copenhagen, Denmark, in 2009, and in Durban, South Africa, in 2011, to continue their discussions, yet failed to reach any breakthroughs.

LEGACY OF ENVIRONMENTAL POLICY

Although often overlooked, nature plays a role in American foreign relations, and American foreign relations have had a tremendous impact on nature. Every time an American buys something fashioned from materials that come from overseas, or drives a car or operates a machine powered by fuels from overseas, he or she is part of an economic network with significant consequences for ecosystems around the world. All resources come from some place, and all pollution and waste must go somewhere. It is also true that American military actions around the world, preparations for military actions, and American overseas economic development programs have reshaped environments around the world and the United States, often, although not always with harmful long-term consequences.

Examining the environmental side of American foreign relations changes the way we understand both foreign relations and environments. It adds a material and ecological context to foreign relations that is often missing and an international side to recent American environmental history that is often overlooked.

See also: **Chapter 31: U.S. Economic and Foreign Relations with the Western Hemisphere; Chapter 33: Europe, the United States, and NATO and Their Roles in the Twenty-first Century; Chapter 34: Diplomatic Milestones, 1992–2000.**

ENDNOTES

1. Richard Tucker, *Insatiable Appetite: The United States and the Ecological Degradation of the Tropical World,* Concise rev. ed. (Lanham, MD: Rowman & Littlefield, 2007), 1.

2. Fairfield Osborn, *Our Plundered Planet* (Boston: Little, Brown, 1948), 136.

3. Dwight D. Eisenhower: "Inaugural Address," January 20, 1953, at Gerhard Peters and John T. Woolley, *The American Presidency Project [online],* available at: http://www.presidency.ucsb.edu/ws/?pid=9600.

4. President Eisenhower's Remarks at Governors' Conference, August 4, 1953, in *Public Papers of the Presidents, 1953* (Washington, DC: U.S. Government Printing Office, 1953), 540.

5. Statement of Secretary Krug Before the Foreign Affairs Committee on the House on the European Recovery Program, January 22, 1948, House Foreign Affairs Committee Folder, Box 66, Julius Krug Papers, Library of Congress.

6. Harry S. Truman, "Inaugural Address," January 20, 1949, in *Public Papers of the Presidents of the United States*, Containing the Public Messages, Speeches, and Statements of the President, Harry S. Truman, January 1 to December 31, 1949 (Washington, DC: U.S. Government Printing Office, 1964), 112–16.

7. Richard Tucker, "Containing Communism by Impounding Rivers," in John McNeill and Corinna Unger, eds., *Environmental Histories of the Cold War* (New York: Cambridge University Press, 2010), 156.

8. Wilfred Owen, *Transport Revolution: Can It Revolutionize Asia?* (Washington, DC: Brookings Institution, 1964).

9. David Potter, *People of Plenty: Economic Abundance and the American Character* (Chicago: University of Chicago Press, 1954), 139.

10. W. W. Rostow, *The Stages of Economic Growth: A Non-Communist Manifesto* (Cambridge, UK: Cambridge University Press, 1960), 4.

11. Donald Worster, *Nature's Economy: A History of Ecological Ideas* (Cambridge, UK: Cambridge University Press, 1994), 342.

12. Stephen Bocking, *Ecologists and Environmental Politics: A History of Contemporary Ecology* (New Haven, CT: Yale University Press, 1997), 89–115; Peter Taylor, "Technocratic Optimism, H. T. Odum, and the Partial Transformation of Ecological Metaphors after World War II," in *Journal of the History of Biology* 21 (1988), 213–44.

13. Fairfield Osborn, "The Lesson Not Yet Learned," in *Bulletin of the New York Zoological Society* 45: 5 (September-October, 1942), 137.

14. David Brower, "Foreword," in Paul Ehrlich, *The Population Bomb* (New York: Ballantine Books, 1968).

15. "Osborn Says We Must Guard Resources, or Face Socialism," in *New York Herald Tribune Forum Section,* October 24, 1948, Folder "Speeches—Our Plundered Planet," Box 1, RG 2, New York Zoological Society Archives, New York, NY.

16. William Vogt, "Let's Examine Our Santa Claus Complex," in *The Saturday Evening Post,* July 23, 1949.

FURTHER READING

Anker, Peder. "The Ecological Colonization of Space," in *Environmental History,* 10:2 (April 2005).

Kinkela, David. *DDT and the American Century: Global Health, Environmental Politics, and the Pesticide That Changed the World.* Chapel Hill: University of North Carolina Press, 2011.

McNeill, John, and Corinna R. Unger, eds. *Environmental Histories of the Cold War.* Washington, DC: German Historical Institute, 2010.

Robertson, Thomas. "'This is the American Earth': American Empire, American Environmentalism." in *Diplomatic History* 32:4 (September 2008), 561–84.

Tucker, Richard P. *Insatiable Appetite: The United States and the Ecological Degradation of the Tropical World.* Concise rev. ed. Lanham, MD: Rowman & Littlefield, 2007.

chapter 33

Europe, the United States, and NATO and Their Roles in the Twenty-first Century

by Andreas Wenger

THE NORTH ATLANTIC TREATY ORGANIZATION (NATO) faced unique issues in the shifting political environment of the late twentieth and early twenty-first centuries. In addition, NATO had to determine how the United States and Europe would react to a set of emerging security challenges that differed radically from those of the Cold War period. During the first decade of the post-Cold War era, the alliance successfully adapted to a fundamentally changed security environment on the continent, and, by 1999, NATO had established itself once again at the core of the new European security order.

In the first decade of the twenty-first century, however, deep cracks opened up in the alliance's foundations when, against the backdrop of President George W. Bush's (2001–2009) "war on terrorism," the United States presented its vision of NATO as a global military alliance of democratic states. Eventually, in 2011, NATO members recognized the political and military limitations of the alliance, and in their newest strategic concept compromised on a globally less ambitious and politically more regional alliance. NATO's resilience in the face of external and internal change owes much to its self-perception as a community of values, to the flexibility of its military structures, and to the adaptability of its political functions as a tool of U.S. influence and leadership in Europe, on the one hand, and of European balance and self-assertion beyond the continent, on the other.

A NEW NATO AT THE CORE OF A NEW SECURITY ORDER IN EUROPE

In the period leading up to 1994, NATO was plagued by internal tension, which by and large crippled the entire organization. Disagreement among the allies concentrated on three key strategic challenges. The first was linked to the disbanding of the Warsaw Pact and the dissolution of the Soviet Union. These dramatic geopolitical changes raised the question of how best to deal with the emerging power vacuum in Central and Eastern Europe.

The discussion about NATO's eastern expansion and the closely related issue of its relations with Russia split the alliance into factions both within and between its member states. The second strategic challenge resulted from the disintegration of the former Yugoslavia and the outbreak of armed conflicts in the Balkans. For some time, the allies were unable to agree on how to end the hostilities, first in Bosnia, and later in Kosovo. The third strategic challenge related to Germany's reunification and the birth of the European Union (EU) in 1993. The critical question here was what this meant for the balance between European autonomy and U.S. leadership. The allies disagreed over burden-sharing, and, politically much more important, they were at odds about whether or not European security and defense policy should be independent of the United States.

NATO's adaptation process in the early post–Cold War years was neither smooth nor straightforward. It was a pragmatic and often controversial reaction to the three key developments outlined above, which were, in practice, interlinked, and which overlapped in many ways. NATO's transformation from the defensive alliance of the Cold War into the security management institution of the twenty-first century was shaped by a complex mix of personal ambition and domestic and bureaucratic politics at the national level; coalition- and network-building at the transnational level; and bargaining among key allied countries at the intergovernmental level. When NATO leaders met in 1999 in Washington to celebrate the fiftieth anniversary of NATO's founding, the alliance had successfully strengthened its political role and radically changed its military structure. The allies generally agreed that NATO had once again become the keystone of the security order in Europe, albeit in a political environment that had changed fundamentally. How did this come about?

Enlarging NATO: Echoes from the Past

The decision to enlarge NATO was made in Madrid in July 1997. The membership invitations extended to the

KEY CONCEPTS

The origins of NATO. The North Atlantic Treaty Organization (NATO) was founded in 1949, when the Cold War set in between the Eastern bloc and Western bloc under the leadership of the two superpowers, the Soviet Union and the United States. Looking back on the Cold War period, which ended in 1991 with the dissolution of the Soviet Union, most contemporary observers recall the alliance primarily as a powerful military structure. NATO's deterrence and defense functions provided the bedrock of Western security and stability in a Europe that was divided between the two blocs. From NATO's founding onward, however, it also performed important political functions as a means of preventing the expansion of Soviet political influence in an economically weak Europe. NATO's first secretary general, Lord Ismay, hit the nail on the head when he stated at the time that NATO existed "to keep the Russians out, the Americans in, and the Germans down."

NATO and the end of the Cold War. More than forty years after NATO's founding, in 1991, the dissolution of the Warsaw Pact and the Soviet Union practically removed the alliance's *raison d'être* overnight. In the midst of jubilant celebrations following the peaceful ending of the Cold War, the alliance faced an existential crisis that continued on into the early 1990s. Prominent academics such as John Mearsheimer and Kenneth Waltz anticipated a weakening of NATO, a re-nationalization of security and defense policy in Europe, and thus a return to a balance-of-power system. Policymakers, too, hotly discussed various blueprints for a European security order without NATO. The options included Russian designs for a restored Concert of Europe, German plans for a pan-European system built around an upgraded Conference on Security and Cooperation in Europe (CSCE), and French hopes of boosting the Western European Union (WEU) as the nucleus of an all-European defense scheme.

Czech Republic, Hungary, and Poland represented a fundamental turning point in U.S. and European policy regarding the geopolitical order in Eastern Europe. The key driving forces behind enlargement were memories of past history and, more particularly, rapidly rising fears, on both sides of the Atlantic, that the strategic vacuum in Central Europe would reactivate the geopolitical competition between Germany and Russia for security in and influence over the zone between their borders. NATO enlargement would reaffirm U.S. leadership in Europe and would ensure that Germany was not driven toward an independent foreign policy. NATO's expansion into Eastern Europe arose from the aspirations of these new democracies to join the Western security community, on the one hand, and Russia's inability to oppose the move, on the other.

German Unification and Germany's Change of Strategy

The history of the alliance's enlargement can be traced back to the "Two Plus Four" negotiations (May to September 1990) that had led to the reunification of Germany. One of the most critical questions of the reunification process was whether the Russians would agree that a unified Germany should remain a member of NATO. U.S. Secretary of State James Baker (in office 1989–1992) convinced Soviet President Mikhail Gorbachev (in office 1985–1991) that it should, asking Gorbachev if he would "prefer a united Germany outside of NATO that is independent and has no U.S. forces," or "a united Germany with ties to NATO and assurances that there would be no extension of NATO's current jurisdiction eastward."[1] Although the diplomatic language used in these negotiations was full of ambiguity, the Russians

never solicited a pledge in writing that the alliance would not expand into Eastern Europe. What this often-quoted episode underlines is the extent to which the fear of German unilateralism influenced the enlargement of the alliance, as well as the process of deepening and widening the European Union.

At the NATO summit in London in mid-1990, the alliance invited the Central and Eastern European states to establish regular diplomatic liaisons with NATO. The overwhelming response of the young democracies left no doubt about their security needs and their political and cultural affiliations with the West. Among NATO members, the Germans were the first to start a heated interagency debate about the merits of enlargement. In the German Foreign Office, skepticism initially prevailed because many diplomats feared Russian opposition and were more concerned with the enlargement of the European Union than with that of NATO. However, driven by personal ambition and bureaucratic competition, German Defense Minister Volker Rühe (in office 1992–1998) soon emerged as the leading advocate of enlargement. Rühe feared, as he put it in October 1993, that if NATO did not "export stability" to Central Europe, it would "import instability" from there.[2] From a military point of view, Rühe argued, Germany was easier to defend from within Poland than from within Germany. Moreover, in the context of the growing crisis in Bosnia, he soon concluded that NATO was better positioned to develop a rapid reaction capability than the Western European Union (WEU) was.

NATO enlargement is a great case of how transnational elites can shape trans-governmental coalitions toward a common position, especially in the context of U.S.-German relations. Rühe realized that a unilateral

German effort to push for enlargement might antagonize Germany's eastern and western neighbors. He decided to reach out to the United States and asked the RAND Cooperation to conceptualize a plan for NATO enlargement and provide advocacy among U.S. and NATO policymakers. After the Pentagon agreed, three leading RAND analysts, Ronald Asmus, Richard Kugler, and F. Stephen Larrabee, began to outline the strategic rationale for enlargement and define options for moving ahead. The result of their work was widely discussed in U.S. government circles.[3] Over time, and influenced by the RAND study, the German Defense Minister began to favor the option according to which NATO enlargement would precede EU enlargement. This led to a major row with the Foreign Office, which still argued that such a course of action would antagonize the Russians and generate disparate zones of security in the European Union. Finally, following his reelection in 1994, German Chancellor Helmut Kohl (in office 1982–1998) stepped in and committed his country to a course that linked NATO enlargement to EU enlargement.

The U.S. Debate: Taking the Lead

The initial reaction of U.S. officials to Rühe's initiative was reserved and skeptical. While the administration of President William J. Clinton (1993–2001) agreed on a "doctrine of enlargement," key officials, including Defense Secretary Les Aspin (in office 1993–1994) and Deputy Secretary of State Strobe Talbott (in office 1994–2001), were primarily concerned with the democratic transition in Russia. Analysts in the State Department prioritized the U.S. relationship with Russia over approaches to Eastern and Central Europe. In the Pentagon, the focus was on securing loose nukes and reducing the stockpiles of aging nuclear weapons.

Pressure to help the young democracies in Eastern Europe increased after President Clinton met the Polish and Czech leaders, Lech Wałęsa (in office 1990–1995) and Václav Havel (in office 1989–2003), in Washington in April 1993. Around this time, the ambitious Richard Holbrooke, U.S. ambassador in Bonn, and Anthony Lake, Clinton's national security adviser, emerged as the key figures who shifted U.S. policy toward enlargement. In October of the same year, however, Secretary of State Warren Christopher (in office 1993–1997) and Defense Secretary Aspin, still holding back, introduced the Partnership for Peace (PfP) as a potential alternative to NATO membership. When Les Aspin presented the initiative to his NATO colleagues in Brussels, he made it clear that PfP was designed to slow down enlargement. The official U.S. view at the time was still behind Volker Rühe, who was not prepared to accept PfP as a substitute for enlargement.

One year later, by the end of 1994, it had become clear that Clinton supported enlargement and was prepared to take the lead in pushing NATO toward a decision. This shift in policy was facilitated by growing Republican pressure, highlighted by a landslide victory in the 1994 congressional elections, which demanded that Clinton provide active leadership in foreign policy. Richard Holbrooke was called back from Bonn to Washington to push the issue forward. Over time, Holbrooke had become convinced of the strategic logic behind enlargement: that without it the classic security dilemma between Germany and Russia would reemerge. While the European agenda could not be held hostage by the slow transition process in Russia, enlargement was an opportunity to establish NATO's preeminence among European security institutions. From a U.S. point of view, it was not acceptable that EU enlargement would precede NATO enlargement, because in practice this would expand the U.S. commitment to the new EU members through the back door. Thus, NATO enlargement not only provided the president with an opportunity to show leadership on foreign policy; it also allowed the United States to reassert its leading role in Europe.

NATO's New Members: The Czech Republic, Hungary, and Poland

In January 1994, after attending his first NATO summit, Bill Clinton declared at a press conference that "the question is no longer whether NATO will take on new members but when and how."[4] The decision to implement a strategy of enlargement had resulted to a large degree from a U.S.-German push. Yet it would still take years before the first former members of the Warsaw Pact joined NATO, namely on the occasion of the Washington summit in 1999. This was because, on the one hand, it took time to overcome initial French and British resistance. On the other hand, the question of exactly which countries should join and under what conditions was highly sensitive, diplomatically speaking, with potentially serious repercussions for bargaining within the alliance and for NATO's relationship with Russia and the states along Russia's periphery.

In 1995, NATO undertook a study to examine the "why and how" of expansion. The study concluded that the end of the Cold War had opened up "a unique opportunity to build an improved security architecture in the whole of the Euro-Atlantic area."[5] As preconditions to membership, the new members would have to settle ethnic and territorial disputes; treat their minorities in accordance with guidelines set forth by the Organization for Security and Cooperation in Europe (OSCE; formerly CSCE); establish democratic control of security instruments; and increase their transparency in defense planning and military budgeting. The allies believed that the stability transfer and transparency building effects of enlargement would be in everyone's interest. Yet Russia remained adamantly opposed to any NATO expansion. Consequently, as an effort complementary to enlargement, and in view of Russia's sharply negative reaction, the allies decided to establish a special institutionalized relationship with Russia. The Founding Act on Mutual Cooperation, signed in May 1997, assured Moscow that NATO had no plans to deploy nuclear weapons or foreign troops on the soil of the new member states. In addition, the act created the Permanent Joint Council (PJC), an official forum for regular consultations between alliance members and Russia. In practice, however, the consultations remained shallow and without much practical meaning, because the mechanism gave Moscow much less influence over NATO decision making than Russian officials had hoped for.

While enlargement was being pursued, the out-of-area debate linked to the developments in the Balkans spurred a discussion about additional candidate countries. The French, after their initial skepticism, began to push for southern enlargement and made a case for the inclusion of Romania, a country with historically close ties to France. The Italians followed suit and argued for extending an invitation to Slovenia. German leaders, in turn, saw the interests of their country limited to its immediate neighbors and were therefore not interested in such an expansion. The final decision thus fell to President Clinton, who decided that, for the time being, enlargement should be limited to the Czech Republic, Hungary, and Poland. The door should remain open for a second round, however, which meant that the issue of enlargement would reappear in the twenty-first century.

The Balkan Wars: A New Type of Challenge

In July 1995, NATO decided for the first time in its history to employ military force outside of its own territory. Massive air strikes were meant to force Serbian leader Slobodan Milošević (in power 1989–2000) to the negotiation table. Together with the deployment of a UN-mandated peacekeeping force (Implementation Force, IFOR), which resulted from the Dayton Peace Agreement, signed in December 1995, the air campaign over Bosnia represented a fundamental turning point in NATO's out-of-area debate: it established a new crisis management and peacemaking role for the alliance in reaction to a new type of complex security challenge on Europe's periphery. Closely linked to the debate about crisis management was the question of who, Europe or the United States, should and could take the lead in dealing with the ethnic wars in the Balkans. NATO's military engagement there proved that the Europeans were not ready to act militarily on their own. The fiasco of the

TABLE 33.1   **Expansion of NATO**

NATO Expansion during the Cold War	NATO Expansion after the Cold War	Candidate Countries Being Reviewed by NATO[a]
1949 (Founding of NATO)	1990	Macedonia
Belgium	East Germany[b]	Montenegro
Canada	1999	Bosnia and Herzegovina
Denmark	Czech Republic	
France	Hungary	
Iceland	Poland	
Italy	2004	
Luxembourg	Bulgaria	
Netherlands	Estonia	
Norway	Latvia	
Portugal	Lithuania	
United Kingdom	Romania	
United States	Slovakia	
1952	Slovenia	
Greece	2009	
Turkey	Croatia	
1955	Albania	
West Germany		
1982		
Spain		

a. Candidate countries are those with a Membership Action Plan (MAP), the procedure during which the applications of candidate countries are reviewed.

b. East Germany did not become a member of NATO itself but reunited with West Germany on October 3, 1990.

United Nations Protection Force (UNPROFOR), led by France and Britain, and the succeeding success of NATO's military campaign under U.S. leadership reestablished the alliance as the core military actor in Europe's shifting security order.

The Hour of Europe: French Ambition and U.S. Diffidence

The breakup of the former Yugoslavia and the outbreak of war in Bosnia exposed European countries to immigration pressure and domestic social tension. It should therefore come as no surprise that the Europeans initially took the lead in determining the form of Western involvement in the Balkans. German initiative was decisive in shaping the diplomatic recognition of Slovenia and Croatia. Once hostilities had escalated in Bosnia, Paris championed the deployment of a Franco-British rapid reaction force and led the establishment of UNPROFOR, whose mission was to protect the civilian population from armed attacks.

European initiative in the Balkans was linked to the process of strengthening the European Union through the Maastricht Treaty. The French, in particular, hoped that Europe could procure crisis management forces at the European level, a development that would potentially facilitate cooperation with Russia through the CSCE. After a meeting in Yugoslavia in June 1991, the chairman of the European Council summarized the general feeling as follows: "This is the hour of Europe. It is not the hour of the Americans."[6] At a meeting of the WEU in June 1992, the member states agreed to jointly deploy their forces and resources in humanitarian, peacekeeping, and peacemaking missions under the authority of the WEU.

The administration of President George H. W. Bush (1989–1993) did not consider the Balkans a foreign policy priority for the United States. Key officials maintained that it constituted a European problem. Secretary of State James Baker was strongly opposed to U.S. involvement, privately declaring that "we don't have a dog in this fight."[7] Thus, to the limited extent that the Bush administration was involved in the Balkans, it tried to operate through NATO. Yet although Washington was able to secure the allies' principal acceptance of an out-of-area mission at the Rome summit in 1991, the absence of any enthusiasm for a NATO role underlined how divided the allies were on the question of a NATO role in the Balkans.

With the arrival of Bill Clinton in the White House in 1993, the United States became more actively involved in the former Yugoslavia. The influential UN Ambassador (and, later, secretary of state) Madeleine Albright (UN ambassador from 1993 to 1997) outlined a strategy of assertive multilateralism and, together with Anthony Lake, argued that the United States should call upon the United Nations to lift its arms embargo against all warring parties and initiate air strikes against the Bosnian Serbs. However, the "lift and strike" proposal was rejected by Joint Chiefs of Staff Chairman Colin L. Powell (in office 1989–1993), who questioned its feasibility. Congressional opposition to a more active role in the Balkans was equally strong for a variety of reasons, including fears of an over-commitment of military forces, opposition to an enhanced UN role, and a general feeling that the United States had more important domestic and foreign policy priorities.

UN Failure: NATO Takes Over

NATO stood on the sidelines as it became more and more obvious that UNPROFOR could not stop ethnic cleansing in Bosnia. The alliance's first involvement came in the form of support for the WEU's maritime monitoring mission of the UN arms embargo, which was approved after a joint session of NATO and the WEU. In Bosnia, however, the UN safe areas could still not be properly protected, and ethnic atrocities proceeded under the eyes of the blue helmets. The situation started to change when France accepted a NATO role in 1993, providing close air support for UNPROFOR, and agreed to assign French aircraft to NATO's integrated military command. In return, the United States accepted UN political control, at least for the time being. On April 10, 1994, NATO delivered air strikes to protect UN safe areas and for the first time in its history actively used military force outside its territory.

Yet the attacks on the safe areas did not stop. On the contrary, Bosnian Serb forces now began to take UN personnel hostage and stepped up their mortar attacks on Sarajevo. The continuing escalation convinced both Paris and Washington that the UN was the wrong organization to implement and oversee peace enforcement operations that had been mandated by the Security Council under Chapter VII of the UN Charter. A common interest emerged that eventually would bring France back into NATO's Military Committee in 1995. Policymakers in Paris and Washington agreed that NATO would have to run military operations to persuade the parties to end the conflict. The massacre of some eight thousand Muslims by Serb troops in Srebrenica in July 1995 focused anti-Serb public opinion in the West, and in Washington it expedited congressional acceptance of a commitment to use ground forces in a NATO operation. On the battlefield, the United States took over, armed the Bosnian Muslims, supported an offensive by the Croatian army, and took the lead in negotiating a cease-fire agreement.

The Dayton Accords: Washington's Preferred Division of Labor

Officials in the Clinton administration justified U.S. involvement in Bosnia as essential to reestablishing NATO as the central security institution in Europe and to ensuring U.S. influence and leadership on the continent. The peace negotiations in Dayton, Ohio, were led by Secretary of State Warren Christopher and negotiator Richard Holbrooke, together with European and Russian representatives. Another key participant was General Wesley Clark, who would later become NATO's supreme allied commander Europe (SACEUR). He made sure that NATO's mission was restricted to imposing order and creating a secure environment. The narrow military responsibility of NATO, together with a presidential premise that U.S. ground troops would stay only one year, provided the basis for congressional and public support for U.S. military engagement in the Balkans.

The Dayton Peace Accords established a division of labor between the various parties that ensured NATO's primacy among Europe's security institutions. The UN provided overall political guidance and an international mandate; the OSCE prepared elections and monitored human rights; and the EU provided economic assistance and training in civilian governance. NATO alone controlled the military mission, and while the United States had contributed half of the overall IFOR contingent, its contribution shrank to about a quarter of the thirty-one thousand troops in the Stabilisation Force (SFOR) when the latter was established in December 1996. This division of labor confirmed that NATO would still be a U.S.-led alliance. At the same time, it limited the alliance's responsibility to the military mission and ensured that the alliance was not overcommitted. Such a division of labor was also acceptable to the Europeans, because it recognized the particular strength of both the EU and the OSCE in the field of soft security.

Adapting NATO's Military Structure: EU-NATO Collaboration

The Dayton Peace Agreement signaled a division of labor between Europe's security institutions and confirmed NATO's preeminence in military security. The Balkans was the arena in which the two key challenges in the process of adapting NATO's military structures played themselves out in practice: the transformation from the deterrence and territorial defense functions that NATO had held in the past to the new role of crisis management and peacemaking, and the rebalancing of the financial and military burden, which would henceforth be shared by the (new) members of the alliance. These issues were closely linked to the political balance between European autonomy and U.S. leadership. With U.S. acceptance of the European Security and Defense Identity (ESDI) in 1996, the allies were able to paper over their differences at the political level, at least for the time being. Of higher practical importance was the allies' experience of working together as a military organization. With all sixteen NATO members operating together in the context of the IFOR/SFOR in Bosnia, France was provided with an acceptable role, bringing it closer to NATO's military structures. Although this newfound sense of purpose carried NATO successfully through its second war in the Balkans, coalition warfare in Kosovo highlighted a series of profound political and military dilemmas. The campaign in Kosovo undermined the stability of the new transatlantic bargain at the very moment at which NATO was celebrating its fiftieth anniversary and its reconstitution as Europe's central security institution.

Adapting NATO's Military Structure

The disbanding of the Warsaw Pact and the dissolution of the Soviet Union made much of the allies' military planning obsolete. As a consequence, large parts of the alliance's nuclear and conventional forces were reduced during the 1990s. NATO ground forces shrank by 35 percent, NATO naval forces by 30 percent, and NATO air forces by 40 percent.[8] U.S. troop strength in Europe fell from 318,700 in 1987 to 107,335 in 1995.[9] The role of nuclear weapons was greatly reduced, and more than 80 percent of U.S. sub-strategic nuclear weapons were withdrawn from Europe. The massive reduction of the alliance's armed forces went along with a reduction of the number of headquarters from sixty-five to twenty. The new NATO was restructured as two strategic commands, one for Europe and the other for the Atlantic region.

Although the Article V commitment to collective defense remained at the core of the alliance, the initial RAND study on alliance enlargement had warned back in 1993 that "NATO must go out of area or it will go out of business."[10] NATO's role in crisis management had already been anticipated in the North Atlantic Treaty. Yet it was the concrete engagement in Bosnia that highlighted the importance of the alliance as an instrument of crisis management in Europe. These new types of operations outside the alliance's traditional territory required more flexible, more mobile, and more interoperable forces. NATO's force planning process was the key, not only to the transformation of the old members' forces toward a crisis management role, but also to the integration of the new member (Warsaw Pact) forces into the West's military structures. To increase the capacity for cooperation with partners, NATO introduced the PfP Planning and Review Process (PARP). The political benefits of the force planning process have increased transparency and trust among and beyond NATO members.

The Rise and Fall of the European Security and Defense Identity (ESDI)

In the early 1990s, the future role of the U.S. in Europe had seemed uncertain, and France and Germany had, for some time, focused on building a common foreign and security policy (CFSP) under the roof of the European Union, reviving and integrating the dormant institutional structure of the WEU. Yet the wars in the Balkans made it painfully obvious that Europe still had a long way to go before it would be capable of managing a crisis such as that in Bosnia. Without an institutional capacity at the European level, and without Franco-British defense cooperation, Europe would remain dependent on the United States and NATO, not just for Article V purposes but also for crisis management tasks along the European periphery.

During the Bosnian crisis, Paris acknowledged that only NATO under U.S. leadership had the political and military clout to force the warring parties to the negotiation table and simultaneously manage the West's relationship with Russia. As a consequence, the allies defined ESDI as a mechanism to square the circle between European autonomy and U.S. leadership. ESDI was launched at the NATO summit in June 1996 as a mechanism that would allow the Europeans to gain access to NATO assets and planning facilities to carry out crisis management missions in which the U.S. did not wish to be involved. The related concept of the Combined Joint Task Forces (CJTF) established new command structures that were to enable the inclusion of non-member countries in NATO operations.

The debate about NATO-EU cooperation was reinvigorated when French President Jacques Chirac (in office 1995–2007) and the newly elected British Prime Minister Tony Blair (in office 1997–2007) announced in Saint-Malo in 1998 that the EU "must have the capacity for autonomous action, backed up by credible military forces, the means to decide to use them, and a readiness to do so, in order to respond to international crises."[11] This Franco-British rapprochement in the field of defense policy initiated a period of remarkable advancement in European Security and Defense Policy (ESDP). At the EU summits in Cologne in June 1999 and in Helsinki in December 1999, the EU declared its intention to create an autonomous military capability in crisis management; integrated the Petersburg tasks of the WEU into the EU; established a permanent political and security committee; and agreed to draw up a rapid reaction force of sixty thousand.

With the rapid development of ESDP, the issue of cooperation between the EU and NATO became politically explosive. While the Europeans were no longer content with the role of a subcontractor to the United States, American leaders feared a weakening of NATO as their forum for political leadership in Europe. Reacting to Saint-Malo, Secretary of State Madeleine Albright (in office 1997–2001) put forward the famous "three D's," which outlined what ESDP should not mean: no duplication, no decoupling, and no discrimination of NATO.[12] U.S. Secretary of Defense William Cohen (in office 1997–2001) demanded a right of first refusal, because the EU would in most cases have to rely on U.S. capabilities. While a U.S. veto over decision-making in the EU was unacceptable to most Europeans, Great Britain facilitated a compromise that allowed the establishment of an ad hoc working group tasked with developing permanent arrangements for EU-NATO consultation and cooperation. The result of the ensuing negotiations was the "Berlin Plus" agreement of March 2003, which highlighted that the crisis management activities and the capability development processes of NATO and the EU were mutually reinforcing and that the EU could use NATO assets, if NATO declined to act.

Kosovo: Europe's Military Failure

The acceleration of ESDP was closely linked to the military failure of the Europeans during the Kosovo war. Serbian leader Slobodan Milošević had infringed on the autonomy that the Kosovars had enjoyed in Yugoslavia for many years. By early 1998, violence was escalating between Serbian police and military forces, on the one hand, and the newly formed Kosovo Liberation Army (KLA), on the other. Yet although the allies threatened to use force, both European and U.S. leaders initially hesitated to take on an additional military commitment. Many European states hesitated because, unlike Bosnia, Kosovo was part of a sovereign state, and the West, in view of Russian and Chinese opposition, could not expect a UN mandate in support of an intervention. In Washington, President Clinton could not hope to get congressional support for a ground operation, because he was weakened by his infamous impeachment trial and thus hesitated to commit to the use of force in Kosovo.

Clinton was, however, sufficiently concerned to send Richard Holbrooke to Belgrade to try to negotiate an end to the spreading violence. As part of a Milošević-Holbrooke agreement, Washington agreed to place two thousand unarmed OSCE observers on the ground in Kosovo and to create a NATO Extraction Force to evacuate OSCE personnel, if necessary. This deal put NATO on a slippery slope toward military engagement. In March 1999, after it had become clear that Serbia did not intend to reach a negotiated peace agreement at Rambouillet, NATO commenced a bombing campaign that eventually ran for seventy-eight days. The United States had decided to take the lead, and both Secretary of State Albright and Secretary of Defense Cohen repeatedly pointed to the need to uphold NATO's credibility as the key motivation for the U.S. campaign. In her memoirs, Madeleine Albright recalls, "Milošević had gambled that Kosovo would split the Alliance and open an unbridgeable gap between Russia and the West." This meant that the "situation was emerging as a key test of American leadership and of the relevance and effectiveness of NATO."[13] The key decision makers in the Clinton administration—Albright, Holbrooke, and General Clark—believed that a limited bombing campaign would coerce Milošević into giving in quickly. They did not anticipate that the Serbian leader would react with an acceleration of the humanitarian disaster. It took almost eleven weeks until Milošević finally capitulated, and the alliance was able to help establish the NATO-led Kosovo Force (KFOR) of forty-five thousand troops under a UN mandate that was tasked with building a secure environment for all of Kosovo's citizens.

The fact that NATO managed to uphold its unity throughout the campaign amid public criticism from many of its member states is no small achievement. Yet unlike the case of Bosnia, the Kosovo engagement undermined the agreed division of labor, producing cracks in the stability of alliance solidarity that would break open during the debate over the war in Iraq. The Europeans were humiliated by their almost total dependence on U.S. military assets: the U.S. air fleet flew close to 75 percent of all NATO assignments, and only about 3 percent of Europe's soldiers were ready for deployment in Kosovo. At the same time, many Europeans were concerned about President Clinton's reluctance to seriously consider the use of ground troops to stop the humanitarian disaster. Conversely, the United States was fed up with making war by committee and unimpressed by Europe's reluctance to share the greater part of the burden in efforts toward long-term peace building while avoiding high-intensity operations.

NATO at Fifty: Back at the Center of the European Security Order

When NATO leaders convened in Washington for the alliance's fiftieth anniversary, there was much reason for celebration: the alliance had successfully adapted to the end of the Cold War and had established itself once again at the core of the new European security order. The debate about NATO's reform had been shaped by the transformation of the post-Soviet democracies in Central Europe, Eastern Europe, and Russia; by the outbreak of war in the Balkans; and by the deepening and widening of the EU integration. The fact that, during the 1990s, the strategic debate in NATO centered on Europe goes a long way toward explaining why the allies were able to define a fairly stable equilibrium for a reformed alliance.

In reaction to these developments, the allies had strengthened and broadened NATO's political role. The traditional political functions of NATO as a transatlantic forum and tool of U.S. leadership in Europe, on the one hand, and as an internal system of peace, embedding a unified Germany into the broader Euro-Atlantic framework, on the other, remained relevant in the post–Cold War era. In addition, NATO took on new political tasks that became more important because of the disintegration of the Warsaw Pact and former Soviet Union. Expanding its membership to three new states, the alliance projected stability into

Eastern and Central Europe. At the same time, NATO offered Moscow an institutionalized dialogue as a means of smoothing Russian opposition to enlargement. The decision to keep the door open to additional members would ensure that the questions regarding NATO's borders would remain on the agenda. After fifty-odd years, NATO retained Article V at its core. At the same time, in its new strategic concept, NATO acknowledged the changes in its security environment and recognized the growing importance of crisis management and peacemaking missions beyond its border.

THE BUSH YEARS: CRACKS IN THE FOUNDATION OF NATO

The question of the geographic and functional expansion of NATO's political and military role had already shaped

SHIFTS IN FOREIGN POLICY: *THE "WAR ON TERRORISM" AND NATO: FROM SOLIDARITY TO RECRIMINATION*

During his presidential campaign, George W. Bush had distanced himself from the humanitarian interventionism of Bill Clinton and had warned against overstretching U.S. military resources by engaging in extensive nation-building missions. It might therefore seem ironic that U.S. foreign policy in Bush's first term was characterized by idealist and interventionist elements, with the result that the U.S. military ended up dangerously overstretched in two costly state-building missions, that in Iraq and that in Afghanistan. This unexpected outcome can only been understood in light of the 9/11 attacks, which evoked a fundamental feeling of vulnerability throughout U.S. society. The attacks on New York and Washington, and the crash of Flight 93 in Pennsylvania, marked the defining moment of the so-called Bush revolution in foreign policy. A dramatic realignment of U.S. foreign policy seemed not only necessary but also possible.

Facing the specter of global terrorists armed with mass casualty weapons, the Bush administration identified the "war on terrorism" as the core mission of U.S. foreign policy. According to the National Security Strategy of 2002, deterrence and containment were no longer sufficient to safeguard the security of the American homeland against terrorist threats with a global reach and so-called rogue states such as Iraq and North Korea. Instead, what was required was an offensive approach that included preventive military operations. At the same time, the full range of U.S. power was to be deployed to facilitate the spread of democracy into the broader Middle East and to guarantee global stability.

THE FIRST PHASE IN AFGHANISTAN: THE POLITICAL SYMBOLISM OF ARTICLE V

For NATO, the "war on terrorism" was a rollercoaster from solidarity to recrimination, with lasting damage to alliance cohesion. In the first phase of the U.S. war on terrorism, the European allies demonstrated extensive solidarity. For the first time in its history, NATO invoked Article V, and the immediate activation of the solidarity clause played an important function in Washington's efforts to build an international coalition against terrorism, though primarily in political, and not in military terms. In fact, the political symbolism of the decision was soon undermined by the negative memories of coalition warfare in Kosovo. U.S. Deputy

Defense Secretary Paul Wolfowitz (in office 2001–2005) traveled to Brussels and told the allies in no uncertain terms that the United States intended to fight the war on terrorism outside NATO's structures and had little interest in the military contributions of the alliance.

Nevertheless, the rapid military victory over the Taliban regime and al Qaeda's paramilitary base in Afghanistan enjoyed robust international support. To counterbalance the marginal role of NATO during the military intervention in Afghanistan and to fend off criticism by NATO skeptics that the alliance was increasingly irrelevant in an age of global terrorism, NATO decided to take command of ISAF, which had been established in parts of Afghanistan by a UN mandate in order to support the Afghan interim government, the reconstruction of the country, and the formation of Afghan security forces. NATO's first mission outside the north Atlantic area was soon expanded to cover the whole of Afghanistan.

THE SECOND PHASE IN IRAQ: TRANSATLANTIC DISCORD AND A DEEP EUROPEAN DIVIDE

Early allied solidarity in the fight against terrorism reached a historic nadir during the 2002–2003 debate over going to war in Iraq. Already in February 2003, France and Belgium, supported by Germany, vetoed protective measures by NATO for Turkey in the event of a possible war with Iraq. This made it plainly obvious that the allies would find it impossible to agree on the legality and strategic wisdom of a policy of military regime change in Iraq. Conversely, the refusal of the Turkish parliament to allow U.S. troops to attack Iraq through their country frustrated and disappointed Washington. How can this complete breakdown of allied solidarity in the run-up to the war in Iraq be explained?

The enormity of the rift among the allies over Iraq can partially be attributed to harsh political rhetoric, incompatible personalities among some of the key leaders, and a charged domestic political atmosphere. The fact that neoconservative circles in Washington seemed to elevate unilateralism to the apex of strategic wisdom infuriated Washington's traditional allies. Conversely, many European leaders were riding the wave of growing anti-Americanism in the alliance's reform debate during the 1990s, albeit with a clear focus on the European periphery. Yet it was clear all along that the United States had a more global understanding of the role of NATO than its European allies. Already in 1998, U.S. Secretary of State Madeleine Albright had advocated a shift away from NATO's traditional role of collective defense toward "the broader concept of the defense of our common interests."[14]

In the 1990s, this debate had arisen primarily in relation to the fight against the proliferation of weapons of mass destruction, although without any clear results. At the turn of the millennium, however, the tragic events of 9/11 propelled the issue of NATO's geographical reach and functional scope to the top of the political agenda in allied capitals. As a consequence of the terrorist attacks on New York and Washington in 2001, the focus of the Euro-Atlantic security debate

shifted from the European periphery to East Asia and the Middle East. The strategic dimension of the threat that emanated from this arc of instability reflected the convergence of regional crises, nuclear proliferation, and the rise of global Islamic terrorism. In response, the United States and a coalition of like-minded states intervened in Afghanistan, toppled the Taliban regime, and dismantled al Qaeda's terrorist infrastructure. While NATO was not at first directly involved in Afghanistan, after the initial intervention had succeeded, the alliance gradually assumed greater responsibility for securing the country's reconstruction. However, this was not without mounting tensions among the allies about the nature of the mission. The changing threat spectrum led to a fundamental reorientation of U.S. foreign policy under President George W. Bush, while the debate about a global NATO opened up deep cracks in the foundation of the alliance.

their public domain and used verbose rhetoric to criticize the simplistic world view of the U.S. "hyperpower." At the same time, the "old" and the "new" Europe were deeply divided and accused each other of undermining EU cohesion and solidarity.

Yet beyond rhetoric, on a strategic level, the glaring differences of opinion over Iraq reflected different threat perceptions, linked to different policy responses, shaped by different strategic cultures. A policy focused on forcible regime change in Iraq lacked legitimacy in the eyes of many Europeans, because the threat of Weapons of Mass Destruction (WMDs) lacked immediacy, and because there was no solid evidence of a close relationship between the al Qaeda network and the Iraqi regime. European analysts and policymakers warned their U.S. colleagues

against putting the military element at the center of their strategy against terrorism. A war in Iraq would destabilize an already unstable region; feed into the dynamics and rhetoric of a clash of civilizations; provide new recruitment opportunities to a defeated al Qaeda in Afghanistan; and push other rogue regimes into accelerating their WMD programs. Conversely, neoconservative circles argued that a change in power in Baghdad would trigger a wave of democratization in the Muslim world, thereby increasing the chances of unblocking the Palestinian-Israeli peace process, depriving Islamist terrorists of a breeding ground, and improving the international framework for a diplomatic solution to the North Korean crisis.

The neoconservative project failed, because, on the one hand, it overestimated the threat of global terrorism, and on the other, it underestimated the difficulties that external actors faced in trying to achieve a democratic transformation of the Arab world. After the remarkably rapid overthrow of Saddam Hussein (in power 1979–2003), Iraq soon sank into civil war across religious and ethnic lines and became a hotbed of recruitment and operations for al Qaeda. The overthrow of Saddam and of the Taliban also resulted in a net gain of influence for Iran and for Shi'ite movements such as Hezbollah, weakening not only the United States as the leading regional power but also Sunni rulers and Arab nationalism in general. The international acceptance of the United States as a political and moral power reached an all-time low in 2004, when photographs became public that depicted U.S. military personnel torturing and abusing the Iraqi inmates of Abu Ghraib prison in Baghdad. The shocking images spread around the world, provoked international outrage, and further weakened the already damaged standing of the United States abroad, particularly in Muslim communities. The departure of key neoconservative players, most notably Secretary of Defense Donald Rumsfeld (in office 2001–2006) and his deputy, Paul Wolfowitz, and the return of the pragmatists (most notably Robert M. Gates as the new secretary of defense) coincided with a shift in the style of conducting foreign policy during President Bush's second term. Bush's symbolic visits to NATO and the EU in Brussels in 2005 inaugurated a period of recuperation for the severely injured transatlantic relationship. However, Bush would be unable to fill the cracks in NATO's foundations.

In Herat, Afghanistan, NATO troops stand guard at the opening of a new police station in September 2011. The troops are charged with providing security for Provincial Reconstruction Teams, small groups of military and civilian workers who are striving to rebuild the war-torn nation's infrastructure.

SOURCE: EPA/Jalil Rezayee/Landov.

Strategic Drift in a Globalizing NATO: The Geographic and Functional Limits of the Alliance

The realignment of U.S. foreign policy in George W. Bush's second term resulted in an improved atmosphere between Washington and the European capitals. The elections of Angela Merkel (in office 2005–) in Germany and Nicolas Sarkozy (in office 2007–) in France expedited the development of a European security strategy that aimed at a rapprochement between EU members in security matters, while also signaling that the Europeans were willing to discuss the new risks and threats in a global context. Within NATO, however, tensions over differing strategic agendas persisted for the remainder of the first decade of the new millennium, as the alliance's center of gravity was recalibrated between a weakened U.S. hegemon and a Europe that once again tried to assert itself as a global actor.

The emergence of at least three different visions for the alliance's future left NATO in a state of strategic drift. First, the United States, with some support from Great Britain, argued for a global NATO that should "open its membership to any democratic state in the world," because global threats "cannot be tackled by a regional organization."[15] A globalizing NATO would branch out into such diverse fields as counter-insurgency, cyber-defense, and energy security. Second, the Eastern European states remained primarily concerned about residual threats emanating from Russia, and as a consequence, they emphasized collective defense. Third, countries such as Germany and France tended toward a middle position that prioritized collective regional security and crisis management along the European periphery. The debate over these differing strategic visions was played out in the two fields where the alliance had to make concrete decisions: the question of further enlargement, which was linked to the debate regarding the geographical reach of the alliance, and the question of strategy and burden sharing in Afghanistan, which was linked to the functional scope of the alliance.

Enlargement: How Far Beyond Northern and Eastern Europe and the Western Balkans?

Since the late 1990s, NATO enlargement had proceeded parallel to the enlargement of the EU on the basis of an open-door policy. On the occasion of its 2002 Prague summit, NATO initiated membership talks with seven additional Northern and Eastern European countries, and in March 2004, Estonia, Latvia, Lithuania, Slovenia, Slovakia, Bulgaria, and Romania joined the alliance. However, the fact that NATO's expansion had reached the Russian border hardened Russian opposition to further expansion: "We view the appearance of a powerful military bloc on our border . . . as a direct threat to the security of our country," stated then-President Vladimir V. Putin (in office

2000–2008) at a press conference after a meeting of the NATO-Russia Council.[16]

The next round of talks turned out to be a turning point in the enlargement debate. The involvement of the Western Balkan states had been an undisputed goal since the Balkan wars of the 1990s. At their Bucharest summit in 2008, the allies decided to accept Croatia and Albania as members and signaled an open door to Macedonia, Bosnia and Herzegovina, Montenegro, and Serbia. Disagreement prevailed among the allies, however, with regard to the question of whether the alliance should expand the Membership Action Plan (MAP) to include Georgia and Ukraine. In an attempt to tie the two states closer to the Euro-Atlantic and to improve the West's access to energy reserves in the Caspian region, the Bush administration recklessly pressed for membership. Germany and France, however, concerned about a Russian backlash and questioning whether these countries were even prepared and willing to join the alliance, successfully opposed the extension of the MAP to Georgia and Ukraine.

Only a few months later, in August 2008, the war in Georgia proved European skepticism to be well-founded. Through its unilateral military and diplomatic action in the Georgia crisis, Russia—strengthened by high energy prices—underscored its role as a regional hegemon in the Caucasus. Announcing the "Medvedev Doctrine" a few days after the intervention, the new Russian President Dimitry A. Medvedev (in office 2008–) opposed a further Western expansion: "Domination is something we cannot allow. . . . [T]here are regions in which Russia has privileged interests."[17] The United States had overplayed its hand, as an astute analyst noted in Washington: "We pushed too far on the periphery of a re-emergent Russia. . . . In the process, we almost certainly played an inadvertent role in convincing a 'rabbit' that it could provoke a 'bear.'"[18]

In the parallel debate on missile defense, Germany and France found themselves once again aligned with Russia in opposition to U.S. plans. Pushing forward its plans to establish a national missile defense system, the Bush administration attempted to install part of the necessary technical infrastructure in Poland and the Czech Republic on the basis of bilateral treaties, a step that would have undermined the principle of collective defense in the Euro-Atlantic region. Yet the German proposal to make missile defense a multilateral project was rejected by the Bush administration. The opposition of "old" Europe to the notion of a unilateral U.S. defense shield over the continent provided Russia with the fuel it needed to fire division in the West. At the Munich security conference in 2007, Putin criticized the U.S. attempt to establish a "unipolar world" and warned of an inevitable "arms race."[19] Gone were the days of the 1990s, when Russia had been too weak to manipulate NATO's enlargement into stalemate.

Crisis Management in Afghanistan: Tensions over Strategy, Burden Sharing, and Command and Control

The mission of the International Security Assistance Force (ISAF) in Afghanistan exposed NATO to additional tensions linked to questions about strategy, burden sharing, and command and control. The allies disagreed over the nature of the mission and the relative weight of military and civilian instruments used to stabilize the country. As Washington's focus shifted to Iraq soon after the toppling of the Islamist Taliban regime, the United States opted for a "light footprint" strategy in Afghanistan, concentrating on antiterrorism activities against remnants of the al Qaeda network and of the Taliban regime. Conversely, many of the European allies focused on governance, reconstruction, and development. Although the allies, at the NATO summit in Bucharest in 2008, opted for a comprehensive approach that integrated civilian and military instruments, the differences of opinion over the nature of what was increasingly turning into a counter-insurgency mission became more pronounced over time.

In short, the security situation began to deteriorate in 2006, initially in the east and south of Afghanistan, but later in the whole country. As NATO became involved in more intensive combat operations against resurgent Taliban, the alliance found itself in what "may be an existential crisis," as U.S. Under Secretary of State for Political Affairs Nicolas Burns noted in 2008.[20] Alliance solidarity and cohesion at times reached breaking point, as NATO struggled to sustain the number of troops deployed in the field and went through rounds of mutual recriminations about a highly uneven distribution of the military burden. Not only was NATO unable to fill the gaps in troop numbers and special capabilities, but national caveats also often undermined the efficient and coherent use of forces stationed in Afghanistan.

During the first decade of the twenty-first century, the allies had come to acknowledge that crisis management and stabilization operations were the most urgent tasks of the alliance. In early 2000, the EU and NATO had begun to set up rapid response capabilities with prospects for a specific division of labor: while the EU battle groups were geared toward preventive tasks in a geographically limited area, the NATO Response Force was able to handle engagements with a higher intensity across the globe. At the level of force planning, the EU and NATO perceived these forces as mutually reinforcing. Yet in practice, the efficiency and legitimacy of these forces depends on a common vision at the political-strategic level, and this was exactly what was missing during much of the first decade of NATO's history in the twenty-first century.

THE OBAMA YEARS: TOWARD A LESS AMBITIOUS NATO

When George W. Bush came into office in 2001, the position of the United States as the leading global power had been undisputed. Until then, its soft power had been robust and

TABLE 33.2   **Defense Spending of All 27 NATO Members, 2010**

Country	Defense Spending as Percentage of GDP (Rank)		Inflation-adjusted Annual Change in Percentage (Rank)	
NATO Europe—total	1.7		−1.4	
Albania	2.0	(4)	39.8	(1)
Belgium	1.1	(22)	−3.9	(16)
Bulgaria	1.7	(9)	−6.3	(19)
Croatia	1.5	(12)	−6.7	(20)
Czech Republic	1.4	(15)	−14.3	(24)
Denmark	1.4	(15)	6.5	(5)
Estonia	1.8	(8)	−1.3	(13)
France	2.0	(4)	−0.5	(11)
Germany	1.4	(15)	−1.2	(12)
Greece	2.9	(2)	−11.5	(23)
Hungary	1.1	(22)	−7.4	(21)
Italy	1.4	(15)	−10.7	(22)
Latvia	1.0	(25)	−19.9	(27)
Lithuania	0.9	(26)	−15.3	(26)
Luxembourg	0.5	(27)	36.5	(2)
Netherlands	1.4	(15)	−3.1	(15)
Norway	1.5	(12)	−2.7	(14)
Poland	1.9	(6)	11.0	(3)
Portugal	1.6	(10)	2.1	(6)
Romania	1.3	(20)	−5.9	(18)
Slovakia	1.3	(20)	−14.9	(25)
Slovenia	1.6	(10)	1.1	(10)
Spain	1.1	(22)	−5.5	(17)
Turkey	1.9	(6)	1.2	(8)
UK	2.7	(3)	1.2	(8)
North America—total	5.0		1.9	
Canada	1.5	(12)	9.0	(4)
USA	5.4	(1)	1.8	(7)
NATO—total	3.3		1.2	

SOURCE: NATO, "Financial and Economic Data Relating to NATO Defence," Press Release, March 10, 2011. Available at http://www.nato.int/nato_static/assets/pdf/pdf_2011_03/20110309_PR_CP_2011_027.pdf.

its military dominance greater than ever. By 2009, the U.S. claim to political leadership had suffered lasting damage, its armed forces were overstretched in two complex wars, and the U.S. economy was in a sorry state as a result of the financial and economic crisis that began in 2007. Incoming President Barack Obama (2009–) had to deal with domestic economic turbulence and, at the same time, with one of the worst foreign policy legacies ever inherited by an incoming U.S. president. While the United States remained indispensable to the solution of most global problems, the country's limited ability to shape global solutions unilaterally had become increasingly obvious.

To renew U.S. leadership around the world, President Obama announced his intention "to rebuild the alliances, partnerships, and institutions necessary to confront common threats and enhance common security."[21] Yet NATO would only be an efficient partnership, Obama reminded his European allies, if member states shared the financial and operational burden and closed the military capability gaps between them. The Europeans were also ready to renew the transatlantic partnership. President Sarkozy was keen to complete the reintegration process of France into the alliance, as Paris was slowly falling behind militarily and was grappling with increased financial pressures. France joined NATO's military structures, excluding the Nuclear Planning Group, on the alliance's sixtieth anniversary. Thus, when the allies convened in Strasbourg and Kehl in 2009, they decided to outline a new strategic concept that would not only readjust the alliance's tasks but at the same time would also rebalance the political equilibrium between U.S. leadership and European self-assertion.

A Phase of Consolidation: The Compromise of New Strategic Concept

By the beginning of 2010, the alliance had entered a phase of introspection and consolidation. The former Danish Prime Minister and new NATO Secretary General Anders Fogh Rasmussen (in office 2009–) asked a group of experts, chaired by Madeleine Albright, to lay the groundwork for a new strategic concept. The process leading up to the final document went through stages of reflection, consultation, and drafting and negotiation. This process was more inclusive and more open to the public than any other before it. The twenty-eight heads of state and government approved the new strategic concept at the Lisbon summit in 2010, when Rasmussen further managed to balance the diverging views among the allies about NATO's future purpose. Despite some ambiguous wording, his concept established a new political consensus on the alliance's "three essential core tasks": collective defense, crisis management, and cooperative security.[22]

Collective Defense: Procuring Combat Assets in a Time of Shrinking Defense Budgets

In 2010, the allies reinforced their commitment to collective defense. This had been the key wish of the Eastern European states. Yet by linking defense to emerging security threats—such as terrorism, nuclear proliferation and missiles, and cyber-attacks—the alliance signaled its understanding that a modern defense could no longer be limited to territorial defense. The U.S. decision to offer its missile defense technology for use as the backbone of a NATO system made a missile defense capability a core element of the alliance's new collective defense. NATO remained a nuclear alliance, a core French interest, but it balanced its commitment to nuclear deterrence with continuing support for nuclear non-proliferation and disarmament, a core German interest.

PUBLIC PORTRAIT: *ANDERS FOGH RASMUSSEN (1953–)*

Anders Fogh Rasmussen became secretary general of NATO in 2009 after serving as prime minister of Denmark for eight years (in office 2001–2009). As the highest-ranking official ever to become NATO secretary general, Rasmussen has considerable political weight in the alliance's internal decision-making process. This fact was borne out in 2010, when NATO members adopted a new strategic concept for the alliance. Instead of limiting himself to merely moderating internal discussions among member states, Secretary General Rasmussen took a leading role in the formulation of the final compromise, which was based, for the first time, on the recommendations of an independent expert group, which he had appointed. His commitment to reform extends to the day-to-day running of the alliance, as well. Immediately after taking office, Rasmussen announced his plan to streamline NATO's cumbersome bureaucracy and make its decision-making process more transparent and efficient. The reform attempts of previous secretary generals were often frustrated by internal resistance; however, Rasmussen's prestige and standing as a former head of government appear to give him more leverage than his predecessors had enjoyed.

During his time as Danish prime minister, Rasmussen was also involved in several important foreign policy matters. In the latter half of 2002, he successfully presided over the Council of the European Union at a time of heated debate on EU enlargement. Further, in 2003, Rasmussen supported the U.S. invasion of Iraq and deployed Danish troops to support coalition operations there. His greatest foreign policy challenge, however, was the international crisis which erupted when Danish newspaper *Jyllands-Posten* published controversial cartoons of the Prophet Mohammed in 2005. Amid angry protests throughout the Muslim world, during which several Danish embassies were set on fire, Anders Rasmussen insisted on the primacy of free speech and free press in Denmark. He regarded the crisis primarily through a domestic lens, not least because his center-right government relied on the parliamentary support of the Danish People's Party, which is highly critical of Muslim influence on Danish cultural values.

The key challenge the allies now face is how best to ensure that they have the full range of capabilities for modern defense. Dwindling defense budgets and the continuing financial and economic crises mean that less money will be available for procurement. Thus, in his farewell speech given on June 10, 2011, U.S. Secretary of Defense Robert Gates (in office 2006–2011) emphasized that if NATO "wanted to avoid the real possibility of collective military irrelevance," the European allies had to "fundamentally change how they set priorities and allocate resources."[23] Pooling military assets and finding smarter ways to procure combat capabilities remains the key challenge for Europe. The new program of defense cooperation between France and Great Britain, which was signed in late 2010, reflects the joint intention of the two strongest military players to improve the collective defense capability of Europe. It remains to be seen whether the initiative can provide a roadmap to more effective European defense cooperation and how inclusive, or exclusive, it will be in practice.

Crisis Management: Withdrawal from Afghanistan, Success in Libya

The new strategic concept confirmed crisis management as the second key task of the alliance and reinforced the need for a comprehensive approach that integrates military and civilian instruments. The fact that there was no discussion about the military and political limitations of current and ongoing operations demonstrated that the allies did not want the strategic concept to be about Afghanistan. At the

summit, the allies instead decided to initiate the withdrawal process from Afghanistan in 2011 and complete the handover of the country's security to the local government by 2014. This decision was driven primarily by domestic political considerations and dwindling public support, on both sides of the Atlantic, for a costly war.

The planned withdrawal from Afghanistan signals the foreseeable end of NATO's engagement in Central Asia, which undermined alliance solidarity and cohesion well into the Obama years. Shifting Washington's attention back from an increasingly secure Iraq to the forgotten war in Afghanistan, President Obama refocused U.S. efforts on al Qaeda's roots in Afghanistan and Pakistan. After the announcement of Obama's new Afghanistan strategy in late 2009, the United States sent thirty thousand additional troops to Afghanistan in an attempt to reverse the momentum the Taliban were enjoying at the time and stabilize the country's government. The Americanization of NATO's mission in 2010 resulted in renewed debates among the allies about strategy, burden sharing, and command and control. While the security situation in Afghanistan has only marginally improved over the past years, dwindling domestic support has increasingly made a reduction of the Western engagement in Central Asia unavoidable.

Just as the decision to withdraw from Afghanistan appeared to indicate that NATO was likely to reduce its level of ambition in crisis management, the "Arab Spring" produced another surprise: a NATO-led bombing campaign in Libya. Even more surprising was the fact that the Europeans were in charge of the operation, with the U.S. military in

IN THEIR OWN WORDS: *SECRETARY GATES'S SPEECH ON NATO'S FUTURE*

In June 2011, Defense Secretary Robert Gates gave a farewell address in Brussels on the future of NATO. Looking back on allied crisis management in Afghanistan and Libya, Gates summarized U.S. frustration with NATO's shortcomings—in military capabilities, and in political will—and warned the Europeans of the possibility of a dismal future for the transatlantic alliance:

> First, a few words on Afghanistan … national caveats that tied the hands of allied commanders in sometimes infuriating ways, the inability of many allies to meet agreed upon commitments and, in some cases, wildly disparate contributions from different member states. …
>
> Turning to the NATO operation over Libya … I've worried openly about NATO turning into a two-tiered alliance: Between members who specialize in "soft" humanitarian, development, peacekeeping, and talking tasks, and those conducting the "hard" combat missions. Between those willing and able to pay the price

and bear the burdens of alliance commitments, and those who enjoy the benefits of NATO membership … but don't want to share the risks and the costs. …

> Looking ahead, to avoid the very real possibility of collective military irrelevance, member nations must examine new approaches to boosting combat capabilities. …
>
> Indeed, if current trends in the decline of European defense capabilities are not halted and reversed, future U.S. political leaders—those for whom the Cold War was *not* the formative experience that it was for me—may not consider the return on America's investment in NATO worth the cost. …

SOURCE: Secretary of Defense Robert M. Gates, "Remarks by Secretary Gates at the Security and Defense Agenda, Brussels, Belgium," June 10, 2011, available at http://www.defense.gov/transcripts/transcript.aspx?transcriptid=4839.

support. Civil unrest broke out in Libya in February 2011. By March, Libyan dictator Mu'ammar al Qaddafi (in power 1969–2011) threatened to recapture the city of Benghazi from rebels, who then faced a massacre at the hand of Qaddafi's troops. To prevent a humanitarian catastrophe, France and Great Britain organized the passing of a UN resolution that authorized the use of military force to "protect civilians and civilian populated areas under threat of attack," but forbade ground occupation.[24] Within hours, French airplanes stopped Qaddafi's heavy weaponry, and soon after, a coalition that included several NATO members was in a position to enforce a no-fly zone.

The United States had spearheaded the initial strikes to eliminate Libya's air defense. However, President Obama and Secretary Gates were reluctant to get involved in another war and demanded that the allies take the lead. Europe did not uniformly accept this challenge, and Germany, notably, as well as many other allies, refused to participate in the operation. Eventually, NATO took command of the entire military operation (the maritime arms embargo, the no-fly zone, and the protection mission). Once again, the alliance proved the value of its well-established military structures and standards. However, the mission was fraught with political risk. The United States accused the non-contributing members of not having usable operational capabilities and of lacking political will. Conversely, some of the non-contributing members criticized NATO for overstepping its mandate. In fact, at the political level, France, Great Britain, and the United States increasingly committed themselves to ousting Qaddafi. As a consequence, NATO began to target Libya's leader and his regime directly. Qaddafi was killed by local forces in Sirte in October. On October 28, 2011, NATO Secretary General Rasmussen announced the successful end of alliance operations in Libya.

Cooperative Security: A Strategic Relationship with Russia

The third key task of the alliance, according to the new strategic concept, emphasized security cooperation through a wide network of partners. The allies wanted to "see a true strategic partnership between NATO and Russia" and indicated that they were determined to encourage political consultations and practical cooperation "in areas of shared interest, including missile defence, counter-terrorism, counter-narcotics, counter-piracy and the promotion of wider international security."[25] The question of how to relate to Russia had divided the allies since the war in Georgia in 2008. While some had rejected closer contacts with what they perceived as an aggressive neighbor, others had searched for ways to reengage Russia.

The chance that a more substantive partnership between NATO and Russia might develop improved, thanks to the gradual advancement of Russia's relations with the United States. President Obama decided to resume the

U.S.–Russian dialogue surrounding nuclear arms control negotiations. The successful conclusion of the New START treaty in April 2011, which reduced the number of deployed strategic warheads and delivery vehicles, represented a significant step toward disarmament. Another important step was President Obama's decision to cancel his predecessor's national missile defense plans. Instead, he offered to develop a missile defense system for the entire alliance.

At the summit in Lisbon, NATO went a step further and invited Russia to jointly review ballistic missile threats and move toward broad cooperation on missile defense. Secretary General Rasmussen highlighted the political importance of the move when he stated that "[for] the first time in history, NATO nations and Russia will be cooperating to defend themselves."[26] Missile defense will remain a sensitive issue, because Russia likely will insist on being treated as an equal partner. The United States, on the other hand, probably will not consider joint command and control and will insist on an American commander.

NATO and the Decline of the West: The Globe's Most Successful Political-Military Alliance

With the formulation of the new strategic concept, the allies were able to mend the cracks that had opened up in NATO's foundations during the first decade of the twenty-first century. The process leading up to the strategic concept provided the allies with an opportunity to renew their alliance as a community of values. Ending a long period of strategic hesitation with a new political compromise, the allies reaffirmed their commitment to preserving NATO's "effectiveness as the globe's most successful political-military Alliance."[27] The fact that the allies were once again willing and able to rebalance the political and military functions of the alliance and recalibrate the political equilibrium between the United States and Europe is no small achievement and is a tribute to NATO's political resilience and institutional flexibility.

Recognizing the military and political limitations of the alliance, NATO members compromised on a globally less ambitious and politically more regional alliance in the process leading up to the strategic concept. NATO is not a global community of democracies; the alliance is a regional organization with an open door to all European democracies. NATO is no substitute for the UN system and the various regional security institutions; it is an internal system of peace, a forum of transatlantic debate and compromise, and an anchor for the West's strategic dialogue with Russia. NATO is not a global policeman; it is the West's central strategic tool for deterring and defending strategic threats against the Euro-Atlantic region and for contributing to crisis management and global stability where such action enhances the security of the alliance.

The geographic reach and the functional scope of NATO must reflect the global shift of power to Asia in order to be effective. Add to this the current severe economic weakness of both the United States and European Union countries and it becomes clear where the critical challenge of NATO lies: Can the European allies muster the political will for a military procurement and resourcing reform that will increase their usable operational capabilities? Can the United States strike the right balance between sharing alliance leadership and its own global interests and responsibilities? NATO is a tool for U.S. influence and leadership in Europe, and for European balance and self-assertion beyond the continent. The alliance's political functions remain closely linked to its military strength; this is the enduring logic of NATO. Precisely because we are living in an increasingly complex and fragmented world, NATO members need to sustain the alliance as a valuable instrument of security in the Euro-Atlantic region and beyond.

See also: **Chapter 34: Diplomatic Milestones, 1992–2000; Chapter 35: The Global War on Terrorism; Chapter 39: U.S. Foreign Policy Goals of the Twenty-first Century; Chapter 40: Diplomatic Milestones, 2001–Present.**

ENDNOTES

1. Baker quoted in Ronald D. Asmus, *Opening NATO's Door: How the Alliance Remade Itself for a New Era* (New York: Columbia University Press, 2002), 5.

2. Rühe quoted in Jane M.O. Sharp, "The Case for Opening up NATO to the East," in *The Future of NATO: Enlargement, Russia, and European Security,* Charles-Philippe David and Jacques Lévesque, eds. (Montreal: McGill-Queen's University Press, 1999), 27.

3. See Ronald D. Asmus, Richard L. Kugler, and F. Stephen Larrabee, "Building a New NATO," in *Foreign Affairs* 72: 4 (September/October 1993), 28–40; Ronald D. Asmus, Richard L. Kugler, and F. Stephen Larrabee, "NATO Expansion: The Next Steps," in *Survival* 37: 1 (Spring 1995), 7–33.

4. William Clinton, "The President's News Conference With Visegrad Leaders in Prague," January 12, 1994, *Public Papers of the Presidents of the United States,* 1994, Book I, 40.

5. NATO. *Study on Enlargement,* September 3, 1995, available at: http://www.nato.int/cps/en/natolive/official_texts_24733.htm.

6. Mark Gilbert, *Surpassing Realism: The Politics of European Integration* (Lanham, MD: Rowman & Littlefield, 2003), 209.

7. Baker quoted in Richard Holbrooke, *To End a War* (New York: Modern Library, 1999), 27.

8. "The Role of Allied Military Force and the Transformation of the Alliance's Defence Posture," NATO Handbook, 69–75, available at: http://www.msz.gov.pl/editor/files/docs/DPB/polityka_bezpieczenstwa/NATO_handbook.pdf.

9. Tim Kane, "U.S. Troop Deployment Dataset," Version of March 1, 2006 (Washington, DC: Heritage Foundation), available at: www.heritage.org/Research/NationalSecurity/troopsdb.cfm.

10. Asmus, Kugler, and Larrabee, "Building a New NATO," 31.

11. "Joint Declaration on European Defence," Declaration Issued at the British-French Summit, Saint-Malo, December 3–4, 1998, available at: http://www.fco.gov.uk/resources/en/news/2002/02/joint-declaration-on-eu-new01795.

12. Madeleine Albright, "The Right Balance Will Secure NATO's Future," in *From St-Malo to Nice: European Defence: Core Documents,* edited by Maartje Rutten, Chaillot Paper 47 (May 2001), 11. Originally published in *Financial Times,* December 7, 1998.

13. Madeleine Albright, *Madam Secretary: A Memoir* (Basingstoke, UK: Macmillan, 2003), 391, 427 (order reversed).

14. Steven Erlanger, "U.S. to Propose NATO Take On Increased Roles," in *The New York Times,* December 7, 1998.

15. Ivo Daalder and James Goldgeier, "Global NATO," in *Foreign Affairs* 85: 1 (January/February 2006), 106, 113.

16. Vladimir Putin, "Press Statement and Answers to Journalists' Questions Following a Meeting of the Russia-NATO Council," April 4, 2008, available at: http://archive.kremlin.ru/eng/speeches/2008/04/04/1949_type82915_163150.shtml.

17. Dimitry Medvedev, "Interview Given by Dmitry Medvedev to Television Channels Channel One, Rossia, NTV," Sochi, August 31, 2008, available at: http://archive.kremlin.ru/eng/speeches/2008/08/31/1850_type82912type82916_206003.shtml.

18. Anthony Cordesman, "The Georgia War and the Century of 'Real Power,'" in *CSIS Commentary,* August 18, 2008, available at: http://csis.org/publication/georgia-war-and-century-real-power.

19. Vladimir Putin, "Speech and the Following Discussion at the Munich Conference on Security Policy," February 10, 2007, available at: http://archive.kremlin.ru/eng/speeches/2007/02/10/0138_type82912type82914type82917type84779_118123.shtml.

20. Burns quoted in Steven Meyers and Thom Shanker, "NATO Expansion, and a Bush Legacy, Are in Doubt," in *The New York Times,* March 15, 2008.

21. Barack Obama, "Renewing American Leadership," in *Foreign Affairs* 86, no. 4 (July/August 2007), 11.

22. NATO, *Strategic Concept for the Defence and Security of the Members of the North Atlantic Treaty Organization,* para 4, available at: http://www.nato.int/lisbon2010/strategic-concept-2010-eng.pdf.

23. Robert Gates, "The Security and Defense Agenda (Future of NATO)," Speech in Brussels, June 19, 2011, available at: http://www.defense.gov/speeches/speech.aspx?speechid=1581.

24. UN Security Council, 6498th Meeting, *Resolution 1973 (2010) [Protection of Civilians in the Libyan Arab Jamahiriya],* March 17, 2011 (S/RES/1973).

25. NATO. *Strategic Concept,* para. 34.

26. Anders Fogh Rasmussen, "Closing Press Conference," Lisbon Summit of NATO Heads of State and Government, November 20, 2010, available at: http://www.nato.int/cps/en/natolive/opinions_68887.htm.

27. NATO, *Strategic Concept,* para. 38.

FURTHER READING

Albright, Madeleine. *Madam Secretary: A Memoir.* London: Macmillan, 2003.

Asmus, Ronald D. *Opening NATO's Door: How the Alliance Remade Itself for a New Era.* New York: Columbia University Press, 2002.

Daalder, Ivo, and James Goldgeier. "Global NATO." In *Foreign Affairs* 85, no. 5 (September/October 2006), 105–13.

Goldgeier, James M. *Not Whether But When: The U.S. Decision to Enlarge NATO.* Washington, DC: Brookings Institution, 1999.

Gordon, Philip, and Jeremy Shapiro. *Allies at War: America, Europe, and the Crisis over Iraq.* New York: McGraw-Hill, 2004.

Holbrooke, Richard C. *To End a War.* New York: Modern Library, 1999.

Kaplan, Lawrence S. *The Long Entanglement: NATO's First Fifty Years.* Westport, CT: Praeger, 1999.

chapter 34

Diplomatic Milestones, 1992–2000

Dilemmas of the Post–Cold War Era

by Henry Brands

THE POST–COLD WAR era was a period of great promise as well as uncertainty in U.S. foreign policy. The end of the Cold War left the United States as the lone superpower and removed the primary threat to American security; it also forced the nation to address the thorny issue of what came next in foreign policy. The answer was by no means obvious, because world politics were nothing if not complex in the 1990s: humanitarian crises in Bosnia, Somalia, Rwanda, and Kosovo; the challenges of world commerce and "globalization"; American relations with Europe, Russia, and China; confrontations with dictatorships in Iraq and North Korea; the dilemmas of the Middle East peace process; and numerous other issues competed for the attention of American policymakers. These issues evoked a need not simply for solutions to specific problems but also for a new overall approach to managing foreign policy in the post–Cold War era.

DEMOCRATIC ENLARGEMENT

The task of reformulating U.S. policy fell largely to the administration of William J. Clinton (1993–2001), which argued that the purpose of American diplomacy should be "democratic enlargement," or the promotion of democracy and free markets abroad. By using America's unparalleled power to promote American values, the administration believed, it could advance U.S. interests while simultaneously bringing about a more humane and prosperous world order.

Enlargement was a bold and ambitious concept, but one that would prove difficult to implement. During the 1990s, President Clinton faced a variety of dilemmas pertaining to enlargement and the broader conduct of foreign policy. When and how should America use force? How should it reconcile competing priorities and allocate finite resources like time and energy? Could the administration build a domestic consensus in support of its

policies? How should it deal with rising threats and the limits of American power? In some cases, Clinton's administration did well in meeting these and additional challenges; in others, it fell short. Ultimately, Clinton would leave an ambiguous legacy as steward of America's post–Cold War foreign policy.

INTO THE POST–COLD WAR ERA

In many ways, the United States was in a truly enviable—indeed, unparalleled—position in the 1990s. The collapse of the Soviet Union in 1991 left the United States without peer in the global hierarchy, and American values seemed to be on the march throughout the world. Democracy was advancing in Eastern Europe, Latin America, and elsewhere; market economics were spreading throughout the developing world and seemed poised to do so in the former Soviet bloc as well. In the phrasing of neoconservative columnist Charles Krauthammer, the world had reached a "unipolar moment": the United States and its values reigned supreme.[1]

In other ways, however, the end of the Cold War left a more troubling legacy. While the United States no longer faced any existential threat to its security, international peace was hardly in the offing during the early 1990s. Rather, the global scene was menaced by post–Cold War disorder: ethnic and civil conflict in Africa and southeastern Europe, the prospect of nuclear proliferation in numerous countries, the specter of chaos or resurgent authoritarianism in the former Soviet Union, lingering regional disputes in the Middle East and South Asia, and the residue of the Persian Gulf War of 1990–1991. Moscow "is no longer the enemy," said President George H. W. Bush (1989–1993) in 1991. "The enemy is uncertainty. The enemy is unpredictability."[2]

Competing Foreign Policy Goals

As the end of the Cold War exposed new instability abroad, it also set off increased debate about U.S. foreign policy at

KEY CONCEPTS

Post–Cold War era. The term is generally used to refer to the period between the fall of the Berlin Wall in 1989 and the terrorist attacks of September 11, 2001. During this period, the overriding theme of American foreign policy was the search for a new diplomatic paradigm to replace the notion of containment that had guided the United States during the Cold War. Upon coming to power in 1993, the Clinton administration would make *democratic enlargement*—the idea that U.S. policy should promote democratization and free trade—a key tenet of its statecraft.

Democratic enlargement. Over the next several years, U.S. foreign policy would involve a number of themes related to enlargement. These included *humanitarian intervention*, or the use of force to prevent or stop gross violations of human rights; efforts to contain *backlash states*, or those authoritarian governments that rejected Clinton's view of a peaceful, democratic world; the promotion of *globalization*, or the increasing integration of national economies, societies, and cultures; and *non-proliferation*, or efforts to prevent the spread of nuclear, chemical, and biological weapons to hostile states or terrorist groups. Also prominent in American foreign policy was *NATO enlargement*, or the expansion of this Cold War–era alliance to include new members in Eastern Europe. Together, these issues constitute some of the major themes of post–Cold War foreign policy.

home. With the Cold War over and the threat from the Soviet Union having vanished, domestic opinion on foreign policy fragmented. Some observers, such as Krauthammer, advocated a robust, interventionist foreign policy aimed at achieving a benevolent global hegemony. Others believed that the end of the Cold War made it possible for the United Nations (UN) to fulfill its role as guarantor of global peace. Still others argued that the primary purpose of post–Cold War foreign policy should be the promotion of democracy. Then there were those who contended that, with no major threats to American security, the United States should retrench, ending its overseas troop deployments and conducting a more restrained diplomacy. It was time, argued conservative spokesman and Republican presidential candidate Patrick Buchanan, to put "America First—and Second, and Third."[3]

In these uncertain circumstances, the administration of George H. W. Bush struggled to articulate a compelling vision of what America's post–Cold War policy should be. At times, Bush spoke grandly of a "new world order" based on collective security and respect for human rights and democracy, but many of his advisers, particularly Joint Chiefs of Staff Chairman General Colin Powell, objected to the notion that military force should be used to advance moral rather than strategic ends. The Defense Department advanced a more muscular vision of American purpose in its 1992 Defense Planning Guidance, a classified document meant to describe the strategic landscape of the 1990s and make recommendations for U.S. defense policy and military expenditures. As initially prepared in the Pentagon, the Defense Planning Guidance called for efforts to cement U.S. supremacy by precluding the rise of any peer challenger on the level of the Cold War–era Soviet Union. Yet the assertive language and unilateral tone of this

document clashed with the multilateral afterglow of the Persian Gulf War, as well as the more restrained foreign policy instincts of top officials like National Security Adviser Brent Scowcroft.

The fact that Bush's post–Cold War policy had yet to congeal was evident in his inconsistent response to a series of international crises in the last 18 months of his presidency. Despite the idealistic rhetoric of the new world order, Bush declined to intervene to reverse a military coup in Haiti in 1991 or to halt civil war and ethnic violence in the former Yugoslavia in 1991–1992. "We don't want to put a dog in this fight," Bush wrote in his diary; human rights were being violated and civilians brutalized, but American strategic interests were not at stake.[4] After being battered by domestic criticism for this seemingly amoral stance, however, the administration did choose to send troops to Somalia in December 1992 after internecine conflict threatened to lead to mass famine. Bush was well aware of the inconsistency in these actions. Amid the complexity of the post–Cold War world, he acknowledged in early 1993, "There can be no single or simple set of guidelines for foreign policy."[5] As Bush left office, America's involvement in the post–Cold War world remained unsettled.

The Clinton Administration and "The Successor to Containment"

In many respects, President William Clinton seemed poorly suited to the task of articulating a post–Cold War foreign policy. Clinton had little background in foreign affairs prior to taking office, and he was skeptical of the idea that any single "grand strategy" could guide America's involvement in a dauntingly complex world. Great leaders like Truman and Roosevelt "just made it up as they went along," he told an adviser early in his presidency.[6]

Despite Clinton's instinctive aversion to grand strategy, he was keenly aware that his administration needed to articulate a persuasive vision of America's role in the world in order to maintain domestic support for a global foreign policy of any sort. "You've still got to be able to crystallize complexity in a way people get right away," he commented.[7] Similarly, advisers like Secretary of State Warren Christopher (in office 1993–1997) and National Security Adviser Anthony Lake (in office 1993–1997) argued that the administration needed to set its bearings lest it become disoriented in the fluid global environment. "We cannot afford to career from crisis to crisis," said Christopher in early 1993.[8]

The foreign policy that thus emerged was rooted in a sense that global politics had reached a crucial tipping point. On the one hand, the end of the Cold War had removed the artificial geopolitical divisions of the postwar era and opened the path to a more humane, prosperous, and secure global order. "America's core concepts—democracy and market economics—are more broadly accepted than ever," Lake noted in a major speech in September 1993. To the extent that these trends could be strengthened and the world made to look more like the United States, American interests would inevitably be advanced. On the other hand, while the United States no longer confronted an existential threat like the Germany of Adolf Hitler (in power 1933–1945) or the Soviet Union, there were myriad troubling phenomena—ethnic conflict; humanitarian disasters; nuclear proliferation; the actions of aggressive rogue states, or "backlash" states (the term used in the Clinton administration), such as Iraq and North Korea; the prospect of renewed authoritarianism or neo-nationalism in Russia and other nations—phenomena that threatened to derail continued progress toward democracy and market economics, or perhaps even to throw the global scene into turmoil and chaos.

Thus arose the relevance of American power. While the Clinton administration generally eschewed the assertive language of the 1992 Defense Planning Guidance, its top officials were quite comfortable with the fact of American preeminence. "We have the world's strongest military, its largest economy and its most dynamic, multiethnic society," Lake declared in 1993. Accordingly, the purpose of American policy should be to use this unique position of power to promote democratization and market reform while simultaneously containing the threats to these trends. "The successor to a doctrine of containment must be a strategy of enlargement," announced Lake in September 1993, "enlargement of the world's free community of market democracies." The United States must support the existing community of market democracies by providing security in crucial regions and deepening free trade; it should support the emergence of new democracies in the former Soviet Union and elsewhere; it should contain "backlash" states that stood athwart the progress toward democracy and markets; and it should consider using military force to address human rights violations, civil wars, and interruptions of democracy in places such as Bosnia and Somalia. By doing so, the United States would simultaneously do good and do well: it would support what were deemed to be the universal aspirations of mankind, while also forging an international environment conducive to the long-term advancement of American security and prosperity.[9]

Enlargement was thus a bold conception of American purpose in the post–Cold War world. In practice, however, its implementation would be attended by a number of potent foreign policy dilemmas. Some Clinton resolved with relative success; others ultimately proved more perplexing.

Humanitarian Intervention and the Use of Force

One of the most prominent dilemmas pertained to the question of under what circumstances the United States would use military force in the post–Cold War world. At the outset, officials such as ambassador to the United Nations (and, later, secretary of state) Madeleine Albright (in office 1993–1997 and 1997–2001) took a relatively permissive position on this issue, arguing that America should use force not simply to protect its vital interests but to advance human rights and democracy as well. "What's the point of having this superb military you're always talking about if we can't use it?" she asked General Colin Powell in one early meeting.[10] Clinton's early ideas on humanitarian intervention reflected this sentiment. He considerably expanded the nation's and the UN's role in Somalia, announcing that the goal of the intervention was not simply to deliver food but also to allow the Somalis to create a democratic civil society. The administration also called for multilateral intervention under UN auspices to halt the ongoing war in the Balkans, proposing to supply the Croats and Bosnian Muslims with arms and to launch air strikes against the Bosnian Serbs, who were deemed to be principally responsible for the bloodshed.

Neither initiative turned out well. Bureaucratic infighting and European opposition killed the idea of multilateral

PUBLIC PORTRAIT: *SECRETARY OF STATE MADELEINE ALBRIGHT (1937–)*

Madeleine Albright served as ambassador to the United Nations from 1993 to 1997 and as secretary of state from 1997 to 2001. She was the first woman to hold the latter position, and she served as a key adviser to Bill Clinton throughout his presidency.

Albright's views on world affairs were shaped long before she became an influential policymaker. Forced to flee her native Czechoslovakia twice—in the late 1930s, to escape Adolf Hitler, and in the late 1940s, to escape Joseph Stalin—she became a strong believer in the idea that the world's leading democracies must act boldly to halt aggression or the persecution of vulnerable minorities. "My mindset is Munich," she would say during the Balkan crises of the 1990s, the implication being that a failure to stand up to Serbia's Slobodan Milošević would be just as disastrous as the West's failure to halt Hitler had been decades earlier.

As an adviser to Clinton, Albright frequently argued that the United States had a responsibility to intervene with the military in order to halt human rights violations abroad. She disagreed strongly with officials such as Joint Chiefs of Staff Chairman Colin Powell, who argued that Washington should use military force only in defense of vital interests, and was particularly active in

calling for multilateral intervention in Bosnia in the early 1990s and in Kosovo in the late 1990s.

Albright was also known as a vigorous defender of American values and a strong proponent of American global leadership. In her years at the United Nations, she was sharply critical of dictatorial regimes in North Korea, Iraq, Cuba, and others. After taking over the State Department, Albright argued that the United States must remain engaged abroad. America was "the indispensable nation," she argued, both in the sense that the United States had the greatest capacity for leadership on global issues, and because, in her view, America's democratic values gave it the moral credibility to lead.

As secretary of state, Albright became the face of American diplomacy. She was involved in intensive negotiations as part of the Middle East peace process, although she worried that the administration was spending too much time and energy on this particular question. She also became the highest-ranking American official to date to visit North Korea in 2000, meeting with Kim Jong Il (in power 1994–2011) in an ultimately failed effort to negotiate an end to the North's nuclear and missile programs. After leaving office in 2001, Albright would remain a vocal contributor to debates on U.S. foreign policy, authoring several books and articles on the subject.

---

intervention in the Balkans, and the killing there would only intensify in the next two years. The experience in Somalia proved even worse for Clinton. As the United States plunged deeper into Somalia's internal politics, it inevitably made enemies of certain of the competing factions in that country. A raid in early October intended to capture one prominent warlord, Mohammed Farah Aideed, backfired, resulting in nineteen American deaths and causing a firestorm of criticism in the United States.

The Limits of Enlargement

The debacle in Somalia revealed two key problems with Clinton's early approach to the use of force. The first was his inattention to the relationship between means and ends. Because of the rising domestic concern at the prospect of American casualties, Clinton had withdrawn the majority of U.S. troops from Somalia in mid-1993, just as he also was embracing an expanded mandate in that country. In effect, he had reduced U.S. forces while simultaneously ordering them to undertake a more difficult mission, with costly results.

Second, Somalia revealed that there was little domestic support for the idea of humanitarian intervention abroad. The notion of saving foreigners' lives was pleasing in principle, but the idea that American troops would be losing *their* lives in missions with no clear tie to the nation's security produced a strong backlash. The

"Black Hawk Down" incident in the Somali capital of Mogadishu led to a new low in public support. Also known as the Battle of Mogadishu, two American Black Hawk helicopters were shot down by Somali opposition forces, and nineteen Americans were killed. After the battle, the bodies of several U.S. troops were mangled and dragged through the streets of Mogadishu by crowds of local civilians and Somali forces. In one poll taken shortly after this confrontation, only 31 percent of respondents favored keeping U.S. troops in Somalia until the UN mission was complete. "Right now the average American doesn't see our interests threatened to the point where we should sacrifice one American life," Clinton admitted.[11] The post–Cold War domestic audience was fundamentally a risk-averse domestic audience, as Clinton discovered to his chagrin.

So searing was the president's experience with humanitarian intervention that he immediately sought to abandon the concept altogether. Clinton quickly wound down the U.S. mission in Somalia, and in the 1994 National Security Strategy, the administration made clear that it would commit American troops to battle only when clear U.S. interests were at stake. As if to make its point, Clinton never even considered intervening to stop the furious ethnic violence that claimed eight hundred thousand lives in Rwanda in early 1994. Having overreached in Somalia, the administration now sat passive in the face of a much larger humanitarian catastrophe.

Intervention in the Balkans

Unfortunately, the issue of humanitarian intervention would not go away. During his remaining years in office, Clinton was confronted by several humanitarian crises. Serb atrocities in Bosnia, which George H. W. Bush had ignored, mounted in 1994 and 1995, punctuated by the murder of around eight thousand civilians in the town of Srebrenica in July 1995. Similarly, during the late 1990s, Serbian repression and atrocities in the Kosovo province attracted worldwide attention. These crises were troubling not simply on moral and humanitarian grounds but also because continued American inaction in resolving them eventually proved an embarrassment to Clinton at home and abroad. If the United States was indeed the world's only superpower, critics asked, why could it not stop a tin-pot dictator like Serbia's Slobodan Milošević (in power 1989–2000) from brutalizing his neighbors? As a result, Clinton reversed course. In 1995, U.S. and NATO forces launched air strikes against Milošević's Serbian forces in an effort to halt the bloodshed in the Balkans. In 1999, Clinton again ordered air attacks against Serb positions in Kosovo and Serbia proper in an effort to compel Milošević's forces to withdraw from that province.

In 1999, President Bill Clinton and Russian President Boris Yeltsin met in the Kremlin as Secretary of State Madeleine Albright looked on. Clinton praised Yeltsin, noting, "Well, I liked him because he was always very [direct] with me. He always did exactly what he said he would do, and he was willing to take chances to try to improve our relationship, to try to improve democracy in Russia."

SOURCE: epa.

Even so, Clinton was ambivalent about the use of American force. In both wars, the administration decided to use force only after a long period of hesitation and delay. Moreover, Clinton was so scarred by Somalia that he explicitly ruled out the introduction of U.S. ground troops into combat situations, instead relying solely on airpower. The restrictions on the use of American power were most pronounced in Kosovo. Clinton publicly announced at the outset of the fighting that ground forces would not be used, and he largely restricted bombing missions to high-altitude attacks meant to keep American pilots safely beyond the range of Serb anti-aircraft weapons. Recognizing that most Americans were casualty-averse, Clinton became casualty-averse as well.

Eventually, in 1995 and again in 1999, the administration's strategy was good enough to defeat Milošević. U.S. intervention helped bring about a peace deal that ended one Balkan war in 1996, and American and NATO air strikes forced Serb forces to withdraw from Kosovo three years later. Rightly, during his presidency and after, Clinton took pride in his role in ending the Balkan conflicts at such a low cost in American casualties.

It thus seemed that Clinton had cracked the riddle of post–Cold War humanitarian intervention. He had done enough to resolve these crises and avoid charges of inaction, while also avoiding the political fallout that might accompany U.S. casualties. Yet the victory was at best a partial one, for while Clinton's airpower-only strategy had worked against Milošević, it would prove less effective in dealing with a more serious danger—the rising threat of international terrorism.

Clashing Priorities in Europe

A second dilemma of post–Cold War foreign policy had to do with the fact that key aspects of enlargement inevitably came into conflict with each other. This particular dilemma was most evident in Clinton's European diplomacy. At the outset of Clinton's presidency, his most important priority in Europe was engaging Russia. The fate of Russian democracy hung in the balance in the early 1990. The country was in political and economic crisis, and radical nationalists and other fringe politicians menaced the political scene. If the United States could help the reform faction, led by President Boris Yeltsin (1991–1999), emerge victorious, it would be a major victory for democratization and would presumably conduce to the establishment of a stable, long-term bilateral relationship. If not, enlargement would suffer a major setback, and a chillier and less stable relationship might be in prospect. Clinton thus provided Yeltsin's government with a $2 billion aid package in 1993, and he supported the embattled leader as Yeltsin contended with numerous crises at home.

Clinton's desire for productive relations with Yeltsin, however, soon came into conflict with another goal: expansion of the North Atlantic Treaty Organization (NATO). Originally formed as an anti-Soviet alliance, NATO appeared to have outlived its usefulness after the Cold War, and the Bush administration promised in 1990 that eastward expansion was not in prospect. The Clinton administration initially reiterated this sentiment, but the president abruptly reversed himself following a meeting with Czech President Vaclav Havel (1989–2003) and Polish leader Lech Wałęsa (1990–1995) in 1993. Moved by these countries' tragic pasts, Clinton surprised many of his own advisers by declaring that enlargement of the alliance was only a question of "when and how."[12]

SHIFTS IN FOREIGN POLICY: *NATO EXPANSION*

The end of the Cold War required American policymakers to rethink old policies and adapt old institutions to the new era. This was particularly the case with the North Atlantic Treaty Organization (NATO), the expansion of which during the 1990s would be a key feature of U.S. policy toward Europe.

NATO was a creation of the Cold War. It was designed to tie the United States to the defense of Western Europe, thereby providing reassurance against both the Soviet threat and the possibility of a German resurgence. The alliance served both purposes well, and as NATO matured, it gradually took on new members during the postwar decades: Turkey and Greece in 1952, West Germany in 1955, and Spain in 1982.

A LACK OF PURPOSE?

At the end of the Cold War, however, NATO's mission became uncertain. The Soviet threat vanished, removing a major rationale for the alliance. Furthermore, President George H. W. Bush and Secretary of State James Baker had imposed curbs on the future role of the alliance in negotiations with the Soviet Union in 1990. In exchange for Moscow allowing a reunited Germany to join NATO, Bush and Baker pledged that the alliance would not expand farther into Eastern Europe. Additionally, NATO's future was called into question by the West's uncertain response to the civil war in the former Yugoslavia in the early 1990s, which seemingly showed the irrelevance of the alliance to emerging security threats in Europe.

EXPANSION TO THE EAST

At the beginning of Clinton's presidency, the future of NATO remained in doubt, and expansion of the alliance certainly did not look to be in prospect. Yet within months, Clinton had committed himself to enlarging the alliance to include several new members in Eastern Europe—Poland, Czechoslovakia (later the Czech Republic), and Hungary—and, in early 1994, the administration made its decision public.

The process by which NATO expanded illustrates the impact that well-placed individual policymakers can have on U.S. foreign policy. Most American officials were opposed to expansion. Leading officials in the Defense and State Departments feared that taking NATO eastward, which would be in violation of Bush's informal 1990 pledge, would alienate the Russian government. That alienation, in turn, might slow Russian disarmament, lead to frostier relations with the West, and even allow ultra-nationalist politicians like Vladimir Zhirinovsky to come to power.

The impetus for expansion thus came mainly from two individuals: National Security Adviser Anthony Lake and President Clinton himself. Lake believed that a larger NATO could calm post–Cold War instability in Eastern Europe. By expanding NATO's protective shield over new members, he believed, the United States would ease Eastern European fears of a Russian resurgence and thus allow those countries to concentrate on economic reforms and democratization. Accordingly, Lake worked diligently to keep the idea of expansion alive, and to implement the decision once it was made.

Clinton supported NATO enlargement mainly for moral reasons. Clinton's interest in the project was piqued by the emotional pleas of Czech President Vaclav Havel and Polish leader Lech Wałęsa at an Oval Office meeting in early 1993. Moved by these countries' tragic pasts, as well as by the ethnic cleansing in the former Yugoslav Republics, which had gone on during Bush's presidency, Clinton developed an attachment to the idea of extending NATO protections into Eastern Europe.

The extent to which support for expansion remained a minority opinion in Washington became clear from the difficulty Clinton had in implementing his decision.

Pentagon officials were unenthusiastic about working with new members who would add little to the military capabilities of the alliance. Leading State Department officials like Assistant Secretary of State Strobe Talbott continued to argue that the project would complicate relations with Moscow. Indeed, Russian leaders reacted strongly to the prospect of a larger NATO. President Boris Yeltsin and others argued that expanding NATO would constitute a direct military threat to Russia, and warned that a "new Cold War" could be the result. In consequence, implementation lagged for much of Clinton's first term.

GAINING IMPETUS

Ultimately, expansion began to gather real momentum only in 1996. With the U.S. presidential elections approaching, and with Clinton under pressure from Republicans for the slow pace of the initiative, he finally began to drive the process through the government bureaucracy. Additionally, NATO's success in resolving the Bosnian war, after Clinton persuaded NATO to initiate a bombing campaign in 1995, had renewed faith in the alliance, giving a boost to those who argued that NATO was ready for additional responsibilities. This intervention also saw NATO go "out of area" (operating militarily beyond the borders of its member states) for the first time, a precedent that would subsequently be repeated in Kosovo in 1999 and Afghanistan after 2001. With the alliance revitalized, formal invitations were soon issued to Poland, the Czech Republic, and Hungary, and these three states would be admitted to the alliance in 1999. Additional rounds of expansion would follow.

NATO expansion constituted a major shift in U.S. foreign policy, the extension and adaptation of a Cold War institution for post–Cold War purposes. Yet it ultimately came at a price. U.S.-Russian relations worsened as NATO expansion proceeded, and while Moscow was too weak to impede the process during the Clinton years, it would later take a more forceful stance. In the mid-2000s, Russia exerted strong diplomatic pressure in an effort to dissuade two former Soviet republics and membership candidates, Ukraine and Georgia, from joining the alliance. The Russian invasion of the latter republic in 2008 was widely seen as an attempt to weaken and intimidate that country before it could be extended NATO protection. Twenty years after the end of the Cold War, the role of NATO remained a sticking point in U.S.-Russia affairs.

While Clinton's conversion was apparently spontaneous, there were decent strategic arguments to be made in favor of NATO enlargement. It would provide a security blanket for Central and Eastern Europe, allowing new members of the alliance (Poland, Hungary, and the Czech Republic) to concentrate on domestic reforms, while also providing insurance against a future Russian resurgence. Yet for precisely this reason, expansion also seemed likely to anger Moscow, empowering neo-nationalist elements and jeopardizing internal reform. Clinton and Lake overrode these concerns, but the angry Russian reaction to plans for enlargement seemed to confirm these warnings. Having long considered the Balkans to be a Russian sphere of influence, observers in Moscow were equally upset by U.S. and NATO intervention in Bosnia in 1995.

Dealing with the Contradictions

Through the mid-1990s, Russian weakness and Clinton's close personal ties to Yeltsin meant that the contradictions of U.S. policies in Europe remained manageable. With Russia effectively dependent on Western economic aid, there was little that Moscow could do to impede NATO expansion or U.S. intervention in the Balkans. Showing a deft diplomatic touch, Clinton even persuaded Yeltsin to support the U.S.-sponsored peace settlement in Bosnia by committing two battalions of troops to the NATO contingent.

Unfortunately, Clinton's early success in reconciling his top three priorities in Europe—ending the Balkan wars, engaging Russia, and expanding NATO—led him to conclude that the contradictions among these goals could be safely ignored. In early 1998, before the first round of NATO expansion was even complete, Clinton announced that Latvia, Lithuania, and Estonia would eventually become members of the alliance as well. The strategic argument for this second round of expansion was harder to make, as the three Baltic states added virtually nothing to the alliance, and the decision to include three former Soviet republics was sure to inflame Russian sensitivities. Nonetheless, Strobe Talbott, Clinton's top Russia adviser, dismissed Moscow's concerns on the subject as "neuralgia." "They need to stop looking at the Baltic region as a pathway for foreign armies or as a buffer zone," he said.[13]

Talbott's comments notwithstanding, the decision to push a historically anti-Soviet alliance up to Russia's borders was manifestly in conflict with Clinton's desire to integrate Russia into post–Cold War Europe. Russian perceptions that the United States was taking advantage of Moscow's weakness created a strong undercurrent of tension in the relationship. Those tensions nearly exploded in 1999, when Clinton overrode Russian objections and bypassed the UN Security Council in leading U.S. and NATO intervention in Kosovo. The air strikes provoked a virulent Russian response, with Yeltsin even hinting that war might result. The immediate crisis passed, however, and Clinton won Russian participation in the post-conflict peacekeeping mission. Then, tensions flared again, as the Russians preemptively deployed into Kosovo, leading to a race (won by Moscow) to seize the airport in the capital of Pristina, as well as close calls between Russian and NATO troops. As the war in Kosovo came to an end, U.S.-Russian relations were at a post–Cold War nadir.

By the late 1990s, in fact, Russian frustration with U.S. policies had given rise to efforts to balance American power. Russian leaders cultivated American enemies like Iraq and Iran, became less cooperative with U.S. initiatives in the UN Security Council, and even initiated a degree of strategic cooperation with China, all in hopes of countering the geopolitical dominance of the United States. Clinton's relationship with Yeltsin kept this growing dissonance muffled, but the downward trend became clearer once the two presidents left office. Indeed, years later, the tensions created by NATO expansion and American intervention in the Balkans continued to plague U.S.-Russian relations.

Clinton's European Dilemma

Overall, Clinton's European diplomacy was successful in two important respects: extending NATO's protective reach into Eastern Europe and resolving the Balkan conflicts. Yet grand strategy also is about managing the conflicts that inevitably arise between a nation's various priorities, and it was here that the president struggled. Clinton initially set out to achieve a stable long-term relationship with Russia, but the subsequent pursuit of American objectives in NATO and the Balkans impeded the realization of that primary goal. Contrary to what he had hoped, Clinton could not have everything, even at a time of great American influence. NATO enlargement and ending the wars in the Balkans were the successes of Clinton's European diplomacy; deteriorating relations with Russia was the price of that success.

The Perils of Distraction

A third dilemma, closely related to the second, involved the issue of how best to allocate finite resources like time and energy in dealing with a complex world of competing demands. This dilemma was most directly related to the foreign policy initiative that was closest to Clinton's heart: the search for peace in the Middle East. Clinton assumed office at a promising time in the peace process. The Madrid Conference of 1991 had opened a dialogue between Israel and the Palestinians, and, two years later, negotiators meeting in Oslo, Norway, agreed on a framework for greater eventual Palestinian self-rule. Seeing a chance to resolve a problem that had long contributed to instability and authoritarian rule in the Middle East, and desperate for a foreign policy victory after early embarrassment in Bosnia and Somalia, Clinton would spend much of his presidency seeking to broker a comprehensive peace.

Diplomatic Efforts in the Middle East

The president's efforts began well; using economic aid as leverage, Clinton helped broker a peace settlement between Israel and Jordan in 1994. Unfortunately, the president also had begun two parallel sets of negotiations—between Israel and Syria, and between Israel and the Palestinians—at precisely the time when the parties involved began showing reluctance to move forward. The Oslo process quickly bogged down amid opposition from hard-liners on both sides, and the Syria-Israel talks faltered over disagreement on security arrangements in the Israeli-occupied Golan Heights. All this was despite intensive U.S. involvement in the negotiations; Secretary of State Warren Christopher made more than two dozen visits to the region during Clinton's first term. The peace process sustained another blow in 1995, when Israeli Prime Minister Yitzhak Rabin (in office 1974–1977, 1992–1995) was assassinated. This setback was devastating to Clinton personally, and it led to the triumph of a right-wing coalition, under Benjamin Netanyahu (in office 1996–1999, 2009–), which opposed the Oslo process, accords that would ultimately cede control over parts of the West Bank and Gaza to the Palestinian Authority.

Undaunted, Clinton dived even deeper during his second term, becoming nearly consumed by the peace process. As one adviser later wrote, Clinton considered himself "a legatee, a political son, of the murdered Yitzhak Rabin, whom he revered above all other leaders," and he kept a number of private shrines to the fallen Israeli.[14] Between 1997 and 2000, Clinton sought to honor Rabin's legacy, and ensure his own, by calling for negotiations on the creation of a sovereign Palestinian state, and by prodding the Syrian and Israeli leadership to resume negotiations. These intensive efforts culminated in 2000, with two marathon, climactic summits, hosted by Clinton, between Israeli and Palestinian leaders.

Peace Efforts Unfulfilled

These efforts were nothing if not well intentioned, and at times President Clinton seemed tantalizingly close to achieving peace. In retrospect, however, his approach to the negotiations suffered from two key flaws. The first was that Clinton wanted peace more than the participants themselves. On the Israeli side, the hawkish Benjamin Netanyahu consistently undermined the negotiations between 1996 and 1999. The election of a more dovish Ehud Barak (1999–2001) in 1999 revived the peace process, but as the subsequent Syrian-Israeli talks showed, neither Barak nor Syrian President Hafiz al-Assad (in power 1971–2000) was willing to take the major political risks necessary to seal an accord.

This problem was even more apparent during the summits between Barak and Palestinian leader Yasser Arafat (1996–2004) in 2000. Despite receiving clear indications beforehand that Arafat did not feel ready to make the concessions necessary to conclude an agreement, Clinton desperately wanted a historic accomplishment before leaving office, and he insisted on forging ahead. Predictably, Arafat rejected the proposed terms, resulting in a high-profile failure of American diplomacy and the collapse of the peace process.

Clinton's failure to achieve peace would not have been so damaging were it not for the second problem: the extent to which his consuming involvement with the negotiations began to distort his broader foreign policy agenda. The negotiations, which involved top-level summits, intensive diplomacy, and numerous trips by U.S. officials like Secretary of State Madeleine Albright to the Middle East, absorbed massive amounts of time on the part of Clinton and Albright, to the point that the latter complained after one trip to the region that "I can't be occupied with this full time."[15]

As his second term wore on, however, Clinton failed to free himself from the allure of Middle East peace. In 2000, Clinton missed part of an economic summit in Okinawa due to the negotiations; at another point, he delayed a diplomatic opening to India on the same grounds. While these were relatively minor distractions, more problematic was the fact that the imperatives of peace process also impeded efforts to deal with two rising threats: North Korea and international terrorism.

The end of the Cold War freed Clinton to devote unprecedented time and energy to issues like the search for Middle East peace, but it did not free him from the reality that intensive involvement in that arena came at a cost in other aspects of American diplomacy. Had Clinton achieved peace, his distraction would surely have been forgiven; had he not become so immersed in the process, his failure to achieve peace would not loom so large. Ultimately, though, it was a combination of disappointment and distraction that characterized Clinton's involvement in the peace process, as he himself admitted. As Clinton told Arafat following their final summit, "I am not a great man. I am a failure, and you have made me one."[16]

BACKLASH STATES AND TERRORISM

Clinton would be no less perplexed by a fourth dilemma: the problem of backlash states, or rogue nations, and international terrorism. Enlargement aimed to bring about a peaceful, democratic world, but backlash states rejected that vision and caused considerable problems for Clinton's statecraft.

Iraq

One state that particularly confounded Clinton was Saddam Hussein's Iraq. Even after being soundly defeated in the Persian Gulf War (1990–1991), Saddam continued to test the United States. His regime sought to assassinate former President George H. W. Bush in 1993, amassed eighty thousand troops on the Kuwaiti border a year later, and frequently interfered with the international inspections regime meant to keep Iraq from redeveloping weapons of mass destruction (WMDs).

The Clinton administration termed regimes like Saddam's "backlash states," the idea being that bellicose, authoritarian regimes represented a sharp, yet ultimately transitory, backlash against the inevitable progression of human affairs. For the time being, the key to dealing with backlash states was to contain them and prevent them from disrupting the international order. Accordingly, Clinton took a threefold approach to dealing with Saddam. He sought to weaken Iraq economically by holding UN economic sanctions in place, to contain the regime militarily by stationing substantial U.S. forces in the gulf, and to punish and weaken Saddam through periodic airstrikes against Iraqi targets.

Containment was a reasonable strategy for dealing with Saddam, but it also had drawbacks. The policy was costly, because it demanded continuous military vigilance, and it was diplomatically problematic, in that it required the stationing of U.S. troops in Saudi Arabia. It was also difficult to sustain. The international coalition that had confronted Saddam in 1990 and 1991 frayed as countries such as France and Russia sought to resume business with oil-rich Iraq, and by 1999, the sanctions and inspections regime was on the verge of collapse. Also, and not least of all, containment was frustrating and indecisive, in that it focused on merely restraining Saddam rather than forcing him from power. In other words, at the very moment when U.S. power seemed greatest, America could still not obtain satisfaction from Saddam short of a major war.

Clinton sought to escape the dilemmas of containment by sponsoring covert action to overthrow Saddam in 1995 and 1996, but this initiative came apart due to infighting among Iraqi opposition groups and last-minute indecision in Washington. As the difficulties of containment piled up, domestic frustration with the stalemate in the gulf boiled over. Republican critics assailed Clinton's policy, charging that the president's vacillation was giving Saddam the upper hand in the confrontation, and calling for more decisive action. In 1998, the House and Senate broke with Clinton by passing the Iraqi Liberation Act. The law committed the United States to supporting various Iraqi opposition groups, officially changed American policy from containment to "regime change," and thereby set the two countries on a path toward an even sharper confrontation in the years to come. Indeed, two years after Clinton left office, President George W. Bush (2001–2009) would discard containment altogether in favor of a far more aggressive approach to the problem.

North Korea

Clinton's relations with another rogue state, North Korea, were equally tumultuous.

The two countries nearly came to blows in 1994. North Korea seemed determined to develop a nuclear weapon; Clinton was convinced that a North Korean bomb would destabilize East Asia and encourage proliferation elsewhere as well. At the height of the crisis, Clinton dispatched more troops to South Korea and appeared to consider a military strike against the North. The crisis was resolved through the mediation of former President Jimmy Carter (1977–1981), but the situation on the Korean Peninsula remained tense.

Recognizing that the enigmatic North Korean regime was unlikely to be toppled anytime soon, Clinton tried another tack during his second term. In 1998, former Defense Secretary William Perry recommended that Clinton offer the North security guarantees, economic aid, and diplomatic recognition in exchange for ending its nuclear and missile programs. Doing so would not put an end to Kim Jong Il's (in power 1994–2011) odious regime—in fact, it would help perpetuate that regime—but it would stabilize the situation on the peninsula and ease a recurring problem in the U.S. defense posture. With North Korea recovering from a devastating famine, Kim indicated that he might be interested in such an accord, and talks between the two sides gathered momentum in 2000. Late in Clinton's presidency, Kim invited him to come to Pyongyang, the North Korean capital, for a summit that might produce a tentative agreement to be formalized under Clinton's successor.

Yet Clinton passed on this opportunity, not because of doubts about Kim's sincerity, or repulsion at his brutal practices, but because he could not tear himself away from another set of last-minute negotiations between Barak and Arafat. Whether a U.S.-North Korea summit would have produced an agreement is impossible to say, but looking back, Clinton conceded that he would have done better to pursue that opportunity than to continue chasing after an increasingly unlikely settlement in the Middle East. Consumed by pursuit of one peace, Clinton missed a chance to negotiate another, and U.S.-North Korea relations deteriorated steadily in the years that followed. On December 18, 2011, Kim Jong Il died and was succeeded by his 28-year-old son, Kim Jong Un, known as the "Great Successor" and an inexperienced but fearsome figure.

The Rise of International Terrorism

Concentration on the Middle East peace process also may have undermined Clinton's efforts to deal with an even more dangerous threat. Jihadist terrorism had been a rising concern for U.S. policymakers since the 1980s, and the threat from one particular group, Osama bin Laden's al Qaeda network, grew considerably during Clinton's presidency. Alleging that Washington was occupying Muslim soil through its military presence in Saudi Arabia, supporting Israel's position to increase

IN THEIR OWN WORDS: *PRESIDENTIAL DECISION DIRECTIVE 39*

The issue of jihadist terrorism was considered a rising threat by many officials within the Clinton administration. In June 1995, Clinton signed Presidential Decision Directive 39, which outlined the administration's view of the dangers posed by terrorism and assigned special priority to preventing terrorist groups from acquiring weapons of mass destruction:

> It is the policy of the United States to deter, defeat and respond vigorously to all terrorist attacks on our territory and against our citizens, or facilities, whether they occur domestically, in international waters or airspace or on foreign territory. The United States regards all such terrorism as a potential threat to national security as well as a criminal act and will apply all appropriate means to combat it....
>
> Furthermore, the United States shall seek to identify groups or states that sponsor or support such terrorists, isolate them and extract a heavy price for their actions.

> It is the policy of the United States not to make concessions to terrorists....
>
> We shall have the ability to respond rapidly and decisively to terrorism directed against us wherever it occurs, to protect Americans, arrest or defeat the perpetrators, respond with all appropriate instruments against the sponsoring organizations and governments and provide recovery relief to victims, as permitted by law ...
>
> The acquisition of weapons of mass destruction by a terrorist group, through theft or manufacture, is unacceptable. There is no higher priority than preventing the acquisition of this capability....

SOURCE: Presidential Decision Directive 39, "U.S. Policy on Counterterrorism," June 21, 1995, available at http://www.fas.org/irp/offdocs/pdd39.htm.

its national security at the expense of its Muslim neighbors, and backing corrupt, authoritarian governments in the Middle East, bin Laden sponsored a series of attacks against the United States and its interests during the 1990s; in fact, he explicitly declared war against America in 1996. Two years later, al Qaeda operatives staged their most devastating attack to date, bombing U.S. embassies in Kenya and Tanzania and taking more than two hundred lives.

The Clinton administration was well aware of the rising threat of international terrorism, and of al Qaeda specifically. In June 1995, Clinton signed a directive that assigned "highest priority" to denying WMDs to terrorist groups. In 1996, a classified report warned that "sooner or later, bin Ladin will attack U.S. interests, perhaps using WMD."[17]

After the 1998 embassy attacks, Clinton responded to this emerging menace by ordering cruise missile strikes against al Qaeda training camps in Afghanistan and a suspected chemical weapons plant in Sudan. These attacks adhered closely to the Balkan template: long-range weapons were used to minimize the potential for American casualties. However, they were also ineffective, failing to inflict any substantial damage on al Qaeda's leadership or infrastructure.

Between 1998 and January 2001, Clinton's administration considered a variety of riskier but potentially more effective measures. The United States could mount a sustained bombing campaign against al Qaeda sanctuaries in Afghanistan, or it could use special forces or other ground assets to attempt to capture or kill bin Laden.

Counter-terrorism specialists within the administration strongly advocated these options, warning that the threat from al Qaeda was metastasizing. Their warnings were seemingly confirmed in 2000, when suicide bombers severely damaged the USS *Cole* while refueling in the Yemeni port of Aden.

Wrapped up in the Israel-Palestinian peace talks, the Clinton administration nixed that idea of a sustained bombing campaign for fear that attacks against a Muslim country would incite popular anger in the Middle East and thereby lessen the prospects for a peace agreement. Also adverse to sustaining U.S. casualties, Clinton rejected plans for a determined effort to kill or capture bin Laden. With Clinton unwilling to alter his cost-averse formula for military intervention or divert attention from his quest for Middle East peace, the threat from al Qaeda persisted.

China and the Limits of Enlargement

Clinton's dealings with Iraq, North Korea, and al Qaeda demonstrated that preeminence was not omnipotence and that American power did not always translate into successful, satisfying policies. The same was true of U.S. relations with China, which demonstrated both the limits of enlargement and the difficulties that Clinton faced in adapting to those limits.

At the outset of his presidency, Clinton viewed China as a prime testing ground for enlargement and America's ability to promote a more humane order. Chinese leaders had brutally repressed their own people during the Tiananmen

Square uprising in 1989, and Clinton, who had severely criticized Bush's tepid reaction to this incident during the 1992 presidential election campaign, hinted that U.S.-China relations would remain circumscribed until human rights conditions improved. The administration initially sought to apply economic leverage to bring these changes about, threatening trade sanctions if China failed to engage in meaningful political liberalization.

Yet, as Clinton soon realized, this was not a winning strategy, because American economic power was insufficient to compel internal reform in China. Chinese leaders were especially sensitive on this count after the upheaval of 1989, and as U.S. officials soon realized, a slowdown in bilateral commerce might hurt Washington as much as Beijing. In the same vein, it was clear by the mid-1990s that China was a rising power, both in East Asia and on the broader world stage. If the United States isolated or sought to coerce China, it might make a powerful future enemy; if it engaged China, it might set the stage for a more stable, mutually beneficial relationship.

Comprehensive Engagement with China

From 1994 on, Clinton pursued a policy of "comprehensive engagement" toward China, seeking expanded trade and greater dialogue on security and political issues. During his second term, he traveled to Beijing for a much publicized summit, and worked to facilitate Chinese entry into the World Trade Organization (WTO). Throughout this period, the administration did its best to ignore the human rights issue, arguing that prudence dictated focusing on areas of convergence in the relationship.

Given the obvious fact of growing Chinese power, and the absence of plausible alternatives, Clinton was probably correct to deemphasize human rights in hopes of building a productive relationship. Nonetheless, Clinton found that his policies remained vulnerable to the vicissitudes of international affairs and U.S. domestic politics. On the former count, Clinton's engagement policy was hindered by U.S. relations with Taiwan. In 1996, China staged missile tests in the Taiwan Strait in an effort to influence Taiwan's first democratic presidential election. To show support for Taiwanese sovereignty, Clinton dispatched two aircraft carrier battle groups to the area. This show of force incensed the Chinese leadership and contributed to Beijing's decision to significantly upgrade its military capabilities during the late 1990s and after. U.S. arms sales to Taiwan also remained a sticking point throughout Clinton's presidency, and the accidental bombing of Beijing's embassy in Belgrade during the Kosovo war further clouded the relationship.

Domestic Criticism

Just as problematic was domestic criticism of Clinton's China policy. Following his change of course in 1994 and 1995, Clinton was continually savaged by those who claimed that he was betraying American principles by putting human rights aside. "There is no moral or practical difference between trading with the People's Republic of China (PRC) dictatorship and trading with the Nazis," argued one Republican congressman.[18] Although some of this criticism appears to have been motivated by sincere dismay, much of it derived from a politically motivated desire to embarrass Clinton. Either way, it intruded on the administration's China policy. Domestic pressure was sufficient to convince Clinton to introduce UN resolutions condemning China's human rights practices in 1997 and 2000, a practice that hardly facilitated the bilateral relationship.

U.S.-China relations under Clinton thus demonstrated two essential truths about the post–Cold War era. First, the relationship showed that there were limits to America's ability to change objectionable regimes abroad, and that pragmatism demanded recognizing this reality. Yet it also showed that this approach was morally discomfiting to many Americans, who had hoped that U.S. preeminence would make such ethical compromises unnecessary. Clinton's recognition of the first reality enabled him to hand a functioning, if hardly frictionless, relationship with China to his successor; the latter reality ensured that U.S. engagement with Beijing would remain a contested issue.

THE PROMISE AND CHALLENGE OF GLOBALIZATION

The problem of selling foreign policy at home was also central to yet another dilemma, which had to do with the promise and perils of economic openness. Challenged by a domestic recession at the outset of his presidency, Clinton and his advisers consistently argued that achieving prosperity at home required broadening and deepening American commerce abroad. "For too long we have made economics the poor cousin of our foreign policy," said Secretary of State Warren Christopher in 1993; the search for export markets and affordable goods must be central to the administration's diplomacy, he said.[19]

Early negotiations meant to pry open the notoriously protectionist Japanese market failed to produce the desired results, but Clinton's trade diplomacy was more successful in other areas. In 1993, the administration concluded the North American Free Trade Agreement (NAFTA) with Mexico and Canada, which created the largest trade bloc in the world (as measured in combined gross domestic product, adjusted for purchasing power parity). Clinton also helped secure the conclusion of the Uruguay Round negotiations of the General Agreement on Tariffs and Trade (GATT), which provided for broad international tariff reductions and led to the creation of the World Trade Organization (WTO), a global body charged with regulating and facilitating international commerce. In addition, the administration concluded a range of bilateral trade deals.

Free Trade: The Balance Sheet

On balance, these agreements clearly benefited the U.S. domestic economy, which enjoyed a period of sustained growth under Clinton. Yet free trade is inevitably a contentious political issue: some groups benefit from having greater access to foreign trade and markets, while others suffer from the competition. It was during the Clinton years that organized labor, a key Democratic voting bloc, strongly opposed Clinton's trade agenda, as did environmental groups who feared that heavy polluters would simply exploit free trade to relocate to countries with laxer laws.

As the 1990s went on, free trade also came under fire from a growing number of conservative Republicans who argued that, by linking itself to the international economy, the United States was also exposing itself to instability caused by economic crises in foreign countries. This sentiment was fueled particularly by the Mexican peso crisis of 1994, during which financial instability to the south forced Clinton to provide a $20 billion bailout to the Mexican government in order to protect U.S. exports and prevent the financial contagion from spreading.

These sentiments created growing opposition to Clinton's trade agenda as the decade went on. The administration secured passage of NAFTA and GATT in 1994, but domestic discomfort with free trade was on the rise. In 1994 and again in 1997, the administration sought fast-track trade authority, or the power to submit international trade agreements to Congress for expedited consideration. In both cases, a coalition of legislators blocked the proposal.

Concerns about Globalization

American concerns about free trade were part of a larger debate regarding globalization: the increasing integration of national economies, societies, and cultures. During the 1990s, the erosion of Cold War–era geopolitical and economic barriers, along with rapid improvements in communications technology, led to a striking growth in global interconnectedness. As globalization gained momentum, there also took hold a sense that this process was to be the inevitable outcome of the coming decades.

The notion of increasing global openness comported well with the logic of enlargement. Clinton and his advisers argued that greater trade would produce increased American and global prosperity; global prosperity, in turn, would ease political disputes, dampen nationalism, and conduce to international peace. Clinton sought to position the United States at the forefront of globalization, taking a leading role in the WTO and global trade negotiations.

Yet globalization brought with it a backlash. Economic interconnectedness meant that a financial breakdown in one region could lead to instability around the globe, as happened when an economic crisis in East Asia spread to Russia and Latin America in 1997 and 1998. Economic openness also had pernicious consequences for groups that had traditionally been protected by tariffs and other barriers, and both poor workers and poor countries often complained that the rules of globalization, as made and enforced by groups like the WTO, were slanted to favor the interests of the rich. Additionally, new technologies disseminated new values and norms across the globe, leading to the fraying of existing customs and identities.

Growing Dissent

During the 1990s, these concerns were evident worldwide in boycotts of foreign goods led by Indian community leaders, in labor activism in Europe and Latin America, and in the protests and riots that rocked every major meeting of the WTO and International Monetary Fund. The United States was hardly immune from this dissent. At the WTO summit in Seattle in 1999, anarchists rioted, while an array of peaceful demonstrators, including members of respected groups like the Sierra Club, the Teamsters, and the American Federation of Labor-Congress of Industrial Organizations (AFL-CIO), protested the proceedings. Clinton acknowledged the dislocations caused by globalization, saying that "if we're going to have an open trading system, we have got to make it work for ordinary folks."[20] He sought to accommodate their concerns by proposing stricter WTO sanctions on countries with insufficient labor protections, but the proposal was anathema to developing countries, and the meeting ended in deadlock.

Free trade and globalization promised macro-level benefits for the American economy, but for many domestic groups in the United States, as elsewhere, these processes engendered more anxiety than confidence. By 2000, a plurality of Americans believed that free trade did more harm than good, and Clinton's undersecretary of commerce conceded that the administration had "not convinced most Americans of the value of trade."[21] At the close of Clinton's presidency, trade policy remained politically contested terrain.

THE POLITICS OF FOREIGN POLICY

Disagreement and indifference plagued the process of foreign policy as a whole; this constituted a final dilemma of the post–Cold War era. One of Clinton's key purposes in formulating enlargement had been to articulate a vision that could elicit strong domestic support for his foreign policy and thereby defeat what Lake derisively referred to as "neo-know nothing isolationism."

Domestic Indifference

In practice, however, consensus was more difficult to come by. The debacle in Somalia, Clinton's ambivalence in Bosnia, and various other missteps led to growing disillusion with the notion of humanitarian intervention. Free trade also proved to be a contentious political issue, and throughout the 1990s, many of the president's policies came under sharp criticism at home.

This situation was not entirely Clinton's fault, contrary to what his detractors suggested. The domestic and international circumstances of his presidency were equally to blame. Internationally, the lack of a clear and present danger such as Nazi Germany or the Cold War–era Soviet Union led to a fragmenting of opinion on what the United States should do in the world, and also to a general lack of interest in the subject. When surveys taken toward the end of Clinton's presidency asked respondents to identify "two or three foreign policy problems facing the nation," the most common answer was "don't know," and only one in nine respondents reported following the war in Kosovo "very closely."[22] Moreover, the increasingly poisonous relations between Clinton and congressional Republicans from 1994 onward militated against bipartisan cooperation on foreign policy.

Whatever its causes, this lack of interest and consensus proved increasingly problematic for Clinton as his tenure wore on. In one sense, public apathy made it difficult for the administration to justify the need for a large diplomatic and foreign aid budget, which the House of Representatives slashed by 15 percent in the summer of 1999. In another sense, the absence of consensus on foreign policy meant that the president's opponents were increasingly able to challenge his diplomatic initiatives.

Political Opposition

During the late 1990s, it was this latter problem that often seemed most pressing for the administration. A group of congressional Republicans, motivated by a sense that Clinton had been overly deferential to the wishes of the international community and insufficiently assertive in using American power, attacked a number of the president's policies. They held hostage the payment of U.S. dues to the United Nations, prevented U.S. participation in the International Criminal Court, defeated the Comprehensive Nuclear Test Ban Treaty, and successfully forced the notion of "regime change" on the administration's Iraq policy in 1998–1999. In each case, the administration sought to defend its stated policy, but in each case, Clinton was unable to muster the support that would allow him to hold his ground.

The culmination of this trend came with the debate over National Missile Defense (NMD). For most of his presidency, Clinton strongly opposed the idea of seeking to construct a shield of anti-missile interceptors that would protect the U.S. homeland from missile attacks by Iran, Iraq, North Korea, or other backlash states. Clinton argued that any real missile threat from these countries was at least a decade away, and that terrorism was a more feasible option

for those who wished to do the United States harm. He also argued that construction of NMD would violate the Anti-Ballistic Missile Treaty signed with the Soviet Union in 1972, and thereby further complicate U.S.-Russia relations.

House and Senate Republicans disagreed. They argued that Clinton was neglecting the imperatives of national defense and charged that his efforts to appease one defeated enemy were hampering efforts to secure the country against attacks by emerging foes. "The Clinton administration wants to negotiate permission from Russia over whether the U.S. can protect itself from ballistic missile attack by North Korea," fumed Senator Jesse Helms (R-NC; in office 1973-2003).[23] Coming amid growing concern at the threat from Pyongyang, and amid increasing frustration at the difficulties of dealing with Iraq and other backlash states, Republican objections found a receptive audience. Helms and his allies kept up the pressure on the White House in the late 1990s, holding hearings devoted to making the case for NMD, and when the Pentagon bowed to this campaign and signaled its support for the project, Clinton was concerned. In 1999, he signed the National Missile Defense Act, which pledged $6.6 billion to research and development and required initial deployment of NMD by 2003. Clinton had hoped that enlargement would help him build a durable consensus on post–Cold War foreign policy, but he ended up struggling to overcome apathy and dissent instead.

THE DILEMMAS OF PREEMINENCE

The end of the Cold War ushered in an era of American global preeminence, a period in which the United States was unmatched in economic and military terms and its vital interests were seemingly safe from attack. At the same time, it compelled American leaders to go beyond the obsolete doctrines of the superpower struggle and fashion new policies for an increasingly complex world. Their task, in a sense, was to rise above the emerging disorder, international and domestic, of the post–Cold War world.

Doing so required American officials to confront a number of challenges, ranging from the need to reconcile competing priorities to the imperative of forging domestic support for foreign policy. The Clinton administration compiled a mixed record in addressing these dilemmas. In a positive sense, America emerged from Clinton's presidency with the same surfeit of global power with which it had entered. Clinton largely avoided foreign policy disasters that might have imperiled the nation's preeminent global position, and on a number of issues—NATO expansion, brokering peace between Israel and Jordan, ending the wars in Bosnia and Kosovo, negotiating new international trade agreements, and others—the administration effectively used American power to achieve the goals it set.

Yet, in retrospect, Clinton never fully cracked the riddle of post–Cold War foreign policy. In some areas, his policies ran up against the inevitable limits of American power and the overly optimistic reading of history on which enlargement was premised. In others, the president struggled to convince the domestic audience that his policies were worth support, or even attention, and in a number of cases, Clinton stumbled because of his own shortcomings. In the Middle East, Clinton failed to manage his commitment to the peace process and prevent that issue from distorting the broader conduct of foreign policy. In dealing with Europe, he allowed his enthusiasm for NATO expansion to undercut his own desire for a stable, long-term relationship with Russia. Clinton disliked the notion of grand strategy, and in these areas, it showed.

Finally, Clinton failed to deal effectively with the one issue, terrorism, that would ultimately shatter America's post–Cold War sense of security. Although Clinton recognized that al Qaeda posed a threat, he was unwilling to pay the costs, both human and diplomatic, of grappling with that threat. As a result, in part, the nation would soon be shaken from its optimism and complacency and thrust into a new era of anxiety and war.

See also: **Chapter 27: Rogue States and the Emergence of Terrorist Tactics; Chapter 31: U.S. Economic and Foreign Relations with the Western Hemisphere; Chapter 33: Europe, the United States, and NATO and Their Roles in the Twenty-first Century; Chapter 35: The Global War on Terrorism.**

ENDNOTES

1. Charles Krauthammer, "The Unipolar Moment," in *Foreign Affairs* 70, no. 1 (Winter 1991).

2. "President George Bush at the NATO Summit Conference in Rome, Italy," Federal News Service Transcript, November 8, 1991.

3. Patrick Buchanan, "America First—And Second, and Third," in *National Interest*, Spring 1990.

4. George Bush, *All the Best, George Bush: My Life in Letters and Other Writings* (New York: Scribner, 1999), 527–28.

5. *Public Papers of the Presidents of the United States, 1992* (Washington, DC: U.S. Government Printing Office, 1993), 2192.

6. Strobe Talbott, *The Russia Hand: A Memoir of Presidential Diplomacy* (New York: Random House, 2002), 133.

7. Talbott, *The Russia Hand*, 133–34.

8. Senate Foreign Relations Committee, *Nomination of Warren M. Christopher to be Secretary of State* (Washington, DC: U.S. Government Printing Office, 1993), 19–21.

9. Lake is quoted in Anthony Lake, *From Containment to Enlargement: Remarks at the Paul Nitze School of International Affairs at Johns Hopkins University, September 21, 1993* (Washington, DC: U.S. Government Printing Office, 1993).

10. Michael Dobbs, *Madeleine Albright: A Twentieth-Century Odyssey* (New York: Macmillan, 2000), 360.

11. Hal Brands, *From Berlin to Baghdad: America's Search for Purpose in the Post-Cold War World* (Lexington: University Press of Kentucky, 2008), 134.

12. Brands, *From Berlin to Baghdad*, 175–76.

13. Stephen Erlanger, "U.S. to Back Baltic Membership in NATO, but Not Anytime Soon," in *The New York Times*, January 12, 1998; Erlanger, "Clinton and 3 Baltic Leaders Sign Charter," in *The New York Times*, January 17, 1998.

14. Sidney Blumenthal, *The Clinton Wars* (New York: Farrar, Straus and Giroux, 2003), 487.

15. Thomas Lippman, "Albright Pessimistic as Mideast Trip Ends," in *The Washington Post*, September 16, 1997.

16. Bill Clinton, *My Life* (New York: Random House, 2005), 944.

17. Brands, *From Berlin to Baghdad*, 242–44.

18. Brands, *From Berlin to Baghdad*, 169.

19. Senate Foreign Relations Committee, *Nomination of Christopher*, 22.

20. Bob Deans, "With Nod to Protests, Clinton Chides WTO," in *Atlanta Journal and Constitution*, December 2, 1999.

21. Brands, *From Berlin to Baghdad*, 156.

22. Brands, *From Berlin to Baghdad*, 255.

23. Quoted in Matthew Rees, "Going Ballistic," in *Weekly Standard*, February 8, 1999, 14.

FURTHER READING

Albright, Madeleine. *Madam Secretary: A Memoir*. London: Macmillan, 2003.

Bacevich, Andrew. *American Empire: The Realities and Consequences of American Diplomacy*. Cambridge, MA: Harvard University Press, 2002.

Blumenthal, Sidney. *The Clinton Wars*. New York: Farrar, Straus and Giroux, 2003.

Brands, Hal. *From Berlin to Baghdad: America's Search for Purpose in the Post-Cold War World*. Lexington: University of Kentucky Press, 2008.

Clinton, Bill. *My Life*. New York: Random House, 2005.

Esposito, John. *Unholy War: Terror in the Name of Islam*. New York: Oxford University Press, 2002.

Goldgeier, James. *Not Whether but When: The U.S. Decision to Enlarge NATO*. Washington, DC: Brookings Institution, 1999.

Halberstam, David. *War in a Time of Peace: Bush, Clinton, and the Generals*. New York: Scribner, 2001.

Herring, George C. *From Colony to Superpower: U.S. Foreign Relations since 1776*. New York: Oxford University Press, 2008.

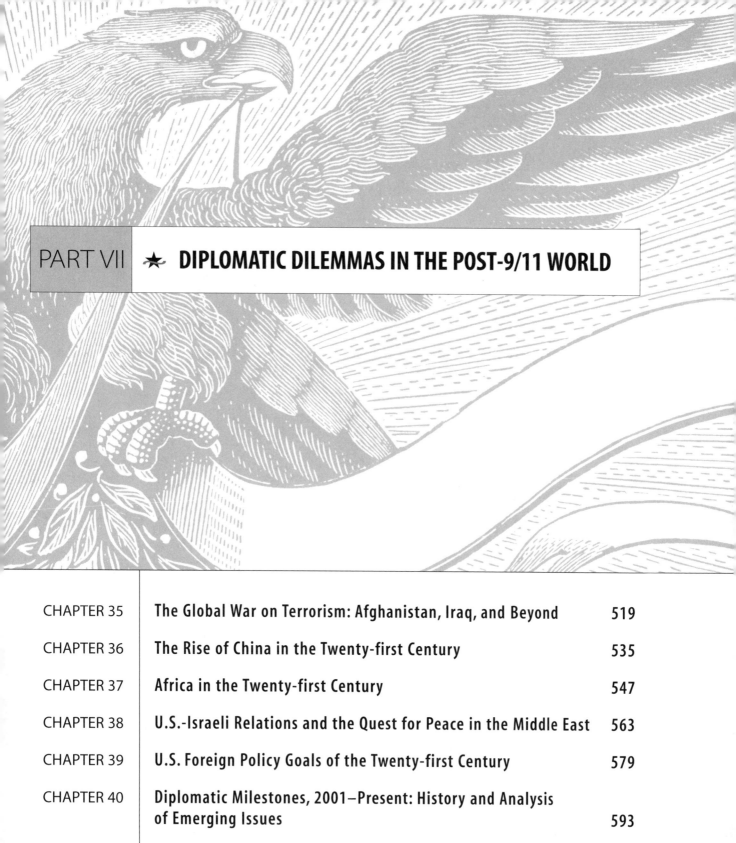

PART VII ★ DIPLOMATIC DILEMMAS IN THE POST-9/11 WORLD

chapter 35

The Global War on Terrorism

Afghanistan, Iraq, and Beyond

by David Zierler

AS A PRESIDENTIAL candidate, and through his first eight months in office, President George W. Bush (2001–2009) specifically and emphatically eschewed many of the interventionist policies that had guided U.S. foreign relations since the Cold War. Among his more famous pronouncements to this effect came during the second presidential debate with Vice President Al Gore, the Democratic candidate, in October 2000. Rebutting Gore's conviction that the United States must embrace its role as a global leader, Bush responded, "I'm not so sure the role of the United States is to go around the world and say this is the way it's got to be. We can help. And maybe it's just our difference in government, the way we view government. I want to empower the people. I want to help people help themselves, not have government tell people what to do. I just don't think it's the role of the United States to walk into a country and say, we do it this way, so should you."[1] As a self-styled "compassionate conservative," Bush staked much of his campaign efforts on domestic and cultural issues. Against the backdrop of the post–Cold War world, foreign policy problems such as the dismemberment of Yugoslavia or instability in places such as Haiti and Somalia could be dealt with at arm's length, if at all, while the containment of such "rogue" regimes such as Saddam Hussein's (in power 1979–2003) Iraq or Kim Jong Il's (in power 1994–2011) North Korea could be maintained through diplomatic sanctions backed up by the threat of military force.

FIRST MONTHS OF THE BUSH ADMINISTRATION

Largely unversed (and arguably incurious) about international affairs, Bush surrounded himself, both as a presidential candidate and later as forty-third president, with foreign affairs "heavyweights," many of whom had served in previous Republican administrations, including that of his father, George H. W. Bush (1989–1993). The core of Bush's inner circle included Vice President Dick Cheney (in office 2001–2009), Secretary of Defense Donald Rumsfeld (in office 2001–2006), Deputy Secretary of Defense Paul Wolfowitz (in office 2001–2007), and Secretary of State Colin Powell (in office 2001–2005). Bush's closest adviser on foreign policy, the noted academic "Sovietologist" Condoleezza Rice, who would go on to be the national security adviser and then secretary of state, was a protégé of Brent Scowcroft, national security adviser to the first President Bush. It was a relatively homogenous foreign policy circle, united around the general idea that the United States needed to maintain a robust defense policy through increases in the size and capabilities of the U.S. armed forces. Noting the difficulty in defining the "national interest" after the Cold War, in a tour d'horizon in the journal *Foreign Affairs* detailing how a hypothetical Bush administration would approach international affairs, Condoleezza Rice emphasized national defense against myriad relatively minor foreign policy threats. Among these threats, Rice included the specter of terrorists gaining access to weapons of mass destruction (WMD), although her reference garnered no more than a bullet point, did not specify the identity of these terrorists, and provided no further explication of how exactly the United States would neutralize the threat they imposed.[2]

The juxtaposition of a young presidential administration unfocused on the looming threat of al Qaeda and the most catastrophic failure in the history of the U.S. intelligence community was best distilled in President Bush's immediate reaction to the attacks, as recounted in his memoir, *Decision Points*. When his adviser Karl Rove "mentioned" on the morning of September 11 that a plane had struck one of the Twin Towers, Bush thought to himself, "That plane must have had the worst pilot in the world."[3] In any other moment, this anecdote would have lent itself well to one of the many satirical caricatures

KEY CONCEPTS

Al Qaeda. The terror attacks of September 11, 2001, executed by nineteen Islamist hijackers who seized control of passenger airplanes and subsequently aimed the planes at buildings as if they were missiles, caught the Bush administration and the U.S. intelligence community completely off guard. It was not the first time the United States was targeted by al Qaeda (Arabic, meaning, "the base") and its leader, Osama bin Laden. The 1998 U.S. embassy bombings in Tanzania and Kenya, as well as the 2000 bombing of the USS *Cole* in Yemen, proved generally that U.S. policies aroused anger among a certain ideological strain of political Islam for which there would be a price, and proved specifically that U.S. interests around the world were vulnerable to terrorist attack.

The American homeland had already been targeted by Islamist radicals connected to bin Laden and 9/11 mastermind Khalid Sheikh Mohammed. The 1993 World Trade Center bombing marked the opening salvo by Islamist terrorists to punish the United States for its support of Israel and deep military and political involvement throughout the Middle East—particularly the presence of U.S. troops and personnel in Saudi Arabia, home to the two holiest sites of Islam, during the first Persian Gulf War. In the minds of President George W. Bush and his key advisers following September 11, the American response undertaken by the Clinton administration to the four previous acts of terror too closely approximated measures of law enforcement; in the "post–9/11 world" those dedicated to attacking the United States and its people were not criminals but enemy combatants engaged in a new kind of war.

Global War on Terrorism: The sheer size and scope of the September 11 operation—nearly three thousand U.S. citizens and foreign nationals murdered—and the potent symbolism of targeting the preeminent symbols of American economic and military might, exhibited by the smoldering ruins of lower Manhattan and the outer ring of the Pentagon, compelled the Bush administration to conceive of a Global War on Terrorism. Although it would be bounded by conventional military conflicts and subsequent peacekeeping operations in Afghanistan and Iraq, by definition it would be a war unlike any conflict Americans had known since the nation's inception: there would be no fixed boundaries, no simple delineation between friend and foe, and no authoritative metrics to determine what "winning" would look like.

At the heart of the War on Terrorism, or any of its semantic relatives, is a logical fallacy far removed from the multifaceted response of the United States and its allies to the threat of Islamist terrorism from the events of September 11 to the present. The foundational basis of the Global War on Terrorism was, and is, to prevent another such attack from taking place. Insofar as it is impossible to correlate a positive action with a negative reaction, it cannot be known if the War on Terrorism has "succeeded." Further, it is highly unlikely that the clearest refutation against the logic of the War on Terrorism—namely, another large-scale terrorist attack on U.S. soil—would oblige the Obama or any subsequent presidential administration to alter radically the basic tenets of the War on Terrorism. Indeed, it is more likely that such an attack would only *intensify* U.S. efforts to secure its borders and track, imprison, or kill adherents to al Qaeda or any of its affiliate organizations wherever they are. To wit: what connection might we draw between the killing of Osama bin Laden by U.S. Special Forces in early May 2011 and the possibility that a terrorist sleeper cell is on the verge of a spectacular assault in a major U.S. city? We can draw many conclusions, no one necessarily more authoritative than the next. In essence, then, the Global War against Terrorism has amounted to a trillion dollar hunch that knows no end, a mission propelled by hazy imperatives such as revenge, justice, vigilance, fear, and, more broadly, the uniquely American impulse to "do something." Even with the war in Iraq winding down, and the year 2014 increasingly firming up as a combat withdrawal deadline from Afghanistan, so long as there remains a commitment on the part of Islamist terrorists to attack the United States, and a consequent American resolve to thwart such attacks, the War against Terror not only will not, but cannot, end.

SOURCE: Timothy Noah, "Why No More 9/11s?" *Slate*, March 5, 2009, available at http://www.slate.com/id/2213025.

of the president as good-natured, aloof, and clueless.[4] However, shortly after this folksy reaction, when news reached Bush that a second plane had hit the other Twin Tower, the president understood, along with the rest of the world in real time, that the United States was under attack. Upon learning of the crash at the Pentagon, the president's reaction was immediate and visceral, even juvenile. Well before he knew who had committed this heinous act, why they did it, and what other attacks might be in the offing, the president laid the foundation for what he would soon call the Global War on Terrorism: "The first plane could have been an accident. The second was definitely an attack. The third was a declaration of war. My blood was boiling. We were going to find out who did this, and kick their ass."[5]

The Administration Reacts to the September 11 Attacks

These were the words of a changed man, a president who, despite having occupied the Oval Office for the previous eight months, had suddenly felt the weight of the world fall on his shoulders, as if he was inaugurated that morning in a Florida classroom. Bush's intellectual disengagement and outsourcing of international security issues to his subordinates ceased immediately. The search to find an overarching

SHIFTS IN FOREIGN POLICY: *THE BEGINNING OF THE GLOBAL WAR ON TERRORISM*

The relatively lowly status accorded by Condoleezza Rice to the interwoven threat of weapons of mass destruction and terrorism serves as a fitting context to the scene at President Bush's extended vacation on his ranch in Crawford, Texas, in August 2001. News footage of the president clearing brush while wearing a cowboy hat projected the idea that the United States was secure and stable, and that its commander in chief could afford such pastoral indulgences. It was at this time that Bush received one of the most important Presidential Daily Briefs (PDB) of his administration. Titled "Bin Laden Determined to Strike in US," the brief, relying on a combination of clandestine and foreign government reporting, and comments made by bin Laden himself, noted that the al Qaeda leader wanted to follow up on the attacks on the U.S. embassies in East Africa with an operation in the United States, possibly by hijacking an aircraft, in an attempt to win the release of the 1993 World Trade Center bombers, among other allies in U.S. custody. The brief further noted the longstanding presence of al Qaeda members on U.S. soil who could aid in bin Laden's attacks. The report concluded that the Federal Bureau of Investigation and the Central Intelligence Agency were investigating all possible leads, both foreign and domestic, that could lead to more information on bin Laden's intentions.

This PDB is a textbook example of one of the inherent challenges in formulating intelligence-derived policy. With the benefit of hindsight and the indelible footage of hijacked airplanes slamming into the World Trade Center (though none as-yet available of the crashes in Shanksville, Pennsylvania, or at the Pentagon) seared into the world's collective consciousness, the brief's specification of bin Laden's focus on airplanes seems remarkably prescient, even "actionable." On closer inspection, however, the brief is more notable for illustrating what the CIA and other intelligence agencies did not know. First and most important, the reference to hijacking airplanes was a far cry from predicting possibly the greatest surprise of the September 11 attacks: instead of overtaking planes and making political demands while holding hostages, as the brief seemed to suggest, the 9/11 hijackers turned passenger jets into missiles. Further, even if the brief could have known of this diabolical plan, it failed to provide information as to the identity of the terrorists preparing for the mission, their location, and their timetable. In short, what President Bush learned was that someone, somewhere, and at some time was planning an attack on the United States. It was not the first time a sitting president received word of a threat to the homeland. The brief's concluding assurance that it would follow leads about bin Laden's intentions proceeded as if the U.S. intelligence community had ample time, perhaps years, to expose and foil an al Qaeda attack. As the journalist Tim Weiner observed, the chasm between what the CIA needed to learn and the amount of time it had to learn it amounted to a "systemic failure" of the U.S. government and specifically an existential indictment of the CIA: September 11 was "a failure to know the enemy. It was the Pearl Harbor that the CIA had been created to prevent."

SOURCE: Timothy Noah, "Why No More 9/11s?" *Slate,* March 5, 2009, available at http://www.slate.com/id/2213025.

meaning to U.S. foreign policy, as Condoleezza Rice had observed in *Foreign Affairs* the previous May, vanished. The president instructed his National Security Council that bringing the terrorists to justice, and preventing future attacks was to be the central mission of the U.S. government. After a chaotic day flying around the country, President Bush concluded September 11, 2001, with an address from the Oval Office, where he was determined to demonstrate that al Qaeda could not scare the president away from Washington.

Building upon his vengeful reaction in the immediate wake of the attacks, the president laid out the strategic basis that would set the War on Terrorism apart from previous attempts by the United States to deter terrorists, which, he believed, tended to treat them in isolation of the states or territories from which they operated: "The search is underway for those who were behind these evil acts," Bush intoned. "I have directed the full resources of our intelligence and law enforcement communities to find those responsible and to bring them to justice. We will make no distinction between the terrorists who committed these acts and those who harbor them."[6] By erasing this distinction, President Bush set in motion the strategic and

legal mechanism that would allow the War on Terrorism to retaliate against stateless adherents of an ideology through a conventional military response against a state. It was, he believed, the only way to satisfy the twin imperatives of this new war: bring the perpetrators to justice, and do whatever possible to ensure that 9/11 would not be repeated. At this early juncture, an attack on Afghanistan was far from preordained and a long way off before either the departments of Defense or State could grapple with the military and diplomatic ramifications of such a response. Still, Bush had committed to principles on that day that would lead U.S. forces indelibly to Afghanistan, Iraq, and all over the globe.

As the international relations theorist Stephen M. Walt observed, "The terrorist attacks that destroyed the World Trade Center and damaged the Pentagon triggered the most rapid and dramatic change in the history of U.S. foreign policy."[7] It was a sober, academic conclusion reached by Walt after months of mulling over the meaning of the September 11 attacks and the U.S. response. It took only two days after September 11 for Thomas L. Friedman, the foreign affairs columnist for *The New York Times,* to make the same analysis, which he put even more bluntly than Walt. Writing from Israel, a nation which had unceasingly grappled with terrorism since its founding, Friedman asked, "Does my country really understand that this is World War III? And if this attack was the Pearl Harbor of World War III, it means there is a long, long war ahead."[8] Friedman did not need any special access to White House sources to make so bold a prognostication. As confirmed in Walt's analysis months later, the immediate posture assumed by the Bush administration told Friedman all he needed to know. In a matter of days, the United States had put the entire world on notice: when it came to cooperating in the War against Terrorism, as the president announced, "You are either with us or against us." In deciding to use the phrase "World War III" (or, alternatively, World War IV, as some commentators likened the Cold War to World War III), Friedman did not mean to equate the sheer intensity of this new conflict with the conflict that engulfed the world from 1939 to 1945; surely the fight against al Qaeda would come nowhere near the staggering human and material cost of World War II. Yet, in another sense, the Bush administration took steps immediately after September 11 to ensure that, theoretically, the War on Terrorism would be even more global than World War II; at least the latter was bounded by the territories controlled by the combatants, all of whom understood that the war would end at some fixed point with a peace treaty and an occupying force of the victors. It was obvious in the days after September 11 that no such markers would ever (or could ever) delimit the War on Terrorism to a fixed time and place in history.

Plans to Find the Perpetrators

With the nation fearful and confused, and the wreckage still a burning gravesite at Ground Zero and at the Pentagon and in Shanksville, the first order of business was for the Bush administration to confirm the source of the attack. On September 12, George J. Tenet, director of the CIA, presented President Bush with intelligence, which he considered conclusive, linking al Qaeda to the nineteen hijackers. The reportage in Tenet's brief finally brought closure, tragically, to the questions that remained outstanding in the Presidential Daily Brief in August. The CIA's linkage was corroborated by comments made by bin Laden during a taped conversation in mid-November 2001. Marveling at the spectacular damage caused by the planes that hit the Twin Towers, bin Laden exclaimed, "We calculated that the floors that would be hit would be three or four floors. I was the most the most optimistic of them all . . . due to my experience in this field, I was thinking that the fire from the gas in the plane would melt the iron structure of the building and collapse the area where the plane hit and all the floors above it only. That is all that we had hoped for."[9]

Although the United States had maintained since 1998 covert operations in Afghanistan supporting anti-Taliban Afghan groups, such as the Northern Alliance and various tribes in southern Afghanistan, Tenet counseled the president that in light of the previous day's events, the CIA's covert operations would require a significant expansion, at a cost of approximately $1 billion. "Whatever it takes," Bush replied.[10] In meetings over the next two days with the National Security Council and intelligence operatives, President Bush made two important decisions that would define the burgeoning War on Terrorism. First, over the objection of Donald Rumsfeld and his deputy, Paul Wolfowitz, the United States would not include Iraq in its initial round of targets. The thinking shared by the top two Pentagon officials, according to the journalist Bob Woodward, was that that the worldwide outpouring of sympathy for the tragedy of 9/11 and subsequent support of America's mission to dismantle al Qaeda would evaporate once the terrorist organization either fell or fled Afghanistan.[11] The president rejected the idea, siding with Secretary of State Colin Powell, who was convinced that the U.S. response should be singularly focused on the source of the attacks, in Afghanistan. While Rumsfeld's reading of world opinion would not be tested in the immediate aftermath of September 11, the overwhelming international rejection of Washington's decision to invade Iraq in March 2003 certainly vindicated Rumsfeld's concern that the United States was constrained within a small window of opportunity with regard to Iraq—if one ever existed in the first place.

On Monday, September 17, President Bush made two more key decisions. He signed a Presidential Finding that authorized the CIA to go after al Qaeda and its affiliate terrorist networks anywhere in the world, and particularly in Afghanistan. The second was the president's decision to issue an ultimatum to the Taliban to hand over Osama bin Laden and the rest of the al Qaeda leadership that had enjoyed safe haven in Afghanistan. The decision to issue the ultimatum was surely the most momentous made by Bush since September 11. First, his intelligence advisers were certain that the Taliban would balk at the request, thereby compelling the United States to launch an overt military attack in Afghanistan (which would complement ongoing and expanded covert operations). Second, Pakistani President Pervez Musharraf, who had committed to supporting the United States, risked the collapse of his government.[12] Sympathy for, and even cultural identification with, the Taliban ran overwhelmingly high in parts of Pakistan, particularly the lawless tribal areas that bordered the two states and served as a primary conduit for arms and materiel during the Soviet occupation of Afghanistan in the 1980s.[13] Bush's advisers wanted to make sure the president understood the risks involved: should the Musharraf government fall, there was a possibility that Pakistan's nuclear arsenal could fall into the hands of Pakistani extremists, who in turn could arm al Qaeda members fleeing the Americans in Afghanistan.[14] It was a shudder-inducing scenario that could have made September 11 seem minor in comparison. Still, President Bush stuck to his "with us or against us" instincts. He issued the ultimatum three days later.

Congressional Support

For all of the dangers and uncertainties inherent in Bush's ultimatum, at a minimum he could be confident of rock-solid support in the chamber in which he issued it. On September 18, Congress issued a Joint Resolution "To Authorize the Use of the United States Armed Forces against Those Responsible for the Recent Attacks Launched Against the United States." The resolution affirmed the president's constitutional authority to "deter acts of international terrorism against the United States" using "all necessary and appropriate force against those nations, organizations, or persons he determines planned, authorized, committed, or aided the terrorist attacks that occurred on September 11, 2001, or harbored such organizations or persons, in order to prevent any future acts of international terrorism against the United States by such nations, organizations, or persons." Additionally, the resolution affirmed that its authorization for the use of force satisfied the statutory requirements of the War Powers Resolution.[15]

At least for a brief moment in time, the bipartisan rancor that had paralyzed Washington since the Supreme Court ruled in favor of Bush following the disputed 2000 presidential election results had disappeared. The resolution embodied one of the strongest expressions of the

IN THEIR OWN WORDS: *PRESIDENT BUSH ADDRESSES CONGRESS, 2001*

Nine days after the 9/11 attacks, President George W. Bush addressed a joint session of Congress. An excerpt of that speech follows:

On September 11th, enemies of freedom committed an act of war against our country. Americans have known wars, but for the past 136 years, they have been wars on foreign soil, except for one Sunday in 1941. Americans have known the casualties of war, but not at the center of a great city on a peaceful morning. Americans have known surprise attacks, but never before on thousands of civilians. All of this was brought upon us in a single day, and night fell on a different world, a world where freedom itself is under attack.

Americans have many questions tonight. Americans are asking, "Who attacked our country?" The evidence we have gathered all points to a collection of loosely affiliated terrorist organizations known as al Qaeda. They are some of the murderers indicted for bombing American embassies in Tanzania and Kenya and responsible for bombing the U.S.S. *Cole*. Al Qaeda is to terror what the Mafia is to crime. But its goal is not making money, its goal is remaking the world and imposing its radical beliefs on people everywhere. The terrorists practice a fringe form of Islamic extremism that has been rejected by Muslim scholars and the vast majority of Muslim clerics; a fringe movement that perverts the peaceful teachings of Islam. The terrorists' directive commands them to kill Christians and Jews, to kill all Americans and make no distinctions among military and civilians, including women and children. This group and its leader, a person named Osama bin Laden, are linked to many other organizations in different countries, including the Egyptian Islamic Jihad and the Islamic Movement of Uzbekistan. There are thousands of these terrorists in more than 60 countries. They are recruited from their own nations and neighborhoods and brought to camps in places like Afghanistan where they are trained in the tactics of terror. They

are sent back to their homes or sent to hide in countries around the world to plot evil and destruction.

The leadership of Al Qaeda has great influence in Afghanistan and supports the Taliban regime in controlling most of that country. In Afghanistan we see Al Qaeda's vision for the world. Afghanistan's people have been brutalized, many are starving and many have fled. Women are not allowed to attend school. You can be jailed for owning a television. Religion can be practiced only as their leaders dictate. A man can be jailed in Afghanistan if his beard is not long enough.

The United States respects the people of Afghanistan—after all, we are currently its largest source of humanitarian aid—but we condemn the Taliban regime. It is not only repressing its own people, it is threatening people everywhere by sponsoring and sheltering and supplying terrorists. By aiding and abetting murder, the Taliban regime is committing murder.

And tonight the United States of America makes the following demands on the Taliban. Deliver to United States authorities all the leaders of Al Qaeda who hide in your land. Release all foreign nationals, including American citizens you have unjustly imprisoned. Protect foreign journalists, diplomats and aid workers in your country. Close immediately and permanently every terrorist training camp in Afghanistan. And hand over every terrorist and every person in their support structure to appropriate authorities. Give the United States full access to terrorist training camps, so we can make sure they are no longer operating. These demands are not open to negotiation or discussion. The Taliban must act and act immediately. They will hand over the terrorists or they will share in their fate.

SOURCE: http://www.washingtonpost.com/wp-srv/nation/specials/attacked/transcripts/bushaddress_092001.html.

The 9/11 Memorial Wall at the World Trade Center site, completed in 2011, features bronze panels inscribed with the names of those who died in the attacks, and soothing waterfalls and reflecting pools. The memorial is a national tribute to the victims of the worst terrorist attack in U.S. history.

SOURCE: Don Emmert//AFP/Getty Images.

American political system's "rally 'round the flag" effect, a mobilization of public opinion not seen since the Japanese attack on Pearl Harbor. It was as close as Congress, representing the will of the American people, could come to issuing the commander in chief a blank check to wage war for the security of the country.

The following day, the Taliban's ambassador to Pakistan announced that his government rejected the Bush ultimatum: "Our position on this is that if America has proof, we are ready for the trial of Osama bin Laden in light of the evidence."[16] It was a curious response for which more questions than answers remain. Was it possible that the Taliban did not believe the trail of evidence that the CIA had amassed linking al Qaeda to the September 11 attacks? If given the opportunity, were its leaders truly prepared to be swayed by this evidence, and then make good on their pledge to hand over bin Laden? Whatever the true intentions of the Taliban, the Bush administration was in no mood to alter the utterly rigid terms of its ultimatum by acquiescing to the ambassador's request. That same day, September 21, Secretary of Defense Rumsfeld signed a massive deployment order of military units and personnel to Persian Gulf and Indian Ocean military installations.[17] The

opening shots in the War on Terrorism had become a foregone conclusion.

By the end of the month, CIA teams had made their way into Afghanistan, where they were authorized to capture or kill bin Laden in Afghanistan. They had linked up with the Northern Alliance and began identifying strategic bombing targets for the coming U.S. military onslaught. On October 7, Secretary Rumsfeld and General Richard B. Myers, chairman of the Joint Chiefs of Staff, gave the first news conference on Operation Enduring Freedom, the code name for the Pentagon's military operation in Afghanistan. In a great twist of history, the operation depended on the support of Russia, which President Vladimir Putin (in office 2000–2008) had recently pledged to President Bush. Only twelve years earlier, the Soviet army withdrew from Afghanistan following a brutal ten-year occupation against U.S.-supported Afghan and Arab *mujahedeen*.

Afghanistan and the Taliban

Myers, sounding a frequent refrain from Bush administration officials, asserted that the military action was not aimed against the Afghan people but al Qaeda and the Taliban. The General noted that the U.S. military had used a variety of land- and sea-based weapons systems against several strategic Taliban defense installations, for the purpose of securing territory in preparation for ground troops.[18] On October 19, Special Forces landed by helicopter into Northern Afghanistan, and by November, approximately fifty thousand U.S. troops had established nearly complete land and air dominance in Afghanistan.[19] The overriding objective of the war, however, remained elusive: in December, Osama bin Laden and several deputies slipped into the Tora Bora mountains near the Pakistan border.[20] It was the last and best opportunity the United States had to capture bin Laden until 2011.

By mid-December, the United States felt sufficiently confident to declare that the Taliban had been defeated, although remarks by Deputy Secretary of Defense Wolfowitz illustrated the equivocal nature of "victory" in this new kind of war: "We've created conditions now, where, I guess, you could say we have accomplished one major objective, which is the defeat of the Taliban government."[21] The tenor of Wolfowitz's comments illustrated what many in the Bush administration understood since the commencement of paramilitary operations in late September: the dismantling of the enemy's defense structure through a conventional military attack was the easy, and largely peripheral, aspect of the broader mission. After all, the United States was willing to forgo an attack on the Taliban had the latter agreed to hand over bin Laden and his al Qaeda subordinates. In an assessment demonstrating extraordinarily poor judgment (rivaling, perhaps, his constant assertions in late 2002 and 2003 that Iraq would be an easily winnable war), Wolfowitz went on to caution, "The American people have to be prepared for the fact that we may be hunting Taliban and Al Qaeda in Afghanistan months from now."[22]

Reaching a Crossroads

President Bush's visceral reaction to the September 11 attacks, which translated so seamlessly into a conventional military response, had reached a crossroads. Although the might of the U.S. armed forces had been unequivocally demonstrated, this was never really the point, and indeed the satisfaction derived by senior administration officials from the lightning victory over the Taliban proved fleeting. Wolfowitz's prognostication of a months-long occupation in Afghanistan, in partnership with the nascent government led by the Afghan Pashtun Hamid Karzai, was quickly revised upward to a timetable that envisioned the U.S. presence in Afghanistan—so long as bin Laden remained at large and the Taliban waged a tenacious guerilla insurgency—as a multi-year proposition. What next? The question, as Secretary Rumsfeld had ensured, was really never shelved since President Bush had determined to focus on Afghanistan.

Perceived Threat from Iraq

The most concise explanation for the defense secretary's insistence (even obsession, after 9/11) on going after Saddam Hussein in short order came from Douglas Feith,

the under secretary of defense of policy at the time. Feith explained that in the wake of the Taliban's defeat, it was clear to Rumsfeld "that the problem is not dealing with one organization in one place. . . . We were not going to solve this problem by focusing narrowly on the perpetrators of 9/11. Rumsfeld wanted some way to organize the military action so that it signaled that the global conflict would not be over if we struck one good blow in Afghanistan."[23] According to Rumsfeld, it was President Bush who revisited the Iraq issue with Rumsfeld, two weeks before the announcement that the Taliban had fallen.[24]

Saddam's record over the previous three years had certainly not inspired confidence in anyone either in Washington or in the international community regarding both his intentions and capabilities with respect to chemical, biological, and nuclear weapons. Between the end of Operation Desert Storm and 1998, the UN Special Commission on Iraq had made significant progress ensuring that Saddam had either dismantled or abandoned his WMD program, but then in late 1998, the Iraqi leader abruptly kicked out all weapons inspectors, thereby leaving the entire nation uninspected from that time through the events of September 11.[25]

Iraq and Weapons of Mass Destruction

In 1998, the Clinton administration, committed to a policy of regime change in Iraq, retaliated for this intransigence with military strikes and the enforcement of no-fly zones. It was a policy followed, albeit half-heartedly, by the Bush administration through the summer of 2001. However, in the wake of September 11, the specter of al Qaeda acquiring WMDs from Saddam's regime, either directly or indirectly, no matter how remote a possibility—or how flimsy the evidence was upon which to make this connection—had become an intolerable variable in the Bush administration's War on Terrorism.[26] Along with Iran and North Korea, Iraq, according to President Bush, was a member of the "Axis of Evil," a phrase the president deployed with much fanfare during his January 2002 State of the Union address. Bush warned: "By seeking weapons of mass destruction, these regimes pose a grave and growing danger. They could provide these arms to terrorists, giving them the means to match their hatred. They could attack our allies or attempt to blackmail the United States. In any of these cases, the price of indifference would be catastrophic."[27]

Bush's decision to group these regimes under one banner, despite the fact that they made no such "axis" alliance in the traditional sense of that word, seemed to suggest that his administration was grappling with the possibility of confronting each regime militarily. In fact, the vast majority of actual war planning and efforts to prime both the U.S. citizenry and the world for a possible war focused exclusively on Iraq. Secretary Rumsfeld, fixated on the idea of transforming the U.S. military into a leaner and more technologically dependent fighting force for the twenty-first century, considered a possible invasion and occupation of Iraq an ideal battleground on which to test his ideas. From the beginning of the first war plans through the invasion in March 2003, Colin Powell was the sole principal in the Bush administration to push back, unsuccessfully, against Rumsfeld's confidence in a small military footprint.[28] Paradoxically, Rumsfeld's insistence on developing a more streamlined U.S. military did not translate into a decrease or even leveling off of government expenditures; in fact, beginning in January 2002, the Pentagon, correctly reading the country's willingness to fund lavishly military programs in furtherance of the War on Terrorism, sought a funding increase of $20 billion for fiscal year 2003, the first in a series of massive defense expenditure increases at a total price tag at present of well over $1 trillion.[29]

War Plans

By summer 2002, the Bush administration had mobilized to full-on war planning mode. The objectives of regime change in Iraq produced vigorous debates throughout the foreign policy establishment in Washington for the better part of the year, and by August, it was clear that President Bush was prepared to embrace an expansive war plan that sought to do more than a military operation that merely ensure the safeguarding of whatever WMDs Saddam had.

The president had come a long way since his days as a presidential candidate scoffing at nation building: on the one hand, with his decision to take out Saddam Hussein, he had committed to finishing the job his father decided to leave unfinished; on the other, he understood that decapitating the country would require that the United States would effectively run Iraq until some provisional government could be formed. These far-reaching goals were embodied in a Department of Defense document titled "Iraq: Goals, Objectives, and Strategy," sent to Bush for his approval in mid-August. The document started from the ideological premise that an Iraq free from Saddam's iron fist would be a cure-all for the multiple security threats Iraq posed both against the region and globally. In a line of thinking that would become known as Bush's "Freedom Agenda," a democratic Iraq would abandon its pursuit of producing and possibly proliferating WMDs; it would cease its territorial designs on, and hostility against, its neighbors; and it would no longer support terrorists, such as Palestinian suicide bombers. These political goals, the document asserted, could be achieved by a military campaign including an aerial bombardment and then rapid ground occupation of Baghdad originating in Kuwait.[30] The basic aim was to prevent Saddam from establishing a "Fortress Baghdad" from which he could launch a protracted urban guerilla war; with an eye toward Mogadishu in 1993, this was precisely the kind of situation the Bush administration wanted to avoid.[31]

Faulty Intelligence

Among the most enduring myths propagated by detractors of President Bush's Iraq policy is that his administration, once it had created a plan of attack to the president's satisfaction, had set itself on an unwavering path to war against Saddam Hussein. While it is true that Rumsfeld's appetite to go after Iraq before all the facts had come in regarding al Qaeda's responsibility for September 11 does raise serious questions about the defense secretary's judgment in a time of crisis, the fact remains that the Bush administration would have preferred a diplomatic resolution to the impasse. However, from fall 2002 to the invasion the following March, three complicated narratives intersected that left the Bush administration to determine that all options short of war had been exhausted. Together, they created a perfect storm of incompetence, misunderstanding, and braggadocio, culminating in the U.S. military's assault on Baghdad. The first and most important narrative is the overarching framework the president and his advisers had constructed since the first days of the War on Terrorism. The prospect of terrorists acquiring WMDs was a "redline" issue (a common term bandied about by government officials at the time) that had to be deterred by any means necessary. The second narrative were two threads of epically flawed intelligence reporting that asserted (1) a connection between Saddam Hussein and al Qaeda going back to the 1990s, and (2) an active and robust WMD program commenced by the Iraqi military shortly after Saddam kicked out the UN weapons inspectors in 1998. The third narrative was Saddam Hussein's dogged insistence (seemingly, even cooperation) *not* to dispel the basic untruths inherent in the first two narratives.

UN Involvement

President Bush's speech on September 12, 2002, before the UN General Assembly laid out his assumptions and priorities for dealing with the Iraqi menace. Although Cheney and Rumsfeld, in particular, had acquired a habit of contemptuousness with regard to building an international alliance against Saddam, the objective of Bush's speech was to remind the international community as a whole that it must live up to its obligation to enforce sanctions against Iraq. The president insisted that the world must believe that Saddam was actively pursuing a chemical, biological, and nuclear weapons capability, that his support for international terrorism continued unabated, and that his ongoing military provocations and brutal treatment of Iraqi citizens were in breach of a number of UN resolutions. Bush's concluding sentences left the unmistakable message that if the United Nations failed to enforce its own resolutions, the United States would: "We cannot stand by and do nothing while dangers gather. We must stand up for our security and for the permanent rights and the hopes of mankind. By heritage and by choice, the United States of America will make that stand. And, delegates to the United Nations, you have the power to make that stand, as well."[32]

Bush's reference to Iraqi transgressions unrelated to WMDs was an early attempt by the administration to make the broadest possible case for regime change in Iraq; one remarkable study found that the Bush administration, between 2002 to the start of the war, made twenty-seven discrete rationales for taking out Saddam.[33] This effort, which speaks to the Bush administration's keen desire to mobilize public support for regime change in Iraq from as many angles as possible, need not obscure the primacy of the one overriding concern about WMDs, the absence of which almost certainly would have dissuaded the United States from attacking Iraq.

To say that the Bush administration's case for war against Saddam Hussein was built upon a lie is to run the risk of conflating the basic veracity of the statement with the notion that a program of willful deception existed, and led directly to the president. Based on the available primary source documentation, paltry as it is, such conflation has no basis in fact. A more accurate description of the events over the course of late 2002 and early 2003 is that the Bush administration, intent not to cross the "redline" that it had established in its efforts to prevent another attack of a magnitude equal or even greater than September 11, determined that Saddam Hussein not only possessed WMDs but also could not be trusted with them. On its face, the logic of the assessment was self-fulfilling: if Saddam had nothing to hide, and in particular if he knew that his survival depended on it, why not open the doors back up to weapons inspectors, who could resume the work they had left in 1998?[34] However, logic would not be enough to make the case for war.

UN Resolution 1441

Following President Bush's speech before the General Assembly, the United Nations Security Council passed, by a unanimous vote of 15 to 0, Resolution 1441, which gave Saddam Hussein one last chance to comply with the numerous resolutions relating to WMD violations and other weapons systems. Although the unanimous vote signaled broad international disapproval of Saddam's record of deception and evasion, it did not amount to a consensus authorizing war should Iraq fail to comply with the mandates of the resolution. As the journalist Fred Kaplan observed on the eve of the war, Resolution 1441 was fatally flawed because it lacked even the pretense of establishing timetables or priorities for the Iraqis to meet.[35] Therefore, even though Saddam did reopen Iraq to UN weapons inspectors in December 2002, the fuzziness of the resolution's mandates essentially ensured that, no matter his level of compliance, the Iraqi dictator could still be considered in material breach of the resolution. More substantively, Hans Blix, the chief

UN weapons inspector, reported in February 2003 that despite laudable cooperation in a number of areas of weapons compliance, on the whole, inspectors, over the previous four months, had failed to ascertain the state of Saddam's WMD program. Blix concluded that Iraq's overall program to disarm as "very limited."[36]

Saddam's intransigence at the eleventh hour only reinforced the intelligence assessments that CIA Director George Tenet infamously characterized as a "slam dunk." A top secret National Intelligence Estimate (NIE), published in October 2002, included this finding: "Baghdad has mobile facilities for producing bacterial and toxin BW [biological warfare] agents; these facilities can evade detection and are highly survivable. Within three to six months these units probably could produce an amount of agent equal to the total that Iraq produced in the years prior to the Gulf War."[37]

On February 5, President Bush dispatched Secretary of State Colin Powell to the United Nations to bring this information to the international stage. The decision to have Powell make the case was no accident: the president understood and appreciated Powell's reputation as a voice of moderation in his administration; his public persona as a soldier of unimpeachable credibility would underscore the seriousness and legitimacy of the charges he would bring to bear against Saddam—this despite Powell's own strong reservations about some of the allegations in his prepared remarks.[38] Still, Powell affirmed the following charges against the Iraqi dictator: Saddam remained in material breach of UN Resolution 1441; U.S. intelligence had incontrovertible evidence, based on multiple and independent sources, of active chemical and biological weapons facilities in Iraq, complete with diagrams and audio recordings; and, perhaps most menacingly, Saddam harbored al Qaeda members, including the notorious Abu Musab Al-Zarqawi. Toward the end of his remarks, Powell explained why Iraq had become what administration officials increasingly called the "central front" in the War on Terrorism: "The United States will not and cannot run that risk to the American people. Leaving Saddam Hussein in possession of weapons of mass destruction for a few more months or years is not an option, not in a post-September 11th world."[39] Although Powell cautioned that failure of the UN to mobilize against Iraq would threaten to turn the UN into an "irrelevant" institution, the United States failed to gain Security Council authorization to use military force against Saddam. Ironically, a presidential administration so often accused of being disdainful of multilateral institutions ultimately went to war in the name of enforcing the UN's demand that Iraq disarm and abandon its WMD program.

Part of the reason the Bush administration failed to gain a broader coalition in its campaign against Saddam, beyond its partnership of the "willing," consisting of the United Kingdom and a number of other countries providing small support roles, was that the evidence that Colin

Powell brought to bear in the UN was based on a lie. The source of nearly all of his testimony was derived from an Iraqi informant, Rafid Ahmed Alwan al-Janabi, codenamed "Curveball," who had fabricated a story in which he claimed to German intelligence officials that he had firsthand knowledge of a biological weapons factory. Although "Curveball" admitted his lies during a 2011 interview on the news program *60 Minutes*, grave doubts about his credibility also were raised by German officials and UN weapons inspectors before Powell's speech at the UN.[40]

The staggering and broad intelligence failure culminating in Powell's speech and, shortly thereafter, President Bush's consequent decision to issue a direct ultimatum that Saddam Hussein must abdicate power or face forcible removal by the U.S. military will be a topic debated by historians for decades to come; indeed it will require the passage of decades' time before a sufficient amount of government documentation is declassified that will allow something approximating a fulsome picture of events as they really occurred. What we do know now is that Saddam remained defiant to the end, and it was only as a result of Operation Iraqi Freedom that U.S. troops and support personnel were afforded the level of unrestricted access to lay bare the two great falsehoods upon which the Bush administration made its case against Saddam: first that he had an active WMD program (he did not); second, that he maintained close links with al Qaeda (he did not). On the former point, the seemingly invincible logic of Saddam's refusal to cooperate fully with UN weapons inspectors (ergo, he must have had an active weapons program) falls flat when one considers that Iraq's foreign policy did not begin and end with a view toward Washington.

In a series of documents released by the FBI in 2009, based on interrogations of Saddam Hussein after his capture by U.S. forces, the former Iraqi leader admitted that, until the last moment, he wanted Iran to believe that he had weapons of mass destruction.[41] Apparently, he did not believe until it was too late that the United States would actually invade; he envisioned ruling Iraq long after 2003, during which he determined that Iraq would need to maintain its deterrent threat against Iran, Iraq's mortal enemy. What more credible deterrent is there, Saddam must have thought, than the ability to signal to the world that the UN and the United States are gravely worried about Iraq's weapons programs, even if it was all based on lies? The second, and equally damning, confirmation of Washington's flawed intelligence came in June 2004, when the September 11th Commission, an independent, non-partisan commission tasked by Congress and the Bush administration in 2002 to create a full accounting of the events surrounding September 11, concluded it had found no evidence of any collaborative relationship of any kind between Saddam Hussein's regime and al Qaeda.[42]

Al Qaeda in Iraq

Ironically, al Qaeda would come to play a prominent role in Iraq, in the wake of the power vacuum created by Saddam's ouster. Documents recovered amid the ruins of the compound of Abu Musab al-Zarqawi, the head of al Qaeda in Iraq, who was killed by a five hundred–pound bomb dropped by U.S. forces in 2006, suggested that al Qaeda leaders saw America's ongoing occupation of Iraq as vital to the ongoing growth and outward reach of al Qaeda throughout the Middle East.[43] Indeed, it was al Qaeda fighters who helped ensure that U.S. forces would face a far more daunting task than what Secretary Rumsfeld (and, for that matter, most government officials involved in war planning) had envisioned in the run-up to the war. One of the reasons the systemic intelligence failures that led the U.S. military to Baghdad have been so emotionally charged is that the chaos and ensuing insurgency that engulfed Iraq for the following four years left a human toll so vast that it caused many people, in Iraq, in the United States, and around the world, to question if leaving Saddam in power, vile as he was, actually would have been preferable. Unlike the actual state of Iraq's WMD program, and, therefore, the truly marginal space Saddam should have occupied on Washington's threat horizon of the War on Terrorism, it is a question that cannot be answered. Still, even with a view to these glaring missteps in U.S. intelligence analysis and policymaking, it is difficult, if not morally obtuse, not to acknowledge that the world is better off without Saddam Hussein, arguably the greatest violator of international norms of the past fifty years.[44]

Challenges for the Future

More than ten years after the September 11 attacks, and with a stable military situation in Iraq and a tenuous, hard-fought progress continuing apace in Afghanistan, it is becoming possible to view these conflicts with some measure of historical detachment. Yet one aspect of the Global War on Terrorism, inextricably linked to these wars as they are, remains inconclusive, seemingly forever stuck in the present.

The United States has yet to confront fully the vexing issue of what to do with "enemy combatants," that legally hazy term the U.S. government affixes to fighters engaged against U.S. troops in the War on Terrorism. The issue can be subdivided into how combatants are treated while in custody, and how they can be tried in a court of law. The fact that prisoner treatment remains stuck in a web of legal, cultural, and moral debates speaks to what President Bush immediately believed in wake of the September 11 attacks: that this was the start of a new kind of war. At the present, the United States still lacks the institutions to grapple with the fundamental issues of extending some form of *habeas corpus,* as well as according both basic human decency and internationally recognized legal

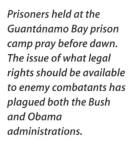

Prisoners held at the Guantánamo Bay prison camp pray before dawn. The issue of what legal rights should be available to enemy combatants has plagued both the Bush and Obama administrations.

SOURCE: AP Photo/Brennan Linsley.

norms for all persons detained under U.S. custody. Now, more than ten years removed from September 11, we remain as unprepared to deal with these issues as the day the "War on Terrorism" began.

Prisoner Abuse

The revelations of horrific treatment suffered by Iraqi prisoners at the hands of U.S. officials at Abu Ghraib prison came to light in April 2004 in a *60 Minutes* expose.[45] Allegations of beatings, ritual humiliations, rapes, and even a homicide were corroborated in reporting conducted by the journalist Seymour Hersh, writing for the *The New Yorker* a month later.[46] These revelations led to other reports of similar abuses taking place at the Guantanamo prison camp in Cuba, and at numerous CIA "black prisons" around the world. Despite the military's swift meting out of justice to a number of personnel found responsible for perpetrating such acts, the horrors of what happened at Abu Ghraib and elsewhere could not be understood just as the actions of low-level soldiers in a highly stressful wartime environment. As a bipartisan Senate report concluded in December 2008, "The abuse of detainees in U.S. custody cannot simply be attributed to the actions of 'a few bad apples' acting on their own. The fact is that senior officials in the United States government solicited information on how to use aggressive techniques, redefined the law to create the appearance of their legality, and authorized their use against detainees. Those efforts damaged our ability to collect accurate intelligence that could save lives, strengthened the hand of our enemies, and compromised our moral authority."[47] Well

before 2008, thanks to the dogged analysis and reporting of journalists such as Mark Danner and Andrew Sullivan, we now know that the abuses at Abu Ghraib can be linked directly to decisions that came from the White House.[48]

Torture or Enhanced Interrogation Techniques

Because the Bush administration explicitly determined that enemy combatants were not to be afforded protections to prisoners of war as specified in the Geneva Convention of 1949, the immediate effect was the beginning of a legal gray zone leading ineluctably to prisoner abuse.[49] The administration's rationale was that, in the War on Terrorism, captured enemy combatants who did not fight for a state, as did prisoners of war in the traditional sense, could be in possession of information that might help thwart a terrorist attack. As battle-hardened zealots, so the thinking went, these combatants might only be compelled to give up such information under extreme duress. While the Bush administration did not want to commit torture overtly, it settled on a policy known as "enhanced interrogation techniques," a remarkably expansive menu of pain-inducing techniques that could be inflicted upon enemy combatants. The options included simulated drowning, known as "waterboarding," stress positions, beatings, subjecting inmates to extreme heat or cold, or endless loud music. In short, the administration determined that any kind of infliction that did not leave lasting physical damage to the prisoner was considered within the bounds of the law. The Bush administration steadfastly held to the position that such measures did not constitute torture.[50]

Wherever the line is separating these techniques from torture, assuming such a line exists in the first place, perhaps more troubling is the fact that no one can say for sure whether enhanced interrogation actually produced the kind of actionable intelligence for which it was designed and tolerated: namely, the ability of the United States to thwart future terrorist attacks. According to a report released by the CIA's inspector general in 2009, the CIA never conducted a systematic review to determine the efficacy of the program.[51] What this means is that almost certainly no "ticking bomb" scenario ever materialized in the history of the interrogation program. This scenario, popularized in our collective imagination by TV shows such as *24*, which often included scenes of a detainee in possession of time-sensitive knowledge of an impending attack (but only divulges the necessary information under extreme physical coercion), has thus far remained solely in the realm of fiction.

THE OBAMA ADMINISTRATION TAKES CONTROL

The Obama administration (2009–) has attempted to cordon off prisoner abuse as an unfortunate and immoral distraction in America's ongoing attempt to protect itself from future terror attacks. Yet this process has proved incomplete at best. On the one hand, President Obama moved swiftly to end prisoner abuse; as president-elect, he directed U.S. intelligence agencies to abide by the Geneva Conventions, while his nominee to lead the Department of Justice, Eric Holder, testified during his confirmation hearings that he considered waterboarding to be torture.[52]

On the other hand, Obama has thus far failed to make good on his campaign pledge to close Guantanamo prison, and has so far declined to seek prosecutions against any of the architects of the enhanced interrogation program, even though his interpretation of the Geneva Conventions would suggest that those architects acted illegally.[53] Whether or not the United States will be prepared at some point in the future for some kind of moral or legal reckoning to confront fully the prisoner abuse issue remains to be seen.

Ongoing Challenges

One ongoing challenge for President Obama regards the question of redressing a past problem for which there is no current solution: what to do with those "enemy combatants" currently in U.S. custody for whom there is either no country to which they can be extradited, or those for whom there is an insufficient amount of evidence to prosecute yet have been determined to be too dangerous to release? Although President Obama abandoned the term "enemy combatant," the legal question marks inherent in the name remain.[54]

Initially, in January 2010, the Obama administration, pledging its confidence in the American legal system, announced its intention to try even the most notorious incarcerated terrorists, such as Khalid Sheikh Mohammed, in criminal courts. The administration encountered a tremendous amount of popular and political pushback against this idea, and, ultimately, the president backed off. Yet the legal conundrum remains: the landmark 2006 Supreme Court ruling in *Hamdan v. Rumsfeld* found that the military trial commission system, which had been used to try enemy combatants in military courts since November 2001, was invalid, because the "military commission at issue lacks the power to proceed because its structure and procedures violate both the UCMJ and the four Geneva Conventions signed in 1949."[55] Therefore, at the present time and for the foreseeable future, the Obama administration (and the prisoners, for that matter) is stuck between the political and moral impetus to close Guantanamo while lacking a domestic jurisdiction in which to try them. Whatever the solution to this legal morass, the answer is certainly not a continuation of the status quo, which would have prisoners die of old age while in U.S. custody without ever having had a criminal charge leveled against them. It is an issue that cuts to the core of the country's founding principles.

Legacy of the War on Terrorism

What of the legacy of the Global War on Terrorism, in the militant terms that President Bush first conceived of it in the hours after the attacks of September 11? Semantically, the Global War on Terrorism ended with the second term of the Bush administration. Like the term "enemy combatant" the Pentagon announced in March 2009 that it was phasing out the Global War on Terrorism, in favor of the more anodyne "Overseas Contingency Operation," which, for obvious reasons, has failed to catch on.[56] Whatever name we attach to the struggle between the United States and its allies against Islamist extremists matters much less then the durability of the policies set in place by the Bush administration, which will ensure that this struggle will know no end for the projected future.

The policies the Obama administration has taken with regard to Iraq and Afghanistan support this proposition. First, with regard to Iraq, Barack Obama had stated publicly his opposition to the war in Iraq, first as a state senator in Illinois in 2002, a stance he carried with him to the White House.[57] Obama's decision to draw down troops from Iraq as quickly and as responsibly as possible reflected his longstanding belief that the Iraq War was from the beginning an unnecessary and dangerous distraction from the core mission of the War on Terrorism: to ensure no repeats of September 11. The post-invasion revelations that Saddam neither had WMDs nor collaborated with al Qaeda

PUBLIC PORTRAIT: *RICHARD C. HOLBROOKE (1941–2010)*

Only a week after winning the presidential election, Barack Obama asked Richard Holbrooke to meet with him in Chicago. The president-elect had decided that Holbrooke should assume leadership over U.S. relations with Afghanistan and Pakistan at the Department of State. With one of the most celebrated diplomatic careers in modern times, and a pointed critic of the Bush administration's Afghanistan policy, Obama felt that Holbrooke was the best person to guide U.S. foreign policy in what was arguably the most intractably dangerous area in the world. Holbrooke agreed to the offer and became "special representative for Afghanistan and Pakistan," a title that recognized that the ongoing threat of al Qaeda in the border region meant that U.S. policy needed to deal with the two countries as two parts of the same problem. As expected, Holbrooke threw himself into the task with full force: he assembled a core team of area experts and experienced diplomats and made frequent trips to the region to ensure that Pakistan was keeping pressure on militants in the tribal areas while searching for ways, in concert with

military commanders in Afghanistan, that the United States could eventually exit the country without it becoming the dreaded "safe haven" for terrorists as it had been before September 11. Holbrooke's experience as a Foreign Service officer in South Vietnam in the early 1960s was never far from his mind; he knew instinctively that the political corruption and warring factions that had doomed U.S. efforts in Vietnam could do the same in Afghanistan. On the other hand, Holbrooke presided over the Dayton Accords in 1995, which marked an end to the war in Bosnia. It was easily the greatest diplomatic achievement of the Clinton presidency, and it is likely that Holbrooke, well aware of his enormous talents, often thought that somehow he could put together some grand peace arrangement that could finally bring stability to the region, despite the grim realities on the ground. He died unexpectedly in December 2010, far too soon to see any potential fruits of his work. Friends and colleagues around Washington, D.C., assumed the Herculean effort he put into his job was ultimately too much stress to bear.

demonstrated unequivocally this fact. Thus, Obama's decision to expedite the drawdown of troops from Iraq, while shifting some of those resources to Afghanistan, should be understood as a validation, not repudiation, of the original terms of the War on Terrorism as President Bush defined them. As planned, the drawdown in Iraq allowed Obama to focus on the region that had remained, since September 11, the true central front on the War on Terrorism. For the new presidential administration, this framework required an intensified military and diplomatic focus on Afghanistan and Pakistan.

One monumental event that Richard Holbrooke would not live to witness was the killing of Osama bin Laden at the hands of Navy Seals Special Team Six. After months of painstaking intelligence collection, on May 1, 2011, the CIA located and shot the al Qaeda leader—not in the tribal border area between Afghanistan and Pakistan, but in the upscale Pakistani town of Abbotabad, some sixty miles outside of Islamabad. The United States did not inform Pakistan of its attack plan, an omission that illustrates the ongoing suspicion in Washington of Pakistan's true loyalties.[58] Although the news of bin Laden's death prompted spontaneous celebrations outside the White House, President Obama emphasized in his announcement that evening that bin Laden's "death does not mark the end of our effort. There's no doubt that al Qaeda will continue to pursue attacks against us. We must—and we will—remain vigilant at home and abroad."[59]

True to form, al Qaeda's number-two commander, Ayman al-Zawahiri, vowed a month later that al Qaeda

would avenge bin Laden's death. "We will pursue the jihad until we expel the invaders from Muslim lands," Zawahiri pledged, thus making clear that the source of al Qaeda's hatred for the United States remained what it had always been.[60] At the time of writing, it is too soon to assess what impact bin Laden's death will have in the ongoing battle between the United States, its allies, and Islamist terrorists. There is little reason to doubt the sincerity of Zawahiri's vow, although President Obama's relentless pursuit of al Qaeda in Pakistan, Afghanistan, Yemen, and beyond does raise questions about Zawahiri's capacity to avenge bin Laden's death. And yet, to return to one of the introductory premises of this essay, the self-perpetuating logic of the War on Terrorism holds there need not be any particular linkages between al Qaeda's strength and the possibility of a major terrorist attack against the United States at some point in the future. Why this has not happened yet may or may not speak directly to the fact that al Qaeda is a shell of its former self.[61] However, in the awful event that a terrorist group does manage to pull off a catastrophic attack at some point in the future, it is likely that the details that emerge on the origins and execution of that attack will be as surprising to us as the day nineteen hijackers seized control of commercial airliners and flew them into buildings.

See also: **Chapter 39: U.S. Foreign Policy Goals of the Twenty-first Century; Chapter 40: Diplomatic Milestones, 2001–Present.**

ENDNOTES

1. A full transcript of the second presidential debate between Al Gore and George W. Bush of October 11, 2000, is reproduced at http://www.debates.org/index.php?page=october-11-2000-debate-transcript.

2. See, for example, Condoleezza Rice, "Campaign 2000: Building the National Interest," in *Foreign Affairs,* v. 79 (January/February 2000), 47, available at http://www.foreignaffairs.com/articles/55630/condoleezza-rice/campaign-2000-promoting-the-national-interest.

3. George W. Bush, *Decision Points* (New York: Crown Publishers, 2010), 126.

4. In his memoirs, President Bush neglected to mention that the entire government, except for the Federal Aviation Administration, was unaware that American Airlines Flight 11 had been hijacked until after it crashed into the World Trade Center at 8:46 a.m. See *The 9/11 Commission Report* (2004), available at: http://govinfo.library.unt.edu/911/report/index.htm (information on what the government knew about AA Flight 11 appears on p. 35).

5. Bush, *Decision Points,* 128.

6. President Bush's address to the nation from the Oval Office on the evening of September 11, 2001, is reproduced in full at http://www.americanrhetoric.com/speeches/gwbush911addresstothenation.htm.

7. Stephen M. Walt, "Beyond bin Laden: Reshaping U.S. Foreign Policy," in *International Security* 26 (Winter 2001/2002): 56.

8. Thomas L. Friedman, "World War III," in *The New York Times,* September 13, 2001, available at http://www.nytimes.com/2001/09/13/opinion/foreign-affairs-world-war-iii.html?src=pm.

9. "Transcript of Usama bin Laden Video Tape," December 13, 2001, accessed at DNSA, http://nsarchive.chadwyck.com/cat/displayItemIdImages.do?queryType=&&ItemID=CTE01435.

10. Bob Woodward, *Bush at War* (New York: Simon & Schuster, 2002), 41.

11. Ibid, 48–49.

12. Musharraf asserts in his memoirs that Pakistan came under extreme pressure to switch its alliance from the Taliban to Washington. Allegedly, Richard Armitage, the deputy secretary of state, threatened the chief of Pakistan's Intelligence Service that if Islamabad sided with the Taliban, Pakistan should be prepared "to be bombed back to the Stone Age." See "Musharraf's Book Says Pakistan Faced U.S. 'Onslaught' If It Didn't Back Terror War," in *USA Today,* September 26, 2006.

13. A poll on Pakistani public opinion, conducted on September 19, found that only 7 percent of respondents favored Washington over the Taliban, with 67 percent siding with the Taliban, while the remaining group registered a neutral opinion. Figures cited in Barry Bearak, "In Pakistan, a Shaky Ally," in *The New York Times,* October 2, 2001, A1.

14. Bin Laden met with two Pakistani nuclear scientists in August 2001 in a purported attempt to acquire nuclear weapons. The meeting is detailed in Douglas Frantz and Catherine Collins, *The Nuclear Jihadist: The True Story of the Man Who Sold the World's Most Dangerous Secrets . . . and How We Could Have Stopped Him* (New York: Hachette, 2007), 263.

15. United States, 107th Congress, Public Law 40, "To Authorize the Use of the United States Armed Forces against Those Responsible for the Recent Attacks Launched against the United States," September 18, 2001, accessed at: http://www.gpo.gov/fdsys/pkg/PLAW-107publ40/html/PLAW-107publ40.htm.

16. "Taliban Defy Bush Ultimatum," in *The Guardian,* September 21, 2001, accessed at: http://www.guardian.co.uk/world/2001/sep/21/september11.usa15.

17. David E. Sanger and Eric Schmitt, "Focus on bin Laden: Officials Say Course of War on Terrorism Is Still to Be Decided," in *The New York Times,* September 22, 2001, A1.

18. "News Transcript: Rumsfeld and Myers News Briefing on Enduring Freedom," October 7, 2001, accessed at DNSA: http://nsarchive.chadwyck.com/cat/displayItemIdImages.do?queryType=&&ItemID=CTE01330.

19. The best operational history on the early days of the war is United States Army, Center of Military History, *American Military History, v. II: The United States Army in a Global Era* (Washington, DC: U.S. Government Printing Office, 2005). Chapter 14, "The Global War on Terrorism," available at: http://www.history.army.mil/books/AMH-V2/AMH%20V2/chapter14.htm.

20. Former CIA operatives have alleged that with the proper resources directed at the Tora Bora cave complex, bin Laden could have been captured in December 2001. See especially, Gary Berntsen and Ralph Pezzullo, *Jawbreaker: The Attack on Bin Laden and Al Qaeda: A Personal Account by the CIA's Key Field Commander* (New York: Broadway, 2006). Tommy Franks, the commanding general at the time, subsequently denied that bin Laden was at any time within the grasp of U.S. forces. See "Document Suggests bin Laden Escaped at Tora Bora," at CNN, March 24, 2005, available at: http://articles.cnn.com/2005-03-24/us/pentagon.binladen_1_tora-bora-bin-john-stufflebeem?_s=PM:US.

21. U.S. Department of Defense, "DoD News Briefing—Deputy Secretary Wolfowitz and Rear Admiral Stufflebeem," December 10, 2001, available at: http://www.defense.gov/transcripts/transcript.aspx?transcriptid=2628.

22. Ibid.

23. Michael R. Gordon and Bernard E. Trainor, *Cobra II: The Inside Story of the Invasion and Occupation of Iraq* (New York: Vintage Books, 2007), 11.

24. Rumsfeld, *Known and Unknown: A Memoir* (New York: Penguin, 2011), 427.

25. A useful primer on Saddam's non-cooperation on WMD inspections is Kenneth Katzman and Alfred B. Prados, "Iraq-US Confrontation," Library of Congress, Congressional Research Service, November 20, 21, accessed at DNSA: http://nsarchive.chadwyck.com/cat/displayItemIdImages.do?queryType=cat&&ItemID=CTE01411.

26. The rationale of zero tolerance of a threat from potential suppliers of WMDs, Saddam or rogue elements in Pakistani, developed in November 2001 and largely attributed to Vice President Dick Cheney, became known among administration officials as the "One Percent Doctrine." See Ron Susskind, *The One Percent Doctrine: Deep Inside America's Pursuit of Its Enemies since 9/11* (New York: Simon & Schuster, 2006).

27. President Bush's 2002 State of the Union Address is reproduced in full at http://edition.cnn.com/2002/ALLPOLITICS/01/29/bush.speech.txt.

28. Among the best narratives describing the massive bureaucratic and ideological battles between Rumsfeld and Powell, and the respective departments they led, is Karen DeYoung, *Soldier: The Life of Colin Powell* (New York: Vintage Books, 2007), especially 446–66.

29. A useful breakdown of congressionally approved funding for the War on Terrorism is Amy Belasco, "The Cost of Iraq, Afghanistan, and Other Global War on Terror Operations since 9/11," Congressional Research Service, March 29, 2011, available at: http://www.fas.org/sgp/crs/natsec/RL33110.pdf.

30. The document is detailed in Gordon and Trainor, *Cobra II,* 83–85.

31. The standard account for the Mogadishu battle is Mark Bowden, *Black Hawk Down: A Story of Modern War* (New York: Grove Press, 2010).

32. President Bush's speech before the United Nations on September 12, 2002, reproduced in full at http://news.bbc.co.uk/2/hi/middle_east/2254712.stm.

33. See Devon Largio, "Uncovering the Rationales for the War on Iraq: The Words of the Bush Administration, Congress and the Media from September 12, 2001, to October 11, 2002," Senior Honors Thesis, University of Illinois, summarized at http://news.illinois.edu/news/04/0510war.html.

34. President Bush poses the same question in his memoirs. He does not hazard an answer. *Decision Points*, 242.

35. Fred Kaplan, "Resolution Dissolution: How the U.S. and France Botched UN Resolution 1441," in *Slate*, March 6, 2003, available at: http://www.slate.com/id/2079746.

36. Blix, quoted in "Blix: Iraq Cooperation Has Been 'Very Limited,'" at CNN, February 28, 2003, available at http://articles.cnn.com/2003-02-28/world/sprj.irq.main_1_weapons-declaration-iraqi-cooperation-weapons-inspector?_s=PM:WORLD.

37. United States, Central Intelligence Agency, National Intelligence Estimate 2002–16HC, "Iraq's Continuing Programs for Weapons of Mass Destruction," October 2002, accessed at DNSA: http://nsarchive.chadwyck.com/cat/displayItemIdImages.do?queryType=&&ItemID=CWM00583.

38. See, for example, DeYoung, *Soldier*, 492–95.

39. Secretary of State Colin Powell's speech at the UN is reproduced in full at *The Washington Post*, February 5, 2003, at http://www.washingtonpost.com/wp-srv/nation/transcripts/powelltext_020503.html.

40. See, for example, Dafna Linzer, "Panel: U.S. Ignored Work of UN Arms Inspectors," in *The Washington Post*, April 3, 2005, at http://www.washingtonpost.com/ac2/wp-dyn/A21854–2005Apr2?language=printer. The "Curveball" interview is available at "Curveball Speaks Out," CBS News/60 Minutes, at http://www.cbsnews.com/video/watch/?id=7359532n.

41. See: *Saddam Hussein Talks to the FBI: Twenty Interviews and Five Conversations with "High Value Detainee #1,"* National Security Archive Electronic Briefing Book No. 279 (July 2009), at http://www.gwu.edu/~nsarchiv/NSAEBB/NSAEBB279/index.htm. See also Kevin Woods, James Lacey, and Williamson Murray, "Saddam's Delusions: The View from the Inside," in *Foreign Affairs* 85 (May/June 2006), available at: http://www.foreignaffairs.com/articles/61701/kevin-woods-james-lacey-and-williamson-murray/saddams-delusions-the-view-from-the-inside.

42. Walter Pincus and Dana Milbank, "Al-Qaeda-Hussein Link Is Dismissed," in *The Washington Post*, June 17, 2004.

43. Dan Murphy, "How Al Qaeda Views a Long War," in *Christian Science Monitor*, October 6, 2006, available at: http://www.csmonitor.com/2006/1006/p01s04-woiq.html.

44. This line of reasoning is perhaps most elegantly made by Christopher Hitchens, "How Did I Get Iraq Wrong? I Didn't," in *Slate*, March 17, 2008, available at: http://www.slate.com/id/2186740.

45. Rebecca Leung, "Abuse of Iraqi POWs by GIs Probed," at CBS News/60 Minutes, February 11, 2009, available at: http://www.cbsnews.com/stories/2004/04/27/60II/main614063.shtml.

46. Seymour M. Hersh, "Torture at Abu Ghraib: American Soldiers Brutalized Iraqis. How Far up Does Responsibility Go?" in *The New Yorker*, May 10, 2004, available at: http://www.newyorker.com/archive/2004/05/10/040510fa_fact.

47. United States, Congress, "Senate Armed Services Committee Inquiry into the Treatment of Detainees in U.S. Custody," December 2008, reproduced at http://media.washingtonpost.com/wp-srv/nation/pdf/12112008_detaineeabuse.pdf (the quote appears on p. xii).

48. See especially Andrew Sullivan's "Atrocities in Plain Sight" (a review of Mark Danner, *Torture and Truth: America, Abu Ghraib, and the War on Terror*), in *The New York Times*, January 13, 2005, available at: http://www.nytimes.com/2005/01/13/books/review/books-sullivan.html; see also Andrew Sullivan's own analysis, "The Architect of Abu Ghraib," in *The Atlantic*, December 15, 2008, available at http://www.theatlantic.com/daily-dish/archive/2008/12/the-architect-of-abu-ghraib/207485.

49. The White House memorandum of February 7, 2002, exempting enemy combatants in the War on Terrorism from the Geneva Convention, is reproduced at http://media.washingtonpost.com/wp-srv/nation/pdf/12112008_detaineeabuse.pdf.

50. See, for example, "Bush: 'We Do Not Torture' Terror Suspects," at MSNBC, November 7, 2005, available at: http://www.msnbc.msn.com/id/9956644/ns/us_news-security/t/bush-we-do-not-torture-terror-suspects.

51. "Interrogation Techniques' Efficacy Wasn't Scrutinized," in *Chicago Tribune*, April 26, 2009, available at: http://articles.chicago-tribune.com/2009-04-26/news/0904250147_1_justice-department-and-cia-director-porter-goss-interrogation.

52. See "Obama names intel picks, vows no torture," at MSNBC, January 9, 2009, available at: http://www.msnbc.msn.com/id/28574408/ns/politics-white_house/ and David Stout; "Holder Tells Senators Waterboarding Is Torture," in *The New York Times*, January 15, 2009, at http://www.nytimes.com/2009/01/16/us/politics/16holdercnd.html.

53. See, for example, Saul Loeb, "Obama's Growing Dilemma on Torture Prosecution," in *Time*, April 22, 2009, available at: http://www.time.com/time/politics/article/0,8599,1893023,00.html.

54. Randall Mikkelsen, "Guantanamo Inmates No Longer 'Enemy Combatants,'" at Reuters, March 14, 2009, available at: http://www.reuters.com/article/2009/03/14/us-obama-security-combatant-idUSTRE52C59220090314.

55. United States, Supreme Court, "Hamdan v. Rumsfeld, et. al.," decided June 26, 2006; available at: http://www.supremecourt.gov/opinions/05pdf/05-184.pdf (the quote appears on p. 4).

56. Scott Wilson and Al Kamen, "'Global War on Terror' Is Given New Name," in *The Washington Post*, March 25, 2009, available at: http://www.washingtonpost.com/wp-dyn/content/article/2009/03/24/AR2009032402818.html.

57. Portions of Obama's famous speech against the Iraq War reproduced at Matt Cover, "Obama in 2002: Toppling Brutal Dictator a 'Dumb War,'" at CNS News, March 30, 2011, available at: http://www.cnsnews.com/news/article/obama-2002-toppling-brutal-dictator-dumb.

58. The best blow-by-blow account of the operation is Christy Choi, "Timeline: How the U.S. Found and Killed Osama bin Laden," in *Time*, May 2, 2011, available at: http://newsfeed.time.com/2011/05/02/timeline-how-the-u-s-found-and-killed-osama-bin-laden.

59. The full text and video of President Obama's remarks is available at http://www.whitehouse.gov/blog/2011/05/02/osama-bin-laden-dead.

60. "Al Qaeda leader Ayman al-Zawahiri vows to avenge Osama bin Laden's death," in *The Telegraph*, June 8, 2011, available at: http://www.telegraph.co.uk/news/worldnews/al-qaeda/8564209/Al-Qaedas-second-in-command-Ayman-al-Zawahiri-vows-to-avenge-Osama-bin-Ladens-death.html.

61. The most comprehensive and fascinating attempt to understand why the September 11 attacks have remained isolated events is Timothy Noah, "Why No More 9/11s?" in *Slate*, March 5, 2009, at http://www.slate.com/id/2213025.

FURTHER READING

Bergen, Peter L. *Holy War Inc.: Inside the Secret World of Osama bin Laden*. New York: Free Press, 2001.

———. *The Longest War: The Enduring Conflict between America and Al-Qaeda*. New York, Free Press, 2011.

Bush, George W. *Decision Points*. New York: Crown, 2010.

Clarke, Richard A. *Against All Enemies: Inside America's War on Terror*. New York: Free Press, 2004.

Coll, Steve. *Ghost Wars: The Secret History of the CIA, Afghanistan, and Bin Laden, from the Soviet Invasion to September 10, 2001*. New York: Penguin, 2004.

Daalder, Ivo. *America Unbound: The Bush Revolution in Foreign Policy*. Washington, DC: Brookings Institution, 2003.

Danner, Mark. *Torture and Truth: America, Abu Ghraib, and the War on Terror*. New York: New York Review of Books, 2004.

DeYoung, Karen. *Soldier: The Life of Colin Powell*. New York: Vintage Books, 2007.

Gellman, Barton. *Angler: The Cheney Vice Presidency*. New York: Penguin, 2008.

Gordon, Michael R., and Bernard E. Trainor. *Cobra II: The Inside Story of the Invasion and Occupation of Iraq*. New York: Vintage Books, 2007.

Mann, James. *Rise of the Vulcans: The History of Bush's War Cabinet*. New York, Viking, 2004.

Mayer, Jane. *The Dark Side: The Inside Story of How the War on Terror Turned into a War on American Ideals*. New York: Anchor, 2009.

Packer, George. *The Assassin's Gate: America in Iraq*. New York: Farrar, Straus and Giroux, 2005.

Preble, Christopher A. *The Power Problem: How American Military Dominance Makes Us Less Safe, Less Prosperous, and Less Free*. Ithaca, NY: Cornell University Press, 2009.

Riedel, Bruce. *Deadly Embrace: Pakistan, America, and the Future of Global Jihad*. Washington, DC: Brookings Institution, 2011.

Rumsfeld, Donald. *Known and Unknown: A Memoir*. New York: Penguin, 2011.

Susskind, Ron. *The One Percent Doctrine: Deep Inside America's Pursuit of Its Enemies since 9/11*. New York: Simon & Schuster, 2006.

Weiner, Tim. *Legacy of Ashes: The History of the CIA*. New York: Anchor, 2008.

Woodward, Bob. *Bush at War*. New York: Simon & Schuster, 2002.

———. *Obama's Wars*. New York: Simon & Schuster, 2010.

Wright, Lawrence. *The Looming Tower: Al-Qaeda and the Road to 9/11*. New York: Vintage Books, 2007.

chapter 36

The Rise of China in the Twenty-first Century

by Yafeng Xia

CHINA, FORMALLY KNOWN as the People's Republic of China (PRC), has risen with amazing speed to become a world economic power. Starting in 1949 as an impoverished, peasant-based, agricultural economy with limited natural resources and a huge population of about 450 million, in about sixty years, China's population reached 1.3 billion, and its real GDP has probably multiplied by more than thirty-seven times. China's annual growth has averaged around 10 percent for the past thirty years. In 1978, when China's paramount leader, Deng Xiaoping (in power 1978–1992), initiated economic reforms, China's GDP barely topped $100 billion; it hit almost $5 trillion in 2011. The United States and China are each other's second-largest trade partner, and trade between the two countries is close to $400 billion annually. In 2010, China's GDP at purchasing power parity per capita income was $7,519, according to International Monetary Fund statistics. China has also steadily increased its level of defense spending over nearly twenty years, especially in the last ten years. China's official 2010 defense budget was about $78 billion, and its military expenditures are now the second-largest in the world, behind the United States. China's rural population continues to move to the cities, and its middle class continues to grow. Now, China has the second-largest national economy and is the second-largest exporter. It has by far the world's largest current account surplus and foreign exchange reserves. According to some estimates, China's economic size will match America's by 2035 and double it by mid-century.[1]

China's rise reflects the long-term growth of its economic and military capabilities. It has aroused endless debate about its implication for international politics and global stability in general, and the dynamics of the U.S. global role in particular. What role will China, as an emerging power, play in global economic and security organizations? Will China use its rising interests in ways that are compatible with U.S. interests, or will it seek to advance interests that undermine the global system, and the peace and prosperity it has provided for so many around the world? Will China emerge as a responsible global stakeholder or not? These are questions of vital concern to U.S. diplomacy in the twenty-first century.

U.S. POLICY TOWARD CHINA EVOLVES DURING THE CLINTON AND BUSH ADMINISTRATIONS

After initially challenging China over its human rights record following the 1989 Tiananmen Square incident, in which hundreds, and perhaps thousands, of Chinese university student-protesters were gunned down by the Chinese military, the Clinton administration (1993–2001) adopted a moderate policy of engagement. Beginning in 1996, the United States sought change in offensive Chinese government practices through a gradual process involving closer Chinese integration with the world economic and political order.[2] However, the Bush administration (2001–2009) started with a tough policy toward China. U.S. policy toward China gradually tempered after the September 11 terrorist attacks on New York City and Washington. In September 2005, a senior U.S. State Department official called on China to become a "responsible stakeholder" on the international stage. In responding to China's rise, the Bush administration adopted a two-pronged strategy toward China: diplomatic engagement and military hedging.

A Rocky Start

The Bush team was initially suspicious of China's growing power, labeling China a "strategic competitor" during the 2000 presidential campaign. Bush stressed the importance of strengthening U.S. alliances in East Asia, codified in the 2000 "Armitage Report," an influential prescriptive analysis of the alliance, written by several future Bush administration officials, including the future deputy secretary of state, Richard Armitage.[3] In contrast to the Clinton administration's perceived tilt toward China, the report called for a "recognition that the time has arrived for renewed attention to improving, reinvigorating, and refocusing the U.S.-Japan

KEY CONCEPTS

Responsible stakeholders. China is the most populous nation in recorded history. It has been gradually emerging as an important economic and military power in Asia and the world. What does the simultaneous rise of China in the twenty-first century mean to the United States? How should U.S. policymakers cope with this rising power? When the Bush team entered office in early 2001, Washington's Asian policy was unsettled. Initially, the Bush administration was tough on China, regarding China as a "strategic competitor." However, after the September 11 terrorist attacks on the United States, Washington's policy toward Beijing gradually changed. By 2005, administration officials called on China to become a "responsible stakeholder" on the international stage. In responding to China's rise, the Bush administration adopted a two-pronged strategy toward China: diplomatic engagement and military hedging. The Obama administration continues much of the Bush era China policy and is searching for a more comprehensive policy toward China.

In sum, the United States enters the twenty-first century hoping to boost its ties to China financially and strategically. Effectively managing this relationship may result in enormous potential rewards. It is important that U.S. leaders wake up to the reality that they will have to deal with China as an equal rather than as a supplicant.

alliance." While arguing against containment, the unstated direction of the report leaned toward a hedging strategy with respect to China. The United States and Japan would work to encourage China's evolution as a responsible regional actor, but should China fail to move in that direction, it would be confronted by a reinvigorated alliance.[4] The Bush administration's approach to China was based in large measure on a fundamental uncertainty: China was rising and becoming more prominent in Asia and world affairs, but U.S. leaders were unsure if China would "emerge" as a friend or foe of the United States, or, perhaps most likely, somewhere in between.[5]

In sharp contrast to the outgoing Clinton administration's engagement policy toward China, the Bush administration lowered China's priority in U.S. foreign policy decision making, placing it well behind Japan and other U.S. allies and even Russia and India for foreign policy attention.[6] Following the April 2001 Hainan incident, in which a Chinese jet fighter collided with an American EP-3 reconnaissance plane over the South China Sea, resulting in the death of the Chinese pilot and the forced emergency landing of the EP-3 on the Chinese island of Hainan, the Bush administration did not resort to high-level envoys or other special arrangements previously used by the Clinton administration to resolve difficult U.S.-China issues. Instead, it insisted on working through normal State Department and Defense Department channels that did not raise China's stature in U.S. foreign policy.[7] The Bush administration was also dedicated to improving Taiwan's defense capabilities. Immediately after the EP-3 crisis, the U.S. government announced its intention to offer a large-scale arms package to Taiwan, and President Bush stated in an interview with Charlie Gibson of *ABC News* on April 25, 2001, that the United States would "do whatever it takes" to help Taiwan defend itself.[8] Taiwan has been under separate rule since 1949, but the PRC claims sovereignty over Taiwan. Thus,

the Taiwan issue has always been contentious in U.S.-PRC relations.

Improving Relations

After the EP-3 incident, U.S.-China relations began to improve with Secretary of State Colin Powell's (in office 2001–2005) trip to China in late July 2001. That process would accelerate after the September 11 terrorist attacks, even though China was somewhat tentative and reserved in supporting the U.S. war in Afghanistan. However, all was not well with U.S.-China relations at the time, as Thomas Christensen, professor of political science at Princeton University and deputy assistant secretary for East Asian and Pacific affairs (2006–2008), argues, because the Bush administration seemed very supportive of Taiwan. During his visits to Shanghai in October 2001 and Beijing in February 2002, Bush repeatedly affirmed his strong support for Taiwan and his firm position regarding human rights issues in China. His aides made clear China's lower priority in the administration's view of U.S. interests, as the Bush administration continued to focus higher priority on relations with Japan and other allies in Asia and the Pacific.[9]

The U.S.-China relationship began to stabilize and improve over the course of 2002. By mid-2001, Chinese leaders seemed to recognize that if U.S.-China relations were to avoid further deterioration, it was up to China to take steps to improve ties. In a period of overall ascendant U.S. influence and leverage in Asian and world affairs, Beijing saw its interests best served by a stance that muted differences and sought common ground. In spring 2002, Hu Jintao, then vice president of the PRC, paid a visit to Washington and had a very productive discussion with Vice President Dick Cheney (in office 2001–2009). This meeting laid the foundation for Deputy Secretary of State Richard Armitage's important trip to Beijing in late August 2002. Three weeks before that trip,

Chen Shui-bian (in office 2000–2008), president of Taiwan, made a speech asserting Taiwan's sovereignty and violating his promises to eschew the pursuit of Taiwan independence while in office, which he made in his moderate inaugural address of May 2000. On August 3, 2002, Chen described relations across the Taiwan Strait as "one country on each side (*yi bian yi guo*)," and suggested that he would pursue a popular referendum to determine Taiwan's status. During his visit to Beijing, Armitage not only clearly distanced himself from the statements by Chen but implicitly labeled them as actions designed to promote Taiwan independence. When answering questions to the press about the statements, Armitage replied simply and firmly that the United States "does not support Taiwan independence." Armitage also treated China as a partner in the War on Terrorism by publicly labeling the East Turkestan Islamic Movement, which seeks independence for China's Xinjiang region, as an international terrorist organization with links to al Qaeda.[10]

Amid continued Chinese moderation and concessions in 2002, and reflecting greater U.S. interest in consolidating relations and avoiding tensions with China at a time of growing U.S. preoccupation with the War on Terrorism and deeper U.S. involvement in Afghanistan and Iraq, the Bush administration broadened cooperation with China and gave U.S. relations with China a higher priority as the year wore on. An October 2002 meeting between President Bush and Chinese President Jiang Zemin (in office 1993–2003) at the U.S. president's ranch in Crawford, Texas, highlighted this trend. At the Crawford summit, Bush told Jiang that his administration was not seeking to change the historical U.S. "one China policy."[11] In December 2003, in the lead-up to the 2004 Taiwan presidential elections, with the visiting Chinese Premier Wen Jiabao (in office 2003-) at his side, Bush clearly and publicly stated that he opposed actions by either side of the Taiwan Strait to unilaterally change the status quo. On the

PUBLIC PORTRAIT: *HU JINTAO (1942–)*

Hu Jintao was born to the family of a tea merchant in Jiangsu in 1942. He graduated with a degree in hydraulic engineering from China's Tsinghua University in 1965. His rise to political power began in 1984, when he was promoted to first secretary of the Communist Youth League Central Committee. In 1992, with the support of China's paramount leader, Deng Xiaoping, Hu became the youngest member of the seven-member Politburo Standing Committee. Hu was the vice president of the People's Republic of China (PRC) from 1998 to 2003, and has been general secretary of the Chinese Communist Party since 2002, president of the PRC since 2003, and chairman of the Central Military Commission since 2004, succeeding Jiang Zemin. He is also the chief of Central Foreign Affairs Leading Small Group, which has overall control over China's foreign and defense policy-making. Hu, a low-key and reserved leader, is expected to step down from the top posts in 2012 and 2013. His rise to political supremacy represented the focus in Chinese politics on technocratic competence rather than revolutionary credential and personality.

Over the last two decades or so, China's foreign and defense policies have been remarkably consistent and reasonably well-coordinated with the country's domestic priorities. Following Deng Xiaoping's teaching of *taoguangyanghui* (hide brightness; nourish obscurity), China has kept a low profile in international affairs. Under Hu Jintao, Beijing has in recent years formulated a new development and social policy geared toward continuing to promote fast economic growth while emphasizing good governance, improving the social safety net, protecting the environment, encouraging independent innovation, lessening social tensions, perfecting the financial system, and stimulating domestic consumption.

In view of the fear of China's rise within the international community, Hu advocates for an approach termed China's "peaceful rise" and "peaceful development," pursuing soft power in international relations and creating "a

harmonious world." In recent years, the Chinese leadership has redefined the purpose of China's foreign policy. Hu announced in July 2009 that China's diplomacy must "safeguard the interests of sovereignty, security, and development." Dai Bingguo, the state councilor for external relations, further defined those core interests in an article in December 2010: first, China's political stability, namely, the stability of the Chinese Communist Party (CCP) leadership and of the socialist system; second, sovereign security, territorial integrity, and national unification; and, third, China's sustainable economic and social development. In fact, for the central government, sovereignty, security, and development all continue to be China's main goals. As long as no grave danger—for example, Taiwan's formal secession—threatens the CCP leadership or China's unity, Beijing will remain preoccupied with the country's economic and social development, including its foreign policy. Along with his colleague Premier Wen Jiabao, Hu presided over nearly a decade of consistent economic growth and development that cemented China as a major world power. Through Hu's tenure, China's global influence in Africa, Latin America, and other developing countries has increased dramatically.

The United States has been China's primary foreign policy concern in the last three decades. Hu Jintao visited the United States as vice president in spring 2002. In September 2005, President Hu attended the High Level Plenary of the United Nations General Assembly in New York and met with President George W. Bush. In April 2006, Hu Jintao arrived in Washington for his first official visit to the United States as China's president. At the invitation of President Bush, President Hu attended the G-20 Summit on Financial Markets and the World Economy in Washington on November 15, 2008. Since the Obama administration took office, President Hu has met with President Obama frequently at the sidelines of international gatherings and when President Obama visited Beijing in November 2009. In January 2011, President Hu made a state visit to the United States.

campaign trail in late 2003, Taiwanese President Chen Shui-bian had suggested that he would pursue "defensive referenda" on aspects of Taiwan's relationship with the mainland during the March 2004 presidential election. He also suggested the need for constitutional reform, and made various assertions of Taiwan's sovereign independence from mainland China. Bush singled out Chen's recent actions and statements for tough and negative comments in his public address.[12]

Debate over China's Rise

China expanded military power along with economic and diplomatic relations in Asian and world affairs at a time of U.S. preoccupation with the wars in Afghanistan and Iraq and other foreign policy problems. Debate over the implications of China's rise for U.S.-China relations was important in Bush administration deliberations for several years, and it remained strong among congressional, media, and nongovernment specialists and interest groups. Within the Bush administration, according to Robert Sutter, a leading scholar on U.S.-China relations, there emerged three viewpoints or schools of thought.

First, some officials argued that China's rise in Asia was designed by the Chinese leadership to dominate Asia, and in the process to undermine U.S. leadership in the region. Second, others contended that China's rise was having an indirect but substantial negative impact on U.S. leadership in Asia. The third school of thought puts less emphasis than the other two on competition with China and more emphasis on cooperation with China to preserve and enhance U.S. leadership and interests in Asia as China rises.[13]

The third school holds that the United States has much to gain from working directly and cooperatively with China to encourage China to use its rising influence in "responsible" ways, in accord with broad American interests in Asian and world affairs. This viewpoint is identified with Deputy Secretary of State Robert Zoellick's important speech at the National Committee on U.S.-China Relations gala dinner on September 21, 2005, a statement that invited China to become a "responsible stakeholder" on the international stage and outlined the philosophy behind the U.S.-China "Senior Dialogue" on security and political affairs.[14] Zoellick emphasized important U.S. and Chinese common interests that can be pursued through cooperation and proclaimed a "shared interest in sustaining political, economic, and security systems that provide common benefits." In the realm of foreign policy, China was considered to have ample opportunities to demonstrate responsibility in dealing with issues such as North Korea, nonproliferation, and counterterrorism. Zoellick praised specific Chinese contributions to stability, while noting that in other cases, such as export controls and dealing with the

Iranian nuclear program, the seriousness of China's commitment was not clear.[15]

A Responsible Stakeholder?

Between 2005 and 2008, the Bush administration adopted a two-pronged strategy: a strong U.S. presence in Asian security and political affairs to discourage the use of coercion by China when resolving its disputes, and active diplomatic engagement to encourage China to seek greater influence through constructive economic and diplomatic policies. First, by maintaining a strong U.S. security presence in Asia in the form of U.S. forces and bases, along with a network of strong alliances and non-allied security partnerships, the United States made it difficult for experts, advisers, and decision-makers within China to advocate the use of coercive force against Taiwan or other regional actors as an inexpensive and effective way for Beijing to address its problems.

The term *hedging* is frequently used, even in official government documents, to describe this role of the U.S. security presence. For instance, the Bush administration's 2006 National Security Strategy encourages China to become a responsible stakeholder in support of the international order, notes the global significance of the U.S.-Japan relationship, and explicitly endorses a hedging strategy toward China.[16] The 2006 *Quadrennial Defense Review* names China as the only country that competes militarily with the United States and points at ways that Washington will try to maintain its strategic supremacy.[17] The military strength of the United States and its allies and security partners in Asia complements positive U.S. diplomacy by channeling China's competitive energies in more beneficial and peaceful directions. The second prong of the strategy, a set of diplomatic dialogues, is designed to urge China to use its growing power constructively and to help Beijing recognize that, if it does so, it will be accorded the greater prestige and influence that it seeks.

The United States has maintained several dozen formal dialogues with the Chinese, the most famous of which have been the Strategic Economic Dialogue on bilateral and global economic and environmental affairs under former secretary of treasury Henry M. Paulson, and the Senior Dialogue on bilateral and global political and security affairs under former deputy secretaries of state John Negroponte and Robert Zoellick. The United States wants the Chinese to adjust their domestic and foreign policies in ways that will foster long-term stability and growth at home, and will foster stability in international economic and political relations.[18]

The goal of this Bush administration initiative was to move the U.S.-China relationship beyond traditional bilateral issues—relations across the Taiwan Strait, human rights, and economic frictions—and toward cooperation on ensuring stability in places such as Northeast Asia, the Persian Gulf,

On April 20, 2006, President and Mrs. Bush welcomed Chinese President Hu Jintao and his wife (second and fourth from right), Liu Yongqing, to the White House. The leaders discussed a full range of regional and international issues, including the War on Terrorism, nonproliferation, advancing freedom, and promoting prosperity in Asia and beyond.

SOURCE: George W. Bush Presidential Library and Museum.

and Africa. As Thomas Christensen puts it, "What was truly innovative in the Bush administration's China policy, however, was the intensive and sustained engagement with Beijing on how better to coordinate U.S. and the People's Republic of China's responses to policy problems around the globe, from a nuclear weapons program in North Korea to pirates in the Gulf of Aden to humanitarian crises in Sudan."[19]

Between 2006 and 2008, China responded moderately to this shift in U.S. policy. Beijing continued to host the six-party talks on North Korea's nuclear program and participated in the crafting of international sanctions against Pyongyang in the UN Security Council. In particular, between late 2006 and early 2007, China also exerted bilateral economic pressure on North Korea, which led to the disablement of its nuclear facilities at Yongbyon, the only concrete progress made to date as part of the six-party talks.

Beijing also shifted policy on Sudan. It went from protecting Sudan's regime against international pressure over human right abuses in Darfur to backing then UN Secretary-General Kofi Annan's (in office 1997–2006) three-phase plan for peace and stability in the region in late 2006. In late 2008, China also agreed to send a naval contingent to the Gulf of Aden to assist in the international effort to counter piracy off the coast of Somalia. The UN resolution authorizing the mission allowed for the pursuit of pirates into Somalia's territorial waters. In endorsing the UN resolution, Beijing was moving away from its traditional foreign policy and softening its long-held and once rigid positions on sanctions

and noninterference in the internal affairs of sovereign states. By making clear to skeptical Chinese audiences that Washington did not view the relationship as a zero-sum game, the Bush administration's initiative was favorable to U.S.-Chinese bilateral relations.[20] However, it was clear that China was not yet the "responsible global stakeholder" that Washington expected by the end of the Bush presidency.

CONTINUITY AND FRICTIONS IN U.S.-CHINA RELATIONS

There is much continuity in U.S. policy toward China from the Bush to the Obama administrations, such as U.S. policy toward Taiwan and continuing U.S.-China high-level dialogues. The Obama administration has attached greater importance to U.S. relations with China and called for "strategic reassurance" from China about its intentions. However, the U.S.-China bilateral relationship has been strained by a series of unexpected events since late 2009.

Strategic Reassurance?

For the first time since 1979 and the Taiwan Relations Act, China policy went almost unmentioned in the 2008 U.S. presidential campaign. The election of Ma Ying-jeou (in office 2008–) to the presidency of Taiwan in March 2008 has greatly reduced the risk of Sino-American conflict over Taiwan. Ma rejected the pursuit of Taiwan independence and has actively sought practical cooperation with the mainland since 2008. Contenders for the 2008 presidential elections hardly disputed the Bush administration's Asia policy. President Barack Obama (2009–) and his team did not strongly take issue with China's trade surplus with the United States. After the inauguration, foreign policy officials have been at pain to point out that they saw nothing wrong with their predecessor's Asia policy and would continue on the same course.

Faced with a rising China, the Obama administration has repeatedly emphasized that it "welcomes a strong, prosperous and successful China that plays a greater role in world affairs."[21] President Obama signaled soon after taking office that he hoped to work with China to address a broad range of global issues, most prominently the global financial crisis, climate change, and nuclear non-proliferation, but also such issues as security in Afghanistan and Pakistan and the threat of pandemic disease. In July 2009, in his remarks at the opening session of the first round of U.S.-China Strategic and Economic Dialogue, a new mechanism to replace the former Senior Dialogue and Strategic Economic Dialogue started under the Bush administration, Obama stated, "The relationship between the United States and China will shape the 21st century, which makes it as important as any bilateral relationship in the world." He argued that partnership between the United States and China was "a prerequisite for progress on many of the most pressing global challenges."[22]

At the same time, the Obama administration has called for "strategic reassurance" from China about its intentions. In a September 2009 speech, Deputy Secretary of State James B. Steinberg asserted, "Just as we and our allies must make clear that we are prepared to welcome China's 'arrival' . . . as a prosperous and successful power, China must reassure the rest of the world that its development and growing global role will not come at the expense of security and well-being of others." Steinberg maintained that supporting that kind of bargain of "reassurance" should be a priority in the U.S.-China relationship. [23]

Ongoing Relations

The Obama administration's emphasis is on two points: preserving security and getting along. The first aspect implies continuity with the Bush years. The second implies a new degree of openness and engagement, and this may have gained unexpected prominence with Secretary of State Hillary Clinton's (in office 2009–) first trip to East Asia in February 2009. On the eve of her visit to Beijing, Clinton declared that pressing China on Taiwan, Tibet, and human rights "can't interfere on the global economic crisis, the global climate change crisis, and the security crisis." [24]

The global economic crisis is creating a historical shift of economic power toward Asia, and within Asia toward China, possibly joined by India, in a longer-term perspective. China's financial rise is even more spectacular, although the accumulation of foreign currency surpluses comes at the cost of the celebrated "dollar trap," with an unavoidable large proportion of China's $2.2 trillion of reserves held in dollars. This was highlighted by the uneven results of President Obama's visit to China in November 2009. In the run-up to the summit, media and think tank pundits had debated the prospects of a U.S.-China "G-2" emerging between the world's two most powerful nations. On the one hand, the visit ended with a detailed joint declaration citing issues for bilateral cooperation. Obama had mentioned a China-U.S. strategic partnership before the visit. He recognized a Chinese role in South Asia, did not refer publicly to the Taiwan Relations Act before a press conference at the end of the visit, and signed on to a statement of respect for the "core interests" of the two countries. The United States agreed with China on its position that the Taiwan issue is at the "core" of bilateral Sino-U.S. relations. This was the first time Washington agreed with China on Taiwan to such an extent. Yet his public expression was kept off the Chinese media on two occasions, and the visit yielded no measurable new commitments by China.[25]

Nonetheless, the Obama administration points to some successes in working with China to address pressing global issues, including coordination of stimulus spending to address the global financial crisis. The administration also stressed cooperation in negotiating new sanctions against North Korea (in 2009) and Iran (in 2010) over their nuclear programs.

A Negative Turn of Events

In the year following President Obama's November 2009 state visit to China, however, the bilateral relationship was strained by a series of troublesome issues. In March 2010, despite U.S. pressure, China declined to condemn its neighbor North Korea for its alleged torpedo attack on U.S. ally South Korea's naval vessel, the *Cheonan*. In July, Chinese Foreign Minister Yang Jiechi protested U.S. plans to hold military exercises in the Yellow Sea in response to North Korea's provocations; the Yellow Sea borders China to the east. At a meeting in Hanoi of the ASEAN (Association of Southeast Asian Nations) Regional Forum the same month, Secretary of State Clinton asserted that the United States had "a national interest" in freedom of navigation and respect for international law in the South China Sea.[26] In spite of earlier warnings by Chinese diplomats, as many as twelve delegates from the region also raised the issue, incurring the wrath of China's Foreign Minister Yang. In September, after a Chinese fishing trawler collided with Japanese coast guard vessels near disputed islands in the East China Sea, the United States

President Barack Obama (left) greets Chinese President Hu Jintao in the Old Family Dining Room of the White House. The leaders of the world's two most powerful nations met in January 2011 to try to find common ground on economic and security issues. Later that year, the two leaders again met at the Asia-Pacific Economic Cooperation (APEC) summit in Honolulu and continued their dialogue.

SOURCE: The White House/Pete Souza.

angered China by voicing its support for Japan in the ensuing China-Japan quarrel, and by clarifying that the disputed islands are among areas covered by the U.S. military alliance with Japan. In November, China declined to condemn North Korea over revelations of its uranium enrichment program and over its shelling of a South Korean island, and later also blocked United Nations action over the uranium program. It again protested U.S.-South Korean joint military exercises in the Yellow Sea.[27] In a recent *Foreign Affairs* article, Thomas Christensen argues, "Rather than a simple assertion of its newfound power, China's negative diplomacy seems rooted in a strange mix of confidence on the international stage and insecurity at home."[28]

Despite these frictions, high-level exchanges continue. In January 2011, China's President Hu Jintao made a state visit to the United States. Both countries' presidents used the trip to reassure each other about their respective intentions, to refocus on their shared interests, and to restate their belief in all that their countries stand to benefit from cooperation and to lose from conflict. Their pledges were contained in a forty-one-point Joint Statement, which also served to update the relationship to "a cooperative partnership based on mutual respect and mutual benefit."[29] The third round of the U.S.-China Strategic and Economic Dialogue, which wrapped up in Washington on May 10, 2011, was seen as a step to carry out and implement agreements and consensus reached between the two countries during President Hu's visit to

Washington. In May and July 2011, General Chen Bingde, PLA chief of the general staff, and Admiral Mike Mullen, chairman of the Joint Chiefs of Staff, exchanged visits. In August, Vice President Joe Biden (in office 2009–) made his first official visit to China. As former secretary of state Henry Kissinger (in office 1973–1977) points out, "What remains to be dealt with is to move from crisis management to a definition of common goals, from the solution of strategic controversies to their avoidance."[30]

Engagement and Hedging

Part of the Obama administration's stated response to China's rise has been an emphasis on "robust regional engagement" by the United States across Asia. In a major address about China policy ahead of President Hu's state visit in January 2011, Secretary of State Clinton noted that the Obama administration had worked to strengthen its security alliances with Japan, South Korea, Thailand, Australia, and the Philippines; stepped up relations with India, Indonesia, Vietnam, Malaysia, Singapore, and New Zealand; and pursued a major free trade agreement with South Korea. She also said that the U.S. had committed itself to strengthening regional institutions.[31] Needless to say, what some view as a power shift toward Asia, and within Asia itself, is likely to be contested. America's successes and difficulties in balancing China's influence while not challenging Beijing directly are as much a front-page story for Asia in 2010 and 2011 as China's sudden rash of assertiveness toward its maritime neighbors. In spite of much outside criticism about Washington's difficulties with Beijing, continuity bodes well for the tests ahead.

Engagement, Integration, and Balancing

In September 2009, the Center for a New American Security (CNAS) issued an important study on how the United States should respond to the rise of China. It recommended that the United States' strategic framework in dealing with China must move beyond the simplistic formula of "engage" or "hedge." Rather, the framework must have a nuanced focus on the need to "engage, integrate, and balance."[32] John Ikenberry, professor of political science at Princeton University, argues that in adjusting to, and promoting, greater regionalism in East Asia, the United States should not block China's entry into the regional order, but, rather, it should attempt to use regional institutions to "shape" the terms of this entry. To do this, Ikenberry suggests, the United States should develop a regional security institution that complements existing U.S. security alliances and binds China to the larger regional order.[33] Abraham Denmark, fellow at CNAS

and former country director for China at the Department of Defense, suggests that China has risen, but that U.S. policy and strategy toward China have not come to grips with the complexity of managing the U.S.-China relationship. He suggests that the current U.S. "engage and hedge" policy formulation unnecessarily feeds the misunderstanding that the United States pursues two virtually separate China strategies: engaging (managed by the Department of State) and hedging (managed by the Department of Defense). The hedging/engagement formula must expand to incorporate engagement, integration, and balancing into a comprehensive approach at the global, regional, bilateral, and unilateral levels that utilizes all elements of U.S. national power.[34]

It seems that the Obama administration has adopted some of these suggestions. The administration has made an effort to embed China in international institutions. The United States and China are fellow permanent members of the UN Security Council and, since President Obama took office in 2009, have worked together successfully in the Security Council to pass sanctions targeting North Korea

---

SHIFTS IN FOREIGN POLICY: *PRESIDENT OBAMA AND U.S. POLICY WITH ASIA*

Since taking office, the Obama administration has worked to renew American leadership and pursue a new era of engagement with the world, based on mutual interests and mutual respect. After years of focusing U.S. time and attention on the Middle East, the Obama administration is seeking to reorient its foreign policy toward Asia, largely as a way to ensure domestic economic growth in the decades ahead. This shift in U.S. foreign policy also is a reaction to the changing security and economic environment in Asia. A decade ago, Asia was an important economic region; today, it is critical for U.S. prosperity. It is no coincidence that the first foreign leader whom Obama welcomed to the White House was Taro Aso (in office 2008–2009), the prime minister of Japan, on February 24, 2009. For the first time in nearly fifty years, the first foreign trip by the new administration's secretary of state, Hillary Clinton, was made to Asia, starting in Japan. It is also no coincidence that the first state visit hosted by President and Mrs. Obama was for an Asian leader, Indian Prime Minister Manmohan Singh, in November 2009.

U.S. leaders actively participate in the activities of Asian regional organizations. President Obama participated in the APEC Summit in Singapore in November 2009, as well as visiting China, Japan, and South Korea; the United States supported the creation of a regular G-20 leaders summit with strong Asian participation reflecting the new global balance of financial and political power; the first-ever U.S.-ASEAN (Association of Southeast Asian Nations) summit was held in November 2009; in February 2009, the U.S. and Japan signed the Guam International Agreement, which helps sustain a strong U.S. military presence in the region. In July 2009, Secretary of State Clinton signed the United States' Instrument of Accession to the Treaty of Amity and Cooperation in Southeast Asia.

A LONG-STANDING COMMITMENT

As Secretary of Defense Robert Gates has noted, "The United States is not a visiting power in Asia, but a resident power." The United States is back in

Asia and intends to take a leadership role. The Obama administration has implemented a three-part strategy to build that strength in international cooperation.

First, the U.S. alliance relationships are the cornerstone of its regional involvement. The United States' alliances with Japan, South Korea, Australia, Thailand, and the Philippines are among the most successful bilateral partnerships in modern history. The Obama administration has reaffirmed its treaty commitments with its Asian allies. On November 16 and 17, 2011, after the APEC Summit, President Obama traveled to Australia, where he announced that the United States is planning to rotate twenty-five hundred marines through a permanent base near Darwin in northern Australia. Some argue that Obama is strategically positioning the United States as counterbalance to China's growth.

Second, beyond its treaty alliances, the United States is committed to strengthening relationships with other key players. Washington is pursuing a strategic dialogue with India, a strategic and economic dialogue with China, and a comprehensive partnership with Indonesia. The United States is working on strengthening its partnerships with newer partners such as Vietnam and long-standing partners such as Singapore. While in Bali, for the ASEAN Summit on November 17 through 19, 2011, President Obama announced that he would send Secretary of State Clinton to Myanmar (also known as Burma), with which the United States has had only limited relations since 1962. Renewed U.S. involvement in Burma has been seen as another regional U.S. bulwark against an expanded China. The Obama administration has focused on strengthening dialogues between these partners, because Washington recognizes that it needs to deepen dialogues with its Asian partners to realize positive-sum benefits and enhance the prospect of successful results over time.

and Iran's nuclear programs, although critics have accused China of taking a minimalist approach to implementation of those sanctions. The United States has worked with China on economic issues in the G-20 grouping, and welcomed a greater Chinese role in the International Monetary Fund (IMF) and the World Bank. It has also sought to resolve trade disputes with China through the rules-based mechanisms of the World Trade Organization (WTO), and brought complaints about China's currency to the IMF.[35]

In an effort to increase clarity about each side's intentions and promote cooperation between officials of the two countries at all levels and across multiple departments, the Obama administration has embraced and added to a broad array of official dialogues inherited from the Bush administration. Its decision to merge the Strategic Economic Dialogue and the Senior Dialogue into the Strategic and Economic Dialogue (SED) was a valuable step toward integrating security and economics. Yet, as Lindsey Ford points out, effective management of the current U.S.-China relationship "will require U.S. policy makers to design effective bureaucratic forums to support the overarching strategic vision for the relationship. The expanding scope and depth of the bilateral relationship will require a proactive effort on the part of U.S. leaders to coordinate the broad array of bureaucratic institutions and actors now invested in our relationship with China."[36]

A FUTURE GLOBAL ORDER

The rise of China has been one of the outstanding developments of the first decade of the twenty-first century. It has raised fundamental questions about the structure of the world economy and the balance of global geopolitical power. The United States retains a dominant position in the world, but the rise of new centers of power, especially Beijing, suggests that the twenty-first century will be multipolar. The best prospects for maintaining U.S. global leadership and general prosperity lie in recognizing the reality that America's unipolar moment has already passed. It is safer and far more advantageous for U.S. national interests to seek peace and cooperation with Beijing than to seek conflict.

Third, the United States recognizes that it is necessary to embed these relationships in broader regional and global cooperation to maximize their chance of leading to success. Another major focus of U.S. efforts has been to strengthen its regional engagement in Asia. During his visit to Tokyo in November 2009, President Obama conveyed the U.S. intention to engage fully with Asia's regional organizations. As part of this strategy, the United States proposes to begin consultations with Asian partners and friends on how it might play a role in the East Asia Summit and how the East Asia Summit fits into the broader institutional landscape. To achieve this goal, President Obama hosted the second U.S.-ASEAN summit in the United States in September 2010. Secretary of State Clinton attended the East Asia Summit in Vietnam in October 2010. With the support of Japan and India, the United States became a member of the East Asia Summit in 2011. President Obama hosted the APEC forum in Honolulu and attended the East Asian Summit in Indonesia in November 2011. All these efforts represent U.S. interest in developing more effective regional cooperation and dealing with common challenges. Equally important, such cooperation allows the United States to embed critical bilateral relationships in a broader context.

AMERICAN LEADERSHIP IN THE TWENTY-FIRST CENTURY

In Asia, the United States intends to project American leadership in three areas: economic growth, regional security, and enduring values. These arenas formed the foundation of American leadership in the twentieth century, and they are as relevant in the twenty-first century.

First, in economic growth, Asia still wants the United States to be an optimistic, engaged, open, and creative partner in its flourishing trade and financial interactions. The Obama administration has set a goal of doubling U.S. exports, and it is important for the U.S. to expand its exports and investment opportunities in the dynamic markets of Asia. Second, sustained economic progress relies on durable investments in stability and security, which the United States will continue to make. The Obama administration believes that the U.S. military presence in Asia has deterred conflict and provided security for sixty years and will continue to support economic growth and political integration. The 2010 Quadrennial Defense Review lays out a plan for the continued presence of U.S. forces in Asia. It reflects three principles: U.S. defense posture will become more politically sustainable, operationally resilient, and geographically dispersed. With these principles in mind, the United States is enhancing its presence in Northeast Asia. The buildup on the U.S. territory of Guam, for example, reflects these ideas, as does the agreement on bases that the United States reached with Japan in January 2010, an agreement that came during the fiftieth anniversary of a U.S.-Japan mutual security alliance. On October 24, 2011, U.S. Defense Secretary Leon Panetta (in office 2011–) called the U.S.-Japan alliance a cornerstone of regional security and stability that was critical to addressing challenges such as North Korea and China. The United States has also adopted new defense guidelines with South Korea to advance their military cooperation into a strategic alliance of bilateral and global scope. Third, the United States maintains that a nation's most precious asset is the persuasive power of its values, in particular, its steadfast belief in democracy and human rights. As the United States deepens its engagement with partners with whom it disagrees on these issues, it will continue to urge them to embrace reforms that would improve governance, protect human rights, and advance political freedoms.

IN THEIR OWN WORDS: *PRESIDENT BARACK OBAMA, NOVEMBER 12, 2011, APEC SUMMIT*

In November 2011, President Obama embarked on an important trip across the Pacific. He hosted the Asia Pacific Economic Cooperation (APEC) forum in Honolulu, signed bilateral defense agreements with Australia, and attended the U.S.-ASEAN Summit and the East Asian Summit in Bali. President Obama attempted to reinforce America's enduring commitment to regional diplomacy, economics, and security. On November 12, President Obama met with President Hu Jintao of China at the sidelines of the APEC summit. Although many countries in the Asia-Pacific region feel uneasy about the rapid ascendance of China, and worry that insufficient American involvement will ultimately enable China to dominate in the region, both Obama and Hu stressed the importance of continuous U.S.-China cooperation. Obama noted that cooperation between the world's two largest countries and largest economies is vital not only to the security and prosperity of American people but also to the world.

President Obama continued:

> Such cooperation is particularly important to the Asia Pacific region, where both China and the United States are extraordinarily active. We are both Pacific powers. And I think many countries in the region look to a constructive relationship between the United States and China as a basis for continued growth and prosperity. As we did at the G20 in Cannes, President Hu and I I'm sure will be discussing issues related to economic growth, how we can continue to rebalance growth around the world, emphasize the importance of putting people back to work, and making sure that the trade relationships and commercial relationships between our two countries end up being a win-win situation. And I look forward to the opportunity to also discuss a range of both regional and global security issues, including nonproliferation and denuclearization of the Korean Peninsula, ways that we can work together

on issues like climate change, and our efforts to jointly assure that countries like Iran are abiding by international rules and norms. And although there are areas where we continue to have differences, I am confident that the U.S.-China relationship can continue to grow in a constructive way based on mutual respect and mutual interests. And I want to extend my appreciation to President Hu for the continuous engagement not only of him but also of the entire Chinese government in addressing a wide range of these issues. . . .

President Hu replied,

> . . . As things stand, the international situation is undergoing complex and profound changes. There is growing instability and uncertainty in the world economic recovery, and regional security threat has become more salient. Under these circumstances, it is all the more important for China and the United States to increase their communication and coordination. China looks forward to maintaining and strengthening dialogue and cooperation with the United States, to respect each other's major concerns, appropriately manage sensitive issues, and ensure that the China-U.S. relationship will continue to grow on a sustainable and stable path. This APEC meeting has drawn a lot of attention worldwide and we appreciate the tremendous work the United States has done in preparing for this meeting. The Asia Pacific region is the most dynamic region in today's world, with the biggest development potential. This region should become a region of active cooperation between China and the United States. . . .

SOURCE: http://www.whitehouse.gov/the-press-office/2011/11/12/remarks-president-obama-and-president-hu-china.

Dealing with the complexity of China requires caution. It remains possible that a prosperous, confident, economically expansive China may develop toward democracy in the coming decades. That prospect will be vastly reduced, or completely lost, however, if Sino-American relations descend into the new Cold War.

With the world's fastest-growing markets, fastest-rising military expenditures, and most volatile hot spots, a resurgent Asia today holds the key to the future global order. Central to Asia's future is the strategic triangle made up of the largest Asian economic and military powers: China, India, and Japan. For its part, the United States will remain a key player in Asia through its security arrangements and other

strategic ties with an array of regional states. Its policies and actions will continue to have an important influence on the strategic calculus of the major Asian actors.[37] While Washington has adopted a policy of engagement and hedging toward China in the first decade of the twenty-first century, in the years ahead, U.S. policymakers will need to reexamine their most fundamental beliefs and assumptions toward China, in the Asia region, and about American power, and then undertake significant changes in strategy and policy.

See also: **Chapter 39: U.S. Foreign Policy Goals of the Twenty-first Century; Chapter 40: Diplomatic Milestones, 2001–Present.**

ENDNOTES

1. Tai Xie and Benjamin Page, "Americans and the Rise of China as a World Power," in *Journal of Contemporary China* 19, no. 65 (June 2010): 479–80; C. Fred Bergsten, Charles Freeman, Nicholas Lardy, and Derek Mitchell, eds., *China's Rise: Challenges and Opportunities* (Washington, DC: Peter G. Peterson Institute for International Economics, 2008), 9–10; Michael D. Swaine, *America's Challenge: Engaging a Rising China in the Twenty-first Century* (Washington, DC: Carnegie Endowment for International Peace, 2011), 162–63; Secretary of State Hillary Rodham Clinton, "Inaugural Richard C. Holbrooke Lecture on a Broad Vision of U.S.-China Relations in the 21st Century," Washington, D.C., January 14, 2011, available at: http://www.state.gov/secretary/rm/2011/01/154653.htm.

2. For good coverage of the Clinton administration's China policy, see Henry Kissinger, *On China* (New York: Penguin, 2011), 461–70.

3. *The Amitage Report: The United States and Japan: Advancing toward a Mature Partnership*, INSS (Institute for National Strategic Studies) Special Report, National Defense University (October 11, 2000), accessed online on May 30, 2011.

4. Thomas Christensen, *Worse Than a Monolith: Alliance Politics and Problems of Coercive Diplomacy in Asia* (Princeton, NJ: Princeton University Press, 2011), 244; James Przystup and Phillip Saunders, "Visions of Order: Japan and China in U.S. Strategy," in *Strategic Forum* (Institute for National Strategic Studies, National Defense University), no. 220, June 2006, accessed online on May 30, 2011.

5. Murray Hiebert, *The Bush Presidency: Implications for Asia* (New York: The Asia Society, January 2001), 5–9.

6. Bonnie Glaser, "First Contact: Qian Qichen Engages in Wide-ranging, Constructive Talks," in *Comparative Connections*, April 2001.

7. John Keefe, *Anatomy of the EP-3 Incident, April 2001* (Alexandria, VA: Center for Naval Analysis, 2001).

8. Christensen, *Worse Than a Monolith*, 245.

9. Ibid., 246–47; Robert Sutter, *U.S.-Chinese Relations: Perilous Past, Pragmatic Present* (Rowman & Littlefield, 2010), 152.

10. Christensen, *Worse Than a Monolith*, 248–49.

11. Sutter, *U.S.-Chinese Relations*, 153; Christensen, *Worse Than a Monolith*, 249.

12. John Pomfret, "China Lauds Bush for Comments on Taiwan," in *The Washington Post*, December 11, 2003; Christensen, *Worse Than a Monolith*, 249.

13. Robert Sutter, "Dealing with a Rising China: U.S. Strategy and Policy," in Zhang Yunlin, ed., *Making New Partnership: A Rising China and Its Neighbors* (Beijing: Social Sciences Academic Press, 2008), 370–74.

14. Remarks of Deputy Secretary of State Robert Zoellick, "Whither China? From Membership to Responsibility?" New York, National Committee for U.S.-China Relations, September 21, 2005, available at: http://usinfo.state.gove/eap/Archive/2005/Sep/22-29048.html.

15. Zoellick, "Whither China?"

16. *The National Security Strategy of the United States of America*, March 2006, available at: http://www.comw.org/qdr/fulltext/nss2006.pdf.

17. Department of Defense, *Quadrennial Defense Review Report*, February 2, 2006, 29, available at: http://www.defense.gov/pubs/pdfs/QDR20060203.pdf.

18. Thomas Christensen, "Shaping the Choices of a Rising China: Recent Lessons for the Obama Administration," in *Washington Quarterly* 32, no. 3 (2009): 90–91.

19. Ibid., 90.

20. Thomas Christensen, "The Advantages of an Assertive China," in *Foreign Affairs*, March/April 2011, 90, no. 2: 54–55.

21. This language appeared in joint statements issued by the U.S. and Chinese presidents in 2009 and 2011.

22. The White House Office of the Press Secretary, "Remarks by the President at the U.S./China Strategic and Economic Dialogue," July 27, 2009, available at: http://www.whitehouse.gov/the-press-office/remarks-president-uschina-strategic-and-economic-dialogue.

23. James B. Steinberg, "China's Arrival: The Long March to Global Power," keynote address to the Center for a New American Security, Washington, D.C., September 24, 2009, available at: http://www.cnas.org/node/3415.

24. Francois Godement, "The United States and Asia in 2009," in *Asian Survey* 50, no. 1: 8–24.

25. Ibid.

26. Comments by Secretary Clinton in Hanoi, July 23, 2010, available at: http://www.america.gov/st/texttrans-english/2010/July/20100723164658su0.4912989.html.

27. For a longer list of Chinese abrasiveness, see Susan V. Lawrence and Thomas Lum, "U.S.-China Relations: Policy Issues," in *Congressional Research Service*, March 11, 2011, 4–5, accessed online, May 29, 2011.

28. Christensen, "The Advantage of an Assertive China," 54–67.

29. Lawrence and Lum, "U.S.-China Relations."

30. Kissinger, *On China*, 513.

31. Hillary Clinton, "Inaugural Richard C. Holbrooke."

32. Abraham Denmark and Nirav Patel, eds., *A Strategic Framework for a Global Relationship* (Washington, DC: Center for New America Security, September 2009), 12.

33. G. John Ikenberry, "Asian Regionalism and the Future of U.S. Strategic Engagement with China," in Denmark and Patel, eds., *A Strategic Framework*, 95–108.

34. Abraham M. Denmark, "China's Arrival: A Framework for a Global Relationship," in Denmark and Patel, eds., *A Strategic Framework*, 157–79.

35. Lawrence and Lum, "U.S.-China Relations."

36. Lindsey Ford, "21st Century Strategy with 19th Century Institutions: The Challenge of Bureaucracies in the U.S.-China Relationship," in Denmark and Patel, eds., *A Strategic Framework*, 153.

37. Brahma Chellaney, *Asian Juggernaut: The Rise of China, India and Japan* (New York: HarperBusiness, 2010), vi–viii.

FURTHER READING

Bergsten, C. Fred. *China's Rise: Challenges and Opportunities.* Washington, DC: Peter G. Peterson Institute for International Economics, 2008.

Sutter, Robert. *U.S.-Chinese Relations: Perilous Past, Pragmatic Present.* Lanham, MD: Rowman & Littlefield, 2010.

Swaine, Michael D. *America's Challenge: Engaging a Rising China in the Twenty-first Century.* Washington, DC: Carnegie Endowment for International Peace, 2011.

chapter 37

Africa in the Twenty-first Century

by John Stoner

MUCH OF ANY nation's foreign policy is predicated upon the concept of *security;* at different times, however, what defines security varies. This is certainly the case with the foreign policy of the United States toward Africa. Its diplomacy in Africa has varied, as has the government's sense of what constitutes security. In the twenty-first century, U.S. policy toward Africa combines an older conceptualization of security for Americans from terrorism or attack with a newer belief that security for the United States may spring from the stability and security of Africans themselves, stability that may come from healthier African populations or more vibrant African economies.

THE UNITED STATES AND NEWLY INDEPENDENT AFRICAN NATIONS

Much early U.S. foreign policy toward newly independent Africa between the 1950s and the 1980s reflected the imperatives of the Cold War. While rarely as central to Cold War struggles as Western Europe, Asia, or even Latin America, Africa bore the brunt of several Cold War–era proxy wars (in which allies or representatives of the United States and Soviet Union engaged in conflict) that caused significant economic and political damage. Most importantly, those conflicts killed, injured, or displaced millions of Africans; their effects are still being felt in the twenty-first century. During the same period, the grip of colonialism on Africa eased, and Africans found themselves struggling to create new states, invigorate fledgling economies, and negotiate the perils of a two-superpower world in which their leaders were expected to choose sides.

With the end of the Cold War, African countries faced being further marginalized; with the exception of crises, what little importance Africa had enjoyed was on the wane. During the 1980s and 1990s, however, it became clear that there were still important reasons for the United States government to remain engaged in Africa. For example, political

chaos in Somalia brought both a U.S.-supported military response and a relatively hasty departure after nineteen American soldiers were killed in 1993. Highly publicized images of dead American soldiers brought scrutiny and criticism to a mission that many Americans neither understood nor supported. The reluctance of the U.S. government to label mass murder in Rwanda in 1994 as genocide helped to guarantee United Nations (UN) inaction; a concerted UN effort may have saved hundreds of thousands of Tutsis killed during the violence.

Throughout the 1990s, instability in Somalia, Kenya, Sudan, Nigeria, and elsewhere raised concerns about regional destabilization and, eventually, radical Islamist connections to international terrorism that became the central focus of American diplomacy during the early part of the century. Even in those states that are inherently more stable or have more representative forms of government, U.S. diplomacy seeks to encourage commitments to multiparty democracy, the end of one-party states, and more transparent political regimes that guarantee certain human and legal rights for all of their citizens.

In addition to more obvious political instability, other factors pushed for new U.S. policies. The growing scourge of HIV/AIDS (Human Immuno-deficiency Virus/Acquired Immune Deficiency Syndrome), which has affected Africa more than any other continent, brought a renewed commitment by both the U.S. government and non-governmental organizations (NGOs) in treating those with the virus, as well as preventing its transmission. In this regard, the presidency of George W. Bush (2001–2009) was a pivotal moment. The Bush administration dramatically increased funds to HIV/AIDS treatment. This commitment has thus far been sustained by the administration of Barack Obama (2009–). The government has been joined in its efforts to improve global health by several powerful new NGOs, such as the Bill and Melinda Gates Foundation and the William Jefferson Clinton Foundation. Other diseases, such as malaria, also are the focus of American campaigns.

KEY CONCEPTS

National security. During the Cold War, security meant one of a few different things to the United States; for example, the physical security of Americans from military attack or espionage by the Soviet Union or its allies. It also meant economic security, the protection of the preeminent position of the United States. With the decline and subsequent end of the Cold War, the United States enjoyed what Charles Krauthammer of *The Washington Post* termed, in a 1991 *Foreign Affairs* article (70:1 [1990/1991]: 22–23), the "unipolar moment," in which the United States appeared to reign supreme. A little more than a decade later, however, the attacks of September 11, 2001, suggested unexpected and unwelcome vulnerability. The resulting war on terrorism under the presidency of George W. Bush singled out terrorists and those people and governments sympathetic to their cause worldwide.

The threat of terrorism in Africa seemed confined to states with pro-Islamist policies, or states in crisis in which many different political groups could operate with relative impunity. Over time, however, older formulations of physical security gave way to more flexible interpretations of how to achieve that security. In Africa, as in other places around the world, people began to recognize that many different kinds of conditions contributed to destabilization and potentially paved the way for the development of anti-American or anti-Western attitudes. In addition to putting a new military focus on Africa through the creation of the first centralized U.S. military command (AFRICOM), other efforts focused on good governance, civil society, health, and economic development. By facilitating access by Africans to various kinds of essential needs (human rights, civil rights, food, health, etc.), American policy in the early twenty-first century sought to achieve security for its own citizens.

Economic growth is another way in which the U.S. government hopes to promote stability in Africa. One of the key ways in which the U.S. government sought to encourage African exports and economic growth was through the Africa Growth and Opportunity Act, first passed in 2000 and signed into law by President William J. Clinton (1993–2001); it since has been extended until 2015. By providing preferential status to African manufacturers, the government hopes to secure not only an improved economic climate for countries that participate but also to foster goodwill.[1] The Millennium Challenge Corporation, another organization created by the U.S. government, seeks to combat poverty by making grants that encourage economic growth.

Political Stability and Good Governance

It is clearly in the interest of the United States (and countries like France and the United Kingdom, which maintain relationships with their former colonies) for African countries to be stable. Stability creates an atmosphere in which political transitions can occur relatively painlessly, economic growth can actually positively benefit the citizens of that nation, and outside governments and other institutions and organizations can ensure that much-needed assistance gets to those who need it.

From the American perspective, stability can be achieved in several ways. One is through a definition of security that stresses the need for well-trained and well-equipped military and police forces to maintain order, ensure the rule of law, and protect against less stable neighbors. In Cold War Africa, American principles favoring representative democracies often gave way to an ideological pragmatism that preferred pro-Western, anti-Communist dictators to more representative or democratic leaders who favored the Soviet Union.

Since the end of the Cold War in late 1991, the United States has been better able to focus on encouraging the growth of more representative forms of government. These efforts have met with some success, but many obstacles remain, not the least of which is that some African leaders have little interest in adopting practices that would likely see them removed from office. In some cases, the United States has sufficient leverage to influence internal political dynamics; in others, such as in Zimbabwe, it has few options except to watch a situation go from bad to worse.

In 2011, Assistant Secretary of State for Africa Johnnie Carson gave testimony before the Senate Foreign Relations Subcommittee on African Affairs. In that testimony, he identified five key areas in which the United States sought to engage with Africans. They were as follows: (1) strengthening democratic institutions and the rule of law; (2) encouraging long-term development and growth, including food security; (3) enhancing access to quality health care and education; (4) assisting in the prevention, mitigation, and resolution of conflicts; and (5) working with Africans to address transnational challenges, including terrorism, maritime security, climate change, narcotics trafficking, and trafficking in persons.

According to Carson, there still existed an ongoing ideological conflict. If the United States were to fail to exploit its opportunities to help Africa, Americans would be "on the defensive in the global competition for influence and ideas."[2]

Good Governance and the Encouragement of Democracy

In many ways, good governance initiatives were casualties of the Cold War. If dictators agreed to help the United

States frustrate alleged Soviet intentions, then they could often continue their dictatorial rule in relative peace, assured of the friendship and assistance of the United States. There were several exceptions to this rule; the moment when popular and congressional pressure overrode the reluctance of the administration of Ronald Reagan (1981–1989) to impose sanctions on apartheid South Africa in 1986 is probably the best known of them. With Soviet communism (or any other kind) no longer a threat, the United States has been more comfortable practicing what it preaches in terms of political change in the last two decades.

The Need for Democracy

Political scientist Joel Barkan identifies Africa as a particularly important region in which the United States needs to advance democracy. He argues that "every U.S. interest in Africa—from security and counterterrorism to economic development, trade, health, and energy—will depend on participatory, capable, and accountable governments with which the United States can partner."[3] This places a significant burden on the U.S. government not only to figure out how to achieve stable and (at least ideally) democratic states where they do not yet exist, but also how to ensure that they will stay that way. It also begs the question of whether or not every African country needs to replicate a certain form of government in order to be stable, prosperous, and ensure better access to rights to its citizens.

Because relatively few less-democratic states (in Africa or elsewhere) can transition easily into more democratic ones, regime change always brings with it the potential for further instability, violence, or other outcomes, which do little to foster good governance or more participatory states. The few successful cases (as in South Africa in the 1990s, when the minority, white-dominated government gave way to a popularly elected one) are greatly outnumbered by cases, as in Zimbabwe or the Ivory Coast, in which autocratic rulers refuse to cede power even after relatively free and fair elections. Therefore, American political leaders have to tread carefully in terms of encouraging regime change, unless and until it becomes patently obvious that change is occurring with or without American assistance. It is especially critical at those moments, however, for the United States to encourage new regimes to be more representative, more transparent, and if not democratic then at least accepting of the goals of U.S. African policy.

In the now fifty-four countries that comprise the African continent, there is a wide range of governmental systems in place, ranging from effectively authoritarian states to multiparty representative democracies. At times, the U.S. government has struggled to know how to encourage the shift from the former to the latter. That struggle will likely continue into the foreseeable future, although recent events in North Africa and in the Ivory Coast, Nigeria, and Tanzania suggest that some progress is being made.

One potentially useful barometer of the degree of freedom in Africa is the scale generated by Freedom House, an NGO dedicated to improving access to democratic forms of government around the world. Each year, using a scale of 1 to 7 (from most free to least), Freedom House rates countries based on both the political rights enjoyed by citizens as well as their enjoyment of civil liberties. It also tracks how (and why) those scores shift over time. Over the last decade, relatively little has changed in terms of the degrees of freedom enjoyed by many Africans. In 2001, nine African countries were considered to be "free"; that number rose to eleven in 2006 and dropped back to ten in 2010. For countries considered by Freedom House to be "partly free," African nations lost ground slightly; the continent had twenty-five partly free nations in 2001, twenty-three in 2006, and twenty-two in 2010. The number of "not free" nations remained static at nineteen in 2001 and 2006, but rose to twenty-one in 2010. While only one African country, Cape Verde, received the lowest (and therefore best) combined average score in 2010, five nations (Equatorial Guinea, Eritrea, Libya, Somalia, and Sudan) received the highest and worst average scores.[4] While neither a perfect measure nor a good way to monitor incremental change, the ratings suggest that many African nations still have a long way to go toward achieving Western ideals of freedom. At the very least, this implies that any American efforts at democracy-building will be a long-term process requiring significant financial and human resources; it also assumes that the United States has the ability to influence events in each country equally, something that is demonstrably not the case.

MILITARY SUPPORT OF U.S. AFRICAN POLICY (AFRICOM)

During the Cold War, there were no major points at which any nation in Africa posed a significant military threat to the United States. Its biggest concern was the presence of military advisers or military forces of the Soviet Union and its satellites, such as the Cuban military presence in Angola in the 1970s and 1980s, or the presence of Soviet advisers in Egypt, Angola, and elsewhere throughout the Cold War. The United States responded in kind, sending military advisers to a variety of countries during the period.

In the post–Cold War world, threats to American security have become less easily identifiable, particularly in the context of the effort to combat international terrorism.

Thus, military efforts have largely been confined to intelligence gathering and assistance in training the military and police in African countries with good relationships with the United States.

Training Peacekeepers

By the late 1990s, the U.S. military had started to take on several new projects in regard to Africa. The African Crisis Response Initiative (ACRI) used special operations personnel to train African peacekeepers. ACRI and a subsequent program have trained roughly two hundred thousand peacekeepers. Early in the new century, the military also tasked a Combined Joint Task Force–Horn of Africa (CJTF-HOA) with helping promote regional security, stability, and economic growth. Within a few years, it was clear to many within the military that a centralized command structure was necessary to coordinate American military efforts in Africa.[5]

The linchpin in this new effort is the first unified American military command specifically devoted to Africa. The United States African Command (AFRICOM) came into being in 2007 in an effort to centralize planning and operations of several different projects. It has an unusual command and advisory structure that the command itself terms "unique." It purposely integrates civilians from the Departments of State, Commerce, Homeland Security, and from the United States Agency for International Development.[6]

AFRICOM's tenure has been controversial, drawing criticism from both inside and outside of the government in the United States, and a fair amount of criticism in Africa as well. Among these concerns are those by the non-governmental community about a significant American military presence on the continent and African concerns about where such a command would be headquartered (after great controversy, it retained its headquarters in Germany, although a new commander in 2011 has expressed openness to reconsidering that decision); AFRICOM faces a major public relations challenge.[7] If its model works, however, it could provide a template not only for military and civilian cooperation in American Africa policy, but it also could throw additional resources into the U.S. attempt to effect positive change on the continent. Despite the criticism, one analyst calls it "the Bush administration's most important innovation with regard to security policy in Africa. This coincided with a shifting focus on the use of military assets in preventive and proactive ways rather than reactive or combat-oriented ones."[8] Another scholar notes AFRICOM's initial missteps but says that "time and effort will still be required to . . . prove AFRICOM's positive place in the United States' approach to Africa."[9]

SHIFTS IN FOREIGN POLICY: *A DISEASE RESHAPES U.S. FOREIGN POLICY*

One of the main ways in which many Americans encountered Africa during the last century was during moments of political strife or human suffering. The famine caused by political upheaval in Biafra (a secessionist state in southeast Nigeria) in the late 1960s and the famine in Ethiopia in the mid-1980s are two such examples. Food aid has been a staple of international assistance to Africa for decades in an effort to ameliorate the worst effects of poor harvest, climate change, or political instability. The American public also was aware of the prevalence of some diseases in Africa. Yet malaria, so-called sleeping sickness, and others were generally diseases confined to the continent or only affecting those who traveled there. In the most prosperous countries of the world, however, there was little impetus to invest significant resources in health more broadly, or disease treatment and prevention more narrowly.

This all changed with growing public awareness of the HIV/AIDS epidemic. While many Americans first perceived AIDS as a disease principally affecting gay men, research being done in Africa at the same time indicated that heterosexual transmission was not only common but perhaps even more prevalent in the African context. Early responses by the U.S. government understandably focused on fighting the effects of the disease domestically and funding research for an AIDS vaccine. Relatively little attention or funding went to supporting the fight against the disease abroad; in 1999, for example, the Clinton administration appropriated $135 million through the United States Agency for International Development to fund HIV/AIDS related efforts (*The Clinton/Gore Administration: A Record of Progress* *on HIV and AIDS,* June 1999, 6, accessed on July 3, 2011, at: http://clinton2.nara .gov/ONAP/pub/hivacc.pdf).

CHANGING RATES OF TRANSMISSION

As rates of transmission slowed in the United States, and as anti-retroviral therapy became much more successful at controlling the disease, it became equally crucial to export resources not only to cut down on the spread of the disease but also to provide medical treatment for those who had already contracted it. The number of those in sub-Saharan Africa who were either HIV-positive or who had developed AIDS was staggering; one estimate of the prevalence of the epidemic in South Africa in 1999 estimated that almost 20 percent of the adult population was living with HIV or AIDS (United Nations, Joint United Nations Programme on HIV/AIDS [UNAIDS] and Economic Commission for Africa, *AIDS in Africa: Country by Country* [Geneva: Joint United Nations Programme on HIV/AIDS, 2000], 195, accessed on July 3, 2011, at: http://data.unaids .org/publications/IRC-pub05/aidsafrica2000_en.pdf). While South Africa and several other southern African countries with large migrant worker populations undoubtedly had higher rates of infection, they also had the infrastructure to begin to document the severity of the problem, infrastructure not always present in their neighbors to the north. By 2000, twenty-five million of the estimated thirty-six million people with HIV/AIDS worldwide lived in Africa. As the cost of antiretroviral therapy dropped, the opportunities for helping other countries struggling with the epidemic increased. One UNAIDS/WHO report indicated that ramping up the international response to Africa's

HEALTH SECURITY

The President's Emergency Plan for AIDS Relief (PEPFAR) has been variously described as either bigger than the Marshall Plan or the largest single foreign assistance program since the Marshall Plan channeled money to European countries shortly after World War II (1939–1945).[10] In either case, it represents an enormous commitment to ameliorating the effects of HIV/AIDS and seeking to roll back the rate of growth of the number of those infected.

Governmental Efforts

Both through direct assistance and through partnerships like those with the Global Fund to Fight AIDS, Tuberculosis and Malaria, and non-governmental organizations, PEPFAR has directly affected the lives of millions of Africans. As of the end of September 2010, PEPFAR was providing antiretroviral therapy to 3.2 million people worldwide; with the exception of approximately 100,000 in Asia and the Caribbean, the rest of the recipients were in sub-Saharan Africa. Certain countries received disproportionate shares of the assistance; more than 900,000 South Africans received assistance in 2010, as did more than 400,000 Kenyans. The Global Fund estimated, however, that as of 2009, more than ten million people in Africa were in need

of antiretroviral therapy. One of the key reasons for seeking greater stability and development in African states is that it makes possible the reliable and potentially increased delivery of treatment.

HIV/AIDS is not the only health focus of American diplomacy. The Bush administration also created the President's Malaria Initiative (PMI) in 2005. Congress extended PMI's funding until fiscal year 2013. Most of the President's Malaria Initiative is administered through the United States Agency for International Development (USAID), with the help of the Centers for Disease Control and Prevention (CDC). PMI focuses on four measures to control malaria; these include indoor spraying of insecticides, the use of treated mosquito nets, "intermittent preventive treatment for pregnant women, and diagnosis of malaria and treatment with artemisinin-based combination therapy (ACT)."[11] Since 2001, the World Health Organization (WHO) has been encouraging the use of ACT in countries in which drug-resistant malaria is endemic. Funding for PMI in fiscal year 2010 was $500 million.

Through its partnership with the Global Fund, the United States government also is seeking to influence outcomes for a number of other health problems that plague much of sub-Saharan Africa. Between 2002 and 2010, the fund's own malaria prevention efforts included

plight was both "imperative and affordable" (United Nations, Joint United Nations Programme on HIV/AIDS and the World Health Organization, *AIDS Epidemic Update: December 2000* [Geneva: UNAIDS/WHO, 2000], 5, accessed on July 3, 2011, at: http://www.aegis.com/files/unaids/waddecember2000_epidemic_report.pdf).

U.S.–SPONSORED INITIATIVES

In many ways confounding those who expected relative apathy from his administration, President George W. Bush was responsible for taking bold new steps and devoting previously unheard-of resources toward fighting HIV/AIDS in Africa. While the U.S. government has increased funding to fight HIV/AIDS through other organizations, the centerpiece of its effort has been the President's Emergency Plan for AIDS Relief (PEPFAR). Announced during President Bush's 2003 State of the Union Address, on January 28, and transcribed in *The Washington Post,* PEPFAR was to be "a work of mercy beyond all current international efforts to help the people of Africa." President Bush originally asked for $15 billion over five years; with additional congressional appropriations, the program spent almost $19 billion in its first five years, the majority of it in Africa (Nieburg, Phillip, and J. Stephen Morrison, "The Big U.S. Leap on HIV/AIDS In Africa: What is the Next Act?" in Cooke, Jennifer G., and J. Stephen Morrison, eds., *U.S. Africa Policy beyond the Bush Years* [Washington, DC: The CSIS Press, 2009], 34–61).

The United States has used a variety of delivery methods to channel money for HIV/AIDS and other health issues to African recipients. In addition to others, it is the single-largest contributor to the Global Fund to Fight AIDS,

tuberculosis, and malaria, which is a joint public-private partnership initially sponsored by the United Nations.

In 2009, President Barack Obama announced the formation of an umbrella program, the Global Health Initiative, which encompasses four U.S. government health programs, including PEPFAR, the President's Malaria Initiative (PMI), Feed the Future (FTF), and the Neglected Tropical Disease Initiative (NTD). In the first years of the Obama administration, the U.S. government continued to emphasize the importance of PEPFAR and other projects devoted to lessening the impact of AIDS and other diseases. In 2010, PEPFAR provided antiretroviral therapy for more than 3.2 million people and testing and HIV counseling for another thirty-three million. Its commitment of $4 billion to the Global Fund for 2011–2013 represents an increase of almost 40 percent more than during the previous period (United States, U.S. President's Emergency Plan for AIDS Relief, "Saving Lives through Smart Investments: Latest PEPFAR Results," accessed on July 5, 2011, at http://www.pepfar.gov/documents/organization/153723.pdf).

Even if external funding results in dramatically lower rates of HIV transmission, tens of millions of people will continue to live with AIDS; with appropriate pharmaceutical therapies, they could live for some time, requiring a sustained commitment from donors to antiretroviral therapy and other forms of assistance. Given the economic downturn at the end of the decade, maintaining steady levels of funding, let alone increasing them, remains uncertain more than a few years into the future. Without a cure in sight, organizations like PEPFAR and the Global Fund must continue to provide therapy or condemn millions to much shorter lives.

the distribution of roughly 110 million treated mosquito nets in sub-Saharan Africa and the treatment of 140 million cases of malaria. In the same period, almost two million Africans received a diagnosis of, and treatment for, tuberculosis. The Global Fund also distributed 1.7 billion condoms.[12]

The distribution of condoms under PEPFAR was somewhat controversial during the Bush administration. PEPFAR's initial strategy called for a three-pronged attack against AIDS transmission; this "ABC" approach included abstinence, being faithful, and condom use. Programmatic rules and policy imperatives placed emphasis on the first two parts of the strategy; critics charged that this ideological weighting of potentially less-realistic goals was harming those at risk of contracting the virus. PEPFAR condom distribution programs focused on higher-risk populations (relationships in which one partner is already HIV-positive, sex workers, and men who are sexually active with other men, among others), thereby effectively denying access to condoms to many. Mandating funding levels at times meant that some countries had to scale back condom distribution to meet the requirements of the plan. The reauthorization of PEPFAR in 2008 made its requirements somewhat more flexible but still pushed the politicized model.[13]

Non-Governmental Organizations

Several U.S.-based non-governmental organizations have become major figures in the global campaign against HIV/AIDS and other diseases. The Bill and Melinda Gates Foundation made grant commitments of more than $22 billion between 1995 and 2009, 58 percent of which targeted health issues. Of that $13 billion, grants went to a variety of efforts including HIV (17 percent), malaria (13 percent), neglected diseases (7 percent), tuberculosis (7 percent), and others. The Gates Foundation's report on its Global Health Program in 2010 cited its belief "that our generation will be judged by how we handle the crisis of global health."[14] The foundation worked in concert with organizations like the Global Fund; its 2009 commitment of $1.8 billion to improve global health ranked it as the third-largest donor in the world, behind only the U.S. government and the Global Fund.[15]

A relatively new foundation headed by former President William J. Clinton also devoted the majority of its 2010 funding to health projects. The William J. Clinton Foundation's Clinton Health Access Initiative (CHAI), formerly the Clinton HIV/AIDS Initiative, received the lion's share of the Foundation's 2010 spending. CHAI focuses on negotiating lower prices for key drugs, improving access to treatment, and reducing mother-to-child transmission of HIV/AIDS; it has also begun to apply some of the same strategies to the prevention and treatment of malaria.[16]

AFRICAN ECONOMIC GROWTH

Central to many of the other integrated goals of American foreign policy in Africa (good governance, democracy, and stability) is economic growth. This argument is hard to refute; the desperate poverty in most African countries, coupled with frequent corruption that further concentrates wealth into the hands of very few, has a number of different consequences, none of which is good. Poor countries cannot generate tax revenue, which limits the ability of those governments to invest in education, infrastructure, economic development, or health care. Poor countries often cannot adequately compensate civil servants or members of the police and military; this can lead to corruption and political instability. Countries that have borrowed money from international multilateral institutions may face significant debt burdens, which they are unlikely to ever repay. In the face of these and other challenges, American efforts to jumpstart African economic growth are key.

While the United States ranks as one of the more prosperous nations in the world, most African countries number among the poorest. Statistics indicating per-capita gross domestic product (GDP), the monetary value of goods and services produced in a year, reflect this poverty. According to 2008 UN statistics, twenty-nine of the then fifty-three African countries had per-capita GDP of less than $1,000. Another ten were between $1,000 and $2,000. Only fifteen countries enjoyed a per-capita GDP greater than $2,000, with only three greater than $10,000.

Improving the economy of another country is often difficult to accomplish. In terms of American policy, the U.S. government has pursued two principal strategies in trying to do so. One, reflected in the African Growth and Opportunity Act (AGOA), effectively subsidizes African exports to the United States, giving preferential access to many African goods. The other strategy is development assistance, which the United States manages in several different ways, one of which is the Millennium Challenge Corporation (MCC). Countries that make progress toward certain benchmarks regarding democracy and transparency have access to assistance through both AGOA and the MCC.

African Growth and Opportunity Act (AGOA)

Initially signed into law by President William J. Clinton in 2000, the African Growth and Opportunity Act has been renewed until at least 2015; the Obama administration has suggested extending it until at least 2025. According to the legislation, the president can declare a sub-Saharan African country eligible if it had or sought a "market-based economy" rooted in private property and limited government. Other requirements included respecting the rule of law and political pluralism, "the elimination of barriers to United States trade and investment," economic policies to combat

TABLE 37.1   **Per Capita Gross Domestic Product (GDP), 2008**

Country or Area	Annual per Capita GDP (US$)
United States (for comparison)	45,230
Equatorial Guinea	27,130
Libyan Arab Jamahiriya	14,430
Seychelles	11,044
Gabon	9,888
Mauritius	7,450
Botswana	6,108
South Africa	5,566
Algeria	4,959
Namibia	4,143
Tunisia	3,876
Cape Verde	3,439
Congo	2,934
Morocco	2,740
Swaziland	2,369
Egypt	2,031
Angola	1,942
Sudan	1,700
Nigeria	1,450
Cameroon	1,218
Djibouti	1,155
Zambia	1,144
Côte d'Ivoire	1,137
São Tomé and Príncipe	1,108
Senegal	1,088
Mauritania	1,017
Comoros	802
Kenya	788
Lesotho	788
Benin	767
Chad	765
Ghana	709
Mali	677
Gambia	636
Burkina Faso	522
Guinea	505
United Republic of Tanzania	502
Uganda	500
Madagascar	488
Afghanistan	466
Central African Republic	464
Rwanda	458
Togo	446
Mozambique	440
Sierra Leone	418
Niger	354
Ethiopia	319
Zimbabwe	314
Eritrea	300
Somalia	298
Malawi	278
Guinea-Bissau	257
Liberia	219
Democratic Republic of the Congo	181
Burundi	138
African average	2,498

SOURCE: Adapted from United Nations, Statistics Division, "Indicators on income and economic activity," updated December 2010, accessed on July 11, 2011, at http://unstats. un.org/unsd/demographic/products/socind/inc-eco.htm#tech.

NOTE: GDP is the combined total of all goods and services produced in a country. It is often used as a gauge of the economic strength of a nation. These figures (while only for one year) suggest that the average African nation's economy is eighteen times less productive than the United States.

poverty and corruption while encouraging access to education, and the guarantee of worker rights.[17] As of September 2010, thirty-eight countries were eligible for AGOA benefits, although not all of them qualified for all benefits potentially available under the legislation. Including AGOA imports, a United States Trade Representative document noted that "almost all African exports to the United States enter duty-free."[18]

It is difficult to quantify how much AGOA is helping Africa, particularly since, at least in monetary terms, the most important import by far from eligible countries was oil. In the first half of 2010, imports from AGOA countries were valued at $22.4 billion, only $1.6 billion of which came from "non-oil" products. The "top five" beneficiary countries included the two oil-producing powerhouse countries of Nigeria and Angola in first and second place, respectively; the third country, South Africa, boasts one of the continent's strongest economies.[19] While AGOA may be helping some African nations, there is no question that in many African countries there has not been sufficient economic development to generate the trade capacity to take advantage of the opportunities afforded by the legislation.[20]

Millennium Challenge Corporation (MCC)

Created in 2004, the Millennium Challenge Corporation (MCC) is funded by the U.S. government and chaired by the secretary of state. In addition to several board members from outside of the government, the secretary of the treasury, the United States Trade Representative, and the administrator of USAID all serve on the board. Its mandate is to approve "compacts" with eligible countries to fund development projects. As with AGOA, countries which hope to receive funds must meet certain benchmarks from three broad categories. These include "ruling justly," "investing in people," and "encouraging economic freedom." The MCC uses outside measures in order to evaluate prospective candidates; its measure for political rights and civil liberties, for example, comes from Freedom House. Other measures come from UNESCO, the World Health Organization, the Brookings Institution, and the World Bank, and IMF.[21]

While not as specifically focused on Africa as some other development assistance programs like PEPFAR or AGOA, many of the early compact countries of the MCC have been in Africa. As of the end of September 2010, the MCC had funded or agreed to fund compacts with twenty-one countries, twelve of which were in Africa. Current commitments totaled more than $7.5 billion, more than $5.1 billion (or roughly 68 percent) of which was headed to African compact countries. The majority of "compact investments" go either to transport or agriculture.

The MCC also made provisions for countries not yet able to meet the benchmarks required of compact countries. Its "threshold" program allocated smaller amounts to

TABLE 37.2   **Total Crude Oil and Products: Top Eight African Exporters to the United States (thousands of barrels)**

	2005	2006	2007	2008	2009	2010	Total	% of Total
All Countries	5,005,541	5,003,082	4,915,957	4,726,994	4,267,110	4,289,772	28,208,456	100.00%
Nigeria	425,440	406,662	413,932	361,659	295,310	374,279	2,277,282	8.07%
Algeria	174,652	239,959	244,605	200,652	180,018	184,969	1,224,855	4.34%
Angola	172,609	195,048	185,652	187,790	167,877	142,531	1,051,507	3.73%
Libya	20,520	31,896	42,801	37,834	28,863	25,717	187,631	0.67%
Chad	35,574	37,143	28,400	38,080	25,134	11,792	176,123	0.62%
Equatorial Guinea	25,385	21,957	21,597	28,439	32,310	21,063	150,751	0.53%
Congo (Brazzaville)	11,592	12,957	23,849	24,943	23,816	26,276	123,433	0.44%
Cameroon	2,923	2,857	10,804	5,341	15,585	18,133	55,643	0.20%
Total Crude Oil and Products from Top 8 African Exporters	868,695	948,479	971,640	884,738	768,913	804,760	5,247,225	18.60%

SOURCE: Distilled from U.S. Energy Information Administration table, Petroleum and Other Liquids, U.S. Imports by Country of Origin, 2005–2010, available at http://www.eia.gov/dnav/pet/pet_move_impcus_a2_nus_ep00_im0_mbbl_a.htm.

countries that committed themselves to eventually reaching compact status. Of the twenty-one threshold countries in late 2010, ten were from Africa; reforms being conducted in Africa focused predominantly on control of corruption and improving educational access for girls.[22]

As with several other of the more integrated forms of assistance and policy thus far under way during the twenty-first century, the jury is still out on the MCC. By its nature, it will likely take years, if not decades, to fairly evaluate its impact. John Hewko, a former MCC staffer, worries that the corporation will fall victim to political pressures; while recognizing early missteps at the under-staffed agency in its first several years, he strongly advocates that the MCC be allowed to improve its policies, to support countries interested in applying for compact status, and to have what he sees as the necessary seven- to ten-year window before evaluating particular country projects. He argues that institutions like the MCC will assist other countries in embracing transparency, good governance, and economic development, while simultaneously being exposed to what he perceives as "core American values."[23] Others are less certain, and worry that countries that graduate from threshold to compact status do not receive adequate oversight or face the same challenges of the initial benchmarks.[24]

One successful form of international assistance and a useful tool for fighting poverty comes from microfinance institutions, organizations that provide very small loans, or micro-loans, to poor people. The recipients of micro-loans are often women who start or expand very small businesses. Through ingenuity and drive, and the support of the lending microfinance institutions, poor people are able to start their journey out of poverty.

REGIONAL SPOTLIGHT

A major difficulty in working with more contemporary historical topics is that events can overwhelm efforts at analyzing the recent past and unduly complicate any efforts to assess the future direction of U.S. diplomacy. Events in North Africa in early 2011 were just one such example of this: the leaders of Tunisia and Egypt, who ruled their respective countries for more than fifty years combined, went out of power following popular mass protests, and Libya's Muammar el-Qaddafi fled Tripoli after more than forty years of autocratic rule. In addition to looking at the programmatic ways in which the State Department and other U.S. government agencies formulate and implement American foreign policy, it is important to at least briefly examine some of the key regions and countries in Africa. Some of those countries are significant because of their relative stability and the ways in which the lack of turmoil within is noteworthy and reflects stated American policy goals; others, such as Libya, are important for the opposite reasons and get attention because of U.S. efforts to prevent conflict or respond to crises. Frequent regime change is rarely positive, but regime change that results in more stable governments with which the United States can cooperate is very useful for the government and NGOs alike.

North Africa

No other African region has experienced as much political upheaval in 2011 as North Africa. The several-decades-old conflict in Sudan has occupied much popular attention, particularly in recent years. In the first several months of 2011, however, uprisings in Tunisia, Egypt, and Libya reshaped the political landscapes of those countries and impressed upon the region's other rulers the need to implement political and economic reform. Concerns remain that new governments may legitimize more extreme Islamist tendencies that many American policymakers view as antithetical to American security interests, particularly if they provide cover for terrorism.

Egypt

For much of the last thirty years, Egypt and its leader, Hosni Mubarak, were important American allies. Next to Israel, Egypt has been the second-largest recipient of American foreign assistance since 1979.[25] Mubarak's rule was a prime example of how American rhetoric and ideals warred with the pragmatic desire of the United States to have Mubarak at the head of a stable Arab nation on Israel's southern border.

This all changed in early 2011, when Egyptians took to the streets in late January demanding political and economic reforms. The initial response of the United States was cautious; the State Department urged restraint on the part of the Egyptian government, but reiterated that the protests represented public interest in having a "role in the decisions that will shape their lives."[26] Mubarak's appointment of a vice-president and promises of political reforms did little to quell growing demands for his resignation. Less than a week after protests began, Mubarak announced he would not "run" again for president in fall elections; this too failed to quell the unrest, and Mubarak announced his resignation ten days later.[27]

Secretary of State Hillary Rodham Clinton (in office 2009–) used Mubarak's vacillation as an opportunity to speak more broadly about the type of change desired by the United States. When asked about what advice she would give to Arab leaders, she responded, "Well, we give the same advice we have given for years. . . . We believe that democracies are more stable than authoritarian regimes. We believe that economic reform that spreads prosperity broadly among the population, that builds a middle class, that doesn't just enrich the elite—we believe measures against corruption are necessary to avoid destroying trust between leaders and their citizens. We have a very consistent American view of this. . . . Some leaders listen better than other leaders. But all leaders have to recognize now that the failure to reform, the failure to open up their economies and their political systems, is just not an option any longer."[28] Mubarak's departure may in fact presage a more open and democratic Egypt, but many questions remain. One in particular surrounds the role of the Islamist Muslim Brotherhood in the Egyptian protests, and what role it will play as Egypt moves forward toward elections; initial State Department reactions were that it was up to Egyptians to determine their own future.

Libya

Muammar el-Qaddafi was in control in Libya since a 1969 coup. His many efforts to lay claim to leadership of the Arab world and the numerous examples of Libyan support for terrorism (including the 1988 bombing of Pan-Am Flight 103 over Lockerbie, Scotland, among others) made Libya a pariah state in the eyes of the American government. More recently, however, the willingness of the Libyan government to take responsibility for its role in the Lockerbie bombing reflected the thawing of U.S.-Libyan relations in the first decade of the twenty-first century. Libya's promise to abandon its nuclear and chemical weapons programs accelerated this process after more than two decades of tense relations and U.S. sanctions.

As in Egypt, Qaddafi proved unable to prevent Libyans from rising up to protest human rights violations and political repression. His intransigence and his willingness to use military force to attack Libyans dedicated to his removal from power highlights some of the limits of the ability of the international community to effect regime change without direct intervention.

Less than a month after uprisings in the eastern and western sections of the country began in mid-February, the international community had moved to isolate Qaddafi and pressure him to resign. The European Union (EU) and UN Security Council imposed sanctions; the U.S. government froze the assets of the government of Libya, as well as those of individuals affiliated with the Qaddafi regime.

When it became clear that Qaddafi would stand and fight, the under-equipped and untrained rebel forces were at a significant disadvantage. UN Security Council Resolution 1973 included in its restrictions the creation of a no-fly zone over the entire country; it authorized member states to "take all necessary measures to enforce compliance."[29] The nations of the North Atlantic Treaty Organization (NATO) agreed to provide military support for the mission and began Operation Unified Protector in order to enforce the no-fly zone and protect Libyan civilians.

The United States was forced to play a secondary role in Operation Unified Protector by domestic political considerations. Public and congressional criticism of getting engaged in a third international conflict (Iraq and Afghanistan being the primary ones) required President Obama to stress the limited nature of American involvement in Libya and to promise that even that would be scaled back. Obama decried the "false choice" posed by the domestic debate over whether or not the United States should support Libya either now or through what is likely to be a lengthy rebuilding process required not only by the military conflict but by forty years of authoritarian rule. "To brush aside America's responsibility as a leader and—more profoundly—our responsibilities to our fellow human beings under such circumstances would have been a betrayal of who we are," Obama averred. He continued, "Some nations may be able to turn a blind eye to atrocities in other countries. The United States of America is different. And as President, I refused to wait for the images of slaughter and mass graves before taking action."[30] Complicating the president's commitment to situations like that in Libya was the fact that the armed conflict has apparently seen atrocities committed not only by the forces loyal to Qaddafi but also by those who sought his removal from power.

Even a limited American involvement in the military operation in Libya created criticism from Congress that the administration failed to abide by the terms of the 1973 War Powers Resolution, which required that the executive branch needed to secure congressional approval for a military operation within sixty days of its commencement. After the Obama administration approached and passed the deadline without seeking congressional approval, critics claimed that he had violated the terms of the resolution. The administration replied that the Justice Department had determined that the level of military operations being conducted by the United States in Libya did not rise to the threshold of "hostilities" as defined by the War Powers Act.[31]

Sudan

Several regions in Sudan have been the subjects of intense focus of both the diplomatic community as well as the broader public. High-profile public campaigns about the ongoing violence in Darfur, where hundreds of thousands of people have been killed and millions displaced, have brought renewed attention to one of the least stable countries in Africa. Sudan more broadly has been subject to various U.S. sanctions for being categorized as a state supporting terrorism and subject to UN sanctions adopted in 2004 and 2005. An African Union and UN-brokered peace agreement in 2006 failed to stop the violence between the Sudanese government and the Janjaweed militia, which supports it on the one hand and anti-government rebels on the other.

The southern part of Sudan has been in a state of almost constant conflict since Sudan's independence in 1956. After various failed efforts to mediate or resolve the conflict, progress finally came in 2005, in the form of the Comprehensive Peace Agreement (CPA) between the Government of Sudan and the Sudan People's Liberation Movement/Army. The agreement called for a referendum in the south on whether or not southerners should split off and form an independent state. The election occurred in January 2011. Almost 99 percent of those who voted chose independence. The United States has enthusiastically

---

IN THEIR OWN WORDS: *STATEMENT OF PRESIDENT BARACK OBAMA—RECOGNITION OF THE REPUBLIC OF SOUTH SUDAN*

On July 9, 2011, the Republic of South Sudan came into being; President Barack Obama's statement embracing the new nation reflects in many ways the imperatives of contemporary U.S. diplomacy by stressing the need for good governance, self-determination, the protection of minority rights, and stability.

. . . After so much struggle by the people of South Sudan, the United States of America welcomes the birth of a new nation.

Today is a reminder that after the darkness of war, the light of a new dawn is possible. . . . The eyes of the world are on the Republic of South Sudan. And we know that southern Sudanese have claimed their sovereignty, and shown that neither their dignity nor their dream of self-determination can be denied.

This historic achievement is a tribute, above all, to the generations of southern Sudanese who struggled for this day. . . .

. . . As Southern Sudanese undertake the hard work of building their new country, the United States pledges our partnership as they seek the security, development and responsive governance that can fulfill their aspirations and respect their human rights.

As today also marks the creation of two new neighbors, South Sudan and Sudan, both peoples must recognize that they will be more secure and prosperous if they move beyond a bitter past and resolve differences peacefully. . . . The safety of all Sudanese, especially minorities, must be protected. Through courage and hard choices, this can be the beginning of a new chapter of greater peace and justice for all of the Sudanese people.

Decades ago, Martin Luther King reflected on the first moment of independence on the African continent in Ghana, saying, "I knew about all of the struggles, and all of the pain, and all of the agony that these people had gone through for this moment." Today, we are moved by the story of struggle that led to this time of hope in South Sudan, and we think of those who didn't live to see their dream realized. Now, the leaders and people of South Sudan have an opportunity to turn this moment of promise into lasting progress. The United States will continue to support the aspirations of all Sudanese. Together, we can ensure that today marks another step forward in Africa's long journey toward opportunity, democracy and justice.

SOURCE: Barack Obama, "Statement of President Barack Obama Recognition of the Republic of South Sudan," July 9, 2011, available at http://www.whitehouse.gov/the-press-office/2011/07/09/statement-president-barack-obama-recognition-republic-south-sudan.

backed the creation of South Sudan, and diplomatic efforts continue to resolve territorial disputes between the two governments.

Central Africa

The unique circumstances of the nations in Central Africa present a different set of challenges for American foreign policy makers. The overriding issues of poverty, corruption, and disease remain paramount, but the region's colonial past has not facilitated democracy in the region.

Democratic Republic of the Congo

Formerly a Belgian colony, the Democratic Republic of Congo (DRC) was a prime example of how not to realize independence. Effectively abandoned by the Belgians, who made little to no effort to oversee a smooth or stable transition to a Congolese government after an often brutal colonial experience, the fledgling nation struggled from the beginning. The murder of popular leader Patrice

Lumumba in a Cold War–influenced environment did little to help. Shortly thereafter, Joseph Mobutu Sese Seko came to power and led the DRC (called Zaire for much of Mobutu's tenure in office) until being deposed in 1997 by a coalition including elements from Rwanda, Burundi, and Uganda, and resulting in Laurent Kabila assuming the presidency. During Mobutu's thirty-two years in office, the United States maintained cordial relationships with Zaire because of its anti-Soviet stance and its rich mineral deposits. Sadly, Kabila's term as president was no more democratic than Mobutu's, and he grew increasingly unpopular.[32]

The Democratic Republic of Congo continues to face a variety of challenges, not the least of which is the human cost of conflict over the past fifteen years. In addition to the deaths caused by strife, the UNHCR estimates that two million Congolese have been displaced; the DRC continues to host more than one hundred thousand refugees from Angola, Rwanda, and elsewhere. Also, a recent public health study has suggested that as many as 1.8 million Congolese women have been victims of sexual violence.[33]

PUBLIC PORTRAIT: *JOSEPH KABILA (1971–)*

In some ways, Joseph Kabila faces some of the biggest challenges of any African leader. As president of the largely landlocked Democratic Republic of Congo (formerly known as the Belgian Congo and Zaire), he oversees the largest country in sub-Saharan Africa; it is also one of the most populous. Because of its history, its geography, and its neighbors, it continues to struggle mightily despite great mineral resources which could prove a source of economic growth and stability.

After his father Laurent Kabila's killing in 2001, Major-General Joseph Kabila became a compromise choice as interim president. Less than ten days after the elder Kabila's death, Joseph Kabila became president. According to François Ngolet, in *Crisis in the Congo: The Rise and Fall of Laurent Kabila* (Palgrave/Macmillan, 2011, 184–188), upon entering office, Kabila said that he would welcome the assistance of the United Nations and honor the 1999 Lusaka Accords, which sought to end the conflict in the DRC. He warned, however, that he would not tolerate the presence of non-Congolese forces in the eastern part of the country, a pledge that would result in conflict over the next several years.

Despite ongoing concerns about human rights violations against political opponents and others in the chaotic DRC, Joseph Kabila proved to be much more interested in reaching out to the international community than his father. After reaching agreements with some of his political opponents, he participated in multiparty elections in 2006, eventually winning the presidency with almost 60 percent of the popular vote in a runoff.

Kabila's willingness to embrace democratic government has earned him accolades from American government officials, who have described the relationship between the United States and the DRC as "very strong." In 2010, the United States provided more than $300 million in assistance and more than $300 million

in support for the newly renamed United Nations Organization Stabilization Mission in the Democratic Republic of the Congo (MONUSCO) [United States, Department of State, Bureau of African Affairs, "Background Note: Democratic Republic of the Congo," April 13, 2011, accessed on July 3, 2011, at: http://www.state.gov/r/pa/ei/bgn/2823.htm].

In a 2009 interview, President Kabila addressed many of the issues facing his country in candid fashion. While at the same time praising them for their assistance, he took the Western democracies to task for not doing more; in particular, he cited arms restrictions on the DRC as hampering its efforts to restore peace, and expressed indignation at being criticized for accepting a controversial development deal with China, which promised the DRC billions of dollars for mining and road infrastructure. When asked about what he had accomplished, Kabila responded:

"We've given back the Congolese people that respect and self respect. . . . And we've made sure that democracy becomes reality in the Congo. Nobody has done that since independence. And maybe the most important thing is the hope that we've given to the Congolese people, hope that there is tomorrow, that there's something that we call tomorrow and that they're not going to die today and that there is a better tomorrow, that tomorrow will be better than today."

Presidential elections are mandated for late 2011; the forty-year-old president is eligible for one additional five-year term but will face existing political opponents as well as other parties that boycotted the election in 2006. In addition to already formidable challenges facing the DRC, the international economic downturn has affected demand for minerals, damaging what had been promising economic growth in the middle part of the decade.

Visiting Ghana in July 2009, U.S. President Barack Obama (left) greets President John Atta Mills of Ghana, one of the most democratic nations in Africa. Later, President Obama spoke to the Ghanian parliament in Accra, the capital. During his address, Obama noted, "I do not see the countries and peoples of Africa as a world apart; I see Africa as a fundamental part of our interconnected world—as partners with America on behalf of the future that we want for all our children. That partnership must be grounded in mutual responsibility...."

SOURCE: AP Photo/Haraz N. Ghanban.

West Africa

Countries in West Africa provide a study in contrasts in terms of recent U.S. diplomacy. Ghana in many ways serves as a template for what American diplomats would like to see in the rest of the continent. Formerly a dictatorship, Ghana now sports a vigorous multiparty system and has weathered peacefully several political transitions since 1992. It has become a Millennium Challenge Corporation grantee.

Other West African nations have not been so lucky. Democracies in Sierra Leone and Liberia are relatively new and still dependent in many ways on international assistance. After almost a decade of political strife and internal conflict, Cote d'Ivoire (the Ivory Coast) seemed to be on the path to peace. Elections in 2010 favored Alassane Ouattara over incumbent President Laurent Gbagbo, who refused to leave office. Six months of pressure from military forces loyal to Ouattara, United Nations forces, and units of the French military finally forced Gbagbo to relinquish power.

Nigeria

Because of its size, its population, and its significant oil resources, Nigeria has always been a regional economic power, and the United States has sought to foster stability in a religiously and ethnically diverse country. Deep divisions remain between north and south, and unrest in the oil-rich Niger Delta region, whose inhabitants feel they have not shared in oil profits, continues to plague the southern part of the country. Despite these challenges and an almost storied problem with corruption, Nigeria has progressed toward a more democratic system. Elections in April 2011 were marred by violence in the north and charges of voter irregularities, but many countries, including the United States, endorsed the outcome as legitimate. Goodluck Jonathan, who had been serving as president since May 2010 after the death of his predecessor, received almost 60 percent of the vote.

While he recognized the problems with the electoral process and signaled that Nigeria still had some ways to go, Assistant Secretary of State Johnnie Carson reaffirmed Nigeria's importance in sub-Saharan Africa and argued that "if Nigeria, with its large size and population, can ... run and manage successful democratic elections, that it is possible for many of the other smaller states to do so as well. It also indicates that the democratic trajectory not only in Nigeria, but across West Africa has not stalled but continues to rise."[34] Nigeria has been one of the prime beneficiaries of the African Growth and Opportunity Act and is an increasingly important source of oil for the United States.

Horn of Africa

Since the 1970s, the Horn of Africa has been one of the most violent regions on the continent. Revolution in Ethiopia in the mid-1970s brought to power a repressive military junta, which ruled until 1991. Boundary disputes with Eritrea frequently resulted in violence. Since independence, Somalia has only enjoyed a brief period of functioning democratic rule. The repressive two-decade reign of Mohamed Siad Barre ended in 1991, as he fled the country. Chaos ensued and would characterize much of the next decade.

Somalia

The turmoil in Somalia in 1993 that resulted in the deaths of nineteen American soldiers was a stark lesson to American policymakers about the need to balance policy imperatives with public opinion. The fractured political calculus of Somalia has resulted in several failed attempts at recreating a stable national government since 2000. With the withdrawal of Ethiopian troops in 2009 after a two-year presence in the country, various groups sought to fill the resulting space and reinvigorated attacks on the tenuous Transitional Federal Government.[35] American government concerns about Somalia include the presence in parts of the country of the militant Islamic organization Al-Shabaab, which has ties to al Qaeda. Coupled with ongoing instability, concerns about Somalia becoming a haven for terrorists continue. Human rights abuses, both by the government and its opponents, have been widespread.[36]

More recently, Somalia has reentered the public eye because of an ongoing problem with piracy off its coast in both the Indian Ocean and the Gulf of Aden, a heavily trafficked gateway to the Red Sea and Suez Canal. Since 2008, Somali pirates have launched increasingly brazen and far-reaching attacks on commercial shipping and recreational vessels. Captured vessels and crew are ransomed, at times for huge amounts of money. Initial claims that Somali pirates had engaged in the practice only after large-scale commercial fishing off the coast of Somalia had exhausted fishing stocks have some merit; as piracy has spread, however, it has clearly degenerated into a cynical money-making venture orchestrated by criminal elements.

Since the Somali state has no capacity to prevent piracy or protect shipping off its coast, the international community has stepped in to do so. In late 2008, the United Nations passed a resolution calling for an international response to the problem. The United States and almost sixty other countries now participate in the Contact Group on Piracy Off the Coast of Somalia, which coordinates efforts to end piracy. This includes antipiracy patrols off of the Somali Coast, including naval ships from a number of different countries.[37] Despite these efforts, piracy continues; as recently as February 2011, pirates killed four Americans aboard a private yacht as negotiations continued with American naval forces that sought the release of the hostages.

East Africa

East Africa has been relatively stable during much of the decade, and its political institutions are all at least somewhat representative. After many years of conflict in the 1970s and 1980s, Uganda has been relatively stable since the mid-1980s and a republic since 1995. Its president, Yoweri Museveni (in office 1986–), has been reelected three times under this new system, most recently in 2011. While there are concerns about his government's attacks on political opponents, Uganda has generally been a close ally of the United States and benefits from the Africa Growth and Opportunity Act.

Kenya

As another potential regional anchor state, Kenya has been of particular interest to the United States. Kenya's common border with Ethiopia, Somalia, and Sudan has made it even more crucial as those countries experienced political upheaval at various points. Since independence, Kenya has mostly enjoyed representative government, at least theoretically. The domination by the ruling Kenya African National Union (KANU) party lasted from 1963 until 1991; even after political reforms went into place, KANU won several more elections before being ousted by an opposition party. Since 2000, elections have been marred by violence and charges of voter fraud. The 2007 disputed election led to more than one thousand deaths and hundreds of thousands of people being displaced from their homes. In late 2010, the International Criminal Court (ICC) announced that six Kenyans would be prosecuted for crimes against humanity. President Obama urged Kenyans to assist the ICC in its investigation and to continue its steps on the "path to lasting peace and prosperity." Human rights violations by the police and security forces have been reported.[38]

Southern Africa

With the exception of Zimbabwe and Swaziland, Southern Africa is the most stable region in Africa. Despite ongoing challenges relating to the worldwide economic downturn and the HIV/AIDS health crisis, Botswana and South Africa have enjoyed peace and stability for many years. By contrast, Swaziland, which is controlled by a hereditary monarchy that suppresses political opposition, and Zimbabwe represent the opposite extreme.

Zimbabwe stands as one of the best examples of how little the United States and other governments can accomplish in the face of intransigence and undemocratic rule.

Zimbabwe's president, Robert Mugabe, has ruled since 1980; in the face of withering international criticism and growing internal opposition, and following the results of a 2008 national election that failed to accurately represent the will of Zimbabwean voters, Mugabe agreed to a power-sharing arrangement with the opposition Movement for Democratic Change (MDC). While this technically elevated MDC head Morgan Tsvangirai to the post of prime minister, Mugabe has continued to marginalize his opponents and wield power in autocratic fashion. The United States, while continuing humanitarian assistance to Zimbabwe, has imposed a variety of sanctions against a number of Zimbabweans and banned direct assistance to the Zimbabwean government.

South Africa

South Africa continues to exhibit one of the strongest economies on the continent; its 2008 per-capita GDP of $10,700 makes it one of the most prosperous in Africa. Despite that, unemployment is higher than 20 percent, and impoverished South Africans continue to agitate for greater economic reform.[39] At least in part because of its large mining industry, which has served as the epicenter for regional migrant workers, South Africans have borne a disproportionate burden of sexually transmitted diseases such as AIDS; more than five million South Africans are HIV-positive. Dealing with South Africa's AIDS crisis has not been easy despite its relatively advanced medical system and the significant international commitment to combating HIV/AIDS in the country. This was largely a result of failed leadership by Thabo Mbeki (in office 1999–2008), who followed Nelson Mandela (in office 1994–1999) as South Africa's second democratically elected leader. In the face of internal and external pressure to provide leadership on the issue, Mbeki refused to universally implement commonly accepted norms for AIDS treatment and the prevention of HIV-transmission. This almost certainly delayed full implementation of effective treatment regimens. Crime remains a serious problem in South Africa; the level of sexual violence is horrifying, and more can be done to assist South Africa in bringing crime and violence under control.

Yet South Africa remains one of Africa's success stories. Its handling of the 2010 FIFA World Cup allayed international concerns of endemic violence, which failed to hamper an impressive showing by the host country. It has one of Africa's most progressive constitutions, and the goodwill generated by the remarkably peaceful political transition in the mid-1990s remains.

THE FUTURE OF AMERICAN AFRICAN POLICY

As the Cold War ended, most analysts agreed that Africa's significance to U.S. policymakers was at a relative nadir. Events in the 1990s, including the 1998 attacks on U.S. embassies in Dar Es Salaam, Tanzania, and Nairobi, Kenya, as well as growing support for terrorist organizations in Sudan and elsewhere, suggested that American inattention to Africa threatened U.S. security. The events of 9/11 convinced many that political instability and poverty in Africa (compounded by the AIDS epidemic) increased the likelihood that terrorist organizations would find new converts in Africa.

Beginning with the Bush administration's efforts to engage Africa in the first decade of the twenty-first century, and following with the Obama administration's interest in continuing or expanding upon those commitments, America's African policy has never been so robust or so well-funded. That said, the problems to which many of those policies responded are major ones; ongoing health and political crises around the continent require even larger commitments in order to begin to bring them under control. As the United States and other countries attempt to recover from the global economic downturn, it remains unclear if there is the political will to fund even more aggressive programs. Even when political will and the necessary appropriations exist, there are all too many examples of the limits of U.S. power. In all likelihood, and given the domestic political pressure to limit rather than expand foreign aid, Africa's new status in American policymaking will recede once again when and if the risk of terrorism is lessened and AIDS is better under control. Some of that loss of status may be mitigated by the ongoing U.S. interest in African energy resources, although that interest involves only a few countries on the continent.

Unless the unlikely confluence of political will and greatly expanded aid budgets remains in the medium to long term, Africa's importance will likely diminish, particularly as economic competition from other parts of the world continues. This is perhaps most notable in the U.S. relationship with a number of countries in South and East Asia. There is little doubt, for example, that China's growing economic and military prowess is of much greater concern; Africa only plays a secondary role in that contest in terms of investments there by Chinese interests.

See also: **Chapter 21: Relations with Nonaligned Nations in Asia and Africa; Chapter 39: U.S. Foreign Policy Goals of the Twenty-first Century; Chapter 40: Diplomatic Milestones, 2001–Present.**

ENDNOTES

1. United States Trade Representative, "Fact Sheet on AGOA," September 2010, accessed on July 10, 2011, at: http://www.ustr.gov/sites/default/files/AGOA%20Fact%20Sheet%202010.pdf.

2. United States, Department of State, Bureau of African Affairs, Testimony by Johnnie Carson, assistant secretary of state for African affairs, before the Senate Foreign Relations Committee Subcommittee on African Affairs, April 14, 2011, on the FY2012 Budget Request for U.S. Policies on Africa, accessed on July 9, 2011, at: http://www.state.gov/p/af/rls/rm/2011/161202.htm.

3. Joel D. Barkan, "Advancing Democratization in Africa," in Jennifer G. Cooke and J. Stephen Morrison, eds., *U.S. Africa Policy beyond the Bush Years: Critical Challenge for the Obama Administration* (Washington, DC: CSIS [Center for Strategic and International Studies], 2009), 91.

4. Statistics averaged from *Freedom in the World* Country Ratings, accessed on April 12, 2012, at: http://www.freedomhouse.org/sites/default/files/inline_images/FIWAllScoresCountries1973-2011.xls; Combined Average Ratings—Independent Countries in *Freedom in the World 2011*, accessed July 3, 2011, at: http://www.freedomhouse.org/sites/default/files/inline_images/CombinedAverageRatings%28IndependentCountries%29FIW2011.pdf.

5. United States, United States Africa Command Office of Public Affairs, *United States Africa Command: The First Three Years. . . .* (Stuttgart: U.S. Africa Command Office of Public Affairs, 2011), accessed on July 3, 2011, at: http://www.africom.mil/research/USAfricaCommand-TheFirstThreeYears-March2011.pdf.

6. United States, United States Africa Command Office of Public Affairs, *United States Africa Command: The First Three Years. . . .* (Stuttgart: U.S. Africa Command Office of Public Affairs, 2011), accessed on July 3, 2011, at http://www.africom.mil/research/USAfricaCommand-TheFirstThreeYears-March2011.pdf.

7. John Vandiver, "AFRICOM leaders to mull headquarters location," *Stars and Stripes,* January 6, 2011 (http://www.stripes.com/news/africom-leaders-to-mull-headquarters-location-1.130831), accessed July 12, 2011. For a broader critique of the way in which AFRICOM came into being and the critical welcome it received, see Burgess, Stephen F. "In the National Interest? Authoritarian Decision-Making and the Problematic Creation of US Africa Command," *Contemporary Security Policy* 30, no. 1 (August 2007): 79–99.

8. William Mark Bellamy, "Making Better Sense of U.S. Security Engagement in Africa," in Jennifer G. Cooke and J. Stephen Morrison, eds., *U.S. Africa Policy beyond the Bush Years: Critical Challenge for the Obama Administration* (Washington, DC: CSIS [Center for Strategic and International Studies], 2009), 23–24.

9. Katherine J. Almquist, "U.S. Foreign Assistance to Africa: Securing America's Investment for Lasting Development," in *Journal of International Affairs* 62, no. 2 (Spring/Summer 2009): 21.

10. The Department of State uses the formulation of the largest foreign assistance program since the Marshall Plan. For example, see United States, "USG Agencies Involved in Human Rights Work," accessed July 11, 2011, at: http://www.humanrights.gov/usg%20agencies/?cat=DOS; the head of PEPFAR since 2009 called the plan "bigger than the Marshall Plan. . . ." see Jim Fisher-Thompson, "U.S. PEPFAR Program Helps Millions with AIDS in Africa," November 19, 2009, accessed July 11, 2011, at: http://iipdigital.usembassy.gov/st/english/article/2009/11/200911191603341ejrehsiF0.2920191.html#axzz1Rns9tiZB.

11. United States, President's Malaria Initiative, "Fast Facts: The President's Malaria Initiative," April 2011, accessed on July 11, 2011, at: http://www.fightingmalaria.gov/resources/reports/pmi_fastfacts.pdf.

12. Global Fund to Fight AIDS, Tuberculosis and Malaria, *Making a Difference: Global Fund Results Report 2011* (Geneva: Global Fund to Fight AIDS, Tuberculosis and Malaria, 2011), 23, accessed on July 3, 2011, at: http://www.theglobalfund.org/en/library/publications/progressreports.

13. John W. Dietrich, "The Politics of PEPFAR: The President's Emergency Plan for AIDS Relief," in *Ethics and International Affairs* 21:3 (Fall 2007), 287–289, accessed on July 11, 2011, at: http://www.carnegiecouncil.org/resources/journal/21_3/essay/001.html; also see Phillip Nieburg and J. Stephen Morrison, "The Big U.S. Leap on HIV/AIDS in Africa: What Is the Next Act?" in Cooke and Morrison, eds., *U.S. Africa Policy beyond the Bush Years*, 34–61.

14. Bill and Melinda Gates Foundation, "Global Health Strategy Overview, September 2010," accessed July 3, 2011 at: http://www.gatesfoundation.org/global-health/Documents/global-health-strategy_overview.pdf.

15. Kimberly Smith, "Statistical Reporting by the Bill and Melinda Gates Foundation to the OECD DAC: Aid to Health Data Now Includes World's Largest Private Foundation," April 2011, accessed July 11, 2011, at: http://www.oecd.org/dataoecd/5/60/47539494.pdf.

16. William J. Clinton Foundation, "Building a Better World: William J. Clinton Foundation Annual Report 2010 Financials," accessed July 3, 2011, at: http://www.clintonfoundation.org/buildingabetterworld/financials_2010.php; also see William J. Clinton Foundation, "Building a Better World: William J. Clinton Foundation Annual Report 2010 Clinton Health Access Initiative," accessed July 11, 2011, at: http://www.clintonfoundation.org/buildingabetterworld/projects.php?initiative=CHAI.

17. United States, House of Representatives, Trade and Development Act of 2000, H.R. 434, 106th Congress (2000), 4, accessed July 3, 2011, at: http://www.agoa.gov/agoa_legislation/agoatext.pdf.

18. United States Trade Representative, "Fact Sheet on AGOA," September 2010, accessed July 10, 2011, at: http://www.ustr.gov/sites/default/files/AGOA%20Fact%20Sheet%202010.pdf.

19. Ibid.

20. Princeton Lyman, "U.S. Foreign Assistance and Trade Policies in Africa," in Cooke and Morrison, eds., *U.S. Africa Policy beyond the Bush Years,* 111–41.

21. United States, Millennium Challenge Corporation, "Guide to the MCC Indicators and the Selection Process Fiscal Year 2011," accessed July 12, 2011, at: http://www.mcc.gov/documents/reports/reference-2010001040503-fy11guidetotheindicators.pdf.

22. United States, Millennium Challenge Corporation, "A New Vision for Development: 2010 Annual Report," 9–20, accessed July 12, 2011, at: http://www.mcc.gov/documents/reports/report-2011001049801-2010annual.pdf.

23. John Hewko, *Millennium Challenge Corporation: Can the Experiment Survive?* (Washington, DC: Carnegie Endowment for International Peace, 2010).

24. Joel D. Barkan, "Advancing Democratization in Africa," in Cooke and Morrison, eds., *U.S. Africa Policy beyond the Bush Years*, 105–06.

25. Jeremy Sharp, "U.S. Foreign Assistance to the Middle East: Historical Background, Recent Trends, and the FY2011 Request," prepared for the Congressional Research Service, June 15, 2010, accessed July 12, 2011, at: http://www.fas.org/sgp/crs/mideast/RL32260.pdf.

26. United States, Department of State, Bureau of Public Affairs, "Press Statement by Philip J. Crowley, Assistant Secretary, Bureau of Public Affairs, January 25, 2011," accessed July 12, 2011, at: http://www.state.gov/r/pa/prs/ps/2011/01/155307.htm.

27. "Timeline: Egypt's Revolution. A Chronicle of the Revolution That Ended the Three-Decade-Long Presidency of Hosni Mubarak," in *Al Jazeera*, accessed July 11, 2011, at: http://english. aljazeera.net/news/middleeast/2011/01/201112515334871490.html.

28. Hillary Rodham Clinton, interview with Michele Kelemen of NPR, Munich, Germany, February 6, 2011, accessed July 12, 2011, at: http://www.state.gov/secretary/rm/2011/02/156050.htm.

29. United Nations Security Council, Resolution 1973 (2011), March 17, 2011, accessed July 12, 2011, at: http://daccess-dds-ny .un.org/doc/UNDOC/GEN/N11/268/39/PDF/N1126839.pdf.

30. United States, White House, Office of the Press Secretary, "Remarks by the President in Address to the Nation on Libya," March 28, 2011.

31. Public Broadcasting Service, transcript of "Libya, War Powers Start White House, Congress on Collision Course," *PBS Newshour*, June 15, 2011, "The Situation in Libya," accessed on July 12, 2011, at: http://www.un.org/Docs/sc/unsc_resolutionsll.htm.

32. François Ngolet, *Crisis in the Congo: The Rise and Fall of Laurent Kabila* (New York: Palgrave Macmillan, 2011), 182.

33. United Nations, Office of the United Nations High Commissioner for Refugees, "2011 UNHCR Country Operations Profile—Democratic Republic of the Congo," accessed on July 12, 2011, at: http://www.unhcr.org/cgi-bin/texis/vtx/page?page=49e45c366; on sexual violence in the DRC, see Jeffrey Gettleman, "Congo Study Sets Estimate for Rapes Much Higher," in *The New York Times*, May 11, 2011, accessed on July 7, 2011, at: http://www.nytimes .com/2011/05/12/world/africa/12congo.html?ref=congothedemocr aticrepublicof.

34. United States, Department of State, Bureau of African Affairs, "The Recent Elections in Nigeria: Special Briefing by Johnnie Carson, Assistant Secretary, Bureau of African Affairs, April 28, 2011," accessed on July 12, 2011, at: http://www.state.gov/p/af/rls/ spbr/2011/161931.htm.

35. "Somali Joy as Ethiopians Withdraw," at BBC News, January 13, 2009, accessed on July 12, 2011, at: http://news.bbc.co.uk/2/hi/ africa/7825626.stm.

36. United States, Department of State, "2010 Country Reports on Human Rights Practices: Somalia," April 8, 2011, accessed on July 12, 2011, at: http://www.state.gov/documents/organization/ 160144.pdf.

37. United States, Department of State, "International Response: Contact Group on Piracy off the Coast of Somalia," accessed on July 12, 2011, at: http://www.state.gov/t/pm/ppa/ piracy/contactgroup/index.htm.

38. United States, White House Office of the Press Secretary, "Statement by President Obama on the International Criminal Court Announcement, December 15, 2010," accessed on July 12, 2011, at: http://www.whitehouse.gov/the-press-office/2010/12/15/ statement-president-obama-international-criminal-court-announ cement; United States, Department of State, Bureau of Democracy, Human Rights, and Labor, "2010 Human Rights Report: Kenya," accessed on July 12, 2011, at: http://www.state.gov/documents/ organization/160127.pdf.

39. Central Intelligence Agency, "South Africa," *The World Factbook*, accessed on July 12, 2011, at: https://www.cia.gov/library/ publications/the-world-factbook/geos/sf.html.

FURTHER READING

Cooke, Jennifer G., and J. Stephen Morrison, eds. *U.S. Africa Policy beyond the Bush Years: Critical Challenge for the Obama Administration*. Washington, DC: CSIS (Center for Strategic and International Studies), 2009.

Copson, Raymond W. *The United States in Africa: Bush Policy and Beyond*. New York: Zed Books, 2007.

Forest, James J., and Matthew V. Sousa. *Oil and Terrorism in the New Gulf: Framing U.S. Energy and Security Politics for the Gulf of Guinea*. Lanham, MD: Lexington Books, 2006.

Francis, David J., ed. *US Strategy in Africa: AFRICOM, Terrorism and Security Challenges*. New York: Routledge, 2010.

chapter 38

U.S.-Israeli Relations and the Quest for Peace in the Middle East

by Michelle Mart

THE CONCLUSION OF the Camp David Accords in 1979 capped a period of tremendous activism in U.S. foreign policy in the Middle East. Not only had American diplomats been actively involved in Middle East diplomacy, but President Jimmy Carter (1977–1981) had been personally involved in the Arab-Israeli conflict in an unprecedented way. Although, the details of U.S. policy toward that Arab-Israeli conflict had changed over the years, there was also a remarkable consistency in overall U.S. policies in the conflict since at least the late 1960s, and in American foreign policy goals in the region as a whole. The post–Camp David period would challenge that consistency and usher in a new era of American policies.

CHALLENGES TO CAMP DAVID

The hopefulness symbolized by the 1979 Camp David Accords and Egyptian-Israeli peace treaty did not last. It soon became apparent that the bilateral peace between Egypt and Israel would *not* lead to a broader, regional peace. Israel's government, under Likud Prime Minister Menachem Begin (in office 1977–1983), made it clear that its policy of settlements in the occupied territories would not be curtailed, and that the Palestinians would not be granted real sovereignty. Egypt became not a regional leader for peace but a pariah state among fellow Arab nations. The country was expelled from the Arab League, and most Arab states broke bilateral relations with the nation. Meanwhile, President Jimmy Carter, who had been sincerely committed to his role as a broker in the peace process, had to shift his attention to what were more pressing issues for the United States in 1979: instability in the Middle East because of the Iranian revolution and in Central Asia after the Soviet invasion of Afghanistan, as well as the domestic crises of a weak economy, high oil prices, and declining popularity for a president facing reelection.

U.S. Policy Reacts to the Iranian Revolution

For the remainder of Jimmy Carter's presidency, the triumph of Camp David and the possibility of achieving peace in the region were overshadowed by instability and thwarted American ambitions in the wake of the Iranian revolution. It is difficult to overestimate the significance of the 1979 Iranian revolution in remaking the strategic map of the Middle East and, indirectly, affecting the course of U.S.-Israeli relations and the possibility of resolving the Arab-Israeli conflict.

Since the 1950s, the United States had relied on the Iranian government as a reliable ally in the Middle East and, especially since the promulgation of the Nixon Doctrine in 1969, a conservative and powerful pillar in the region. The militarily modern, non-Arab nation also had built an extensive bilateral relationship with another American ally, Israel. The longstanding American support for Mohammad Reza Shah Pahlavi (in power 1941–1979), who ruled Iran as a dictator, left a bitter legacy for many Iranians, leading to street protests past the American embassy in Tehran. Once the shah was overthrown by the coalition of revolutionary groups, he went into exile in a variety of countries, including Egypt, Morocco, and Mexico, but soon sought entry into the United States for treatment of non-Hodgkin's lymphoma. The situation for the United States went from bad to worse in November 1979, when hundreds of militants, angry at Carter's reluctant decision two weeks earlier to admit the shah to the United States for medical treatment, stormed the U.S. embassy, seizing its personnel as hostages. At first, Carter followed the advice of his secretary of state, Cyrus Vance (in office 1977–1980), and responded through a series of diplomatic maneuvers to the crisis. By April 1980, with little progress to show for his efforts, Carter switched tacks to the policies of his national security adviser, Zbigniew Brzezinski (in office 1977–1981), and attempted a military rescue of the hostages. The mission was an unmitigated failure and resulted in the accidental death

KEY CONCEPTS

Oil and stability. Ever since World War II (1939–1945), the most important goals of U.S. foreign policy in the Middle East have been relatively stable: provide a continual flow of affordable oil and establish strategic relationships with allies in the region. The American presence in the region increased beginning in the late 1950s—including its financial and military role—but the basic goals remained the same.

In some respects, U.S. policy toward the Arab-Israeli conflict has been similarly consistent. From the founding of Israel in 1948, the United States has always supported its survival and promoted an end to the Arab-Israeli conflict through negotiation and compromise. American policymakers played an increasingly active role seeking an end to the conflict, especially after the 1973 Yom Kippur War and the 1979 Iranian revolution changed the political dynamic in the region.

Opposing extremism. The most important shift over time in U.S. policy, both in the region and toward the Arab-Israeli conflict, has been the growing opposition to radicalism, as first seen in so-called non-aligned governments during the Cold War, such as Egypt in the 1950s and 1960s; second, as seen in religiously fundamentalist governments, such as in revolutionary Iran after 1979; and, finally, as seen in groups viewed as terrorists, such as al Qaeda.

The increasing opposition to radicalism has, in turn, strengthened the ties between the United States and Israel and, thus, affected American policy toward the Arab-Israeli conflict. The consequences of this last shift became plain by the start of the twenty-first century, when the United States no longer was seen as an honest broker in the search for peace between the Arabs and the Israelis.

of eight soldiers in the Iranian desert, when one of the American helicopters crashed into a transport plane. Administration policymakers resumed efforts to negotiate a release through back channels, but this was not achieved until the day that Ronald Reagan (1981–1989) was inaugurated in January 1981.

At the same time that the U.S. strategic position in the Middle East was deteriorating, following the Iranian revolution and during the hostage crisis, the country's long-term interests also were being challenged in Central Asia. In late 1979, the Soviet Union, worried about nationalists within Afghanistan challenging the friendly government there, invaded and occupied the country. Carter unhesitatingly condemned the invasion as a serious threat to world peace and responded with a variety of measures, ranging from a boycott of the 1980 Moscow Olympics to the promulgation of the "Carter Doctrine," a public commitment to use force if necessary to protect the Persian Gulf region. His policies in Afghanistan were as ineffective as they were in Iran, and Soviet forces did not budge from the occupation, demonstrating the weakness of the United States' actions.

Further Moves Away from Camp David under Ronald Reagan

When Ronald Reagan became president in 1981, he brought with him none of Carter's determination to negotiate an enduring peace. Even if he had, circumstances in the Middle East had become less conducive to compromise and negotiation. Prime Minister Menachem Begin's government in Israel became more conservative after he was rewarded for his preemptive strike at an Iraqi nuclear reactor with an electoral victory. In addition to Carter being thrown out of office, two of the architects of the Camp David Accords died

in 1981: Israel's former foreign minister Moshe Dayan, from cancer, and Egypt's President Anwar Sadat, from an assassin's bullet. The year ended with Begin's support in the Knesset for a bill annexing the Golan Heights, a violation of the Camp David Accords, as well as previously accepted formulations of trading land for peace to end the Arab-Israeli conflict.

Although Reagan and his advisers came to office uninterested in active American involvement in the Arab-Israeli conflict, changing circumstances drew them into a peacemaking role. In June 1982, an emboldened Israeli Minister of Defense Ariel Sharon (in office 1981–1983) took the ambivalence of U.S. Secretary of State Alexander Haig (in office 1981–1982) as a green light for Israeli war plans in Lebanon. With only a tenuous cease-fire on the border between Israel and Lebanon, where the Palestine Liberation Organization (PLO) was based, Begin's government was eager to destroy the Palestinian organization, weaken the threat from Syrian forces in Lebanon, and ensure that Maronite leader Bashir Gemayel ascend to the Lebanese presidency (and possibly sign a peace treaty with Israel). Sharon was commanding officer in the invasion of Lebanon and quickly exceeded the cabinet's authorization to advance up to forty kilometers into the country. Instead, Sharon reached north to Beirut, and worked with Christian militia forces to threaten PLO fighters in the city.

President Reagan reacted angrily to the Israeli offensive, accepting the resignation of his secretary of state, whose conversations with Sharon may have encouraged Israeli aggression, and pressed Prime Minister Begin to change course. American envoy Philip Habib helped to achieve a settlement, which included the evacuation of PLO forces from Lebanon, under the supervision of American, French, and Italian troops.

Although PLO forces departed by September 1, 1982, Israeli forces remained in Lebanon, reoccupying parts of Beirut when President-elect Bashir Gemayel was assassinated in the middle of the month. Israeli cooperation with the Maronite (Phalangist) militias allowed them to massacre hundreds of Palestinian civilians in the Sabra and Shatila refugee camps, neighborhoods first established by the United Nations in 1949, but which had increased in population following the fighting in southern Lebanon.

New American Attempts at Mediation

Following the dangerous escalation of violence in the 1982 Lebanon War, President Ronald Reagan attempted to lead a new peace effort that would recognize Palestinian autonomy under Jordanian control, but deny the PLO or other Palestinians statehood. Arab leaders collectively affirmed the necessity of PLO involvement in any peace deal, while Israel rejected the territorial aspects of Reagan's proposal. Failing to get any progress on a broader peace deal, by the following spring, Secretary of State George Shultz (in office 1982–1989) negotiated an end to the war between Israel and Lebanon, with the continued occupation of forty kilometers of southern Lebanon by Israeli troops and the introduction of UN peacekeeping troops stationed north of them. The American-negotiated solution did not bring true stability, however. Israeli troops remained for another twenty years, and internal factions in Lebanon continued intermittent fighting.

As Arab leaders in the region rebuffed President Reagan's peace initiative in 1982, since it did not include any role for the PLO, so Reagan rejected peace initiatives in the mid-1980s from within the region. In 1985, PLO chief Yasser Arafat (in power 1968–2004) and Jordanian King Hussein (reigned 1952–1999) proposed to enter a federation that would negotiate with Israel once it withdrew from the occupied territories. Reagan insisted that the PLO first recognize Israel by accepting UN Resolution 242; in addition, the president was not eager to allow a Soviet role at the proposed international peace conference. Another attempt to move the peace process forward was also spurned by Reagan in 1987. King Hussein worked with leaders of Israel's Labor Party to propose an international conference, but this was rejected by both the Likud leaders (then in a power-sharing government with Labor) and by Reagan, who said that the United States could not side with one Israeli party over another.

THE INTIFADA

With possible peace initiatives stymied, ordinary Palestinians took matters into their own hands and launched an uprising in December 1987. The *Intifada* ("shaking off" in Arabic) included street protests, sometimes violent, in which mainly young Palestinians hurled rocks and Molotov cocktails at Israeli forces. Israelis closed universities, instituted curfews,

arrested masses of people, and fought back with various means, including water cannons, batons, and live ammunition. A year and a half after the start of the uprising, Israelis had killed more than eight hundred Palestinians (including two hundred children), and more than two hundred Palestinians were murdered by other Palestinians as suspected collaborators with the Israelis. The PLO moved to take charge of and coordinate the resistance, which had begun as a grassroots movement. Arafat's organization, though, was soon challenged for leadership in the occupied territories by a new radical religious group coming out of the Intifada, Hamas.

Meanwhile, on the international stage, the PLO gained more legitimacy in mid-1988, when Jordan formally renounced any claim to the West Bank and any representation for the Palestinians. By the end of 1988, the Palestine National Council voted to accept UN Resolutions 242 and 338, and, thus, the 1947 partition of Palestine and the existence of Israel; the vote was accompanied by a declaration of a Palestinian state.

The United States on the Periphery

U.S. actions at the time remained largely irrelevant to the unfolding events. Secretary of State George Shultz attempted to organize a UN-sponsored conference in 1988 to restart the Camp David process; he remained wedded to the idea of a joint Jordanian-Palestinian delegation, while Likud leader Yitzhak Shamir and Jordan's King Hussein seemed uninterested in the proposal. On another issue, Shultz agreed with Shamir: he did not accept the PLO affirmation of UN Resolutions 242 and 338 as sufficient criteria for the organization to gain legitimacy. U.S. pressure on Yasser Arafat continued, finally leading to a new statement from the Palestinian leader, in December 1988, explicitly renouncing terrorism, whereupon the United States agreed to speak to the PLO.

Other Regional Conflicts

Separate from the Arab-Israeli conflict, the United States also was brought into a Middle Eastern war during the Reagan administration. Iraq, along with other countries in the region, was worried about the export of religious fundamentalism from the revolutionary regime in Iran; Iraq also had a long-standing dispute with Iran over their common border and the title to disputed oil lands. Under the leadership of Saddam Hussein (in office 1979–2003), Iraq invaded Iran in 1980, launching a bloody eight-year war between the two nations. Fortune at first favored Iraq, but then switched sides more than once. The official neutrality of the United States masked strategic support for Iraq, including its championing an international arms embargo against Iran. Between mid-1987 and mid-1988, the United States was directly involved in military skirmishes with the Iranian navy as part of its operation to reflag and convoy Kuwaiti oil tankers through the Persian Gulf in order to protect them from Iranian attack. This naval war ended when U.S. forces tragically downed an Iranian civilian airliner in July 1988, killing 290 people. The Iran-Iraq War (1980–1988) was finally brought to an end two weeks later under the auspices of a UN cease-fire resolution.

At the same time that American policymakers were attempting to broker peace in the Middle East and weaken Iran in its conflict with Iraq, the United States was much more aggressive in neighboring Central Asia. When Ronald Reagan came into office, he sought to challenge Soviet positions in places such as Afghanistan through strong covert military support for the rebels fighting the occupation. Reagan articulated his policy in the "Reagan Doctrine," which asserted the American commitment to support anti-Soviet forces, freedom, and democracy. The United States sent advisers and aid to Afghan rebels, including Stinger antiaircraft missiles in 1986. Two years later, the battered Soviets announced that their forces would be withdrawn from Afghanistan.

Although Reagan's policies in the Middle East were publicly more decisive than those of Jimmy Carter, behind the scenes, Reagan's policies were sometimes strategically confused. Despite the president's declaration of an arms embargo against Iran and a vow never to negotiate with terrorists ("We make no concessions. We make no deals," the president avowed in 1985), the administration secretly supplied Iran with arms in 1985 and 1986 in an effort to gain help for the release of American hostages taken in Lebanon.[1] (Profits of these sales were then funneled to rebel groups in Nicaragua, violating the congressional ban on arming rebels in that country.) When these dealings came to light in 1986, the strategic confusion undermined the reputation of the president and the strength of U.S. foreign policy in the region.

Reagan's policies with respect to Israel were less confused, but certainly no more successful in addressing the Arab-Israeli conflict. Reagan strengthened ties to the Likud party and encouraged its hard-line stance in the peace process, but remained more distant from the Labor party and had little pretense of acting as a fair broker between the Israelis and the Palestinians. In contrast to his predecessor Jimmy Carter, who earnestly sought to end the Arab-Israeli conflict, Reagan was determined to support the interests of Israel as an American ally, whether or not it helped to further the peace process.

Continuity and Transition under George H. W. Bush

The Middle East foreign policy of George H. W. Bush's administration (1989–1993) was dominated by the Persian Gulf War (1991), but both before and after this conflict with Iraq, the administration seized the opportunity of the Cold War's end to build multilateral support for an Arab-Israeli

peace process. In response to continued Israeli settlement activity in the West Bank and a refusal to negotiate with the PLO, U.S. Secretary of State James Baker (in office 1989–1992) publicly exhorted Israel to change course and tried, in summer 1989, to arrange a meeting between Israelis and Palestinians, only to be rebuffed by Israeli Prime Minister Yitzhak Shamir (in office 1983–1984, 1986–1992). Baker's speech to an AIPAC (American Israel Public Affairs Committee) meeting in 1989, which was intended to restore the American role as a fair broker, only succeeded in angering Shamir and his supporters. Baker called on Israel to "Foreswear annexation. Stop settlement activity.... Reach out to Palestinians who deserve political rights."[2] Terrorist acts from both sides and retaliations in spring 1990 brought any further U.S. attempts to foster peace to an end until after the Persian Gulf War.

The U.S. triumph in the Gulf War created a serious opportunity for peace. Conservative Arab leaders were grateful that an expansionist Iraq had been checked, the Palestinians and Jordanians who sympathized with Iraq had made a poor political calculation and were eager to cooperate with the United States, and the lack of Soviet opposition in the Gulf War encouraged the idea of American-Russian cooperation on other issues. With much persuasion and arm twisting, Secretary of State Baker succeeded in organizing the multilateral Madrid conference in October 1991, with delegations including Palestinians and Israelis meeting face to face for the first time. The conference itself merely reaffirmed UN Resolutions 242 and 338 and established a framework for future negotiations. Progress after this point was slow, especially since the Likud-led Israeli government moved ahead with settlement construction in the occupied territories, which threatened the Palestinian plan to build their future state in those same territories. The Bush administration pressed Israel to change course by withholding U.S. aid for housing construction, an acute need at the time as thousands of Russians were immigrating to Israel after the collapse of the Soviet Union in 1991.

In June 1992, Yitzhak Rabin (in office 1974–1977, 1992–1995) was again elected prime minister with a new Labor government. Although he initially made moderate moves, such as reducing settlement construction and freeing some Palestinian prisoners, renewed violence from Hamas led the Israeli government to deport Palestinian prisoners and seal its borders with the West Bank and Gaza Strip. Progress on the public peace-making front had reached a wall which would only be breached with the secret negotiations that would create a new peace process.

Because the Persian Gulf War was at the center of Bush's Middle East policies, the administration's impact on the Arab-Israeli conflict was predictably minor. Nevertheless, there were a couple of notable developments in U.S.-Israeli relations during Bush's term. First, the construction of the Madrid Conference signaled the U.S. commitment to the international process established by President Carter at Camp David, including the methods of trading land for peace and the idea that the United States should be a fair broker between the parties. Second, Bush's ill-fated attempt to withhold housing aid in order to force Israel to change course demonstrated his sincerity in being a fair broker. However, more importantly, the domestic political price that Bush paid for the policy demonstrated to his contemporaries and successors that the consensus of the political establishment was that the United States was not a fair broker, but rather an ally of Israel. Israelis and their U.S. supporters looked forward to repairing the relationship between their two countries under Bush's successor.

THE OSLO PEACE PROCESS: A NEW BEGINNING?

Although American policymakers had tried over many decades to encourage a resolution to the Arab-Israeli conflict, it was in the mid-1990s that the chances of success seemed greatest. Beginning in 1993, with eight months of secret meetings between Israelis and Palestinians sponsored by Norwegian diplomats, the Oslo process promised a breakthrough, because it was based on bilateral negotiations between the principal antagonists in the dispute. The Oslo Accords appeared to change everything.

The United States had been officially committed to the peace process which it had helped design at the Madrid Conference, and was at first uninvolved in the secret 1993 negotiations. Very quickly, though, the new president, William J. Clinton (1993–2001), embraced and championed the Oslo process, which was first made public with the initialing of the Declaration of Principles on Interim Self-Government Arrangements (Oslo I Accord) in August 1993. President Clinton hosted a formal signing ceremony of the accord on the White House lawn in September 1993. The crowd of dignitaries and an international television audience had high hopes following the dramatic ceremony.

For the next two years, there was tremendous progress in the peace process. In May 1994, Israeli troops withdrew from parts of the Gaza Strip and from Jericho in the West Bank. Within two months of the departure, PLO leader Arafat returned to Gaza from exile to establish the Palestinian Authority (PA). The PA soon began to build a state structure through such actions as the establishment of a police force and new government bureaucracies such as a postal system.

The examples of progress, though, masked the inadequacies of the Oslo structure that American policymakers preferred to ignore, and that seemed completely invisible in the hopeful stories in the American press. For example, because the most difficult issues were postponed in Oslo I

until "final status" talks, the American press paid more attention to the partial withdrawal from Gaza and less to the continuing construction of Israeli settlements in the West Bank, which was contrary to the spirit though not the letter of the agreement. Similarly, the hopefulness of building a Palestinian police force was more of a focus than that the force had limited powers under the Israeli military, and that it would become a militia used to fight the Israelis when the peace process unraveled. Moreover, many of the funds pledged from foreign governments to support the new Palestinian entity were withheld due to rampant corruption and a lack of accountability, as all funds were directly controlled by Arafat. Meanwhile, economic conditions worsened in Gaza and the West Bank as a whole remained tense.

Oslo II

A little more than a year later, in October 1995, Yasser Arafat and other political leaders signed the next formal agreement in the peace process, the Israeli-Palestinian Interim Agreement on the West Bank and Gaza, also known as Oslo II or the Taba Accord. This agreement affirmed that Israeli forces would be withdrawn from nine major Palestinian towns, and it established a complicated plan and staged withdrawal with a three-tiered system of zones in the West Bank. Zone A was made up of eight West Bank cities already controlled by Palestinians (including Jericho); Palestinians here would be responsible for internal security and public order. Zone B comprised other West Bank cities in which Israel would retain authority for security, but Palestinians would eventually be responsible for order. Zone C was made up of Jewish settlements, unoccupied land, or areas that Israelis deemed to be strategic; here, Israel would retain full control of security until otherwise changed by "final status" talks. Palestinian police and Israel soldiers were to go on joint patrols, and Israel would build bypass roads for settlers and soldiers connecting Israeli zones of responsibility. The map designed in the accords was confusing indeed. Also in the accords, Palestinians were to elect a president and an eighty-eight-member council.

Secretary of State Warren Christopher (in office 1993–1997) and other American diplomats realized that a new Palestinian state would need tremendous financial aid to establish itself. The Americans hosted a conference in Washington at which forty-six countries pledged $2.5 billion in economic aid to the Palestinian Authority. The Palestinians took one more step closer to statehood in January 1996 with the election of the new legislature and Arafat as president. Another hurdle was cleared away in April, when the Palestine National Council voted to eliminate from its charter the call for the destruction of Israel; with this vote, the Labor Party in Israel said it no longer opposed Palestinian statehood.

Israeli Relations with Arab States

Along with progress on the Israeli-Palestinian front, there was progress in Israel's relationships with other nations. Within a month after the signing of Oslo I, leaders of Jordan and Israel began negotiations to end the state of hostilities between the two nations. By July 1994, King Hussein and Prime Minister Rabin traveled to Washington to announce an end to hostilities; they followed their announcement three months later with the signing of a formal peace treaty, witnessed by President Clinton, and the opening of diplomatic relations a month after that. In addition to acting as a witness, the United States encouraged dialogue in different ways, including with the appropriation of $900 million in economic and military aid to Jordan. Morocco and Tunisia also began negotiations with Israel, and Saudi Arabia and the multilateral Gulf Cooperation Council weakened its economic boycott of Israel.

American efforts to encourage improved relations between Israel and Syria, however, were not as successful. Despite the repeated personal involvement of Secretary of State Warren Christopher, and even a visit by President Clinton to Damascus, Syrian leader Hafiz al-Assad (in office 1971–2000) refused to negotiate with Israel until it withdrew unconditionally from the Golan Heights. In contrast, a month before the signing of Oslo I, Rabin had proposed a gradual withdrawal from the Golan over five years in exchange for peace and normalization between the two countries. State Department attempts to facilitate Israeli-Syrian negotiations at the Wye River meetings in Maryland in December 1995 and January 1996 failed as well. This attempt was followed by the exchange of fire between Hezbollah and Israel across the Lebanon border, where occupying Syrian troops played an important role. Negotiations between Syria and Israel did not resume again until January 2000, at the insistence of the United States, and with American efforts to mediate an exchange at Shepherdstown, Virginia. Neither that meeting nor a follow-up meeting two months later in Geneva resulted in a successful agreement to establish relations and resolve the dispute over the Golan Heights. In many ways, the collapse of peace efforts was predictable. Both Israeli and American leaders underestimated the importance for Syria of an unconditional return of its territory in the Golan, as well as the impact of simmering tensions in Lebanon, where both Syrians and Israelis had long had occupying troops, each trying to shape the internal politics of the country.

Collapse of the Oslo Process

The peace process was not just doomed by intractable animosities between nation states. Perhaps more importantly, non-state extremist groups and individuals used violence to inflame and alienate popular sentiments on all sides, eventually making further compromise seem politically impossible. A few months after the signing of Oslo I, in February 1994, an American-born Jewish settler killed twenty-nine Palestinians as they prayed at a mosque in Hebron. Another Jewish extremist shocked the world in November 1995 by assassinating Prime Minister Yitzhak Rabin after he finished speaking at a peace rally in Tel Aviv. The settler, Yigal Amir, reported that he was acting on God's orders to make sure that the Holy Land was not taken away from the Jews.

Meanwhile, religiously motivated extremists from Hamas and Islamic Jihad also attacked the peace process from the other side with suicide bombings on Israeli buses. Four attacks between October 1994 and August 1995 killed scores of Israelis; another four attacks took place in the two months following the election of Yasser Arafat as president in January 1996 and killed fifty-nine Israelis.

In the face of escalating violence from various sides of the dispute, and with the lack of tangible progress in reaching a political settlement, many ordinary Israelis and Palestinians became less supportive of the entire Oslo proposition. A little more than six months after the assassination of Rabin, Israelis narrowly elected as prime minister Likud leader Benjamin Netanyahu (in office 1996–1999, 2009–), a man known as a hard-liner who had already publicly criticized Oslo.

It is worth noting that the Oslo process faced other critics in addition to violent extremists. The Labor government under Rabin was in the unusual situation of facing opposition to its policies from within the organized American Jewish community. Many of the American Jewish establishment organizations had long-standing ties to the earlier Likud governments, and had a more conservative approach to the Arab-Israeli conflict than did the Labor leaders. Rabin spoke out against the efforts of organized Jewry to pressure the U.S. Congress against support for the Oslo process: "... never before have we witnessed an attempt by U.S. Jews to pressure Congress against the policy of a legally, democratically elected government."[3] Despite Rabin's admonitions, American Jewish organizations never fully embraced the Oslo process.

Wye River Memorandum

Encouragement from Secretary of State Madeleine Albright (in office 1997–2001) and Middle East envoy Dennis Ross, who had already played a pivotal role in helping broker the existing agreements between Israel and its neighbors, did little to stem the deterioration of the peace process. In October 1998, Bill Clinton hosted a meeting at the Wye River center in Maryland, hoping to persuade Arafat and Netanyahu to make real progress. Each leader made promises at the meeting to continue the process and to restart final status negotiations before May 1999. More specifically, in the Wye River Memorandum, Israelis agreed to transfer more land in the West Bank to Palestinian control, to provide safe passage between the West Bank and the Gaza Strip, and to release certain Palestinian prisoners from jail. The Palestinians, for their part, promised to try to prevent violent attacks against Israel, to arrest certain people whom Israel had judged to be responsible for violence, and to hold a meeting of the PNC at which it would actually amend its charter to eliminate the passages calling for the destruction of Israel (previously, the Palestinians had vowed to amend the charter but had not yet done so). Clinton journeyed to Gaza two months later, in December 1998, to watch the fulfillment of one of the pledges made at Wye River, the PNC's vote to remove from its charter the call for the destruction of Israel. Clinton rewarded Arafat with a visit to the White House three months later.

Camp David II

Although the May 1999 deadline came and went, American diplomats continued to prod and cajole the adversaries, pressing Israel to make concessions about occupied lands and the PLO to stop violence. Although Israel increasingly blamed Arafat and the Palestinian security forces for the violence, the PLO forces had less and less hope of controlling Hamas and curbing that violence. In September 1999, Secretary of State Albright got consensus on the Sharm al-Sheikh Agreement, which called for a Declaration of Principles by February 2000 and a final settlement in September 2000. By mid-2000, it was obvious to all observers that the September 2000 deadline would not be met without a serious change in course.

Dennis Ross and Madeleine Albright worked to push forward on final status talks, but to no avail. A frustrated Arafat warned that if agreement could not be reached by the September deadline, Palestinians might unilaterally declare their state, and that there was danger of more violence.

President Clinton attempted to rescue the whole process, and perhaps repeat the dramatic success of Jimmy Carter two decades before, with intensive negotiations at Camp David in July 2000. Clinton spent two weeks meeting with both Yasser Arafat and Israeli Prime Minister Ehud Barak (prime minister 1999–2001), the relatively more moderate successor to Benjamin Netanyahu, trying to draw concessions from both. Top American policymakers Ross and Albright participated, as did National Security Adviser Sandy Berger (in office 1997–2001). One positive aspect of the meeting was that the principals, including Arafat and Barak, met face to face to discuss the most difficult issues of the Arab-Israeli conflict, topics that always had been avoided before. Moreover, the earnest negotiations indicated that the leaders involved were genuinely trying to reach accommodation. Their efforts, though, did not achieve what they had hoped.

The dramatic failure of the meeting at Camp David revealed not just the weaknesses of the Oslo process or the intransigence of the individual leaders involved, but also the flaws of long-term U.S. policy in the region and the bedrock assumptions used to shape that policy. The story of the Camp David meeting, told in contemporary press accounts, in most subsequent American histories, and in the recollections of Bill Clinton and other American participants,

---

IN THEIR OWN WORDS: *PRESIDENT CLINTON'S COMMITMENT TO PEACE AT SIGNING OF ISRAELI-PALESTINIAN INTERIM AGREEMENT, 1995*

When Bill Clinton came into office as president in 1993, he had no special foreign policy expertise or knowledge about the Arab-Israeli conflict. However, within months of his inauguration, news of the secret negotiations between Israel and the Palestinians changed the dynamic within the region and opened up a new chapter in the peace process. As president, Clinton worked hard to encourage and cajole all sides into making progress and to regain the U.S. role of fair broker in the conflict. Here, in an excerpt of his speech at the signing of the Israeli-Palestinian Interim Agreement in 1995, Clinton shows his commitment to the peace process and his optimism for its success:

You, the children of Abraham, have made a peace worthy of your great forebear. Abraham, patriarch of both Arabs and Jews, sacrificed power for peace when he said to his nephew, Lot, "Let there be no strife between thee and me. If thou will take the left hand, then I will go to

the right." Patience and persistence, courage and sacrifice—these are the virtues, then as now, that set peacemakers apart.

Mr. Prime Minister and Mr. Chairman, you are showing that it is not by weapons, but by will and by word, that dreams best become reality. Your achievement shines as an inspiration to others all around this world who seek to overcome their own conflicts and to secure for themselves the blessings of peace....

All those who doubt the spirit of peace should remember this day and this extraordinary array of leaders who have joined together to bring a new era of hope to the Middle East. The United States is proud to stand with all of them....

SOURCE: http://clinton6.nara.gov/1995/09/1995-09-28-remarks-at-israeli-palestinian-interim-agreement.html, accessed October 3, 2011.

emphasized that Barak offered dramatic, unprecedented concessions that were spurned by a stubborn Arafat. To be sure, the Israeli offer went further than any previous discussions, including recognition of Palestinian sovereignty in much of East Jerusalem, and Israeli withdrawal from about 90 percent of the West Bank, along with compensation for those parts of the territory that would be retained by Israel. Arafat held out for full sovereignty over all of East Jerusalem and, more importantly, Israeli withdrawal to the 1967 borders and the right of return for Palestinian refugees. Although on the face of it, Barak's position appeared eminently more reasonable than Arafat's, the latter's refusal to accept the offered 90 percent of the West Bank must be understood as a reflection of the fact that the territory Israel proposed to return would not have been contiguous. It would have been divided by Israeli controlled roads and bounded in the east by an Israeli controlled area along the border with Jordan. Moreover, the "country" of Palestine would not have control over its water supply, borders, immigration, or airspace, and would be prohibited from acquiring defensive arms. Finally, no curbs were placed on the population of existing Jewish settlements, which had continued to grow in population (and geographic size) throughout the Oslo process; by the end of 2000, there were more than two hundred thousand Jewish settlers in the West Bank and Gaza.

American understanding of the events at Camp David also differed from the Palestinian perspective for another reason. The Camp David meeting was brokered by Bill Clinton and American policymakers who imagined themselves as impartial facilitators. While it was clear that they sincerely sought to reach an enduring peace in the Arab-Israeli conflict, that desire could not overcome a long-standing relationship with Israel, which biased U.S. policy in the region at least since the late 1960s, if not before. Thus, the events at Camp David reflected two bedrocks of American policy in the region: unflappable support for Israeli interests, and support for status quo or conservative powers over dramatic change.

Before the end of his presidency, Clinton made one last attempt to broker a deal between Israelis and Palestinians. He proposed that the future Palestinian state would get about 95 percent of the West Bank following a staged withdrawal of Israeli troops, and that there would be a compromise on the right of return. Barak signed on, but Arafat called for an immediate withdrawal and no compromise on the refugee issue. The participants met in Sharm al-Shakh and Taba, both cities located on the Sinai Peninsula, in their attempt to reach an agreement. In the end, Clinton's "Bridging Document" was not enough to overcome the differences among the various positions.

Bill Clinton happened to be president during the high point of the Israeli-Palestinian peace process, when optimism about the future ran high. In such an atmosphere, he could easily assert the role of the United States as a fair broker, while also continuing to support the "special relationship" between Americans and Israelis. As the peace process unraveled after 1995, it became increasingly difficult for Americans to simultaneously play both roles. Thus, Clinton, like his predecessors, affirmed the iron-clad American support for Israel, while criticizing the demands of Palestinians as too radical and Arafat as unwilling to compromise. This tilt is illustrated by the events of Camp David II in 2000, where the president and his negotiators endorsed the Israeli position and rejected the demands of Arafat. Under Clinton, then, the American-Israeli relationship remained strong, even at the expense of progress in the peace process.

THE AL-AQSA OR SECOND INTIFADA

Looking at these events in a broader context, it is perhaps no surprise that the negotiations of 2000 failed. The Oslo peace process, whose high point was between 1993 and 1995, was weakened and struggling since Rabin's assassination. It was effectively over by the time that the Al-Aqsa Intifada began in September 2000.

For most Palestinians, day-to-day life had not improved since the start of the Oslo process, and by 2000, they were pessimistic that this would change or that they would soon see an independent Palestinian state. Similarly, many Israelis were also disillusioned with the peace process, and a number were voicing more conservative sentiments that they should retain not only the Golan Heights but also the West Bank. An undeniable part in the background of the whole situation was that the Oslo process had been built with one group of Palestinians under PLO leadership, but soon after, that leadership was challenged and under siege from another group, Hamas.

In September 2000, Ariel Sharon, former Defense Minister and then Likud leader, led an entourage of police to the Temple Mount in Jerusalem, where the Al-Aqsa mosque stood. His assertion of continuing Israeli sovereignty over this holy Muslim site provoked rioting throughout the West Bank, including attacks on Jewish settlements with rocks and sometimes guns. The Israeli response was swift and large, with raids that killed hundreds and injured thousands. Houses were blown up, fruit trees were uprooted, tear gas was used against whole villages, and demonstrators were shot. Fighting even broke out between Israeli Arab citizens and the Israel Defense Forces (IDF) in Nazareth. Border crossings between the West Bank, Gaza, and Israel were closed, preventing many Palestinians from reaching their jobs in Israel. Israel reoccupied the Gaza Strip, used air strikes against PLO and other buildings, and imprisoned Palestinians without trial.

Meanwhile, support for Arafat among Palestinians was drying up, with many viewing him as corrupt and ineffectual. Hamas and Hezbollah stepped into the vacuum, escalating the situation with suicide attacks against Israel and attacks on settlements.

The violence of the Second or Al-Aqsa Intifada led Israeli voters rightward, and they elected Ariel Sharon (in power 2001–2006) prime minister, along with his Likud party, in February 2001. Sharon made no pretense of supporting the Oslo process and declared that there would be no concessions on Jerusalem, territory, or refugees; he further asserted that Israel's goal was to suppress the violence, rather than reach a comprehensive peace with the Palestinians. Most Palestinians and other Arabs were not surprised, as many viewed Sharon as a war criminal for his role in allowing the Phalangist militias to carry out the massacres in the Sabra and Shatilla refugee camps during the 1982 Lebanon War. Most Arabs supported the uprising of the Palestinians, and many states broke diplomatic and commercial ties with Israel. (Egypt and Jordan continued a formal, though chilly, relationship with Israel, since they had official and hard-won peace treaties.)

American Reaction to the Second Intifada

Reactions in the United States were predictably different from those in the Arab world. American press coverage included graphic images of the fighting but overall tended to balance out the actions taken on each side. Nevertheless, probably more graphic images of the aftermath from suicide bombs appeared on American televisions than did images of devastated Palestinian villages or frustrated Palestinians at border crossings. In the end, images of the new intifada led many Americans to throw up their hands at the seemingly insoluble Arab-Israeli conflict, in which the participants seemed determined to fight each other forever.

Predictably, with the public failure of the Camp David meeting, Bill Clinton's ability to negotiate an end to the fighting was not great. In January 2001, the administration of George W. Bush (2001–2009) also pushed for an end to the violence and supported an initiative that had been started under Clinton, a commission under the leadership of former Senator George Mitchell (D-ME; in office 1980–1995).

In May 2001, the Mitchell Commission proposed a three-step plan to resurrect the peace process. The plan was deceptively simple but unrealistic, since it did not change any of the factors that had led to the intifada in the first place. The plan called first for the reaffirmation of agreements already made, an end to violence, and security cooperation between the sides. It next called for "confidence-building measures," including a denunciation of terrorism

PUBLIC PORTRAIT: *GEORGE MITCHELL (1933–)*

George Mitchell had been a senator from Maine for more than fifteen years and had risen through the leadership to become majority leader. He had retired from the Senate by the time he was tapped by President Bill Clinton to lead a commission to address the escalating violence in the Middle East. During Clinton's second term, Mitchell had proved his diplomatic abilities as a special envoy to Northern Ireland. His efforts there helped lead to the signing of the Belfast Peace Agreement (or Good Friday Agreement) in 1998, which established principles of non-violence and led to all-party negotiations.

The Mitchell Commission, established in 2000, was charged with reporting on the state of the Arab-Israeli conflict and making recommendations to move forward. By the time the commission finished its work in the Bush administration, the Al-Aqsa Intifada had already been under way for eight months, and the prospects for peace looked bleak. The commission's report (also known as the Sharm el-Sheikh Fact Finding Committee Report) had three parts to it, none of which was new. First, it called for a confirmation of past agreements, controlling violence, and reinstating security cooperation. Next, it said each side should offer "confidence-building measures," such as ending settlements and renouncing terrorism. Finally, it called for peace negotiations to be restarted. Although Ariel Sharon and Yasser Arafat paid lip service to the Mitchell plan, the intifada and responses to it did not cease. The report became the basis of the "Roadmap" process introduced during the Bush administration, but that, too, did not achieve its goals of ending the Arab-Israeli conflict.

For the remainder of the Bush administration, Mitchell practiced law in the private sector and burnished his image as an impartial arbiter of disputes by leading an investigation into steroid use in professional baseball. In January 2009, President Barack Obama and Secretary of State Hillary Clinton (in office 2009–) asked him to return to government service as special Middle East envoy for peace, with the hope that he would be able to bring the warring factions together as he had done in Northern Ireland. He left for his first trip to the Middle East within a week of his appointment, visiting five countries, as well as the West Bank. His role was intended to demonstrate to all observers that Obama was serious about trying to address the ongoing conflict, and that intervention seemed necessary in light of the unstable situation following the newly concluded cease-fire in the Gaza-Israel fighting of 2008–2009.

Yet Mitchell did not radically change U.S. policy or the American approach to the conflict. In some ways, this meant that his mission had little chance of success. For example, he continued the American policy of refusing to speak or meet with Hamas, labeled a terrorist organization by the U.S. government. By only dealing with the Fatah faction of the PLO, he ignored a key player in the region that enjoyed popular support and controlled the Gaza Strip. In addition, he did not propose any substantially new policies for the region, nor press Israel to stop or reduce settlements in the West Bank. By the time he resigned his post in May 2011, peace was no closer than it had been at the start of his appointment, and the Arab-Israeli conflict seemed like it would go on indefinitely.

and an end to settlements. In the third stage, the plan called for the resumption of peace negotiations. President Bush sent CIA Director George Tenet (in office 1997–2004) to formulate a plan for implementation; he was followed by retired Marine Corps General Anthony Zinni, who pushed Arafat and Sharon to accept the Tenet plan.

George W. Bush and the Middle East before 9/11

Although some observers argued that U.S. policy had long sided with Israel, American policymakers had continued to assert that they were unbiased and that the interests of each side must be respected. By the time that George W. Bush became president, this changed. Bush's views of the Arab-Israeli conflict were shaped in part by neoconservative advisers like Paul Wolfowitz, who were iron-clad defenders of Israel, and by realist advisers like Condoleezza Rice, who also believed that American interests lay with the Israelis. The change of orientation in the Bush administration was reflected in open hostility to Arafat, who was isolated by the Israelis and the Americans as a supporter of terrorism. While policymakers in the Bush administration did not openly renounce the idea that they wanted a fair solution for both sides, the pretense that the United States was an honest broker in the conflict was weaker than ever.

The change in U.S. policy was illustrated in the American reaction to the barrier that Israel built to separate itself from parts of the territory it occupied on the West Bank. Although the idea of a barrier had first been introduced by Yitzhak Rabin, it was not until after 2000 when construction began in earnest. The wall roughly followed the Green Line, the border that had separated Israel and the occupied territories since the 1967 war, but it was built mainly on occupied land and veered away from the 1967 line in a number of places, enclosing many Jewish settlements on the Israeli side of the divide and separating Palestinians from their agricultural lands and from other towns. Thus, as the barrier was being constructed, it appropriated occupied West Bank territory into Israel proper without waiting for status negotiations on the borders of a Palestinian state. Israel maintained an extensive presence on the supposedly Palestinian side of the barrier, controlling access roads, checkpoints, settlements and outposts, and vast swaths of the West Bank that had been designated as Area C under the Oslo Accords. The barrier was almost uniformly condemned by the Palestinians, most countries, the UN, and many international organizations as an illegal absorption of occupied land. The Israeli Supreme Court and the International Court of Justice also handed down decisions in 2004 saying that the parts of the wall constructed within the West Bank were illegal and should be moved. The Bush administration, meanwhile, completely accepted the defense

put forward by first the Barak government and then by the Sharon and Netanyahu governments, that the barrier was a necessary defense to stop terrorists from entering Israel. By the end of the Bush administration in early 2009, the Israeli barrier was still being constructed, unchallenged by American policymakers.

There were other examples of American deference to Israeli interests. In 2004, George W. Bush announced that Israel could keep its major settlement blocs in the West Bank, and that it need not be concerned with the right of return for Palestinian refugees. Such a decision was contrary to international law and reversed decades of American policy. Another example was seen in 2006, when border skirmishes between Hezbollah in Lebanon and Israel escalated into war during the summer. The United States refused to push for an end of the fighting when the Israeli government said that it needed more time to achieve its objectives of weakening Hezbollah.

The reaction of Bush officials to Palestinian political changes also illustrated the trend of Middle East policy in the administration. Americans and Israelis continued to isolate Yasser Arafat in his West Bank compound. By 2003, Bush journeyed to the Middle East to meet with various leaders in support of a renewed peace process, including the American-sponsored "Roadmap." The 2002 Roadmap was an American plan to revive the dormant peace process, even though it was sponsored by the "Quartet" (the United States, Russia, the European Union [EU], and the UN). Bush championed the Roadmap as a new way of reaching peace, but there was little new in the three-stage proposal to create a Palestinian state living next door to Israel, following a period in which each side made concessions, such as halting settlements and preventing violence. Of the Palestinian leadership, though, President Bush would only meet with moderate Prime Minister Mahmoud Abbas (in office 2003; president, PNA, 2005–), who would be elected president of the PNA following Arafat's death in 2004. The proposed Roadmap was not much different from earlier propositions and almost seemed to go backward to the Madrid process, because it was promoted by the Quartet, introducing outside powers back into the process. Importantly, though, the Roadmap did not propose any new solutions to address the key issues that had ended the Oslo process.

One of the goals in Phase Two of the Roadmap was the establishment of a democratic government for the Palestinians. In 2006, the Palestinians elected the Palestinian Legislative Council, but to the shock of Americans, Israelis, and Abbas' Fatah party, the Hamas-affiliated party won a majority of delegates, seventy-four to Fatah's forty-five (with thirteen going to other minor parties). The Bush administration and the Israeli government chose not to recognize the results of the election, charging that Hamas was a terrorist organization. Hamas took control of the Gaza Strip, while Abbas ruled in the West Bank, with the support of Israel and the United States. Meanwhile, Israel and the United States imposed sanctions on the Hamas government. Subsequent missile attacks from Gaza into Israel were militarily ineffective but heightened fear in Israel and provoked both counterattacks and a tightening of the Israeli blockade of Gaza, which had been in effect in some form since 2001, following the spread of the Al-Aqsa Intifada.

9/11 AND THE "WAR ON TERROR"

At the start of the twenty-first century, it is very difficult to understand U.S. policy toward the Arab-Israeli conflict and the search for peace in the Middle East without understanding the impact of the al Qaeda terror attacks on the United States on September 11, 2001, and how this event reshaped American priorities. The launch of the War on Terror had a profound impact on U.S. policy in the Arab-Israeli conflict for at least two reasons. First, many policymakers in the Bush administration identified with the longstanding Israeli fight against terrorism and believed that their two countries were on the same side of this broader struggle. This identification in the fight against terrorism further eroded the idea that the United States could be a fair broker between the Palestinians and Israelis. Second, with the War on Terror defining the purpose and priorities for U.S. foreign policy, everything else seemed somehow less important, including the Arab-Israeli conflict.

Shifting Strategic Goals

Aside from attitudes toward the Arab-Israeli conflict, the goals of American foreign policy, especially in the Middle East, changed following the events of 9/11. The greatest disjuncture between pre- and post-9/11 policies lay in the assertion of a new war paradigm. From the days immediately following the attack, policymakers in the Bush administration framed the event as the start of a war instead of as a horrible crime whose perpetrators should be punished. The president's immediate reaction was to tell Vice President Dick Cheney, "Somebody's going to pay."[4] The war, moreover, was promulgated as a moral crusade whose goal was to defeat evil itself. President George W. Bush explained the War on Terror to Americans on September 20, 2001: "This is civilization's fight. This is the fight of all who believe in progress and pluralism, tolerance and freedom."[5]

To be sure, the scale and symbolism of the 9/11 attacks were unique, a circumstance that bolstered international condemnation and the judgment that the events were a crime against humanity. Yet terrorism had been a familiar weapon that had targeted many peoples and nationalities in the past, and had been used, especially, to make symbolic statements in Middle Eastern political disputes. Thus it was not preordained that such an attack would initiate an American War on Terror. Instead of following the lead of international public opinion, though, Bush policymakers chose to launch a broad-based, open-ended war against a method and an ideology that existed outside of the borders of a nation state and a particular ethnic group.

The second reason that the 9/11 attacks constituted a cleavage in American foreign policy in the Middle East was the way in which the Bush administration decided to wage the war and what it was designed, ultimately, to prove. The assertion of an unbridled unilateralism that could reshape the power dynamics of the Middle East without the check of other powers illustrated the assumptions of Bush policymakers and their unwillingness to compromise goals or American dominance where it asserted itself.

U.S. Army vehicles pass through Baghdad, Iraq, on their way to Kuwait, thus signaling an end to the seven-and-a-half-year war. President Obama called the troops' withdrawal a "milestone in the Iraq War" and noted, "I hope you'll join me in thanking them, and all of our troops and military families, for their service." The Iraq War defined the presidency of George W. Bush, leaving more than forty-four hundred American service members and tens of thousands of Iraqis dead.

SOURCE: Mario Tama/Getty Images.

The third important foreign policy change in the Bush administration's response to 9/11 was the decision to elevate national security over domestic protections of civil liberties and international laws banning torture and inhumane treatment. Not since the Cold War's Red Scare had a national security threat been used as a blatant excuse to disavow protections to civil liberties, excusing intrusions such as wiretapping and surveillance of religious and civic groups. The public sanctioning of torture, or what administration personnel referred to as "enhanced interrogation techniques," brought condemnation from around the world and quickly eroded any remaining sympathy for the United States.

Going to War in Afghanistan and Iraq

U.S. strategic goals had very specific consequences. Less than a month after the 9/11 attacks, the United States, along with the United Kingdom and Afghan rebel fighters, went to war against al Qaeda groups in Afghanistan and the Taliban government that supported them. The war in Central Asia was a direct response to 9/11 and initially enjoyed popular and political support in the United States as a just war. Moreover, ordinary Americans initially believed that

the war was spectacularly successful, since the Taliban regime fell and the focus of American policymakers shifted to the Middle East. The war, though, was far from over more than a decade later, and its success was in doubt.

The decision of U.S. policymakers to go to war in Iraq in 2003 was far more complex than that to go to war in Afghanistan in 2001. Although Bush administration policymakers linked the Iraq War to 9/11, that connection was and remains controversial. The Bush administration argued that war against Iraq was necessary because of the imminent danger from Iraqi weapons of mass destruction (WMDs), weapons that could not be found by the UN inspectors who were being hoodwinked by Saddam Hussein's government. Furthermore, administration members hinted and implied that Iraq was somehow linked to 9/11 and the broader War on Terrorism. Bush asserted in his ultimatum to Iraq on the eve of war, "Terrorists and terror states do not reveal these threats with fair notice. . . . The security of the world requires disarming Saddam Hussein now."[6]

Contemporary and subsequent observers have discounted these reasons, instead arguing that policymakers from the president down were motivated by other goals. First was the familiar U.S. goal of ensuring ready access to

President Barack Obama (right) met with Benjamin Netanyahu, the prime minister of Israel, in the Oval Office on May 20, 2011. The two leaders have had a sometimes rocky relationship, but they exchanged cordial words during their meeting. In his remarks during the session, the prime minister noted, "We share your hope and your vision for the spread of democracy in the Middle East. I appreciate the fact that you reaffirmed once again now and in our conversation, and in actual deed, the commitment to Israel's security. We value your efforts to advance the peace process."

SOURCE: Doug Mills/*The New York Times*/Redux.

affordable oil in the Middle East. Such a goal had been a concern for American foreign policy since World War II, and its importance was self-evident in an administration led by two former oil executives, President George W. Bush and Vice President Dick Cheney.

The second goal represented a new direction, introduced by neoconservatives in the Bush administration who were intent on changing the power dynamics in the Middle East; they included Paul Wolfowitz, Richard Perle, and Douglas Feith. They advised that the United States should prevent any rival to its superpower status, and that it should act unilaterally in the Middle East and elsewhere. Moreover, they argued that the United States should maintain unquestioned support for Israel, and that real American power was demonstrated through military might, not through diplomacy. Many of these policymakers believed that it was a mistake to have allowed Saddam Hussein to stay in power following the 1991 Gulf War. Even before the election of George W. Bush, some of these policymakers supported what they called the Project for the New American Century in a letter to President Bill Clinton in 1998, calling on the United States to remove Saddam Hussein from power. This group was supported by a number of conservative and pro-Israeli organizations in Washington. Although staunch support for Israel had long been a pillar of American policy, the neoconservatives, led by Paul

Wolfowitz, sought to overthrow or change regimes that most forcefully opposed U.S. and Israeli interests in the region. From this perspective, the interests of the United States and Israel were one and the same.

Along with the strategic calculations of the neoconservatives, there were other policymakers in Washington who were concerned about the possibility of weapons of mass destruction in Iraq. Before the 1991 Gulf War, the United States had sold arms to Iraq, and secretly took its side in the Iran-Iraq War. The start of Iraq's biological weapons program came from the United States, as did satellite technology used in conventional and gas weapons in the Iran-Iraq War. After the Gulf War, the United States and its allies maintained sanctions against Iraq, while investigating, looking for, and disarming weapons of mass destruction (nuclear, biological, and chemical), and also enforced two no-fly zones in the northern and southern thirds of the country. Thus, long before 2003, American policymakers had been determined to prevent Iraq from keeping weapons of mass destruction.

Results of American Policy in Iraq and Afghanistan

Early in the war in 2003, United States forces were militarily successful with the use of overwhelming firepower and very few American casualties. In twenty-one days' time, the American forces, along with British forces and small contingents from minor allies, demolished Saddam Hussein's

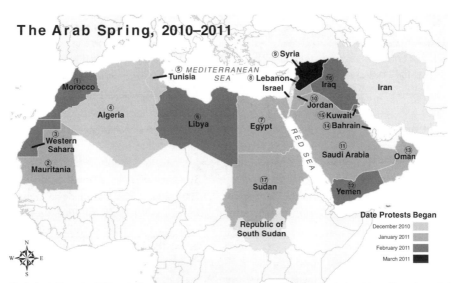

Beginning in December 2010, and with mixed results, popular protests began throughout the Arab world, as citizens demanded reforms in their respective governments.

1   February 20, 2011   King Mohammad VI grants political concessions; vows to end corruption
2   January 17, 2011   Protests curbed by government
3   February 26, 2011   Protests, but no changes in government
4   December 28, 2010   Mass protests result in lifting a 19-year-old state of emergency
5   December 18, 2010   President Ben Ali ousted; elections held on October 23, 2011
6   February 17, 2011   Civil war; government overthrown in October 2011
7   January 25, 2011   Government overthrown; protests continue
8   January 12, 2011   Limited protests bring a 40 percent increase in wages
9   March 15, 2011   Widespread protests lead to severe government crackdown; thousands killed
10   January 14, 2011   King Abdullah dismisses two governments to speed up reforms
11   January 21, 2011   King Abdullah grants concessions; male-only elections in 2011; women allowed to vote in municipal elections in 2015
12   February 3, 2011   President Ali Abdullah Saleh agrees to step down
13   January 17, 2011   Sultan Qaboos grants economic concessions and gives law-making powers to the legislature
14   February 14, 2011   King Hamad grants economic concessions
15   February 18, 2011   Resignation of nation's cabinet
16   February 10, 2011   Prime Minister Nouri al-Malaki announces he will not run for third term; resignations of local authorities
17   January 17, 2011   President Omar al-Bashir announces he will not seek a third term in 2015

SHIFTS IN FOREIGN POLICY: *THE STRUGGLE AGAINST VIOLENT EXTREMISM*

Barack Obama campaigned for president asserting that the administration of George W. Bush had made terrible mistakes in many areas of the nation's foreign policy, most dramatically in the war against Iraq. In addition, he said in the campaign, and continued to say after he was elected, that keeping the nation secure did not mean that its values should be compromised by using methods such as torture. He and his advisers also disagreed with one of the fundamental premises of the Bush administration, that the United States was engaged in a "War on Terror." Following Obama's inauguration in January 2009, he and his policymakers no longer used the term, instead referring to specific engagements or more generally to "the struggle against violent extremism."

Another criticism that President Obama and his advisers voiced against the outgoing administration was that U.S. policies had unnecessarily antagonized and alienated many people throughout the Muslim world. Obama pledged to repair that rift, a change that was eagerly awaited by many Muslims abroad whose opinion of the United States and George W. Bush had plummeted by 2008.

Obama's new approach was presented in a widely viewed speech that the president gave at Cairo University in Egypt in June 2009. The president addressed several themes in the speech, but highlighted three. He assured his audience that he sought "a new beginning" between the United States and Muslims around the world based on respect and the truth that "Islam is a part of America." In reaching out, Obama firmly condemned violent extremism and explained that he would work to end the wars in Afghanistan and Iraq. The second major issue that he addressed was the Arab-Israeli conflict. He attempted to regain the earlier American role of being a fair and honest broker by acknowledging the legitimate aspirations of both the Palestinians and the Israelis, and asserted that the only solution to the conflict was two states living in security, side by side. In a departure from the Bush administration positions, he said directly that all Israeli settlements were illegitimate, violating previous agreements.

The third major issue that Obama addressed was the American-Iranian relationship. He acknowledged the "tumultuous history" between the two countries and admitted that the United States had in the past helped overthrow a democratically elected government in Iran. He asserted that the United States wanted to move forward in the relationship "without preconditions on the basis of mutual respect," but he gave no ground on American opposition to Iran acquiring nuclear weapons, which he said might lead to an arms race in the Middle East.

FULFILLING THE CAIRO INITIATIVES

In the two years after this speech, the Obama administration followed up on its outreach to the Muslim world, but in many ways, the promise of the rhetoric remained unfulfilled. His administration banned torture, but his attempts to close the U.S. prison at Guantanamo Bay, opened in 2002 as a holding place for suspected terrorists, were stymied by strong congressional opposition and the inability to resolve the status and placement of the detainees.

The United States fulfilled Obama's promise to wind down and "responsibly" end the Iraq War, with the combat mission officially over by August 2010 and the remaining combat troops removed by December 2011. Military operations continued in Afghanistan, and the president fulfilled his promise to send more troops to the country and to reenergize the fight against al Qaeda and the Taliban. More than one hundred thousand U.S. troops were in Afghanistan in mid-2011. Although the administration asserted that the U.S. had been successful in drastically weakening al Qaeda and the Taliban, the country remained extremely unstable and violent in 2011. The most dramatic victory in Central Asia in mid-2011 was the killing of Osama bin Laden by U.S. Navy commandos, but that same operation also illustrated the deteriorating relations between the United States and Pakistan, since bin Laden had been sought out and killed in his hiding place in Pakistan without the knowledge of that country's government.

Obama's policies toward Iran did not fulfill the idealism of his Cairo speech. Iran continued to give support to Hezbollah in Lebanon, Hamas in Palestine, and

military, occupied the country, and forced Saddam into hiding. Uncounted thousands of Iraqi soldiers and civilians were killed, and the infrastructure and countryside were devastated.

Very quickly, though, after the fall of Saddam's government, with the country in chaos and the Americans doing little to control or rebuild it, a strong insurgent movement formed against the foreign occupiers. Sunni Muslims who had enjoyed a privileged position under Saddam rebelled and fought bitterly in the towns northwest of Baghdad, while Shiites in the south also rebelled against the American occupation. New groups formed, such as al Qaeda in Iraq, which recruited people to fight the Americans. The chaotic situation could be traced, in part, to strategic blunders made by U.S. policymakers, including the decision to disband the Iraqi army, police force, and Ba'ath party, the lack of planning for occupation, and the determination to hold the occupation force to a skeleton number of about 140,000 U.S. soldiers in a country of 29 million Iraqis. Despite relentless searching by the U.S. forces, there was never any evidence of weapons of mass destruction uncovered in Iraq.

As the war continued to drag on, neoconservatives and Secretary of Defense Donald Rumsfeld (in office 1975–1977, 2001–2006), who had made so many strategic mistakes, left the U.S. government. By 2007, the Bush administration tried to rescue the situation with a "surge" of American troops to defeat the insurgents. Apart from the new military force, though, violence declined, due more to the United States giving financial support to Sunni leaders to turn them away from fighting the Americans and toward defeating terrorists, to the decision to separate Sunnis and Shiites in urban neighborhoods to prevent sectarian killings, and to the decision by Iran to greatly increase its own strategic position in Iraq by using its influence to stabilize the country and its Shiite government.

By mid-2011, more than forty thousand U.S. troops remained in Iraq, though the combat mission had officially ended and the political situation in Iraq had stabilized in comparison with the previous few years; remaining U.S.

fighters opposing the American occupation in Iraq. Such policies, though to be expected from an Iranian perspective, are for many American policymakers threatening. The harsh anti-Iranian rhetoric of the Bush administration and the examples of American willingness to invade sovereign nations made many Iranians worry that their country might be next.

The strongest American criticisms of Iran and justifications for anti-Iranian policies were for the country's nuclear energy program. American policymakers in both the Bush and Obama administrations accused Iran of working toward production of a nuclear bomb. Although there was no concrete evidence that this was the case, Iran was capable of enriching uranium for a weapon, and it was unclear whether or not it planned to build a weapon.

The United States first placed sanctions on Iran in response to the 1979 revolution, and strengthened these in the 1990s and 2000s, focusing on nuclear and weapons systems, and international financial transactions. With strong American pressure, the UN imposed new sanctions in 2006, 2007, 2008, and 2010; the European Union and other nations also imposed their own sanctions. Under the Obama administration, policymakers such as Dennis Ross and others argued that their efforts to open a dialogue with Iran and defuse the tensions under the Bush administration were rebuffed, so the United States had to maintain a tough stance to prevent the Iranian acquisition of nuclear weapons.

For many in the Middle East, probably the most disappointing aspect of the first two years of Obama's regional policy was that toward the Arab-Israeli conflict. The appointment of former Senator George Mitchell as special envoy for Middle East peace raised expectations, as did the rhetoric of the president, that resolving the Arab-Israeli conflict would be a priority for the administration. Although Mitchell participated in many personal meetings with various Israeli and Palestinian leaders, neither he nor the administration was willing to change long-standing U.S. policy to shun contact with Hamas or to press Israel too hard on settlement construction. Little changed in the standoff between Israelis and

Palestinians in the first two years of the Obama administration, and there was no end in sight to the conflict.

THE IMPACT OF THE ARAB SPRING

In 2011, two years into the Obama administration, the Middle East was rocked by the tumultuous events of the "Arab Spring." Beginning with popular revolts in Tunisia and Egypt, uprisings rippled through Arab countries in the region, eventually reaching Bahrain, Syria, Yemen, and Libya. Ordinary Arabs rose up against the authoritarian regimes that had ruled their lives. The revolts empowered many new challengers to the status quo, including secular democratic and Islamist groups. The response from the Obama administration was mixed. For example, in Egypt, the United States reluctantly abandoned the reliable ally Hosni Mubarak when his people turned him out of office; in Syria, the United States used rhetoric and political pressure to attempt to force out President Bashar al-Assad when he violently suppressed protests; and in Libya, the United States, along with its allies, used military air power to aid the rebellion against leader Muammar el-Qaddafi. In contrast, U.S. policymakers were silent about demonstrations in Bahrain, not wanting to upset their Saudi allies who opposed the protests.

In terms of the Arab-Israeli conflict, the most significant impact of the Arab Spring was in the ousting of Mubarak. Whether or not this regime change would threaten the survival of the Israeli-Egyptian peace remained an open question in 2011, because the peace with Israel was highly unpopular among many ordinary Egyptians.

In 2011, disappointment with the Obama administration was widespread in the Middle East, and public opinion of the United States even lower in some areas than it had been at the end of the Bush administration. The ability of ordinary Arabs to upend the status quo probably lowered that estimation even further, as many Arabs believed that they could reshape the region without the assistance of major powers such as the United States.

combat troops left the country by December 2011. It was still difficult to predict the long-term stability of a post-Saddam Iraq. At the same time, Afghanistan remained highly unstable, and U.S. troops were actively engaged in combat operations almost a decade after the start of fighting there; more than one hundred thousand U.S. troops remained in the country in 2011. The Taliban had made military gains in parts of the country, and other factions continued to challenge a weak central government.

For American foreign policy, the consequences of the wars in the Middle East and Central Asia went beyond military instability and continued war spending. International criticism of the American decision to go to war in Iraq and to continue its war in Afghanistan was great and eroded the sympathy and goodwill expressed after the 9/11 attacks. The wars were unpopular among other governments as well as ordinary people around the world, serving, many observers felt, as recruiting tools for anti-American insurgent or terrorist groups. The criticisms of American policy stemmed, in part, from the military tactics used, which sometimes

killed or wounded civilians, and from the limited use of torture in interrogation and in abusive imprisonment.

Probably one of the most significant impacts of the Iraq War was on the position of Iran and on the Iranian-American relationship. Many neoconservative policymakers had originally championed the overthrow of Saddam Hussein in part because they believed that he represented a continuing threat to Israeli interests in the region. In some ways, though, this strategy backfired, since the overthrow of the Sunni-based regime in Iraq and the subsequent political instability in the country led to the increase of Iranian influence in the majority Shiite country. The continued and overt hostility between the United States and Iran remained one of the biggest unresolved regional problems at the end of the Bush administration.

Finally, the wars also had a significant impact on U.S. foreign policy in the Middle East, and especially toward the Arab-Israeli conflict. With respect to the Arab-Israeli conflict, the American preoccupation with Iraq and Afghanistan crowded out any other regional concerns and initiatives. The tepid, intermittent American support for the Roadmap process during the Bush administration conveyed to all in the region that resolving the Arab-Israeli conflict was not a top priority for the United States. The increasingly obvious U.S. disinterest in solving the Arab-Israeli conflict, ironically, strengthened the U.S.-Israeli relationship. Despite the public assertions to the contrary, the succession of right-of-center Israeli governments during the Bush administration had little interest in pursuing peace with a weak Fatah faction or Hamas, which they considered to be a terrorist organization. Policymakers from both countries happily affirmed that the strength of the U.S.-Israeli bond and that the interests of the nations in the Middle East were synonymous. By the time George W. Bush left office, the U.S.-Israeli relationship had never been stronger.

See also: **Chapter 18: Middle East Diplomacy; Chapter 39: U.S. Foreign Policy Goals of the Twenty-first Century; Chapter 40: Diplomatic Milestones, 2001–Present.**

ENDNOTES

1. Quoted in H. W. Brands, *Into the Labyrinth: The United States and the Middle East, 1945–1993* (New York: McGraw-Hill, 1994), 183.

2. Quoted in Elizabeth Stephens, *US Policy towards Israel: The Role of Political Culture in Defining the 'Special Relationship'* (Portland, OR: Sussex Academic Press, 2006), 213.

3. Ibid., 238.

4. Quoted in Peter Hahn, *Crises and Crossfire: The United States and the Middle East since 1945* (Washington, DC: Potomac Books, 2005), 121.

5. Dennis Merrill and Thomas Paterson, *Major Problems in American Foreign Relations, Volume II: Since 1914* (Boston: Wadsworth, 2009), 556.

6. Quoted in Hahn, p. 175.

FURTHER READING

Anderson, Terry H. *Bush's Wars.* New York: Oxford University Press, 2011.

Bacevich, Andrew. *The Limits of Power: The End of American Exceptionalism.* New York: Metropolitan Books, 2008.

Bickerton, Ian, and Carla Klausner. *A Concise History of the Arab-Israeli Conflict.* Upper Saddle River, NJ: Pearson, 2002.

Brands, H. W. *Into the Labyrinth: The United States and the Middle East, 1945–1993.* New York: McGraw-Hill, 1994.

Gardner, Lloyd C., and Marilyn B. Young. *Iraq and the Lessons of Vietnam: Or, How Not to Learn from the Past.* New York: The New Press, 2007.

Hahn, Peter L. *Crisis and Crossfire: The United States and the Middle East since 1945.* Washington, DC: Potomac Books, 2005.

Meyerowitz, Joanne. *History and September 11th.* Philadelphia: Temple University Press, 2003.

Miller, Aaron David. *The Much Too Promised Land: America's Elusive Search for Arab-Israeli Peace.* New York: Bantam Books, 2008.

Quandt, William B. *Peace Process: American Diplomacy and the Arab-Israeli Conflict since 1967.* Washington, DC, and Berkeley: The Brookings Institution and University of California Press, 2005.

U.S. Foreign Policy Goals of the Twenty-first Century

by William B. McAllister[1]

THE GLOBAL FOREIGN policy environment of the twenty-first century features both old and new elements; while some aspects of international affairs have changed little for centuries, other recent developments are unprecedented. In that regard, the United States is no different from other governments, which also face their challenges on this same altered playing field. Moreover, because each nation's domestic political arrangements contribute to how (and how well) those challenges are addressed, it is important to consider the role that U.S. governance structures play in determining national policy. How the decisions of American policymakers shape, and are shaped by, those external and internal factors will be of crucial importance over the course of the twenty-first century because the United States is likely to play a special role as *primus inter pares* in the international system.

OLD WINESKINS: THE INHERITANCE OF THE EIGHTEENTH CENTURY

A key domestic factor in U.S. foreign policy making is the distinctive nature of the nation's political organization. In essence, the United States functions with a political system created in the eighteenth century. Although many aspects of this governance structure have evolved, certain fundamental elements remain intact. Twenty-first century problems will be addressed through the unique amalgam of constitutional, national, federal, local, and extra-governmental components that comprise the U.S. policymaking apparatus.

An apt aphorism that describes the dynamic that inheres in the policy process is: "The losers always scream louder than the winners say thank you." Encapsulated in that statement is an understanding that no policy is intrinsically permanent; all programs are subject to revision. In foreign affairs, for example, a three-part cycle recurs: domestic policy formulation, international policy negotiation, and domestic/international policy implementation. First, a state must determine national policy on a given issue through internal procedures specific to its governance structure. Officials espousing that policy then negotiate with representatives of other governments, typically forging a compromise agreement. Once an international policy is determined, it must be interpreted and implemented by national officials. At all three stages, losers from the previous round may attempt to redress their losses, while winners maneuver to protect their gains. By the time policy implementation occurs, both winners and losers may already be engaged in the next round of policy formulation and negotiation. The United States is no exception to the rule that a wide variety of "constituents" wish to influence the policy creation, negotiation, and implementation cycle.

The Limitations of Presidential Leadership

The U.S. system places great responsibility on one person, the president, but also limits the president's capacity to direct the nation's affairs. In contrast to most parliamentary systems, the president serves as both head of state and head of government, but not necessarily as head of party. In many other democratic systems, the largely ceremonial head of state function is performed by a monarch or other figurehead considered above political debates. Consequently, more of the head of government's time is available to deal with strategic management of the nation's business. In the United States, the president must fulfill both those functions. Moreover, in parliamentary systems, the prime minister is typically the leader of the majority party and can call upon fellow party members for legislative support. Because of the diffuse nature of the U.S. party system, however, the president cannot necessarily enforce party discipline. Additionally, divided government is common in the United States; when a president from one party faces a majority from the other party in one or both houses of Congress, forging a consensus sufficient to enact significant policy change often is difficult to achieve. Taken altogether, those factors limit the president's capacity both to make and to enforce decisions.

KEY CONCEPTS

Relative decline of U.S. power. Since the height of U.S. influence in the early decades of the Cold War, other states have gained power relative to U.S. capabilities. Once the unparalleled leader in military strength, economic production, financial resources, cultural capital, and diplomatic prowess, the United States now contends on a more level playing field. In fact, some countries have surpassed the United States in widely recognized standard-of-living measures such as per-capita income, educational proficiency, provision of minimum health care standards for all citizens, support for the elderly, or child welfare.

Leading European states (as well as the European Union acting as a whole), China, India, Japan, Brazil, South Korea, and a potentially resurgent Russia all challenge various aspects of U.S. supremacy. While some states exert at least as much influence in their regions as the United States, others wield considerable economic power or hold significant U.S. debt, or control strategic materials, and still others exercise leadership on important global issues. Even if, by many measures, the United States remains the "greatest power in the world," that hegemony has diminished in relative terms, because multiple nations have accelerated the pace of their own growth and capacities at a rate greater than the United States. Moreover, a plethora of international organizations also curb the capacity of even the strongest states to act independently. Although the United States remains central to resolving foreign policy dilemmas, North American policymakers address the challenges of the twenty-first century in a world over which they exercise less control than their predecessors in the half-century after 1945.

Congressional Crosscurrents

Congress, of course, plays a significant role in negotiating and implementing foreign policy. Both houses exercise budgetary oversight, pass legislation, and hear testimony from administration officials and other knowledgeable individuals. The Senate approves treaties and confirms or vetoes high political appointments, including ambassadors. Congressional representatives, in turn, juggle the interests of multiple constituencies that often advocate contradictory positions. The fixed election cycle, with its concomitant fundraising requirements, the practice of lobbying, and a legislative committee system featuring overlapping areas of interest all create multiple opportunities to influence the positions of House and Senate members. Under this type of system, especially when coupled with the limitations on the president's capacity to direct the agenda, radical departures in the trajectory of policy are difficult to achieve. Gradual, evolutionary changes are the norm, allowing other actors to play a role in policymaking and implementation.

Other Participants

Executive branch agencies, intended both to inform presidential decision-making and to carry out directives, comprise another key factor that impacts the trajectory of U.S. policy. This unelected bureaucracy (though key officials must be confirmed by the Senate) exercises significant influence, because it is the principal mechanism through which problems are both defined and addressed. Certain entities, such as the White House staff and the National Security Council (NSC), serve a type of coordinating function that also reflect presidential preferences. Cabinet-level organizations and other agencies are tasked with executing governmental policy, but they also represent constituencies

in certain respects, and therefore can exercise an important influence on the formulation of policy. Post-1945, the principal stakeholder foreign affairs agencies have included the Department of State, the Department of Defense, the Treasury Department, the Central Intelligence Agency (CIA), and the National Security Council. However, an increasing number of other cabinet departments, such as Health and Human Services, Justice, Homeland Security, Agriculture, and Commerce, also vie for a place at the table.

In the realm of foreign affairs, the president is usually too busy to address all but immediate concerns, the most important long-term issues, and ceremonial duties. In the course of accomplishing the everyday business of implementing directives under constantly changing circumstances, executive branch organizations also reinterpret standing policy and encounter new issues. This is especially important with regard to the emerging, global-level concerns that increasingly populate the policy landscape. Bureaucracies encountering new phenomena naturally attempt to define the problem and craft solutions. Those topics of sufficient import move up the chain to higher authorities, but it is not uncommon for the initial assessment of the nature of the problem and the choice of policy options to be embedded quite early in the process. For example, when an unprecedented wave of drug abuse erupted across the world in the late 1960s and early 1970s, governmental responses to the crisis were predetermined by a longstanding emphasis on supply-control strategies built into an international drug regulatory regime that had developed over the previous seven decades with little input from high authorities.[2] It is likely that in the twenty-first century, the number of topics requiring attention will increase, and the pace of this policy response process will accelerate, which highlights the influence of executive branch agencies over the formulation, as well as the implementation, of policy.

The federal nature of the U.S. system also affords multiple opportunities for sub-national political entities to have an impact on foreign policy. At the state level, governors and other officials have traditionally promoted overseas trade, tourism, cultural exchange, and governmental interaction. More recently, states have also attempted to address issues previously reserved for national-level policy, such as immigration, pollution control, and measures to combat climate change.[3] In much the same way, some local jurisdictions, such as counties and cities, increasingly attempt to entice business or deal with acute local issues not addressed by higher authorities. Other special actors in the U.S. system, such as Native American tribal governments, complicate matters further, both because they may attempt to forge their own arrangements with governments abroad, and also because their quasi-independent status can lead to problems of domestic jurisdiction.[4]

Non-State Actors

Finally, owing to the relatively open nature of the U.S. political system, a variety of non-state actors also have the capacity to influence the policy process. For-profit corporations have multiple avenues of entrée. Philanthropic organizations, old-line large funders (including the Carnegie, Ford, and Rockefeller foundations) as well as newer mega-funders such as the Gates Foundation, can alter the trajectory of foreign aid, bring new issues to the attention of foreign affairs officials, and act independently of governments. Private voluntary organizations, smaller philanthropies, religious organizations, and special-issue advocacy groups make up another category of actors that can have a significant impact on issues of international concern.

Because it is unlikely that any fundamental changes will occur in U.S. political and governance structures, the extant system will impact *how* decisions are made, which in turn makes an impact on *what* decisions are made. The process will result in a continued undulation of winners and losers. This constant jostling to protect gains or redress losses in the battle over the direction of foreign policy is not new, although the number of players has expanded. What is new, or at least significantly modified, is the international context in which that decision-making process must operate.

NEW WINE: THE CIRCUMSTANCES OF THE TWENTY-FIRST CENTURY

The twenty-first-century international landscape encompasses an array of features that is in several respects unique and unprecedented. Foreign policy makers face a global balance of power, vastly increased numbers and types of

PUBLIC PORTRAIT: *WILLIAM HENRY "BILL" GATES III (1955–)*

William Henry (Bill) Gates III represents a twenty-first-century combination of inventor, entrepreneur, business magnate, and philanthropist who exerts a significant impact on global affairs. In 1976, Gates co-founded the Microsoft Corporation, which grew into one of the world's largest and most influential companies. Operating systems and programs developed by Microsoft proved crucial to a revolution in computing that has touched all aspects of modern life. The growth of the Internet magnified Microsoft's influence, and the company's Windows software became the industry standard. Selling its products worldwide, Microsoft prospered and Gates grew rich; by the 1990s, he rose to the ranks of the world's wealthiest individuals.

Gates established charitable foundations that grew in scope and scale, culminating with the creation of the Bill and Melinda Gates Foundation in 2000. In 2008, Gates retired from active management of the Microsoft Corporation in order to devote his energies to the foundation. The foundation ranks as the largest private philanthropy in the world, far outstripping long-established funds such as Ford, Carnegie, and Rockefeller. The Bill and Melinda Gates Foundation (http://www.gatesfoundation.org) held assets valued at more than $35 billion in 2009. The foundation's giving focuses primarily on initiatives outside North America designed to improve health, alleviate poverty, foster sustainable development,

and improve education. In 2009, the Bill and Melinda Gates Foundation disbursed approximately $3 billion. That figure dwarfed the contributions of any other individual charitable organization.

Moreover, the foundation's giving also surpassed the foreign aid budgets of more than 180 countries; the Organization for Economic Cooperation and Development calculates that in 2009, only the Overseas Development Assistance programs of the United States, France, Germany, the United Kingdom, Japan, Spain, the Netherlands, Sweden, Norway, Canada, and Italy exceeded Gates Foundation donations (http://webnet.oecd.org/oda2009). The Microsoft Corporation can exert considerable influence on the choices that businesses and governments make. Similarly, the size and scope of the foundation's programs can play an important role in determining the direction of foreign assistance in many countries. Gates's success and wealth have also gained him entrée into the halls of power. He is a featured presenter at major conferences of business, academic, and government leaders; he consults with prominent politicians and international organization officials; and he collaborates with celebrities to promote philanthropic causes. Both Microsoft and the Bill and Melinda Gates Foundation can act as independent forces, separate from the prerogatives of governments as well as international organizations.

participants, a rapidly expanding set of issues, and the prospect of fundamental transformations in the basis of international relations. Although the adaptability of the decision-making institutions and processes will significantly affect the extent to which these formidable challenges will be addressed successfully by the United States, certain fundamental dynamics are beyond the capacity of any individual government to control.

Global Power Relationships

The twenty-first-century world can be characterized as an era of emerging global balance of power that mimics, on a world scale, the regional balance of power that existed between the European states in the seventeenth through nineteenth centuries. For several hundred years, the greater and lesser nations of Europe contested with each other in shifting coalitions. Several European states expanded overseas, drawing on colonial resources in large measure to support the metropole's position within Europe. This multi-polar European rivalry of long-lasting, competitive character, encompassing a wide geographical area, prevented any single state or alliance from gaining hegemony over the continent. Additionally, in the nineteenth century, the major European powers attempted to constrain their own behavior, at least to some degree, through informal cooperative arrangements intended to lessen the prospect of Great Power conflict. In the first half of the twentieth century, rising tensions sparked two major wars that destroyed this Europe-centered, multi-polar balance. The second half of the twentieth century featured a unique period of bipolar struggle on a world scale; nothing similar in scope or scale to the Cold War has occurred in world history.[5] At the dawn of the twenty-first century, the Cold War ended. In subsequent years, the power of not only the former Soviet Union but also the United States decreased relative to other players such as China, Japan, India, and the collective nations that comprise the European Union (EU).[6] Those actors, regional powers such as Brazil and South Africa, and no doubt some additional contestants that emerge in the course of the twenty-first century will all attempt to exert power well beyond neighboring territories by offering aid, fostering trade, exerting economic pressure, wielding military power, and applying political influence. This global, de-centered balance of power and the accompanying worldwide influence of mediating supra-national institutions are unique in modern history.

A Surfeit of Actors

An increasing, and increasingly diverse, cast of characters vie for "voice opportunities" on this multifaceted global stage. Because the U.S. domestic system is relatively open, it is possible for many external constituencies to secure a hearing. International organizations, corporations, non-profits, transnational citizens' groups, collections of experts, and other states all can influence the direction of policy. The scope and scale of these "external" interventions into the U.S. policymaking process likely will increase as the century progresses.[7]

At its inception in 1945, the United Nations Organization (UN) membership totaled fifty-one states. In ensuing years, that number has burgeoned to 193 members—an increase of 278 percent. Because the United States wishes to promote its interests in all parts of the world, the sheer number of diplomats necessary to service this vastly enhanced population of states multiplies the inputs into, and therefore the size and complexity of, the policy apparatus.

Moreover, the number of International Governmental Organizations (IGOs) and International Non-Governmental Organizations (INGOs) has skyrocketed, especially since the 1960s. INGO numbers have risen exponentially, surpassing twelve thousand.[8] Although many of those entities are small, with limited influence on the policymaking process, a sizeable subset interacts with governmental representatives on a sustained and substantial basis. For example, approximately seventy-five IGOs and INGOs enjoy standing invitations to participate as observers in the sessions and the work of the UN General Assembly.[9] In addition to more than 180 chiefs of mission accredited to other nations, the United States maintains approximately twenty ambassadorial-rank representatives to UN agencies, IGOs, and other international organizations.[10]

Others with a stake in the outcome of policy debates also will promote their interests. In addition to direct lobbying of governments, multinational for-profit corporations utilize international organization pathways to advocate positions on issues of importance. Foreign governments also routinely attempt to influence the decisions of other states. Informal or formal amalgamations of issue-area experts (often referred to as epistemic communities) and transnational advocacy groups promote policies from both within governments and without. The realm of environmental policy illustrates the interaction of these multiple constituencies. Since the landmark 1972 United Nations Conference on the Human Environment, many agreements have been forged to foster scientific research, to enhance technical cooperation in reducing pollution, to protect non-human species, and to raise standards for cleaner water, air, and land. Most actors have focused on how best to promote the idea of sustainable development, a concept that enables all parties to promote their agendas: governments continue to support growth-oriented policies with some modification, preservationists advocate for stricter regulations, scientists conduct more sophisticated studies, and corporations pursue profit by taking advantage of market opportunities created by new incentives.[11]

The Growing Role of Non-Governmental Actors

The role of these extra-domestic entities has expanded as well. Once confined to observation and consultation, it is now common for non-governmental actors to play a direct part in negotiating agreements, treaty language, and interpreting rules. An interesting example is the consortium of IGOs that forged the WHO Framework Convention on Tobacco Control. This agreement is the first treaty inaugurated by the World Health Organization (WHO). Beginning in 1971, the WHO issued guidelines and recommendations concerning tobacco control. In the 1980s, the EU attempted to institute tobacco-usage reduction targets by regulating internal commerce among its member states. In 1986, the World Health Assembly of the WHO adopted a resolution recommending that governments develop a comprehensive suite of tobacco-reduction policies. In the 1990s, the World Bank initiated a series of warnings about the danger that tobacco usage posed to overall progress in economic development. In that same decade, the United Nations Children's Fund supported international tobacco control initiatives under its mandate to protect children. By the early 1990s, more than two dozen countries had banned smoking on domestic commercial air carrier flights, causing the International Civil Aviation Organization to recommend a smoking ban on all international flights commencing in 1996. After consultations with governments and other parties, the WHO opened the Framework Convention for signature in June 2003, and it entered into force only twenty months later. An impressive 168 governments have adhered to this treaty, originated and supported by a transnational coalition of non-state actors.[12]

Perhaps most importantly, this plethora of agreements, organizations, memberships, cooperative arrangements, and rules bind states to an interlocking set of relationships with other states as well as non-state actors that not only limit governmental autonomy but also foster more stable, predictable outcomes. In a few cases, NGOs may even appear to take on some of the attributes of states. For example, in 2000, the non-profit Nature Conservancy purchased most of the Palmyra Atoll.[13] Administered by the U.S. government as an unorganized incorporated territory, and designated a Natural Wildlife Refuge, it is the only entirely privately owned territory within U.S. jurisdiction. In other cases, states themselves may cede some of their authority to supranational entities; the European Union is the most salient instance to date.

As those many external factors exert influence via the multiple entry points available in the U.S. system, officials must deal with the attendant choices and consequences. Formulating policy includes not only considering domestic constituencies, but also attention to treaties, IGO and INGO rules, and other arrangements to which the United States already adheres. These additional considerations slow the policymaking process and constrain options. Moreover, when the United States embeds its preferences within larger organizations and networks of commitment, the resultant policies are more likely to become entrenched. Those influences are not intrinsically good or bad; they simply embody the tilted playing field upon which twenty-first-century decision makers must operate.

Illicit Actors

Further complicating matters, policymakers also must take account of illicit actors in the international system. Traffickers in all manner of contraband occupy interstitial spaces in an increasingly connected world. Many peddle wares traditionally associated with the underground economy: prostitution, stolen property, arms, drugs, and black marketing of legal commodities. Others take advantage of (relatively) new global rules by acquiring and selling items more recently regulated on an international level, such as endangered species, intellectual property, or fissile material. From remote locations, thieves exploit technology to steal money, information, identities, intellectual property, and secrets. The scale of this activity is, by its very nature, difficult to quantify. Nevertheless, it seems apparent that as the global governance system becomes more rule-bound, illegal entrepreneurs will continue to devise profitable ways to purvey items of value. Many policymakers will spend considerable amounts of time combating such non-state, non-licit activities, which usually requires coordinated international effort.

Failed States and Fragile States

An additional calculation of increasing importance in the twenty-first century is the effect of "failed states" or "fragile states" on international affairs. Throughout history, regions remote from power centers have escaped the reach of governments. These zones have always served as sites of illicit activity, lawlessness, and rebellion. The ever-present potential for such instability to spread, however, was limited to nearby areas; it made no difference to a ruler in Pomerania whether pirates operated off the coast of Penang. However, in a world that features instant global communication, worldwide commercial interconnections, and rapid movement of people over long distances, a governmental "black hole" practically anywhere can reverberate planet-wide. Terrorist groups, computer hackers, and others opposed to fundamental elements of the modern world can train recruits and direct operations from very remote locales. The array of responses available to policymakers (historical examples include punitive expeditions, quarantine, sanctions, and nation-building campaigns intended to deny unregulated operations by promoting rule of law and integration with supra-national governance arrangements) almost invariably require substantial international cooperation.

An Expanding Universe of Issues

Added to this multi-polar, fully globalized power structure and vastly expanded list of participants is a dizzying array of issues requiring negotiation. Policymakers will continue to confront all the traditional topics of diplomatic intercourse, such as state-to-state relations and commercial affairs. Moreover, new issues, for example environmental protection and space law, have arisen in recent decades, with the prospect of more concerns in the offing. Finally, it is not beyond the realm of possibility that the dilemmas posed by one or more transformative issues will generate a fundamental reorientation of international relations over the course of the twenty-first century.

Much of diplomatic activity will continue to focus on issues of longstanding concern. Mediating trade disagreements, protecting citizens abroad, forging alliances, and reducing international tensions remain essential governmental tasks. States will promote their interests and attempt to garner support for those positions in the international arena. The markedly increased number of states and nongovernmental entities that require persuasion adds to the complexity of the task, but the essential work is in many ways unchanged from a century ago. Of particular note here are newer applications of the longstanding issue of arms control; in a world featuring nuclear, chemical, and biological weapons that can be wielded by both governments and non-state actors, securing international cooperation to stem proliferation and coordinate protective measures is of paramount concern.

New Diplomatic Concerns

The traditional work of diplomacy has undergone significant modification in recent decades, and in all likelihood that trend will continue. Technological innovations have literally expanded the negotiating sphere. By the 1970s, the deep sea, Antarctica, and outer space all became new areas requiring negotiation because technological advances made it possible to exploit those regions. More recently, the advent of computers, cellular telephones, and the Internet has created a need to develop procedures, standards, rules, and norms for a previously non-existent electronic universe. Additionally, topics previously considered "domestic" and therefore not susceptible to international interference have entered the diplomatic arena. In an interconnected world, other states' policies concerning population growth, migration, policing, education, public health, labor practices, human rights, and even road safety can have international implications.[14]

Despite those many pressing problems, the greatest challenges of the twenty-first century may well center on the resource base of the increasingly extractive modern world. Since at least the time of the French Revolution, the driving factor for Western industrial powers (and the increasing multitudes who wished to emulate them) was the assumption that sustained per-capita economic growth was both achievable and desirable. Exactly what political and economic arrangements could best foster growth, the definition of how that material gain should be distributed, and the role that government should play were all very much disputed.

The essence of the Cold War competition, for example, centered on which system was superior in, literally, delivering the goods. The general assumption reigned that "development" was desirable and that the capacity to grow was limited primarily by human-imposed impediments; material resources were presumed to be abundant, and any shortages could be circumvented through application of technological innovation. Beginning in the last third of the twentieth century, however, those fundamental assumptions about the planet's limitless carrying capacity came into question. Concerns about environmental pollution, overfishing, soil degradation, water contamination, chemical toxins, and nuclear waste disposal grew as research unveiled the previously unrecognized costs of economic development. Moreover, it gradually became apparent that the carbon energy regime fueling the industrial revolution also manufactured global climate change.

These transformative issues portend the possibility of significant resource scarcities and profound alterations in the planetary environment that challenge the assumptions upon which modernist growth-oriented socio-economic-political interaction patterns are based. Put straightforwardly, how will democratic governments and market-based economies fare if the populace comes to doubt that those systems can deliver continually improving standards of living, and if the prospects of a better future for one's children seem increasingly unlikely?[15]

An Altered Playing Field

In sum, the playing field for twenty-first-century international contests is altered in key respects. Nations will continue, of course, to exercise power. Yet the conditions under which that power is wielded will be bounded in significant ways. Traditional national borders of all types (physical, ideological, financial) will be increasingly difficult to police. States also must cross topical borders to address previously unrecognized issues. Governments must be prepared to integrate policies across regions and issues, which increases the likelihood that power will be ceded to intermediary institutions such as IGOs and INGOs. States must interact with dissimilar actors in the international arena, both subnational and supranational, some of which are not recognized as licit entities. The success of any national policy in the twenty-first century will rest in large measure on how well constituencies, elected representatives, and bureaucracies adapt to continued rapid changes in this evolving international environment. Ultimately, states must have viable mechanisms for reconsidering the fundamental construct of "national interest" in light of changing circumstances, additional knowledge, and competing priorities. The United States faces a particularly unique set of questions given its diffuse domestic governance structure, its global leadership position, and the historical American approach to overseas involvement.

THE BIG QUESTIONS

U.S. policymakers and their many constituencies face a variety of potential problems in the immediate and medium-term future. Given the factors discussed previously, the questions outlined here highlight some of the major categories of dilemmas that U.S. policymakers, their supporting apparatus, and others impacting the system may have to address.

United States Involvement in Non-Traditional Elements of Diplomacy

The United States has well-established mechanisms for interacting with governments recognized as legitimate and will no doubt continue to conduct state-to-state relations in the conventional manner. Diplomacy in the twenty-first century, however, entails making significant choices about interaction with other entities in the international arena.

International Organizations

How much authority should the United States cede to IGOs, INGOs, and other extra-state actors? How are those organizations, which vary greatly in size, mission, structure, and capability, to be held accountable for the programs they institute and the money they spend?

Pariah States

How should the United States deal with governments that eschew widely accepted rules of international behavior? It will be necessary to calculate carefully the full global ramifications of whether to act unilaterally or in concert with other nations or international organizations.

Fragile States

When governments are clearly faltering or have collapsed entirely, should the United States respond, and, if so, how? In addition to engaging in relations with existing states, should U.S. government agencies involved in foreign affairs be configured to engage in nation-building? What is the role of non-state international organizations in such reclamation projects?

Illicit Non-State Actors

What are the best strategies for reducing the capacities of terrorist groups, information pirates, money launderers, traffickers in contraband, black marketers, and other shadow-profiteers? Adopting strategies that heavily emphasize law enforcement are intrinsically problematic in an integrated world that nevertheless features multiple legal systems, jurisdictions, and policing mechanisms. Are there approaches that can complement, or serve as alternatives to, law-and-order regimes? What role should licit non-state actors play in developing and implementing those alternatives?

Response to Significant Political Instability

In its first century of existence, instability in other parts of the world (with the partial exception of the Caribbean basin) did not engender major interventions by the United States. For example, between 1830 and 1913, a series of revolts, undulations between monarchical and representative forms of government, and national unification wars roiled Europe, yet the United States largely stood aloof from those events. During the nineteenth century, the imperial Chinese government's capacity to rule steadily deteriorated, but the United States exerted little influence on events in East Asia.

During this same period, U.S. leaders sometimes fomented instability and initiated warfare to achieve foreign policy objectives. The United States wrested considerable territories from Mexico and Native American tribes, and in the 1890s acquired overseas colonial holdings. The culmination of this advantageous use of destabilization occurred when the United States secured the right to build a canal in Panama, intended to cement maritime defense and facilitate commerce.

After that point, the United States increasingly favored stability abroad in order to reduce defense costs and foster trade. Interventions in the affairs of other nations continued, but with the goal of supporting the status quo. This was especially the case in the Caribbean basin, where the United States interposed itself frequently. The 1914 war that began in Europe and aggression in the 1930s that began in East Asia eventually presented fundamental threats that drew the United States into global wars.

After 1945, the nation engaged in a significant debate about the extent to which the United States should commit itself to promote interests in far-flung locales. A consensus emerged that an unprecedented level of engagement overseas was necessary to preserve the American way of life. The principal goal was to ensure a stable, predictable world open to receiving American goods and American ideas. In the post-1945 period, then, the United States deployed both the capacity and the will to play a major role on the world stage.

Twenty-first-Century Challenges

The question for the twenty-first century is whether the United States possesses the capability to wield significant power, and whether the electorate wishes to do so. The scenarios presented below indicate the range of potentially destabilizing events that might occur in the foreseeable future. Whether any of these specific scenarios will come to pass is impossible to predict, but they do indicate the types of dilemmas that U.S. policymakers are likely to encounter in some fashion. Questions along the following lines will no doubt arise: Should the United States take the lead in attempting to adjudicate disputes, and, if so, how? Should the United States act in concert with other states and non-state actors, or are there instances in which the U.S. should go it alone? How much capacity does the United States have to direct events? Are there cases in which the United States should withdraw? Are the American people willing to support the expenditure of treasure, and perhaps blood, on this issue? What are the consequences of inaction?

Unification Conflicts

A desire to reshape African political boundaries to correspond more closely to the ethnic, religious, and cultural groups that occupy the region could lead to civil wars or wars between states. Should the United States support maintenance of current African borders and, if so, how? If not, what principles of political-social-economic organization for Africa should guide U.S. actions?

Disruptions in East Asia

China could enter another "warring states" period under the centripetal forces of political disunity, economic inequity, linguistic differences, or perhaps foreign interference. Alternately, if China remains unified and strong, the increasingly depopulated Asiatic Russian territories, or Taiwan, might appear attractive targets for acquisition. Current disputes over oil drilling, fishing rights, or national security perimeters that trouble the East Asian waters touching upon China, Japan, and the Philippines, as well as the ongoing threat of a nuclear North Korea, could spill over into open conflict. What options do U.S. policymakers face, and how do they calculate the U.S. capacity to impact events?

Disunity in Europe

The United States has benefited from a quiescent Europe for two generations. A collapse of the Euro currency in a time of economic crisis, the success of sub-national groups in attaining increasing autonomy (such as Scotland or Wales, or the Basque regions of Spain and France), increased ethnic tensions, or internal political disunity (Belgium is a suggestive case)[16] might derail the centrifugal forces encouraging greater European unity since 1945. If Europe reverts to the type of internecine restiveness that fomented significant global instability in previous centuries, how should U.S. policymakers respond?

In this era in which international policymakers seek a global, de-centered balance of power, world leaders gathered in New York in September 2011 for the annual meeting of the UN General Assembly. Here, addressing the media on post-Qaddafi Libya and other issues, are Mustafa Abdul Jalil, chairman of the Libyan National Transitional Council; Ban Ki-moon, secretary-general of the United Nations; and B. Lynn Pascoe, under-secretary-general of the United Nations for political affairs.

SOURCE: EPA/Allan Tannenbaum/Pool/Landov.

German Chancellor Angela Merkel and her husband, Joachim Sauer, greet President Barack Obama and First Lady Michelle Obama on April 3, 2009, in Baden-Baden, Germany. The two world leaders were meeting prior to a summit meeting of the twenty-eight NATO member countries.

SOURCE: AP Photo/Michel Euler.

Congenitally Dysfunctional States

The structure and ideology of the nation state as developed since the 1648 Peace of Westphalia does not necessarily graft itself well in all parts of the world. For example, neither imperial Russian nor British attempts to control Afghanistan in the nineteenth century, nor various incursions into Afghan lands in the twentieth century, yielded a stable, self-perpetuating national government capable of consistently exercising authority within its territorial borders. Much the same could be said elsewhere, including several areas in Africa, the Southeast Asian uplands, and at least a few cases in the Western Hemisphere, such as Haiti. One or more of those areas might continue to resist functional incorporation into the international system of states and the concomitant interlocking web of binding agreements, international organizations, capital flows, and legal regimes to control cross-border phenomena, such as immigration, terrorism, arms control, and various illicit activities. How will the United States address the issue of systemic instability in certain locales?

Global Epidemic

Interdependent world systems might be visited by a highly contagious infection: a disease that causes rapid death, a computer virus, or a massive attack on the world's electronically dependent financial systems. If, for example, it were determined that the danger could only be curtailed by cessation of trade and transportation, would the United States impose, and could it enforce, a quarantine?

The Advent of Uncooperative Democracies

A wave of regime-changing revolts could sweep through a region or spread in an uneven fashion across the globe. The subsequent popularly elected governments might adopt policies inimically opposed to the secular, capitalist, free-trade preferences espoused by the United States. Will the United States support the legitimacy of democratically elected governments under all circumstances, even if some pursue positions disadvantageous to U.S. interests?

U.S. Options in Light of Systemic Resource Scarcities

If it becomes increasingly evident that climate change, or environmental degradation, or shrinking carbon-based energy resources are causing stagnation, perhaps even decline, in living standards, how will peoples and governments react? Major disputes could break out over basic necessities, such as water, or arable land, or access to oceanic resources. Will the United States get involved in peaceful dispute resolution? Might the United States craft policies that would enable its citizens to preserve a higher standard of living at the expense of others? For example, spheres-of-influence arrangements have been common in past instances of resource-stressed, international, multi-polar power balances.[17] The fundamental issue is that large-scale Western democracy developed in a time when it was possible to practice distributive politics, because sustained per-capita growth was demonstrably achievable. Because the pie was getting bigger, owing largely to the consumption of previously untapped resources from the Western Hemisphere and utilization of carbon-based energy reserves, it was possible to keep most people happy (or at least hopeful). If the general populace concludes that it is no longer plausible to promise a better material future, what will happen to the assumptions about the bases of civil society that animate all aspects of Western democratic political systems?

LEGACY AND INHERITANCE

There is no shortage of reports, blueprints, warnings, and recommendations about the United States' place in the twenty-first-century world.[18] Few contemplate a radical U.S. withdrawal from its role as a significant player in world affairs. Given the extent of U.S. interests abroad, and the interconnected nature of financial, trade, communications, governmental, and cultural networks, it seems unlikely that a return to a distanced "City upon a Hill" approach to promoting American ideals is in the offing. Most would agree

SHIFTS IN FOREIGN POLICY: *THE DEFICIT CEILING DEBATE OF 2011*

In the summer of 2011, the culmination of a remarkable series of events brought the U.S. government within a few hours of declaring a default, unable to pay its debts. Albeit averted at the eleventh hour, the impasse highlights many of the domestic and international issues discussed in this chapter. This episode illustrates themes that may recur throughout the twenty-first century, signaling important shifts in the relationships between the multiple constituent factors that contribute to the formation and implementation of foreign policy.

A long-brewing dispute became acute when a vocal element of politically active U.S. citizens articulated increasing concern about the size of the national debt that supported, in their assessment, an overly intrusive federal government role in certain aspects of American life. A sizeable number of House and Senate members pledged to reduce expenditures while refusing to raise taxes. Some even asserted that a default, although painful, would provide a necessary corrective to curb what they judged the dangerously out-of-control spending habits of the U.S. government. Another coalition of Americans objected to multiple elements of that agenda. They believed that the deficit could be reduced by raising taxes, thereby ensuring that essential services for needy citizens were not imperiled. They countered that the immediate needs of an anemic economic recovery mitigated in favor of continued government expenditures, justifying increased borrowing in the short term in order to stimulate a more rapid recovery that would enhance government revenues in the long term. A stalemate developed between the two houses of the representative branch, with the president unable to negotiate a resolution. In the last phase of the crisis, dire warnings about the deleterious effects of downgrading the credit rating of U.S. debt securities provided sufficient incentive to break the impasse. The House and Senate forged a compromise bill that the president signed, but an uneasy tension remained as it became evident that this incident appeared to usher in an era of increasingly acrimonious dispute over the size and purpose of the federal government. By the end of the week, one of the major domestic credit rating agencies took the unprecedented step of downgrading the creditworthiness of federal government bonds, citing primarily the inability of the U.S. political system to resolve the country's debt dilemma.

Although direct discussion about U.S. foreign policy remained in the background of this budgetary debate, the implications for the American role in world affairs are not difficult to discern. If previous historical examples are any guide, bankruptcy represents an unmistakable sign of Great Power

decline. Imperial Spain and royal France both suffered multiple defaults, which eventually crippled their efforts to retain their status as first-rank powers. The British government, on the other hand, despite massive debts accumulated during the French Revolutionary and Napoleonic wars, continued to maintain its creditworthiness. London became the center of nineteenth and early twentieth century world finance. In the aftermath of World War I, British expenditures caused the pound sterling to lose its status as the world's preferred "safe haven" currency, and the locus of world finance shifted to New York. Whether the United States will suffer ill effects in global credit markets from this essentially voluntary descent to the precipice of default remains to be seen, but the likelihood of relative U.S. decline is high if the dollar loses its status as the world's leading currency.

At the same time, however, most of the principal competitors that might be expected to supplant the United States appeared to fare little better. Several states in the European Union suffered debt crises of their own, and the viability of the Euro currency came into some question. The Japanese economy remained stagnant after twenty years of negligible growth. China's growth rate continued to be quite high, and most observers anticipated that the Chinese economy would become the world's largest, but per-capita income remained very low by Western standards, and the capacity of the Chinese economy to produce sufficient increases in living standards while improving fundamental business practices such as the fiscal transparency and protection for intellectual property rights remained in doubt. In the short term, Americans benefited from a perception that few viable alternatives existed to a continued reliance on the United States as the world's lynchpin economy.

In its largest aspect, what these difficulties among the world's leading economies may portend is an increasing level of disagreement over resource allocation. The redistributive politics of the modern era, especially the last century, in which higher standards of living are promised to the citizenry based on the assumption that economic growth will exceed per-capita population increase, appear to be coming under increasing stress. The growing acknowledgement that resource limitations (arable land, clean water and air, ocean resources, etc.) coupled with significant climate change and population pressures are altering the basic living conditions of the planet suggests that some will opt for a more zero-sum calculation in determining the distribution societal goods. The traditional human strategy to overcome resource constraints, reliance the United States should not, and indeed cannot, extricate itself from world affairs. Rather, the principal points of debate turn on whether the country should pursue an independent strategy that features more freedom of action at potentially higher cost, or promote a burden-sharing, consensus-building, cooperative approach that risks slowness of decision and dissolution of purpose. In reality, policymakers will doubtless adopt the former strategy in certain instances and the latter under different circumstances. As a practical matter, U.S. options also will be limited by budgetary constraints, which may become acute at some point. It is entirely possible that a significant retrenchment, especially of substantial U.S. military commitments overseas, will become a necessary cost-saving measure. The State Department's Quadrennial Diplomacy and Development Review presents an ambitious, comprehensive program that envisions a significant U.S. diplomatic presence abroad, but it is likely that fiscal stringency and domestic opposition to such substantial involvement overseas will result in less than complete implementation. Nevertheless, it is hard to imagine the country retreating into some twenty-first-century version of a "Fortress America" posture.

on technological enhancements, may continue to provide sufficient improvements to alleviate at least the most disruptive effects of this disjunction between needs, wants, and assets. Political mediation will, therefore, be essential in arbitrating the claims of competing constituencies. That profound domestic political disagreement almost caused the world's leading power to renege on its obligations indicates that intense negotiations about who gets what, both within and between states, are likely to feature prominently in twenty-first-century domestic and international affairs.

The quotes below, from U.S. political leaders on the day the debt ceiling legislation was signed, indicate profound differences in perspective and priorities. Similar disputes can be observed in many other societies around the globe.

> ... [T]his legislation caps spending over the next 10 years, with a mechanism that ensures that these cuts stick. It protects the American people from a government default that would have affected every single one of them in one way or another. It puts in place a committee that will recommend further cuts and much-needed reforms. It doesn't include a dime in job-killing tax hikes at a moment when our economy can least afford them. And, crucially, it ensures the debate over a balanced budget amendment continues, and that it gets a vote.... [S]lowing down the big-government freight train from its current trajectory will give us the time we need to work toward a real solution, or give the American people the time they need to have their voices heard.

SOURCE: Senate Minority Leader Mitch McConnell (R-KY), August 2, 2011, available at http://www.realclearpolitics.com/video/2011/08/02/mcconnell_agreement_will_slow_down_the_big_government_freight_train.html.

> This is a positive step forward that begins to rein in federal spending, but it's only a step. We should save the celebration for when a Balanced Budget Amendment is ratified, the deficit is fixed, and our economy has returned to creating jobs.

SOURCE: House Majority Leader John Boehner (R-OH), August 2, 2011, available at http://johnboehner.house.gov/News/DocumentSingle.aspx?DocumentID=254837.

If there's continual talk by the Republicans from the House and the Senate that there will be no revenue, then there would be no bill. They have to understand today, right now, the day we passed the bill, that we will have no legislation that will come out of that joint committee unless revenues are part of the mix. It's a fact of life. And if they don't like that and they can look forward to the huge cuts that will take place in sequestration dealing with defense and some other programs would be cut, including mandatory programs, foreign programs and things of that nature.

SOURCE: Senate Majority Leader Harry Reid (Democrat, Nevada), National Public Radio interview, August 2, 2011, available at http://www.npr.org/2011/08/02/138935765/reid-discusses-now-passed-debt-bill.

> And since you can't close the deficit with just spending cuts, we'll need a balanced approach where everything is on the table. Yes, that means making some adjustments to protect health care programs like Medicare so they're there for future generations. It also means reforming our tax code so that the wealthiest Americans and biggest corporations pay their fair share. And it means getting rid of taxpayer subsidies to oil and gas companies, and tax loopholes that help billionaires pay a lower tax rate than teachers and nurses.
>
> I've said it before; I will say it again: We can't balance the budget on the backs of the very people who have borne the biggest brunt of this recession. We can't make it tougher for young people to go to college, or ask seniors to pay more for health care, or ask scientists to give up on promising medical research because we couldn't close a tax shelter for the most fortunate among us. Everyone is going to have to chip in. It's only fair. That's the principle I'll be fighting for during the next phase of this process.

SOURCE: President Barack Obama, statement on the debt compromise, August 2, 2011, available at http://www.whitehouse.gov/blog/2011/08/02/putting-americans-back-work-president-obama-speaks-debt-compromise.

IN THEIR OWN WORDS: *LEADING THROUGH CIVILIAN POWER: THE FIRST QUADRENNIAL DIPLOMACY AND DEVELOPMENT REVIEW, 2010 (QDDR)*

Initiated by Secretary of State Hillary Clinton (2009–), the QDDR is modeled after the longstanding quadrennial review process conducted by the Department of Defense. It serves as a type of detailed mission statement, enabling strategic planning and providing guidance for determining budgeting priorities. This ambitious document envisions an active role for the United States in world affairs, while also recognizing that the United States must engage state and non-state partners to share the burdens of maintaining stability. The QDDR focuses on adapting diplomatic practices and priorities to twenty-first-century conditions, revitalizing foreign aid programs, enhancing capacities for crisis prevention or early intervention in crisis situations, and improving management techniques, personnel procedures, organization, and recruiting.

> Civilian power is the combined force of civilian personnel across all federal agencies advancing America's core interests in the world. Leading through civilian power is required by the nature of problems

we face in the 21st century. Even the world's finest military cannot defeat a virus, stop climate change, prevent the spread of violent extremism, or make peace in the Middle East. Moreover, civilian power is the most cost-efficient investment in a time of constrained resources. Much of the work that civilians do around the world is the work of prevention, investing proactively in keeping Americans safe and prosperous through cooperation and partnerships with other countries, and building the capabilities of other governments to address problems of violent extremism and criminal networks at home before they are exposed abroad. And prevention is almost always cheaper and more effective than response.

SOURCE: "Introduction," in *Leading through Civilian Power: The First Quadrennial Diplomacy and Development Review* (2010), 1, available at http://www.state.gov/documents/organization/153108.pdf.

After World War II (1939–1945), at the apex of U.S. power, American policymakers strove to construct a postwar world that they hoped would ensure peace, stability, and growth. Despite the many faults of the regime that emerged, it is nevertheless defensible to conclude that they succeeded to a significant extent. The world not only avoided a global nuclear war (albeit only just on at least one or two occasions) but also engineered a sustained general growth in living standards and life expectancy, despite a tripling of the planet's population. The system even survived the demise of one of its key elements, the Bretton Woods agreements, designed to foster a stable international economic order. Yet U.S. leaders' greatest accomplishment may have been to implement a suite of arrangements sufficiently appealing and sufficiently flexible to adapt as conditions changed. Indeed, perhaps the most important non-event of the postwar era was the creation of conditions under which the Soviet empire could expire without sparking a general war. In attempts to stave off decline in previous eras, various German, Austrian, French, Spanish, Japanese, and Russian empires initiated widespread, profoundly destructive hostilities. Assurances of NATO restraint, the U.S. capacity to influence Chinese and Japanese policy, provision of significant financial support, the attractions of a functional world market, and the presence of international mediating institutions all contributed to an environment that made possible not only the termination of Soviet satellite regimes in Eastern Europe but also the dissolution of the Soviet Union itself without igniting a major conflagration.

What remains to be seen is whether the system is sufficiently robust to accommodate the relative decline of its own founding hegemon. In a world where the United States no longer wields preponderant influence, can a more diverse array of principal actors manage conflicts and devise solutions to pressing problems, especially if the general level of turmoil increases? Has the United States, however imperfectly, fostered conditions that mimic on a global level the essential elements of the "ethos of compromise" that suffuse the American system of governance? If so, that outcome is not only a notable legacy to the world but also the best guarantor of a continued American capacity to wield material influence throughout the twenty-first century.

See also: **Chapter 16: The Legacy of World War II; Chapter 18: Middle East Diplomacy; Chapter 27: Rogue States and the Emergence of Terrorist Tactics; Chapter 31: U.S. Economic and Foreign Relations with the Western Hemisphere; Chapter 32: The Environment and International Diplomacy; Chapter 35: The Global War on Terrorism; Chapter 36: The Rise of China in the Twenty-first Century; Chapter 37: Africa in the Twenty-first Century; Chapter 38: U.S.-Israeli Relations and the Quest for Peace in the Middle East.**

ENDNOTES

1. The interpretations in this article are the author's and do not necessarily represent those of the U.S. government or the Department of State.

2. William B. McAllister, *Drug Diplomacy in the Twentieth Century: An International History* (New York: Routledge, 2000).

3. See, for example, the *Arizona Support Our Law Enforcement and Safe Neighborhoods Act of 2010,* which attempts to regulate immigration (2010 Arizona Session Laws, Chapter 113, Forty-ninth Legislature, Second Regular Session, Senate Bill 1070, House Engrossed Senate Bill, Arizona State Legislature, and, 2010 Arizona Session Laws, Chapter 211, Forty-ninth Legislature, Second Regular Session, House Bill 2162, Conference Version, Arizona State Legislature); the *California Global Warming Solution Act of 2006* (California, Assembly Bill 32, Chapter 488, Statutes of 2006) and the *California Sustainable Communities and Climate Protection Act of 2008* (California Senate Bill 375, Statutes of 2008), both designed to reduce emissions and other climate change agents; and, the Regional Greenhouse Gas Initiative, a market-based, greenhouse gas reduction agreement among a consortium of Northeast and Mid-Atlantic states (available at: http://www.rggi.org/home).

4. See, for example, the U.S. Department of Interior website (http://www.doi.gov/index.cfm); entering "Indian water rights" into the search box yields a list of current cases about access to water that highlight the many disputes over Native American sovereignty. For other jurisdictional issues within the United States, see Wade Davies and Richmond L. Clow, *American Indian Sovereignty and Law: An Annotated Bibliography* (Lanham, MD: Scarecrow Press, 2009). For international aspects of the sovereignty issue, see S. James Anaya, *Indigenous Peoples in International Law* (New York: Oxford University Press, 2004).

5. There are some instances in world history that might be characterized as featuring bipolar rivalry on a regional scale. China's Southern and Northern period (420–581 CE) and Southern Song period (1127–1279 CE) may be the best examples. There is nothing similar in scope or scale, however, to the global bipolar Great Power rivalry of the Cold War period.

6. The classic treatment of the importance of relative change in assessing state military and political-economic capacities is Paul Kennedy, *The Rise and Fall of the Great Powers: Economic Change and Military Conflict from 1500–2000* (New York: Vintage Books, 1989).

7. For an analysis of the relationship between openness of governmental systems and "voice opportunities" for multiple types of actors to express preferences, see G. John Ikenberry, *After Victory: Institutions, Strategic Restraint, and the Rebuilding of Order after Major Wars* (Princeton, NJ, and Oxford, UK: Princeton University Press, 2001).

8. *Yearbook of International Organizations,* 43rd Edition, Volume 5 (Munich: K. G. Saur, 2006–2007), 33–37.

9. See: http://www.un.org/en/members/intergovorg.shtml.

10. Department of State, chiefs of mission list (available at: http://www.state.gov/m/dghr/cm). Although the number of non-chief of mission ambassadorial-level appointments vary, and therefore the Department of State does not maintain a regularly updated comprehensive list, a representative array of current examples include: four ambassadors to the United Nations; the U.S. representative on the Council of the International Civil Aviation Organization; the special envoy for North Korean human rights issues; the coordinator for Threat Reduction Programs; the U.S. representative to the Conference on Disarmament; the special representative and coordinator for Burma; and several ambassadors at large for various issues.

11. The 1992 United Nations Conference on Environment and Development, also known as the Earth Summit or the Rio Summit, produced several important agreements and initiatives that have generated continuing attention to the issues of environmental protection, climate change, and sustainable development. The *United Nations Framework Convention on Climate Change* (http://unfccc.int/2860.php) established principles for combating global warming and instituted regular meetings to review progress. The *Convention on Biological Diversity* (http://www.cbd.int) focuses on the conservation of biological diversity and the sustainable and equitable use of products derived there from. *Agenda 21* (http://www.un.org/esa/dsd/agenda21) outlines a detailed action plan for sustainable development. The *Rio Declaration on Environment and Development* enunciated guidance for action on environmental protection and development United Nations (United Nations General Assembly, *Report of the United Nations Conference on Environment and Development, Annex I, Rio Declaration on Environment and Development,* UN Document A/Conf.151/26 Vol. I). The *Statement of Principles for the Sustainable Management of Forests* outlines general principles for the protection and management of forest resources (United Nations General Assembly, *Report of the United Nations Conference on Environment and Development, Annex III, Non-Legally Binding Authoritative Statement of Principles for a Global Consensus on the Management, Conservation, and Sustainable Development of all Types of Forests,* U.N. Document A/Conf.151/26, Vol. III). See also Luc Reydams, ed., *Global Activism Reader* (New York and London: Continuum, 2011), especially Part IV for international environmental activism.

12. World Health Organization, *WHO Framework Convention on Tobacco Control* (Geneva: WHO Press, 2003; updated reprint, 2005); Donley T. Studlar, *Tobacco Control: Comparative Politics in the United States and Canada* (Peterborough, ON: Broadview Press, 2002), Ch. 7; A. L. Holm and R. M. Davis, "Clearing the Airways: Advocacy and Regulation for Smoke-free Airlines," in *Tobacco Control* 13: Supplement I (2004), 30–36.

13. http://www.nature.org.

14. See, for example, the longstanding dispute between Mexico and the United States over trucking issues related to the North American Free Trade Agreement (United States Department of Commerce, International Trade Administration, Current Retaliatory Actions, Mexico Trucking Retaliation, available at: http://www.trade.gov/mas/ian/tradedisputes-enforcement/retaliations/tg_ian_002094.asp).

15. Two works of history that address this issue in insightful ways are J. R. McNeill, *Something New under the Sun: An Environmental History of the Twentieth-century World* (New York: Norton, 2001), and Kenneth Pomeranz, *The Great Divergence: China, Europe, and the Making of the Modern World Economy* (Princeton, NJ: Princeton University Press, 2001). McNeill discusses the unprecedented environmental effects of human activity in the twentieth century that may be irreversible. Pomeranz explains how European states escaped the resource-limited "economic cul de sac" facing all societies in the early modern era by appropriating new resources from the Western Hemisphere, an option no longer available.

16. Divided into three regions, with governmental authority devolved onto a complex arrangement involving federal, regional, and linguistic community elements, at the time of this writing, the Belgian political parties had failed to form a government for over a year.

17. Such a statement may appear problematic, because sphere-of-influence arrangements, whether in the guise of formal agreements or informal mutual acquiescence, always entail continued competition. Nevertheless, these spheres of influence are often

characterized by a laissez-faire understanding that enables multiple parties to enhance power without threatening others. Relevant modern examples include the Eastern Powers' partitions of Poland in 1772, 1793, and 1795; post-Napoleonic French interventions in Spain and Austrian interventions in Italy; the post-1880 Scramble for Africa; general European Great Power acceptance of U.S. prerogatives in the Caribbean; and relative Western acquiescence to post-1945 Soviet dominance of Eastern Europe. In addition to classical Greece, pre-modern non-European examples, insofar as the evidence allows us to judge, might include the Mahajanapadas period in India (c. 600 BCE) and the classic Mayan period (c. 300–c. 900 CE).

18. Examples include: Joseph S. Nye Jr., *The Future of Power* (New York: PublicAffairs, 2011); Allison Stanger, *One Nation, under Contract: The Outsourcing of American Power and the Future of Foreign Policy* (New Haven, CT, and London: Yale University Press, 2009); Robert Kagan, *The Return of History and the End of Dreams* (New York: Alfred A. Knopf, 2008); Anne-Marie Slaughter, *The Idea That Is America: Keeping Faith with Our Values in a Dangerous World* (New York: Basic Books, 2008); Andrew J. Bacevich, *The Limits of Power* (New York: Metropolitan Books, 2008); Thomas R. Pickering and Chester A. Crocker, *America's Role in the World: Foreign Policy*

Choices for the Next President (Washington, DC: Georgetown University Edmund A. Walsh Institute for the Study of Diplomacy, 2008); Richard L. Armitage and Joseph S. Nye Jr., *A Smarter, More Secure America: Report of the CSIS Commission on Smart Power* (Washington, DC: Center for Strategic and International Studies, 2007); G. John Ikenberry and Anne-Marie Slaughter, *Forging a World of Liberty under Law: U.S. National Security in the 21st Century, Final Report of the Princeton Project on National Security* (Princeton, NJ: Woodrow Wilson School of Public and International Affairs, 2006); and Joseph S. Nye Jr., *Soft Power: The Means to Success in World Politics* (New York: PublicAffairs, 2005).

FURTHER READING

Kennedy, Paul. *The Rise and Fall of the Great Powers: Economic Change and Military Conflict from 1500–2000.* New York: Vintage, 1989.

McNeill, John R. *Something New under the Sun: An Environmental History of the Twentieth-century World.* New York: Norton, 2001.

Nye, Joseph S., Jr. *Soft Power: The Means to Success in World Politics.* New York: PublicAffairs, 2005.

chapter 40

Diplomatic Milestones, 2001–Present

History and Analysis of Emerging Issues

by George C. Herring

I N THE FIRST decade of the twenty-first century, America's world position experienced a transformation as profound as in any comparable period in its history. The United States entered the new century as the world's lone superpower, its military and economic strength unrivaled, its ideals and institutions the standard for other nations across the globe. The administration of William J. Clinton (1993–2001) had never quite resolved the issue of how and for what purposes America's vast power should be used. Horrific terrorist attacks on New York City and Washington, D.C., on September 11, 2001, seemed to clarify in the most gruesome way the urgency of asserting U.S. power forcefully in a suddenly menacing world. Yet after two stalemated and enormously costly wars and what came to be called the Great Recession, an overextended and debt-burdened United States began to talk about scaling back its international obligations and focusing on domestic revival. The salient facts of the new international system after the first decade of the twenty-first century appeared to be the decline of the United States from its *fin de siécle* preeminence, the rise of China as the new economic superpower, and a new and even more complex and challenging world.

The national mood at the turn of the century was one of triumphalism and insularity. In opinion polls, Americans ranked foreign policy twentieth in terms of significance. Aping cable television, the networks increasingly favored entertainment over hard news and slashed coverage of overseas events. In the educational system, the teaching of foreign languages declined sharply. Defense spending remained remarkably high through the 1990s, exceeding much of the rest of the world combined, but foreign affairs spending was heavily reduced. The United States was deeply in debt to the United Nations (UN). Because of budget cuts, the State Department closed thirty embassies and twenty-five U.S. Information Agency (USIA) libraries. Foreign policy played a minor role in the campaign of 2000. To people abroad, Americans seemed to revel in their singular prosperity, a minority of the world's population recklessly consuming a large part of its resources. The United States was both admired and feared. Some saw its unique ability to project its values as a threat to their own identities. The fearsome display of American military strength in Kosovo worried potential enemies, and allies. A top German official fretted about the possibility of a rising U.S. unilateralism. A French diplomat speculated in early 1999 that the major problem in international politics was the American "hyperpower."[1]

U.S. DIPLOMACY IN THE TWENTY-FIRST CENTURY

The administration of Texan George W. Bush (2001–2009) took on the unexpectedly difficult challenges of the new century. The younger Bush had won only a minority of the popular vote against Vice President Al Gore in 2000, but he was elevated to the White House by a 5–4 vote of the Supreme Court after a bitterly contested election. Compared to his internationalist father, the new president's background was notably parochial. He had traveled little, worked mostly in business, and held only the office of governor of Texas. His campaign gave little hint of what he might do. He attacked Clinton for not framing a coherent foreign policy, but when questioned about his own "guiding principles," he responded only that he would do what was in U.S. interests. He did express skepticism about humanitarian interventions and disdain for nation building. He promised humility rather than arrogance in dealing with other nations.

Bush sought to make up for his lack of foreign policy experience by appointing a team of experienced veterans. Former Joint Chiefs of Staff chairman Colin Powell was named secretary of state, the first African American to hold

KEY CONCEPTS

Preemptive/preventive war. A preemptive war is launched against an enemy assumed to be ready to attack. It seeks thereby to gain strategic advantage. Preventive war is mounted before an enemy has the means or opportunity to strike. It is considered tantamount to aggression and therefore illegitimate. Less stigma is attached to preemption. An example of preventive war is the Japanese attack on Pearl Harbor on December 7, 1941, and of preemptive war, Israel's 1967 attack on Egypt after that nation positioned troops along Israel's border.

After 9/11, the Bush administration claimed the right to deal with terrorist threats preemptively. Many observers agree that since Iraq had neither the intent nor the capability of attacking the United States, the U.S. war against it was instead preventive and of dubious legality.

Unilateralism/multilateralism. Unilateralism is a go-it-alone foreign policy approach that stresses avoiding alliances and international organizations and even working informally with other nations to achieve desired goals. Multilateralism involves seeking maximum support from allies, the international community, and international institutions for any foreign policy initiative.

Until World War II, the United States generally followed a unilateralist path (often mistakenly labeled isolationism). After 1941, it shifted to multilateralism.

The George W. Bush administration verbally endorsed multilateralism in its War on Terror but made clear that the United States would act on its own if necessary. In going to war with Iraq, it put together a "coalition of the willing," but the administration's heavy-handed diplomacy and determination to do things its own way provoked charges of arrogant unilateralism.

---

that position. However, the duo of Vice President Dick Cheney and Secretary of Defense Donald Rumsfeld (in office 2001–2006) quickly established themselves as the dominant force in the framing and execution of foreign policy. These men had worked together for nearly thirty years. They had been profoundly affected by the outcome of the Vietnam War, which they had experienced while serving in the administration of Gerald R. Ford (1974–1977). Aggressive nationalists, they believed that the United States must maintain its military and economic primacy and single-mindedly promote its interests, without concern for the opposition of allies or the niceties of diplomacy. The presence in important second-tier position of men like Paul Wolfowitz, Douglas Feith, John Bolton, and other so-called neoconservatives, many of them former liberals and ardent supporters of Israel who believed that the United States must use its power to promote democracy throughout the world, would have a crucial impact on Bush administration policies.

In its first months, the new administration was no better able than Clinton to frame a cohesive foreign policy. In domestic policy, it followed Republican orthodoxy, seeking to roll back government regulation and enacting a massive $1.35 trillion tax cut that would have enormous consequences at home and abroad. It resolved skillfully and through quiet diplomacy a potentially explosive crisis with China, provoked when an American aircraft was shot down in Chinese air space. It gave top foreign policy priority to creating a missile defense shield, although many experts doubted its practicality, and its implementation would require abrogation of Cold War treaties with Russia. The United States summarily withdrew from the 1997 Kyoto Protocol on global warming and scrapped talks aimed at

stopping North Korea from developing long-range missiles. Hinting at a major change in direction, Bush privately indicated that the United States would no longer be an honest broker in Middle East peace talks but would side with Israel. Top officials gave little attention to the threat of terrorism, even though scattered signals, in several cases potentially quite alarming, pointed to a possible attack on the United States. From the outset, however, they did discuss the desirability of getting rid of Iraqi dictator Saddam Hussein (in power 1979–2003). State Department spokesperson Richard Haass called the administration's approach "a la carte multilateralism"; critics in the United States and abroad warned that its abrupt manner and go-it-alone approach signaled a new isolationism.[2]

The September 11 Attacks

Early on the morning of September 11, 2001, nineteen al Qaeda jihadists, operating under the direction of Saudi terrorist leader Osama bin Laden, at this time based in Afghanistan, easily slipped through the minimal airport security system then in place, hijacked four commercial airliners, and used them as missiles to attack two of the foremost symbols of U.S. power, New York's landmark World Trade Center and the Pentagon in Washington, D.C. An additional attack, presumably on the Capitol or White House, was thwarted when courageous passengers on a fourth plane revolted and forced a crash on Pennsylvania farmland. After two enormous explosions, the famed Twin Towers of the World Trade Center crumbled into a massive pile of rubble. The attack caused major damage at the Pentagon. Nearly three thousand innocent people were killed.

The September 11 attacks worked dramatic changes in American life. In one fiery moment, the intellectual and emotional baggage left from the nation's failure in Vietnam seemed swept aside in a surge of fear and anger. Foreign policy once again became the highest national priority; anti-terrorism jumped to the top of foreign policy concerns. An already ailing economy fell into what economists finally conceded was a recession. With but one dissenting vote, Congress gave the president sweeping authority to "use all necessary and appropriate force" to combat the new enemy of terrorism. Through the Patriot Act, passed in October, it granted the president additional authority to detain and deport immigrants and search telephone and e-mail records. The administration went beyond this in a secret executive order that permitted the government to listen in on phone calls and read e-mails without court orders. Nine-eleven, as it came to be called, worked a sea change in a national mindset shaped by Vietnam and Watergate.

The "War on Terror"

An administration that had appeared in its first months to be floundering suddenly seemed to find purpose and direction, and with broad popular support launched a global "War on Terror." It defined the war broadly against all terrorists rather than narrowly against al Qaeda, a move that gave the White House license to decide who was the enemy. It also portrayed the war as a long-term struggle between good and evil, giving it a powerful rallying cry to gain and hold popular support. Seemingly confounding those who had dismissed him as a lightweight, Bush, on September 20, gave a rousing address before a joint session of Congress to rally the nation. The September 11 attacks evoked an outpouring of sympathy from abroad: "*Nous somme tous Americains,*" the French daily *Le Monde* proclaimed.

Under the guidance of Powell, an administration that had only recently seemed to shun multilateralism began putting together a broad coalition of old allies like Great Britain and France, former enemies such as China and Russia, and even the pariah state Pakistan, to attack in different ways and on multiple fronts a new kind of non-state foe and its sources of support. Behind the scenes, Cheney, Rumsfeld, and the neo-cons also made clear their determination to take out Saddam Hussein. "Go massive," the secretary of defense insisted, "Sweep it all up. Things related and not."[3] The administration's early actions hinted, mistakenly as it turned out, that the summer's unilateralism was a thing of the past. The president's stark warning that "Every nation in every region" must decide whether it was "with us, or . . . with the terrorists" reflected more accurately the direction his administration would take.[4]

Afghanistan

The first phase of the war in Afghanistan astounded some experts. Throughout history, Afghanistan had acquired a reputation as the graveyard of empires for its fierce resistance to outside intruders, most recently the Soviet Union, and some pessimists predicted that it could become for the United States a Vietnam with snow. The administration mobilized disparate forces to strike at bin Laden's al Qaeda and the fundamentalist Taliban regime that sheltered them in Afghanistan. Bush put a $25 million price on bin Laden's head. In the parlance of the Old West, he vowed to bring back the "evil one" dead or alive.

The United States applied on a much larger scale and again with stunning results the high-tech methods of warfare employed in Kosovo in 1999. CIA operatives and a handful of Special Forces on the ground in Afghanistan dispensed millions of dollars to buy the loyalty of tribes hostile to the ruling Taliban. They used global positioning devices to lock in bombers on key targets. With support from numerous allies, the United States eliminated in less than four months the despised and surprisingly weak Taliban, destroyed bin Laden's training camps, and sent the leader and his surviving followers fleeing into the rugged mountain region of Tora Bora near the border with Pakistan. In early December, the allied coalition installed an interim government headed by Hamid Karzai. Administration backers cheered the victory and sneered at those who had foreseen a quagmire.

In fact, the United States made crucial errors that transformed smashing tactical success into a major strategic failure. Understandably nervous about prolonged warfare in Afghanistan and conflict with the local population, concerned about heavy American casualties, and set on reforming the armed forces for twenty-first-century warfare, Rumsfeld relied on air power and local proxies to do what would have required large numbers of U.S. ground forces. Less than five thousand Americans were sent to secure Afghanistan. Osama bin Laden and al Qaeda appear to have been trapped and in desperate shape at Tora Bora in early December. Yet Washington, already focusing on Iraq, turned down requests for additional troops. Bin Laden either paid off or eluded those Afghans charged with killing or capturing him. Pakistan failed to seal its border. In mid-December, he and his chief lieutenants, along with Taliban leader Mullah Omar, fled into the tribal areas of western Pakistan. In time, a reconstituted Taliban would mount an insurgency that threatened the Karzai government. Never enthusiastic about nation building, the Bush administration made inadequate preparations and provided insufficient funds and people for a truly monumental task. Local warlords controlled much of the country. Opium production resumed and helped fund the Taliban's revival. Afghanistan soon disappeared from the front pages.

The "War on Terror" Expands

In 2002, the Bush administration spelled out its concepts for waging a global War on Terror, setting forth in the process the most cohesive strategic design since the Cold War. The new strategy was based on the premise that the United States faced dire threats to its security and its way of life. The two greatest dangers were the proliferation of weapons of mass destruction and the existence of terrorist networks hostile to the United States. Deterrence had not worked on 9/11; it could not be depended on in the future in dealing with unstable dictators and terrorists. The United States must be ready to head off threats before they full materialized, mobilize all its resources to eliminate such threats, and spread democracy to prevent the creation of states where terrorism might flourish.

In his January 2002 State of the Union Address, the president warned that the war was just beginning. Directing the nation's attention to Iraq, Iran, and North Korea, he spoke of an "axis of evil" that threatened the peace of the world. Curiously, he identified three nations that had nothing to do with 9/11, and by using the word "axis" suggested a unity of purpose that simply did not exist. In a speech at West Point on June 1, he enunciated what became known as the Bush Doctrine, affirming that the sort of containment that had been practiced in the Cold War would not work against "unbalanced dictators" and terrorists who might have access to weapons of mass destruction. Such threats must be thwarted by preemptive action, he said.

The administration put it all together in a national security strategy paper made public in September 2002. The document used 9/11 and the War on Terror to set forth as doctrine ideas that conservatives and neo-cons had been discussing for years. It drew heavily on the 1992 Defense Planning Guidance Document repudiated by the elder Bush. It reflected a born-again president's taste for moral absolutes and manifested the influence of the neo-cons, who sought to promote democracy abroad. It combined ringing affirmation of Wilsonian ideals with hard-nosed statements about the uses of American power. Admitting to but one "sustainable model for national success: freedom, democracy, and free enterprise," it promised to "use this moment of opportunity to extend the benefits of freedom across the globe." It insisted that the United States must maintain its military preeminence. It spoke of multilateralism but made clear that the nation would "act apart when our interests and unique responsibility require." Nor could it wait for "absolute proof" of danger from weapons of mass destruction. Such threats must be stopped before they reached American shores.

The principles of military preeminence, unilateralism, and preemptive or even preventive war departed sharply from the Cold War strategy of containment and deterrence. Although praised by conservatives, the national security strategy document was denounced by critics as arrogant and high-handed.[5]

Even as it was developing the new strategy, the Bush administration instituted important foreign policy initiatives to advance the aims of the War on Terror. Because of its location, Pakistan became an important ally, despite its long record of providing assistance to rogue nations seeking nuclear weapons and its support for the Taliban. The United States turned a blind eye to Uzbekistan's horrid human rights record to secure bases crucial for waging war in the region. The administration pushed an agreement with Russia to reduce nuclear arsenals on both sides. Surprisingly, it negotiated a rapprochement with Libya's dictator, Muammar el-Qaddafi, a long-time promoter of terrorism, in order to secure a halt to that nation's nuclear program. The United States even approached Iran in what predictably turned out to be a fruitless gambit.

Iraq

Months before it made public the new doctrine, the Bush administration had decided to launch a preemptive war to force regime change in Iraq. Saddam Hussein had miraculously survived the disastrous defeat of 1991 and a decade of United Nations sanctions. Upon taking office, top Bush administration officials had been fixated on getting rid of Saddam, and after 9/11 they strained mightily to link him to an attack for which he had no responsibility. Although there was no firm evidence to support it, they were certain that Saddam had or would soon have weapons of mass destruction and might share them with terrorists, thus providing a cause for war. Even before the Afghan war was won, the administration diverted its attention to Iraq, perhaps facilitating bin Laden's escape. By July 2002, it had determined to go to war with Iraq, without searching internal debate or close examination of the possible consequences. The issue was settled, a British official reported to London: "the intelligence and facts were being fixed around the policy."[6]

The reasons for this fateful decision seem clear. Cheney and Rumsfeld saw an opportunity to complete the unfinished business of 1991, rid the world of a perceived nuisance and possible threat, promote vital U.S. interests in the Middle East, and, through a demonstration of U.S. military superiority, deter other threats such as al Qaeda. For the neo-cons, war satisfied deep philosophical convictions and immediate practical concerns. In their view, the United States had a moral obligation to stop tyranny, spread democracy, and impose a global "benign hegemony." They were closely tied to Israel, and the democratization of Iraq would promote that vital ally's security. They fantasized through a sort of reverse domino theory that the implantation of democracy in Iraq would promote its spread through the Middle East. The president had his own reasons for war: getting rid of Saddam would enable Bush to succeed where his father had failed, and to avenge the dictator's 1993 attempt on his father's life. Neither a deep thinker nor particularly curious, Bush saw the world in terms of good and evil and was absolutely certain that he had been "called" to defend the United States and extend "God's gift of liberty" to "every human being in the world."[7] In his simplistic world view, war would advance U.S. security, eliminate a source of evil, and expand freedom.

In a strange, even surreal way, the administration in the second half of 2002 took the nation toward war with very little dissent. Exploiting still-vivid memories of 9/11, it created a culture of fear that helped it run roughshod over all opposition. Employing evidence that turned out to be exaggerated or just plain wrong, it repeated time and again solemn warnings of the consequences of inaction. "We don't want the smoking gun to be a mushroom cloud," was the clinching mantra.[8] Military officers who raised questions about troop levels or postwar planning were ignored or marginalized. The Democrats were badly divided and nervous about opposing a war president at the height of his power, especially with midterm elections approaching, and they failed to muster effective opposition. Some opposition leaders, like Senators Hillary Clinton and John Kerry, actually supported war. In October 2002, Congress resoundingly passed a resolution authorizing the president to "use the armed forces of the United States as he determines necessary and appropriate . . . against the continuing threat posed by Iraq." By early December, large numbers of U.S. troops were en route to the Middle East.

The Bush administration was not similarly successful abroad, and its heavy-handed pressure to drag other nations into war with Iraq squandered much of the goodwill the United States had earned after 9/11. Powell persuaded a reluctant president to take the issue to the United Nations. Among leading countries, however, only Great Britain went along, although the Eastern European nations did back the United States to secure aid as they were integrated into NATO. France and Germany actively opposed the United States, provoking much bad feeling on both sides. In early February, an estimated eight million people on five continents protested against war with Iraq, according to one scholar, the "largest global opposition to an American foreign policy in history."[9] After months of arrogant and occasionally brutish bullying, and a much ballyhooed February 2003 Powell speech at the UN, later shown to have included numerous false and misleading statements, failed to produce a resolution endorsing military action, the administration

plunged ahead on its own. Gathering a "coalition of the willing" composed of Britain and twenty-five smaller nations, most of whom provided token assistance in return for generous incentives, the United States in March 2003 launched Operation Iraqi Freedom.

As with Afghanistan, the war with Iraq was a spectacular short-term success, and an enormously costly long-term disaster. A massive "shock and awe" bombing campaign shut down Iraqi communications and destroyed key military installations. In one of the most rapid military advances in history, U.S. forces sped from Kuwait to Baghdad in less than three weeks. Although Saddam remained at large, the toppling of his statue in the capital on April 11 symbolized the demise of his regime. The United States suffered only 122 killed, most of them from accidents or friendly fire; the British, 43. On May 10, Bush, in full flight regalia, landed on the deck of the aircraft carrier USS *Abraham Lincoln* in San Diego Harbor. Standing beneath an enormous banner proclaiming "Mission Accomplished," the commander in chief hailed the success of his troops.

The excitement of victory soon turned into haunting fears of a Vietnam-like quagmire. Largely because of decisions made by Rumsfeld, the coalition had sufficient forces to win the war but not enough to secure the peace. In an act of remarkable fecklessness, the Pentagon made few preparations for the postwar period and spurned plans developed by other agencies. Rumsfeld and Wolfowitz naively insisted that the United States could invade Iraq, dump the regime, turn the government over to Iraqis, and get out, all in three months. The result instead was an outbreak of lawlessness, violence, and looting, including the theft of millions of dollars and Euros from the national bank and priceless antiquities from the museum. Rumsfeld's flippant remarks that "stuff happens" and freedom was "untidy" appeared to highlight the administration's callousness.

Rise of the Insurgency

The rampant lawlessness and inability of the victors to put a shattered infrastructure back together increased the rage of the occupied. The U.S. occupation authority compounded the chaos by purging an already dysfunctional government of members of Saddam's political party, thereby bringing the ministries to a halt; by disbanding the army, putting four hundred thousand men, many of them with guns, out of work; and, through conservative "shock doctrine," seeking to replace a state-run system with a market economy.[10] Many of the Americans sent to assist in Iraq were young Republican loyalists and campaign workers who had no language skills, knew nothing about Iraq or the Middle East, and had no experience dealing with the problems they confronted. Anarchy quickly evolved into violent and sustained guerrilla opposition to what most Iraqis now viewed as a hostile foreign occupation. Support for the United States among the coalition nations began to wither away.

During the ensuing years, the insurgency grew in strength and the war dragged on.

Patched together after World War I (1914–1918) by British imperial planners, a country in name only, Iraq had a long history of religious, tribal, and ethnic struggle. Sunni Muslim followers of Saddam were joined in opposition to the United States by some dissident Shiites and also by al Qaeda and other jihadists who flocked into Iraq across porous borders. What was supposed to be a bastion of democracy became instead a battleground and training camp for terrorists. Using car bombs and improvised explosive devices (IEDs) with lethal effectiveness, the insurgents took a growing toll of U.S. and coalition troops, as well as Iraqi security forces hastily pressed into service. The war made refugees of an estimated 4.7 million Iraqis. In 2004, the United States transferred governance to a fragile Iraqi government, but it was crippled by corruption and could not bring a divided nation together. After 2006, with the insurgency still thriving, a full-scale civil war erupted between Sunnis and Shiites, with already weary U.S. troops caught in the middle. U.S. prestige plummeted among Arabs and indeed around the world.

As the costs escalated, Americans increasingly soured on what became commonly known as "Bush's War." U.S. forces found no evidence of weapons of mass destruction, completely undermining the administration's case for war. Meanwhile, critics discredited other evidence used to justify going to war with Iraq. Official spokespersons now insisted that the deposition of Saddam had removed a bloody tyrant and made the world safer. However, the abuse of captives at Baghdad's Abu Ghraib prison by U.S. guards, the alleged widespread use of torture, including the notorious water boarding, and the detention of prisoners at Guantanamo Bay and in friendly foreign countries without charges or trial raised questions at home and abroad about American claims to a higher morality. Bush eked out a reelection victory over Democratic Senator John Kerry in 2004. Four years later, six in ten Americans believed that the nation should have stayed out of Iraq. Only 23 percent approved the president's handling of the war.

Diplomatic Initiatives of Bush's Second Term

Midway through his second term, Bush changed course in Iraq with positive results. Following crushing Democratic victories in the 2006 elections, giving the opposition control of both houses of Congress, he replaced the abrasive and ineffectual Rumsfeld with the quiet and pragmatic national security veteran Robert Gates. Flatly rejecting demands for withdrawal from Democrats, and some

Republicans, he gambled on a "surge" that sent thirty-five thousand additional U.S. troops to Iraq. His commanders belatedly implemented a counterinsurgency strategy that focused on protecting the Iraqi population rather than killing insurgents. The new strategy, along with the defection of large numbers of Sunnis from the insurgency into an alliance of expediency with the United States, changed the war. The immediate result was a spike in violence: 940 Americans were killed in 2007. Gradually, however, the security situation improved, the United States regained the initiative, and al Qaeda was weakened.

As the Bush administration began to stabilize a war it belatedly admitted it was losing, it also came to recognize that it was losing a war in Afghanistan it presumed to have won. Karzai seemed to be effective in his first years and, in a reasonably honest election in 2004, won another term. Kabul came to life, and women experienced new freedoms. However, the United States repeated in Afghanistan the mistakes made in Iraq. It had far fewer troops than were needed to maintain security. Its distaste for nation building was crippling. As in Iraq, no plans were made for reconstruction, and Afghanistan was the most poorly funded reconstruction program since World War II (1939–1945). Given sanctuary in Pakistan, sometimes trained in Iraq, and well funded through the opium trade, the Taliban filled the vacuum and began to reconstitute strongholds in southern and eastern Afghanistan. The fighting intensified. In 2008, the United States suffered more killed in action in Afghanistan than in Iraq. In its last months, the administration undertook a full review of a situation that was rapidly spiraling out of control.

The tone if not the essential direction of Bush's foreign policy changed in his second term. Powell was replaced by National Security Adviser Condoleezza Rice. Stephen Hadley took over the National Security Council (NSC). Former CIA director Robert Gates brought broad experience and strong leadership to the Defense Department. Given this lineup and her close ties with Bush and Gates, Rice took the lead in foreign policy. Not surprisingly, in view of the debacles in Iraq and Afghanistan, Bush's second inaugural pledge to spread democracy died aborning. Quite the contrary, elections in the Palestinian territory and Lebanon resulted in victories for Hamas and Hezbollah, two terrorist movements tied closely to Iran. Under Rice's leadership, the United States set out to rebuild good relations with the European allies. Against strong opposition from neo-cons like Bolton, the administration offered concessions to North Korea that made possible a tenuous agreement to halt its nuclear program.

A major late-term initiative was to reinvigorate the Middle East peace process. In his first term, Bush had refused to involve himself in discussions, and his public statements generally favored Israel. The rise of Iran as a major regional and possibly nuclear power and its ties with terrorist groups Hezbollah and Hamas frightened Sunni nations, such as Saudi Arabia, a key ally and oil supplier. The secretary of state thus visited the Middle East numerous times during 2007 and brought Israeli and Palestinian delegates to a conference in Maryland in November. The two sides did agree to work together, but they were firmly deadlocked on the issues, and the weakness of their leaders along with Bush's continuing unwillingness to get involved brought no solutions. The Middle East was as conflict-ridden as ever.

A Tarnished Legacy

The Bush foreign policy legacy could not escape the burden of Iraq and Afghanistan. Nearly four thousand Americans had been killed in Iraq by early 2008. Thousands more whose lives were spared by modern medicine suffered lasting physical wounds and severe trauma. The two wars strained the U.S. armed forces to the point of raising questions about the viability of the volunteer army concept. The financial costs were staggering, an estimated $800 billion as of 2008. The addition of postwar health costs for veterans was calculated to raise the long-term price tag as high as $3 trillion. The war in Iraq helped revive al Qaeda, at least temporarily, and fulfilled bin Laden's dream of getting the United States bogged down in a quagmire in the Arab world. It sparked anti-Americanism through much of the Middle East and strengthened the position of Iran. It cost the support of key American allies. The way the administration chose to wage the wars had the effect of undermining at home the very freedoms it professed to be defending abroad. Its absorption with the wars through much of its eight years in office limited its ability to deal with other pressing foreign policy issues.

The United States of 2008 bore little resemblance to the global behemoth of the millennial year. The national debt nearly doubled during the Bush years, from $5.5 trillion in 2001 to about $11 trillion by 2008. A banking collapse in Bush's final months triggered the worst U.S. economic crisis since the Great Depression of the 1930s. It is supremely ironic that an administration passionately committed to maintaining U.S. primacy and using it to spread American values squandered the nation's world position by its arrogant unilateralism, reckless misuse of its

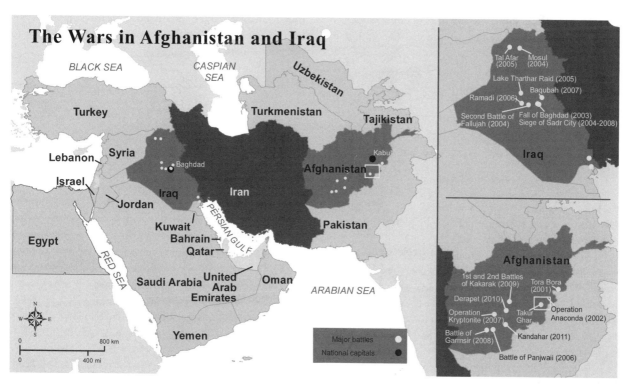

The wars in Afghanistan and in Iraq are two of the longest wars in American history. The Afghan War, which began in October 2001, quickly toppled the ruling Taliban who were shielding al Qaeda leader Osama bin Laden. However, an increasingly powerful insurgency has prevented a resolution to the conflict. The Iraq War, begun in March 2003, removed long-time Iraqi dictator Saddam Hussein from power. Soon afterward, however, conflict between the Shia and Sunni Muslims in the country, as well as ethnic rivalries, led to civil war. An increase of twenty thousand American troops in 2007 restored some semblance of order to the country, and, at the end of 2011, American troops finally left Iraq.

power, and the betrayal of its own ideals. Among the punditry, talk of a unipolar moment gave way to warnings about a nation in decline. The emergence of China as an economic giant, predicted to surpass the United States in the near future and already holding a large share of the U.S. debt, even prompted speculation about the rise of the East and the decline of the West.

THE OBAMA ADMINISTRATION TAKES POWER

Bush's successor, Illinois Senator Barack Hussein Obama (2009–), brought to the presidency a quite different background and worldview. Born in Hawaii to a Kenyan father and an American mother, he spent part of his youth in Indonesia. His biracial and multi-continental biography gave him broad exposure to other peoples and cultures. The election of an African American won for the United States acclaim across the world. While running for president, Obama sought foreign policy instruction from idealists such as Susan Rice and prize-winning author Samantha Power, and from Democratic realists such as Zbigniew Brzezinski, Jimmy Carter's (1977–1981) national security adviser.

He sometimes spoke the language of American idealism and on occasion seemed to endorse the notion of American exceptionalism. Yet he was also a disciple of Protestant theologian Reinhold Niebuhr, who conceded that evil would always exist in the world and warned of the limits of U.S. power to eradicate it. Obama vowed to break free from the ideologies of an earlier era. His background bespoke sensitivity, compromise, and a pragmatic approach to problem-solving. His appointment of New York Senator Hillary Clinton, once his bitter rival for the Democratic nomination, to the post of secretary of state, and his retention of veteran Republican national security operative Robert Gates as secretary of defense signified his tendency toward compromise and reconciliation. Obama expressed admiration for George H. W. Bush (1989–1993) as a diplomatist, and even modeled his national security apparatus after the elder Bush, giving the NSC control over the policy process.

Substantial Changes in Foreign Policy

In office, President Obama proposed to change U.S. foreign policy in style and substance. While reserving the nation's right to act alone if necessary, he vowed to replace the blustery unilateralism of the early Bush years with a civil tone. The United States would continue to play the role of world leader, he insisted, but it could no longer do the job by itself. He hoped to work closely with the traditional European allies and establish partnerships with rising powers such as Brazil, Russia, India, and China to

PUBLIC PORTRAIT: *HILLARY RODHAM CLINTON (1947–)*

Secretary of State Hillary Rodham Clinton was First Lady of the United States (1993–2001), Democratic U.S. senator from New York (2001–2009), and, since 2009, secretary of state, the third woman to hold that position. In all of these posts, she focused on women's issues.

A native of Chicago, Clinton was born on October 26, 1947. She was educated at Wellesley College, where she gave a controversial graduation speech opposing the Vietnam War, and at the Yale Law School, where she was one of twenty-seven female students out of a total of 262. On October 11, 1975, she married ambitious Arkansas politician William Jefferson Clinton. While serving as First Lady of the state during his several governorships, she raised eyebrows by continuing to practice law.

An admirer of activist First Lady Eleanor Roosevelt, Clinton, in the White House, took on a prominent role, sparked controversy, and became a sort of lightning rod for her husband. In 1993, she chaired an ill-fated task force created to draft proposals to submit to Congress to reform the nation's health care system. Her recommendations were rejected by the legislators. She also became an outspoken advocate for women's rights internationally. Over the objections of some of her husband's foreign policy advisers, she made a stirring speech in Beijing at the 1995 Fourth World Conference on Women, proclaiming that "human rights are women's rights and women's rights are human rights once and for all." The speech attracted much attention and persuaded her that she could have influence in this area.

Although, as a student, Clinton had vocally protested against the Vietnam War, in later life she adopted more hawkish foreign policy views. To the consternation of liberal Democrats, she voted for the Bush administration's proposed war with Iraq in the fall of 2002. In the 2008 presidential nomination debates with Illinois Senator Barack Obama, she took consistently hard lines on foreign policy issues and questioned his lack of experience and toughness. A surprise appointment as secretary of state, she supported the surge in Afghanistan in the summer/fall review of 2009. On the basis of human rights' concerns, she also strongly endorsed U.S. intervention in Libya in the spring of 2011.

Clinton traveled farther than any of her predecessors in the State Department and visited seventy-nine countries in her first two and one-half years. She continued to promote international women's rights, "the unfinished issue of the 21st century," she called it. During the protests that formed throughout the Middle East in the Arab Spring, she was especially sensitive to and concerned about the rights and welfare of women and children. She also saw to it that those issues had a prominent place in the State Department's Quadrennial Diplomatic and Development Review.

Diplomats gather for a meeting of the Organization of American States (OAS). The world's oldest regional organization, dating back to 1889, the OAS today includes all thirty-five nations in the Western Hemisphere. The OAS is the main political, juridical, and governmental forum in the Hemisphere and strongly supports the protection of human rights.

SOURCE: Organization of American States (OAS).

address a broad range of world problems. He aimed to reduce the U.S. role in the Middle East and focus more on the surging region of East Asia and the Pacific. He abandoned the Bush commitment to spreading democracy. Evoking John Quincy Adams (1825–1829) in the nineteenth century, he spoke eloquently of rebuilding the United States as an example to the world and promised that the United States would not seek to impose democracy by force. He publicly admitted that the United States had made mistakes. He conceded that other nations had legitimate interests, while urging those nations to abandon their "reflexive" anti-Americanism.

To the dismay of hard-line critics, he offered the possibility of "engagement" to rogue states such as Iran and North Korea, insisting that it "strengthens our hand to reach out to enemies." He was even photographed shaking the hand of the notorious Yankee-baiter Hugo Chavez of Venezuela. In a much publicized and widely applauded June 2009 speech in Cairo, he offered rapprochement with Islam. He proposed a "reset" in relations with Russia to reduce the arsenals of the world's two leading nuclear powers. His conciliatory and worldly demeanor won him the Nobel Peace Prize for 2009, an award he himself admitted he had not earned through tangible accomplishment. Typical of his approach, in his acceptance speech he took a Niebuhrian line by affirming that while seeking peace the United States would also respond forcibly to threats to its vital interests.

On key national security issues, Obama's administration charted a pragmatic and distinctly nuanced path. He

UN peacekeepers patrol a road in Darfur, Sudan, the center of a civil war that has raged since 2003. Estimates of the number of casualties range from fewer than twenty thousand to several hundred thousand dead, either from direct combat or the starvation and disease brought about by the conflict. Labeled as an example of genocide, the ongoing conflict remains a challenge for American and world diplomats in the twenty-first century.

SOURCE: Reuters/Louis Charbonneau.

continued to assign a high priority to the war against terrorism, but he also made clear that the United States was at war with extremist groups such as al Qaeda and the Taliban, not with Islam. He also emphasized the importance of addressing issues such as climate change and emphasized that rebuilding the economy and upgrading education were vital components of the nation's security. He sought to balance military needs with the preservation of American

IN THEIR OWN WORDS: *NATIONAL SECURITY STRATEGY, MAY 2010*

In May 2010, President Barack Obama presented a paper outlining the national security strategy of the United States. The president defined how the nation will respond to security challenges in an era of financial distress at home and a reordering of political power abroad.

...For nearly a decade, our Nation has been at war with a far-reaching network of violence and hatred.... This is part of a broad, multinational effort that is right and just, and we will be unwavering in our commitment to the security of our people, allies, and partners.... [A]s we face multiple threats ... we will maintain the military superiority that has secured our country, and underpinned global security, for decades....

Our strategy starts by recognizing that our strength and influence abroad begins with the steps we take at home. We must grow our economy and reduce our deficit. We must educate our children to compete in an age where knowledge is capital, and the marketplace is global. We must develop the clean energy that can power new industry, unbind us from foreign oil, and preserve our planet. We must pursue science and research that ... unlocks wonders as unforeseen to us today as the surface of the moon and the microchip were a century ago....

The burdens of a young century cannot fall on American shoulders alone.... We are clear-eyed about the challenge of mobilizing collective action, and the shortfalls of our international system. But America has not succeeded by stepping outside the currents of international cooperation. We have succeeded by steering those currents in the direction of liberty and justice....

[W]e will be steadfast in strengthening those old alliances that have served us so well.... [W]e will build new and deeper partnerships in every region, and strengthen international standards and institutions. This engagement is not an end in itself. The international order we seek is one that can resolve the challenges of our times ... while also healing its wounds....

SOURCE: http://whitehouse.gov/sites/default/files/rss_viewer/ national_security_strategy.pdf.

values by ending torture and the harshest methods of interrogation.[11] To the disappointment of many of his supporters, he did not close the prison at Guantanamo Bay or stop warrantless wiretaps. He also employed Predator drones relentlessly, and with devastating effect, against al Qaeda and the Taliban in Pakistan and Afghanistan.

Ongoing Challenges

Managing two ongoing wars posed enormous challenges. A critic of the conflict in Iraq since its inception, Obama had vowed during the campaign to get American combat forces out as quickly as possible. He did so in summer 2010, leaving thirty-five thousand troops behind to train Iraqis to defend themselves. He had also pledged to fight more vigorously and effectively what he called the "necessary war" in Afghanistan. By the time he took office, a resurgent Taliban controlled or threatened almost half the country. In some areas, it had actually created a shadow government. To hold the line, Obama early approved twenty-one thousand new troops in addition to the twelve thousand already committed by Bush. The military pushed for a surge approach comparable to Iraq, calling for forty thousand more troops, implementation of a counterinsurgency strategy, and a 2013 date before troops would begin to be removed. Only 32 percent of Americans approved additional troops, and there was especially strong opposition within the president's own party. After an extended summer/fall 2009 policy review that provoked nasty bureaucratic infighting and exposed sharp civil-military tensions, Obama agreed to send thirty thousand additional troops and approved the counterinsurgency strategy. He also scaled back U.S. objectives from defeating to "degrading" the enemy, while pointing toward the beginning of troop removals from Afghanistan as soon as 2011.

The administration's initial foreign policy accomplishments were limited. In its first two years, the Great Recession dominated policymaking and politics. Obama had also set an ambitious domestic agenda, and the passage of a large economic stimulus package, landmark (and highly contentious) health care legislation, and a financial reform bill consumed much of his first year. An eloquent speechmaker with a keen analytical mind, the president sometimes seemed disengaged and unable to explain his policies in terms that resonated with people. People across the world applauded his conciliatory demeanor, and he began to rebuild U.S. prestige. However, especially on economic issues, other nations pursued their own interests and did not automatically follow the U.S. lead. The Europeans not surprisingly went their own way while applauding Obama's conciliatory overtures. Neither Russia nor China went along with his idea of forming a global partnership. The administration did negotiate and with considerable difficulty secure Senate approval of a nuclear arms reduction agreement with Russia, but the proposed "reset" did not get much further.

Progress in the wars also was at best uncertain. Obama got U.S. combat forces out of Iraq expeditiously, but it remained quite unclear whether the still shaky Iraqi government could stand by itself, revive its battered economy, or reconcile the bitter ethnic and sectarian conflicts within a diverse population. The United States and NATO launched a major counterinsurgency program in Afghanistan by moving against Marjah in Helmland, the center of opium growing, and Kandahar, the spiritual home of the Taliban. They appeared to score some early gains. The Taliban was weakened, not destroyed, and Obama's timetable for departure offered them the tempting option of waiting out the United States. "You have the watches, we have the time," one insurgent told a reporter.[12] An increasingly corrupt and incompetent Karzai government, the safe havens enjoyed by insurgents in Pakistan, and the stubborn persistence of the insurgency rendered long-term success at best dubious. "The gains are fragile, and they are tenuous," top U.S. generals said of both Iraq and Afghanistan.[13]

Elsewhere as well, there was frustration. North Korea and Iran resisted offers of engagement and threats of sanctions alike. In summer 2009, an obviously rigged election provoked widespread demonstrations in Iran. Obama's initial silence and subsequently mild verbal support for the protesters while the demonstrations were being crushed raised questions about his commitment to U.S. values. The president attempted to return to the role of honest broker in Israeli-Palestinian peace discussions, but to no avail. The Great Recession refused to go away. What Obama himself labeled a "shellacking" in the 2010 midterm elections significantly weakened his hands both at home and abroad.

Mixed Responses to the Arab Spring

An unanticipated uprising among oppressed Arab peoples in winter/spring 2011 brought U.S. focus squarely back to a region Obama had originally hoped to downplay. For years, the United States had tolerated and even abetted authoritarian regimes in the Middle East to advance key foreign policy goals, such as access to vital oil supplies and the security of Israel. Indeed, such regimes in Egypt and Saudi Arabia had been the twin pillars of U.S. Middle East policy. The so-called Arab Spring caught the United States between its vital interests and the values it professed to uphold. U.S. officials recognized that a more democratic Middle East in time could be a more prosperous and stable region more in line with American ideals. A historical study commissioned by the president also concluded that revolutions were notoriously unpredictable and uncontrollable. The fear of a replay of the Iranian revolution lurked in the back of officials' minds.

The uprising began almost inadvertently with the individual action of a Tunisian fruit vendor, Mohamed Bouazizi, who immolated himself to protest official corruption in his country. This act of desperation and conscience sparked a popular uprising that led to the overthrow of the Tunisian government. The revolt spread to Egypt, a key American ally, and subsequently to Bahrain, Yemen, Syria, and Libya.

True to its pragmatist bent, the Obama administration responded to each of the revolts on its own merits and in terms of the importance of U.S. interests. Obama praised the "victory of the will of the people" in Tunisia, where U.S. interests were negligible. Eighty-two-year-old Egyptian dictator Hosni Mubarak (in power 1981–2011) had been a close U.S. ally for years, and his acceptance of Israel was sufficiently important that the United States had generally ignored his corruption and oppression. The revolt in late January was led by Egypt's middle class. It was largely secular, and included numerous women. The protesters naturally looked to the United States for support. The Obama administration first responded as it had to the Iranian uprising in 2009, remaining conspicuously silent in the face of broadening and unrelenting demonstrations in Cairo's Tahrir Square. As Mubarak's demise seemed increasingly likely, the administration quietly urged him to step down while seeking a smooth transition through the instrumentation of the army. The U.S. response was necessarily clumsy; while seeking to play both sides of the struggle, Obama satisfied neither. Ultimately, after Mubarak reluctantly resigned, the president could take some comfort in seeming to be on the right side of history.

In other countries, the United States took varied approaches depending on the severity of the oppression and the extent of its interests. In tiny Bahrain, where a Sunni royal family ruled a largely Shiite population (and where the U.S. Sixth Fleet was based), the administration encouraged restraint on the part of the rulers and reforms to appease the protesters, while keeping quiet when neighboring Saudi Arabia sent military forces to contain the rebellion, a clear case of vital interests over values. The United States tried various options including sanctions to stop Syrian dictator Bashar al-Assad's (in power 2000–) brutal suppression of popular protests; by February 2012, an estimated 7,500 had been killed. Yet, it also worried what a new government might look like and feared a sectarian bloodbath should Assad be forced out. Fragile Yemen was a failed state and the center of al Qaeda activity, but its government assisted the United States in the fight against terrorism. The administration said and did nothing.

A revolt against Libya's maniacal, corrupt, and brutal dictator Muammar el-Qaddafi (in power 1969–2011) presented similar challenges but brought forth a unique response. Qaddafi had been a leading exporter of terrorism in the 1980s, but he had reached an accommodation with the Bush administration on stopping his nuclear program. From his ascent to power, he had ruthlessly maintained his position, however, and his removal could be justified on grounds of human rights alone. European nations who relied on Libyan oil pushed for his removal. Idealists in the Obama administration, such as UN ambassador Susan Rice and NSC official Samantha Power, supported by Secretary Clinton, pushed for U.S. intervention. Gates strenuously objected on the grounds that an already overextended United States had no vital interests in Libya. Obama eventually split the difference: he encouraged international intervention through NATO and the UN, initially through the institution of a no-fly zone to prevent Qaddafi from using aircraft to massacre civilians, later expanded to forcing his removal. He insisted that the approval of the UN and the Arab League be secured first. The result was a NATO intervention in which the United States played only a supporting role. After six months of sometimes heavy fighting, Qaddafi was driven from power and killed. One official called it "leading from behind"; pundits debated whether in authorizing limited action in Libya the president had enunciated a new "Obama Doctrine" of limited international intervention.[14]

Death of bin Laden

As the Arab Spring ground toward a still quite uncertain outcome, Obama got to enjoy one of those rare moments of triumph that most chief executives can only imagine. On the night of May 1, 2011, U.S. Navy Seals in Chinook and Black Hawk helicopters slipped into a compound in Abbottabad, Pakistan, broke through locked gates, and stormed the residence, killing fugitive al Qaeda leader Osama bin Laden. After more than nine years, Bush's vow to take out the "evil one" was fulfilled. Obama had approved the bold and risky mission, and its success gave him a huge boost in prestige and approval ratings. Americans took pride in the remarkable achievements of their men in uniform. The nation enjoyed a rare moment of unity.

The success, at least for a moment, countered the image of the United States as an ailing superpower. Experts acknowledged that the death of bin Laden did not mean the end of al Qaeda. However, along with the killing of other top terrorist leaders and its obvious irrelevancy in the Arab Spring, it was plainly weakened. The United States had not informed Pakistan of this violation of its sovereignty for fear of leaks, and this blatant exposure of a widening rift with a key ally seemed the only negative in a cause for national celebration.

The G-20 London Summit was the second meeting of G-20 heads of state to discuss the condition of the world's financial markets and the global economy. Held in 2009, world leaders agreed to several commitments to encourage economic growth and pledged to make the G-20 meetings "the premier forum for discussing, planning and monitoring international economic cooperation."

SOURCE: Eric Ferferberg/AFP/Getty Images.

SHIFTS IN FOREIGN POLICY: *A TURNING INWARD*

Throughout much of its history, the United States has veered between periods of global interventionism in foreign policy and times of turning inward. Such shifts have been made possible, at least in part, by America's geographical position, which has allowed greater freedom of action than is possible for most nations.

Following an outburst of overseas imperialist ventures in the early twentieth century, and a protracted war to subdue Filipino insurgents fighting U.S. colonial rule, the United States pulled back to focus on domestic reform and consolidate the territories already held. Woodrow Wilson's "great crusade" during World War I was followed by the Senate's rejection of his proposed League of Nations and a decade in which the United States assisted other nations in solving some world problems but scrupulously avoided binding commitments. Between 1931 and 1941, the era of the Great Depression, U.S. foreign policy was more truly isolationist than at any time in the nation's history. A long period of global activism followed. In World War II, the United States assumed leadership of the Grand Alliance. During the Cold War, the threat of the Soviet Union and communism evoked unprecedented U.S. global involvement. The end of the Cold War and the collapse of the Soviet Union brought a decade of sharply lowered interest in the world and reluctance to intervene militarily. The dramatic events of 9/11, of course, sparked yet another time of global interventionism, including two wars in far-flung areas.

In this cyclical process, wars or other foreign threats spurred periods of global activism, sometimes taking the form of crusades to defend perceived threats to the American way of life by seeking to spread U.S. values abroad. On the other hand, disillusion with existing wars, the easing of foreign threats, or the emergence of urgent problems at home usually produced lowered interest in world affairs and focus on domestic issues.

By the summer of 2011, the United States appeared once more turning inward after a decade of intensive foreign involvement. In its causes, this shift followed established historical patterns: war weariness, a soaring national debt, and pressing economic issues at home.

By this time, the nation was burned out with war. The United States had been involved in Afghanistan since October 2001 and Iraq since March 2003. Total costs were estimated to reach as high as $3 trillion. To be sure, the nation as a whole had not shared in the sacrifice; most Americans had benefited from tax cuts. The volunteer military establishment represented only a small cross-section of the public. However, the costs of war burdened an already sagging economy and added to a soaring national debt. The military itself was perilously overextended. And for all this, Americans could see few gains. Iraq was still politically unstable and economically dysfunctional. The insurgency dragged on in Afghanistan.

The apparent easing of the threat from al Qaeda also contributed to America's turning inward. The killing of Osama Bin Laden in the spring of 2010 and the apparent crippling of his organization seemed to lessen the danger to the

United States to a greater extent than at any time since 9/11. The absence of any major attacks on the United States appeared to confirm this trend, permitting a reversal of the major shift in priorities brought forth by the awful scenes of destruction in New York, Washington, and Pennsylvania in September 2001.

Above all, pressing economic problems drove the turning inward. The Great Recession provoked the worst economic crisis in the United States since the 1930s, causing a collapse of the housing market, a rash of foreclosures, and unemployment that refused to drop below 9 percent. By 2011, the deficit had risen above $14 trillion and had become the focus of political attention. The truly crucial issue was jobs.

For many Americans, the persisting economic crisis called for drastic cuts in spending, including even defense spending. For many others, President Barack Obama included, the times called for a concentrated program of national renewal to rebuild the nation's crumbling infrastructure, reform and upgrade a faltering educational system, and stimulate research and development to put the United States back at the forefront of global innovation. President Obama repeatedly stressed rebuilding America as an essential component of national security. Recalling how the Soviet launch of the first satellite in 1957 awakened the United States to the challenges of a new era, he called for a "Sputnik moment" to once again regenerate the nation.

Signs of turning inward were abundant by the summer of 2011. A poll taken in June indicated that 56 percent of Americans wanted U.S. troops out of Afghanistan as soon as possible. Another poll indicated that solid majorities in each of the major political parties believed that the United States should "pay less attention to problems overseas and concentrate on problems at home." Since the Vietnam War, Democrats and especially liberals had been less interventionist than Republicans, allowing the GOP to smear the opposition as weak on national defense. What was striking about the new majority was a major shift among conservative Republicans, since the 1970s the most hawkish group in U.S. politics. To be sure, neoconservatives like Senators John McCain of Arizona and Marco Rubio of Florida still held strongly interventionist views. However, a sizeable majority of conservative Republicans, including many of the so-called Tea Party faction, agreed that the nation should pay less attention to problems overseas, a dramatic change since 2004.

A historic shift away from the globalist mood of post-9/11 thus seemed under way. It was not clear what direction the change would take or how far it would go. Predictions of a new "isolationism" were surely exaggerated. The shift might yet be aborted or blunted by new terrorist attacks on the United States or as yet unseen changes in world politics and economics. A change was well under way, however, and very much in keeping with the nation's historical cycles of interventionism and retraction.

The Impact of Recurring Domestic Issues

As with most triumphant moments, the boost to Obama and America's fortunes was short-lived. The U.S. economy went into another tailspin in summer 2011; unemployment rose again, and consumption fell. A terminally divided and rampantly politicized Congress went right up to the deadline to

pass legislation raising the nation's debt limit, thus avoiding a possible default with potentially dire economic consequences. Even then, it could only patch together a makeshift solution that did nothing to address the nation's fundamental budget problems. By rashly cutting government spending, the deal seemed likely to delay rather than promote recovery from the recession. Foreign observers expressed doubt that the United States had a strategy for recovery and growth, and even wondered whether the nation, only recently the world's greatest superpower, had the ability or will to lead the world out of economic crisis and play its customary role of world stabilizer. Economic mega-power China had come through the recession better than any of the developed nations, and its public chiding of the United States for irresponsibility during the debt ceiling crisis highlighted the dramatic changes that had occurred in the international system.

A little more than a year before the 2012 elections, U.S. foreign policy appeared to be at another major turning point. The seeming endlessness of the wars in Iraq and Afghanistan, the killing of bin Laden and apparent weakening of al Qaeda, constitutional squabbles over the president's power to intervene in Libya, and the emergence of increasingly urgent budget and debt problems seemed to have

fostered a growing consensus in Congress and the country that the United States should play a reduced role in world affairs. Even Secretary of Defense Gates, near the end of his tenure at the Pentagon, insisted, "Let's finish the wars we're in and keep focused on that instead of signing up for other wars of choice."[15] President Obama seemed to agree, and in the aftermath of the debt limit fight also proclaimed that it was time to focus on rebuilding America. The new consensus could be shaken by events abroad, of course, but for the moment the direction of U.S. foreign policy seemed distinctly inward.

See also: **Chapter 35: The Global War on Terrorism; Chapter 36: The Rise of China in the Twenty-first Century; Chapter 37: Africa in the Twenty-first Century; Chapter 38: U.S.-Israeli Relations and the Quest for Peace in the Middle East; Chapter 39: U.S. Foreign Policy Goals of the Twenty-first Century.**

ENDNOTES

1. G. John Ikenberry, "The Costs of Victory: American Power and the Use of Force in the Contemporary Order," in Albrecht Schnabel and Ramesh Thakur, eds., *Kosovo and the Challenge of Humanitarian Intervention: Selective Indignation, Collective Action, and International Citizenship* (Tokyo: United Nations, 2000), 97.

2. *The New York Times,* July 31, 2000.

3. Terry H. Anderson, *Bush's Wars* (New York: Oxford University Press, 2011), 70.

4. Bush speech to a Joint Session of Congress and the Nation, September 20, 2001, *The Washington Post,* September 20, 2001.

5. "The National Security Strategy" Paper, September 2002, available at: http://georgewbush-whitehouse.archives.gov/nsc/nss/2002; see also *The New York Times,* September 20, 2002.

6. This so-called Downing Street Memo was first published in the *(London) Sunday Times,* May 1, 2005.

7. Howard Fineman, in *Newsweek,* March 10, 2003.

8. The statement was first used by Rice, then by Bush himself: Bryan Burroughs et al., "The Path to War," in *Vanity Fair* (May 2004), 282.

9. Anderson, *Bush's Wars,* 127.

10. The Republican idea of privatization through a "shock doctrine" is developed in the book by Naomi Klein of the same name. For its application in Iraq, see Paul Krugman, *The New York Times,* February 24, 2011.

11. "National Security Strategy, May 2010," available at: http://www.whitehouse/gov/sites/default/files/rss_viewer/national_security_strategy.pdf.

12. Anderson, *Bush's Wars,* 224.

13. Ibid., 225.

14. Ryan Lizza, "The Consequentialist," in *The New Yorker* (May 2, 2011), 55.

15. *Los Angeles Times,* June 18, 2011.

FURTHER READING

Anderson, Terry H. *Bush's Wars.* New York: Oxford University Press, 2011.

Bergen, Peter L. *The Longest War: The Enduring Conflict between America and Al-Qaeda.* New York: Free Press, 2011.

Bush, George W. *Decision Points.* New York: Crown, 2010.

Drezner, Daniel. "Does Obama Have a Grand Strategy?" In *Foreign Affairs* (July 2011), 57–68.

Lizza, Ryan. "The Consequentialist: How the Arab Spring Remade Obama's Foreign Policy." In *The New Yorker* (May 2, 2011), 44–55.

Mann, James. *Rise of the Vulcans: The History of Bush's War Cabinet.* New York: Viking Adult, 2004.

Packer, George. *The Assassins' Gate: America in Iraq.* New York: Farrar, Straus and Giroux, 2005.

Ricks, Thomas E. *Fiasco: The American Military Adventure in Iraq.* New York: Penguin, 2006.

Zakaria, Fareed. *The Post-American World.* New York: W. W. Norton, 2008.

THE HANDBOOK OF KEY DIPLOMATIC TERMS, EVENTS, AND ORGANIZATIONS

T his handbook is a guide to identifying and understanding the essential concepts, rationales, incidents, and treaties that have been a part of and that have shaped U.S. diplomatic history since the nation's beginning. The handbook also defines nongovernmental players, international organizations or groups that often influence American foreign policy. Dates are included throughout to help the reader recognize the historical context of each term. For additional explanation, each entry is cross-referenced to the chapter(s) in which it is also discussed.

A

Adams-Onís Treaty (1819): Also known as the Transcontinental Treaty, agreement reached between the governments of Spain and the United States. U.S. Secretary of State John Quincy Adams and the Spanish Minister to the United States, Don Luis de Onís y Gonzalez, negotiated the agreement in order to settle differences between the two nations. Under the terms of the treaty, Spain ceded East Florida to the United States. In exchange, the United States assumed payment of Americans' claims against the Spanish government, up to $5 million, for damages caused by Native American raids. The treaty also established the border between the western edge of the Louisiana Territory and Spanish Mexico. The boundary was established beginning at the Sabine River north from the Gulf of Mexico to the thirty-second parallel north, then due north to the Red River, west along the Red River to the one-hundredth meridian west, north to the Arkansas River, west to its headwaters, north to the forty-second parallel, and finally westward along that parallel to the Pacific Ocean. *See also* Chapter 2.

African Union (AU): Launched in 2002, international organization of fifty-three independent African nations which replaced the Organization of African Unity (OAU) and is based loosely on the European Union (EU). The AU is Africa's foremost institution and major organization for the promotion of socioeconomic assimilation of the continent, leading to greater unity and solidarity among African countries and peoples. It is based on the common vision of a united and strong Africa; the need to build a partnership between governments and all segments of civil society, including women, youth, and the private sector; and the objective of establishing the necessary conditions that enable the continent to play its rightful role in the global economy and international negations. As a continental organization, it focuses on the promotion of peace, security, and stability for the implementation of the development of Africa. *See also* Chapter 37.

al Qaeda: Established in 1988, international terrorist organization, founded by the fundamentalist militant Osama bin Laden, which calls for global jihad. *Al Qaeda* transliterates from the Arabic as "the base." Al Qaeda ideologues envision the complete elimination of any foreign, namely Western, influences in Muslim nations and the creation of a new Islamic caliphate. Among the organization's reported beliefs are that a Christian-Jewish alliance is conspiring to destroy Islam and that the killing of civilians is religiously justified. Al Qaeda has attacked civilian and military targets in numerous nations, including Tanzania, Kenya, Turkey, Great Britain, and Spain. Most notably, al Qaeda was responsible for the September 11 attacks on New York City and Washington, D.C., in 2001, to which the U.S. government responded by launching a War on Terror. In May 2011, bin Laden was killed at his hideout in Abbottabad, Pakistan, by U.S. Navy Seals. Other al Qaeda members are presumed to be based in the mountainous tribal border region between Afghanistan and Pakistan. Known al-Qaeda affiliates operate in Iraq, the Arabian Peninsula, Yemen, Somalia, Libya, Egypt, the Maghreb, and the far western regions of China. *See also* Chapters 34 and 40.

***Alabama* Claims:** A disagreement between the United States and Great Britain concerning the capture, damage, or destruction of a number of Union merchant ships during the American Civil War (1861–1865). The CSS *Alabama* and other Confederate raiders were built in British ports, and the British government allowed the Confederacy to buy these vessels, after which the British-built ships attacked Northern shipping and helped break the Union blockade of Southern ports. The North claimed that these actions violated Britain's official stance of neutrality. After the war, the United States demanded that Britain pay for the damage. Discussion of the issue dragged on for several years. Finally, in 1872, after international arbitration supported the American position, Britain settled the issue by paying the United States $15.5 million for the damages inflicted by the warships built in Britain and sold to the Confederacy, thus ending the dispute and ensuring friendly relations. The use of arbitration led to a movement to codify international law with the hope of finding peaceful solutions to international disputes. *See also* Chapter 3.

Allied powers: Name given to the nations of Great Britain, France, and Russia during World War I (1914–1918). These first three Allied powers were also known as the Triple Entente. Joining the Triple Entente's fight against the Central powers of Germany, Austria-Hungary, the Ottoman Empire, and Bulgaria, were Japan, Italy, and, in 1917, the United States, as well as numerous other nations. The Allies defeated the Central powers when Germany agreed to an armistice on November 11, 1918. The name was used again during World War II (1939–1945) to describe the nations fighting the Axis powers of Germany, Italy, and Japan. The victorious Allied powers included Great Britain, France, Poland, Denmark, Norway, Belgium, Luxemburg, and many other European nations. The Soviet Union joined the Allies on June 22, 1941, after Adolf Hitler's armies invaded. The United States joined the Allies after the December 7, 1941, Japanese attack on Pearl Harbor, Hawaii, and numerous other nations joined the Allies as the war progressed. Italy surrendered unconditionally to the Allies in September 1943, and Germany surrendered unconditionally on May 8, 1945. Japan continued fighting until after the United States dropped atomic bombs on the cities of Hiroshima and Nagasaki. Japan surrendered on August 14, 1945. *See also* Chapters 8 and 9.

ambassador: The highest ranking diplomat representing a nation, an ambassador who has plenipotentiary authority. In modern usage, most ambassadors on foreign postings carry the full title of ambassador extraordinary and plenipotentiary. *See also* Chapter 2.

America First Committee (AFC): Organization opposed to U.S. involvement in World War II (1939–1945), which insisted on a policy of isolationism as the war spread through western Europe. Founded in September 1940 by two Yale University scholars, R. Douglas Stuart and Kingman Brewster, the group drew upon the widespread noninterventionist sentiment present in the United States after World War I (1914–1918). The AFC eventually grew to include about 850,000 members. Among its backers were Robert McCormick, the wealthy and influential publisher of the *Chicago Tribune,* and Robert Wood, chairperson of the board of Sears Roebuck and Co. One of the most prominent and outspoken members of the AFC was Charles A. Lindbergh, who, in 1927, had become the first pilot to fly solo across the Atlantic. The AFC also gained the support of many members of Congress, including senators William Borah of Idaho, Burton Wheeler of Montana, and Gerald Nye of North Dakota. Rather than military intervention, the AFC supported the development of homeland defenses to make the United States invulnerable to foreign attack. After the Japanese attack on Pearl Harbor, Hawaii, on December 7, 1941, the AFC promptly disbanded. *See also* Chapter 13.

apartheid: A legally sanctioned system of racial segregation and oppressive government policies in South Africa, enforced between 1948 and 1994 by the ruling National Party. The term *apartheid* comes from the Afrikaans word meaning "apartness." It was coined in the 1930s, but the policy dates back to white settlement in 1652. Following the general election of 1948, new legislation classified inhabitants into racial groups ("white," "black," "coloured," and "Indian"), and residential areas were segregated, sometimes by forced removals. Apartheid sparked significant internal resistance and violence as well as a long trade embargo against South Africa. Beginning in the 1980s, popular uprisings and protests were met with the banning of opposition and imprisoning of antiapartheid leaders. As unrest spread and became more turbulent, state organizations responded with increasing repression and state-sponsored violence. Although reforms to apartheid in the 1980s failed to quell opposition, in 1990, President Frederik Willem de Klerk began negotiations to end apartheid, culminating in 1994 in a multiracial democratic election. The African National Congress (ANC), under Nelson Mandela who became South Africa's first black president, won the 1994 elections. *See also* Chapter 21.

appeasement: The strategy of settling conflicts by meeting the demands of an opponent. The concept or policy of appeasement is associated most often with the 1938 Munich Agreement, in which British and French leaders conceded German control of a region of western Czechoslovakia known as the Sudetenland, which had a large ethnic German population. *See also* Chapters 12 and 14.

arbitration: A dispute resolution process in which the disputing parties submit to a neutral third party who examines all the appropriate evidence and then makes a decision that resolves the dispute. An early example of proposed arbitration in U.S. diplomatic history is the 1794 Jay Treaty, in which the British agreed to settle a number of disagreements through arbitration, thus helping establish the precedent. *See also* Chapters 2 and 4.

armistice: The cessation of fighting between warring parties, which may be temporary or which may lead to a permanent end of the war. World War I (1914–1918) ended with the armistice of November 11, 1918, which led to an uneasy peace under the Treaty of Versailles (1919). The fighting of the Korean War (1950–1953) terminated with the armistice of July 27, 1953. Technically, a state of war still exists between the Koreas, because the countries have not signed a formal peace treaty. *See also* Chapters 9 and 19.

arms race: The competition for military superiority between two or more nations to build the best armed forces, which includes increasing the size of the army and navy, stockpiling larger numbers of weapons, and improving military technology. In general, no absolute goal exists, only the relative goal of remaining ahead of the competitors. Beginning about 1890, an arms race occurred among the European Powers of Germany, France, Russia, and Great Britain. One of the primary causes of World War I was an arms race. After 1933, Japan, Italy, and Germany steadily developed their armed forces to make them equal or superior to the existing forces of France, Britain, and the United States. At the beginning of the Cold War, a nuclear arms race broke out between the United States and the Soviet Union. *See also* Chapters 21 and 24.

Atlantic Charter (1941): Agreement reached between President Franklin D. Roosevelt (1933–1945) and British Prime Minister Winston Churchill on August 9, 1941. Meeting secretly on the British battleship *Prince of Wales* off the Newfoundland coast, the two leaders framed and announced the charter, which set out the joint aims of Great Britain and the United States, including a common set of principles against Nazi aggression. The charter renounced territorial aggrandizement and proclaimed "the rights of all peoples" to choose their form of government. It also affirmed freedom of the seas and expressed hope for the "abandonment of the use of force" in international affairs. It further promised "freedom from fear and want" and called for the establishment of an international body to serve as an arbiter of disputes and protector of the peace, thus laying the foundation for the Charter of the United Nations (UN) in 1945. *See also* Chapter 13.

Axis powers: During World War II (1939–1945), the nations of Germany, Italy, and Japan, who fought and lost against the Allies—Great Britain, France, the United States, the Soviet Union, China, and a host of other nations. Italy surrendered unconditionally to the Allies in early September 1943; Germany surrendered unconditionally on May 8, 1945; Japan continued fighting until August 1945. *See also* Chapter 14.

B

balance of power: The existence of parity and stability between competing nations. Preserving a balance of power between nations has probably existed since ancient times. In 1815, after the Napoleonic Wars, Austrian Chancellor Klemens von Metternich organized what became known as the Concert of Europe, or the Congress of Vienna, to prevent the rise of a single dominant state or coalition and to establish a balance of power in Europe. In the later years of the Cold War, the United States and the Soviet Union, two superpowers, attempted to attain a balance of power through détente. *See also* Chapter 1.

Bay of Pigs: Failed invasion of Cuba in April 1961 by anti-Castro forces who were aided secretly by the United States. The covert military operation had the approval of the outgoing administration of President Dwight D. Eisenhower (1953–1961). Soon after President John F. Kennedy (1961–1963) took office, a group of Cuban émigrés, who had been planning to overthrow the Communist regime of Fidel Castro, invaded Cuba at the Bahia de Cochinos (Bay of Pigs). They hoped, with the help of uprisings in Cuba, to oust Castro and establish a more democratic government. They were disastrously defeated. Castro's forces were forewarned and well armed, and the uprisings within Cuba did not occur. In addition, the invading exiles did not have adequate weapons and almost no air cover for their landing. Most of the invaders, more than eleven hundred, were captured, and 114 were killed. *See also* Chapter 31.

Berlin airlift: The American and British response to the Soviet blockade of Berlin, Germany, which began in summer 1948. After World War II (1939–1945), Germany was divided into four zones with the Soviet Union, the United States, Great Britain, and France each occupying one zone. Similarly, the German capital of Berlin was divided into four occupation zones. After the United States, Britain, and France set up a common German government (which later became West Germany) in the zones they controlled in summer 1948, the Soviets blockaded all roads, railroads, and canals leading from West Germany to Berlin. Were the blockade successful, two million Berliners in the western sector would either starve or succumb to communism. Fearing that war might result if the Western powers sent armed forces to relieve Berlin, the United States and Britain decided to airlift food and supplies to the city. Through summer 1948 and winter 1948–1949, American and British planes flew about 2.5 million tons of food and supplies, including coal, to the West Berliners. On May 12, 1949, after establishing a separate government in East Berlin, the Soviets finally ended the blockade. Berlin, however, remained a contentious issue between the West and the Soviet Union until the fall of the Berlin Wall in 1989. *See also* Chapter 24.

Berlin Wall: Barrier between East Berlin and West Berlin (in East Germany), construction of which began in August 1961 at the direction of the Soviet Union. The wall, built of concrete and wire, became one of the most significant symbols of the Cold War; erected in the middle of a politically divided city, it was supposed to stop the emigration of East Germans to the freer and more prosperous West. In response to the Soviet's provocative action, President John F. Kennedy (1961–1963) enlarged all branches of the military and sent additional troops to Europe. He also sent Vice President Lyndon Johnson to West Berlin to assure its citizens of the determination of the United States to protect the city. Later in July 1963, Kennedy himself went to West Berlin to demonstrate U.S. solidarity with the city. The Berlin Wall remained a potential hot spot until the fall of communism in Eastern Europe in 1989. The wall was demolished that same year. *See also* Chapters 24 and 28.

big stick diplomacy: Foreign-policy principle associated with President Theodore Roosevelt (1901–1909), especially concerning his policies in Latin America. The term originated from the African proverb, "Speak softly and carry a big stick." Wielding his "big stick," Roosevelt used force or the implication of force throughout the Caribbean region to obtain rights to build the Panama Canal, to control Cuba's internal affairs through the Platt Amendment, and to protect U.S. interests by deploying American troops to several Latin American nations. *See also* Chapters 7 and 9.

bilateral: Of or referring to an agreement between two agencies, parties, or nations. Bilateralism is a foreign policy strategy that describes the political and cultural relations between two nations; for example, the United States and Canada cooperate bilaterally on issues of defense. The vast majority of diplomatic relations takes place on the bilateral level. *See also* Chapters 14 and 19.

Boxer Rebellion: In China, a 1900 uprising by a secret organization called the Boxers (in Chinese, "righteous, harmonious fists"). The Boxers took over foreign property, massacred about 300 foreigners, and besieged other outsiders in Peking (now Beijing), China's capital. The four major European powers, Great Britain, France, Germany, and Russia, joined by the United States and Japan, sent a joint expeditionary force to protect their nationals and their property. Many believed that China would be carved up as each nation established its own Chinese colonies. U.S. Secretary of State John

Hay announced that it was the policy of the United States to preserve Chinese territory and safeguard the principles of the open door policy. Reluctantly, the other powers agreed and China was not occupied. However, China was forced to pay a huge indemnity of $333,000,000 for damage sustained during the rebellion. The U.S. share was about $24,000,000; realizing that this sum was too much, American officials gave back half of it to provide for education for Chinese students coming to the United States. *See also* Chapter 6.

Bretton Woods system: An organized method of global monetary management that established the ground rules for international trade and finance among the world's major industrial nations. The Bretton Woods system was the first example of agreed-upon financial policies and institutions designed to govern monetary affairs among independent nations. As World War II (1939–1945) was still raging, 730 delegates from all forty-four Allied nations gathered in Bretton Woods, New Hampshire, at the Mount Washington Hotel, for the United Nations Monetary and Financial Conference. During the first three weeks of July, the delegates deliberated upon and signed the Bretton Woods agreements, thus laying the groundwork to rebuild a stable international economic system and establishing the International Monetary Fund (IMF) and the International Bank for Reconstruction and Development (IBRD), which today is part of the World Bank Group. In 1945, these organizations became operational after the required number of countries ratified the agreement. Based on a stable U.S. dollar with a value fixed in gold, the agreements became obsolete by March 1973, as foreign economies grew stronger and the dollar grew relatively weaker. *See also* Chapter 16.

brinkmanship: The art or practice, especially in international affairs, of seeking advantage over opponents by creating the impression that one is willing and able to push an extremely dangerous situation to the brink of disaster, rather than concede. In 1956, after ten years of Cold War with the Soviet Union, Secretary of State John Foster Dulles, who served under President Dwight D. Eisenhower (1953–1961), pointed out the paradoxical situation: "The ability to get to the verge without getting into the war is the necessary art. If you cannot master it, you inevitably get into war. If you try to run away from it, if you are scared to go to the brink you are lost." Perhaps the most infamous example of brinkmanship was the Cuban Missile Crisis of 1962. *See also* Chapters 21 and 24.

C

capitalism: Economic system based on free enterprise in which individuals or businesses, rather than government, own the means of production: land, labor, and capital. In a capitalist society, where there is an unrestricted exchange of ideas, individuals or businesses also contribute entrepreneurship. The system was proposed by Scottish philosopher Adam Smith in *The Wealth of Nations*. *See also* Chapter 10.

Central Intelligence Agency (CIA): Independent federal agency created at the beginning of the Cold War and charged with gathering and providing national security intelligence to senior U.S. foreign policymakers. President Harry S. Truman (1945–1953) signed the National Security Act of 1947, officially establishing the agency. The National Security Act charged the CIA with coordinating the nation's intelligence activities and correlating, evaluating, and disseminating intelligence affecting national security. The agency is organized into four basic parts: the National Clandestine Service, the Directorate of Intelligence, the Directorate of Science & Technology, and the Directorate of Support. Together, these groups carry out the intelligence cycle, the process of collecting, analyzing, and distributing intelligence information about foreign governments, corporations, and individuals to U.S. government officials. The director of the agency is nominated by the president with the advice and consent of the Senate and serves to manage the CIA's operations, personnel, and budget. In addition, the director has several staffs who deal with public affairs, human resources, protocol, congressional affairs, and legal issues. CIA operations are usually secret and sometimes create scandals when revealed; an example of this is President Richard M. Nixon's (1969–1974) pressuring the agency to cover up ex-agents' break-in at the Democratic Party's headquarters in 1972. On December 17, 2004, President George W. Bush (2001–2009) signed the Intelligence Reform and Terrorism Prevention Act, which restructured the intelligence community by abolishing the positions of director of central intelligence and deputy director of central intelligence. In their stead, the act created the positions of the director of the Central Intelligence Agency and director of National Intelligence (DNI), which oversee the Intelligence Community and the National Counterterrorism Center (NCTC). *See also* Chapter 18.

Central powers: Name given to the nations of Germany, Austria-Hungary, Turkey, and Bulgaria, who fought against the Allies—Great Britain, France, Italy, the United States, and others—during World War I (1914–1918). *See also* Chapter 8.

Citizen Genêt Affair: A 1793 incident in which Edmond Charles Genêt, the recently appointed ambassador of the new French Republic (proclaimed after the 1789 French Revolution), failed to present his credentials to President George Washington (1789–1797) in Philadelphia, then the nation's capital. Genêt landed instead at Charleston, South Carolina, where he was greeted with great enthusiasm. He ignored Washington's recently issued Proclamation of Neutrality, which declared the United States to be at peace with Great Britain and France and warned the citizenry to perform no hostile acts against either nation. Genêt persuaded Americans to aid the French cause and hired American ships to serve as privateers to attack British ships. Because Spain was also fighting against France, he encouraged frontier leaders to attack the Spanish in Louisiana and Florida. His actions were a flagrant violation of U.S. neutrality. When Genêt finally arrived in Philadelphia, Washington received him with cold formality and refused his requests for aid. Undaunted by the president's rebuff, Genêt continued to appeal to the American people to help the French. Washington, now thoroughly provoked, asked the French government to recall its irresponsible envoy. *See also* Chapter 1.

Cold War: The sharp tensions between the United States and the Soviet Union and their allies from about 1946 until the fall of the Soviet Union in 1991, which entailed diplomatic, ideological, and indirect military confrontations. Joseph Stalin (the leader of the Soviet Union from 1924 to 1953) believed it impossible for his Communist nation to exist side by side with the imperialist West. The Soviet Union, and later the People's Republic of China, precipitated crises around the globe in central Europe, Asia, and Africa. The issue facing the West became how to contain and prevent the spread of communism and a major war. Thus there began a cold war between the two sides which was characterized by a nuclear arms race and proxy wars. *See also* Chapters 17, 20, and 24.

communism: A political and economic system in which communal property is owned by the state and the state controls the economy, often through a single political party such as the Communist Party of the (former) Soviet Union. The Marxist-Leninist version of communism that was practiced in the Soviet Union in the twentieth century called for the abolition of class structures and advocated the overthrow of the capitalist system, based on private ownership, by the proletariat. *See also* Chapter 18.

Communist Party: Political organization that advocates the principles of communism through a Communist form of government. Hundreds of Communist parties exist throughout the world; in some nations, such as the People's Republic of China, Cuba, the Democratic People's Republic of Korea (North Korea), and the Socialist Republic of Vietnam, the Communist Party maintains absolute control of the state, including the rights of its citizens. In the United States, the Communist Party is a minor third party. *See also* Chapters 16 and 17.

containment: U.S. foreign policy designed to prevent the Soviet Union and its allies from spreading communism to other nations. In July 1947, in an anonymous article, State Department official George F. Kennan expressed the basic and guiding idea behind American activity in the Cold War. He wrote, "The main element of any United States policy toward the Soviet Union must be that of long-term patient but firm and vigilant containment of Russian expansive tendencies. . . ." *See also* Chapter 17.

Convention of 1800: Treaty reached between the United States and France which abrogated all earlier treaties between the two nations, thus formally releasing the United States from its defensive alliance with the French Republic. The Convention also ended the Quasi War with France (which occurred between 1798 and 1800), restoring peace between the two nations. *See also* Chapter 1.

covert aid: Military or political assistance given to a nation, rebel group, or other faction in such a way that the parties giving the aid may be known, but their responsibility cannot be proved. *See also* Chapter 38.

cowboy diplomacy: Term used derisively by critics of U.S. policy, which they view as heavy-handed and which may include the use of threats, intimidation, or direct military action. The term was used first to describe the big stick policies of Theodore Roosevelt (1901–1909); more recently, critics have used the term in reference to the policies of Ronald Reagan (1981–1989) and George W. Bush (2001–2009). *See also* Chapters 7 and 28.

Cuban Missile Crisis: Critical confrontation between the United States and the Soviet Union precipitated when the Soviets began establishing missile bases in Cuba in 1962; also the development that is generally considered the incident that almost moved the Cold War into a nuclear conflict. The Soviets had been sending Cuba military supplies and weapons, but the installation of missiles that could be launched against the United States, threatening its security and military superiority, brought dramatic American reaction. President John F. Kennedy (1961–1963) immediately declared a quarantine against all arms shipments to Cuba and sent naval and air units to intercept incoming Soviet vessels. He announced that the launching of a missile attack against any nation in the Western Hemisphere would bring "full retaliatory response upon the Soviet Union." The United States and the Soviet Union stood at the brink of war. After several tense days, Soviet leader Nikita Khrushchev (in power 1953–1964) declared that "in the interest of peace," the Soviet Union would destroy its missile sites in Cuba and withdraw its missiles. Kennedy praised Khrushchev's "statesmanlike decision" and agreed not to invade Cuba, as well as to remove certain types of missiles from Europe and Turkey. *See also* Chapter 20.

D

D-Day: June 6, 1944, the day the Allied invasion of Normandy (in France) began in an effort to liberate mainland Europe from Nazi occupation. Planning for the operation, code-named "Overlord," began two years in advance under the direction of Dwight D. Eisenhower, the Allied Supreme Commander. Before the D-Day landings, Allied planes heavily bombed the French region and smashed German lines of communication all the way to Paris. A fleet of more than 4,500 warships, freighters, and other landing craft carried the initial force of 176,000 American, British, and Canadian troops. Allied forces recaptured Paris in August 1944, and, aiming at the heart of Germany, slowly but steadily advanced toward Berlin, the German capital. *See also* Chapters 14 and 15.

Demilitarized Zone (DMZ): Buffer area separating two enemy nations in which soldiers, weapons, and military installations are forbidden. In the twentieth century, one well-known DMZ was at the seventeenth parallel, which separated North Vietnam from South Vietnam. Also, since the 1953 armistice ending the Korean War (1950–1953), the DMZ along the thirty-eighth parallel has separated North Korea from South Korea. *See also* Chapter 19.

Department of Homeland Security (DHS): Created in 2003, the cabinet department charged with preventing terrorist attacks on American soil. The department's establishment was a direct result of the terrorist attacks of September 11, 2001. Proposed by President George W. Bush (2001–2009) in June 2002, Congress approved the new department later that year, and it began operation in January 2003. The DHS coordinates various security functions that were handled previously by several different federal departments and agencies. In addition to working to prevent terrorist attacks within the United States, the DHS is responsible for coordinating information about terrorist threats and reviewing the vulnerability of the nation's infrastructure to possible attack. The department also enforces trade and immigration laws and protects against financial crimes, such as preventing counterfeiting of the nation's money. *See also* Chapter 39.

Department of State, United States: The oldest executive department of the U.S. government, established in 1781 under the Articles of Confederation as the Department of Foreign Affairs. After the ratification of the Constitution in 1788, the department was reorganized as the Department of State, and President George Washington (1789–1797) appointed Thomas Jefferson the first secretary of state. The secretary of state is the president's official adviser on foreign affairs and international diplomacy and is the highest ranking member of the cabinet. The secretary is in charge of State Department operations and is responsible for the overall direction, coordination, and supervision of American foreign policy. *See also* Chapters 16 and 17. **détente:** A French term that literally means a "relaxation of tension." It was used to describe the easing of Cold War tensions among the United States, the Soviet Union, and the People's Republic of China in the 1970s under President Richard M. Nixon (1969–1974) and President Gerald R. Ford (1974–1977). *See also* Chapter 25.

disarmament: The policy and process of limiting, reducing, or destroying weapons. Disarmament may refer to the elimination of one type of weapon, such as nuclear warheads; complete disarmament refers to the removal of all weaponry, including conventional arms. States or groups may be compelled to disarm or negotiate disarmament through agreements. *See also* Chapters 11, 20, and 39.

Dollar Diplomacy: An American policy, often associated with President William Howard Taft (1909–1913), which used the economic power of the United States to further the nation's business and political interests in Latin America and East Asia. The term, coined by President Theodore Roosevelt (1901–1909), involved American banks providing loans to foreign nations, thus increasing U.S. leverage within those nations. Taft, as well as his secretary of state, Philander C. Knox, believed that a major goal of foreign policy was political and economic stability abroad, which in turn would benefit American business interests. For example, dollar diplomacy was in evidence during the construction of the Panama Canal, the protection of which was behind many American interventions in the early twentieth century. *See also* Chapter 7.

domino theory: The concept, popular from the 1950s to the 1980s, that if one crucial nation in an area fell under Communist control, neighboring states would do so as well, falling like dominos. The theory, first cited by President Dwight D. Eisenhower (1953–1961), was behind the American policy of containment during the Cold War and was used to justify American intervention around the globe. *See also* Chapter 23.

E

embargo: A governmental ban or prohibition of trade with a particular nation, intended to isolate and weaken the other nation. Examples include the Arab oil embargo of 1973

against nations that supported Israel in the Yom Kippur War and the American embargo against exports to Cuba that has been in effect since 1960. *See also* Chapters 1 and 26.

embassy: The building that houses an ambassador and staff, most often located in the nation's capital; also, the diplomatic mission to a nation, usually permanent in nature. Embassies (the building and grounds) do not enjoy full extraterritorial status and are not sovereign territory of the represented state; the premises of diplomatic missions remain under the jurisdiction of the host state while enjoying special privileges, such as immunity from most local laws, by the Vienna Convention on Diplomatic Relations (1961). Diplomats themselves retain full diplomatic immunity, and the host country may not enter the premises of the mission without permission of the represented country. *See also* Chapter 27.

envoy: A representative of a sovereign government, often with a rank below that of an ambassador, sent on a special diplomatic mission. *See also* Chapter 1.

European Union (EU): A cooperative league of twenty-seven (as of 2012) European member states whose goals include promoting economic growth, removing trade and immigration barriers, and maintaining peace. The roots of the EU go back to the 1949 Council of Europe, an agreement among Western European nations to cooperate further among themselves. Starting with six original members, the organization officially became the European Union in 1992, when the founding nations signed the Treaty of Maastricht. EU citizens may travel between member nations without a passport or other documentation. The organization has eliminated trade barriers among member nations and, in 2002, introduced the euro as a unit of common currency (although some member nations have opted not to use the euro). In late March 2003, troops from EU nations took over NATO's peacekeeping activities in the Balkan Peninsula. *See also* Chapter 31.

expansionism: A national policy to extend control over additional territory, either peacefully or through military aggression. The Louisiana Purchase in 1803 is an example of peaceful expansionism; the policies of Nazi Germany and Fascist Italy in the 1930s are examples of militaristic expansionism. *See also* Chapter 2.

F

failed states: Nations that are perceived to have fallen far short of providing some of the basic conditions and responsibilities of a sovereign government. Among the characteristics of failed states are the loss of physical control of its territory, the erosion of legitimate authority to make decisions, the inability to provide minimal public services, and the inability to interact with other states in the international community. In addition, usually, failed states are plagued by widespread corruption and criminal activity, refugees, and sharp economic decline. Political observers differ in determining whether a nation is a failed state; however, most consider Somalia, Chad, Sudan, Zimbabwe, Democratic Republic of the Congo, Afghanistan, and Haiti to be failed states. *See also* Chapters 27, 34, and 35.

fascism: Radical type of government that promotes extreme nationalism and promises to improve the nation, usually through military conquest. Political and economic power are in the hands of a dictator or a powerful central government; however, unlike communism or socialism, the government does not legally control ownership of all property. In World War II (1939–1945), fascist regimes arose in Mussolini's Italy, Hitler's Germany, and Imperial Japan. *See also* Chapter 11.

Fascist Party: Founded in 1919, a political party that supports fascism, a national dictatorial movement that emphasizes the state over the individual and is opposed to both communism and democracy. Italy's Fascist Party rose in the 1920s under Benito Mussolini (in power 1922–1943). *See also* Chapter 14.

Federalists: Government leaders and other individuals who supported ratification of the proposed Constitution of the United States between 1787 and 1789. The *Federalist Papers* are documents that lay out the reasons for their support. Those opposed to the ratification of the Constitution were known as Antifederalists. Later, in the 1790s, when the first political parties emerged, the Federalist Party founded by Alexander Hamilton controlled the new government during the administrations of presidents George Washington (1789–1797) and John Adams (1797–1801). In opposition to the Federalist Party, the Democratic-Republican Party was founded by Thomas Jefferson and James Madison. Note, however, that the Federalists who supported the ratification of the Constitution are not necessarily synonymous with the members of the Federalist Party. For example, James Madison, known as "the Father of the Constitution," was a strong ratification supporter; later, he became a staunch Democratic-Republican. *See also* Chapter 1.

First Continental Congress: First governing body of the thirteen united colonies, established to present a single voice of opposition to Great Britain's taxation policies, especially the Coercive Acts (1774), which were passed in response to the Boston Tea Party (1773). Delegates from all the colonies except Georgia attended the First Continental Congress, which assembled in Philadelphia on September 5, 1774. The congress endorsed the Suffolk Resolves, which declared that the Coercive Acts were not to be obeyed, that Massachusetts collect taxes but withhold them from the royal governor until the Coercive Acts were repealed, and that strict economic sanctions be put into effect against Britain. The resolves also called for the people to arms themselves and form militias, and they pledged that all the colonies would support Massachusetts if attacked. To implement the economic sanctions, the congress adopted the Continental Association, a strict and extremely successful boycott against Britain which included imports and exports. In response, many British merchants angrily petitioned Parliament to repeal the Coercive Acts. British leaders, however, viewed the boycott as a symbol of rebellion for which the colonists must be punished. Tensions continued to rise between Great Britain and the colonies, leading to the battles of Lexington and Concord (1775). *See also* Chapter 1.

Five Power Treaty: Agreement among the United States, Great Britain, France, Italy, and Japan to limit naval armaments. Also known as the Washington Naval Treaty, it was negotiated in Washington, D.C., between November 1921 and February 1922. An attempt to limit the naval arms race that began after World War I (1914–1918), the treaty enjoyed limited success; at first, the signatories limited new naval construction and decommissioned many vessels, but by 1936, Japan declared that it would no longer abide by the treaty's terms. *See also* Chapter 11.

foreign minister: A member of the cabinet who helps form foreign policy for a sovereign head of state. In the United States, this position is occupied by the secretary of state; the position in other nations may be known as the minister of foreign affairs, minister for external affairs, or the minister of foreign relations. *See also* Chapter 11.

Fourteen Points: Promulgated by President Woodrow Wilson (1913–1921) in January 1918, a set of principles designed to serve as a blueprint for peace at the end of World War I (1914–1918). In his ambitious Fourteen Points, Wilson called for an end to secret diplomacy, the removal of economic barriers to trade, freedom of the seas, reduction of armaments, and the adjustment of colonial claims. He also pressed for the German evacuation of Russian, Belgian, Serbian, and Romanian territories; the German return of the Alsace-Lorraine to France; adjustment of the Italian frontier; self-determination for all national groups; and the recreation of an independent Poland. His final point advocated the formation of "a general association of nations" to guarantee the "political independence and territorial integrity of great and small states alike." Realization of this proposal was Wilson's highest goal during the Paris Peace Conference, which resulted in the 1919 Treaty of Versailles;

however, following strong opposition from isolationists in the U.S. Senate, the treaty failed to be ratified. *See also* Chapters 9 and 10.

free trade: A policy of international commerce in which merchants are permitted to trade with minimal interference from their respective governments. For example, The North American Free Trade agreement (NAFTA) is a trilateral agreement among the United States, Canada, and Mexico which seeks to remove barriers to commerce; it went into effect on January 1, 1994. Another massive free trade bloc is the European Union (EU), which, as of 2012, includes twenty-seven members and has taken on political, social, and diplomatic functions. The EU pursues free trade among its members, but not with outsiders. *See also* Chapters 31 and 34.

G

GATT: Signed in 1947, the General Agreement on Tariffs and Trade was a multilateral accord designed to regulate trade, and especially to reduce tariffs, among more than one hundred countries. According to the preamble of the founding document, the purpose of the GATT was the "substantial reduction of tariffs and other trade barriers and the elimination of preferences, on a reciprocal and mutually advantageous basis." In 1995, GATT was superseded by the World Trade Organization (WTO). *See also* Chapters 16 and 34.

Geneva Conventions: Formulated in international meetings in Geneva, Switzerland, a series of four treaties and three protocols of international law that require the humanitarian treatment of civilians in a war zone, as well as the same treatment for the sick, wounded, and prisoners of war (POWs). The First Geneva Convention, held in 1864, laid the foundations of humanitarian law whereby participants agreed to universal written rules to protect the victims of conflicts; the obligation to extend care without discrimination to wounded and sick military personnel; and respect for and the marking of medical personnel, vehicles, and other equipment using a red cross on a white background. In 1906, additional agreements to govern the treatment of sick, wounded, or shipwrecked armed forces at sea were reached and signed in The Hague in the Netherlands. The third Geneva Convention, held in 1929, addressed the treatment of prisoners of war, calling also for the release and repatriation of POWs at the end of hostilities. The Fourth Geneva Convention (1949) required the humanitarian treatment of civilians in a war zone and outlawed total war, in addition to expanding upon earlier protections. The singular term *Geneva Convention* is used often to refer to the 1949 agreements.

Three subsequent protocols have amended the 1949 agreements. Protocol I, adopted in 1977, calls for increased protections of civilians in international conflicts, including outlawing indiscriminate attacks on civilian populations and the destruction of food, water, and other items needed for survival. It also forbids conscription of children under the age of fifteen but allows for voluntary participation by persons under that age. Protocol II, also adopted in 1977, addresses issues of internal conflicts (as opposed to international conflicts), and, in deference to the sovereignty of national governments, it is more limited in scope. It requires that persons taking no active part in hostilities should be treated humanely, including military personnel who are no longer active as a result of sickness, injury, or detention. Approved in 2005, Protocol III added the Red Crystal as an emblem to be used by medical or religious personnel. This symbol may be used in place of the Red Cross. International law prohibits the misuse of these emblems. *See also* Chapter 29.

genocide: Systematic murder of a national, racial, religious, political, or ethnic group with the intent of annihilating that group. The term *genocide* was coined in 1944 by Raphael Lemkin, a Polish-Jewish legal scholar. In his *Axis Rule in Occupied Europe*, published by the Carnegie Endowment for International Peace in 1944, Lemkin includes an extensive legal analysis of German rule in countries occupied by Nazi Germany during World War II (1939–1945), along with a definition of *genocide*: "the destruction of a nation or of an ethnic group." Lemkin's concept of genocide as an offense against international law was widely accepted by the international community. It became one of the legal bases of the Nuremberg Trials, during which twenty-four Nazi leaders were charged with conducting "deliberate and systematic genocide—namely, the extermination of racial and national groups. ..." Following the Holocaust, the extermination of more than six million European Jews by the Nazis, Lemkin pushed for international laws to define and forbid genocide. In 1946, the first session of the United Nations General Assembly adopted a resolution that affirmed that genocide was a crime under international law but did not provide a legal definition of the crime. Then, in 1948, the UN General Assembly adopted the *Convention on the Prevention and Punishment of the Crime of Genocide*, which, in Article 2, legally defines the crime as: " ... any of the following acts committed with intent to destroy, in whole or in part, a national, ethnical, racial or religious group, as such: (a) killing members of the group; (b) causing serious bodily or mental harm to members of the group; (c) deliberately inflicting on the group conditions of life calculated to bring about its physical destruction in whole or in part; (d) imposing measures intended to prevent births within the group; and (e) forcibly transferring children of the group to another group." Horrific incidents of genocide have occurred recently in Rwanda, the former Yugoslavia, and Darfur in Sudan. *See also* Chapter 30.

Gentlemen's Agreement (1907): An informal agreement between the United States and the Japanese Empire which limited immigration from Japan and reversed the segregation of Japanese schoolchildren in San Francisco, California. In 1906 and 1907, diplomatic relations between the United States and Japan grew strained when San Francisco attempted to segregate Japanese children in its schools. At this time, American public opinion, especially in California, strongly opposed further Japanese emigration to the United States. The Empire of Japan looked upon this development as an insult and demanded equal treatment as a world power, especially after its 1905 victory over Russia. President Theodore Roosevelt (1901–1909) brought pressure to stop the segregation of schoolchildren and obtained from Japan an agreement to end the emigration of Japanese agricultural workers. *See also* Chapter 7.

Gilded Age: Lasting roughly from the end of the Civil War (1861–1865) to about 1900, a period of rapid change and economic growth in the United States. The term *Gilded Age* was coined by Mark Twain and Charles Dudley Warner in their book, *The Gilded Age: A Tale of Today* (1873). The era was characterized by new inventions, rapid industrialization, the growth of big business, the accumulation of wealth by entrepreneurs and industrialists, and ostentatious displays of prosperity by the rich. At the same time, the rate of urbanization increased significantly, city living conditions worsened, and workers toiled long hours under unsafe and often filthy conditions. The unionization of workers also increased during this time. By the beginning of the twentieth century, the nation had become the world's leading industrial power, surpassing Great Britain and Germany. The economic and social ills of this era led to the rise of the Progressive Era. *See also* Chapter 4.

glasnost: Social policy of free and open discussion of economic and political problems initiated by Soviet Premier Mikhail Gorbachev (in power 1985 to 1991) in the late 1980s in an attempt to save the Soviet Union from collapse. The then new policy of political and cultural openness produced unintended consequences. Gorbachev had weakened the nation's system of internal political repression, greatly limiting the ability of the central Communist government to impose its will on the Soviet Union's fifteen member republics. Ultimately, with an end to seventy-five years of single-party rule by the Communist Party, glasnost was a determining factor leading to the dissolution of the Soviet Union in December 1991. *See also* Chapter 29.

globalization: The effect produced when regional economies, societies, and cultural traditions become globally interconnected through a vast system of complex interactions, ranging from formal treaties to international investments and social networking. The foundation of globalization is economic expansion and connectivity; the goal is to create a single, universal market for goods and services, and this economic activity then spills over into the environment, culture, political systems, economic development, and physical well-being in societies worldwide. In the years since World War II (1939–1945), and especially during the past two decades, many governments have adopted free-market economic systems, thus greatly increasing their own productive potential and creating new opportunities for international trade and investment. In addition, governments have negotiated remarkable reductions of trade barriers and established international agreements, such as NAFTA and the EU, to promote globalized trade in goods, services, and investment. Technology has been the other major force in globalization. Advances in information science have given consumers, investors, and businesses valuable new tools for identifying and pursuing economic opportunities, including faster and more informed analyses of economic trends around the world, easy transfers of assets, and collaboration with worldwide partners. Still, globalization remains controversial, with proponents arguing that it allows poor countries to develop economically and opponents claiming that the creation of an unregulated international free market has benefited multinational corporations in the West at the expense of local enterprises, local cultures, and common citizens. *See also* Chapter 34.

Good Neighbor Policy: Embraced by President Franklin D. Roosevelt (1933–1945), an essentially successful U.S. foreign policy indicating that the United States would cooperate, rather than forcibly intervene, in the affairs of Latin American nations. The policy aimed to promote friendly relations and mutual defense arrangements among the nations of the Western Hemisphere. After World War I (1914–1918), American public opinion turned against imperialism and intervention in Latin America. In 1931, President Herbert Hoover (1929–1933) did not intervene when several Latin American countries filed to pay their debts, and in 1932, he withdrew U.S. marines from Nicaragua. Under Roosevelt, relations grew friendlier, and Secretary of State Cordell Hull arranged reciprocal tariff reductions in Latin America. In 1936, Roosevelt withdrew the last American marines from Haiti, and in that same year, he made a triumphal tour of Latin America. Cooperation from Latin American neighbors helped the United States win World War II (1939–1945). *See also* Chapter 12.

Great Depression: The worldwide economic collapse in the 1930s. In the United States, the Great Depression began with the stock market crash of October 29, 1929, and ended with World War II (1939–1945). During the Depression, trade, income, prices, profits, and tax revenues declined sharply; almost all nations of the world were affected. President Franklin D. Roosevelt's (1933–1945) New Deal was designed to pull the United States out of the Depression. Most countries set up relief programs to aid their citizenry and many endured some sort of political upheaval. In some nations, desperate citizens turned toward nationalist demagogues, the most infamous being Adolf Hitler (in power 1933–1945), setting the stage for World War II (1939–1945). *See also* Chapters 12 and 13.

Guantánamo: U.S. detention facility in southeastern Cuba. The southern portion of Guantánamo Bay has been under U.S. control since the 1903 Cuban-American Treaty, which granted the United States a perpetual lease of the area. Since then, the United States has operated a naval base there, nicknamed "Gitmo," which covers about forty-five square miles (about 116 square kilometers). The facility, established in 2002 by the administration of George W. Bush (2001–2009), detains captured al-Qaeda personnel, as well as detainees from the wars in Afghanistan and Iraq. Operated by the U.S. military under the Joint Task Force Guantánamo, the detention facility has come under severe criticism from human rights groups and much of the international community because of allegations of torture and other prisoner abuses, which the U.S. government denies. Although President Barack Obama (2009–) signed an order on January 22, 2009, to suspend the proceedings at Guantánamo and to have the controversial facility shut down within the year, the U.S. Senate would not support the administration. Instead, the Senate passed an amendment to the Supplemental Appropriations Act of 2009 (by a 90–6 vote) to block funds needed for the transfer or release of prisoners held at the detention camp. On January 7, 2011, President Obama signed the 2011 Defense Authorization Bill, which contains provisions preventing the transfer of Guantánamo prisoners to the mainland or to other foreign countries, thus effectively stopping the closure of the camp. However, the president strongly objected to many of the bill's provisions and stated that he would work with Congress to rectify the measure. As of February 2011, more than 150 detainees remained at Guantánamo. *See also* Chapter 35.

Gulf of Tonkin Resolution (1964): Authorization passed by a joint session of Congress that granted President Lyndon B. Johnson (1963–1969) as commander in chief, almost unlimited power to conduct the war in Vietnam and to repel or prevent any future attacks against the U.S. military. On August 2, 1964, North Vietnamese gunboats allegedly attacked a U.S. destroyer, the USS *Maddox,* in the Gulf of Tonkin off the coast of North Vietnam, and two days later, another U.S. ship was supposedly attacked. In response, President Johnson ordered retaliatory attacks on North Vietnamese coastal bases. On August 7, Congress authorized the president to take "all necessary steps, including the use of armed forces" to assist any nation that requested aid in defense of its freedom under the provisions of the Southeast

Asia Collective Defense Treaty. During fall 1964, Johnson sent larger and larger numbers of troops and equipment to help repel the North Vietnamese and the Viet Cong. By mid-1966, the number of U.S. troops had grown to about 350,000. Seeking to restore limits on presidential authority to engage American forces without a formal declaration of war, the Resolution was repealed in 1971, and Congress passed the War Powers Resolution in 1973, over the veto of President Richard M. Nixon (1969–1974), who also had used the Gulf of Tonkin Resolution to escalate U.S. involvement in Vietnam. The War Powers Resolution, which is still in effect, requires the president to consult with Congress regarding decisions that send U.S. forces into hostilities or imminent hostilities.

In 2005, a declassified National Security Agency study concluded that the *Maddox* had engaged the North Vietnamese Navy on August 2, but there may not have been any North Vietnamese Naval vessels present on August 4. The report stated, "It is not simply that there is a different story as to what happened; it is that *no attack* happened that night. . . In truth, Hanoi's navy was engaged in nothing that night but the salvage of two of the boats damaged on August 2." *See also* Chapter 23.

Gulf War: *See* Persian Gulf War.

H

Hay-Pauncefote Treaty (1901): Agreement between the United States and Great Britain, which was negotiated by U.S. Secretary of State John Hay and the British ambassador to the United States, Lord Pauncefote. Under the terms of the Hay-Pauncefote Treaty, Britain agreed to give the United States the right to build a canal across Panama, if the canal was to be open to all nations at equal charges. The Hay-Pauncefote Treaty negated the 1850 Clayton-Bulwer Treaty, in which both nations renounced building a canal under the control of one nation. *See also* Chapter 7.

Holocaust: The systematic, state-sponsored genocide of more than six million European Jews by the Nazi regime and its collaborators. The term *holocaust* comes from the Greek, meaning "sacrifice by fire." In 1933, when the Nazi Party came to power, the Jewish population of Europe stood at more than nine million. By 1945, the Nazis and their collaborators had killed nearly two out of every three European Jews as part of Adolph Hitler's so-called "Final Solution." With organized executions and mass exterminations, Nazi leaders also targeted religious dissenters, the disabled, gypsies, and some Slavic peoples. *See also* Chapter 14.

House Un-American Activities Committee (HUAC): From 1938 to 1975, powerful but controversial committee of the

United States House of Representatives, organized to investigate suspected disloyalty and subversive activities on the part of private citizens, public employees, and organizations suspected of having Communist ties. Through its power to subpoena witnesses and hold people in contempt of Congress, HUAC often pressured witnesses who testified to surrender names and other information that could lead to the apprehension of communists and Communist sympathizers. Most Americans agreed, especially after World War II (1939–1945) and with the growing fear of communism, that the U.S. government should expect that its secrets, particularly those of a military and diplomatic nature, were to be guarded closely. However, there was widespread disagreement over the necessity or desirability for limitations on freedom of speech and action.

In 1947, on President Harry S. Truman's (1945–1953) order, loyalty boards investigated all federal employees. Of the three million employees, about two hundred were dismissed, some on flimsy evidence, and about two thousand resigned. New revelations of actual or alleged Soviet spying along with Communist successes in Europe and Asia accentuated the concern of many people. In 1948, a former State Department official, Alger Hiss, was accused of having given State Department secrets to the Soviet Union in 1938 and 1939. During dramatic HUAC hearings, Hiss was convicted of perjury. Significantly, the accusatory interrogation employed by HUAC served as the model upon which the notorious Senator Joseph McCarthy (R-WI) would conduct his controversial investigative hearings in the early 1950s. Following Senator McCarthy's censure in late 1954, however, and his subsequent departure from the Senate, the American public grew increasingly wary of the outrageous "redbaiting" techniques employed by the HUAC, which was finally abolished in 1975. See also Chapter 17.

human rights: The basic political, economic, and social rights and freedoms to which all people are entitled. The modern concept of human rights can be traced to the aftermath of World War II (1939–1945) and the subsequent founding of the United Nations (UN). In 1948, the UN adopted the Universal Declaration of Human Rights; although the declaration was a nonbinding UN resolution, some people hold that it carries the force of international law. The declaration was framed by members of the Human Rights Commission, which was chaired by former First Lady Eleanor Roosevelt. Of the thirty articles, Articles 1 through 6 of the Universal Declaration of Human Rights state: "*Article 1.* All human beings are born free and equal in dignity and rights. They are endowed with reason and conscience and should act toward one another in a spirit of brotherhood. *Article 2.* Everyone is entitled to all the rights and freedoms set forth in this Declaration, without distinction of any kind, such as race, color, sex, language, religion, political or other opinion, national or social origin, property, birth or other status. Furthermore, no distinction shall be made on the basis of the political, jurisdictional or international status of the country or territory to which a person belongs, whether it be independent, trust, non-self-governing or under any other limitation of sovereignty. *Article 3.* Everyone has the right to life, liberty and security of person. *Article 4.* No one shall be held in slavery or servitude; slavery and the slave trade shall be prohibited in all their forms. *Article 5.* No one shall be subjected to torture or to cruel, inhuman or degrading treatment or punishment. *Article 6.* Everyone has the right to recognition everywhere as a person before the law." Beginning with the administration of President Jimmy Carter (1977–1981), the acceptance of human rights stands as a keystone of American foreign policy. See also Chapter 34.

I

immigration and foreign policy: The process of entering and settling in another country or area and the impact of such movement upon international relations. Other than the Native Americans, all people in the United States are immigrants or are descended from immigrants. Since the mid-nineteenth century and earlier, immigration, along with its impact on the nation, has been considered a foreign-policy issue. In the early years of the Republic, fewer than eight thousand people a year migrated to the United States, but after 1820, immigration gradually increased. From 1850 to 1930, the foreign-born population of the United States increased from 2.2 million to 14.2 million. During this era, few restraints on immigration existed as the rapidly expanding industrialized economy demanded more and more cheap labor.

Two notable exceptions to the open immigration policy were the Chinese Exclusion Act of 1882 and President Theodore Roosevelt's (1901–1909) Gentlemen's Agreement (1907) with Japan. Both of these measures reflected Americans' deep mistrust of nonwhite immigrants. Nonetheless, the highest percentage of foreign-born people in the United States was found in this period, peaking in 1890 at 14.7 percent.

Between 1880 and 1924, more than twenty-five million Europeans migrated to the United States. Following this period, immigration fell after Congress passed the Immigration Act of 1924, which favored European source countries that had already sent many migrants to the United States. This law reflected Americans' anti-immigration views of the time.

Immigration patterns of the 1930s were dominated by the Great Depression, and, in the early 1930s, more people emigrated from the United States than immigrated to it; immigration continued to fall throughout the 1940s and 1950s but increased again afterwards.

The Immigration and Nationality Act Amendments of 1965 (which abolished the Immigration Act of 1924) removed immigration quotas and legal immigration to the United States surged, especially from nations in Asia and Latin America. By the 1980s, only 11 percent of new U.S. immigrants were European. The 1990 Immigration Act (IMMACT) modified and expanded the 1965 act; it significantly increased the total immigration limit to 700,000. After 2000, immigrants to the United States numbered about one million per year. Also, despite tougher border scrutiny after the September 11, 2001, attacks, nearly eight million immigrants came to the United States between 2000 and 2005—more than in any other five-year period in the nation's history. Almost half entered illegally. Mexico has been the leading source of new U.S. residents for more than two decades, and, since 1998, China, India, and the Philippines have been among the top four countries sending immigrants every year.

In 1990, President William J. Clinton (1989–2001) appointed the U.S. Commission on Immigration Reform, led by Barbara Jordan, which lasted until 1997. The commission made the most thorough examination of the impact of U.S. immigration policies on American life of any federal commission to date. One key recommendation called for reducing legal immigration to about 550,000 people a year. The commission's recommendations have yet to be implemented, however. Immigration policies and their effects on the nation remain extremely controversial issues and they are likely to remain so for years to come, thereby affecting the nation's foreign policy and relations with the rest of the world. *See also* Chapters 2, 4, and 31.

imperialism: An expansionist policy of a stronger state's imposing political and economic control on weaker foreign colonies and possessions. The concept of American imperialism arose after the Spanish-American War (1898) and often refers to the military, economic, social, and cultural influences of the United States. The term was first widely applied to U.S. foreign policy by the American Anti-Imperialist League, founded in 1898 to oppose the Spanish-American War and the subsequent postwar military occupation of the Philippines. *See also* Chapters 6 and 7.

impressment: Seizing by force, by a person or government; first used in U.S. history to describe the British practice of forcibly taking sailors from American ships. The impressment issue grew to crisis proportions during the wars with France (1793–1815), when Britain needed all the men that could be found and was careless about whom they impressed, often taking any able-bodied English-speaking sailor. The American government tried to help its sailors by providing them with documents attesting to their American citizenship, but the British largely ignored these papers. Impressment

was a major issue that contributed to the U.S. declaration of war against Great Britain in 1812. The Treaty of Ghent (1814), which ended the War of 1812 (1812–1814), failed to address the issue of impressment. The British stopped the practice in 1814, after the defeat of the French emperor Napoleon Bonaparte. *See also* Chapter 1.

international law: A body of law—treaties, customs, resolutions, conventions, principles of law, and declarations of international organizations—that governs the conduct of independent nations in their relations with one another. Two basic categories of international law exist, public and private. Public international law focuses on governing relationships between or among different nations or between a nation and persons from another country. Private international law generally deals with individual concerns, such as civil or human rights issues, not only between a government and its own citizens but also in how its citizens are treated by other nations. The concept of international law has existed since the Middle Ages; in the mid-nineteenth century, international law became increasingly codified with the international acceptance of various agreements such as the Geneva Conventions. In the mid-twentieth century, the League of Nations was replaced by the United Nations, which today has become the center of researching and applying international law. Article 13 of the UN Charter obligates the General Assembly to initiate studies and make recommendations to encourage the development of international law and its codification. *See also* Chapter 16.

International Monetary Fund (IMF): An organization of 187 member countries that work to foster global monetary cooperation, secure financial stability, facilitate international trade, promote high employment and sustainable economic growth, and reduce poverty around the world. The IMF was conceived in July 1944, when representatives of forty-five countries meeting in the picturesque town of Bretton Woods, New Hampshire, agreed on a framework for worldwide economic cooperation that was to be established after World War II (1939–1945). These economic leaders believed that such a plan was necessary to avoid a repetition of the catastrophic economic policies that had contributed to the Great Depression and to assist with the rebuilding of the international economy after the war. The IMF came into formal existence in December 1945, when its first twenty-nine-member countries signed the Articles of Agreement. It began operations on March 1, 1947, functioning as a bank from which members could borrow money. Later that year, France became the first country to borrow from the IMF. Since its creation, the IMF has supervised the international monetary system to ensure exchange rate stability; it therefore encourages members to eliminate exchange restrictions that hinder trade. Since the worldwide economic downturn in 2008, the IMF has lent billions of dollars to countries to help boost the global economy that suffered from the deepest economic crisis since the Great Depression. *See also* Chapter 16.

internationalism: A policy that advocates strong relations among nations, including economic and political cooperation, to the benefit of all involved. Since its involvement in World War II (1939–1945), before which its foreign policy was isolationist, the United States has been unabashedly internationalist in its policy and world view. As one of two superpowers after World War II, and as the world's sole superpower since the end of the cold war, the United States has worked to assist democratic movements, arbitrate disputes between nations, foster free trade, and defend human rights. *See also* Chapters 15 and 16.

Iraq War: U.S.-led invasion of Iraq, which began on March 20, 2003, to overthrow Saddam Hussein. Based on mistaken intelligence that Hussein was stockpiling weapons of mass destruction (WMDs), prior to the war, President George W. Bush (2001–2009) and his administration had argued that the Iraqi dictator posed a serious threat to the United States and other nations. However, after the capitulation of Hussein's government, coalition forces found no WMDs, revealing that the intelligence information used to justify the invasion was faulty.

After the combat phase of the controversial invasion, coalition forces and the UN established a provisional government to rule Iraq until a democratic government could be established, and after the fall of Hussein's dictatorship, racial and religious tensions that had smoldered for decades exploded in the streets as widespread looting and violence erupted. Guerrilla forces, often called the insurgency, attacked civilians and soldiers alike.

Violence raged through 2003 and increased during 2004, with al-Qaeda-affiliated Abu Musab al-Zarqawi helping to drive the insurgency. In January 2005, the Iraqis elected the Iraqi Transitional Government to draft a permanent constitution. Although some violence and a widespread Sunni boycott marred the event, most of the eligible Kurd and Shia populace participated in the election. In a referendum held on October 15, 2005, a new Iraqi constitution was ratified; an Iraqi national assembly was elected in December, with participation from the Sunnis as well as the Kurds and Shia. Despite the slow steps toward self-government, insurgent attacks increased through 2005, and conditions in Iraq continued to deteriorate as bombings and attacks between Sunni and Shia sects raged throughout the following year. A December 18 Pentagon report found that insurgent attacks were averaging about 960 per week. In January 2007, President Bush proposed sending 21,500 more troops to combat the insurgency, as well as a job program for Iraqis, more reconstruction proposals, and $1.2 billion for

these programs. By mid-2008, violence declined, and most of the American people called for the complete withdrawal of U.S. military force in Iraq. On December 4, 2008, the Iraqi government approved the U.S.-Iraq Status of Forces Agreement. It established that U.S. combat forces would withdraw from Iraqi cities by June 30, 2009, and that all U.S. forces would be completely out of Iraq by December 31, 2011. Since 2003, more than 5,000 American troops have died in Iraq. On February 27, 2009, President Barack Obama (2009–) announced at Marine Corps Base Camp Lejeune in North Carolina that the U.S. combat mission in Iraq would end by August 31, 2010. The president added that a transitional force of up to 50,000 troops tasked with training the Iraqi Security Forces, conducting counterterrorism operations, and providing general support may remain until the end of 2011, when all U.S. military in fact left Iraq. *See also* Chapters 35 and 40.

iron curtain: Following World War II, term used by Winston Churchill to describe the political and economic division of Europe into western democracies and eastern communist bloc nations dominated by the Soviet Union. Although the term was coined in 1945 in a speech by Nazi propaganda minister Joseph Goebbels, it is more closely associated with Churchill's 1946 speech in Fulton, Missouri, when he described the realities of Soviet policy: "From Stettin in the Baltic to Trieste in the Adriatic an iron curtain has descended across the Continent [of Europe]. . . I do not believe that Soviet Russia desires war. What they desire is the fruits of war and the indefinite expansion of their power and doctrines." The popularized phrase "behind the iron curtain" was used to describe nations under Soviet control for more than forty years. *See also* Chapter 16.

isolationism: Also known as noninterventionism, a foreign policy of political, economic, and cultural seclusion from alliances with other nations except to achieve specific short-term goals, such as winning a war. After World War I (1914–1918), American public opinion grew increasingly isolationist, a view that was reflected in the nation's elected officials. Thus, throughout the 1920s and 1930s, the United States rejected the League of Nations, negotiated treaties that promoted peace or outlawed war, and passed several neutrality acts that prevented or severely limited U.S. aid to warring nations. American isolationism ended on December 7, 1941, after the Japanese attack on Pearl Harbor, Hawaii, which brought the United States into World War II (1939–1945). *See also* Chapter 11.

J

Jay Treaty (1794): Agreement reached between the United States and Great Britain which attempted to resolve several issues that remained after the signing of the Treaty of Paris of 1783, which ended the War for Independence (1775–1783). Under the terms of the Jay Treaty, the British agreed to abandon their posts in the Northwest Territory on or before June 1, 1796; permit American vessels of less than seventy tons to trade in the British West Indies; and grant some trading privileges in the British East Indies. However, the British did not promise to stop seizing the cargoes of American ships trading with France, and no provision of the treaty addressed the ongoing British impressment of American sailors on the high seas. Significantly, the British did agree that a number of other disagreements would be settled by arbitration, thus establishing the important precedent of using arbitration as a means of settling international disputes. *See also* Chapter 1.

jingoism: Extreme patriotism in the form of an aggressive foreign policy. The term is often used in reference to the foreign policy of President Theodore Roosevelt (1901–1909). *See also* Chapter 6.

K

Kellogg-Briand Pact (1928): Signed in Paris, a multilateral international agreement that attempted to ensure world peace by renouncing war. In 1928, the U.S. Secretary of State, Frank B. Kellogg, entered into negotiations with the foreign minister of France, Aristide Briand, to secure a treaty that would outlaw war as an "instrument of national policy" between their two nations. Jointly, the two leaders crafted a treaty for other nations to sign as well. Under the terms of the pact, the signing nations, sixty-two in total, agreed to settle differences peacefully. The Kellogg-Briand Pact, also known as the Pact of Paris, was only a declaration of intentions; most nations were quite willing to say they supported peace, especially because no means to enforce the pact were established. *See also* Chapter 11.

Korean War (1950–1953): Armed conflict between the Communist Democratic People's Republic of Korea (North Korea) and the democratic Republic of Korea (South Korea) and a proxy war between the Soviet Union and the United States. The war was the first military action taken to enforce the U.S. Cold War policy of containing communism.

At the end of World War II (1939–1945), Korea was divided at the thirty-eighth parallel, with the north ruled by Soviet-backed communists and the south in the hands of a government favorable to and aided by the United States. Allied leaders had made the division with the intention that the two regions eventually would be joined to form one independent nation. In spite of repeated efforts to unite the country, Korea remained divided, as neither the Soviet Union nor the United States would consent to unification that gave the other dominance. Suddenly, on June 25, 1950, Soviet-armed North Korea invaded South Korea, swept down the peninsula, and almost wholly occupied it. President Harry S. Truman (1945–1953) immediately asked for action by the UN Security Council and promptly dispatched American military aid to South Korea in what he called a "police action," intending to justify his sending troops without a declaration of war. The Security Council was able to act because the Soviet Union was temporarily boycotting it, and its representative was not present to veto the council's actions. The council condemned the attack and asked the North Koreans to withdraw behind the thirty-eighth parallel; it also called on member nations of the UN to send assistance to the South. When the North's army did not withdraw, troops from seventeen nations participated in driving them back, although most of the fighting was done by South Korean and U.S. troops, who together made up 90 percent of the UN's forces. With the backing of the UN, Truman appointed General Douglas MacArthur as commander in chief of all UN forces. The North Korean offensive continued through fall 1950, when UN troops pushed them back to the thirty-eighth parallel. Then a major question arose: Would the Chinese communists send troops to help the North Koreans? At first, the Chinese intervened with "volunteers" and aircraft, and then launched a massive counter offensive in November 1950, driving back UN forces. MacArthur wanted to bomb Chinese supply lines in the northern province of Manchuria, but Truman refused because of the likelihood that such an action would lead to full-scale war with China. By June 1951, both sides indicated their willingness to negotiate an end to hostilities, and negotiations dragged on for months. A permanent armistice finally was signed on July 27, 1953, establishing a demilitarized zone on either side of the thirty-eighth parallel. As a formal peace treaty was never signed, technically, state of war still exists between the two Koreas. *See also* Chapter 17.

Kyoto Protocol (2005): Linked to the United Nations Framework Convention on Climate Change, an international agreement that sets binding targets for thirty-seven industrialized countries and the European community for reducing greenhouse gas (GHG) emissions. The Kyoto Protocol was adopted in Kyoto, Japan, on December 11, 1997, and entered into force on February 16, 2005. Under its terms, countries' actual emissions must be monitored, and precise records are required of the trades carried out. By the end of the first commitment period of the Protocol, in 2012, a new international framework will need to be negotiated and ratified if the controls on greenhouse gas emissions are to continue to be reduced. *See also* Chapter 32.

L

League of Nations: A precursor of the United Nations, an international organization established by the Treaty of Versailles (1919) after the end of World War I (1914–1918). The idyllic vision of President Woodrow Wilson (1913–1921), the League's goal was to provide postwar order and maintain world peace. At the Paris Peace Conference, Wilson headed a committee to draft the plan for the League, a plan ultimately accepted as part of the Treaty of Versailles. Article X of the League's Covenant provided that member nations would "respect and preserve . . . against external aggression the territorial integrity and existing independence of all members. . . ." The league largely failed in its goals, as the European powers joined, but the United States did not. Many members of the U.S. Senate, which must ratify treaties, were staunchly opposed to the League, especially Article X, believing that it would commit U.S. troops to foreign conflicts. Senate leaders proposed drastic changes to the plan, but Wilson refused to compromise. In 1919, and again in 1920, the Senate voted on the League and both times the vote fell short of the required two-thirds majority. *See also* Chapters 9, 10, and 11.

Lend-Lease Act (1941): Law proposed by President Franklin D. Roosevelt (1933–1945) and passed by Congress as a means to aid Great Britain's war effort in the fight against Nazi Germany prior to American entry into the conflict. Under the terms of the act, the United States would sell, transfer, lend, or lease war materials and supplies to any nation "whose defense was considered vital to the defense of the United States." Any country would be aided in the way "the President deems satisfactory," and repayment was to be made on the same terms. During spring and summer 1941, the United States provided assistance to Britain in multiple ways. Military officers of the two nations held talks on possible joint actions; American arms and planes went to Britain in ever-increasing quantities; the American navy began to patrol the North Atlantic to search for German submarines and report their presence to the British; and the United States turned over oil tankers to the British. Lend-lease was later extended to the Soviet Union, China, Australia, New Zealand, and other Allied nations. However, it also became an initial point of contention in the emerging Cold War when the Truman administration inadvertently cut off the aid to the USSR (and then restored it) in 1945. The total approximate amount of U.S. lend-lease during World War II was $50 billion. The act expired in September 1945, after the surrender by Japan. *See also* Chapter 14.

Lusitania: British ship torpedoed off the southern coast of Ireland on May 7, 1915, by a German submarine, resulting in the loss of nearly twelve hundred lives, including 128 Americans.

In early 1915, Germany had declared it would sink on sight every enemy merchant ship in the war zone around Great Britain and had warned Americans to stay out of the area. President Woodrow Wilson (1913–1921) protested the German policy without result, and after the sinking of the Lusitania, issued three notes of vigorous protest, to no avail. Later, in August 1915, two more Americans were killed when a German submarine sunk the British liner Arabic, after which, Germany promised that liners would not be sunk without warning and consideration for the lives of noncombatants. However, in spring 1916, a German submarine torpedoed the French ship, *Sussex. See also* Chapter 13.

M

mandates: In foreign policy, a term used to describe the legal status of former territories of the defeated Central powers (chiefly Imperial Germany and the Ottoman Empire) after World War I (1914–1918), which were to be administered by the governments of the victorious Allies. These lands were to be governed with due consideration of the inhabitants, under the supervision of the League of Nations. The nations administering mandated lands were forbidden to construct fortifications or raise an army within the mandates' territory. *See also* Chapters 9 and 10.

manifest destiny: The idea held to be true by many Americans in the pre–Civil War era that the United States was meant to expand across the North American continent, stretching from the Atlantic in the east to the Pacific in the west. Although the term *manifest destiny* was first used by John L. O'Sullivan in 1845 in the *United States Magazine and Democratic Review* in an article titled "Annexation," the concept of westward expansion dates back to the time of the thirteen colonies and was expanded in the early years of the Republic. In the 1820s, Representative Francis Baylies of Massachusetts noted, ". . . our natural boundary is the Pacific Ocean. The tide of our population must roll on until that mighty ocean interposes its waters, and limits our territorial empire." The term itself fell into disuse in the mid-nineteenth century, but the idea that the United States has a mission to promote and defend democracy throughout the world continues to have an influence on American political ideology and policy even today. *See also* Chapter 2.

Marshall Plan: Foreign aid proposal put forth in 1947 by Secretary of State George C. Marshall to provide vast amounts of economic assistance to facilitate the recovery of Europe after World War II (1939–1945) and prevent further Soviet expansion into a weakened Western Europe. Officially known as the European Recovery Program (ERP), the plan stated that the United States would aid any government in recovery measures directed against "hunger, poverty, desperation, and chaos." To this end, from 1949 to 1952, the United States poured more than $13 billion into sixteen European countries. The Soviet gains in Europe stopped as the Western European nations rapidly regained their economic health. *See also* Chapters 16 and 17.

***Mayagüez* Incident:** In May 1975, a military excursion usually considered the last official battle of the Vietnam War. After the last U.S. military forces departed from South Vietnam in April 1975, in what President Gerald R. Ford (1974–1977) called "a humiliating withdrawal," U.S. military involvement in Southeast Asia was to have officially ended. On May 12, 1975, however, an American merchant ship, the SS *Mayagüez,* was in a regular shipping lane in the Gulf of Thailand, about sixty miles from the coast of Cambodia but only about eight miles from the island of Poulo Wai, claimed by Cambodia, Thailand, and Vietnam. Gunboats of the Cambodian navy seized the *Mayagüez* and then began towing the ship to the Cambodian mainland. When word reached the White House, President Ford was determined to prevent the situation from deteriorating. In addition, after the embarrassing withdrawal from South Vietnam after the fall of Saigon, it was believed to be diplomatically important to counter a growing perception among U.S. allies and adversaries that America was "a helpless giant" and an unreliable ally.

After intense deliberation in the White House, an extravagant plan that employed two destroyers, one aircraft carrier, two marine units with twelve helicopters, and a huge array of Air Force fighters, bombers, and reconnaissance aircraft was approved. President Ford believed that it was better to use too much force rather than too little, and military operations began on the morning of May 15. The destroyer USS *Holt* was directed to seize the *Mayagüez,* while Marines, airlifted and supported by the Air Force, would rescue the crew. At the same time, the aircraft carrier *Coral Sea* would launch four bombing strikes on military targets on the Cambodian mainland to convince the Khmer Rouge, the Communist government of Cambodia, that the United States was serious; the bombing apparently convinced the Khmer Rouge leaders that they had underestimated U.S. resolve. As the American assault on nearby Kho-Tang Island was raging, a fishing boat approached another American ship with white flags flying. Aboard were the thirty-nine crew members of the *Mayagüez.* Although the ship and its crew were rescued, eighteen Marines and airmen were killed or missing in the assault and withdrawal from Kho-Tang, and twenty-three others were killed in a helicopter crash. The names of the Americans killed in this incident are among the last carved into the Vietnam Veterans Memorial in Washington, D.C. *See also* Chapter 23.

Mexican-American War (1846–1848): Conflict between the United States and Mexico that began as a dispute over the southern boundary of Texas and concluded with an American victory. After the United States annexed the Republic of Texas in 1845, Mexico responded by breaking diplomatic relations. Mexico claimed that the southern boundary of Texas was the Nueces River, but Texas and the United States insisted that the border was farther south, at the Rio Grande. In early 1846, President James K. Polk (1845–1849), an ardent expansionist, ordered General Zachary Taylor to take up a position on the Rio Grande; thus, Polk purposely ordered Taylor to move into the disputed area. After several weeks, Mexican troops attacked the American soldiers. On May 11, 1846, Polk sent his war message to Congress, and two days later, Congress asserted that, "by act of the Republic of Mexico, a state of war exists between that government and the United States." Fighting raged through the rest of 1846 and 1847, until the American troops under General Winfield Scott occupied Mexico City, the national capital, in September 1847. In 1848, representatives of the two nations signed the Treaty of Guadalupe Hidalgo, in which Mexico was forced to recognize the annexation of Texas and the Rio Grande boundary. It also ceded California and New Mexico to the United States, helping to fulfill the concept of Manifest Destiny. This vast territory includes what is today the states of California, Nevada, Utah, most of Arizona and New Mexico, and small parts of Colorado and Wyoming—nearly half of Mexico's land. In return for this huge land cession, the United States paid Mexico $15 million and agreed to assume debts that Mexico owed citizens of the United States, which totaled about $3.25 million. *See also* Chapter 2.

military-industrial complex: Coined by President Dwight D. Eisenhower (1953–1961) in his final speech to the nation, term used to describe the growing influence of the military on U.S. economy and culture. As one of the generals of World War II (1939–1945), Eisenhower was opposed to an independent role for the military in shaping defense policy. He warned against the consequences of a close connection between America's military establishment and the huge arms industry, predicting a misallocation of power. In his speech he noted, "We must never let the weight of this [military-industrial] combination endanger our liberties or democratic processes." *See also* Chapter 24.

Monroe Doctrine (1823): Foreign policy principle warning European powers against involvement in the Western Hemisphere. Expressed by President James Monroe (1817–1825) in his December 1823 annual message to Congress, this policy became known as the Monroe Doctrine. It consists of two principle sections, the first aimed at Russia. It declared " . . . that the American continents, by the free and independent condition which they have assumed and maintain, are henceforth not to be considered as subject to future colonization by any European powers. . . ." The second section was aimed at those powers that might intervene in Latin America, stating, "that we should consider any attempt on their [European powers] part to extend to any portion of this hemisphere as dangerous to our peace and safety." Monroe also made it clear that the United States would not interfere in European affairs, saying, "Our policy in regard to Europe . . . [is] not to interfere in the internal concerns of any of its powers . . . [but] to cultivate friendly relations . . . and to preserve those relations by a frank, firm, and manly policy, meeting in all instances the just claims of every power, submitting to injuries from none." Although the doctrine was neither binding nor part of international law, it lasted because it asserted a policy that the United States found to be profitable for many years to come. Later, the Monroe Doctrine would become the cornerstone of American foreign policy in the Western Hemisphere, establishing a precedent for future administrations. *See also* Chapters 1 and 2.

most-favored-nation status: In international economic relations, a level of treatment accorded by one state to another for the purposes of international trade. In the early days of international trade, most-favored-nation status was attributed usually on a bilateral, state-to-state basis; one nation could enter into a most favored nation treaty with another nation. For example, under the terms of the 1794 Jay Treaty, the United States granted most-favored-nation trading status to Great Britain. Since the end of World War II (1939–1945), all members of the World Trade Organization (WTO) have most-favored-nation status, and all receive the same trade benefits as all other members. *See also* Chapter 16.

multilateral: Of or referring to an agreement among three or more parties, agencies, or national governments. In international relations, the term *multilateralism* refers to a foreign policy strategy in which multiple countries work in concert on global issues. International organizations such as the United Nations (UN) and the World Trade Organization (WTO) are multilateral in nature. *See also* Chapters 16 and 33.

Munich Conference: Meeting held in Munich, Germany, in September 1938, attended by representatives from Germany, Great Britain, France, the Soviet Union, and Italy. The Munich Pact, concluded at the conference, allowed Nazi Germany to annex the Sudetenland region of Czechoslovakia, where a majority of the population was ethnic German. Thus, the Allies allowed Germany to erase the boundaries established by the Versailles Treaty (1919) without taking military action. Upon his return to Britain, Prime Minister

Neville Chamberlain (in power 1937–1940) delivered his famous "peace for our time" speech to delighted crowds in London. At the conference, it was also agreed that the sovereignty of Poland would be protected; Nazi Germany violated this part of the agreement by invading Poland on September 1, 1939, leading to the outbreak of World War II (1939–1945). Today, the conference is generally considered a failed act of appeasement toward Nazi Germany. *See also* Chapter 15.

Mutually Assured Destruction (MAD): A national security policy and military strategy in which two opposing sides recognize that the full-scale use of nuclear weapons would result in the total destruction of both the attacker and the defender, and therefore agree not to attack. A policy based on MAD assumes that a war would have no victory nor armistice but only annihilation. It is based on the theory of deterrence, which calls for the deployment of powerful weapons as essential to threaten the enemy and prevent the opposing party's use of the same weapons. After World War II (1939–1945), both the United States and the Soviet Union gained a greater ability to deliver nuclear weapons into the interior of the opposing country. In the United States, the official nuclear policy was one of "massive retaliation," a term coined by Secretary of State John Foster Dulles, who served under President Dwight D. Eisenhower (1953–1961). This policy called for a massive attack against the Soviet Union if it were to invade Europe, regardless of whether the attack was conventional or nuclear. This policy was considered viable throughout the 1950s, 1960s, and 1970s.

The original idea of MAD was modified in mid-1980, when President Jimmy Carter (1977–1981) adopted the concept of countervailing strategy. According to Secretary of Defense Harold Brown (in office 1977-1981), countervailing strategy's response to a Soviet attack was not to include the bombing of Russian population centers and cities, but first to kill the Soviet leadership and then attack military targets. This would be done in the hope of a Soviet surrender before that nation's total annihilation and the destruction of the United States. This modified version of MAD was seen as a winnable nuclear war, while still maintaining the possibility of assured destruction for at least one party. This policy was developed further during the presidency of Ronald Reagan (1981–1989) with the announcement of the Strategic Defense Initiative (SDI), intended to develop space-based technology to destroy Soviet missiles before they could reach the United States. Since the fall of communism and the collapse of the Soviet Union in 1991, MAD has become irrelevant, as the United States and Russia have generally maintained a strategy of cooperation. During the administration of President William J. Clinton (1993–2001), another strategy was proposed: mutual assured safety. *See also* Chapter 20.

N

NAFTA: Trade agreement among the United States, Canada, and Mexico which went into effect on January 1, 1994. The North American Free Trade Agreement has led to greatly increased trade between the United States and its NAFTA partners. NAFTA created the world's largest free trade area, linking 450 million people producing $17 trillion worth of goods and services. *See also* Chapters 31 and 34.

nation building: The process of creating a national identity using the power of the state so that eventually the unified nation and people create a stable government. After World War II (1939–1945), the term referred to the building of national identities in newly independent countries, especially in Africa, where colonial powers had drawn random borders without any sense of tribal loyalties or animosities. Nation building included creating all the trappings of a national identity— national flag, national airline, national stadium, national myths, as well as building infrastructure. More recently, the term *nation building* has come to be used in a different context, namely the use of military forces in the aftermath of a conflict to effect a transition to democracy. In this sense, the term describes the efforts of a foreign power to construct or install the institutions of a national government. *See also* Chapter 40.

national interest: A plan that dictates a country's goals or ambitions, whether economic, political, cultural, or military. Nicoló Machiavelli is often considered the first political thinker to develop the concept of national interest. Today, the concept of "the national interest" is most often associated with political realists, as opposed to idealists, who seek to inject a sense of morality into foreign policy. In most countries, which goals and objectives constitute the national interest is a subject of much debate and controversy. *See also* Chapters 35 and 39.

National Security Council (NSC): In the United States, the president's primary forum for coordinating foreign policy and national security issues. Established in 1947, and chaired by the president, the council advises the president on "the integration of domestic, foreign, and military policies relating to national security." Policymakers created the NSC, convinced that the diplomacy of the Department of State was no longer adequate to contain the Soviet Union in light of the increasing tensions between that nation and the United States. Members include the vice president, the secretary of state, and the secretary of defense. The head of the Joint Chiefs of Staff is the military adviser to the council, and the director of National Intelligence is the intelligence adviser. The chief of staff to the president, counsel to the president, and the assistant to the president for economic policy are also invited to attend any NSC meeting. Other high-ranking government officials may be invited as necessary. The president appoints and the Senate confirms the national security adviser, who directs the various activities of the NSC staff. In 2009, President Barack Obama (2009–) merged the White House staff supporting the Homeland Security Council (HSC) and the National Security Council into one National Security Staff (NSS). Other nations have a similar advisory body. *See also* Chapters 16, 17, and 40.

nationalism: A pride and passionate belief in one's country (often also a particular race, religion, or culture). Nationalists tend to believe their nation and its leaders can do no wrong, beliefs that have resulted in episdoes of genocide and ethnic cleansing. Germany under Adolf Hitler (in power 1933–1945) and Serbia under Slobodan Milošević (in power 1997–2000) were nations that fueled extreme nationalist sentiment. *See also* Chapter 33.

Nazi Party: National Socialist German Workers' Party, active in Germany from 1919 to 1945 under Adolf Hitler. After taking power in 1933, Hitler proclaimed himself fürher, or leader, and with the support of the Nazi Party he rapidly transformed Germany into a police state. He advanced the idea that the Germans were a "master race" and that it was Germany's destiny to rule the world. The Nazis persecuted religious and cultural minorities imagined to be racially inferior and forced millions into death camps. Hilter's "final solution" was to exterminate more than six million European Jews in the Holocaust, a systematic campaign of genocide. With Germany's defeat in World War II, the Nazi Party collapsed. *See also* Chapter 12.

Neutrality Acts: A series of laws passed by Congress in the 1930s, the decade before World War II (1939–1945), designed to keep the United States out of another conflict in Europe. These laws included a prohibition on the sale of arms to foreigners and of loans to European nations that still owed money from World War I (1914–1918), though restrictions were eased as the war in Europe loomed. *See also* Chapter 13.

Nine-Power Treaty: Agreement reached in 1922, which was signed by nine nations: the United States, Great Britain, France, Belgium, Italy, Japan, China, the Netherlands, and Portugal. It was intended to make the 1899 Open Door Policy into international law. The treaty was unsuccessful as it lacked any means of enforcement; it was abrogated in 1931 when Japan invaded and seized Manchuria, a northern province of China, and established the puppet state of Manchukuo. *See also* Chapter 11.

nonintervention: The foreign policy of avoiding conflict (not directly connected to self-defense) and alliances with other nations while still maintaining diplomatic relations.

In the early years of the Republic, U.S. foreign policy was essentially noninterventionist as the nation's political leaders followed the advice of President George Washington (1789–1797) to avoid "entangling alliances." After the nation's participation in World War I (1914–1918), American public opinion strongly supported a policy of nonintervention, which was reflected in the nation's relations with other countries. *See also* Chapter 13.

nonstate actors: Groups or organizations that are not nations but play a role in international relations. The number of nonstate actors has grown significantly since the end of World War II (1939–1945), and several types operate in the international community. Nongovernmental organizations (NGOs) are groups, such as the United Nations (UN) or Doctors without Borders, which are typically considered a part of civil society. Multinational corporations (MNCs) are for-profit organizations that operate in three or more sovereign nations. Often the international media are considered nonstate actors because of the influence they exert on international issues. Violent nonstate actors are armed groups, including groups such as al Qaeda, Hamas, and Hezbollah. Criminal organizations, such as drug cartels or the Mafia are also nonstate actors. Religious groups, such as the Quakers, often are considered to be nonstate actors. For example, the Quakers are active in their international advocacy efforts and have in part founded other nonstate actors such as Amnesty International, Greenpeace, and OXFAM. Finally, transnational diaspora communities, such as the Roma in Europe, may be nonstate actors. *See also* Chapter 40.

normalcy: Term coined by Republican Warren G. Harding during his campaign for the presidency in 1920. During the campaign, Harding noted, "America's present need" was not nostrums [reforms], but normalcy." "The world," he said, "needs to be reminded that all human ills are not curable by legislation." Harding may have been alluding to the pleasant, peaceful life he had lived in Marion, Ohio, and in Washington, D.C., during his years as a senator. *See also* Chapter 11.

North American Aerospace Defense Command (NORAD): A binational military command between the United States and Canada established in May 1958 to defend North American airspace by monitoring human-made objects in space. With its command center located at Cheyenne Mountain in Colorado, the headquarters are responsible for detecting, substantiating, and warning of attack against North America by aircraft, missiles, or spacecraft. Through exceptional binational cooperation, NORAD has proven itself effective in its roles of watching, warning, and responding, and thus continues to play an important role in the defense of Canada and the United States by evolving to meet today's threats of domestic and international attack. The

events of September 11, 2001, confirmed NORAD's relevance to North American security by providing civil authorities with a powerful military response capability. In May 2006, the NORAD Agreement was renewed for the eighth time and a maritime warning mission was added. This aspect of the command entails a shared knowledge and understanding of the activities conducted in U.S. and Canadian maritime areas and inland waterways. *See also* Chapters 16, 31, and 35.

North Atlantic Treaty Organization (NATO): Signed in spring 1949, alliance among the United States, Canada, and ten European nations, for collective defense against a possible attack by the Soviet Union. From its founding, NATO encouraged political, military, economic, and cultural cooperation among its members. In addition to the United States and Canada, the other original members included the United Kingdom, France, Norway, Denmark, Belgium, the Netherlands, Luxemburg, Portugal, Italy, and Iceland. In 1952, Greece and Turkey joined the alliance; West Germany was admitted in 1955 and Spain in 1982. After the reunification of Germany in 1990, the former East Germany was incorporated as well. After the fall of communism in Eastern Europe, several former Communist nations also joined the alliance. Poland, the Czech Republic, and Hungary joined in 1999; Slovakia, Slovenia, Romania, and Bulgaria, as well as the former Soviet Republics of Estonia, Latvia, and Lithuania, joined in 2004; and Croatia and Albania in 2009. After the collapse of the Soviet Union in 1991, NATO turned essentially to crisis management, sending peacekeeping troops into Bosnia, Herzegovina, Afghanistan, and Iraq. *See also* Chapters 16 and 33.

Nuclear Non-proliferation Treaty (1968): Agreement to limit the spread of nuclear weapons and to promote the peaceful use of nuclear technology across the world. The treaty was proposed by Ireland and Finland, the first member states to sign, and it went into effect in 1970. More than 185 nations have signed the treaty, including the five recognized nuclear-weapon states: the United States, Russia, Great Britain, France, and China. Under the terms of the treaty, nuclear weapons states are permitted to keep their nuclear arsenals provided they do not transfer nuclear weapons to non-nuclear weapons states nor assist them in developing nuclear weapons. Three nations known to possess nuclear weapons are not part of the treaty: India, Pakistan, and North Korea. (North Korea acceded to the treaty, violated it, and in 2003 withdrew from it.) Israel, which has also refused to sign the treaty, maintains an official policy of "nuclear ambiguity," meaning it has never admitted to having nuclear weapons. Instead, Israel has stated repeatedly that it would not be the first country to "introduce" nuclear weapons to the Middle East. Nonetheless,

Israel is believed to possess between seventy-five and four hundred nuclear warheads and the ability to deliver them by missile, aircraft, or submarine. *See also* Chapters 16 and 40.

nuncio: A permanent representative of the pope, vested with both political and ecclesiastical powers, appointed to the court of a sovereign or assigned to a definite territory. The special character of a nuncio, as distinguished from other papal envoys (such as legates) is that the office is specifically defined and limited to a definite district (his nunciature), where he must reside. His mission is general, embracing the interests of the Holy See. The office requires the appointment of a successor when the incumbent is recalled or dies. *See also* Chapter 14.

O

Open Door Policy: Proposed in 1898 by President William McKinley (1879–1901), guiding principle of U.S. economic strategy that the United States as well as Japan and the European powers have equal trading opportunities in China. In 1898, Great Britain suggested that the United States join with it in supporting equal trading opportunities in China, an open-door policy regardless of which countries held spheres of influence in China. Secretary of State John Hay responded, in 1899, by sending identical notes to Britain, Germany, France, Russia, Italy, and Japan, asking each nation to grant equal trade privileges to the other nations. Hay's proposal was not well received in Europe. Only Britain agreed, and with exceptions. Nevertheless, in July 1900, Hay boldly announced that all nations had given "final and definite" approval and that the Open Door Policy was, therefore, in effect. After 1899, the Open Door Policy merged into a doctrine with more general applicability, one that stated America's interest in providing equal opportunity and nondiscrimination for trade and investment worldwide. *See also* Chapter 6.

Oregon Treaty (1846): Agreement between the United States and Great Britain which peaceably settled the Oregon question. By the 1840s, considerable dissension had developed between the United States and Great Britain over control of the Oregon Country. The United States claimed all of the territory south of Parallel 54 degrees 40 minutes north. Britain claimed the territory north of the forty-second parallel. In reality, however, the contested area was essentially the region between the Columbia River on the south and the forty-ninth parallel on the north. After the election of 1844, President James K. Polk (1845–1849), a fervent expansionist, accepted a British proposal to extend the international boundary along the forty-ninth parallel west to Puget Sound and south of Vancouver Island to the Pacific.

Polk wisely avoided a possible war with Great Britain when war with Mexico seemed imminent. The U.S. states of Oregon, Washington, Idaho, and parts of Montana and Wyoming were carved from the land received by the United States. The British area became the Canadian province of British Columbia. *See also* Chapter 2.

Organization of American States (OAS): Designed to address security issues and settle disputes, multinational organization made up of all thirty-five nations of the Western Hemisphere. The world's oldest regional organization, the OAS dates back to the First International Conference of American States, held in Washington, D.C., from October 1889 to April 1890. The International Union of American Republics was established at that conference, setting the stage for interhemispheric cooperation. The OAS came into being in 1948, with the signing of the OAS Charter in Bogotá, Colombia; the charter has been amended numerous times. The goal of the OAS, as stated in Article 1 of its Charter, is to establish among its member states "an order of peace and justice, to promote their solidarity, to strengthen their collaboration, and to defend their sovereignty, their territorial integrity, and their independence." Today, the OAS comprises the thirty-five independent states of the Americas, and it has granted observer status to sixty-three states, as well as to the European Union (EU). It is the primary political, juridical, and social governmental forum in the Western Hemisphere. *See also* Chapter 31.

Oslo Accords (1993): Officially known as the Declaration of Principles on Interim Self-Government Arrangements, or simply the Declaration of Principles (DOP), a milestone in the ongoing Palestinian-Israeli conflict. The accords marked the first direct, face-to-face agreement between the government of Israel and the Palestine Liberation Organization (PLO). The accords were intended to be the framework for future negotiations and relations between the Israeli government and the Palestinians within which all outstanding "final status issues" between the two sides would be addressed and resolved. Negotiated in secret in Oslo, Norway, the accords were officially signed at a public ceremony in Washington, D.C., on September 13, 1993, in the presence of PLO chairman Yasser Arafat, Israeli Prime Minister Yitzhak Rabin, and President William J. Clinton (1993–2001). Most significant was the PLO's acceptance of the right of Israel to exist and its renouncing its claim to most of the territory on which Israel had been founded. In return, Israel agreed to gradually withdraw its forces from parts of the Gaza Strip and the West Bank and affirmed a Palestinian right of self-government within those areas; a Palestinian Interim Self-Government Authority was also created. Palestinian rule was to last for a five-year interim period during which permanent status negotiations would commence, no later than May 1996, to reach a final agreement. Major issues such as Israeli security and borders, the status of Jerusalem, Palestinian refugees, and the future of Israeli settlements were to be decided at these permanent status negotiations. However, the accords have not been implemented fully and their future as a template for peace has become increasingly clouded. *See also* Chapter 38.

P

Pan-American Congress (1889): The first of a series of conferences held among nations of the Western Hemisphere. U.S. Secretary of State James G. Blaine initiated the conference in 1889 to establish closer ties between the United States and Latin America, hoping that improved relations would open Latin American markets to U.S. trade. Gathered together in Washington, D.C., eighteen nations founded the International Union of American Republics. The Ninth International Conference of American States, held in Bogotá, Colombia, between March and May 1948, was led by U.S. Secretary of State George C. Marshall. At this meeting, member nations pledged to fight communism in the Americas. This event led to the birth of the Organization of American States (OAS) as it stands today. *See also* Chapter 4.

peace dividend: Term used to describe the benefits that would arise from the decrease in defense spending after the end of the Cold War in the early 1990s. After the collapse of the Soviet Union in December 1991, many Western nations significantly cut military spending, thus freeing public money for other programs. *See also* Chapters 28, 29, and 30.

peace with honor: Phrase used by President Richard M. Nixon (1969–1974) in a January 23, 1973, speech, announcing the Paris Peace Accord that ended American involvement in the Vietnam War (1945–1975). The accord specified that a cease-fire would take place four days later and that within sixty days of the cease-fire, the North Vietnamese would release all U.S. prisoners of war (POWs) and all American troops would withdraw from South Vietnam. The phrase is a variation of a campaign promise Nixon made in 1968, "I pledge to you that we shall have an honorable end to the war in Vietnam." The phrase is considered euphemistic by critics, as Saigon, the capital of South Vietnam, fell to the North in April 1975. *See also* Chapter 23.

peaceful coexistence: Concept promulgated by Soviet leader Nikita Khrushchev (in power 1953–1964) that stated that Communist nations could peacefully exist with capitalist nations, as opposed to the Marxist-Leninist principle that communism and capitalism could never coexist in peace. The policy arose to reduce hostility between the Soviet Union and the United States, particularly as their growing arsenals led to the increased possibility of nuclear war. Khrushchev tried to demonstrate his commitment to peaceful coexistence by attending international peace conferences such as the Geneva Summit in 1955 and by traveling internationally. The policy also reflected a key shift in the Soviet Union's strategic military position—the move away from large, and possibly politically provocative, military ventures toward armed forces focused on proxy wars and the development of a strategic nuclear missile force. *See also* Chapters 16 and 17.

peacekeeping: Term defined by the United Nations (UN) as "a unique and dynamic instrument developed by the Organization as a way to help countries torn by conflict create the conditions for lasting peace." Peacekeepers observe peace processes in postconflict areas and help ex-combatants in implementing the peace agreements they may have signed. UN peacekeeping assistance may come in many forms, including confidence-building measures, power-sharing provisions, electoral support, and economic and social development. Thus, UN peacekeepers can include soldiers, police officers, and civilian personnel. *See also* Chapters 16, 34, and 40.

Pentagon: Five-sided office building located in Arlington County, Virginia, and home to the U.S. Department of Defense. The Pentagon is the largest office building in the world by floor area. Completed in 1943, the building itself, as well as the term *Pentagon*, has come to symbolize America's military might. On September 11, 2001, al-Qaeda terrorists hijacked American Airlines Flight 77 and crashed it into the western side of the Pentagon at 9:37 A.M., killing 189 people: fifty-nine innocent civilians aboard the plane, 125 people working in the building, and the five hijackers. *See also* Chapter 35.

perestroika: A policy of economic and political "restructuring" begun by Soviet Premier Mikhail Gorbachev (in power 1985–1991) in the late 1980s in an attempt to revive the languishing Soviet economy. Perestroika is considered to be a key factor in the fall of communism in the Soviet Union and Eastern Europe, as well as a cause of the end of the Cold War. *See also* Chapter 29.

Persian Gulf War (1991): Conflict between Iraq and a U.S.-led coalition of more than thirty nations, including Great Britain, France, Egypt, and Saudi Arabia. The goal of the war was to drive the Iraqi army out of neighboring Kuwait, which Iraq had invaded on August 2, 1990, claiming that Kuwait was stealing Iraqi oil. Iraq then annexed Kuwait, which it had long claimed as its nineteenth province. During the Iraqi occupation, about one thousand Kuwaiti civilians were killed, and more than 300,000 people fled the country. The United Nations Security Council condemned the invasion and called for Iraq to withdraw immediately from Kuwait, which Iraq ignored; on November 29, the UN set January 15, 1991, as the deadline for Iraqi withdrawal. When Iraqi dictator Saddam Hussein refused to comply, the UN-sanctioned invasion, known as Operation Desert Storm, was launched on January 17, 1991, under the leadership of U.S. General Norman Schwarzkopf. The U.S.-led coalition began a massive air campaign, flying more than 100,000 sorties, dropping 88,500 tons of bombs, and widely destroying military and civilian infrastructure. In response, Iraq launched Scud missiles at Israel (in an unsuccessful attempt to widen the war and break up the coalition) and at Saudi Arabia. Coalition forces invaded Kuwait and Iraq on February 24, and over the next four days, encircled and defeated the Iraqis and liberated Kuwait. When President George H. W. Bush (1989–1993) declared a cease fire on February 28, most of the Iraqi forces in Kuwait had either surrendered or fled. Although the exact number of Iraqi combat casualties is unknown, it is believed to have been between twenty thousand and thirty-five thousand fatalities. As of February 2011, the United States Department of Defense reported that U.S. forces suffered 148 battle-related deaths and another 145 deaths in noncombat accidents. *See also* Chapters 38 and 39.

Pinckney's Treaty (1795): Also known as the Treaty of Madrid or the Treaty of San Lorenzo, agreement reached by the United States and Spain which settled several key disagreements between the two nations. Thomas Pinckney, then the U.S. ambassador to Great Britain, negotiated the treaty for the United States, and Don Manuel de Godoy represented Spain. Under the terms of Pinckney's Treaty, the lower Mississippi River was opened to navigation by Americans, and New Orleans was established as a "port of deposit" for American goods. Spain also recognized the borders of the United States as established by the Treaty of Paris of 1783, namely the Mississippi River as the western boundary and the thirty-first parallel as the southern boundary. *See also* Chapter 1.

ping-pong diplomacy: Term that refers to the visit of ping pong players from the United States to the People's Republic of China (PRC) in the early 1970s. The friendly games initiated a thaw in the relations between the United States and China, which at the time was considered one of America's staunchest foes. The games paved the way to a visit to China by President Richard M. Nixon (1969–1974) in 1972. The U.S. Table Tennis team was in Nagoya, Japan, in 1971, for the Thirty-first World Table Tennis Championship when, on April 6, they received an invitation to visit China. On April 10, 1971, the team became the first American sports delegation

to set foot in Beijing, the Chinese capital, since 1949. In addition to playing friendly games of ping pong, the Americans also toured the Great Wall and the Summer Palace. President Nixon's subsequent visit to the People's Republic of China was an important step in formally normalizing relations between the two nations. During the week of June 9, 2008, a three-day Ping Pong Diplomacy event was held at the Richard Nixon Presidential Library and Museum in Yorba Linda, California. Original members of both the Chinese and American ping pong teams from 1971 were present and played. *See also* Chapter 35.

Platt Amendment: A rider attached to the Army Appropriations Act passed by Congress in 1901, after victorious U.S. forces occupied Cuba following the Spanish-American War (1898). The amendment stipulated the conditions for the withdrawal of U.S. troops remaining in Cuba, declared that Cuba could make no agreement that would affect its independence, stated that the United States could intervene to keep order, and stipulated that the United States was to be given land, by sale or lease, for naval bases. Guantánamo became one of these bases. Thus, although Cuba became independent in name, the nation in many ways remained under control of the United States. The amendment defined Cuban-U.S. relations until the 1934 Treaty of Relations. *See also* Chapters 6 and 7.

Potsdam Conference (1945): Final meeting of the three great powers—the United States, Great Britain, and the Soviet Union—in July and August 1945, held in Potsdam, near Berlin. As in other such meetings, Joseph Stalin (in power 1924–1953) represented the Soviet Union, but President Harry S. Truman (1945–1953) took the place of the late Franklin D. Roosevelt (1933–1945), and Clement B. Attlee (1945–1951), as the new prime minister of Great Britain, replaced Winston Churchill (1940–1945, 1951–1955) as the talks went forward. The goal was to determine the fate of Germany and the lands it had invaded during World War II (1939–1945). By this time, Soviet armies occupied most of Eastern Europe, Bulgaria, Hungary, Poland, and Romania, and it became clear at this conference that Stalin was determined to retain control of these nations and make them satellites of the Soviet Union. Although the leaders of the Allied powers were determined to eliminate Nazi influence and prevent Germany from again becoming a military threat, little was accomplished at the conference. Germany and Austria were divided into four zones, with the Soviet Union, the United States, Britain, and France each occupying one zone. Western access to Berlin was acknowledged, but the Soviet Union refused to conclude any official agreement about the future of Germany. As there was no agreement on specific peace treaties, negotiations continued; not until 1947 were treaties worked out for Italy, Bulgaria, Finland,

and Hungary. Significantly, the three leaders did agree to the prosecution of Nazi war criminals, leading to the Nuremburg Trials that began in November 1945 and lasted until October 1946. *See also* Chapter 16.

Powell Doctrine: A term, created by the media, used to describe a list of specific questions promulgated by General Colin L. Powell before the beginning of the Persian Gulf War (1991). These diplomatic questions, which must be answered (in the affirmative) before military action is undertaken, are: "Is a vital national security interest threatened? Do we have a clear attainable objective? Have the risks and costs been fully and frankly analyzed? Have all other nonviolent policy means been fully exhausted? Is there a plausible exit strategy to avoid endless entanglement? Have the consequences of our action been fully considered? Is the action supported by the American people? Do we have genuine broad international support?" The Powell Doctrine is similar to a set of principles defined by Caspar Weinberger, defense secretary (in office 1981-1987) during the administration of Ronald Reagan (1981–1989). Although Powell rarely advocated force as the first solution to international conflict, he later expanded upon the doctrine, asserting that when a nation is at war, every resource should be used against the enemy, while at the same time minimizing U.S. casualties. In a 2009 interview, Powell noted that the doctrine also calls for the exhausting of all "political, economic, and diplomatic means," before a nation should resort to military force. *See also* Chapter 35.

prisoner of war (POW): In or after an armed conflict, an individual, either civilian or combatant, who is held by an enemy power. The earliest recorded usage of the phrase is in 1660. The Hague Convention (1907), the subsequent Geneva Convention (1929), and the 1949 update to the 1929 convention, covered the treatment of prisoners of war in detail. One of the major provisions of the convention makes it illegal to torture prisoners and states that prisoners can only be required to give their name, date of birth, rank, and service number. During the twentieth century, Imperial Japan and Nazi Germany were known to commit atrocities against prisoners of war during World War II (1939–1945). The German military used the Soviet Union's refusal to sign the Geneva Convention as a reason for not providing the necessities of life to Soviet POWs. North Korean and North and South Vietnamese forces regularly killed or mistreated prisoners taken during those conflicts. Since the Vietnam War (1945–1975), the official U.S. military term for enemy POWs is Enemy Prisoner of War (EPW). This change was introduced to distinguish between enemy and U.S. captives. *See also* Chapters 9, 14, and 23.

proxy war: A war in which two nations support military action between other parties, rather than fighting each other directly. During the Cold War era, the Korean War (1950–1953) and the Vietnam War (1945–1975) were proxy wars between the United States and the Soviet Union. *See also* Chapters 19 and 23.

puppet state: A nation that is controlled by another more powerful nation. A puppet state lacks independence, but the controlling power preserves all the external trappings of independence, such as a national flag, currency, and leadership. In the twentieth century, for example, Imperial Japan invaded Manchuria, a northern province of China, and established the puppet state of Manchukuo. *See also* Chapters 12 and 13.

Q

Quasi War: Lasting from 1798 to 1800, an undeclared war between the United States and France. After the XYZ Affair, indignation rose and many Americans called for war against France. Although President John Adams (1797–1801) was committed to peace, the United States and France fought each other at sea where American ships captured several French vessels and harassed French commerce in the Caribbean region. In 1800, after the French foreign minister, the Duc de Talleyrand, indicated that ministers from the United States would be received with all due respect, Adams sent a commission to France. By that time, First Consul Napoleon Bonaparte had assumed power and offered a more conciliatory diplomatic stance. As a result, the commission worked successfully with the French and signed the Convention of 1800 on September 30, ending the Quasi War. *See also* Chapter 1.

R

Reconstruction: Period in U.S. history immediately following the Civil War (1861–1865) to 1877, when President Rutherford B. Hayes (1877–1881) ordered the removal of federal troops from the vanquished South. After the turmoil of civil war, the South was in ruins, governmental functions stopped, and the economy was in shambles. Reconstruction-era laws, supported by northern radical Republicans, attempted to restore the seceded states to the Union, establish new governments, and secure the rights of the recently freed slaves. After Hayes withdrew federal troops from the South in 1877, white supremacy was restored throughout the region. The Democratic Party took control of state and local governments and quickly passed laws, known as Jim Crow laws, which restricted the rights of African Americans and denied them many of the rights they had gained during Reconstruction, including the right to vote. Politically, the region became known as the "Solid South," as it overwhelmingly supported the Democratic Party and was vital to the party's success. Many later foreign policy issues have their roots in the Reconstruction period. For example, during Reconstruction, the number of immigrants, mostly European, began to increase, thus creating a cheap labor force for rapid industrialization and improved agriculture, which later made the United States a world economic power. While Europeans were welcomed, for the most part, Asian immigrants were not. Anti-Chinese sentiments in California and the west ultimately resulted in the passage of the 1882 Chinese Exclusion Act. Later, the informal 1907 Gentlemen's Agreement greatly limited Japanese immigration. *See also* Chapters 3 and 4.

red scare: Term used after both World War I (1914–1918) and World War II (1939–1945) to describe the fear of rising communism in the United States. Near the end of World War I, a Communist revolution occurred in Russia, and its leaders supported revolution worldwide. The fear of communism mounted in the United States, especially after a wave of strikes and several isolated bombings in 1919 and 1920. The strikes and bombings were blamed on the communists and led the federal government to vigorously search for "Reds." During this time, several hundred aliens were imprisoned and deported, often without due process of law. After World War II, a fear of communists infiltrating the government seized the nation, and the term *red scare* was again applied to this panic. Senator Joseph McCarthy's widespread accusations that the State Department was "thoroughly infested with Communists," which he claimed posed a threat to national security, epitomized the red scare of the early 1950s. For more than three years, McCarthy and his zealous supporters mounted a paranoid crusade searching for Communist influences on American culture, even falsely accusing Republican officials in the administration of Dwight D. Eisenhower (1953–1961) of favoring communism. McCarthy lost his following after the nation saw him on television tearing into witnesses during a hearing in which he accused the U.S. army of "softness on communism." In December 1954, the U.S. Senate censured McCarthy for acting "contrary to senatorial ethics" and obstructing the "constitutional processes of the Senate." *See also* Chapters 16 and 17.

refugee: A person who has been forced to leave his or her home country and seek refuge elsewhere. The 1951 United Nations Convention Relating to the Status of Refugees defined a refugee as a person who "owing to a well-founded fear of being persecuted for reasons of race, religion, nationality, membership of a particular social group, or political opinion, is outside the country of his nationality, and is unable to or, owing to such fear, is unwilling to avail himself of the protection of that country." Under U.S. law, to apply for refugee status, the applicant must be located physically outside the United States. One year after legally being granted refugee status in the United States, the applicant may apply for a Green Card, indicating lawful permanent residence, and eventually for U.S. citizenship. *See also* Chapters 16 and 23.

rivalries: In international relations, competition between nations or groups of nations. During the Cold War, the Soviet Union and its satellite states and the United States and its allies exhibited worldwide rivalry, which led to competition in influencing nonaligned nations, a costly arms race, the space race, and a struggle to develop superior technologies. *See also* Chapters 17, 26, and 28.

rogue states: Nations that reject international law and are considered to be threats to world peace. Rogue states are known to restrict human rights, sponsor terrorism, and seek weapons of mass destruction (WMDs). In the 1990s, the U.S. government considered North Korea, Cuba, Iran, Iraq, Afghanistan, Syria, Sudan, and Yugoslavia to be rogue states. Yugoslavia was removed from the list after the overthrow of Slobodan Milošević in 2000. Afghanistan was removed from the list after the 2001 U.S.-led invasion of that nation; Iraq was removed in 2003 after U.S.-led forces invaded and Saddam Hussein fled from power. Using diplomacy, Libya worked to remove itself from the list of rogue states. Rogue states are feared and condemned by the international community but are differentiated from "pariah states," such as Zimbabwe and Myanmar (Burma), which restrict and abuse the human rights of their citizenry but are not perceived as threats beyond their own borders. *See also* Chapter 35.

Roosevelt Corollary: Foreign policy pronouncement made by President Theodore Roosevelt (1901–1909) in his 1904 annual message to Congress in which he expanded upon the Monroe Doctrine (1823) in order to stipulate American involvement in Latin America. Asserting America's right to maintain order and protect American interests, Roosevelt declared: "If a nation [in Latin America] shows that it knows how to act with reasonable efficiency and decency in social and political matters, if it keeps order and pays its obligations, it need fear no interference from the United States. Chronic wrongdoing, or an impotence which results in a general loosening of the ties of civilized society, may in America, as elsewhere, ultimately require intervention by some civilized nation, and in the Western Hemisphere the adherence to the Monroe Doctrine may force the United States, however reluctantly, in flagrant cases of such wrongdoing or impotence, to the exercise of international police power." Implicitly, Roosevelt was warning Europeans to stay out of Latin America. Throughout the early years of the twentieth century, the United States intervened in the affairs of several Latin American nations to protect property and lives and to collect debts. The United States took over the actual control of finances in Cuba, the Dominican Republic, Haiti, Honduras, and Nicaragua. To enforce its will, the

United States sent marines to Nicaragua and Haiti. This policy was renounced by the Good Neighbor Policy initiated in 1934 by President Franklin D. Roosevelt (1933–1945). *See also* Chapter 7.

Root-Takahira Agreement (1908): Accord between the United States and Japan in which the two nations agreed to support "by all pacific means" the "independence and integrity of China" and to maintain the "principle of equal opportunity for commerce and industry of all nations," that is, the Open Door Policy. *See also* Chapter 7.

S

Second Continental Congress (1775–1781): The de facto governing body of the thirteen united colonies during the War for Independence (1775–1783). Delegates to the First Continental Congress (1774) had agreed to hold another meeting in 1775 if Great Britain failed to end colonial grievances. Three weeks after the battles of Lexington and Concord (April 1775), twelve colonies sent representatives to the Second Continental Congress in Philadelphia. (Georgia did not send delegates until the following autumn.) The Congress assumed responsibility for the colonial troops around Boston and, by unanimous vote, appointed George Washington as commander in chief of the Continental Army. Tensions with Great Britain were high. In mid-1775, the Congress drew up a Declaration of Causes and Necessity of Taking Up Arms. In it, the delegates resolved to " . . . die freemen rather than live slaves," but went on to note, "We have not raised armies with ambitious designs of separating from Great Britain and establishing independent states." In July 1775, Congress adopted the Olive Branch Petition, reasserting the colonists' loyalty to the Crown, but the following month King George III (reigned 1760–1820) refused to accept the petition and declared that the colonies were in a state of rebellion.

In December 1775, Parliament forbade all trade with the colonies, leading John Adams (then one of the Massachusetts representatives) to declare that this act "makes us independent in spite of supplications and entreaties." After much debate, Congress adopted a resolution for independence, drawing up the declaration that Congress adopted on July 4. The Second Continental Congress then assumed directing the conduct of the War for Independence. The Congress requested that each colony send money to finance the war and printed nearly $250 million to that end. During the course of the war, the Congress also borrowed money from European nations: $5 million from France, $1.25 million from the Netherlands, and $200,000 from Spain. In 1778, delegates from the Congress negotiated an alliance with France, which ultimately led to the American victory at Yorktown in 1781. After more than a year of debate, on November 15, 1777, Congress passed and sent to the states for ratification the Articles of Confederation. Virginia was the first to ratify the Articles, on December 16, 1777, and Maryland became the last to do so, on February 2, 1781. Finally, on March 1, 1781, the Articles of Confederation were signed and Congress declared them ratified. On the next day, the same congressional delegates met as the new Congress of the Confederation. The Second Continental Congress established the American precedent of conducting diplomatic relations through foreign ministers and other governmental representatives. *See also* Chapter 1.

sectionalism: Term used to describe the growing differences among the regions of the United States prior to the Civil War (1861–1865). In the early 1800s, while the North grew more industrialized and favored high tariffs to protect domestic industries, the South remained agricultural and opposed high tariffs, wanting to keep the cost of imported goods, upon which it depended, low. Southerners and northerners showed fierce loyalty to their regions rather than to the nation as a whole. The settlers of the West were mostly small farmers who wanted cheap land and demanded that the federal government make it available on easy terms. The Northern states had abolished slavery, and law prohibited slavery in the West; the South, however, increased its reliance on slave labor, especially after the 1793 invention of the cotton gin made cotton an extremely profitable crop. Slavery became a bitter sectional issue that ultimately led to the secession of the South and the Civil War. *See also* Chapter 3.

self-determination: In international law, the principle that free nations have the right to develop their own economic, social, and cultural destinies. The right to self-determination is embodied in several international documents, including the Charter of the United Nations, the International Covenant on Civil and Political Rights, and the International Covenant on Economic, Social, and Cultural Rights. *See also* Chapter 14.

September 11, 2001: Date on which nineteen Islamic fundamentalists, members of the international terrorist group al Qaeda, hijacked four American airliners and crashed two planes into the twin towers of New York's World Trade Center and the third plane into the Pentagon in Washington, D.C. The fourth plane, which the hijackers had directed toward either the White House or the Capitol, crashed into a field near Shanksville, Pennsylvania, as the crew and some of the passengers attempted to retake control of the plane. There were no survivors from any of the flights; nearly three thousand innocent people and the nineteen hijackers died. Among the 2,752 victims who died in the World Trade

Center attacks were 343 firefighters and sixty police officers from New York City and the Port Authority as well as people from more than seventy countries.

The United States responded to the attacks by launching a so-called War on Terror and invading Afghanistan to depose the Taliban regime, which had harbored Osama bin Laden, the leader of al Qaeda, and other terrorists. The U.S. Congress also passed the controversial USA PATRIOT Act, signed into law by President George W. Bush (2001–2009) on October 26, 2001, which greatly expanded the ability of law enforcement agencies to search telephone and e-mail communications as well as procure financial and other personal records. It also eased restrictions on foreign intelligence gathering within the United States and expanded the secretary of the treasury's power to regulate financial transactions, especially those involving foreign individuals and entities. The law further expanded the discretion of law enforcement officers and immigration authorities to detain and deport immigrants suspected of terrorism. Responses to the 9/11 terrorist attacks marked a crucial turning point in domestic and international policies, including not only the constriction of civil liberties but also two costly wars in Afghanistan and Iraq. Since 9/11, terrorist activities have increased around the globe. *See also* Chapter 35, 39, and 40.

sharia law: The sacred law of Islam, which is based on the Quran. Examples are believed to have been set by the Prophet Mohammed. Muslims differ as to what exactly sharia requires. Sharia law deals with many of the same topics addressed by secular law, including crime, economics, and politics; it also addresses personal matters such as sexuality, hygiene, diet, prayer, and fasting. Where it has official status, sharia law is applied by Islamic judges. The reintroduction of sharia law is a longstanding goal for Islamist movements in Muslim countries. In the international media, it has come under significant criticism, particularly when punishments move away from established principles of international human rights. As examples, sharia law calls for the application of the death penalty for the crimes of adultery, blasphemy, apostasy, and homosexuality; amputations for the crime of theft; and flogging for fornication or public intoxication. *See also* Chapters 38, 39, and 40.

shock and awe: A military doctrine based on the use of overwhelming power, dominant maneuvers, and spectacular displays of force, all designed to destroy the enemies' will to fight and force them into submission. The doctrine was developed by Harlan K. Ullman and James P. Wade of the National Defense University (NDU) in 1996. The United States used a shock-and-awe strategy in the launching of the 2003 Iraq War. The term is used to describe the beginning of the invasion, not the long-lasting war nor the insurgency. *See also* Chapter 35.

shuttle diplomacy: Term used in international diplomacy to describe the actions of a third-party intermediary between (or among) parties involved in a dispute. Usually, the intermediary travels, or shuttles, between the parties' locations. The term became associated with U.S. Secretary of State Henry Kissinger's efforts to end the fighting during the 1973 Yom Kippur War between Israel and a coalition of Arab nations led by Egypt and Syria. *See also* Chapter 26.

small state diplomacy: The concept that small states must use particularly wise and strategic diplomatic means in the global arena to ensure that common goals, issues, and problems are addressed, given that they lack the power, resources, and population to otherwise assert themselves. Iceland provides an example of successful small state diplomacy. In the early 1950s, Iceland's government, reacting to a trend in world affairs, extended its fisheries limits from four miles to twelve miles. Over the next quarter of a century, Iceland supported international organizations to extend fisheries limits aggressively and progressively to the now universally accepted two hundred miles. The principal asset of this small state was the skill, persistence, and thorough knowledge of its diplomatic corps. *See also* Chapter 40.

Smoot-Hawley Tariff (1930): Tax law passed by the United States Congress in 1930. Also known as the Tariff Act of 1930, the law raised tariffs on more than 200,000 imported goods. In return, U.S. trading partners passed retaliatory tariffs that ultimately reduced American exports and imports by more than half. At the time, most economists opposed the law, and today many economists believe that the Smoot-Hawley Tariff contributed to the severity of the Great Depression around the world. *See also* Chapter 12.

socialism: A type of social and economic organization that advocates communal or public ownership of all property and control of the means of production. In Marxist theory, socialism is the type of governmment that arises after the proletariat takes over the means of production but before the state withers away and true communism is achieved. In a socialist society, the state controls the economy. *See also* Chapters 11 and 14.

sovereignty: Term used to describe the quality of having supreme authority over a geographic region. Sovereign nations are independent and free to determine their own foreign policy with respect to other nations. *See also* Chapter 16.

space race: Cold War competition between the United States and the Soviet Union to gain technological superiority in exploring outer space. The space race began on October 4, 1957, after the Soviets launched *Sputnik I*, the first artificial satellite to orbit the earth, a launch that was immediately perceived as a threat to U.S. security. One direct effect of the launch was a significant increase in educational spending in the United States, as the nation attempted to "catch up" to the Soviet Union. About four months after the launch of *Sputnik,* the United States successfully launched the *Juno I* rocket, which carried the satellite *Explorer I.* The next phase of the race focused on sending a human into space; here, again, the Soviet Union was first, sending cosmonaut Yuri Gagarin into space on April 12, 1961. Alan Shepard became the first American in space three weeks later, on May 5, 1961. On May 25 of the same year, President John F. Kennedy (1961–1963) announced the race to the moon in a special joint session of Congress: "I believe that this nation should commit itself to achieving the goal, before this decade is out, of landing a man on the moon and returning him safely to the earth." This feat was achieved by the United States on July 20, 1969, when astronaut Neil Armstrong disembarked from the lunar module, *Eagle,* and set foot on the surface of the moon. Although much of the technology that runs modern society was developed as a result of the space race, its legacy is mixed. *See also* Chapter 17.

Spanish-American War (1898): Conflict between Spain and the United States which occurred as tensions between the two nations increased, especially over Spain's harsh treatment of Cuban rebels, which the yellow journalism of the time magnified. The spark that ignited the war was the sinking of the U.S. battleship *Maine,* which was docked in Havana to protect American lives and property. More than 260 sailors lost their lives. No one knows why the *Maine* exploded, but the American public, urged on by New York newspaper editors William Randolph Hearst and Joseph Pulitzer, quickly jumped to the conclusion that the Spanish had done it with a submarine mine. Public opinion nationwide demanded action. On April 11, 1898, although he was personally opposed to war, President William McKinley (1897–1901) asked Congress for authority to send American troops to Cuba to end the fighting there. On April 19, 1898, as Congress was considering McKinley's request, Senator Henry M. Teller of Colorado proposed the Teller amendment to ensure that the United States would not establish permanent control over Cuba after the war. The amendment, disavowing any intention of annexing Cuba, quickly passed both houses of Congress. The resolution also demanded Spanish withdrawal and authorized the president to use as much military force as he thought necessary to help Cuba gain independence from Spain.

McKinley signed the joint resolution on April 20, 1898, and the ultimatum was sent to Spain. In response, Spain broke off diplomatic relations with the United States on April 21. On the same day, the U.S. Navy began a blockade of Cuba. Spain declared war on April 23; on April 25, Congress declared that a state of war between the United States and Spain had existed since April 21, the day the blockade had begun.

Fighting lasted less than three months and hostilities ended on August 12. After more than two months of negotiations, the Treaty of Paris was signed on December 10, 1898, and ratified by the U.S. Senate on February 6, 1899. Under the terms of the peace treaty, the United States gained almost all of Spain's colonies, including the Philippines, Guam, and Puerto Rico. Cuba formed its own government and attained independence on May 20, 1902. However, the United States imposed several restrictions on the new government, including prohibiting alliances with other countries, and it reserved the right to intervene. The United States also established a perpetual lease of Guantánamo Bay. The war is considered a turning point in U.S. foreign relations. *See also* Chapter 6.

spheres of influence: An area or region over which another usually more powerful nation exerts significant economic, cultural, or political influence. Before the implementation of the Open Door Policy in 1900, China was divided into spheres of influence among Russia, Japan, Germany, Great Britain, and France. During the Cold War, Cuba, Eastern Europe, North Korea, Vietnam, and the People's Republic of China (until the Sino-Soviet split in 1961) were said to be under the Soviet sphere of influence. In a similar fashion, Japan, South Korea, Western Europe, and Oceania were often said to be under the sphere of influence of the United States. *See also* Chapter 7.

Sputnik I: The first artificial satellite launched into outer space. With this achievement on October 4, 1957, the Soviet Union initiated the space race with the United States. A surprise to the United States, the launch created a sense of panic among many experts who believed that the Soviets could soon deploy a nuclear missile capable of reaching the United States. *See also* Chapter 17.

START I (1991): A bilateral treaty between the United States and the Soviet Union which was signed in 1991, just before the collapse of the Soviet Union, and went into effect in 1994. The first Strategic Arms Reduction (START) proposal was made in 1982 by President Ronald Reagan (1981–1989). One of the most complex nuclear arms treaties ever negotiated, it reduced the number of nuclear warheads by about 80 percent. A second Strategic Arms Reduction Treaty (START II) was signed by President George H.W. Bush (1989–1993) and Russian President Boris Yeltsin (1991–1999) in early January 1993. The U.S. Senate ratified the treaty, but the Russian Duma did not. In 2001, the START II treaty was bypassed by the Strategic Offensive Reductions Treaty (SORT), signed by presidents George W. Bush (2001–2009) and Vladimir Putin (2000–2008) in May 2002. The START I treaty expired on December 5, 2009; in April 2010, a new START treaty was signed in Prague by Presidents Barack Obama (2009–) and Dmitri Medvedev (2008–). *See also* Chapters 29, 39, and 40.

Strategic Arms Limitation Talks (SALT): Between November 1969 and May 1979, a series of discussions, held alternatively in Helsinki, Finland, and Geneva, Switzerland, between the United States and the Soviet Union to negotiate limits on armaments. In the Treaty on the Limitation of Anti-Ballistic Missile Systems (ABMs), the two moved to end a competition to develop additional defensive systems. In an Interim Agreement on Certain Measures with Respect to the Limitation of Strategic Offensive Arms, both superpowers took the first steps to reduce their most powerful land- and submarine-based offensive nuclear weapons. On January 20, 1969, the day that President Richard M. Nixon (1969–1974) assumed office, the Soviet foreign minister expressed an interest in discussing strategic arms limitations. In turn, the new president initiated, under the guidance of the National Security Council (NSC), an extensive review of the strategic, political, and verification aspects of the issues. In October, it was announced that the Strategic Arms Limitation Talks would begin in Helsinki on November 17, 1969, "for preliminary discussion of the questions involved." The talks led to two-and-a-half years of SALT I negotiations.

In a summit meeting in Moscow, the first round of SALT ended on May 26, 1972, when President Nixon and General Secretary Brezhnev (in power 1964–1982) signed the ABM Treaty and the Interim Agreement on strategic offensive arms. SALT II negotiations began in November 1972 in Geneva. The primary goal of SALT II was to replace the Interim Agreement with a long-term treaty providing broad limits on strategic offensive weapons systems. A major breakthrough occurred at the Vladivostok meeting in November 1974 between President Gerald R. Ford (1974–1977) and General Secretary Brezhnev when both sides agreed to a basic framework for the SALT II agreement. President Jimmy Carter (1977–1981) and General Secretary Brezhnev signed the completed SALT II treaty in Vienna on June 18, 1979, and Carter transmitted it to the U.S. Senate on June 22 for ratification. On January 3, 1980, however, the president requested the Senate delay consideration of the treaty in response to the Soviet invasion of Afghanistan in December 1979. In May 1982, President Ronald Reagan (1981–1989) stated he would not act to undercut the SALT agreements as long as the Soviet Union showed equal restraint. The Soviet Union again agreed to abide by the unratified treaty. *See also* Chapter 25.

Strategic Defense Initiative (SDI): Developed in 1983 by President Ronald Reagan (1981–1989), plan that sought to end the threat of nuclear missiles with the use of land- and satellite-based systems to protect the United States from nuclear attacks. The initiative focused on strategic defense, rather than mutual assured defense (MAD). The elaborate plan was criticized as being unrealistic and quickly dubbed "Star Wars," a reference to the popular movie of the 1970s. During the administration of President William J. Clinton

(1993–2001), the program was renamed the Ballistic Missile Defense Organization (BMDO), which in turn was renamed the Missile Defense Agency in 2002. The United States has spent more than $100 million on space-based missile defense system research and holds a commanding lead in the field of space technology and warfare. *See also* Chapter 29.

Strategic Offensive Reductions Treaty: Officially, the Treaty Between the United States of America and the Russian Federation on Strategic Offensive Reductions (SORT), better known as the Moscow Treaty, signed by presidents George W. Bush (2001–2009) and Vladimir Putin (2000–2008) in May 2002. Under the terms of this agreement, the parties agreed to reduce their nuclear arsenals to between 1,700 and 2,200 operational warheads each. The treaty went into effect on May 24, 2002, and expires on December 31, 2012. *See also* Chapters 39 and 40.

summit meetings: Conferences of governments' heads of state, often with a high level of media coverage, a prearranged agenda, and tight security, to attempt to satisfy mutual demands through negotiation rather than warfare. During the Cold War era, meetings held between U.S. presidents and Soviet or Chinese leaders were termed *summits*. Since that time, the number and types of summit meetings have significantly increased, with topics ranging from global warming to the world economy. *See also* Chapters 30 and 33.

***Sussex* Pledge:** Statement issued on May 4, 1916, by the German Imperial government promising once again to abandon unrestricted submarine warfare during World War I (1914– 1918). The pledge came about after the French ship, *Sussex,* was torpedoed in the English Channel, resulting in the injury of several Americans. The pledge temporarily averted U.S. participation in the war. In January 1917, Germany concluded that it could win the war if it resumed unrestricted warfare against the Allies before the United States could enter the war. Thus, the *Sussex* Pledge was rescinded. Resumption of unrestricted warfare by Germany and the interception of the Zimmermann Note led the U.S. Congress to declare war on Germany on April 6, 1917. *See also* Chapters 8 and 9.

T

Taliban: An Islamist militia group that ruled large parts of Afghanistan between 1996 and 2001 and practiced an extreme Sunni Muslim political and religious ideology. Although the Taliban controlled Kabul, Afghanistan's capital, and most of the country for more than five years, the Taliban's Islamic Emirate of Afghanistan received diplomatic recognition from only three nations: Pakistan, Saudi Arabia, and the United Arab Emirates. In the areas under their control, the Taliban imposed their strict interpretation of Islam. For example, women were required to wear the all-covering *burqa*, they were banned from public life, denied access to health care and education, and were forbidden to laugh in a manner that could be heard by others. Windows were required to be covered so that women could not be seen from the outside. The Taliban also imposed strict Islamic justice, amputating people's hands or arms when they were accused of stealing. Taliban hit squads carefully monitored the streets, conducting brutal public beatings.

During Taliban rule, Afghanistan was home to the international terrorist organization al Qaeda. After the terrorist attacks of September 11, 2001, Mullah Omar, the Taliban leader, refused the demand of the United States to turn over Osama bin Laden, the leader of al Qaeda, who claimed responsibility for the attacks. The Taliban regime was overthrown quickly after the U.S.-led invasion of Afghanistan in October 2001, known as Operation Enduring Freedom, but many of their leaders remain at large. Most of the Taliban fled to neighboring Pakistan, where they reorganized as an insurgency movement to fight against NATO-led forces and the democratic Islamic Republic of Afghanistan that had been established in late 2001. The Taliban routinely engage in terrorist acts against the civilian population of Afghanistan. According to a report by the United Nations, the Taliban were responsible for 76 percent of civilian casualties in Afghanistan in 2009. *See also* Chapters 35, 39, and 40.

Tehran Conference (1943): The meeting of Joseph Stalin (in power 1924–1953), Franklin D. Roosevelt (1933–1945), and Winston Churchill (1940–1945, 1951–1955), between November 28 and December 1, 1943, most of which was held at the Soviet Embassy in Tehran, Iran. It was the first World War II (1939–1945) conference among the Big Three: the Soviet Union, the United States, and the United Kingdom. The primary aim of the meeting was to plan the final strategies in the war against Nazi Germany and its allies, and much of the discussion focused on the opening of a second front in Western Europe. In addition, the wartime leaders discussed relations with Turkey and Iran, operations in Yugoslavia and against Japan, and the postwar settlement. They agreed that Operation Overlord, the invasion of Normandy, would be launched during May 1944; that the military staffs of the three powers should keep in close touch with each other to ensure cooperation against the enemy; and that the borders of postwar Poland would be reconfigured to meet Stalin's demands. The three leaders also tentatively agreed to form a united nations organization, and the Soviet Union agreed to declare war against Japan once Germany was defeated. *See also* Chapters 14 and 15.

Torrijos-Carter Treaties (1977): Two agreements between the United States and Panama, signed in Washington, D.C.,

on September 7, 1977, and abrogating the Hay-Bunau Varilla Treaty of 1903. The treaties are named after the two signers, U.S. President Jimmy Carter (1977–1981) and the Commander of Panama's National Guard, General Omar Torrijos, the *de facto* leader of Panama from 1968 to 1981. The treaties specified that Panama would gain control of the Panama Canal after 1999, ending U.S. control of the canal, which it had held since 1903. This first treaty, officially titled "The Treaty Concerning the Permanent Neutrality and Operation of the Panama Canal" and commonly known as the Neutrality Treaty, declared that the United States retained the permanent right to defend the canal from any threat that might interfere with its neutral service to ships of all nations. The second treaty, titled "The Panama Canal Treaty," provided that as of noon on December 31, 1999, Panama would assume full control of canal operations and become principally responsible for its defense. Both treaties were ratified in Panama by a two-thirds vote held on October 23, 1977. The U.S. Senate ratified the first treaty on March 16, 1978, and the second treaty on April 18 by votes of sixty-eight to thirty-two. The treaties specified a timetable for the transfer of the canal, leading to a total handover of all land and buildings in the canal area to Panama. The most immediate consequence of this treaty was that the Canal Zone ceased to exist on October 1, 1979. The final phase of the treaty was completed on December 31, 1999. On this date, the United States relinquished control of the Panama Canal and all areas in what had been the Panama Canal Zone. *See also* Chapter 31.

sanctions: In international relations, actions taken by nations or international organizations, such as the United Nations (UN), against others for political reasons, either unilaterally or multilaterally. There are several types of sanctions. Diplomatic sanctions are political measures taken to express disapproval or displeasure of a certain action through diplomacy or other political means, rather than affecting economic or military relations. Measures include limitations or cancellations of high-level government visits or expelling or withdrawing diplomatic missions. Economic sanctions can vary from imposing import duties on goods from the target nation, or blocking the export of certain goods to the target country, to a full naval blockade of a nation's ports in an effort to block specific goods, such as armaments. Two well-known examples of economic sanctions include the UN sanctions against Iraq (1990–2003) and the U.S. embargo against Cuba (1962–present). Military sanctions may range from targeted military strikes to degrade a nation's military capabilities, to an arms embargo to cut off supplies of arms. Sports sanctions are used as a way to crush morale of the general population in the target country. The only incident of sports sanctions being applied was the international sanctions against the Federal Republic of Yugoslavia between 1992 and 1995, enacted by UN Resolution 757. *See also* Chapters 16 and 31.

torture: According to the United Nations Convention Against Torture (an advisory measure of the UN General Assembly), "... any act by which severe pain or suffering, whether physical or mental, is intentionally inflicted on a person for such purposes as obtaining from him, or a third person, information or a confession, punishing him for an act he or a third person has committed or is suspected of having committed, or intimidating or coercing him or a third person, or for any reason based on discrimination of any kind, when such pain or suffering is inflicted by or at the instigation of or with the consent or acquiescence of a public official or other person acting in an official capacity. It does not include pain or suffering arising only from, inherent in, or incidental to, lawful sanctions." Torture is prohibited under international law and the domestic laws of most countries in the twenty-first century. Torture is a violation of human rights, and it is deemed to be unacceptable by Article 5 of the UN Universal Declaration of Human Rights. Signatories of the Third Geneva Convention (1929) and Fourth Geneva Convention (1949) officially agree not to torture prisoners captured in armed conflicts. Torture is also prohibited by the United Nations Convention Against Torture, which has been ratified by more than 140 nations. *See also* Chapters 14, 15, and 40.

Treaty of Ghent (1814): Agreement between the United States and Great Britain which ended the War of 1812 (1812–1814). In January 1814, President James Madison (1809–1817) learned that the British were willing to conclude a treaty. Consequently, American and British negotiators met at Ghent in what is now Belgium. The Americans demanded the abandonment of impressments, recognition of the rights of neutrals, and compensation for the loss of merchant vessels. The British wanted to use a part of the American Northwest as a buffer state between Canada and the United States, large cessions of American territory, and the surrender of American fishing rights off the Canadian coast. The final treaty, however, did not mention any of these issues. It simply provided for the end of hostilities and left each side with the same territory it held before the war. Not a word was included about impressment or neutral rights. Finally, it was agreed that any disputed boundaries between Canada and the United States would be settled through arbitration. *See also* Chapter 1.

Treaty of Guadalupe Hidalgo (1848): Agreement between the United States and Mexico which ended the Mexican-American War (1846–1848). Under the terms of this treaty, Mexico was forced to recognize the annexation of Texas and the Rio Grande as Texas' southern boundary. It also ceded the provinces of California and New Mexico to the United States, which includes the present-day states of California, Nevada, and Utah; most of Arizona and New Mexico; and parts of Colorado and Wyoming. Thus, Mexico gave up nearly half of its territory. The United States agreed to pay Mexico $15 million and to assume Mexico's debts to Americans, a sum totaling about $3.25 million. After much debate, the U.S. Senate ratified the treaty by a vote of thirty-eight to fourteen. *See also* Chapter 2.

Treaty of Manila (1946): Agreement between the United States and the Philippines which granted full independence to the Philippines and relinquished American sovereignty over the islands. It was signed in Manila, the capital of the Philippines, on July 4, 1946. *See also* Chapter 16.

Treaty of Paris of 1783: Agreement between the United States and Great Britain ending the War for Independence (1775–1783). Following the American victory at Yorktown (1781), American and British representatives in Paris discussed peace terms between September and November 1782. The principle American negotiators were Benjamin Franklin, the American minister to France; John Jay, the American minister to Spain; and John Adams, the American minister to the Netherlands. Under the terms of the treaty, Britain recognized American independence, and the boundaries of the new nation were extended from Canada and the Great Lakes in the north to the Mississippi River on the west and to the thirty-first parallel and Spanish Florida to the south. In addition, Britain agreed to return Florida to Spain and gave American fishers the right to fish off the coast of Newfoundland and Nova Scotia. Both sides agreed to pay lawful debts to the other side, and the United States agreed to stop further confiscation of the property of loyalists (who had sided with the British during the war). The treaty was signed in Paris in September 1783. *See also* Chapter 1.

Treaty of Versailles (1919): Agreement between the Allies and Germany which ended World War I (1914–1918) and essentially redrew the map of Europe. The term *Treaty of Versailles* inaccurately came to represent the series of treaties that ended the hostilities with the Central Powers: the Treaty of St. Germaine with Austria; the Treaty of Trianon with Hungary; the treaty of Neuilly with Bulgaria; and the Treaty of Sevres with the Ottoman Empire. As a result of these peace settlements, France recovered the provinces of Alsace and Lorraine, which Germany had taken after the Franco-Prussian War (1870–1871). France also gained control of the rich coal deposits in Germany's Saar Basin for fifteen years. In the west, Germany gave up small areas to Belgium and Denmark. In the east, Germany lost large areas to the recreated Poland; included in the new Poland was a narrow strip of land along the Vistula River to the seaport of Danzig, which cut Germany in two. The new Poland also included lands formerly controlled by Austria-Hungary and Russia, and both Austria and Hungary were separated and greatly reduced in size and power. Italy received lands around the northern Adriatic Sea. Romania gained territory at the expense of Hungary, Bulgaria, and Russia. Finland, Estonia, Latvia, and Lithuania were recreated out of Russian territory, even though Russia, engaged in civil war, was not represented in Paris, where representatives met from Britain, France, and the United States. Germany lost all of its overseas possessions, and the Ottoman Empire lost its Arab lands in Asia. The devastated European countries no longer possessed the unrivaled global power they had once known.

At the insistence of President Woodrow Wilson (1913–1921), most of these areas became mandates and not possessions of the victorious powers. The mandates were to be administered by the victorious nations under the supervision of the new League of Nations, established to maintain peace and avoid future wars. The Treaty of Versailles placed huge reparations on Germany and forced Germany, Austria, and Hungary to disarm almost completely; Germany was not allowed to manufacture or obtain war materials. There were 440 articles; Article X of the League's covenant provided that member nations would "respect and preserve . . . against external aggression the territorial integrity and existing independence of all members. . . ." This provision was unacceptable to a majority of Republican senators, who asserted that it would involve "entangling alliances" and drag the nation into foreign wars. Democratic-leaning Irish Catholics and German Americans also opposed the treaty, because they believed that the treaty favored the British. Despite Wilson's efforts to sway public opinion in favor of the treaty, he refused to compromise on the inclusion of the League of Nations. Thus, the U.S. Senate never ratified the Treaty of Versailles. Congress passed the Knox-Porter Resolution, which brought a formal end to hostilities between the United States and the Central Powers. It was signed into law by President Warren G. Harding (1921–1923) on July 21, 1921. *See also* Chapters 9, 10, and 11.

treaty power: The ability to conclude an accord with another sovereign state, usually concentrated in the executive authority of a government. Article II of the United States Constitution empowers the President of the United States to propose and negotiate agreements between the United States and other countries. These agreements become treaties between the United States and other countries after ratification by the United States Senate. *See also* Chapters 1, 9, and 14.

Triple Alliance: Formed in May 1882 among Germany, Austria-Hungary, and Italy, agreement in which each member promised mutual support in the event of an attack by any two other great powers, or for Germany and Italy, an attack by France alone. At the outbreak of World War I (1914–1918), Italy refused to join its two allies, noting that the Triple Alliance was a defensive pact and that Germany and Austria-Hungary took the offensive. Later, in 1915, Italy joined the Allies against the Central Powers of Germany, Austria-Hungary, Bulgaria, and the Ottoman Empire. *See also* Chapters 8 and 9.

Triple Entente: Alliance among Great Britain, France, and Russia formed in 1907 as a counter-weight to the Triple Alliance of Germany, Austria-Hungary, and Italy. At the outbreak of World War I (1914–1918), Italy did not join its two allies; in 1915, it joined Great Britain, France, and Russia against the Central Powers of Germany, Austria-Hungary, Bulgaria, and the Ottoman Empire. *See also* Chapters 8 and 9.

truce: An agreement between opposing sides to cease hostilities for a specific period of time; cease fire. *See also* Chapters 9 and 19.

Truman Doctrine: Policy articulated by President Harry S. Truman (1945–1953) on March 12, 1947, pledging U.S. support of Greece and Turkey with military and economic aid to prevent those nations from falling under Soviet influence. In February 1946, George F. Kennan, an American diplomat in Moscow, sent to Truman his "Long Telegram," in which he predicted that the Soviet Union would only respond to force and that the best way to respond to that nation's aggressive moves would be through a long-term strategy of containment; he hoped to prevent the spread of communism in Europe. In March 1947, Truman appeared before Congress and used Kennan's recommendations as the basis for what became known as the Truman Doctrine, the first in a series of containment moves by the United States. The doctrine was followed by economic restoration of Western Europe through the Marshall Plan (1947–1951) and the creation of NATO (1949) and served to buttress American Cold War policy in Europe and around the world. *See also* Chapter 17.

U

U-boat: Anglicized version of the German *U-boot*, itself shorthand for *unterseeboot* (undersea boat), the German submarines used against Allied warships and merchant ships during World War I (1914–1918) and again in World War II (1939–1945). The primary targets of U-boats were the merchant marine bringing supplies from the United States and the British Empire to the British Isles. Germany's unrestricted use of U-boats during World War I was a major cause of U.S. entry into that conflict. *See also* Chapters 8, 9, and 10.

unconditional surrender: The complete surrender of a nation at the end of a war in which the defeated nation or party is prevented from dictating any terms once fighting ends. In the twentieth century, the most famous examples were the unconditional surrender of Germany and Japan, the leading Axis Powers at the end of World War II (1939–1945). *See also* Chapters 9, 10, and 14.

unilateral: Undertaken by one party or nation only, when a second party or nation could or should have had input. Although unilateral action usually generates a backlash of international anger and opposition, it is the least complicated foreign-policy action, requiring no diplomacy, no consensus, and no multilateral support. Supporters of American unilateralism maintain that the United States is free to act alone to protect its interests and security. *See also* Chapter 35.

United Nations (UN): International organization established after the end of World War II (1939–1945) to maintain world peace; the successor organization to the League of Nations. Late in 1944, representatives of four major Allied powers—the United States, Great Britain, the Soviet Union, and China—met at Dumbarton Oaks, an estate near Washington, D.C., to develop concrete proposals for a united nations. In spring 1945, representatives from more than fifty nations met in San Francisco to set up the UN, and the fifty founding members signed the charter on June 26, 1945. (Poland, which was not represented at the meeting, signed the charter later and became one of fifty-one members.) The UN officially came into existence on October 24, 1945, after the United States, Great Britain, France, the Soviet Union, China, and a majority of the signatory nations approved the charter. Today, the number of UN member states exceeds 190, each of whom has one vote in the General Assembly. The UN also includes a judicial branch, the International Court of Justice, and a peacekeeping body, the Security Council, which also can authorize military action, as well as the Secretariat, the Trusteeship Council, and the Economic and Social Council (ECOSOC). *See also* Chapters 16 and 17.

unrestricted submarine warfare: During wartime, the use of armed submarines to attack enemy merchant vessels without warning. This form of attack was used by German submarines, known as U-boats, during World War I (1914–1918) and World War II (1939–1945). It was a major reason for U.S. entry into World War I. During World War II, German submarines were extremely successful in the North Atlantic, sending more than eight million tons of shipping to the bottom of the sea in the first eleven months after the attack on Pearl Harbor. *See also* Chapters 8, 9, and 14.

V

Vietnam War (1945–1975): Conflict between Communist North Vietnam and non-Communist South Vietnam, and a proxy war between the Soviet Union and the United States. More than two million troops fought in one of the most costly wars in American history. Before World War II (1939–1945), most of Southeast Asia was ruled by the French, and during the war, the Japanese occupied the area. At the end of the war, Communist leader Ho Chi Minh proclaimed Vietnam's independence; from his stronghold in the north, he led a war against the French and their Vietnamese supporters, which resulted in a French defeat in 1954. According to the Geneva Accords that ended the fighting, Vietnam was temporarily divided, pending elections. A Communist government was established in the north and a non-Communist regime in the south. When the leader of the south refused to hold the promised elections, opposition forces, the Viet Cong, began a guerrilla war against the South Vietnamese government.

The United States had been supporting the south with military and economic aid since 1950. In 1961, President John F. Kennedy (1961–1963) sent in about sixteen thousand troops as advisers, but they had little impact on the situation. In 1965, Lyndon B. Johnson (1963–1969), with authorization from Congress under the Gulf of Tonkin Resolution (1964), escalated the military action against the communists. Subsequently, the number of American troops rapidly rose to more than one-half million. Despite the increased ground fighting, the heavy U.S. bombing of the north, and the destruction of about 20 percent of the area's landscape with toxic chemicals, the north would not capitulate. After lengthy negotiations, an unsteady peace was achieved in 1973, leading to the withdrawal of most U.S. forces. In 1975, the communists captured Saigon, the South Vietnamese capital, and unified the country, and remaining U.S. personnel were evacuated hurriedly from the country.

Domestically, the war divided the American people; antiwar protestors demonstrated against the U.S. role in Vietnam. Internationally, many viewed the fall of South Vietnam as a major defeat for the United States. Beginning in 1975, with the defeat of the United States, many political pundits and some government officials began to use the term Vietnam syndrome to describe the less interventionist and more cautious foreign policy of the nation. *See also* Chapters 23 and 24.

W

War of 1812: Conflict between the United States and Great Britain waged from 1812 through 1814. Among the causes of the war were the Americans' belief that the British were supplying arms and munitions to the Native Americans on the western frontier, British interference with American trade on the high seas, and the impressment of American sailors to serve on British ships. With increased tensions between the two nations, Congress declared war on Great Britain on June 19, 1812. In January 1814, upon learning that the British were willing to negotiate a treaty, President James Madison (1809–1817) sent Albert Gallatin, Henry Clay, and John Quincy Adams to Ghent, in what is today Belgium, as the American peace commissioners. The Treaty of Ghent was finally signed on December 24, 1814. The Battle of New Orleans, the final major battle of the war, which occurred on January 8, 1815, was a stunning American victory but had no effect on the war's outcome. *See also* Chapters 1 and 2.

War on Terrorism: A term used by President George W. Bush (2001–2009) following the terrorist attacks of September 11, 2001, to describe an ongoing international military campaign to end state-supported terrorism. The so-called war began in 2001 with the U.S.-led invasion of Afghanistan to topple the Taliban, the fundamentalist Islamic regime that supported and sheltered al Qaeda leader Osama bin Laden, and continued in 2003 with the U.S.-led invasion of Iraq. In an effort to reduce the power of al Qaeda and its affiliates, the war is also waged in the Philippines, the Horn of Africa, and Saharan Africa. To refer to those efforts today, the administration of President Barack Obama (2009–) replaced the term with "Overseas Contingency Operations." *See also* Chapters 35, 39, and 40.

War for Independence (1775–1783): Waged against the British, war in which the thirteen colonies won independence from Great Britain, then the most powerful nation on earth, resulting in the establishment of the United States of America. Tensions had been increasing since 1763, when Great Britain began imposing new and tighter restrictions on the colonies. In particular, the colonists objected to the passage of new tax laws without having representation in the British Parliament in London. On April 19, 1775, fighting broke out in the towns of Lexington and Concord in the Massachusetts colony. In July 1776, the Second Continental Congress, the governing body of the united colonies, issued a formal declaration of independence. A 1777 American victory at the Battle of Saratoga, in New York, brought France into the war as America's ally. The final major battle occurred in 1781 at Yorktown, Virginia, where American and French troops defeated the British and the French fleet prevented British naval units from reinforcing its army. The Treaty of Paris of 1783, signed in September of that year, officially ended the war. *See also* Chapters 1 and 4.

War Powers Act (1973): Resolution passed by Congress, declaring its authority to share with the president decisions about declaring war and military involvements. Under the terms of this act, the president must report to Congress within forty-eight hours after committing forces to combat abroad, explaining the circumstances of the commitment. If Congress does not approve the action within sixty to ninety days, the president is required to withdraw the troops. The act was passed over the veto of President Richard M. Nixon (1969–1974), who believed it was unconstitutional on the grounds that the president is commander in chief of the armed forces. Since the act's passage, all presidents have complied with its terms. *See also* Chapters 23 and 35.

war reparations: Payment required from a defeated nation to make amends for loss of life and property damages during wartime. For example, the 1919 Treaty of Versailles obligated Germany to pay huge war reparations, ultimately set at the equivalent of $33 billion. Germany, however, impoverished by the cost of World War I (1914–1918), and despite financial adjustments made during the 1920s, could not pay. Therefore, in 1931, under the recommendation of President Herbert Hoover (1929–1933), the Allies agreed to suspend Germany's reparation payments, canceling them at the 1932 Lausanne Conference. The harsh reparations imposed on Germany are cited often as a factor in the rise of Adolf Hitler (in power 1933–1945). *See also* Chapters 9 and 13.

Washington Consensus: Term used to describe several policies outlined by economist John Williamson in 1989 in order to provide a set of directions for nations in need of economic assistance. Neither new nor novel, the ideas included in the Washington Consensus were a distillation of advice commonly provided by the World Bank, the U.S. Treasury, the International Monetary Fund, and other lending organizations. The term has come to be used derisively by critics of free market basics. *See also* Chapter 31.

weapons of mass destruction (WMDs): Any weapon that can cause widespread loss of life and catastrophic damage to infrastructure. During the Cold War era, the term primarily referred to nuclear weapons, but today it also refers to chemical, biological, and radiological weaponry. In 2003, President George W. Bush (2001–2009) insisted that Iraqi dictator Saddam Hussein was stockpiling weapons of mass destruction, thus posing a threat to Iraq's neighbors and the United States. After the March 2003 U.S.-led invasion of Iraq, however, no WMDs were found to support the president's and his advisers' claims and faulty intelligence. In the United States, indictments and convictions have been obtained for possession and use of WMDs, such as shoe bombs, pipe bombs, and truck bombs. In the 2006 trial of Zacarias Moussaoui, the "20th hijacker" in the 9/11 terrorist attacks, the judge included aircraft used as missiles as WMDs and sentenced Moussaoui to life without parole. *See also* Chapter 35.

Webster-Ashburton Treaty (1842): Agreement reached between the United States and Great Britain that established a permanent boundary between Maine and Canada. This boundary had been in dispute since the signing of the Treaty of Paris of 1783, which ended the War for Independence (1775–1783). The outbreak of fighting between Maine settlers and trappers and Canadian lumberjacks in the late 1830s made it clear that a resolution was needed to avoid war. The treaty, negotiated by Secretary of State Daniel Webster and Alexander Baring (also known as Lord Ashburton, the British minister to the United States), resulted in the United States' receiving about seven thousand square miles of the disputed area and Britain's receiving about five thousand square miles. Also, the treaty established a fixed boundary west from Lake Superior to the Lake of the Woods. *See also* Chapter 2.

World Bank: Established in 1944, international organization that serves as a source for economic and technical assistance to developing nations. Not a bank in the traditional sense, it is made up of two bodies, the International Bank for Reconstruction and Development (IRBD) and the International Development Association (IDA), which are owned by the 187 member countries. Headquartered in Washington, D.C., and charged with promoting sustainable economic development worldwide, the bank provides low-interest loans, interest-free credits, and grants for a wide array of purposes including health and education, infrastructure, and natural resource management. It also has evolved into an instrument that imposes rules and reforms on nations suffering from economic problems such as debt. *See also* Chapters 15 and 16.

World Court: Term used to refer to the International Court of Justice (ICJ), as the International Criminal Court (ICC), and the Permanent Court of Arbitration (PCA), all of which are located at The Hague in the Netherlands. The ICJ was established in 1945 by the UN Charter and is the successor to the Permanent Court of International Justice, which had been established in 1922 and attached to the League of Nations. The main purpose of the ICJ, as the primary judicial organ of the United Nations (UN), is to settle legal disputes submitted by member nations and to provide opinions on legal questions submitted by the UN General Assembly and certain other international agencies. The ICC is a permanent tribunal established in 2002 to prosecute individuals for genocide, war crimes, crimes against humanity, and the crime of aggression. The PCA, established in 1899, is an administrative organization with the means to arbitrate international disputes, including disagreements over treaties, maritime and territorial boundaries, trade matters, and human rights. *See also* Chapters 35 and 40.

World War I (1914–1918): Global conflict that launched a new era of total war that was ignited in June 1914 when a Serbian nationalist assassinated Archduke Franz Ferdinand, the heir to the Austro-Hungarian throne, as well as his pregnant wife. The incident occurred in Sarajevo, the capital of the Austrian province of Bosnia. At the time, few expected a major war to result, but the incident sparked worldwide conflagration. On July 23, Austria-Hungary sent an ultimatum to Serbia that, if accepted, would have humiliated Serbia and given Austria-Hungary dominance in the Balkans. Germany gave Austria-Hungary *carte blanche*, with a promise of full support. In turn, Russia informed Serbia of its support. Serbia rejected the ultimatum, and on July 28, Austria-Hungary declared war on Serbia and found itself at war with Russia as well. France backed Russia, and Germany fulfilled its promise by supporting Austria-Hungary. When Germany invaded Belgium in order to attack France, Great Britain joined France and Russia. Later, Italy joined the war against Germany and Austria-Hungary. Fighting raged in Europe and spread across the globe as the colonies of the belligerents became involved.

By 1917, the war in Europe reached a stalemate, settling into desperate trench warfare. To keep war material from reaching Britain, Germany implemented unrestricted submarine warfare, a move that caused the loss of innocent civilians, including Americans. Although protests from President Woodrow Wilson (1913–1921) led Germany to abandon its policy for a time, in early 1917, the Imperial German government resumed unrestricted submarine warfare in the hope of victory before the United States would enter the war. This resumption, plus the publication of the so-called Zimmermann Note, in which Germany encouraged Mexico to make war on the United States in return for lands lost in the Mexican War (1846–1848), led to Congress' declaring war on Germany on April 6, 1917.

The arrival of American troops turned the tide of the war in favor of the Allies. In November 1918, the disillusioned German people forced their ruler, Kaiser Wilhelm II (in power 1888–1918), to abdicate and flee to the Netherlands. The armistice signed on November 11, 1918, marked the end of the fighting, and the war officially ended with the Treaty of Versailles (1919). The Russian, Ottoman, and Austro-Hungarian empires were replaced by a number of smaller states, and the United States took on its new role as a global power. *See also* Chapters 8, 9, and 10.

World War II (1939–1945): The most extensive global conflict in history, waged in Europe, Asia, and Africa, which began with the German invasion of Poland on September 1, 1939. During the 1930s, Japan, Italy, and Germany became increasingly aggressive, demanding territory and building up of their respective militaries. As soon as Adolf Hitler took power in 1933, he began to rearm Germany in spite of the limitations imposed on German armed forces by the Treaty of Versailles (1919). He reorganized Germany into a military state in which all citizens were "coordinated" to fit the Nazi military machine. In 1936, he moved German troops into the demilitarized zones of the Rhineland and, when France and Great Britain did not react, he kept troops there. A year earlier, Italian troops under the Fascist dictator Benito Mussolini (in power 1922–1943) had invaded Ethiopia, and while the League of Nations protested ineffectually, the Italian troops easily conquered the weak African nation. In 1931, Japan took over the northern Chinese province of Manchuria and established the puppet state of Manchukuo, and in July 1937, Japanese troops again invaded northern China. Imperial Japan aimed to control eastern Asia from Korea to the East Indies and the entire western Pacific area, to create a "Greater East Asia Co-Prosperity Sphere." By the late 1930s, the nations of Germany, Italy, and Japan had formed a military alliance, becoming known as the Axis powers. In Europe, Hitler demanded the Sudetenland, a region of Czechoslovakia. To avoid war, France and Great Britain appeased Hitler in the infamous Munich Pact of 1938. The following spring, Germany annexed all of Czechoslovakia. In 1939, Germany and the Soviet Union signed the Ribbontrop-Molotov Pact, an understanding in which the two nations agreed not to attack each other and divide Poland between them.

Temporarily assured of Soviet neutrality, Hitler invaded Poland on September 1, 1939. France and Britain declared war on Germany on September 3. Belgium, the Netherlands, France, Denmark, and Norway quickly succumbed to Nazi armies.

In the United States, public opinion was strongly against intervening in the war. However, President Franklin D. Roosevelt (1933–1945) realized that Hitler's ambitions knew no bounds and, if not stopped, Germany would someday attack the United States. As a result, Roosevelt sought to make the United States "an arsenal of democracy" and pushed for measures "short of war" to prepare the nation, including the first peacetime draft and the 1941 Lend-Lease Act to supply materiel to the Allies. In June 1941, Nazi armies invaded the Soviet Union, violating the Ribbontrop-Molotov Pact and bringing the Soviet Union into the war. On the early morning of December 7, 1941, the Empire of Japan launched an attack on the U.S. base at Pearl Harbor, Hawaii; the U. S. Congress declared war on Japan the next day. Three days later, on December 11, Germany and Italy declared war on the United States. Throughout most of 1942, the Axis powers easily achieved new victories: Japan in the Pacific, Germany in the Soviet Union and southeastern Europe, and Germany and Italy in North Africa. Then in November 1942, Britain and the United States invaded North Africa, pushing back the Axis troops. In 1943, Allied troops moved north on the Italian peninsula, and in September of that year, Italy surrendered unconditionally. On June 6, 1944, D-Day, American, British, and Canadian troops landed on the Normandy coast of France, thus beginning a push across France to the German capital of Berlin. As Allied forces moved east, Soviet troops moved west; soldiers from the two armies met in Germany in late April 1945, and Germany surrendered unconditionally on May 8. In the Pacific, war still raged and the Japanese refused to surrender.

In August 1945, President Harry S. Truman (1945–1953), who assumed the presidency after Roosevelt's death on April 12, authorized the dropping of the world's first atomic bombs on Japan. On August 6, the *Enola Gay*, a B-29 bomber, dropped the first atomic bomb on the Japanese city of Hiroshima; three days later, a second atomic bomb was dropped on the city of Nagasaki. The two bombs killed more than 100,000 Japanese and permanently injured thousands more. Still, the Japanese military refused to capitulate. The Emperor Hirohito forced the issue and insisted on an immediate surrender to avoid more bloodshed. The Empire of Japan surrendered unconditionally on August 14. *See also* Chapters 14 and 15.

WTO: The only global international organization dealing with the rules of trade between nations. The goal of the World Trade Organization is to help producers of goods and services, exporters, and importers conduct business. Member nations, more than one hundred fifty, abide by a complex set of trade agreements that are mutually beneficial. The WTO came into being in 1995; it is the successor to the General Agreement on Tariffs and Trade (GATT), which had been established in the wake of World War II. Since 1999, meetings of the WTO have sparked widespread, and often violent, protests against free trade and globalization. *See also* Chapters 31 and 34.

X

XYZ Affair: Diplomatic affront to the United States committed by the Duc de Talleyrand, the French foreign minister, and his agents. The French government viewed the Jay Treaty (1794) with Great Britain as a repudiation of the 1778 Franco-American alliance. As a result, the French ordered the seizure of American ships bound for British ports. In response, many members of the pro-British Federalist Party demanded war against France. In 1797, determined to keep the nation out of war, President John Adams (1797–1801) sent a special commission, consisting of Charles C. Pinckney, John Marshall, and Elbridge Gerry, to negotiate with the French government. However, Talleyrand's agents refused to meet with the American delegation unless assured that the United States would adopt a friendlier attitude toward France. Unofficially, they also demanded a bribe of $240,000. After months of wrangling, the American mission gave up. Adams, when reporting the incident to Congress, referred to the French agents as Messieurs X, Y, and Z and declared that he would "never send another minister to France without assurances that he will be received, respected, and honored as the representative of a free, powerful, and independent nation." The incident became known as the XYZ Affair and sparked indignation across the United States. *See also* Chapter 1.

Y

Yalta Conference (1945): Meeting of the leaders of the Allied powers in February 1945, when the defeat of Germany seemed imminent. Held in the Crimean resort of Yalta, British Prime Minister Winston Churchill (1940–1945, 1951–1955), Soviet leader Joseph Stalin (in power 1924–1953), and President Franklin D. Roosevelt (1933–1945), the "Big Three," tried to arrive at basic arrangements for the postwar world. Often referred to as the beginning of the Cold War, the conference was instrumental in the secret division of the continent and other regions into competing spheres of influence: the Western bloc (led by the United States) and the Eastern bloc (led by the Soviet Union). Roosevelt pressed for Soviet intervention in the war against Japan. The Soviet Union was to have dominance in Mongolia and occupy the Kurile Islands north of Japan. The Soviet Union was allotted eastern Poland, which it already held, while Poland, as compensation, was to receive land from Germany. In the European lands formerly conquered by Germany, new governments were to be established through free elections under the auspices of the three powers. Germany was to be divided into military zones and occupied by the armed forces of the major Allied nations, Great Britain, France, the United States, and the Soviet Union. *See also* Chapters 14 and 15.

yellow journalism: A type of press that presents little or no well-researched news, often using attention-grabbing headlines and wild exaggeration. Yellow journalism is often opinion masquerading as fact. The term comes from an 1890s comic, "Hogan's Alley," which featured a character, dressed in yellow, known as the "yellow kid" and was published by Joseph Pulitzer in the *New York World*. Rival William Randolph Hearst, who published the *New York Journal*, was determined to compete; he hired away the "Hogan's Alley" cartoonist. In response, Pulitzer hired another artist to draw a second "yellow kid." Quickly, the sensationalist stories published by the opposing newspapers became known as "yellow journalism." The yellow journalism of New York's rival newspapers was a key factor leading to the Spanish-American War (1898). *See also* Chapter 6.

Z

Zimmermann Note: A diplomatic proposal by the German Imperial government to Mexico to make war against the United States. In January 1917, British cryptographers deciphered a telegram from the German foreign minister Arthur Zimmermann to the German minister to Mexico, Heinrich von Eckhardt, offering U.S. territory, the states of Texas, Arizona, and New Mexico, to Mexico in return for joining the German cause. Mexico declined the proposal, but the publication of the telegram enraged the American public and helped draw the United States into World War I (1914–1917). *See also* Chapters 8 and 9.

★ CHAPTER ACRONYMS AND INITIALISMS

AAA: Agricultural Adjustment Act [Chapter 12]

ABM: Anti-Ballistic Missile System [Chapter 25]

AC: Advisory Council [Chapter 14]

ACC: Allied Control Commission [Chapter 14]

ACRI: African Crisis Response Initiative [Chapter 37]

ACT: Artemisinin-Based Combination Therapy [Chapter 37]

AFC: America First Committee [Chapter 13]

AFL-CIO: American Federation of Labor–Congress of Industrial Organizations [Chapter 34]

AFRICOM: African Command [Chapter 37]

AGOA: African Growth and Opportunity Act [Chapter 37]

AIOC: Anglo-Iranian Oil Company [Chapter 18]

AMG: Allied Military Government [Chapter 14]

ANC: African National Congress [Chapter 21]

ANZUS: Australia, New Zealand, and United States Treaty [Chapter 19]

APOC: Anglo-Persian Oil Company [Chapter 18]

ARAMCO: Arabian-American Oil Company [Chapter 18]

ARVN: Army of the Republic of Vietnam [Chapter 23]

ASEAN: Association of Southeast Asian Nations [Chapters 21 and 36]

AU: African Union [Chapter 37]

CAAA: Comprehensive Anti-Apartheid Act [Chapter 21]

CAFTA: Central American Free Trade Agreement [Chapter 31]

CBD: Convention on Biological Diversity [Chapter 32]

CBI: Caribbean Basin Initiative [Chapter 31]

CCC: Civilian Conservation Corps [Chapters 12 and 16]

CCP: Communist Chinese Party [Chapter 36]

CDAAA: Committee to Defend America by Aiding the Allies [Chapter 15]

CDC: Centers for Disease Control and Prevention [Chapter 37]

CFCs: Chlorofluorocarbons [Chapter 32]

CHAI: Clinton Health Access Initiative [Chapter 37]

CIA: Central Intelligence Agency [Chapters 16, 17, 20, 22, 24, 27, 29, 35, 38, and 39]

CJTF: Combined Joint Task Forces [Chapter 33]

CJTF-HOA: Combined Joint Task Force-Horn of Africa [Chapter 37]

CNAS: Center for a New American Security [Chapter 36]

COMECON: Council for Economic Assistance [Chapter 29]

Comintern: Communist International [Chapter 11]

CPA: Comprehensive Peace Agreement [Chapter 37]

CPSU: Communist Party of the Soviet Union [Chapter 25]

CPV: Chinese People's Volunteers [Chapter 19]

CSA: Confederate States of America [Chapter 3]

CSCE: Conference on Security and Cooperation in Europe [Chapter 25]

DMZ: Demilitarized Zone [Chapter19]

DOD: Department of Defense [Chapter 32]

DOS: Department of State [Chapter 4]

DPRK: Democratic People's Republic of Korea [Chapters 19 and 27]

DRC: Democratic Republic of Congo [Chapter 37]

DRV: Democratic Republic of Vietnam [Chapter 23]

EAC: European Advisory Commission [Chapter 14]

EAM: National Liberation Front (Greece) [Chapter 16]

ECLA: Economic Commission for Latin America [Chapter 22]

ERP: European Recovery Program [Chapter 32]

ESDI: European Security and Defense Identity [Chapter 33]

ESDP: European Security and Defense Policy [Chapter 33]

EU: European Union [Chapters 37, 38, and 39]

FBI: Federal Bureau of Investigation [Chapters 17 and 35]

FCDA: Federal Civil Defense Administration [Chapter 20]

FEC: French Expeditionary Corps [Chapter 23]

FTF: Feed the Future [Chapter 37]

GATT: General Agreement on Tariffs and Trade [Chapter 34]

GDP: Gross Domestic Product [Chapters 29, 36, and 37]

GNP: Gross National Product [Chapters 12 and 24]

HIV/AIDS: Human Immuno-deficiency Virus/Acquired Immune Deficiency Syndrome [Chapter 37]

HUAC: House Un-American Activities Committee [Chapter 17]

ICBMs: Intercontinental Ballistic Missiles [Chapters 20 and 30]

ICC: International Criminal Court [Chapter 37]

IDF: Israel Defense Forces [Chapters 26 and 38]

IEDs: Improvised Explosive Devices [Chapter 40]

IFOR: Implementation Force [Chapter 33]

IGOs: International Governmental Organizations [Chapter 39]

IMF: International Monetary Fund [Chapters 16, 21, 36, and 37]

INF: Intermediate Nuclear Forces [Chapters 29 and 30]

INGOs: International Non-Governmental Organizations [Chapter 39]

IPCC: Intergovernmental Panel on Climate Change [Chapter 32]

ISAF: International Security Assistance Force [Chapter 33]

ITT: International Telephone and Telegraph [Chapter 22]

IUCN: International Union for the Conservation of Nature [Chapter 32]

JCS: Joint Chiefs of Staff [Chapters 19 and 23]

KANU: Kenya African National Union [Chapter 37]

KFOR: Kosovo Force [Chapter 33]

KLA: Kosovo Liberation Army [Chapter 33]

KMAG: Korean Military Advisory Group [Chapter 19]

KPA: Korean People's Army [Chapter 19]

LAFTA: Latin America Free Trade Area [Chapter 31]

LEP: League to Enforce Peace [Chapter 8]

MAD: Mutually Assured Destruction [Chapters 16, 20, 25, and 29]

MAP: Membership Action Plan [Chapter 33]

MCC: Millennium Challenge Corporation [Chapter 37]

MDC: Movement for Democratic Change [Chapter 37]

MFN: Most Favored Nation [Chapter 12]

MIRV: Multiple Independently Targeted Re-Entry Vehicle [Chapter 25]

MNR: Nationalist Revolutionary Movement [Chapter 22]

MONUSCO: United Nations Organization Stabilization Mission in the Democratic Republic of the Congo [Chapter 37]

MPLA: Movement for the Liberation of Angola [Chapter 25]

NAACP: National Association for the Advancement of Colored People [Chapter 10]

NAFTA: North American Free Trade Agreement [Chapters 31 and 34]

NAM: Non-Aligned Movement [Chapter 21]

NASA: National Aeronautics and Space Administration [Chapter 32]

NATO: North Atlantic Treaty Organization [Chapters 15, 16, 17, 18, 19, 20, 21, 24, 25, 27, 29, 30, 33, 34, 37, 39, and 40]

NGOs: Non-Governmental Organizations [Chapters 30, 32, and 37]

NIRA: National Industrial Recovery Act [Chapter 12]

NLF: National Liberation Front [Chapters 21 and 23]

NMD: National Missile Defense [Chapter 34]

NNSC: Neutral Nations Supervisory Commission [Chapter 19]

NORAD: North American Aerospace Defense Command [Chapter 41]

NPT: Nuclear Non-Proliferation Treaty [Chapter 25]

NRA: National Recovery Administration [Chapter 12]

NSC: National Security Council [Chapters 16, 17, 19, 29, 39, and 40]

NSC-68: National Security Council Report 68 [Chapters 17, 20, 23, and 24]

NSD 26: National Security Directive 26 [Chapter 27]

NSDD 138: National Security Decision Directive [Chapter 27]

NSL: National Security League [Chapter 8]

NTBT: Partial Nuclear Test Ban Treaty [Chapter 25]

NTD: Neglected Tropical Disease Initiative [Chapter 37]

OAS: Organization of American States [Chapters 22 and 40]

OAU: Organization of African Unity [Chapter 21]

OPEC: Organization of Petroleum Exporting Companies [Chapters 21 and 26]

OSCE: Organization for Security and Co-operation in Europe [Chapter 33]

PA: Palestinian Authority [Chapter 38]

PARP: PfP Planning and Review Process [Chapter 33]

PCA: Permanent Court of Arbitration [Chapter 41]

PDBs: Presidential Daily Briefs [Chapter 35]

PDPA: People's Democratic Party of Afghanistan [Chapter 25]

PEPFAR: President's Emergency Plan for AIDS Relief [Chapter 37]

PFLP-GC: Palestinian Front for the Liberation of Palestine—General Command [Chapter 27]

PfP: Partnership for Peace [Chapter 33]

PKI: Communist Party of Indonesia [Chapter 21]

PLO: Palestine Liberation Organization [Chapters 18, 26, 27, and 38]

PMI: President's Malaria Initiative [Chapter 37]

PNW: Prevention of Nuclear War agreement [Chapter 25]

POWs: Prisoners of War [Chapters 19 and 23]

PRC: People's Republic of China [Chapters 17, 19, 21, 25, 34, and 36]

PWA: Public Works Administration [Chapter 12]

QDDR: Quadrennial Diplomacy and Development Review [Chapter 39]

ROC: Republic of China [Chapter 21]

ROK: Republic of Korea [Chapters 19 and 27]

RTA: Reciprocal Trade Agreements Act [Chapter 12]

RVN: Republic of Vietnam [Chapter 23]

SACEUR: Supreme Allied Commander Europe [Chapter 33]

SALT I: Strategic Arms Limitations Treaty [Chapters 25 and 30]

SALT II: Strategic Arms Limitation Talks [Chapters 25 and 30]

SCAP: Supreme Commander of the Allied Powers [Chapter 16]

SDI: Strategic Defense Initiative [Chapters 29 and 30]

SDS: Students for a Democratic Society [Chapter 23]

SEATO: Southeast Asia Treaty Organization [Chapters 21 and 27]

SED: Strategic and Economic Dialogue [Chapter 36]

SFOR: Stabilization Force [Chapter 33]

SLBM: Submarine Launched Ballistic Missiles [Chapter 20]

START: Strategic Arms Reduction Treaty [Chapter 29]

SVN: State of Vietnam [Chapter 23]

TVA: Tennessee Valley Authority [Chapter 12, 32]

UFCO: United Fruit Company [Chapter 22]

UN 242: United Nations Resolution 242 [Chapter 26]

UN: United Nations [Chapters 15, 16, 17, 18, 19, 20, 21, 22, 23, 26, 27, 29, 34, 35, 36, 37, 38, 39, and 40]

UNC: United Nations Command [Chapter 19]

UNEF: United Nations Emergency Force [Chapter 26]

UNEP: United Nations Environment Programme [Chapter 32]

UNESCO: United Nations Educational, Scientific and Cultural Organization [Chapters 27 and 37]

UNFCCC: UN Framework Convention on Climate Change [Chapter 32]

UNHCR: United Nations High Commissioner for Refugees [Chapter 37]

UNPROFOR: United Nations Protection Force [Chapter 33]

UNRRA: United Nations Relief and Rehabilitation Agency [Chapter 16]

USAID: United States Agency for International Development [Chapters 32, 37]

USAMGIK: U.S. Army Military Government in Korea [Chapter 19]

USIA: U.S. Information Agency [Chapter 40]

WEU: Western European Union [Chapter 33]

WHO: World Health Organization [Chapters 32, 37, and 39]

WMDs: Weapons of Mass Destruction [Chapters 34, 35, and 38]

WMO: World Meteorological Organization [Chapter 32]

WTO: World Trade Organization [Chapters 31 and 34]

★ BIBLIOGRAPHY

PART I: THE DEVELOPMENT AND GROWTH OF AMERICAN FOREIGN POLICY

Adams, Ephraim D. *Great Britain and the American Civil War*. 2 vols. New York: Longmans, 1925.

Adams, Henry. *History of the United States of America during the Administrations of Thomas Jefferson and James Madison* [1889–1891]. 2 vols. New York: Library of America, 1986.

Adams, William Howard. *Gouverneur Morris: An Independent Life*. New Haven, CT: Yale University Press, 2003.

Adelman, Jeremy, and Stephen Aron. "From Borderlands to Borders: Empires, Nation-States, and the Peoples in between in North American History." In *American Historical Review* 104, no. 3 (1999): 814–41.

Adickes, Sandra E. "Sisters, Not Demons: The Influence of British Suffragists of the American Suffrage Movement." In *Women's History Review* 11, no. 4 (2002): 675–90.

Alonso, Harriet Hyman. *Peace as a Women's Issue: A History of the U.S. Movement for World Peace and Women's Rights*. Syracuse, NY: Syracuse University Press, 1993.

Ammon, Harry. *The Genet Mission*. New York: W. W. Norton, 1973.

———. *James Monroe: The Quest for National Identity*. New York: McGraw-Hill, 1971.

Anderson, Stuart. *Race and Rapprochement: Anglo-Saxonism and Anglo-American Relations, 1895–1904*. Madison, NJ: Fairleigh Dickinson University Press, 1981.

Armstrong, William M. *E. L. Godkin and American Foreign Policy, 1865–1900*. New York: Bookman, 1957.

Baker, Paula. "The Domestication of Politics: Women and American Political Society, 1780–1920." In *American Historical Review* 89, no. 3 (1984): 620–47.

Barnby, H. G. *The Prisoners of Algiers: An Account of the Forgotten American-Algerian War 1785–1797*. New York: Oxford University Press, 1966.

Barney, William L. *The Passage of the Republic: An Interdisciplinary History of Nineteenth-Century America*. Lexington, MA: D. C. Heath, 1987.

Beckert, Sven. "Emancipation and Empire: Reconstructing the Worldwide Web of Cotton Production in the Age of the American Civil War." In *American Historical Review* 109, no. 5 (2004): 1405–38.

Bederman, Gail. *Manliness and Civilization: A Cultural History of Gender and Race in the United States, 1880–1917*. Chicago: University of Chicago Press, 1995.

Beirne, Francis J. *The War of 1812*. New York: E. P. Dutton, 1949.

Beisner, Robert L. *From the Old Diplomacy to the New, 1865–1900*. Wheeling, IL: Harlan Davidson, 1986.

Bemis, Samuel Flagg. *The Diplomacy of the American Revolution*. Rev. ed. Bloomington: Indiana University Press, 1957.

———. *Jay's Treaty: A Study of Commerce and Diplomacy*. Rev. ed. New Haven, CT: Yale University Press, 1962.

———. *John Quincy Adams and the Foundations of American Foreign Policy*. New York: Alfred A. Knopf, 1949.

———. *Pinckney's Treaty: America's Advantage from Europe's Distress, 1783–1800*. Rev. ed. New Haven, CT: Yale University Press, 1960.

Ben-Atar, Doron S. *The Origins of Jeffersonian Commerical Policy and Diplomacy*. New York: St. Martin's, 1993.

Bender, Thomas. *A Nation among Nations: America's Place in World History*. New York: Hill & Wang, 2006.

Bishel, William V. "Fall from Grace: U.S. Business Interests versus U.S. Diplomatic Interests in Peru, 1885–1890." In *Diplomatic History* 20, no. 2 (1996): 163–83.

Black, Jeremy. *European International Relations 1648–1815*. New York: Palgrave, 2002.

Blackett, Richard J. M. *Divided Hearts: Britain and the American Civil War*. Baton Rouge: Louisiana State University Press, 2001.

Blake, Nelson M. "The Olney-Pauncefote Treaty of 1897." In *American Historical Review* 50, no. 2 (1945): 228–43.

Blondheim, Menahem. *News over the Wires: The Telegraph and the Flow of Public Information in America, 1844–1897*. Cambridge, MA: Harvard University Press, 1994.

Bock, Carl H. *Prelude to Tragedy: The Negotiation and Breakdown of the Tripartite Convention of London, October 31, 1861*. Philadelphia: University of Pennsylvania Press, 1966.

Bogue, Margaret Beatti. "To Save the Fish: Canada, the United States, the Great Lakes, and the Joint Commission of 1892." In *Journal of American History* 79, no. 4 (1993): 1429–54.

Boisseau, T. J. "White Queens at the Chicago World's Fair, 1893: New Womanhood in the Service of Class, Race, and Nation." In *Gender & History* 12, no. 1 (2000): 33–81.

Bolkhovitinov, Nikolai N. *Russia and the American Revolution*. C. Jay Smith, trans. Tallahassee, FL: Diplomatic Press, 1976.

Bowman, Albert Hall. *The Struggle for Neutrality: Franco-American Diplomacy during the Federalist Era*. Knoxville: University of Tennessee Press, 1974.

Brant, Irving. *James Madison*. 6 vols. Indianapolis, IN: Bobbs-Merrill, 1941–1961.

Brauer, Kinley J. "The United States and British Imperial Expansion, 1815–60." In *Diplomatic History* 12, no. 1 (1988): 19–37.

Brawley, Mark R. *Liberal Leadership: Great Powers and Their Challengers in Peace and War*. Ithaca, NY: Cornell University Press, 1993.

Brecher, Frank W. *Negotiating the Louisiana Purchase: Robert Livingston's Mission to France, 1801–1804*. Jefferson, NC: McFarland, 2006.

———. *Securing American Independence: John Jay and the French Alliance*. Westport, CT: Praeger, 2003.

Brown, Gordon S. *Toussaint's Clause: The Founding Fathers and the Haitian Revolution*. Jackson: University of Mississippi Press, 2005.

Brown, Ralph A. *The Presidency of John Adams*. Lawrence: University Press of Kansas, 1975.

Brown, Roger Hamilton. *The Republic in Peril: 1812*. New York: W. W. Norton, 1971.

Butler, Leslie. *Critical Americans: Victorian Intellectuals and Transatlantic Liberal Reform*. Chapel Hill: University of North Carolina Press, 2007.

Calhoun, Charles W. "Rehearsal for Anti-Imperialism: The Second Cleveland Administration's Attempt to Withdraw from Samoa, 1893–1895." In *Historian* 48, no. 2 (1986): 209–24.

Campbell, Charles Soutter. "The Anglo-American Crisis in the Bering Sea, 1890–1891." In *Mississippi Valley Historical Review* 48, no. 3 (1961): 393–414.

———. *From Revolution to Rapprochement: The United States and Great Britain, 1783–1900*. New York: Wiley, 1974.

———. *The Transformation of American Foreign Relations, 1865–1900*. New York: Harper & Row, 1976.

Campbell, Duncan A. *English Public Opinion and the American Civil War*. Woodbridge, Suffolk, UK; Rochester, NY: Royal Historical Society/Boydell, 2003.

Carrigan, William D., and Clive Webb. "The Lynching of Persons of Mexican Origin or Descent in the United States, 1838–1928." In *Journal of Social History* 37, no. 2 (2003): 411–38.

Carroll, Charles Griffin. *The United States and the Disruption of the Spanish Empire 1810–1822: A Study of the Relations of the United States with Spain and with the Rebel Spanish Colonies*. New York: Columbia University Press, 1937.

Carroll, Daniel B. *Henri Mercier and the American Civil War*. Princeton, NJ: Princeton University Press, 1971.

Case, Lynn M., and Warren F. Spencer. *The United States and France: Civil War Diplomacy*. Philadelphia: University of Pennsylvania Press, 1970.

Cassell, Frank A. "The Columbian Exposition of 1893 and United States Diplomacy in Latin America." In *Mid America* 67, no. 3 (1985): 109–24.

Castle, Alfred L. "Tentative Empire: Walter Q. Gresham, U.S. Foreign Policy, and Hawai'i, 1893–1895." In *Hawaiian Journal of History*, no. 29 (1995): 83–96.

Casto, William R. *Foreign Affairs and the Constitution in Age of Fighting Sail*. Columbia: University of South Carolina Press, 2006.

Chambers, John Whiteclay. "The American Debate over Modern War, 1870–1914." In *Anticipating Total War: The German and American Experiences, 1871–1914*, Manfred F. Boemeke, Roger Chickering, and Stig Förster, eds. 241–80. New York: Cambridge University Press, 1999.

Chang, Gordon H. "Whose 'Barbarism'? Whose 'Treachery'? Race and Civilization in the Unknown United States-Korea War of 1871." In *Journal of American History* 89, no. 4 (2003): 1331–65.

Chavez, Thomas E. *Spain and the Independence of the United States: An Intrinsic Gift*. Albuquerque: University of New Mexico Press, 2002.

Chin, Carol C. "Beneficent Imperialists: American Women Missionaries in China at the Turn of the Twentieth Century." In *Diplomatic History* 27, no. 3 (2003): 327–52.

Claussen, Cathryn L. "Gendered Merit: Women and the Merit Concept in Federal Employment, 1864–1944." In *American Journal of Legal History* 40, no. 3 (1996): 229–52.

Colby, Jason M. "Race, Empire, and New England Capital in the Caribbean, 1890–1930." In *Massachusetts Historical Review*, no. 11 (2009): 1–25.

Coles, Harry L. *The War of 1812*. Chicago: University of Chicago Press, 1965.

Combs, Jerald A. *The Jay Treaty: Political Battleground of the Founding Fathers*. Berkeley: University of California Press, 1970.

Conn, Steven. "An Epistemology for Empire: The Philadelphia Commercial Museum, 1893–1926." In *Diplomatic History* 22, no. 4 (1998): 533–63.

Cook, Adrian. *The Alabama Claims: American Politics and Anglo-American Relations, 1865–1872*. Ithaca, NY: Cornell University Press, 1975.

Cooper, Jerry M. *The Rise of the National Guard: The Evolution of the American Militia, 1865–1920*. Lincoln: University of Nebraska Press, 1998.

Cox, LaWanda. *Lincoln and Black Freedom: A Study in Presidential Leadership*. Columbia: University of South Carolina Press, 1981.

Crapol, Edward P. *America for Americans: Economic Nationalism and Anglophobia in the Late Nineteenth Century*. Westport, CT: Greenwood, 1973.

———. "Coming to Terms with Empire: The Historiography of Late-Nineteenth-Century American Foreign Relations." In *Diplomatic History*, no. 16 (Fall 1992): 573–97.

———. *James G. Blaine: Architect of Empire*. Wilmington, DE: Scholarly Resources, 2000.

———. *John Tyler: The Accidental President*. Chapel Hill: University of North Carolina Press, 2006.

Crook, D. P. *Diplomacy during the Civil War*. New York: Wiley, 1975.

———. *The North, the South, and the Powers, 1861–1865*. New York: Wiley, 1974.

Cusick, James G. *The Other War of 1812: The Patriot War and the American Invasion of Spanish East Florida*. Gainesville: University Press of Florida, 2003.

D'Agostino, Peter. "Craniums, Criminals, and the 'Cursed Race': Italian Anthropology in American Racial Thought." In *Comparative Studies in Society and History* 44, no. 2 (2002): 319–43.

Dangerfield, George. *Chancellor Robert R. Livingston of New York, 1746–1813*. New York: Harcourt, 1960.

DeConde, Alexander. *Entangling Alliance: Politics and Diplomacy under George Washington*. Durham, NC: Duke University Press, 1958.

———. *The Quasi-War: The Politics and Diplomacy of the Undeclared War with France, 1797–1801*. New York: Charles Scribner's and Sons, 1966.

———. *This Affair of Louisiana*. New York: Charles Scribner's and Sons, 1976.

DeLay, Brian. *War of a Thousand Deserts: Indian Raids and the U.S.-Mexican War*. New Haven, CT: Yale University Press, 2008.

Downs, Jacques M. *The Golden Ghetto: The American Commercial Community at Canton and the Shaping of American China Policy*. Bethlehem, PA: Lehigh University Press, 1997.

Dull, Jonathan R. *A Diplomatic History of the American Revolution*. New Haven, CT: Yale University Press, 1985.

———. *Franklin the Diplomat: The French Mission*. Philadelphia: The American Philosophical Society, 1982.

Eckes, Alfred E., Jr., and Thomas W. Zeiler. *Globalization and the American Century*. New York: Cambridge University Press, 2003.

Edling, Max M. "'So Immense a Power in the Affairs of War': Alexander Hamilton and the Restoration of Public Credit." In *William and Mary Quarterly*, 3rd ser., 64, no. 2 (April 2007): 285–326.

Edmunds, R. David. *Tecumseh and the Quest for Indian Leadership*. Boston: Little, Brown, 1984.

Egan, Clifford L. *Neither Peace nor War: Franco-American Relations, 1803–1812*. Baton Rouge: Louisiana State University Press, 1983.

Egnal, Marc. *A Mighty Empire: The Origins of the American Revolution*. Ithaca, NY: Cornell University Press, 1988.

Elkins, Stanley, and Eric McKitrick. *The Age of Federalism: The Early American Republic, 1788–1800*. New York: Oxford University Press, 1993.

Endy, Christopher. "Travel and World Power: Americans in Europe, 1890–1917." In *Diplomatic History* 22, no. 4 (1998): 565–94.

Ernst, Robert. *Rufus King: American Federalist*. Chapel Hill: University of North Carolina Press, 1968.

Estes, Todd. *The Jay Treaty Debate, Public Opinion and the Evolution of Early American Political Culture*. Amherst: University of Massachusetts Press, 2006.

Ettinger, Patrick. "'We Sometimes Wonder What They Will Spring on Us Next': Immigrants and Border Enforcement in the

American West, 1882–1930." In *Western Historical Quarterly* 37, no. 2 (2006): 159–81.

Faust, Drew G. *This Republic of Suffering: Death and the American Civil War*. New York: Alfred A. Knopf, 2008.

Ferris, Norman B. *Desperate Diplomacy: William H. Seward's Foreign Policy, 1861*. Knoxville: University of Tennessee Press, 1976.
———. *The Trent Affair: A Diplomatic Crisis*. Knoxville: University of Tennessee Press, 1977.

Fiege, Mark. *Irrigated Eden: The Making of an Agricultural Landscape in the American West*. Seattle: University of Washington Press, 2000.

Field, James A., Jr. *America and the Mediterranean World 1776–1882*. Princeton, NJ: Princeton University Press, 1969.

Flexner, James Thomas. *George Washington*. 4 vols. Boston: Little, Brown, 1965–1972.

Foos, Paul. *A Short, Offhand, Killing Affair: Soldiers and Social Conflict during the Mexican-American War*. Chapel Hill: University of North Carolina Press, 2002.

Frank, Alison. "The Petroleum War of 1910: Standard Oil, Austria, and the Limits of the Multinational Corporation." In *American Historical Review* 114, no. 1 (2009): 16–41.

Franklin, John Hope. *The Emancipation Proclamation*. Garden City, NY: Doubleday, 1963.

Freeman, Douglas Southall. *George Washington*. 7 vols. New York: Charles Scribner's and Sons, 1948–1957.

Fry, Joseph A. *Dixie Looks Abroad: The South and U.S. Foreign Relations, 1789–1973*. Baton Rouge: Louisiana State University Press, 2002.
———. "Phases of Empire: Late Nineteenth-Century U.S. Foreign Relations." In *The Gilded Age: Perspectives on the Origins of Modern America*, Charles W. Calhoun, ed.: 307–32. Lanham, MD: Rowman and Littlefield, 2007.

Gallagher, Gary W., ed. *Antietam: Essays on the 1862 Maryland Campaign*. Kent, OH: Kent State University Press, 1989.
———, ed. *The Richmond Campaign of 1862: The Peninsula and the Seven Days*. Chapel Hill: University of North Carolina Press, 2000.

Gantt, Jonathan. *Irish Terrorism in the Atlantic Community, 1865–1922*. New York: Palgrave, 2010.

Gardiner, A. G. *The Life of Sir William Harcourt*. 2 vols. New York: George H. Doran, 1923.

Gardner, Martha Mabie. *The Qualities of a Citizen: Women, Immigration, and Citizenship, 1870–1965*. Princeton, NJ: Princeton University Press, 2005.

Garroutte, Eva Marie. "The Racial Formation of American Indians: Negotiating Legitimate Identities within Tribal and Federal Law." In *American Indian Quarterly* 25, no. 2 (2001): 224–39.

Gibb, Paul. "Unmasterly Inactivity? Sir Julian Pauncefote, Lord Salisbury, and the Venezuela Boundary Dispute." In *Diplomacy & Statecraft* 16, no. 1 (2005): 23–55.

Gilbert, Arthur N. "The American Indian and United States Diplomatic History." In *History Teacher* 8, no. 2 (1975): 229–41.

Gilbert, Felix. *To the Farewell Address: Ideas of Early American Foreign Policy*. Princeton, NJ: Princeton University Press, 1961.

Gilderhus, Mark T. "The Monroe Doctrine: Meanings and Implications." In *Presidential Studies Quarterly* 36, no. 1 (2006): 5–16.

Gismondi, Michael, and Jeremy Mouat. "Merchants, Mining and Concessions on Nicaragua's Mosquito Coast: Reassessing the American Presence, 1893–1912." In *Journal of Latin American Studies* 34, no. 4 (2002): 845–80.

Goldberg, Joyce S. "Consent to Ascent: The 'Baltimore' Affair and the U.S. Rise to World Power Status." In *Americas* 41, no. 1 (1984): 21–35.

Graebner, Norman A. "Isolation and Antifederalism: The Ratification Debates." In *Diplomatic History* 11, no. 4 (Fall 1987): 337–53.

Greenberg, Amy S. *Manifest Manhood and the Antebellum American Empire*. New York: Cambridge University Press, 2005.

Haller, John S., Jr. *Outcasts from Evolution: Scientific Attitudes of Racial Inferiority, 1859–1900*. Carbondale: Southern Illinois University Press, 1971.

Hanna, Alfred J., and Kathryn A. Hanna. *Napoleon III and Mexico: American Triumph over Monarchy*. Chapel Hill: University of North Carolina Press, 1971.

Hausman, William J., Peter Hertner, and Mira Wilkins. *Global Electrification: Multinational Enterprise and International Finance in the History of Light and Power, 1878–2007*. New York: Cambridge University Press, 2008.

Headrick, Daniel R. *The Invisible Weapon: Telecommunications and International Politics, 1851–1945*. New York: Oxford University Press, 1991.

Healy, David. *James G. Blaine and Latin America*. Columbia: University of Missouri Press, 2001.
———. *U.S. Expansionism: The Imperialist Urge in the 1890s*. Madison: University of Wisconsin Press, 1970.

Heckscher, Eli F. *The Continental System: An Economic Interpretation*. Washington, DC: Carnegie Endowment for International Peace, 1922.

Heidler, David S., and Jeanne T. Heidler, eds. *Manifest Destiny*. Westport, CT: Greenwood, 2003.

Hendrickson, David C. *Peace Pact: The Lost World of the American Founding*. Lawrence: University of Kansas Press, 2003.

Herring, George C. *From Colony to Superpower: U.S. Foreign Relations since 1776*. New York: Oxford University Press, 2008.

Hickey, Donald. *The War of 1812: A Forgotten Conflict*. Urbana: University of Illinois Press, 1989.

Hietala, Thomas R. *Manifest Design: American Exceptionalism and Empire*. Ithaca, NY: Cornell University Press, 2003.

Higham, John. *Strangers in the Land: Patterns of American Nativism, 1860–1925*. Piscataway, NJ: Rutgers University Press, 1955.

Hill, Peter P. *Napoleon's Troublesome Americans: Franco-American Relations 1804–1815*. Dulles, VA: Potomac Books, 2005.

Hixson, Walter L. *The Myth of American Diplomacy: National Identity and U.S. Foreign Policy*. New Haven, CT: Yale University Press, 2008.

Hoganson, Kristin. *Consumers' Imperium: The Global Production of American Domesticity, 1865–1920*. Chapel Hill: University of North Carolina Press, 2007.
———. *Fighting for American Manhood: How Gender Politics Provoked the Spanish-American and Philippine-American Wars*. New Haven, CT: Yale University Press, 1998.
———. "Stuff It: Domestic Consumption and the Americanization of the World Paradigm." In *Diplomatic History* 30, no. 4 (2006): 571–94.

Holton, Sandra Stanley. "'To Educate Women into Rebellion': Elizabeth Cady Stanton and the Creation of a Transatlantic Network of Radical Suffragists." In *American Historical Review* 99, no. 4 (1994): 1112–36.

Horsman, Reginald. *The Causes of the War of 1812*. Philadelphia: University of Pennsylvania Press, 1962.
———. *The Diplomacy of the New Republic, 1776–1815*. Wheeling, IL: Harlan Davidson, 1985.
———. *Expansion and American Indian Policy 1783–1812*. East Lansing: Michigan State University Press, 1967.
———. *Race and Manifest Destiny: The Origins of American Racial Anglo-Saxonism*. Rev. ed. Cambridge, MA: Harvard University Press, 1986.
———. *The War of 1812*. New York: Alfred A. Knopf, 1969.

Howe, Daniel W. *What Hath God Wrought: The Transformation of America, 1815–1848*. New York: Oxford University Press, 2007.

Hunt, Michael H. *American Ascendancy: How the United States Gained and Wielded Global Dominance*. Chapel Hill: University of North Carolina Press, 2007.

———. *Ideology and U.S. Foreign Policy*. New Haven, CT: Yale University Press, 1987.

Hutson, James H. *John Adams and the Diplomacy of the American Revolution*. Lexington: University Press of Kentucky, 1980.

Ilchman, Warren Frederick. *Professional Diplomacy in the United States, 1779–1939: A Study in Administrative History*. Chicago: University of Chicago Press, 1961.

Immerman, Richard H. *Empire for Liberty: A History of American Imperialism from Benjamin Franklin to Paul Wolfowitz*. Princeton, NJ: Princeton University Press, 2010.

Jacobson, Matthew Frye. *Barbarian Virtues: The United States Encounters Foreign Peoples at Home and Abroad, 1876–1917*. New York: Hill & Wang, 2000.

———. *Whiteness of a Different Color: European Immigrants and the Alchemy of Race*. Cambridge, MA: Harvard University Press, 1998.

Jenkins, Brian. *Britain and the War for the Union*. 2 vols. Montreal: McGill-Queen's University Press, 1974, 1980.

Jensen, Merrill. *The New Nation: A History of the United States during the Confederation 1781–1789*. New York: Alfred A. Knopf, 1950.

Jones, Howard. *Abraham Lincoln and a New Birth of Freedom: The Union and Slavery in the Diplomacy of the Civil War*. Lincoln: University of Nebraska Press, 1999.

———. *Blue and Gray Diplomacy: A History of Union and Confederate Foreign Relations*. Chapel Hill: University of North Carolina Press, 2010.

———. *Union in Peril: The Crisis over British Intervention in the Civil War*. Chapel Hill: University of North Carolina Press, 1992.

Jones, Raymond A. *The British Diplomatic Service, 1815–1914*. Waterloo, ON: Wilfrid Laurier University Press, 1983.

Jordan, Donaldson, and Edwin J. Pratt. *Europe and the American Civil War*. Boston: Houghton Mifflin, 1931.

Kagan, Robert. *Dangerous Nation*. New York: Alfred A. Knopf, 2006.

Kaminski, John P. "Honor and Interest: John Jay's Diplomacy during the Confederation." In *New York History* 33, no. 3 (Summer 2002): 293–327.

Kammen, Michael G. *A Rope of Sand: The Colonial Agents, British Politics and the American Revolution*. Ithaca, NY: Cornell University Press, 1968.

Kaplan, Lawrence S. *Alexander Hamilton: Ambivalent Anglophile*. Wilmington, DE: Scholarly Resources, 2002.

———. *Colonies into Nation: American Diplomacy, 1763–1801*. New York: Macmillan, 1972.

———. *Entangling Alliances with None: American Foreign Policy in the Age of Jefferson*. Kent, OH: Kent State University Press, 1987.

———. *Jefferson and France: An Essay on Politics and Political Ideas*. New Haven, CT: Yale University Press, 1967.

———. *Thomas Jefferson: Westward the Course of Empire*. Wilmington, DE: Scholarly Resources, 1999.

Kaufman, Burton Ira, ed. *Washington's Farewell Address: The View from the 20th Century*. Chicago: Quadrangle Books, 1969.

Kelley, Robert. *The Transatlantic Persuasion: The Liberal-Democratic Mind in the Age of Gladstone*. New York: Alfred A. Knopf, 1969.

Kenkel, Joseph F. *Progressives and Protection: The Search for a Tariff Policy, 1866–1936*. Lanham, MD: University Press of America, 1983.

Kennedy, Charles Stuart. *The American Consul: A History of the United States Consular Service, 1776–1914*. Westport, CT: Greenwood, 1990.

Kennedy, Paul. *The Rise and Fall of the Great Powers: Economic Change and Military Conflict from 1500 to 2000*. New York: Random House, 1987.

Kern, Stephen. *The Culture of Time and Space, 1880–1918*. Cambridge, MA: Harvard University Press, 1983.

Ketcham, Ralph L. *James Madison: A Biography*. New York: Macmillan, 1971.

Kloppenberg, James T. *Uncertain Victory: Social Democracy and Progressivism in European and American Thought, 1870–1920*. New York: Oxford University Press, 1986.

Kluger, Richard. *Seizing Destiny: How America Grew from Sea to Shining Sea*. New York: Alfred A. Knopf, 2007.

Koht, Halvdan. "The Origin of Seward's Plan to Purchase the Danish West Indies." In *American Historical Review* 50, no. 4 (1945): 762–67.

Kramer, Paul. "Empires, Exceptions, and Anglo-Saxons: Race and Rule between the British and U.S. Empires, 1880–1910." In *Journal of American History* 88, no. 4 (2002): 1315–53.

Kukla, Jon. *A Wilderness So Immense: The Louisiana Purchase and the Destiny of America*. New York: Alfred A. Knopf, 2003.

Kusmer, Kenneth L. "Toward a Comparative History of Racism and Xenophobia in the United States and Germany, 1865–1933." In *Bridging the Atlantic: The Question of American Exceptionalism in Perspective*, Elisabeth Gläser and Hermann Wellenreuther, eds.: 145–80. Washington, DC: Cambridge University Press for the German Historical Institute, 2002.

LaFeber, Walter. *The American Age: U.S. Foreign Policy at Home and Abroad since 1750*. New York: W. W. Norton, 1989.

———. *The Cambridge History of American Foreign Relations. Vol. 2: The American Search for Opportunity, 1865–1913*. New York: Cambridge University Press, 1993.

———. *The New Empire: An Interpretation of American Expansion, 1860–1898*. Ithaca, NY: Cornell University Press, 1998.

Lambert, Frank. *The Barbary Wars: American Independence in the Atlantic World*. New York: Hill & Wang, 2005.

Lang, Daniel G. *Foreign Policy in the Early Republic: The Law of Nations and the Balance of Power*. Baton Rouge: Louisiana State University Press, 1985.

Latimer, Jon. *1812: War with America*. Cambridge, MA: Harvard University Press, 2007.

Lee, Erika. *At America's Gates: Chinese Immigration during the Exclusion Era, 1882–1943*. Chapel Hill: University of North Carolina Press, 2003.

———. "Enforcing the Borders: Chinese Exclusion along the U.S. Borders with Canada and Mexico, 1882–1924." In *Journal of American History* 89, no. 1 (2002): 54–86.

Leonard, Thomas M. *United States–Latin American Relations, 1850–1903: Establishing a Relationship*. Tuscaloosa: University of Alabama Press, 1999.

Lewis, James E., Jr. *The American Union and the Problem of Neighborhood: The United States and the Collapse of the Spanish Empire 1783–1829*. Chapel Hill: University of North Carolina Press, 1998.

Limerick, Patricia Nelson. *The Legacy of Conquest*. New York: W. W. Norton, 1987.

Long, David Foster. *Gold Braid and Foreign Relations: Diplomatic Activities of U.S. Naval Officers, 1798–1883*. Annapolis, MD: Naval Institute Press, 1988.

Love, Eric Tyrone Lowery. *Race over Empire: Racism and U.S. Imperialism, 1865–1900*. Chapel Hill: University of North Carolina Press, 2004.

Lycan, Gilbert L. *Alexander Hamilton & American Foreign Policy*. Norman: University of Oklahoma Press, 1970.

Lyon, E. Wilson. *Louisiana in French Diplomacy*. Norman: University of Oklahoma Press, 1974.

Mahon, John K. *The War of 1812*. Gainesville: University Press of Florida, 1972.

Malone, Dumas. *Jefferson and His Time*. 6 vols. Boston: Little, Brown, 1948–1981.

"Manifest Destiny" at http://www.enotes.com/american-history-literature-cc/manifest-destiny (accessed December 28, 2010).

Marks, Frederick W., III. *Independence on Trial: Foreign Affairs and the Making of the Constitution.* 2nd ed. Lanham, MD: Rowman & Littlefield, 1997.

Masterson, William H. *Tories and Democrats: British Diplomats in Pre-Jacksonian America.* College Station: Texas A&M University Press, 1985.

Mathews, Joseph J. "Informal Diplomacy in the Venezuelan Crisis of 1896." In *Mississippi Valley Historical Review* 50, no. 2 (1963): 195–212.

Matthew, H. C. G. *Gladstone, 1809–1874.* New York: Oxford University Press, 1986.

Matthewson, Tim. *A Proslavery Foreign Policy: Haitian-American Relations during the Early Republic.* Westport, CT: Praeger, 2003.

Mattox, Henry E. *The Twilight of Amateur Diplomacy: The American Foreign Service and Its Senior Officers in the 1890s.* Kent, OH: Kent State University Press, 1989.

May, Ernest R. *Imperial Democracy: The Emergence of America as a Great Power.* New York: Harcourt, 1961.

May, Robert E. "Epilogue to the Missouri Compromise: The South, the Balance of Power, and the Tropics in the 1850s." In *Plantation Society*, no. 1 (June 1979): 201–25.

———. "Power, Pride, and Purse: Diplomatic Origins of the Constitution." In *Diplomatic History* 11, no. 4 (Fall 1987): 303–19.

———. *The Southern Dream of a Caribbean Empire, 1854–1861.* Athens: University of Georgia Press, 1989.

McCoy, Drew R. *The Elusive Republic: Political Economy in Jeffersonian America.* Chapel Hill: University of North Carolina Press, 1980.

McDougall, Walter A. *Promised Land, Crusader State: The American Encounter with the World since 1776.* Boston: Houghton Mifflin, 1997.

McFadden, Margaret. *Golden Cables of Sympathy: The Transatlantic Sources of Nineteenth-Century Feminism.* Lexington: University Press of Kentucky, 1999.

McKay, Derek, and H. M. Scott. *The Rise of the Great Powers 1648–1815.* New York: Longmans, 1983.

McKeown, Adam. "Ritualization of Regulation: The Enforcement of Chinese Exclusion in the United States and China." In *American Historical Review* 108, no. 2 (2003): 377–403.

McMichael, Andrew. *Atlantic Loyalties: Americans in Spanish West Florida, 1785–1810.* Athens: University of Georgia Press, 2008.

McPherson, James M. *Battle Cry of Freedom: The Civil War Era.* New York: Oxford University Press, 1988.

———. *Crossroads of Freedom: Antietam.* New York: Oxford University Press, 2002.

———. *For Cause and Comrades: Why Men Fought in the Civil War.* New York: Oxford University Press, 1997.

———. *Tried by War: Abraham Lincoln as Commander in Chief.* New York: Penguin, 2008.

———. *What They Fought For, 1861–1865.* Baton Rouge: Louisiana State University Press, 1994.

Mead, Russell Walter. *Special Providence: American Foreign Policy and How It Changed the World.* New York: Alfred A. Knopf, 2001.

Merk, Frederick. *History of the Westward Movement.* New York: Alfred A. Knopf, 1978.

Merli, Frank J. *The Alabama, British Neutrality, and the American Civil War.* David M. Fahey, ed. Bloomington: Indiana University Press, 2004.

———. *Great Britain and the Confederate Navy, 1861–1865.* 1970. Reprint with new introduction by Howard Jones. Bloomington: Indiana University Press, 2004.

Mihm, Stephen. *A Nation of Counterfeiters: Capitalists, Con Men, and the Making of the United States.* Cambridge, MA: Harvard University Press, 2007.

Miller, Melanie Randolph. *Envoy to the Terror: Gouverneur Morris & the French Revolution.* Dulles, VA: Potomac Books, 2005.

Miller, Sally M. "For White Men Only: The Socialist Party of America and Issues of Gender, Ethnicity and Race." In *Journal of the Gilded Age & Progressive Era* 2, no. 3 (2003): 283–302.

Mitchell, Nancy. *The Danger of Dreams: German and American Imperialism in Latin America.* Chapel Hill: University of North Carolina Press, 1999.

Monaghan, Jay. *Abraham Lincoln Deals with Foreign Affairs: A Diplomat in Carpet Slippers.* Introduction by Howard Jones. Lincoln: University of Nebraska Press, 1997. Originally published as *Diplomat in Carpet Slippers: Abraham Lincoln Deals with Foreign Affairs.* Indianapolis, IN: Bobbs-Merrill, 1945.

Moreno, Gary. "Rage against the Monarchy: American Reaction to French Intervention in Mexico." In *Journal of the West* 47, no. 3 (2008): 48–55.

Morgan, William Michael. "The Anti-Japanese Origins of the Hawaiian Annexation Treaty of 1897." In *Diplomatic History* 6, no. 1 (1982): 23–44.

Morris, Richard B. *The Peacemakers: The Great Powers and American Independence.* New York: Harper & Row, 1965.

Moses, L. G. *Wild West Shows and the Images of American Indians, 1883–1933.* Albuquerque: University of New Mexico Press, 1996.

Murphy, Charles T. *Charles Gravier, Compte de Vergennes: French Diplomacy in the Age of Revolution, 1719–1787.* Albany: State University of New York Press, 1982.

Neuman, Gerald L. *Strangers to the Constitution: Immigrants, Borders, and Fundamental Law.* Princeton, NJ: Princeton University Press, 1996.

Newman, Louise Michele. *White Women's Rights: The Racial Origins of Feminism in the United States.* New York: Oxford University Press, 1999.

Ngai, Mae M. "The Architecture of Race in American Immigration Law: A Reexamination of the Immigration Act of 1924." In *Journal of American History* 86, no. 1 (1999): 67–92.

———. *Impossible Subjects: Illegal Aliens and the Making of Modern America.* Princeton, NJ: Princeton University Press, 2004.

Ninkovich, Frank A. *Global Dawn: The Cultural Foundation of American Internationalism, 1865–1890.* Cambridge, MA: Harvard University Press, 2009.

Nugent, Walter. *Habits of Empire: A History of American Expansion.* New York: Alfred A. Knopf, 2008.

Nuxoll, Elizabeth Miles. *Congress and the Munitions Merchants: The Secret Committee of Trade during the American Revolution 1775–1777.* New York: Garland, 1985.

Ogawa, Manako. "The 'White Ribbon League of Nations' Meets Japan: The Trans-Pacific Activism of the Woman's Christian Temperance Union, 1906–1930." In *Diplomatic History* 31, no. 1 (2007): 21–50.

Onuf, Peter, and Nicholas Onuf. *Federal Union, Modern World: The Law of Nations in an Age of Revolution, 1776–1814.* Madison, WI: Madison House, 1993.

O'Sullivan, John. "Annexation." In *United States Magazine and Democratic Review* 17, no. 1 (July–August 1845): 5–10.

Ott, Thomas O. *The Haitian Revolution 1789–1804.* Knoxville: University of Tennessee Press, 1973.

Owsley, Frank L. *King Cotton Diplomacy: Foreign Relations of the Confederate States of America.* Revised by Harriet C. Owsley. Chicago: University of Chicago Press, 1959. Reprint with new introduction by Howard Jones. Tuscaloosa: University of Alabama Press, 2009.

Owsley, Frank Lawrence, Jr., and Gene A. Smith. *Filibusters and Expansionists: Jeffersonian Manifest Destiny, 1800–1821.* Tuscaloosa: University of Alabama Press, 1997.

Palen, Marc-William. "Protection, Federation, and Union: The Global Impact of the McKinley Tariff upon the British Empire, 1890–94." In *Journal of Imperial and Commonwealth History* 38, no. 3 (2010): 395–418.

Pares, Richard. *Colonial Blockade and Neutral Rights 1739–1763*. New York: Oxford University Press, 1938.

Park, James William. *Latin American Underdevelopment: A History of Perspectives in the United States, 1870–1965*. Baton Rouge: Louisiana State University Press, 1995.

Parker, Richard B. *Uncle Sam in Barbary: A Diplomatic History*. Gainesville: University Press of Florida, 2004.

Paterson, Thomas G. "American Businessmen and Consular Service Reform, 1890s to 1906." In *Business History Review* 40, no. 1 (1966): 77–98.

Patrick, Rembert W. *Florida Fiasco: Rampant Rebels on the Georgia-Florida Border*. Athens: University of Georgia Press, 1954.

Pegler-Gordon, Anna. "Chinese Exclusion, Photography, and the Development of U.S. Immigration Policy." In *American Quarterly* 58, no. 1 (2006): 51–77.

Perkins, Bradford. *Castlereagh and Adams: England and the United States, 1812–1823*. Berkeley: University of California Press, 1964.

———. *The Creation of a Republican Empire, 1776–1865*, Vol. I of *The Cambridge History of American Foreign Relations*. New York: Cambridge University Press, 1993.

———. *The First Rapprochement: England and the United States, 1795–1805*. Berkeley: University of California Press, 1955.

———. *Prologue to War: England and the United States, 1805–1812*. Berkeley: University of California Press, 1961.

Peterson, Merrill D. "Thomas Jefferson and Commercial Policy, 1783–1793." In *William and Mary Quarterly*, 3rd ser., 22, no. 4 (October 1965), 584–610.

———. *Thomas Jefferson and the New Nation: A Biography*. New York: Oxford University Press, 1970.

Phelps, Nicole Marie. "Sovereignty, Citizenship, and the New Liberal Order: U.S.-Habsburg Relations and the Transformation of International Politics, 1880–1924." PhD diss., University of Minnesota, 2008.

Platt, D. C. M. *The Cinderella Service: British Consuls since 1825*. New York: Longmans, 1971.

Pletcher, David M. *The Diplomacy of Annexation: Texas, Oregon, and the Mexican War*. Columbia: University of Missouri Press, 1973.

———. *The Diplomacy of Trade and Investment: American Economic Expansion in the Hemisphere, 1865–1900*. Columbia: University of Missouri Press, 1998.

———. "Reciprocity and Latin America in the Early 1890s: A Foretaste of Dollar Diplomacy." In *Pacific Historical Review* 47, no. 1 (1978): 53–89.

Plischke, Elmer. *U.S. Department of State: A Reference History*. Westport, CT: Greenwood, 1999.

Potts, Louis W. *Arthur Lee: A Virtuous Revolutionary*. Baton Rouge: Louisiana State University Press, 1981.

Pratt, Julius W. *Expansionists of 1812*. New York: Macmillan, 1925.

Price, Jacob M. *France and the Chesapeake: A History of the French Tobacco Monopoly, 1674–1791, and of Its Relationship to the British and American Tobacco Trades*. 2 vols. Ann Arbor: University of Michigan Press, 1973.

Rakove, Jack M. *The Beginning of National Politics: An Interpretive History of the Continental Congress*. New York: Alfred A. Knopf, 1979.

Remini, Robert V. *Andrew Jackson and His Indian Wars*. New York: Penguin, 2001.

———. *Henry Clay: Statesman for the Union*. New York: W. W. Norton, 1991.

Richardson, Heather Cox. *The Death of Reconstruction: Race, Labor, and Politics in the Post–Civil War North, 1865–1901*. Cambridge, MA: Harvard University Press, 2001.

Ridley, Jasper Godwin. *Maximilian and Juárez*. New York: Ticknor & Fields, 1992.

Rigby, Barry. "The Origins of American Expansion in Hawaii and Samoa, 1865–1900." In *International History Review* 10, no. 2 (June 1988): 221–37.

Ritcheson, Charles R. *Aftermath of Revolution: British Policy toward the United States, 1783–1795*. Dallas: Southern Methodist University Press, 1969.

Rodgers, Daniel T. *Atlantic Crossings: Social Politics in a Progressive Age*. Cambridge, MA: The Belknap Press of Harvard University Press, 1998.

Roediger, David R. *Working toward Whiteness: How America's Immigrants Became White*. New York: Basic Books, 2005.

Rolde, Neil. *Continental Liar from the State of Maine: James G. Blaine*. Gardiner, ME: Tilbury House Publishers, 2006.

Rosenberg, Emily S. *Spreading the American Dream: American Economic and Cultural Expansion, 1890–1945*. New York: Hill & Wang, 1982.

Rothman, David J. *Politics and Power: The United States Senate, 1869–1901*. Cambridge, MA: Harvard University Press, 1966.

Rupp, Lelia J. *Worlds of Women: The Making of an International Women's Movement*. Princeton, NJ: Princeton University Press, 1997.

Rutland, Robert Allen. *The Presidency of James Madison*. Lawrence: University Press of Kansas, 1990.

Rydell, Robert W. *All the World's a Fair: Visions of Empire at American International Expositions, 1876–1916*. Chicago: University of Chicago Press, 1984.

Salyer, Lucy. *Laws Harsh as Tigers: Chinese Immigrants and the Shaping of Modern Immigration Law*. Chapel Hill: University of North Carolina Press, 1995.

Sampson, Robert D. *John L. O'Sullivan and His Times*. Kent, OH: Kent State University Press, 2003.

Saul, Norman. *Distant Friends: The United States and Russia, 1763–1867*. Lawrence: University Press of Kansas, 1991.

Savelle, Max. *The Origins of American Diplomacy*. New York: Macmillan, 1967.

Schiff, Stacy. *A Great Improvisation: Franklin, France and the Birth of America*. New York: Henry Holt, 2005.

Schonberger, Howard B. *Transportation to the Seaboard; the Communication Revolution and American Foreign Policy, 1860–1900*. Westport, CT: Greenwood, 1971.

Schulte, Nordholt, and Jan Willem. *The Dutch Republic and American Independence*. Herbert H. Rowen, trans. Chapel Hill: University of North Carolina Press, 1982.

Schulzinger, Robert D. *The Making of the Diplomatic Mind: The Training, Outlook, and Style of United States Foreign Service Officers, 1908–1931*. Middletown, CT: Wesleyan University Press, 1975.

Setser, Vernon G. *The Commercial Reciprocity Policy of the United States, 1774–1829*. Philadelphia: University of Pennsylvania Press, 1937.

Sexton, Jay. *Debtor Diplomacy: Finance and American Foreign Relations in the Civil War Era, 1837–1873*. Oxford, England: Clarendon, 2005.

———. *The Monroe Doctrine: Empire and Nation in Nineteenth-Century America*. New York: Hill & Wang, 2011.

Shackleford, George Green. *Jefferson's Adopted Son: The Life of William Short, 1759–1848*. Lexington: University Press of Kentucky, 1993.

Shanks, Cheryl. *Immigration and the Politics of American Sovereignty, 1890–1990*. Ann Arbor: University of Michigan Press, 2001.

Shumsky, Neil Larry. "'Let No Man Stop to Plunder!' American Hostility to Return Migration, 1890–1924." In *Journal of American Ethnic History* 11, no. 2 (1992): 56–75.

Silbey, Joel H. *The American Political Nation, 1838–1893*. Palo Alto, CA: Stanford University Press, 1991.

Skeen, C. Edward. *John Armstrong Jr. 1758–1843: A Biography*. Syracuse, NY: Syracuse University Press, 1981.

Skowronek, Steven. *Building a New American State: The Expansion of National Administrative Capacities, 1877–1920.* New York: Cambridge University Press, 1982.

Smith, Daniel M. *The American Diplomatic Experience.* Boston: Houghton Mifflin, 1972.

Smith, David A. "From the Mississippi to the Mediterranean: The 1891 New Orleans Lynching and Its Effects on United States Diplomacy and the American Navy." In *Southern Historian,* no. 19 (1998): 60–85.

Smith, Robert W. *Keeping the Republic: Ideology and Early American Diplomacy.* DeKalb: Northern Illinois University Press, 2004.

Smith, Rogers M. *Civic Ideals: Conflicting Visions of Citizenship in U.S. History.* New Haven, CT: Yale University Press, 1997.

Smith, Shannon. "From Relief to Revolution: American Women and the Russian-American Relationship, 1890–1917." In *Diplomatic History* 19, no. 4 (1995): 601–16.

Snay, Mitchell. "The Imagined Republic: The Fenians, Irish American Nationalism, and the Political Culture of Reconstruction." In *Proceedings of the American Antiquarian Society* 112, no. 2 (2002): 291–313.

Sneider, Allison L. *Suffragists in an Imperial Age: U.S. Expansion and the Woman Question, 1870–1929.* New York: Oxford University Press, 2008.

Spalding, Matthew, and Patrick J. Garraty. *A Sacred Union of Citizens: George Washington's Farewell Address and the American Character.* Lanham, MD: Rowman & Littlefield, 1996.

Spickard, Paul R. *Almost All Aliens: Immigration, Race, and Colonialism in American History and Identity.* New York: Routledge, 2007.

Spivak, Burton. *Jefferson's English Crisis: Commerce, Embargo, and the Republican Revolution.* Charlottesville: University Press of Virginia, 1979.

Stagg, J. C. A. *Borderlines in Borderlands: James Madison and the Spanish American Frontier 1776–1821.* New Haven, CT: Yale University Press, 2009.

———. *Mr. Madison's War: Politics, Diplomacy and Warfare in the Early American Republic 1783–1830.* Princeton, NJ: Princeton University Press, 1983.

Stahr, Walter. *John Jay.* New York: Hambleton and London, 2005.

Stephanson, Anders. *Manifest Destiny: American Expansion and the Empire of Right.* New York: Hill & Wang, 1995.

Stinchcombe, William C. *The American Revolution and the French Alliance.* Syracuse, NY: Syracuse University Press, 1969.

———. *The XYZ Affair.* Westport, CT: Greenwood, 1980.

Stockley, Andrew. *Britain and France at the Birth of America: The European Powers and the Peace Negotiations of 1782–83.* Exeter, England: University of Exeter Press, 2001.

Stourzh, Gerald. *Benjamin Franklin and American Foreign Policy.* Chicago: University of Chicago Press, 1969.

Strand, Wilson. "Opening the Hermit Kingdom." In *History Today* 54, no. 1 (2004): 20–26.

Stremlau, Rose. "'To Domesticate and Civilize Wild Indians': Allotment and the Campaign to Reform Indian Families, 1875–1887." In *Journal of Family History* 30, no. 3 (2005): 265–86.

Stuart, Graham H. *The Department of State: A History of its Organization, Procedure, and Personnel.* New York: Macmillan, 1949.

Sword, Wiley. *President Washington's Indian War: The Struggle for the Old Northwest, 1790–1795.* Norman: University of Oklahoma Press, 1985.

Takaki, Ronald T. *Iron Cages: Race and Culture in Nineteenth-Century America.* Rev. ed. New York: Oxford University Press, 1979.

Tate, Merze. "Canada's Interest in the Trade and Sovereignty of Hawaii." In *Canadian Historical Review* 44, no. 1 (March 1963): 20–42.

Tilby, A. Wyatt. *Lord John Russell: A Study in Civil and Religious Liberty.* London: Cassell, 1930.

Torpey, John. *The Invention of the Passport: Surveillance, Citizenship and the State.* New York: Cambridge University Press, 2000.

Trachtenberg, Alan. *The Incorporation of America: Culture and Society in the Gilded Age.* New York: Hill & Wang, 1982.

Tucker, Robert W., and David C. Hendrickson. *Empire of Liberty: The Statecraft of Thomas Jefferson.* New York: Oxford University Press, 1990.

Tucker, Spencer C. *The Jeffersonian Gunboat Navy.* Columbia: University of South Carolina Press, 1993.

Tucker, Spencer C., and Frank T. Reuter. *Injured Honor: The Chesapeake-Leopard Affair, June 22, 1807.* Annapolis, MD: Naval Institute Press, 1996.

Tuffnell, Stephen. "'Uncle Sam Is to Be Sacrificed': Anglophobia in Late Nineteenth-Century Politics and Culture." In *American Nineteenth Century History* 12, no. 1 (2011): 77–99.

Tyrrell, Ian. *Woman's World/Woman's Empire: The Woman's Christian Temperance Union in International Perspective, 1880–1930.* Chapel Hill: University of North Carolina Press, 1991.

Van Doren, Carl. *Benjamin Franklin.* New York: Viking, 1938.

Varg, Paul A. *Foreign Policies of the Founding Fathers.* East Lansing: Michigan State University Press, 1963.

Wahlstrom, T. William. "A Vision for Colonization: The Southern Migration Movement to Mexico after the U.S. Civil War." In *Southern Historian,* no. 30 (2009): 50–66.

Wallace, Anthony F. C. *The Long Bitter Trail: Andrew Jackson and the Indians.* New York: Hill & Wang, 1993.

Walt, Stephen. *Taming American Power: The Global Response to American Primacy.* New York: W. W. Norton, 2006.

Warren, Gordon H. *Fountain of Discontent: The Trent Affair and Freedom of the Seas.* Boston: Northeastern University Press, 1981.

Watts, Steven. *The Republic Reborn: War and the Making of Liberal America, 1790–1820.* Baltimore, MD: Johns Hopkins University Press, 1987.

Webb, Clive. "The Lynching of Sicilian Immigrants in the American South, 1886–1910." In *American Nineteenth Century History* 3, no. 1 (2002): 45–76.

Weil, Martin. *A Pretty Good Club: The Founding Fathers of the U.S. Foreign Service.* New York: W. W. Norton, 1978.

Weitz, Eric D. "Race and Nation: An Intellectual History." In *A Century of Genocide: Utopias of Race and Nation:* 16–52. Princeton, NJ: Princeton University Press, 2003.

Welke, Barbara Young. *Law and the Borders of Belonging in the Long Nineteenth Century United States.* New York: Cambridge University Press, 2010.

———. *Recasting American Liberty: Gender, Race, Law and the Railroad Revolution, 1865–1920.* New York: Cambridge University Press, 2001.

Werking, Richard Hume. *The Master Architects: Building the United States Foreign Service, 1890–1913.* Lexington: University Press of Kentucky, 1977.

Whitaker, Arthur Preston. *The Mississippi Question 1795–1803: A Study in Trade, Politics and Diplomacy.* Washington, DC: American Historical Society, 1934.

White, Richard. "Information, Markets, and Corruption: Transcontinental Railroads in the Gilded Age." In *Journal of American History* 90, no. 1 (2003): 19–43.

Wiebe, Robert H. *The Search for Order.* New York: Hill & Wang, 1967.

Wilentz, Sean. *Andrew Jackson.* New York: Times Books, 2005.

Wilkins, David E. *American Indian Sovereignty and the U.S. Supreme Court: The Masking of Justice.* Austin: University of Texas Press, 1997.

———. "The U.S. Supreme Court's Explication of 'Federal Plenary Power': An Analysis of Case Law Affecting Tribal Sovereignty, 1886–1914." In *American Indian Quarterly* 18, no. 3 (1994): 349–68.

Williams, T. Harry. *Lincoln and His Generals.* New York: Alfred A. Knopf, 1952.

Williams, William Appleman. *The Roots of Modern American Empire: A Study of the Growth and Shaping of Social Consciousness in a Marketplace Society.* New York: Vintage Books, 1969.

———. *The Spanish-American Frontier 1783–1795: The Westward Movement and the Spanish Retreat in the Mississippi Valley.* Boston: Houghton Mifflin, 1927.

———. *The Tragedy of American Diplomacy.* Cleveland, OH: World Publishing, 1959.

———. *The United States and the Independence of Latin America, 1800–1830.* Baltimore, MD: Johns Hopkins University Press, 1941.

Wooster, Robert. *The Military and United States Indian Policy, 1865–1903.* New Haven, CT: Yale University Press, 1988.

Wyman, Mark. *Round-Trip to America: The Immigrants Return to Europe, 1880–1930.* Ithaca, NY: Cornell University Press, 1993.

Zimmerman, James F. *Impressment of American Seamen.* New York: Columbia University Press, 1925.

Zolberg, Aristide R. *A Nation by Design: Immigration Policy in the Fashioning of America.* Cambridge, MA: Harvard University Press, 2006.

PART II: THE UNITED STATES ON THE INTERNATIONAL STAGE

Ambrosius, Lloyd E. *Wilsonian Statecraft: Theory and Practice of Liberal Internationalism during World War I.* Wilmington, DE: Scholarly Resources, 1991.

———. *Wilsonianism: Woodrow Wilson and His Legacy in American Foreign Relations.* New York: Palgrave, 2002.

———. "Woodrow Wilson." In *American National Biography,* John A. Garraty and Mark Carnes, eds., no. 23: 604–12. New York: Oxford University Press, 1999.

———. *Woodrow Wilson and the American Diplomatic Tradition: The Treaty Fight in Perspective.* New York: Cambridge University Press, 1987.

———. "Woodrow Wilson and *The Birth of a Nation:* American Democracy and International Relations." In *Diplomacy & Statecraft,* no. 18 (December 2007): 689–718.

Article 3, "Convention for the Construction of a Ship Canal (Hay-Baunau-Varilla Treaty), November 18, 1903." http://avalon.yale.edu/20th_century/pan001.asp (accessed December 14, 2011).

Atkins, Edwin F. *Sixty Years in Cuba.* New York: Arno, 1980.

Bederman, Gail. *Manliness and Civilization: A Cultural History of Gender and Race in the United States, 1880–1917.* Chicago: University of Chicago Press, 1995.

Beisner, Robert L. *Twelve against Empire: The Anti-Imperialists, 1898–1900.* New York: McGraw-Hill, 1968.

Benjamin, Jules R. *The United States and the Origins of the Cuban Revolution: An Empire of Liberty in an Age of National Liberation.* Princeton, NJ: Princeton University Press, 1990.

Blum, Howard. *The Floor of Heaven: A True Tale of the Last Frontier and the Yukon Gold Rush.* New York: Crown, 2011.

Blum, John Morton, *The Republican Roosevelt.* Cambridge, MA: Harvard University Press, 1977.

Bogle, Lori Lyn. "TR's Use of PR to Strengthen the Navy." In *Naval History* 21, no. 6 (December 2007): 6–31.

Bonker, Dirk. "Admiration, Enmity and Cooperation: U.S. Navalism and the British and German Empires before the Great War," In *Journal of Colonialism and Colonial History* 2, no. 1 (Spring 2001).

Bradley, James. *The Imperial Cruise: A Secret History of Empire and War.* New York: Little, Brown, 2009.

Brands, H. W. *The Selected Letters of Theodore Roosevelt.* New York: Cooper Square, 2001.

———. *T. R.: The Last Romantic.* New York: Basic Books, 1997.

Braur, Kinley. "The Slavery Problem in the Diplomacy of the American Civil War." In *Race and U.S. Foreign Policy in the Ages of Territorial and Market Expansion, 1840 to 1900,* Michael Krenn, ed.: 117–47. New York: Garland, 1998.

Briggs, Laura. *Reproducing Empire: Race, Sex, Science, and U.S. Imperialism in Puerto Rico.* Berkeley: University of California Press, 2002.

Coogan, John W. *The End of Neutrality: The United States, Britain, and Maritime Rights, 1899–1915.* Ithaca, NY: Cornell University Press, 1981.

Cooper, John Milton, Jr. *Woodrow Wilson: A Biography.* New York: Alfred A. Knopf, 2009.

Crapol, Edward. *James G. Blaine: Architect of Empire.* Wilmington, DE: Scholarly Resources, 1999.

DeRoche, Andrew. *Andrew Young: Civil Rights Ambassador.* Wilmington, DE: Scholarly Resources, 2003.

Du Bois, W. E. B. "Returning Soldiers." In *The Crisis* (May 1919), no. 13. http://www.yale.edu/glc/archive/1127.htm.

———. *The Souls of Black Folk.* New York: Signet, 1982.

Duffy Burnett, Christina, and Burke Marshall, eds. *Foreign in a Domestic Sense: Puerto Rico, American Expansion, and the Constitution.* Durham, NC: Duke University Press, 2001.

Espinosa, Mariola. *Epidemic Invasions: Yellow Fever and the Limits of Cuban Independence, 1878–1930.* Chicago: University of Chicago Press, 2009.

Faragher, John Mack. *Rereading Frederick Jackson Turner: "The Significance of the Frontier in American History" and Other Essays.* New Haven, CT: Yale University Press, 1994.

Ferrer, Ada. *Insurgent Cuba: Race, Nation, and Revolution, 1868–1898.* Chapel Hill: University of North Carolina Press, 1999.

Fogelsong, David S. *America's Secret War against Bolshevism: U.S. Intervention in the Russian Civil War, 1917–1920.* Chapel Hill: University of North Carolina Press, 1995.

Gardner, Lloyd C. *Safe for Democracy: The Anglo-American Response to Revolution, 1913–1923.* New York: Oxford University Press, 1984.

Grant, James. *Mr. Speaker! The Life and Times of Thomas B. Reed.* New York: Simon & Schuster, 2011.

Greene, Julie. *The Canal Builders: Making America's Empire at the Panama Canal.* New York: Penguin, 2009.

Helg, Aline. *Our Rightful Share: The Afro-Cuban Struggle for Equality, 1886–1912.* Chapel Hill: University of North Carolina Press, 1995.

Herring, George C. *From Colony to Superpower: U.S. Foreign Relations since 1776.* New York: Oxford University Press, 2008.

Hoganson, Kristin L. *Consumers' Imperium: The Global Production of American Domesticity, 1865–1920.* Chapel Hill: University of North Carolina Press, 2007.

———. *Fighting for American Manhood: How Gender Politics Provoked the Spanish-American and Philippine-American Wars.* New Haven, CT: Yale University Press, 1998.

Hunt, Michael H. *The Making of the Special Relationship: The United States and China to 1914.* New York: Columbia University Press, 1914.

Jentleson, Bruce, and Thomas Paterson, eds. *Encyclopedia of U.S. Foreign Relations.* New York: Oxford University Press, 1997.

Johnson, Robert David. *The Peace Progressives and American Foreign Relations.* Cambridge, MA: Harvard University Press, 1995.

Kennedy, Philip W. "Race and American Expansion in Cuba and Puerto Rico, 1895–1905." In *Journal of Black Studies* 1, no. 3 (March 1971): 306–16.

Kennedy, Ross A. *The Will to Believe: Woodrow Wilson, World War I, and America's Strategy for Peace and Security.* Kent, OH: Kent State University Press, 2009.

Knock, Thomas J. *To End All Wars: Woodrow Wilson and the Quest for a New World Order.* Princeton, NJ: Princeton University Press, 1995.

Kramer, Paul A. *The Blood of Government: Race, Empire, the United States, and the Philippines.* Chapel Hill: University of North Carolina Press, 2006.

LaFeber, Walter. *The American Age: U.S. Foreign Policy at Home and Abroad since 1898.* New York: W. W. Norton, 1994.

———. *The American Search for Opportunity, 1865–1913.* New York: Cambridge University Press, 1993.

———. *Inevitable Revolutions: The United States in Central America.* New York: W. W. Norton, 1993.

———. *The New Empire: An Interpretation of American Expansion, 1860–1898.* Ithaca, NY: Cornell University Press, 1998.

Lauren, Paul Gordon. *Power and Prejudice: The Politics and Diplomacy of Racial Discrimination.* Boulder, CO: Westview, 1996.

Levin, N. Gordon, Jr. *Woodrow Wilson and World Politics: America's Response to War and Revolution.* New York: Oxford University Press, 1968.

Lewis, David Levering. *W. E. B. Du Bois: Biography of a Race, 1868–1919.* New York: Henry Holt, 1993.

Link, Arthur S. *The Higher Realism of Woodrow Wilson, and Other Essays.* Nashville, TN: Vanderbilt University Press, 1971.

———, ed. *The Papers of Woodrow Wilson.* 69 vols. Princeton, NJ: Princeton University Press, 1966–1994.

———. *Wilson.* 5 vols. Princeton, NJ: Princeton University Press, 1947–1965.

———. *Woodrow Wilson: Revolution, War, and Peace.* Wheeling, IL: Harlan Davidson, 1979.

Linn, Brian McAllister. *Guardians of Empire: The U.S. Army and the Pacific, 1902–1940.* Chapel Hill: University of North Carolina Press, 1997.

Love, Eric T. L. *Race over Empire: Racism and U.S. Imperialism, 1865–1900.* Chapel Hill: University of North Carolina Press, 2004.

MacMillan, Margaret. *Paris 1919: Six Months That Changed the World.* New York: Random House, 2001.

Madden, Ryan. *Alaska: On-the-Road Histories.* Northampton, MA: Interlink Books, 2005.

Manela, Erez. *The Wilsonian Moment: Self-Determination and the International Origins of Anticolonial Nationalism.* New York: Oxford University Press, 2007.

Martí, José. *Selected Writings.* Esther Allen, ed. New York: Penguin Books, 2002.

Morris, Edmund. *Theodore Rex.* New York: Random House, 2001.

Morton, Louis. "War Plan 'Orange': The Evolution of a Strategy." In *World Politics* 11, no. 2 (January 1959): 221–50.

Ninkovich, Frank. *The United States and Imperialism.* Malden, MA: Blackwell, 2001.

Offner, John L. *An Unwanted War: The Diplomacy of the United States and Spain over Cuba, 1895–1898.* Chapel Hill: University of North Carolina Press, 1992.

Paterson, Thomas G., et al., eds. *American Foreign Relations: A History, Volume 1: To 1920.* 6th ed. Boston: Houghton Mifflin, 2005.

Pérez, Louis. *Cuba and the United States: Ties of Singular Intimacy.* Athens: University of Georgia, 2003.

———. *Cuba between Empires, 1878–1902.* Pittsburgh, PA: University of Pittsburgh Press, 1983.

———. *Cuba under the Platt Amendment, 1902–1934.* Pittsburgh, PA: University of Pittsburgh Press, 1986.

———, ed. *José Martí in the United States: The Florida Experience.* Tempe: Arizona State University Center for Latin American Studies, 1995.

———. *On Becoming Cuba: Identity, Nationality, and Culture.* Chapel Hill: University of North Carolina Press, 1999.

———. "The Pursuit of Pacification: Banditry and the United States Occupation of Cuba, 1889–1902." In *Journal of Latin American Studies* 18, no. 2 (November 1986): 313–32.

———. *The War of 1898: The United States and Cuba in History and Historiography.* Chapel Hill: University of North Carolina Press, 1998.

Roberts, Priscilla. "The Anglo-American Theme: American Visions of an Atlantic Alliance, 1914–1933." In *Diplomatic History*, no. 21 (Summer 1997): 333–64.

Robinson, Michael, and Frank Schubert. "David Fagen: An Afro-American Rebel in the Philippines, 1899–1901." In *Race and U.S. Foreign Policy in the Ages of Territorial and Market Expansion, 1840 to 1900*, Michael Krenn, ed.: 300–15. New York: Garland, 1998.

Rosenberg, Emily. *Financial Missionaries to the World: The Politics and Culture of Dollar Diplomacy, 1900–1930.* Durham, NC: Duke University Press, 2003.

———. "From Colonialism to Professionalism: The Public-Private Dynamic in United States Foreign Financial Advising, 1898–1929." In *Journal of American History* 74, no. 1 (June 1987): 59–82.

———. *Spreading the American Dream: American Economic and Cultural Expansion, 1890–1945.* New York: Hill & Wang, 1982.

Salvatore, Nick. *Eugene V. Debs: Citizen and Socialist.* Urbana: University of Illinois, 1984.

Schulzinger, Robert D. *U.S. Diplomacy since 1900.* New York: Oxford University Press, 2008.

Schwabe, Klaus. *Woodrow Wilson, Revolutionary Germany, and Peacemaking, 1918–1919: Missionary Diplomacy and the Realities of Power.* Chapel Hill: University of North Carolina Press, 1985.

Scott, Rebecca J. "A Cuban Connection: Edwin F. Atkins, Charles Francis Adams Jr., and the Former Slaves of the Soledad Plantation." In *Massachusetts Historical Review*, no. 9 (2007): 7–34.

———. *Degrees of Freedom: Louisiana and Cuba after Slavery.* Cambridge, MA: Harvard University Press, 2005.

———. "Race, Labor, and Citizenship in Cuba: A View from the Sugar District of Cienfuegos, 1886–1909." In *Hispanic American Historical Review* 78, no. 4 (November 1998): 687–728.

———. *Slave Emancipation in Cuba: The Transition to Free Labor, 1860–1899.* Princeton, NJ: Princeton University Press, 1985.

Small, Melvin. *Democracy and Diplomacy: The Impact of Domestic Politics on U.S. Foreign Policy, 1789–1994.* Baltimore, MD: Johns Hopkins University Press, 1996.

Stevenson, David. *Cataclysm: The First World War as Political Tragedy.* New York: Basic Books, 2004.

Strong, Josiah. *Our Country: Its Possible Future and Present Crisis.* New York: Baker & Taylor, 1885.

Suárez Findlay, Eileen J. *Imposing Decency: The Politics of Sexuality and Race in Puerto Rico, 1870–1920.* Durham, NC: Duke University Press, 1999.

Takaki, Ronald. *Pau Hana: Plantation Life and Labor in Hawaii.* Honolulu: University of Hawaii, 1983.

Thomas, Evan. *The War Lovers: Roosevelt, Lodge, Hearst, and the Rush to Empire, 1898.* New York: Back Bay Books, 2010.

Tone, John Lawrence. *War and Genocide in Cuba, 1895–1898.* Chapel Hill: University of North Carolina Press, 2006.

Tucker, Robert W. *Woodrow Wilson and the Great War: Reconsidering America's Neutrality, 1914–1917.* Charlottesville: University of Virginia Press, 2007.

Twain, Mark. *Following the Equator and Anti-Imperialist Essays.* New York: Oxford University Press, 1996.

Widenor, William C. *Henry Cabot Lodge and the Search for an American Foreign Policy.* Berkeley: University of California Press, 1980.

Williams, Walter L. "United States Indian Policy and the Debate over Philippine Annexation: Implications for the Origins of American Imperialism." In *Journal of American History* 66, no. 4 (March 1980): 810–31.

Wilson, Woodrow. *The Public Papers of Woodrow Wilson: The New Democracy,* Ray Stannard Baker and William E. Dodd, eds. New York: Harper & Brothers, 1926.

———. *The Public Papers of Woodrow Wilson: War and Peace,* Ray Stannard Baker and William E. Dodd, eds. New York: Harper & Brothers, 1927.

Zeiler, Thomas. *Ambassadors in Pinstripes: The Spalding World Baseball Tour and the Birth of the American Empire.* Lanham, MD: Rowman & Littlefield, 2006.

PART III: DIPLOMACY AND FOREIGN POLICY BETWEEN THE WARS

Adler, Selig. *The Uncertain Giant: 1921–1941.* New York: Macmillan, 1965.

Anderson, Martin, and Annelise Anderson. *Reagan's Secret War: The Untold Story of His Fight to Save the World from Nuclear Disaster.* New York: Crown, 2009.

Asada, Sadao. "Between the Old Diplomacy and the New, 1918–1922: The Washington System and the Origins of Japanese-American Rapprochement." In *Diplomatic History* 30, no. 2 (April 2006): 211–30.

Ashby, LeRoy. *The Spearless Leader: Senator Borah and the Progressive Movement in the 1920s.* Urbana: University of Illinois Press, 1972.

Baker, James A. *The Politics of Diplomacy: Revolution, War & Peace, 1989–1992.* New York: G. P. Putnam's Sons, 1995.

Berg, A. Scott. *Lindbergh.* New York: G. P. Putnam's Sons, 1998.

Berle, Beatrice B., and Travis B. Jacobs, eds. *Navigating the Rapids, 1918–1971: From the Papers of Adolf A. Berle.* New York: Harcourt, 1973.

Bernstein, Barton, ed. *The Atomic Bomb: The Critical Issues.* Boston: Little, Brown.

Berthon, Simon, and Joanna Potts. *Warlords.* Cambridge, MA: Da Capo, 2006.

Billington, Ray Allen. "The Origins of Middle Western Isolationism." In *Political Science Quarterly* 60, no. 1 (March 1945): 44–64.

Bolt, Ernest C. *Ballots before Bullets: The War Referendum Approach to Peace in America, 1914–1941.* Charlottesville: University Press of Virginia, 1977.

Borgwardt, Elizabeth. *A New Deal for the World: America's Vision for Human Rights.* Cambridge, MA: Harvard University Press, 2005.

Braeman, John. "Power and Diplomacy: The 1920s Reappraised." In *Review of Politics* 44, no. 3 (July 1982): 342–69.

Braumoeller, Bear F. "The Myth of American Isolationism." In *Foreign Policy Analysis* 6, no. 4 (2010).

Buckley, John. "The Icarus Factor: the American Pursuit of Myth in Naval Arms Control, 1921–36." In *The Washington Conference, 1921–22: Naval Rivalry, East Asian Stability and the Road to Pearl Harbor,* Erik Goldstein and John Maurer, eds.: 124–46. London: Frank Cass, 1994.

Buckley, Thomas H. *The United States and the Washington Conference, 1921–1922.* Knoxville: University of Tennessee Press, 1970.

Bulmer-Thomas, Victor. *The Economic History of Latin America since Independence.* 2nd ed. New York: Cambridge University Press, 2003.

Burk, Kathleen. "The Lineaments of Foreign Policy: The United States and a 'New World Order,' 1919–39." In *Journal of American Studies* 26, no. 3 (1992): 377–91.

Burns, E. Bradford. *The Poverty of Progress: Latin America in the Nineteenth Century.* Berkeley: University of California Press, 1980.

Bush, George. "Remarks to Citizens in Hamtramck, Michigan," April 17, 1989, and "Remarks at the Texas A&M University Commencement Ceremony in College Station," May 12, 1989, in *The Public Papers of the Presidents, George Bush, 1989, The American Presidency Project.* http://www.presidency.ucsb.edu/ws/index.php?pid=16935&st=&st1=#axzz1MuomV5oo, and www.presidency.ucsb.edu/ws/index.php?pid=17022&st=&st1=#axzz1MuomV5oo (accessed May 19, 2011).

Carroll, John M. "American Diplomacy in the 1920s." In *Modern American Diplomacy,* John M. Carroll and George C. Herring, eds.: 61–79. Wilmington, DE: Scholarly Resources, 1996.

———. "Owen D. Young and German Reparations." In *U.S. Diplomats in Europe, 1919–1941,* Kenneth Paul Jones, ed. Santa Barbara, CA: CLIO, 1981.

Chadwin, Mark Lincoln. *The Warhawks: American Interventionists before Pearl Harbor.* New York: W. W. Norton, 1970.

Chernyaev, Anatoly. *The Diary of Anatoly Chernyaev 1985–89.* The National Security Archive. http://www.gwu.edu/~nsarchiv/NSAEBB/index.html#Europe (accessed May 2011).

Chester, Edward W. *The Scope and Variety of U.S. Diplomatic History, Readings since 1900.* Vol. 2. Englewood Cliffs, NJ: Prentice Hall, 1990.

Cohen, Warren I. "America and the World in the 1920s." In *Calvin Coolidge and the Coolidge Era: Essays on the History of the 1920s,* John Earl Haynes, ed.: 233–43. Washington, DC: Library of Congress, 1998.

———. *America's Response to China: A History of Sino-American Relations.* 4th ed. New York: Columbia University Press, 2000.

———. *Empire without Tears: America's Foreign Relations, 1921–1933.* Philadelphia: Temple University Press, 1987.

Cohrs, Patrick. *The Unfinished Peace after World War I: America, Britain and the Stabilisation of Europe, 1919–1932.* New York: Cambridge University Press, 2006.

Cole, Wayne S. *America First! The Battle against Intervention, 1940–1941.* Madison: University of Wisconsin Press, 1953.

———. *Roosevelt and the Isolationists 1932–1945.* Lincoln: University of Nebraska Press, 1983.

Connell-Smith, Gordon. "Latin America in the Foreign Relations of the United States." In *Journal of Latin American Studies* 8, no. 1 (May 1976): 137–50.

———. *The United States and Latin America: An Historical Analysis of Inter-American Relations.* London: Heinemann, 1974.

Costigliola, Frank. *Awkward Dominion: American Political, Economic, and Cultural Relations with Europe, 1919–1933.* Ithaca, NY: Cornell University Press, 1984.

———. "The United States and the Reconstruction of Germany in the 1920s." In *Business History Review* 50, no. 4 (Winter 1976): 477–502.

Current, Richard. "Henry L. Stimson." In *An Uncertain Tradition: American Secretaries of State in the Twentieth Century,* Norman A. Graebner, ed.: 168–83, 319–20. New York: Oxford University Press, 1964.

———. *Secretary Stimson: A Study in Statecraft.* Piscataway, NJ: Rutgers University Press, 1954.

Dallek, Robert. *Franklin D. Roosevelt and American Foreign Policy, 1932–1945.* 2nd ed. New York: Oxford University Press, 1995.

Danelski, David J., and Joseph S. Tulchin, eds. *The Autobiographical Notes of Charles Evans Hughes.* Cambridge, MA: Harvard University Press, 1973.

Daniels, Roger. *Guarding the Golden Door: American Immigration Policy and Immigrants since 1882.* New York: Hill & Wang, 2004.

De Grazia, Victoria. *Irresistible Empire: America's Advance through Twentieth-Century Europe.* Cambridge, MA: The Belknap Press of Harvard University Press, 2005.

DeBenedetti, Charles. *Origins of the Modern American Peace Movement, 1915–1929.* Millwood, NY: KTO, 1978.

Dilks, David, ed. *The Diaries of Sir Alexander Cadogan, 1938–1945.* New York: G. P. Putnam's Sons, 1972.

Dingman, Roger. *Power in the Pacific: The Origins of Naval Arms Limitations, 1914–1922.* Chicago: University of Chicago Press, 1976.

Divine, Robert A. *The Illusion of Neutrality.* Chicago: University of Chicago Press, 1962.

Doenecke, Justus D., ed. *The Diplomacy of Frustration: The Manchurian Crisis of 1931–1933 as Revealed in the Papers of Stanley K. Hornbeck.* Stanford, CA: Hoover Institution, 1981.

———. "Recent Explorations Concerning the Interwar Period." In *A Companion to American Foreign Relations,* Robert D. Schulzinger, ed.: 168–87. Malden, MA: Blackwell, 2003.

———. *Storm on the Horizon: The Challenge to American Intervention, 1939–1941.* Lanham, MD: Rowman & Littlefield, 2000.

——— and Mark Stoler. *Debating Franklin D. Roosevelt's Foreign Policies 1933–1945,* Lanham, MD: Rowman & Littlefield, 2005.

Eckes, Alfred E., Jr., and Thomas W. Zeiler. *Globalization and the American Century.* New York: Cambridge University Press, 2003.

Edmonds, Robin. *The Big Three: Churchill, Roosevelt, and Stalin in Peace and War.* New York: W. W. Norton, 1991.

Ellis, L. Ethan. *Republican Foreign Policy, 1921–1933.* Piscataway, NJ: Rutgers University Press, 1968.

Eubank, Keith. *The Summit Conferences: 1919–1960.* Norman: University of Oklahoma Press, 1966.

Falkus, M. E. "United States Economic Policy and the 'Dollar Gap' of the 1920s." In *Economic History Review* 24, no. 4 (November 1971): 599–623.

Fanning, Richard W. *Peace and Disarmament: Naval Rivalry and Arms Control, 1922–1933.* Lexington: University Press of Kentucky, 1995.

Farnham, Barbara. *Roosevelt and the Munich Crisis: A Study of Political Decision-Making.* Princeton, NJ: Princeton University Press, 1997.

Feis, Herbert. *Churchill, Roosevelt, and Stalin: The War They Waged and the Peace They Sought.* Princeton, NJ: Princeton University Press, 1957.

Ferrell, Robert H., ed. *Off the Record, The Private Papers of Harry S. Truman.* New York: Harper & Row, 1980.

Ferris, John R. "The Symbol and the Substance of Seapower: Great Britain, the United States and the One-Power Standard, 1919–1921." In *Anglo-American Relations in the 1920s: The Struggle for Supremacy,* Brian J. C. McKercher, ed.: 55–80. Edmonton: University of Alberta Press, 1991.

Foglesong, David S. *The American Mission and the "Evil Empire": The Crusade for a "Free Russia" since 1881.* New York: Cambridge University Press, 2007.

Gaddis, John Lewis. *Russia, the Soviet Union, and the United States: An Interpretive History.* 2nd ed. New York: McGraw-Hill, 1990.

Garson, Robert, and Stuart Kidd, eds. *The Roosevelt Years—New Perspectives on American History 1933–1945.* Edinburgh: Edinburgh University Press, 1998.

Glad, Betty. *Charles Evans Hughes and the Illusions of Innocence: A Study in American Diplomacy.* Urbana: University of Illinois Press, 1966.

Glantz, Mary E. *FDR and the Soviet Union: The President's Battles over Foreign Policy.* Lawrence: University Press of Kansas, 2005.

Gobat, Michel. *Confronting the American Dream: Nicaragua under U.S. Imperial Rule.* Durham, NC: Duke University Press, 2005.

Gorbachev, Mikhail. "Excerpts from Address by Mikhail Gorbachev, 43rd U.N. General Assembly Session," December 7, 1988. http://isc.temple.edu/hist249/course/Documents/gorbachev_speech_to UN.htm (accessed May 15, 2011).

Gormly, James. *From Potsdam to the Cold War: Big Three Diplomacy, 1945–1947.* Wilmington, DE: Scholarly Resources, 1990.

Grachev, Andrei. *Gorbachev's Gamble: Soviet Foreign Policy and the End of the Cold War.* Cambridge, England: Polity Press, 2008.

Grandin, Greg. *Fordlandia: The Rise and Fall of Henry Ford's Forgotten Jungle.* New York: Metropolitan Books, 2009.

Guinsburg, Thomas N. *The Pursuit of Isolationism in the United States from Versailles to Pearl Harbor.* New York: Garland, 1982.

Habib, Douglas F. "Chastity, Masculinity, and Military Efficiency: The United States Army in Germany, 1918–1923." In *International History Review* 28, no. 4 (December 2006): 737–57.

Harbutt, Fraser. *Yalta 1945: Europe and America at the Crossroads.* New York: Cambridge University Press, 2010.

Herken, Gregg. *The Winning Weapon: The Atomic Bomb in the Cold War 1945–1950.* New York: Alfred A. Knopf, 1980.

Herring, George C. *From Colony to Superpower: U.S. Foreign Relations since 1776.* New York: Oxford University Press, 2008.

Hess, Gary R. *The United States at War, 1941–1945.* 2nd ed. Wheeling, IL: Harlan Davidson, 2000.

Hicks, John D. *Republican Ascendancy, 1921–1933.* New York: Harper & Row, 1960.

Hirobe, Izumi. *Japanese Pride, American Prejudice: Modifying the Exclusion Clause of the 1924 Immigration Act.* Palo Alto, CA: Stanford University Press, 2001.

Hoag, C. Leonard. *Preface to Preparedness: The Washington Disarmament Conference and Public Opinion.* Washington, DC: American Council on Public Affairs, 1941.

Hoenicke-Moore, Michaela. *Know Your Enemy: The American Debate on Nazism, 1933–1945,* New York: Cambridge University Press, 2009.

Hoff, Joan. *American Business and Foreign Policy, 1920–1933.* Lexington: University Press of Kentucky, 1971.

———. *Ideology and Economics: U.S. Relations with the Soviet Union, 1918–1933.* Columbia: University of Missouri Press, 1974.

Hogan, Michael J. "Corporatism." In *Explaining the History of American Foreign Relations,* Michael J. Hogan and Thomas G. Paterson, eds.: 137–48. New York: Cambridge University Press, 2004.

———. *Informal Entente: The Private Structure of Cooperation in Anglo-American Economic Diplomacy, 1918–1928.* Columbia: University of Missouri Press, 1977.

Holden, Robert H., and Eric Zolov. *Latin America and the United States: A Documentary History.* 2nd ed. New York: Oxford University Press, 2011.

Hornbeck, Stanley K. *The Diplomacy of Frustration: The Manchurian Crisis of 1931–1933.* Stanford, CA: Hoover Institution, 1981.

Hull, Cordell, with Andrew Berding. *The Memoirs of Cordell Hull.* Vol. II. New York: Macmillan, 1948.

Hunt, Michael H. *Ideology and U.S. Foreign Policy.* New Haven, CT: Yale University Press, 1987.

INF Treaty and the Washington Summit. The National Security Archive. http://www.gwu.edu/~nsarchiv/NSAEBB/index.html#Europe (accessed May 12, 2011).

Iriye, Akira. *After Imperialism: The Search for a New Order in the Far East, 1921–1931.* Cambridge, MA: Harvard University Press, 1965.

Jankowitsch, Odette, and Karl P. Sauvant, eds. *The Third World Without Superpowers: The Collected Documents of the Non-Aligned Countries,* Vols. I-V. Dobbs Ferry, NY: Oceana, 1978.

Jenner, Robert E. *FDR's Republicans: Domestic Political Realignment and Foreign Policy.* Lanham, MD: Lexington Books, 2010.

Jespersen, T. Christopher. *American Images of China, 1931–1949.* Palo Alto, CA: Stanford University Press, 1999.

Johnson, Robert David. *The Peace Progressives and American Foreign Relations.* Cambridge, MA: Harvard University Press, 1995.

Jonas, Manfred. *Isolationism in America.* Ithaca, NY: Cornell University Press, 1966.

Josephson, Harold. *James T. Shotwell and the Rise of Internationalism in America*. Madison, NJ: Fairleigh Dickinson University Press, 1974.

Kennan, George Frost. *Russia and the West under Lenin and Stalin*. Boston: Little, Brown, 1961.

Kennedy, David M. *Freedom from Fear: The American People in Depression and War, 1929–1945*. New York: Oxford University Press, 1999.

Kennedy, Greg. *Anglo-American Strategic Relations and the Far East, 1933–1939*. London: Frank Cass, 2002.

Kent, Bruce. *The Spoils of War: The Politics, Economics, and Diplomacy of Reparations, 1918–1932*. New York: Oxford University Press, 1989.

Keynes, John Maynard. *The Economic Consequences of the Peace*. New York: Harcourt, 1920.

Kimball, Warren. *Cultural Internationalism and World Order*. Baltimore, MD: Johns Hopkins University Press, 1997.

———. *The Globalizing of America, 1913–1945*. Warren I. Cohen, ed. 4 vols. Vol. 3, Cambridge History of American Foreign Relations. New York: Cambridge University Press, 1993.

———. *The Juggler: Franklin Roosevelt as Wartime Statesman*. Princeton, NJ: Princeton University Press, 1991.

———. *The Origins of the Second World War in Asia and the Pacific*. New York: Longmans, 1987.

Kissinger, Henry. *White House Years*. Boston: Little, Brown, 1979.

Krasner, Stephen D. *Defending the National Interest: Raw Materials Investments and United States Foreign Policy*. Princeton, NJ: Princeton University Press, 1978.

Kroes, Rob. "American Empire and Cultural Imperialism: A View from the Receiving End." In *Diplomatic History* 23, no. 3 (Summer 1999): 463–77.

Kuisel, Richard. "Americanization for Historians." In *Diplomatic History* 24, no. 3 (Summer 2000): 509–15.

LaFeber, Walter. *The Clash: U.S.-Japanese Relations throughout History*. New York: W. W. Norton, 1997.

———. *Inevitable Revolutions: The United States in Central America*. 2nd ed. New York: W. W. Norton, 1993.

Leffler, Melvyn P. *The Elusive Quest: America's Pursuit of European Stability and French Security, 1919–1933*. Chapel Hill: University of North Carolina Press, 1979.

———. "Expansionist Impulses and Domestic Constraints, 1921–1932." In *Economics and World Power*, William H. Becker and Samuel F. Wells Jr., eds.: 225–76. New York: Columbia University Press, 1984.

———. *The Specter of Communism: The United States and the Origins of the Cold War, 1917–1953*. New York: Hill & Wang, 1994.

Leuchtenburg, William E. *The Perils of Prosperity, 1914–32*. Chicago: University of Chicago Press, 1958.

Little, Douglas. "Antibolshevism and American Foreign Policy, 1919–1939: The Diplomacy of Self-Delusion." In *American Quarterly* 35, no. 4 (Fall 1983): 376–90.

Louria, Margot. *Triumph and Downfall: America's Pursuit of Peace and Prosperity, 1921–1933*. Westport, CT: Greenwood, 2001.

Luce, Henry. "The American Century." In *Life Magazine*, February 7, 1941. Reprinted in *Diplomatic History* 23, no. 2 (January 1999): 159–71.

Lundestad, Geir. "'Empire by Invitation' in the Twentieth Century." In *Diplomatic History* 23, no. 2 (Spring 1999): 189–217.

Lynch, Cecelia. *Beyond Appeasement: Interpreting Interwar Peace Movements in World Politics*. Ithaca, NY: Cornell University Press, 1999.

Maddox, Robert James. "Another Look at the Legend of Isolationism in the 1920s." In *Mid America*, no. 53 (January 1971): 35–43.

Mann, James. *The Rebellion of Ronald Reagan: A History of the End of the Cold War*. New York: Penguin, 2009.

Masland, John W. "The 'Peace' Groups Join Battle." In *Public Opinion Quarterly* 4, no. 4 (December 1940): 664–73.

Maurer, John H. "Arms Control and the Washington Conference." In *The Washington Conference, 1921–22: Naval Rivalry, East Asian Stability and the Road to Pearl Harbor*, Erik Goldstein and John Maurer, eds.: 267–93. London: Frank Cass, 1994.

McDonald, J. Kenneth. "The Washington Conference and the Naval Balance of Power, 1921–22." In *Maritime Strategy and the Balance of Power: Britain and America in the Twentieth Century*, John B. Hattendorf and Robert S. Jordan, eds.: 189–213. New York: St. Martin's, 1989.

Miller, Karen A. *Populist Nationalism: Republican Insurgency and American Foreign Policy Making, 1918–1925*. Westport, CT: Greenwood, 1999. Reprint, 1925.

Moser, John E. *Twisting the Lion's Tail: American Anglophobia between the World Wars*. New York: New York University Press, 1999.

Murfett, Malcolm. "Look Back in Anger: The Western Powers and the Washington Conference of 1921–22." In *Arms Limitation and Disarmament: Restraints on War, 1899–1939*, Brian J. C. McKercher, ed.: 83–103. Westport, CT: Praeger, 1992.

"National Security Directive 23," September 22, 1989, The George Bush Presidential Library and Museum. http://bushlibrary.tamu.edu/research/pdfs/nsd/nsd23.pdf (accessed May 22, 2011).

"National Security Review-3," February 15, 1989, The George Bush Presidential Library and Museum. http://bushlibrary.tamu.edu/research/pdfs/nsr/nsr3.pdf (accessed May 22, 2011).

Nevins, Allan. *The United States in a Chaotic World: A Chronicle of International Affairs, 1918–1933*. New Haven, CT: Yale University Press, 1950.

Ninkovich, Frank, *The United States and Imperialism*. Malden, MA: Blackwell, 2001.

O'Brien, Thomas F. *Making the Americas: The United States and Latin America from the Age of Revolutions to the Era of Globalization*. Albuquerque: University of New Mexico Press, 2007.

Palazchenko, Pavel. *My Years with Gorbachev and Shevardnadze: The Memoirs of a Soviet Interpreter*. University Park: Pennsylvania State University Press, 1997.

Parrini, Carl. *Heir to Empire: United States Economic Diplomacy, 1916–1923*. Pittsburgh, PA: University of Pittsburgh Press, 1969.

Perlmutter, Amos. *FDR and Stalin: A Not So Grand Alliance, 1943–1945*. Columbia: University of Missouri Press, 1993.

Phillips, Hugh. "Mission to America: Maksim M. Litvinov in the United States." In *Diplomatic History*, no. 12 (Summer 1988): 261–76.

Plesch, Dan. *America, Hitler and the UN: How the Allies Won the War and Forged a Peace*. New York: I. B. Tauris, 2010.

Powaski, R. *Toward an Entangling Alliance: American Isolationism and Europe, 1901–1950*. Westport, CT: Greenwood, 1991.

Prashad, Vijay. *The Darker Nations: A People's History of the Third World*. New York: Free Press, 2007.

Quint, Howard H., and Robert H. Ferrell, eds. *The Talkative President: The Off-the-Record Press Conferences of Calvin Coolidge*. Amherst: University of Massachusetts Press, 1964.

Reagan, Ronald. "Address to the Nation and Other Countries on United States-Soviet Relations," January 16, 1984, in *The Public Papers of the Presidents, Ronald Reagan, 1984*, The American Presidency Project. http://www.presidency.ucsb.edu/ws/index (accessed May 12, 2011).

———. "Memorandum of Conversation between Thatcher and Reagan," December 28, 1985, The Margaret Thatcher Foundation. http://www.margaretthatcher.org/document/109185 (accessed May 4, 2011).

———. *The Reagan Diaries*. Douglas Brinkley, ed. New York: Harper & Row, 2007.

———. "Remarks and a Question-and-Answer Session with the Students and Faculty at Moscow State University," May 31, 1988, in *The Public Papers of the Presidents, Ronald Reagan, 1988, The American Presidency Project*. http://www.presidency.ucsb.edu/ws/index.php (accessed May 20, 2011).

Reagan, Bush, and Gorbachev at Governor's Island. The National Security Archive. http://www.gwu.edu/~nsarchiv/NSAEBB/index.html#Europe (accessed May 17, 2011).

Renda, Mary A. *Taking Haiti: Military Occupation and the Culture of U.S. Imperialism*. Chapel Hill: University of North Carolina Press, 2001.

Rhodes, Benjamin D. *United States Foreign Policy in the Interwar Period, 1918–1941: The Golden Age of American Diplomatic and Military Complacency*. Westport, CT: Praeger, 2001.

Reykjavik File. The National Security Archive. http://www.gwu.edu/~nsarchiv/NSAEBB/index.html#Europe (accessed May 7, 2011).

Rofe, J. Simon. *Franklin Roosevelt's Foreign Policy and the Welles Mission*. New York: Palgrave Macmillan, 2007.

Rosenberg, Emily. *Financial Missionaries to the World: The Politics and Culture of Dollar Diplomacy, 1900–1930*. Durham, NC: Duke University Press, 2003.

Rossini, Daniela, ed. *From Theodore Roosevelt to FDR: Internationalism and Isolationism in American Foreign Policy*. Edinburgh: Edinburgh University Press, 1995.

Rupp, Leila J. *Worlds of Women: The Making of an International Women's Movement*. Princeton, NJ: Princeton University Press, 1997.

Sainsbury, Keith. *Churchill and Roosevelt at War: The War They Fought and the Peace They Hoped to Make*. New York: New York University Press, 1994.

Saul, Norman E. *Friends or Foes? The United States and Soviet Russia, 1921–1941*. Lawrence: University Press of Kansas, 2006.

Schmitz, David F. *Henry L. Stimson: The First Wise Man*. Wilmington, DE: SR Books, 2001.

———. *Triumph of Internationalism: Franklin D. Roosevelt and a World in Crisis, 1933–1941*, Dulles, VA: Potomac Books, 2007.

———. *The United States and Fascist Italy, 1922–1940*. Chapel Hill: University of North Carolina Press, 1988.

Schortemeier, Frederick E., ed. *Rededicating America: Life and Recent Speeches of Warren G. Harding*. Indianapolis, IN: Bobbs-Merrill, 1920.

Schoultz, Lars. *Beneath the United States: A History of U.S. Policy toward Latin America*. Cambridge, MA: Harvard University Press, 1998.

Schuker, Stephen A. *American "Repatriations" to Germany, 1919–33: Implications for the Third-World Debt Crisis*. Princeton, NJ: International Finance Section, Department of Economics, Princeton University, 1988.

———. *The End of French Predominance in Europe: The Financial Crisis of 1924 and the Adoption of the Dawes Plan*. Chapel Hill: University of North Carolina Press, 1976.

Schulzinger, Robert D. *The Making of the Diplomatic Mind: The Training, Outlook, and Style of United States Foreign Service Officers, 1908–1931*. Middletown, CT: Wesleyan University Press, 1975.

———. *U.S. Diplomacy since 1900*. 6th ed. New York: Oxford University Press, 2008.

Sherwin, Martin J. *A World Destroyed: The Atomic Bomb and the Grand Alliance*. New York: Vintage Books, 1977.

Shultz, George. *Turmoil and Triumph: My Years as Secretary of State*. New York: Charles Scribner's and Sons, 1993.

Siegel, Katherine A. S. *Loans and Legitimacy: The Evolution of Soviet-American Relations, 1919–1933*. Lexington: University Press of Kentucky, 1996.

Small, Melvin. *Democracy and Diplomacy: The Impact of Domestic Politics on U.S. Foreign Policy, 1789–1994*. Baltimore, MD: Johns Hopkins University Press, 1996.

Smith, Gaddis. *American Diplomacy during the Second World War*. 2nd ed. New York: McGraw-Hill, 1985.

Smith, Robert Freeman. "American Foreign Relations, 1920–1942." In *Towards a New Past: Dissenting Essays in American History*, Barton J. Bernstein, ed.: 232–62. New York: Pantheon, 1967.

———. "Republican Policy and Pax Americana, 1921–1932." In *From Colony to Empire: Essays in the History of American Foreign Relations*, William Appleman Williams, ed.: 253–92. New York: Wiley, 1972.

———. *The United States and Revolutionary Nationalism in Mexico, 1916–1932*. Chicago: University of Chicago Press, 1972.

Smith, Tony. *America's Mission—The United States and the Worldwide Struggle for Democracy in the Twentieth Century*, Princeton, NJ: Princeton University Press, 1994.

Steele, Richard W. *The First Offensive 1942: Roosevelt, Marshall and the Making of American Strategy*. Bloomington: Indiana University Press, 1973.

Steiner, Zara. *The Light That Failed: European International History 1919–1933*. New York: Oxford University Press, 2005.

Stimson, Henry L., and McGeorge Bundy. *On Active Service in Peace and War*. New York: Harper & Row, 1948.

Stoler, Mark C. "A Half Century of Conflict: Interpretations of U.S. World War II Diplomacy." In *Diplomatic History*, no. 18 (Summer 1994): 375–403.

Stone, Ralph A. *The Irreconcilables: The Fight against the League of Nations*. Lexington: University Press of Kentucky, 1970.

Thatcher, Margaret. "Television Interview for the BBC," December 17, 1984. The Margaret Thatcher Foundation. http://www.margaretthatcher.org/document/105592 (accessed May 1, 2011).

Thorp, Rosemary. "Latin America and the International Economy from the First World War to the World Depression." In *The Cambridge History of Latin America Vol. 4, c. 1870 to 1930*, Leslie Bethell, ed.: 57–81. New York: Cambridge University Press, 1985.

Threlkeld, Megan. "The Pan American Conference of Women, 1922: Successful Suffragists Turn to International Relations." In *Diplomatic History* 31, no. 5 (November 2007): 801–28.

de Tocqueville, Alexis. *Democracy in America*. New York: Langley, 1840.

Trachtenberg, Marc. *Reparation in World Politics: France and European Economic Diplomacy, 1916–1923*. New York: Columbia University Press, 1980.

Trumpbour, John. *Selling Hollywood to the World: U.S. and European Struggles for Mastery of the Global Film Industry, 1920–1950*. New York: Cambridge University Press, 2002.

Tulchin, Joseph S. *The Aftermath of War: World War I and U.S. Policy toward Latin America*. New York: New York University Press, 1971.

U.S. Department of State. *Foreign Relations of the United States, 1942, Volume I, The British Commonwealth, the Far East*. Washington, DC: Government Printing Office, 1960.

———. *Foreign Relations of the United States: The Conferences at Cairo and Tehran, 1943*. Washington, DC: Government Printing Office, 1961.

———. *Foreign Relations of the United States. The Conference of Berlin, 1945*. 2 vols. Washington, DC: Government Printing Office, 1960.

Utley, Jonathan G. *Going to War with Japan, 1937–1941*. Knoxville: University of Tennessee Press, 1985.

Van Meter, Robert H., Jr. "The Washington Conference of 1921–1922: A New Look." In *Pacific Historical Review* 46, no. 4 (November 1977): 603–24.

Vinson, J. Chalmers. *The Parchment Peace: The United States Senate and the Washington Conference, 1921–1922*. Athens: University of Georgia Press, 1955.

Walker, Thomas W. *Nicaragua: Living in the Shadow of the Eagle*. 4th ed. Boulder, CO: Westview, 2011.

Walker, William O. "Crucible for Peace: Herbert Hoover, Modernization, and Economic Growth in Latin America." In *Diplomatic History* 30, no. 1 (January 2006): 83–117.

Walton, Whitney. "Internationalism and the Junior Year Abroad: American Students in France in the 1920s and 1930s." In *Diplomatic History* 29, no. 2 (April 2005): 255–78.

Watt, Donald Cameron. "American Isolationism in the 1920s. Is It a Useful Concept?" In *Bulletin of the British Association of American Studies:* 3–19. London: British Association for American Studies, 1962.

Weil, Martin. *A Pretty Good Club: The Founding Fathers of the U.S. Foreign Service.* New York: Norton, 1978.

Weinberg, Albert K. "The Historical Meaning of the American Doctrine of Isolation." In *American Political Science Review* 34, no. 3 (June 1940): 539–47.

Weissman, Benjamin. *Herbert Hoover and Famine Relief to Soviet Russia, 1921–1923.* Stanford, CA: Hoover Institution, 1974.

Welles, Sumner. *Naboth's Vineyard: The Dominican Republic 1844–1924.* Vol. 2. Mamaroneck, NY: Paul P. Appel, 1966.

Westad, Odd Arne. *The Global Cold War: Third World Interventions and the Making of Our Times.* New York: Cambridge University Press, 2006.

White, Christine A. *British and American Commercial Relations with Soviet Russia, 1918–1924.* Chapel Hill: University of North Carolina Press, 1992.

Wilkins, Mira. *The Maturing of Multinational Enterprise: American Business Abroad from 1914 to 1970.* Cambridge, MA: Harvard University Press, 1974.

Williams, William Appleman. "The Legend of Isolationism in the 1920s." In *Science and Society* 18, no. 1 (Winter 1954): 1–20.

Wood, Bryce. *The Making of the Good Neighbor Policy.* New York: Columbia University Press, 1961.

Zubok, Vladislav M. *A Failed Empire: The Soviet Union in the Cold War from Stalin to Gorbachev.* Chapel Hill: University of North Carolina Press, 2007.

PART IV: DIPLOMACY STRETCHED TO ITS LIMITS—THE EARLY COLD WAR ERA

Acheson, Dean G. *Present at the Creation: My Years in the State Department.* New York: W. W. Norton, 1969.

Alexander, Bevin. *Korea: The First War We Lost.* New York: Hippocrene, 1986.

Allen, Thomas. "No Winners, Many Losers: The End of the Korean War." In *Security in Korea: War, Stalemate, and Negotiation,* Phil Williams, Donald M. Goldstein, and Henry L. Andrews Jr., eds.: 110–26. Boulder, CO: Westview, 1994.

Ambrose, Stephen E. *Eisenhower, Vol. II: The President.* New York: Simon & Schuster, 1984.

Anders, Roger M. "The Atomic Bomb and the Korean War: Gordon Dean and the Issue of Civilian Control." In *Military Affairs* 52, no. 1 (January 1988): 1–6.

Anderson, David L. *Trapped by Success: The Eisenhower Administration and Vietnam, 1953–61.* New York: Columbia University Press, 1991.

Appleman, Roy E., *East of Chosin: Entrapment and Breakout in Korea.* College Station: Texas A&M University Press, 1987.

———. *Escaping the Trap: The U.S. Army X Corps in Northeast Korea, 1950.* College Station: Texas A&M University Press, 1987.

———. *Ridgway Duels for Korea.* College Station: Texas A&M University Press, 1990.

———. *South of the Naktong, North to the Yalu (June–November 1950).* Washington, DC: Center of Military History, 1961.

Asselin, Pierre. "Choosing Peace: Hanoi and the Geneva Agreement on Vietnam, 1954–1955." In *Journal of Cold War Studies* 9, no. 2 (Spring 2007): 95–126.

Associated Press. "Atomic Bomb Erased All Life in Hiroshima." *Miami Daily News,* August 8, 1945: 1.

Atkins, G. Pope. *Encyclopedia of the Inter-American System.* Westport, CT: Greenwood, 1997.

Attwood, William. *The Reds and the Blacks: A Personal Adventure.* New York: Harper & Row, 1967.

Badash, Lawrence. *Scientists and the Development of Nuclear Weapons: From Fission to the Limited Test Ban Treaty, 1939–1963.* Amherst, NY: Humanity Books, 1998.

Bailey, Sydney D. *The Korean Armistice.* New York: St. Martin's Press, 1992.

Bajanov, Evgueni. "Assessing the Politics of the Korean War, 1949–1951." In *Cold War International History Project Bulletin,* nos. 6–7 (Winter 1995/1996): 54, 87–91.

Bates, Milton J., et al., eds. *Reporting Vietnam: Part One: American Journalism 1959–1969.* New York: Library of America, 1998.

Berger, Carl. *The Korean Knot: A Military-Political History.* Philadelphia: University of Pennsylvania Press, 1957.

Bernstein, Barton J. "New Light on the Korean War." In *International History Review* 3, no. 2 (April 1981): 256–77.

———. "The Policy of Risk: Crossing the 38th Parallel and Marching to the Yalu." In *Foreign Service Journal,* no. 54 (March 1977): 16–22, 29.

Black, Jan K. *United States Penetration of Brazil.* Philadelphia: University of Pennsylvania Press, 1977.

Blair, Clay. *The Forgotten War: America in Korea, 1950–1953.* New York: Times Books, 1987.

Bohlen, Charles. *Witness to History, 1929–1969.* New York: W. W. Norton, 1973.

Boose, Donald W., Jr. "The Korean War Truce Talks: A Study in Conflict Termination." In *Parameters* 30, no. 1 (Spring 2000): 102–16.

———. "Portentous Sideshow: The Korean Occupation Decision." In *Parameters* 25, no. 4 (Winter 1995): 112–29.

Borstelmann, Thomas. *Apartheid's Reluctant Uncle: The United States and Southern Africa in the Early Cold War.* New York: Oxford University Press, 1993.

———. *The Cold War and the Color Line: American Race Relations in the Global Arena.* Cambridge, MA: Harvard University Press, 2001.

Bradley, Mark Philip. *Vietnam at War.* New York: Oxford University Press, 2009.

Brands, H. W., Jr. *Into the Labyrinth: The United States and the Middle East, 1945–1993.* New York: McGraw-Hill, 1994.

———. *The Specter of Neutralism: The United States and the Emergence of the Third World, 1947–1960.* New York: Oxford University Press, 1989.

Brands, Hal. *Latin America's Cold War.* Cambridge, MA: Harvard University Press, 2010.

Buhite, Russell D. *Douglas MacArthur: Statecraft and Stagecraft in America's East Asian Policy.* Lanham, MD: Rowman & Littlefield, 2008.

———. "'Major Interests': American Policy toward China, Taiwan, and Korea, 1945–1950." In *Pacific Historical Review* 47, no. 3 (August 1978): 425–51.

Bundy, McGeorge. *Danger and Survival: Choices about the Bomb in the First Fifty Years.* New York: Random House, 1988.

Calingaert, David. "Nuclear Weapons and the Korean War." In *Journal of Strategic Studies* 11, no. 2 (June 1988): 177–202.

Caridi, Ronald J. *The Korean War and American Politics: The Republican Party as a Case Study.* Philadelphia: University of Pennsylvania Press, 1968.

Casey, Steven. *Selling the Korean War: Propaganda, Politics, and Public Opinion in the United States, 1950–1953.* New York: Oxford University Press, 2008.

Catton, Philip. *Diem's Final Failure: Prelude to America's War in Vietnam.* Lawrence: University Press of Kansas, 2002.

Chang, Laurence, and Peter Kornbluh, eds. *The Cuban Missile Crisis, 1962: A National Security Archive Documents Reader.* New York: The New Press, 1992.

Chapman, Jessica M. "The Sect Crisis of 1955 and the American Commitment to Ngô Đình Diệm." In *Journal of Vietnamese Studies* 5, no. 1 (February 2010): 37–85.

Chen Jian. *China's Road to the Korean War: The Making of the Sino-American Confrontation.* New York: Columbia University Press, 1994.

Childs, Marquis. "Atomic Bomb Marks Beginning—or End." *Miami Daily News,* August 7, 1945: 6-A.

Cho, Soon Sung. *Korea in World Politics, 1940–1950: An Evaluation of American Responsibility.* Berkeley: University of California Press, 1967.

Clark, Mark W. *From the Danube to the Yalu.* New York: Harper & Row, 1954.

Clemens, Peter. "Captain James Hausman, U.S. Army Military Advisor to Korea, 1946–1948: The Intelligent Man on the Spot." In *Journal of Strategic Studies* 25, no. 1 (March 2002): 163–98.

Cockcroft, James D. *Latin America: History, Politics, and U.S. Policy.* 2nd ed. Belmont, CA: Wadsworth Group/Thomson Learning, 1996.

Coll, Steve. *Ghost Wars: The Secret History of the CIA, Afghanistan, and Bin Laden, from the Soviet Invasion to September 10, 2001.* New York: Penguin, 2004.

Collins, J. Lawton. *War in Peacetime: The History and Lessons of the Korean War.* Boston: Houghton Mifflin, 1969.

Condit, Doris. *History of the Office of the Secretary of Defense. Vol. 2: The Test of War, 1950–1953.* Washington, DC: Office of the Secretary of Defense, 1988.

Cowell, Alan. "Guinea Is Slowly Breaking Out of Its Tight Cocoon." In *The New York Times,* December 3, 1982.

———. "In Revolutionary Guinea, Some of the Fire Is Gone." In *The New York Times,* December 9, 1982.

Craig, Campbell. *Destroying the Village: Eisenhower and Thermonuclear War.* New York: Columbia University Press, 1998.

——— and Fredrik Logevall. *America's Cold War: The Politics of Insecurity.* Cambridge, MA: The Belknap Press of Harvard University Press, 2009.

——— and Sergey Radchenko. *The Atomic Bomb and the Origins of the Cold War.* New Haven, CT: Yale University Press, 2008.

Crane, Conrad. "'No Practical Capabilities': American Biological and Chemical Warfare Programs During the Korean War." In *Perspectives in Biology and Medicine* 45, no. 2 (Spring 2002): 241–49.

———. "To Avert Impending Disaster: American Military Plans to Use Atomic Weapons during the Korean War." In *Journal of Strategic Studies* 23, no. 2 (June 2000): 72–88.

Cullather, Nick. *The Hungry World: America's Cold War Battle against Poverty in Asia.* Cambridge, MA: Harvard University Press, 2010.

Cumings, Bruce, ed. *Child of Conflict: The Korean-American Relationship, 1943–1953.* Seattle: University of Washington Press, 1983.

———. *The Origins of the Korean War.* 2 vols. Princeton, NJ: Princeton University Press, 1981, 1990.

Dingman, Roger. "Atomic Diplomacy during the Korean War." In *International Security* 13, no. 3 (Winter 1988/1989): 61–89.

Divine, Robert A. *Eisenhower and the Cold War.* New York: Oxford University Press, 1981.

Dobbs, Michael. *One Minute to Midnight: Kennedy, Khrushchev, and Castro on the Brink of Nuclear War.* New York: Alfred A. Knopf, 2008.

Donovan, Robert. *Conflict and Crisis: The Presidency of Harry S Truman, 1945–1948.* New York: W. W. Norton, 1977.

———. *Tumultuous Years: The Presidency of Harry S Truman, 1949–1953.* New York: Norton, 1952.

Dower, John W. *War without Mercy: Race and Power in the Pacific War.* New York: Random House, 1986.

Dudziak, Mary L. *Cold War Civil Rights: Race and the Image of American Democracy.* Princeton, NJ: Princeton University Press, 2000.

"Dulles Shifts on Neutrality." In *The Washington Post,* July 12, 1956: 8.

Eden, Lynn. *Whole World on Fire: Organizations, Knowledge, and Nuclear Weapons Devastation.* Ithaca, NY: Cornell University Press, 2004.

Editorial. "Neutral Is Left." In *National Review* 31, no. 39 (September 28, 1979): 1197.

Eisenhower, Dwight D. *The White House Years. Vol. I: Mandate for Change, 1953–1956.* Garden City, NY: Doubleday, 1963.

Ekbladh, David. *The Great American Mission: Modernization and the Construction of an American World Order.* Princeton, NJ: Princeton University Press, 2010.

Endicott, Stephen, and Edward Hagerman. *The United States and Biological Warfare: Secrets from the Early Cold War and Korea.* Bloomington: Indiana University Press, 1998.

Fehrenbach, T. R. *This Kind of War: A Study of Unpreparedness.* New York: Macmillan, 1963.

Foot, Rosemary J. "Nuclear Coercion and the Ending of the Korean Conflict." In *International Security* 13, no. 3 (Winter 1988/1989): 92–112.

———. *A Substitute for Victory: The Politics of Peacemaking at the Korean Armistice Talks.* Ithaca, NY: Cornell University Press, 1990.

———. *The Wrong War: American Policy and the Dimensions of the Korean Conflict, 1950–1953.* Ithaca, NY: Cornell University Press, 1985.

Friedman, Edward. "Nuclear Blackmail and the End of the Korean War." In *Modern China* 1, no. 1 (January 1975): 75–91.

Fursenko, Aleksandr, and Timothy Naftali. *Khrushchev's Cold War: The Inside Story of an American Adversary.* New York: W. W. Norton, 2006.

Gaddis, John Lewis. *The Long Peace: Inquiries into the History of the Cold War.* New York: Oxford University Press, 1987.

———. *Strategies of Containment: A Critical Appraisal of American National Security Policy during the Cold War.* Rev. ed. New York: Oxford University Press, 2005.

———. *The United States and the Origins of the Cold War.* New York: Columbia University Press, 2000.

———. *We Now Know: Rethinking Cold War History.* New York: Oxford University Press, 1997.

Gallicchio, Marc. *The Scramble for Asia: U.S. Military Power in the Aftermath of the Pacific War.* Lanham, MD: Rowman & Littlefield, 2008.

Gasiorowski, Mark J. *U.S. Foreign Policy and the Shah: Building a Client State in Iran.* Ithaca, NY: Cornell University Press, 1991.

Gittings, John. "Talks, Bombs and Germs: Another Look at the Korean War." In *Journal of Contemporary Asia* 5, no. 2 (Spring 1975): 205–17.

Gleijeses, Piero. *Shattered Hope: The Guatemalan Revolution and the United States, 1944–1954.* Princeton, NJ: Princeton University Press, 1991.

Goncharov, Sergei N., John W. Lewis, and Xue Litai. *Uncertain Partners: Stalin, Mao, and the Korean War.* Palo Alto, CA: Stanford University Press, 1993.

Goodman, Allen E., ed. *Negotiating while Fighting: The Diary of Admiral C. Turner Joy at the Korean Armistice Negotiations.* Stanford, CA: Hoover Institution, 1978.

Goodrich, Leland M. *Korea: A Study of U.S. Policy in the United Nations.* New York: Council on Foreign Relations, 1956.

Hahn, Peter L. *Caught in the Middle East: U.S. Policy toward the Arab-Israeli Conflict, 1945–1961.* Chapel Hill: University of North Carolina Press, 2004.

———. *Crisis and Crossfire: The United States and the Middle East since 1945.* Washington, DC: Potomac Books, 2005.

———. *The United States, Great Britain, and Egypt, 1945–1956: Strategy and Diplomacy in the Early Cold War*. Chapel Hill: University of North Carolina Press, 1991.

Halberstam, David. *The Best and the Brightest*. New York: Random House, 1969.

Halliday, Jon, and Bruce Cumings. *Korea: The Unknown War*. New York: Pantheon, 1988.

Hao Yufan and Zhai Zhihai. "China's Decision to Enter the Korean War: History Revisited." In *The China Quarterly*, no. 121 (March 1990): 94–115.

Harry S. Truman Library and Museum. "Proclamation 2914." http://www.trumanlibrary.org/proclamations/index.php?pid=473&st=&st1=.

Hasegawa, Tsuyoshi. *Racing the Enemy: Stalin, Truman, and the Surrender of Japan*. Cambridge, MA: The Belknap Press of Harvard University Press, 2005.

Hastings, Max. *The Korean War*. New York: Simon & Schuster, 1987.

Haynes, John Earl, and Harvey Klehr. *The Soviet World of American Communism*. New Haven, CT: Yale University Press, 1998.

———. *Venona: Decoding Soviet Espionage*. New Haven, CT: Yale University Press, 1999.

Heinl, Robert D. *Victory at High Tide: The Inchon-Seoul Campaign*. Philadelphia: Lippincott, 1968.

Heiss, Mary Ann. *Empire and Nationhood: The United States, Great Britain, and Iranian Oil, 1950–1954*. New York: Columbia University Press, 1997.

Henderson, Gregory. *Korea: The Politics of the Vortex*. Cambridge, MA: Harvard University Press, 1968.

Hermes, Walter G., Jr. *Truce Tent and Fighting Front*. Washington, DC: Center of Military History, 1966.

Herring, George C. *America's Longest War: The United States and Vietnam, 1950–1975*. 4th ed. New York: McGraw-Hill, 2002.

———. *From Colony to Superpower: U.S. Foreign Relations since 1776*. New York: Oxford University Press, 2008.

Hewlett, Richard G., and Jack M. Holl. *Atoms for Peace and War, 1953–1961: Eisenhower and the Atomic Energy Commission*. Berkeley: University of California Press, 1989.

Higgins, Trumbull. *Truman and the Fall of MacArthur: A Precis on Limited War*. New York: Oxford University Press, 1960.

Holloway, David. *Stalin and the Bomb: The Soviet Union and Atomic Energy, 1939–1956*. New Haven, CT: Yale University Press, 1996.

Hunt, Michael H. "Beijing and the Korean Crisis, June 1950–June 1951." In *Political Science Quarterly* 107, no. 3 (Fall 1992): 453–78.

———. *A Vietnam Reader: A Documentary History from American and Vietnamese Perspectives*. Chapel Hill: University of North Carolina Press, 2010.

Immerman, Richard. *The CIA in Guatemala: The Foreign Policy of Intervention*. Austin: University of Texas Press, 1982.

Isaacson, Walter, and Evan Thomas. *Kissinger: A Biography*. New York: Simon & Schuster, 1992.

———. *The Wise Men: Six Friends and the World They Made*. New York: Simon & Schuster, 1997.

Jacobs, Seth. *America's Miracle Man in Vietnam: Ngo Dinh Diem, Religion, Race, and U.S. Intervention in Southeast Asia, 1950–1957*. Durham, NC: Duke University Press, 2004.

James, D. Clayton. *The Years of MacArthur, Vol. III: Triumph and Disaster, 1945–1964*. Boston: Houghton Mifflin, 1985.

Jankowitsch, Odette, and Karl P. Sauvant, eds. *The Third World without Superpowers: The Collected Documents of the Non-Aligned Countries*. Vols. I–V. Dobbs Ferry, NY: Oceana, 1978.

Jervis, Robert. "The Impact of the Korean War on the Cold War." In *Journal of Conflict Resolution* 24, no. 4 (December 1980): 563–92.

Jones, Howard. *Death of a Generation: How the Assassinations of Diem and JFK Prolonged the Vietnam War*. New York: Oxford University Press, 2003.

Joseph, Gilbert M., and Daniela Spenser, eds. *In from the Cold: Latin America's New Encounter with the Cold War*. Durham, NC: Duke University Press, 2008.

Joy, C. Turner. *How Communists Negotiate*. New York: Macmillan, 1955.

Kaufman, Burton I. *The Korean Conflict*. Westport, CT: Greenwood, 1999.

———. *The Korean War: Challenges in Crisis, Credibility, and Command*. Philadelphia: Temple University Press, 1986.

Keefer, Edward C. "President Dwight D. Eisenhower and the End of the Korean War." In *Diplomatic History* 10, no. 3 (Summer 1986): 267–89.

Kennan, George. *Memoirs, 1925–1950*. New York: Pantheon, 1983.

———. *Memoirs, 1950–1963*. New York: Pantheon, 1983.

Kissinger, Henry. *White House Years*. Boston: Little, Brown, 1979.

Kuniholm, Bruce R. *The Origins of the Cold War in the Near East: Great Power Conflict and Diplomacy in Iran, Turkey, and Greece*. Princeton, NJ: Princeton University Press, 1980.

LaFeber, Walter. "Crossing the 38th: The Cold War in Microcosm." In *Reflections on the Cold War: A Quarter Century of American Foreign Policy*, Lynn H. Miller and Ronald W. Pruessen, eds.: 71–90. Philadelphia: Temple University Press, 1974.

———. *Inevitable Revolutions: The United States in Central America*. 2nd ed. New York: W. W. Norton, 1993.

Langley, Lester D. *America and the Americas: The United States in the Western Hemisphere*. 2nd ed. Athens: University of Georgia Press, 2010.

Lawrence, Mark Atwood. *The Vietnam War: A Concise International History*. New York: Oxford University Press, 2008.

Leffler, Melvyn. *A Preponderance of Power: National Security, the Truman Administration, and the Cold War*. Palo Alto, CA: Stanford University Press, 1993.

———. *The Specter of Communism: The United States and the Origins of the Cold War, 1917–1953*. New York: Hill & Wang, 1994.

Leitenberg, Milton. "The Korean War Biological Weapon Allegations: Additional Information and Disclosures." In *Asian Perspective* 24, no. 3 (2000): 159–72.

Lichterman, Martin. "To the Yalu and Back." In *American Civil-Military Decisions: A Book of Case Studies*, Harold Stein, ed.: 569–642. Tuscaloosa: University of Alabama Press, 1963.

Little, Douglas. *American Orientalism: The United States and the Middle East since 1945*. Chapel Hill: University of North Carolina Press, 2002.

Logevall, Fredrik. *The Origins of the Vietnam War*. Hoboken, NJ: Pearson Education, 2001.

Longley, Kyle. *In the Eagle's Shadow: The United States and Latin America*. 2nd ed. Wheeling, IL: Harlan Davidson, 2009.

———. *The Sparrow and the Hawk: Costa Rica and the United States during the Rise of José Figueres*. Tuscaloosa: University of Alabama Press, 1997.

Louis, Wm. Roger. *The British Empire in the Middle East, 1945–1951: Arab Nationalism, the United States, and Postwar Imperialism*. New York: Oxford University Press, 1984.

MacArthur, Douglas. *Reminiscences*. New York: McGraw-Hill, 1964.

MacDonald, Callum A. *Korea: The War before Vietnam*. New York: The Free Press, 1986.

Macdonald, Donald Stone. *The Koreans: Contemporary Politics and Society*. Boulder, CO: Westview, 1988.

Mahoney, Richard D. *JFK: Ordeal in Africa*. New York: Oxford University Press, 1983.

Malloy, Sean L. "A 'Paper Tiger?': Nuclear Weapons, Atomic Diplomacy and the Korean War." In *The New England Journal of History*, no. 60 (Fall 2003–Spring 2004): 227–52.

Mandelbaum, Michael. *The Nuclear Question: The United States and Nuclear Weapons, 1946–1976*. New York: Cambridge University Press, 1979.

Mart, Michelle. *Eye on Israel: How America Came to View Israel as an Ally.* Albany: State University of New York Press, 2006.

Martini, Edwin A. *Invisible Enemies: The American War on Vietnam, 1975–2000.* Amherst: University of Massachusetts Press, 2007.

Massie, Robert K. *Loosing the Bonds: The United States and South Africa in the Apartheid Years.* New York: Doubleday, 1997.

Mastny, Vojtech. "The Soviet Union's Partnership with India." In *Journal of Cold War Studies* 12, no. 3: 50–90.

Matray, James I. "Dean Acheson's National Press Club Speech Reexamined." In *Journal of Conflict Studies* 22, no. 1 (Spring 2002): 28–55.

———. "Hodge Podge: U.S. Occupation Policy in Korea, 1945–1948." In *Korean Studies*, no. 19 (1995): 17–38.

———. "Truman's Plan for Victory: National Self-Determination and the Thirty-Eighth Parallel Decision in Korea." In *Journal of American History* 66: no. 2 (September 1979): 314–33.

May, Ernest R. *"Lessons of the Past": The Use and Misuse of History in American Foreign Policy.* New York: Oxford University Press, 1973.

McCormack, Gavan. *Cold War/Hot War.* Sydney, NSW: Hale and Iremonger, 1983.

McCullough, David. *Truman.* New York: Simon & Schuster, 1992.

McCune, George M., and Arthur L. Grey Jr. *Korea Today.* Cambridge, MA: Harvard University Press, 1950.

McGlothen, Ronald L. *Controlling the Waves: Dean Acheson and U.S. Policy in East Asia.* New York: Norton, 1993.

McMahon, Robert J. *The Cold War: A Very Short Introduction.* New York: Oxford University Press, 2003.

———. *Cold War on the Periphery: The United States, India, and Pakistan.* New York: Columbia University Press, 1994.

———. *The Limits of Empire: The United States and Southeast Asia since World War II.* New York: Columbia University Press, 1999.

Meade, E. Grant. *American Military Government in Korea.* New York: King's Crown, 1951.

Memorandum, David Newsom to Henry Kissinger, October 5, 1973, in Department of State, *FRUS, 1969–1976, Vol. E–6, Documents on Africa, 1973–1976,* doc. 11, http://history.state.gov/historicaldocuments/frus1969-76ve06/d11.

Memorandum, G. Mennen Williams to Dean Rusk, November 23, 1963, in Department of State, *FRUS, 1961–1963, Vol. 21, Africa.* Washington, DC: Government Printing Office, 1995: 338–40.

Memorandum, Robert Komer to McGeorge Bundy, January 16, 1963, in Department of State, *FRUS, 1961–1963, Vol. 23: Southeast Asia.* Washington, DC: Government Printing Office, 1995: 656–58.

Memorandum of Conversation, May 27, 1970, in Department of State, *FRUS, 1969–1976, Vol. 20, Southeast Asia, 1969–1972.* Washington, DC: Government Printing Office, 2006: 642–45.

Millett, Allan R. "Captain James H. Hausman and the Formation of the Korean Army, 1945–1950." In *Armed Forces and Society* 23, no. 4 (Summer 1997): 503–39.

———. *The War for Korea, 1945–1950: A House Burning.* Lawrence: University of Press Kansas, 2005.

———. *The War for Korea, 1950–1951: They Came from the North.* Lawrence: University Press of Kansas, 2010.

Morgan, Joseph. *The Vietnam Lobby: The American Friends of Vietnam, 1955–1975.* Chapel Hill: University of North Carolina Press, 1997.

Mossman, Billy C. *Ebb and Flow: November 1950–July 1951.* Washington, DC: Center of Military History, 1990.

National Security Archive. http://www.gwu.edu/~nsarchiv.

Nehru, Jawaharlal. *India's Foreign Policy: Selected Speeches, September 1946–April 1961.* New Delhi: Ministry of Information, 1961.

Newsom, David. *The Imperial Mantle: The United States, Decolonization, and the Third World.* Bloomington: University of Indiana Press, 2001.

Nicosia, Gerald. *Home to War: A History of the Vietnam Veterans Movement.* New York: Crown, 2001.

Noer, Thomas J. *Cold War and Black Liberation: The United States and White Rule in Africa, 1948–1968.* Columbia: University of Missouri Press, 1985.

Offner, Arnold. *Another Such Victory: President Truman and the Cold War, 1945–1953.* Palo Alto, CA: Stanford University Press, 2002.

Oh, Bonnie B. C., ed. *Korea under the American Military Government, 1945–1948.* Westport, CT: Praeger, 2002.

Olmsted, Kathryn. *Red Spy Queen: A Biography of Elizabeth Bentley.* Chapel Hill: University of North Carolina Press, 2002.

Osgood, Kenneth. *Total Cold War: Eisenhower's Secret Propaganda Battle at Home and Abroad.* Lawrence: University Press of Kansas, 2006.

Oshinsky, David. *A Conspiracy So Immense: The World of Joseph McCarthy.* New York: Oxford University Press, 2005.

Paige, Glenn D. *The Korean Decision, June 24–30, 1950.* New York: Free Press, 1968.

Paterson, Thomas G. *On Every Front: The Making of the Cold War.* New York: W. W. Norton, 1979.

Patterson, James. *Grand Expectations: The United States, 1945–1974.* New York: Oxford University Press, 1997.

Pearlman, Michael D. *Truman and MacArthur: Policy, Politics, and the Hunger for Honor and Renown.* Bloomington: Indiana University Press, 2008.

Perret, Geoffrey. *Old Soldiers Never Die: The Life of Douglas MacArthur.* New York: Random House, 1996.

Pierpaoli, Paul G., Jr. *Truman and Korea: The Political Culture of the Early Cold War.* Columbia: University of Missouri Press, 1999.

Pollack, Jonathan D. "The Korean War and Sino-American Relations." In *Sino-American Relations, 1945–1955,* Harry Harding and Yuan Ming, eds.: 213–37. Wilmington, DE: Scholarly Resources, 1989.

Prashad, Vijay. *The Darker Nations: A People's History of the Third World.* New York: Free Press, 2007.

Public Papers of the Presidents. Washington, DC: Government Printing Office.

Rabe, Stephen G. *The Most Dangerous Area in the World: John F. Kennedy Confronts Communist Revolution in Latin America.* Chapel Hill: University of North Carolina Press, 1999.

Radosh, Ronald, and Joyce Milton. *The Rosenberg File: A Search for the Truth.* New York: Holt, Rinehart, and Winston, 1983.

Reagan, Ronald. "Remarks to Members of the World Affairs Council and the Foreign Policy Association," July 22, 1986, in *Public Papers of the Presidents, Ronald Reagan, 1986, Book II—June 28 to December 31, 1986,* Washington, DC: Government Printing Office, 1989: 948–88.

Rees, David. *Korea: The Limited War.* New York: Macmillan, 1964.

Rhodes, Richard. *Dark Sun: The Making of the Hydrogen Bomb.* New York: Simon & Schuster, 1995.

———. *The Making of the Atomic Bomb.* New York: Simon & Schuster, 1986.

Ridgway, Matthew B. *The Korean War.* Garden City, NY: Doubleday, 1967.

Roberts, Sam. *The Brother: The Untold Story of Atomic Spy David Greenglass and How He Sent His Sister, Ethel Rosenberg, to the Electric Chair.* New York: Random House, 2001.

Rotter, Andrew J. *Comrades at Odds: The United States and India, 1947–1964.* Ithaca, NY: Cornell University Press, 2000.

———. *The Path to Vietnam: Origins of the American Commitment to Southeast Asia.* Ithaca, NY: Cornell University Press, 1987.

Rovere, Richard, and Arthur M. Schlesinger Jr. *The General and the President and the Future of American Foreign Policy.* New York: Farrar, Straus, and Giroux, 1951.

Rubin, Barry. *Paved with Good Intentions: The American Experience and Iran.* New York: Oxford University Press, 1980.

Ruetten, Richard T. "General Douglas MacArthur's 'Reconnaissance in Force': The Rationalization of a Defeat in Korea." In *Pacific Historical Review* 36, no. 1 (February 1967): 79–94.

Sandusky, Michael C. *America's Parallel.* Alexandria, VA: Old Dominion, 1983.

Sawyer, Robert K., and Walter G. Hermes Jr. *Military Advisors in Korea: KMAG in War and Peace.* Washington, DC: Office of the Chief of Military History, 1962.

Schaller, Michael. *Douglas MacArthur: The Far Eastern General.* New York: Oxford University Press, 1989.

Schlesinger, Arthur M. *Journals: 1952–2000.* New York: Penguin, 2007.

———. *A Thousand Days: John F. Kennedy in the White House.* Boston: Houghton Mifflin, 1969.

Schmidt, Elizabeth. *Cold War and Decolonization in Guinea, 1946–1958.* Athens: Ohio University Press, 2007.

Schmitz, David F. *The United States and Right-Wing Dictatorships.* New York: Cambridge University Press, 2006.

Schnabel, James F. *Policy and Direction: The First Year.* Washington, DC: Office of the Chief of Military History, 1972.

———, and Robert J. Watson. *The Joint Chiefs of Staff and National Policy, Vol. III: The Korean War.* Wilmington, DE: Michael Glazier, 1979.

Schrecker, Ellen. *Many Are the Crimes: McCarthyism in America.* New York: Little, Brown, 1998.

Schulzinger, Robert D. *A Time for War: The United States and Vietnam, 1941–1975.* New York: Oxford University Press, 1997.

Shaw, Tony. *Hollywood's Cold War.* Amherst: University of Massachusetts Press, 2007.

Shen Zhihua. "China and the Dispatch of the Soviet Air Force: The Formation of the Chinese-Soviet-Korean Alliance in the Early Stage of the Korean War." In *Journal of Strategic Studies* 33, no. 2 (April 2010): 211–30.

———. "Sino-Soviet Relations and the Origins of the Korean War." In *Journal of Cold War Studies* 2, no. 2 (Spring 2000): 44–68.

Sheng, Michael M. *Battling Western Imperialism: Mao, Stalin, and the United States.* Princeton, NJ: Princeton University Press, 1997.

Sherwin, Martin J., and Kai Bird. *American Prometheus: The Triumph and Tragedy of J. Robert Oppenheimer.* New York: Alfred A. Knopf, 2005.

Sibley, Katherine. *Red Spies in America: Stolen Secrets and the Dawn of the Cold War.* Lawrence: University Press of Kansas, 2004.

Simmons, Robert R. *The Strained Alliance: Peking, Pyongyang, Moscow and the Politics of the Korean Civil War.* New York: Free Press, 1975.

Simpson, Bradley R. *Economists with Guns: Authoritarian Development and U.S.-Indonesian Relations, 1960–1968.* Palo Alto, CA: Stanford University Press, 2008.

Smith, Peter H. *Talons of the Eagle: Dynamics of U.S.-Latin American Relations.* 2nd ed. New York: Oxford University Press, 2000.

Smoke, Richard. *National Security and the Nuclear Dilemma: An Introduction to the American Experience.* 2nd ed. New York: Random House, 1987.

Spanier, John W. *The Truman-MacArthur Controversy and the Korean War.* New York: W. W. Norton, 1959.

Spurr, Russell. *Enter the Dragon: China's Undeclared War against the U.S. in Korea, 1950–1951.* New York: Newmarket, 1988.

Stanley, Elizabeth A. *Paths to Peace: Domestic Coalition Shifts, War Termination and the Korean War.* Palo Alto, CA: Stanford University Press, 2009.

Stueck, William. *The Korean War: An International History.* Princeton, NJ: Princeton University Press, 1995.

———, ed. *The Korean War in World History.* Lexington: University Press of Kentucky, 2004.

———. *Rethinking the Korean War: A New Diplomatic and Strategic History.* Princeton, NJ: Princeton University Press, 2002.

———. *The Road to Confrontation: American Policy toward China and Korea, 1947–1950.* Chapel Hill: University of North Carolina Press, 1981.

Taffet, Jeffrey F. *Foreign Aid as Foreign Policy: The Alliance for Progress in Latin America.* New York: Taylor & Francis, 2007.

Telegram 1120, Cairo to Washington, February 6, 1955, in Department of State, *Foreign Relations of the United States (FRUS), 1955–1957, Vol. 12, Near East Region; Iran; Iraq.* Washington, DC: Government Printing Office, 1991: 15–16.

Telegram 1579, Jakarta to State Department, December 6, 1975, National Security Archive. http://www.gwu.edu/~nsarchiv/NSAEBB/NSAEBB62/doc4.pdf.

Telegram 104050, State Department to All Diplomatic Posts, May 17, 1974, in Department of State, *FRUS, 1969–1976 Vol. E–14, Part 1, Documents on the United Nations, 1973–1976,* Doc. 14. http://history.state.gov/historicaldocuments/frus1969-76ve14p1/d14.

Truman, Harry S. *Foreign Relations of the United States. The Conferences at Cairo and Tehran 1943.* Washington, DC: Government Printing Office, 1961.

———. *Memoirs.* 2 vols. Garden City, NY: Doubleday, 1955, 1956.

———. *1950.* Vol. VII: *Korea.* Washington, DC: Government Printing Office, 1976.

———. *1951.* Vol. VII: *Korea and China.* Part 1. Washington, DC: Government Printing Office, 1983.

———. *1952–1954.* Vol. XV: *Korea.* 2 parts. Washington, DC: Government Printing Office, 1984.

Tulchin, Joseph. *Argentina and the United States: A Conflicted Relationship.* Boston: Twayne's, 1990.

United Nations. *International Statistical Yearbook 2007.* New York: United Nations Statistical Office, 2008.

United Nations. *Yearbook of International Trade Statistics.* New York: United Nations Statistical Office, various years.

United Nations Conference on Trade and Development. *World Investment Report.* Geneva: UNCTAD, various years.

Usdin, Steve. *Engineering Communism: How Two Americans Spied for Stalin's Secret Service and Founded the Soviet Silicon Valley.* New Haven, CT: Yale University Press, 2005.

Vatcher, William H., Jr. *Panmunjom: The Story of the Korean Military Armistice Negotiations.* Westport, CT: Praeger, 1958.

Walker, J. Samuel. *Prompt and Utter Destruction: Truman and the Use of the Atomic Bombs against Japan.* Rev. ed. Chapel Hill: University of North Carolina Press, 2004.

Weathersby, Kathryn. "Deceiving the Deceivers: Moscow, Beijing, Pyongyang, and the Allegations of Bacteriological Weapons Use in Korea." In *Cold War International History Project Bulletin,* no. 11 (Winter 1998): 176–85.

———. "Korea, 1949–50: To Attack or Not to Attack: Stalin, Kim Il Sung, and the Prelude to War." In *Cold War International History Project Bulletin,* no. 5 (Spring 1995): 1–9.

———. "New Findings on the Korean War: Translation and 'Commentary." In *Cold War International History Project Bulletin,* no. 3 (Fall 1993): 1, 14–18.

———. "The Soviet Role in the Early Phase of the Korean War: New Documentary Evidence." In *Journal of American–East Asian Relations* 2, no. 4 (Winter 1993): 425–58.

Weinraub, Bernard. "Reagan in Toast to Suharto Names an Envoy." In *The New York Times,* October 13, 1982.

Weinstein, Allen. *The Haunted Wood: Soviet Espionage in America—The Soviet Era.* New York: Random House, 1999.

———. *Perjury: The Hiss-Chambers Case.* New York: Vintage Books, 1978.

Weintraub, Stanley. *MacArthur's War: Korea and the Undoing of an American Hero.* New York: Free Press, 2000.

Wenger, Andreas. *Living with Peril: Eisenhower, Kennedy, and Nuclear Weapons.* Lanham, MD: Rowman & Littlefield, 1997.

Westad, Odd Arne. *The Global Cold War: Third World Interventions and the Making of Our Times.* New York: Cambridge University Press, 2005.

White, G. Edward. *Alger Hiss's Looking Glass Wars.* New York: Oxford University Press, 2004.

Whiting, Allen S. *China Crosses the Yalu: The Decision to Enter the Korean War.* Palo Alto, CA: Stanford University Press, 1970.

Wilkinson, Mark F., ed. *The Korean War at Fifty: International Perspectives.* Lexington: Virginia Military Institute, 2004.

Williams, William Appleman. *The Tragedy of American Diplomacy.* New York: W. W. Norton, 1988.

Williams, William J., ed. *A Revolutionary War: Korea and the Transformation of the Postwar World.* Chicago: Imprint, 1993.

Winham, Gilbert R. "The Evolution of the Global Trade Regime." In *Global Political Economy* 3, John Ravenhill, ed.: 137–72. New York: Oxford University Press, 2011.

Winkler, Allan M. *Life under a Cloud: American Anxiety about the Atom.* New York: Oxford University Press, 1993.

Wittner, Lawrence S. *The Struggle against the Bomb.* 3 vols. Palo Alto, CA: Stanford University Press, 1993–2003.

Xia Yafeng. *Negotiating with the Enemy: U.S.-China Talks during the Cold War, 1949–1972.* Bloomington: Indiana University Press, 2006.

Young, Marilyn B. *The Vietnam Wars, 1945–1990.* New York: HarperCollins, 1991.

Zeiler, Thomas W. *Unconditional Defeat: Japan, America, and the End of World War II.* Wilmington, DE: Scholarly Resources, 2004.

Zhang Shu Guang. *Mao's Military Romanticism: China and the Korean War, 1950–53.* Lawrence: University Press of Kansas, 1995.

PART V: THE END OF THE COLD WAR

Ahmed, Nafeez Mosaddeq. *Behind the War on Terror: Western Secret Strategy and the Struggle for Iraq.* Gabriola Island, BC: New Society, 2003.

American Embassy in Riyadh. Telegram to Secretary of State. "Examining Our Military Options." October 29, 1990. Folder, "Working Files-Iraq, 10/90." OA/ID CF1478 [2 of 6]. Richard Haass. Subject File. National Security Council Bush Presidential Records. George Bush Presidential Library.

Anderson, Martin, and Annelise Anderson. *Reagan's Secret War: The Untold Story of His Fight to Save the World from Nuclear Disaster.* New York: Crown, 2009.

Andrianopoulos, Gerry A. *Kissinger and Brzezinski. The NSC and the Struggle for Control of U.S. National Security Policy.* New York: Macmillan, 1991.

Armbrister, Trevor. *A Matter of Accountability: The True Story of the Pueblo Affair.* 2nd ed. Guilford, CT: Lyons, 2004.

Aslund, Anders. *How Capitalism Was Built: The Transformation of Central and Eastern Europe, Russia, and Central Asia.* New York: Cambridge University Press, 2007.

Assistant Secretary of State for Inter-American Affairs (Rubottom), Memo to the Under Secretary of State (Dillion), December 29, 1959. *Foreign Relations of the United States, 1958–1960, Volume VI, Cuba, Document 414.* http://history.state.gov/historicaldocuments/frus1958–60v06/d414

Baker, James A. *The Politics of Diplomacy: Revolution, War & Peace, 1989–1992.* New York: G. P. Putnam's Sons, 1995.

Banca Nazionale Del Lavoro (BNL). [n.d.] Folder, "USDAGSM 102–3 Credits to Iraq." OA/ID 06375. Files of Clair Sechler, Cabinet Affairs, Bush Presidential Records. George Bush Presidential Library.

Berend, Ivan T. *From the Soviet Bloc to the European Union.* New York: Cambridge University Press, 2009.

Bianco, Mirella. *Gadafi: Voice from the Desert.* Margaret Lyle, trans. New York: Longmans, 1975.

Bitar, Salah. Letter to the Secretary-General of the United Nations (Hammarskjold), October 15, 1957. In *The Arab States and the Arab League: A Documentary Record Vol. II International Affairs,* Muhammad Khalil, ed.: 342–43. Beirut: Khayats, 1962.

Building Up Our Deterrent Capabilities. [n.d.], Folder, "Meetings NSC 293: 325–80." Box 32. Files: Brzezinski collection. Jimmy Carter Presidential Library.

Bundy, William. *A Tangled Web: The Making of Foreign Policy in the Nixon Presidency.* New York: Hill & Wang, 1998.

Burnett, Stanton H. Memo to the Director and Deputy Director. April 15, 1986. Folder, "Libya: USIA." Box 30, Oliver L. North Files. Ronald Reagan Presidential Library.

Burr, William, ed. *The Kissinger Transcripts: The Top Secret Talks with Beijing and Moscow.* New York: New Press, 1999.

Bush, George H. W. "Address before a Joint Session of the Congress on the State of the Union," January 28, 1992. *The American Presidency Project* [online]. Santa Barbara, CA. http://www.presidency.ucsb.edu/ws/index.php?pid=20544&st=grace+of+god&st1=#axzz1NhfY.

———. Memo of National Security Directive 26 to the Vice President, the Secretary of State, the Secretary of the Treasury, The Secretary of Defense, the Attorney General, the Secretary of Energy, the Director of the OMB, the Assistant to the President for National Security Affairs, the Director of Central Intelligence, the Chairman of the Joint Chiefs of Staff, The Director of the United States Arms Control and Disarmament Agency, and the Director of the USIA. Oct. 2, 1989. Folder, "Working Files-Iraq Pre-8/2/90." OA/ID CF01043 [1 of 6]. Richard Haass. Subject File. National Security Council. Bush Presidential Records. George Bush Presidential Library.

———. "The President's News Conference on the Persian Gulf Crisis, January 9, 1991." John T. Woolley and Gerhard Peters, *The American Presidency Project* [online]. Santa Barbara, CA. http://www.presidency.ucsb.edu/ws/index.php?pid=19202#axzz1PH7sRFJv (accessed June 9, 2011).

———. "Remarks to Citizens in Hamtramck, Michigan," April 17, 1989, and "Remarks at the Texas A&M University Commencement Ceremony in College Station," May 12, 1989, in *The Public Papers of the Presidents, George Bush, 1989, The American Presidency Project.* http://www.presidency.ucsb.edu/ws/index.php?pid=16935&st=&st1=#axzz1MuomV5oo and http://www.presidency.ucsb.edu/ws/index.php?pid=17022&st=&st1=#axzz1MuomV5oo (accessed May 19, 2011).

Bush, George H. W., and Brent Scowcroft. *A World Transformed.* New York: Alfred A. Knopf, 1998.

Cahn, Anne Hessing. *Killing Détente. The Right Attacks the CIA.* University Park: Pennsylvania State University Press, 1998.

Carter, Jimmy. "American Federation of Labor and Congress of Industrial Organizations Remarks at the 13th Constitutional Convention, November 15, 1979." John T. Woolley and Gerhard Peters, *The American Presidency Project* [online]. Santa Barbara, CA. http://www.presidency.ucsb.edu/ws/index.php?pid=31691axzz1PH7sRFJv (accessed June 9, 2011).

Chamberlin, Paul. *The Global Offensive: The United States, the PLO, and the Making of the New International Order, 1967–1975.* New York: Oxford University Press, Forthcoming.

Chen Jian. *China's Road to the Korean War: The Making of the Sino-American Confrontation.* New York: Columbia University Press, 1994.

Chernyaev, Anatoly. *The Diary of Anatoly Chernyaev 1985–89.* The National Security Archive. http://www.gwu.edu/~nsarchiv/NSAEBB/index.html#Europe (accessed May 2011).

Chernyaev, Anatoly, et al. *My Six Years with Gorbachev.* University Park: Pennsylvania State University Press, 2000.

Committee on Armed Services. Inquiry into the USS *Pueblo* and Ec-121 Plane Incidents. H. R. Doc. No. 91–12, at 639–40 (1969).

Dallek, R. *Nixon and Kissinger: Partners in Power.* New York: HarperCollins, 2007.

Department of State Briefing Paper: Central America. February 1, 1983. Folder, "Briefing Book, Ambassador Kirkpatrick Visit to Central and South America, February 3–12, 1983 [1 of 3]." Box 90500, Files of Jacqueline Tillman. Ronald Reagan Library.

Dominguez, Jorge I. *To Make a World Safe for Revolution: Cuba's Foreign Policy.* Cambridge, MA: Harvard University Press, 1989.

Drachman, Edward R., and Alan Shank. *Presidents and Foreign Policy: Countdown to 10 Controversial Decisions.* Albany: State University of New York Press, 1997.

Dyke, Nancy Berg. Memo through Admiral Murphy to Vice President. March 25, 1982. Folder, "Narco-Terrorism [3 of 5]." OA/ID 19850. Bush Vice Presidential Records. National Security Affairs. George Bush Presidential Library.

Eisenhower, Dwight D. "Special Message to the Congress on the Situation in the Middle East, January 5, 1957."

El Saadany, Salah. *Egypt and Libya from Inside, 1969–1976,* Mohamed M. El-Behairy, trans. Jefferson, NC: McFarland, 1994.

Engel, Jeffrey. *The Fall of the Berlin Wall: The Revolutionary Legacy of 1989.* New York: Oxford University Press, 2009.

Fergusson, Ian F., Robert D. Shuey, Craig Elwell, and Jeanne Grimmett. "Export Administration Act of 1979 Reauthorization," March 2002, Order Code RL30169, Congressional Research Service. http://www.fas.org/asmp/resources/govern/crs-RL30169.pdf (accessed June 1, 2011).

Fitzwater, Marlin, "Statement on the Attack against the USS *Stark*," May 19, 1987. John T. Woolley and Gerhard Peters, *The American Presidency Project* [online]. Santa Barbara, CA. http://www.presidency.ucsb.edu/ws/?pid=34294.

Flores, David E. "Export Controls and the U.S. Effort to Combat International Terrorism." In *Law and Policy in International Business,* no. 13 (1981): 521–90.

Foot, Rosemary. *The Practice of Power: U.S. Relations with China since 1949.* New York: Oxford University Press, 1995.

Ford, Gerald A. "Address at a Tulane University Convocation," April 23, 1975. *The American Presidency Project* [online]. Santa Barbara, CA. http://www.presidency.ucsb.edu/ws/index.php?pid=4859&st=&st1=#axzz1SknMRHfh.

Foreign Policy: Coherence in Sense of Direction. [n.d.] Folder, "Meetings SSC 293: 325–80." Box 32. Files: Brzezinski collection. Jimmy Carter Presidential Library.

Fosdick, Dorothy, ed. *Staying the Course: Henry M. Jackson and National Security.* Seattle: University of Washington Press, 1987.

Gaddafi, Muammar. *My Vision: Conversations and Frank Exchanges of Views with Edmond Jouve.* Angela Parfitt, trans. London: John Black, 2005.

Gaddis, John. *Strategies of Containment: A Critical Appraisal of Postwar American National Security Policy.* New York: Oxford University Press, 1982 (revised and updated 2005).

Garthoff, R. L. *Détente and Confrontation: American-Soviet Relations from Nixon to Reagan.* Washington, DC: Brookings Institution, 1994.

———. *The Great Transition: American-Soviet Relations and the End of the Cold War.* Washington, DC: Brookings Institution, 1994.

Gates, Robert M. *From the Shadows: The Ultimate Insider's Story of Five Presidents and How They Won the Cold War.* New York: Simon & Schuster, 1996.

Ginat, Rami. *Syria and the Doctrine of Arab Nationalism: From Independence to Dependence.* East Sussex, UK: Sussex Academic, 2005.

Gleijeses, Piero. *Conflicting Missions: Havana, Washington, and Africa, 1959–1976.* Chapel Hill: University of North Carolina Press, 2002.

Goldgeier, James G. "NATO Expansion: Anatomy of a Decision." In *Washington Quarterly* 21, no. 1 (Winter 1998): 85–102.

Goode, James. *The United States and Iran, 1946–51: The Diplomacy of Neglect.* New York: St. Martin's, 1989.

Gorbachev, Mikhail. *At the Summit: How the Two Superpowers Set the World on a Course for Peace.* New York: Richardson, Steirman & Black, 1988.

———. "Excerpts from Address by Mikhail Gorbachev, 43rd U.N. General Assembly Session," December 7, 1988. Temple University. http://isc.temple.edu/hist249/course/Documents/gorbachev_speech_to_UN.htm (accessed May 15, 2011).

Goren, Roberta. *The Soviet Union and Terrorism.* Edited by Jillian Becker. London: George Allen and Unwin, 1984.

Grachev, Andrei. *Gorbachev's Gamble: Soviet Foreign Policy and the End of the Cold War.* Cambridge, UK: Polity, 2008.

Greene, John Robert. *The Presidency of Gerald R. Ford.* Lawrence: University of Kansas Press, 1995.

———. *The Limits of Power: The Nixon and Ford Administrations.* Bloomington: Indiana University Press, 1992.

Hahn, Peter L. *Caught in the Middle East: U.S. Policy toward the Arab-Israeli Conflict, 1945–61.* Chapel Hill: University of North Carolina Press, 2004.

Haig, Alexander. Memorandum for the Record. NSC Meeting on North Korean Downing of U.S. EC-121 Reconnaissance Aircraft, National Security Council Institutional Files. Folder, "NSC Minutes Originals 1969." Box 109. National Archives: Richard Nixon Presidential Library and Museum. Accessed through the National Security Archives, Document Code KT00018.

Hanhimäki, Jussi M. *The Flawed Architect: Henry Kissinger and American Foreign Policy.* New York: Oxford University Press, 2004.

Hanhimäki, Jussi, and Odd Arne Westad. *The Cold War: A History in Documents and Eyewitness Accounts.* New York: Oxford University Press, 2003.

Herring, George C. *From Colony to Superpower: U.S. Foreign Relations since 1776.* New York: Oxford University Press, 2008.

Hickey, Edward V., Jr. Memo to the White House for Baker, Deaver, and McFarlane. October 23, 1983. Folder, "Lebanon Bombing/Airport October 23, 1983," Box 91353, Executive Secretariat, National Security Council: Records: Country File. Ronald Reagan Library.

Huntington, Samuel, Michel Crozier, and Joji Watanuki. *The Crisis of Democracy: A Report on the Governability of Democracies to the Trilateral Commission.* New York: New York University Press, 1975.

Hutchings, Robert. *American Diplomacy and the End of the Cold War.* Washington, DC: Woodrow Wilson Center Press, 1997.

Hyland, William G. *Mortal Rivals: Superpower Relations from Nixon to Reagan.* New York: Random House, 1987.

INF Treaty and the Washington Summit. The National Security Archive. http://www.gwu.edu/~nsarchiv/NSAEBB/index.html#Europe (accessed May 12, 2011).

International Convention Against the Taking of Hostages. G.A. Res. 146 (XXXIV). U. N. GAOR. 34th Sess. Supp. No 46 at 245. U.N. Doc. A/34/46 (1979), entered into force June 3, 1983. University of Minnesota Human Rights Library. http://www1.umn.edu/humanrts/instree/takinghostages.html (accessed June 14, 2011).

Jenkins, Philip. *Images of Terror: What We Can and Can't Know about Terrorism.* New York: De Gruyter, 2003.

Jones, Howard. *Crucible of Power: A History of American Foreign Relations from 1897.* Wilmington, DE: Scholarly Resources, 2001.

Jordan, David C. *Revolutionary Cuba and the End of the Cold War.* Lanham, MD: University Press of America, 1993.

Jordan, Hamilton. Memo to President Carter. [n.d.]. Folder, "11/79." Box 34. Office Files of Hamilton Jordan. Jimmy Carter Presidential Library.

Kaufman, Robert G. *Henry M. Jackson: A Life in Politics.* Seattle: University of Washington Press, 2000.

Key Facts on "Iraqgate." [n.d.] Folder, "Iraq [1], OA/ID CFO1992. Files of John Schmitz. Counsel's Office. Bush Presidential Records. Bush Presidential Library.

Kimball, Jeffrey. *Nixon's Vietnam War.* Lawrence: University Press of Kansas, 1998.

Kissinger, Henry. *White House Years.* New York: Little, Brown, 1979.

———. *Years of Upheaval.* Boston: Little, Brown, 1982.

Korn, David A. *Assassination in Khartoum.* Bloomington: Indiana University Press, 1993.

Kotkin, Stephen. *Uncivil Society: 1989 and the Implosion of the Communist Establishment.* New York: Modern Library, 2009.

Kutler, Stanley I. *The Wars of Watergate.* New York: W. W. Norton, 1990.

Leffler, Melvyn. *For the Soul of Mankind: The United States, the Soviet Union, and the Cold War.* New York: Hill & Wang, 2008.

Leffler, Melvyn P., and Jeffrey W. Legro, eds. *In Uncertain Times: American Foreign Policy after the Berlin Wall and 9/11.* Ithaca, NY: Cornell University Press, 2011.

Leffler, Melvyn, and Odd Arne Westad, eds. *The Cambridge History of the Cold War.* 3 vols. New York: Cambridge University Press, 2010.

Lerner, Mitchell. *The Pueblo Incident: A Spy Ship and the Failure of American Foreign Policy.* Lawrence: University Press of Kansas, 2002.

Lesch, David. *The Arab-Israeli Conflict: A History.* New York: Oxford University Press, 2007.

Libya under Qadhafi: A Pattern of Aggression. [n.d.] Folder, "Libya Sensitive 1986 [7 of 7]." Box 91668. Files of Howard Teicher. Ronald Reagan Presidential Library.

Little, Douglas. *American Orientalism: The United States and the Middle East since 1945.* Chapel Hill: University of North Carolina Press, 2002.

Mann, James. *About Face: A History of America's Curious Relationship with China, from Nixon to Clinton.* New York: Vintage Books, 1998.

———. *The Rebellion of Ronald Reagan: A History of the End of the Cold War.* New York: Penguin, 2009.

Maresca, John. *To Helsinki: The Conference on Security and Cooperation in Europe, 1973–1975.* Durham, NC: Duke University Press, 1985.

Marshall Plan. Featured Documents Library, National Archives and Records Administration. http://www.archives.gov/exhibits/featured_documents/marshall_plan/images/marshall_plan_page_1.jpg (accessed June 13, 2011).

Mastny, Vojtech, and Malcolm Byrne. *A Cardboard Castle? An Inside History of the Warsaw Pact, 1955–1991.* Budapest: Central European University Press, 2005.

Maynard, Christopher. *Out of the Shadow: George H. W. Bush and the End of the Cold War.* College Station: Texas A&M University Press, 2008.

McFarlane, Robert C. Memo to Edwin Meese III, August 15, 1984. Folder, "Terrorism, Vol II 4/1/84–831/84, [8404913]." Box 91400. Executive Secretariat, National Security Council: Records: Subject File. Ronald Reagan Presidential Library.

McKinzie, Richard D. Oral History Interview with Richard D. Weigle, June 11, 1973. Harry S. Truman Presidential Library.

Memorandum. The Seizure of the Saudi Arabian Embassy in Khartoum. Intelligence. Washington, June 1973. Foreign Relations of the United States, 1969–1976 Volume E-6, Documents on Africa, 1973–1976, Document 217.

Memorandum of telephone conversation between Joseph Alsop and Secretary of State Kissinger. Kissinger Telephone Conversation Transcripts (Telcons). Chronological Files. Folder, "April 15–22, 1969." Box 1. National Archives: Richard Nixon Presidential Library and Museum. Accessed at the National Security Archives, Document Code KA00525.

Memorandum of telephone conversation between Ambassador Yost and Secretary of State Kissinger. Kissinger Telephone Conversation Transcripts (Telcons). Chronological Files. Folder, "April 15–22, 1969." Box 1. National Archives: Richard Nixon Presidential Library and Museum. Accessed at the National Security Archives, Document Code KA00522.

Memorandum of telephone conversation between President Nixon and Secretary of State Kissinger. Kissinger Telephone Conversation Transcripts (Telcons). Chronological Files. Folder, "April 15–22, 1969." Box 1. National Archives: Richard Nixon Presidential Library and Museum. Accessed at the National Security Archives, Document Code KA00524.

Memorandum of telephone conversation between President Nixon and Henry Kissinger. Kissinger Telephone Conversation Transcripts (Telcons). Chronological Files. Folder, "April 15–22, 1969." Box 1. National Archives: Richard Nixon Presidential Library and Museum. Accessed at the National Security Archives, Document Code KA00529.

Metz, Steven. *Iraq and the Evolution of American Strategy.* Washington, DC: Potomac Books, 2008.

Minutes of a Meeting of the National Security Council, Washington, September 23, 1970. *Foreign Relations of the United States, 1969–1976, Volume E-10, Documents on American Republics, 1969–1972,* Document 226.

Moses, Russell. *Freeing the Hostages: Reexamining U.S.-Iranian Negotiations and Soviet Policy, 1979–1981.* Pittsburgh, PA: University of Pittsburgh Press, 1996.

National Security Archives and Records Administration. RG 59, Central Files 1967–69, POL 33–6 KOR N-US. Secret; Nodis. Drafted by Brown on December 2. In Person, J (2010). *New Evidence on North Korea.* North Korea International Documentation Project, Doc No. 47. http://www.wilsoncenter.org/topics/pubs/New-Evidence-North-Korea-Reader.pdf (accessed June 1, 2011).

"National Security Directive 23," September 22, 1989. The George Bush Presidential Library and Museum. http://bushlibrary.tamu.edu/research/pdfs/nsd/nsd23.pdf (accessed May 22, 2011).

"National Security Review-3," February 15, 1989. The George Bush Presidential Library and Museum. http://bushlibrary.tamu.edu/research/pdfs/nsr/nsr3.pdf (accessed May 22, 2011).

Nelson, Keith L. *The Making of Détente: Soviet-American Relations in the Shadow of Vietnam.* Baltimore, MD: Johns Hopkins University Press, 1995.

Nixon, Richard. "The President's News Conference, March 2, 1973." *Public Papers,* Document 63. John T. Woolley and Gerhard Peters, *The American Presidency Project* [online]. Santa Barbara, CA. http://www.presidency.ucsb.edu/ws/index.php?pid=4123axzz1PH7sRFJv (accessed June 9, 2011).

———. "The President's News Conference, April, 18, 1969." *Public Papers,* Document 156. John T. Woolley and Gerhard Peters, *The American Presidency Project* [online]. Santa Barbara, CA. http://www.presidency.ucsb.edu/ws/index.php?pid=2004axzz1PH7sRFJv (accessed June 9, 2011).

———. "Remarks at a Ceremony Honoring Slain Foreign Service Officers," March 6, 1973. John T. Woolley and Gerhard Peters, *The American Presidency Project* [online]. Santa Barbara, CA. http://www.presidency.ucsb.edu/ws/index.php?pid=4132 (accessed June 5, 2011).

Notes of the President's Lunch Meeting with Senior American Advisors, Special Files Collection. Folder, "Tom Johnson's Notes of Meetings." Box 2. January 9, 1968. Accessed from the National Security Archive, Document Code HN01566.

Office of the Press Secretary. Letter from George Herbert Walker Bush to Ronald Reagan, 2 June 1987. Folder, "Letter from VP to Reagan on Terrorism, June 2, 1987." OA/ID 23352. Office files of Emily Mead. Office of Policy Development. Bush Vice Presidential Records. George Bush Presidential Library.

Ostermann, C., and James F. Person, eds. *Crisis and Confrontation on the Korean Peninsula: A Critical Oral History.* Washington, DC: Woodrow Wilson International Center for Scholars. www.wilsoncenter.org/topics/pubs/NKIDP_Critical_OralHist_textL.pdf (accessed June 1, 2011).

Ouimet, Matthew J. *The Rise and Fall of the Brezhnev Doctrine in Soviet Foreign Policy.* Chapel Hill: University of North Carolina Press, 2003.

Paczkowski, Andrzej. *Spring Will be Ours.* Jane Cave, trans. University Park: Pennsylvania State University Press, 2003.

Palazchenko, Pavel. *My Years with Gorbachev and Shevardnadze: The Memoirs of a Soviet Interpreter.* University Park: Pennsylvania State University Press, 1997.

Pipes, Richard. *Vixi: Memoirs of a Non-belonger.* New Haven, CT: Yale University Press, 2003.

Prados, Alfred B. "Syria: U.S. Relations and Bilateral Issues." *CRS Issue Brief for Congress.* IB92075. July 27, 2006.

President's Assistant for National Security Affairs (Kissinger), Memo to President Nixon, Washington, D.C., February 7, 1969. *Foreign Relations of the United States, 1969–1976, Volume E-10, Documents on American Republics, 1969–1972,* Document 196.

Quandt, William. *Peace Process.* Washington, DC: Brookings Institution, 2005.

Reagan, Ronald. *The Reagan Diaries.* Douglas Brinkley, ed. New York: Harper, 2007.

———. "President's News Conference, April, 9, 1986." John T. Woolley and Gerhard Peters, *The American Presidency Project* [online]. Santa Barbara, CA. http://www.presidency.ucsb.edu/ws/index.php?pid=37105axzz1PH7sRFJv (accessed June 9, 2011).

———, "Address to the Nation and Other Countries on United States-Soviet Relations," January 16, 1984, in *The Public Papers of the Presidents, Ronald Reagan, 1984, The American Presidency Project.* http://www.presidency.ucsb.edu/ws/index.php?pid=39806&st=&st1=#axzz1MAYmizuY (accessed May 12, 2011).

———. "Interview with Foreign Journalists," April 22, 1986. John T. Woolley and Gerhard Peters, *The American Presidency Project* [online]. Santa Barbara, CA. http://www.presidency.ucsb.edu/ws/index.php?pid=37173#axzz1PYWTZlOv (accessed June 9, 2011).

———. "Memorandum of Conversation between Thatcher and Reagan," December 28, 1985, The Margaret Thatcher Foundation. http://www.margaretthatcher.org/document/109185 (accessed May 4, 2011).

———. "The President's News Conference Following the Soviet-United States Summit Meeting in Moscow." June 1, 1988. *The American Presidency Project* [online]. Santa Barbara, CA. http://www.presidency.ucsb.edu/ws/index.php?pid=35903&st=evil+empire&st1=#ixzz1SM9zdE.

———. "Radio Address to the Nation on the Iran Arms and Contra Aid Controversy," December 22, 1986. *The American Presidency Project* [online]. Santa Barbara, CA. http://www.presidency.ucsb.edu/ws/index.php?pid=36788#axzz1PYWTZlOv (accessed June 9, 2011).

———. "Remarks Announcing the Release of the Hostages from Trans World Airlines Hijacking Incident, June 30, 1985." John T. Woolley and Gerhard Peters, *The American Presidency Project* [online]. Santa Barbara, CA. http://www.presidency.ucsb.edu/ws/index.php?pid=38841axzz1PH7sRFJv (accessed June 9, 2011).

———. "Remarks and a Question-and-Answer Session with the Students and Faculty at Moscow State University," May 31, 1988, in *The Public Papers of the Presidents, Ronald Reagan, 1988, The American Presidency Project.* (http://www.presidency.ucsb.edu/ws/index.php?pid=35897&st=&st1=#axzz1MjC5f47Z (accessed May 20, 2011).

Reagan, Bush, and Gorbachev at Governor's Island. The National Security Archive. http://www.gwu.edu/~nsarchiv/NSAEBB/index.html#Europe (accessed May 17, 2011).

Reykjavik File. The National Security Archive. http://www.gwu.edu/~nsarchiv/NSAEBB/index.html#Europe (accessed May 7, 2011).

Rubin, Barry. "The United States and Iraq: From Appeasement to War." In *Iraq's Road to War,* Amatzia Baram and Barry Rubin, eds.: 255–72. New York: St. Martin's, 1993.

Saadany, S. E. *Egypt and Libya from Inside, 1969–1976: The Qaddafi Revolution and the Eventual Break in Relations, by the Former Egyptian Ambassador to Libya.* Mohamed M. El-Behairy, trans. Jefferson, NC: McFarland, 1994.

Sarotte, Mary Elise. *1989: The Struggle to Create Post-Cold War Europe.* Princeton, NJ: Princeton University Press, 2009.

Schulzinger, Robert D. *Henry Kissinger: Doctor of Diplomacy.* New York: Columbia University Press, 1989.

Schweizer, Peter, *Reagan's War: The Epic Story of His Forty-year Struggle and Final Triumph over Communism.* New York: Doubleday, 2002.

Shlaim, Avi. *The Iron Wall.* New York: W. W. Norton, 2000.

Shultz, George. *Turmoil and Triumph: My Years as Secretary of State.* New York: Charles Scribner's and Sons, 1993.

Sick, Gary. *All Fall Down: America's Tragic Encounter with Iran.* New York: Random House. 1985.

Small, Melvin. *The Presidency of Richard Nixon.* Lawrence: University Press of Kansas, 1999.

Smith, Charles D. *Palestine and the Arab-Israeli Conflict.* Boston: Bedford St. Martin's, 2001.

Smith, G. *Morality, Reason, and Power: American Diplomacy in the Carter Years.* New York: Hill & Wang, 1986.

Smith, Gerard C. *Doubletalk: The Story of the First Strategic Arms Limitation Talks.* Garden City, NY: Doubleday, 1980.

Simpson, Christopher. *National Security Directives of the Reagan and Bush Administrations: The Declassified History of U.S. Political and Military Policy, 1981–1991.* Boulder, CO: Boulder, 1995.

Snyder, Sarah. *Human Rights Activism and the End of the Cold War: A Transnational History of the Helsinki Network.* New York: Cambridge University Press, 2011.

St. John, Ronald B. *Qaddafi's World Design: Libyan Foreign Policy, 1969–1987.* London: Saqi, 1987.

Statement Signed at Panmunjom, Rusk's Explanation and McCloskey's Remarks. In *New York Times* (December 23, 1968): 2. http://media/proquest.com/media/pq/hnp/doc/76922322/fmt/ai/rep/NONE?hl=statements.

Stivers, William. *America's Confrontation with Revolutionary Change in the Middle East.* New York: St. Martin's, 1986.

Suri, Jeremi. *Power and Protest: Global Revolution and the Origins of Détente.* Cambridge, MA: Harvard University Press, 2003.

Ta'if Accord. http://www.al-bab.com/arab/docs/lebanon/taif.htm (accessed June 5, 2011).

Telegram to Ambassador Lang, Feb. 1980. Folder, "Iran 2/80." Box 34. Office Files of Hamilton Jordan. Jimmy Carter Presidential Library.

Terrorist Attacks and U.S.-Libyan Relations. [n.d.] Folder, "Libya Sensitive 1986, 1 of 7," Box 91668. Files of Howard Teicher. Ronald Reagan Presidential Library.

Thatcher, Margaret. "Television Interview for the BBC," December 17, 1984. The Margaret Thatcher Foundation. http://www.margaretthatcher.org/document/105592 (accessed May 1, 2011).

Thomas, Daniel C. *The Helsinki Effect: International Norms, Human Rights and the Demise of Communism.* Princeton, NJ: Princeton University Press, 2001.

Thornton, Richard C. *The Carter Years: Toward A New Global Order.* New York: Paragon, 1992.

Truman, Harry S. "The President's News Conference, November 17, 1949." John T. Woolley and Gerhard Peters, *The American Presidency Project* [online]. Santa Barbara, CA. http://www.presidency.ucsb.edu/ws/index.php?pid=13361axzz1PH7sRFJv (accessed June 9, 2011).

———. "Special Message to the Congress on Greece and Turkey: The Truman Doctrine, March 12, 1947," John T. Woolley and Gerhard Peters, *The American Presidency Project* [online]. Santa Barbara, CA. http://www.presidency.ucsb.edu/ws/index.php?pid=12846axzz1PH7sRFJv (accessed June 9, 2011).

Tucker, Nancy Bernkopf. *China Confidential: American Diplomats and Sino-American Relations, 1945–1996.* New York: Columbia University Press, 2001.

Tyler, Patrick. *A Great Wall: Six Presidents and China.* New York: Century Foundation, 1999.

U.S. Department of State. Cuba's Renewed Support for Violence in Latin America, Special Report No. 90, December 14, 1981.

———. The Iranians and the PFLP-GC: Early Suspects in the Pan Am 103 Bombing, November 15, 1990. Folder, "Pan Am 103." CF 00703. Press Office/Foreign Affairs, Bush Presidential Records. George Bush Presidential Library.

———. Syrian Support for International Terrorism: 1983–86, Special Report No. 157, December 1986.

Vandewalle, Dirk. *A History of Modern Libya.* New York: Cambridge University Press, 2006.

Walsh, Lawrence E. *Iran-Contra: The Final Report.* New York: Times Books, 1993.

Wandycz, Piotr. *The United States and Poland.* Cambridge, MA: Harvard University Press, 1980.

Westad, Odd Arne. *The Global Cold War.* New York: Cambridge University Press, 2005.

Winkler, Carol K. *In the Name of Terrorism: Presidents on Political Violence in the Post-World War II Era.* Albany: State University of New York Press, 2006.

Woolley, John T., and Gerhard Peters. *The American Presidency Project* [online]. Santa Barbara, CA. http://www.presidency.ucsb.edu/ws/index.php?pid=11007#axzz1P0DZeIhR (accessed June 9, 2011).

Yaqub, Salim. "The Weight of Conquest: Henry Kissinger and the Arab Israeli Conflict." In *Nixon and the World,* Fredrik Logevall and Andrew Preston, eds. New York: Oxford University Press, 2008.

Zubok, Vladislav M. *A Failed Empire: The Soviet Union in the Cold War from Stalin to Gorbachev.* Chapel Hill: University of North Carolina Press, 2007.

PART VI: NEW THRESHOLDS OF DIPLOMACY

Albright, Madeleine. *Madam Secretary: A Memoir.* New York: Macmillan, 2003.

Anker, Peder. "The Ecological Colonization of Space." In *Environmental History* (April 2005).

Asmus, Ronald D. *Opening NATO's Door: How the Alliance Remade Itself for a New Era.* New York: Columbia University Press, 2002.

———, Richard L. Kugler, and F. Stephen Larrabee. "Building a New NATO." In *Foreign Affairs* 72, no. 4 (September/October 1993): 28–40.

———. "NATO Expansion: The Next Steps." In *Survival* 37, no. 1 (Spring 1995): 7–33.

Azpuru, Dinorah, and Carolyn M. Shaw. "The United States and the Promotion of Democracy in Latin America: Then, Now, and Tomorrow," In *Orbis* 54, no. 2 (2010): 252–67.

Bacevich, Andrew. *American Empire: The Realities and Consequences of American Diplomacy.* Cambridge, MA: Harvard University Press, 2002.

Begley, Sharon. "The Truth about Deniers." In *Newsweek* (August 3, 2007).

Biglaiser, Glen, and Joseph L. Staats, "Do Political Institutions Affect Foreign Direct Investment? A Survey of U.S. Corporations in Latin America." In *Political Research Quarterly* 63, no. 3 (2010): 508–22.

Blumenthal, Sidney. *The Clinton Wars.* New York: Farrar, Straus, and Giroux, 2003.

Brands, Hal. *From Berlin to Baghdad: America's Search for Purpose in the Post-Cold War World.* Lexington: University of Kentucky Press, 2008.

Buchanan, Patrick. "America First—And Second, and Third." In *National Interest* (Spring 1990).

Bush, George. *All the Best, George Bush.* New York: Charles Scribner's and Sons, 1999.

———. *Public Papers of the Presidents of the United States, 1992.* Washington, DC: Government Printing Office, 1993.

Cardoso, Fernando Henrique. "Development under Fire." In *The New International Economy, Sage Studies in International Sociology,* Harry Makler, Alberto Martinelli, and Neil Smelser, eds.: 141–65. Beverly Hills, CA: Sage, 1982.

Chamberlin, Paul. *The Global Offensive: The United States, the PLO, and the Making of the New International Order, 1967–1975.* New York: Oxford University Press, Forthcoming.

Clark, Wesley. *Waging Modern War.* New York: Perseus, 2001.

Clarke, Richard. *Against All Enemies: Inside America's War on Terror.* New York: Free Press, 2004.

Clinton, Bill. *My Life.* New York: Random House, 2005.

———. "The President's News Conference with Visegrad Leaders in Prague." In *Public Papers of the Presidents of the United States, 1994,* Book I.

Congressional Budget Office. *The Effects of NAFTA on U.S.-Mexican Trade and GDP.* Washington, DC: Government Printing Office, January 1994.

Connelly, Matthew. *Fatal Misconception: The Struggle to Control World Population.* Cambridge, MA: Harvard University Press, 2008.

Cook, Colleen W. "Mexico's Drug Cartels." CRS Report for Congress, October 2007.

Cordesman, Anthony. "The Georgia War and the Century of 'Real Power.'" In *CSIS Commentary* (August 18, 2008). http://csis.org/publication/georgia-war-and-century-real-power.

Cox, Ronald W. "Transnational Capital, the U.S. State and Latin American Trade Agreements." In *Third World Quarterly* 29, no. 8 (2008): 1527–44.

Crandall, Russell. *The United States and Latin America after the Cold War.* New York: Cambridge University Press, 2008.

Daalder, Ivo, and James Goldgeier. "Global NATO." In *Foreign Affairs* 85, no. 5 (September/October 2006): 105–13.

Deans, Bob. "With Nod to Protests, Clinton Chides WTO." In *Atlanta Journal and Constitution,* December 2, 1999.

Dobbs, Michael. *Madeleine Albright: A Twentieth-Century Odyssey.* New York: Macmillan, 2000.

Domingue, Jorge I. *Contemporary U.S.-Latin American Relations: Cooperation or Conflict in the 21st Century.* New York: Routledge, 2010.

Dorsey, Kurkpatrick. "Environmental Diplomacy." In *Encyclopedia of American Foreign Policy.* 2nd ed. Vol. 2. Alexander DeConde, Richard Burns, and Fredrik Logevall, eds.: 49–62. New York: Charles Scribner's and Sons, 2002.

Dowie, Mark. *Conservation Refugees: The Hundred-Year Conflict between Global Conservation and Native Peoples.* Cambridge, MA: Massachusetts Institute of Technology Press, 2009.

Eckes, Alfred E., Jr. *The Contemporary Global Economy: A History since 1980.* New York: Wiley, 2011.

Erlanger, Stephen. "Clinton and 3 Baltic Leaders Sign Charter." In *The New York Times,* January 17, 1998.

———. "U.S. to Back Baltic Membership in NATO, but Not Anytime Soon." In *The New York Times,* January 12, 1998.

———. "U.S. to Propose NATO Take on Increased Roles." In *The New York Times,* December 7, 1998.

Esposito, John. *Unholy War: Terror in the Name of Islam.* New York: Oxford University Press, 2002.

Evenden, Matthew. "Aluminum, Commodity Chains, and the Environmental History of the Second World War." In *Environmental History* 16, no. 1 (January 2011): 69–93.

Finlay, Mark R. *Growing American Rubber: Strategic Plants and the Politics of National Security.* Piscataway, NJ: Rutgers University Press, 2009.

Gates, Robert. "The Security and Defense Agenda (Future of NATO)," Speech in Brussels, June 19, 2011. http://www.defense.gov/speeches/speech.aspx?speechid=1581.

Gilbert, Mark. *Surpassing Realism: The Politics of European Integration.* Lanham, MD: Rowman & Littlefield, 2003.

Goldgeier, James. *Not Whether but When: The U.S. Decision to Enlarge NATO.* Washington, DC: Brookings Institution, 1999.

Gore, Al. *Earth in the Balance: Ecology and the Human Spirit.* Boston: Houghton Mifflin, 1992.

Gordon, Philip, and Jeremy Shapiro. *Allies at War: America, Europe, and the Crisis over Iraq.* New York: McGraw-Hill, 2004.

Greider, William. *One World, Ready or Not: The Manic Logic of Global Capitalism.* New York: Simon & Schuster, 1997.

Grow, Michael. *U.S. Presidents and Latin American Interventions: Pursuing Regime Change in the Cold War.* Lawrence: University Press of Kansas, 2008.

Grugel, Jean, Pia Riggirozzi, and Ben Thirkell-White. "Beyond the Washington Consensus? Asia and Latin America in Search of More Autonomous Development." In *International Affairs* 84, no. 3 (2008): 499–517.

Halberstam, David. *War in a Time of Peace: Bush, Clinton, and the Generals.* New York: Charles Scribner's and Sons, 2001.

Hamblin, Jacob. "Environmental Dimensions of the Second World War." In *A Companion to the Second World War,* Thomas W. Zeiler, ed. New York: Wiley, forthcoming.

Handelman, Howard. *The Challenge of Third World Development.* Englewood Cliffs, NJ: Prentice Hall, 1996.

Herring, George C. *From Colony to Superpower: U.S. Foreign Relations since 1776.* New York: Oxford University Press, 2008.

Holbrooke, Richard C. *To End a War.* New York: Modern Library, 1999.

"Joint Declaration on European Defence," Declaration Issued at the British-French Summit, Saint-Malo, December 3–4, 1998. http://www.fco.gov.uk/resources/en/news/2002/02/joint-declaration-on-eu-new01795.

Kane, Tim. "U.S. Troop Deployment Dataset." Version of March 1, 2006. Washington, DC: Heritage Foundation. http://www.heritage.org/Research/NationalSecurity/troopsdb.cfm.

Kaplan, Lawrence S. *The Long Entanglement: NATO's First Fifty Years.* Westport, CT: Praeger, 1999.

Kinkela, David. *DDT and the American Century: Global Health, Environmental Politics, and the Pesticide That Changed the World.* Chapel Hill: University of North Carolina Press, 2011.

Kohli, Atul. "Nationalist versus Dependent Capitalist Development: Alternate Pathways of Asia and Latin America in a Globalized World." In *Studies in Comparative International Development* 44, no. 1 (2009): 386–410.

Krauthammer, Charles. "The Unipolar Moment." In *Foreign Affairs* 70, no. 1 (Winter 1991).

Lake, Anthony. *From Containment to Enlargement: Remarks at the Paul Nitze School of International Affairs at Johns Hopkins University, September 21, 1993.* Washington, DC: Government Printing Office, 1993.

Lippman, Thomas. "Albright Pessimistic as Mideast Trip Ends." In *Washington Post,* September 16, 1997.

Manwaring, Max G. "Non-State Actors in Colombia: Threats to the State and to the Hemisphere." In *Small Wars and Insurgencies* 13, no. 2 (2002): 68–80.

Martinez-Diaz, Leonardo. "Latin America: Coming of Age." In *World Policy* 25, no. 3 (2008): 221–27.

McNeill, John. *Something New under the Sun: An Environmental History of the Twentieth-century World.* New York: W. W. Norton, 2000.

McNeill, John, and Corinna R. Unger. *Environmental Histories of the Cold War.* Washington, DC: German Historical Institute, 2010.

Medvedev, Dimitry. "Interview Given by Dmitry Medvedev to Television Channels Channel One, Russia, NTV." *Sochi,* August 31, 2008. http://archive.kremlin.ru/eng/speeches/2008/08/31/1850_type82912type82916_206003.shtml.

Meyers, Steven, and Thom Shanker. "NATO Expansion, and a Bush Legacy, Are in Doubt." In *The New York Times,* March 15, 2008.

Moran, Theodore. *Multinational Corporations and the Politics of Dependence.* Princeton, NJ: Princeton University Press, 1974.

NATO. *Study on Enlargement.* September 3, 1995. http://www.nato.int/cps/en/natolive/official_texts_24733.htm.

NATO. *Strategic Concept for the Defence and Security of the Members of the North Atlantic Treaty Organization.* Para 4. http://www.nato.int/lisbon2010/strategic-concept-2010-eng.pdf.

NATO. "The Role of Allied Military Force and the Transformation of the Alliance's Defence Posture." In *NATO Handbook.* http://www.msz.gov.pl/editor/files/docs/DPB/polityka_bezpieczenstwa/NATO_handbook.pdf.

Obama, Barack. "Renewing American Leadership." In *Foreign Affairs* 86, no. 4 (July/August 2007): 11.

Perkins, John H. *Geopolitics and the Green Revolution: Wheat, Genes, and the Cold War.* New York: Oxford University Press, 1997.

Pollack, Kenneth. *The Gathering Storm: The Case for Invading Iraq.* New York: Random House, 2002.

Putin, Vladimir. "Press Statement and Answers to Journalists' Questions Following a Meeting of the Russia-NATO Council." April 4, 2008. http://archive.kremlin.ru/eng/speeches/2008/04/04/1949_type82915_163150.shtml.

———. "Speech and the Following Discussion at the Munich Conference on Security Policy." February 10, 2007. http://archive.kremlin.ru/eng/speeches/2007/02/10/0138_type82912type82914type82917type84779_118123.shtml.

Rasmussen, Anders Fogh. "Closing Press Conference." Lisbon Summit of NATO Heads of State and Government, November 20, 2010. http://www.nato.int/cps/en/natolive/opinions_68887.htm.

Ravenhill, John, ed. "Regional Trade Agreements." In *Global Political Economy* 3. : 173–212. New York: Oxford University Press, 2011.

Rees, Matthew. "Going Ballistic." In *Weekly Standard,* February 8, 1999.

Reyes, Javier, Stefano Schiavo, and Giorgio Fagiolo. "Assessing the Evolution of International Economic Integration Using Random Walk Betweeness Centrality: The Cases of East Asia and Latin America." In *Advances in Complex Systems* 11, no. 5 (2008): 685–702.

Rodrik, Dani. *Has Globalization Gone Too Far?* Washington, DC: Institute for International Economics, 1997.

Robertson, Thomas. "'This Is the American Earth': American Empire, American Environmentalism." In *Diplomatic History* 32, no. 4 (September 2008): 561–84.

Russell, Edmund. *War and Nature: Fighting Humans and Insects with Chemicals from World War I to Silent Spring.* New York: Cambridge University Press, 2001.

Senate Foreign Relations Committee. *Nomination of Warren M. Christopher to Be Secretary of State.* Washington, DC: Government Printing Office, 1993.

Sharp, Jane M. O. "The Case for Opening up NATO to the East." In *The Future of NATO: Enlargement, Russia, and European Security,* Charles-Philippe David and Jacques Lévesque, eds. Montreal: McGill-Queen's University Press, 1999.

Slater, Jerome. "The United States and Latin America: The New Radical Orthodoxy." In *Economic Development and Cultural Change* 25, no. 4 (1977): 747–61.

Spero, Joan E., and Jeffrey A. Hart. *The Politics of International Economic Relations.* 6th ed. Florence, KY: Thomson Wadsworth, 2003.

Steinberg, Ted. "Can Capitalism Save the Planet?: On the Origins of Green Liberalism." In *Radical History Review,* no. 107 (Spring 2010): 7–24.

Stewart, Mart. "Swapping Air, Trading Places: Carbon Exchange, Climate Change Policy, and Naturalizing Markets." In *Radical History Review,* no. 107 (Spring 2010): 25–43.

Talbott, Strobe. *The Russia Hand: A Memoir of Presidential Diplomacy.* New York: Random House, 2002.

Tucker, Richard P. *Insatiable Appetite: The United States and the Ecological Degradation of the Tropical World.* Concise rev. ed. Lanham, MD: Rowman & Littlefield, 2007.

United Nations. *International Statistical Yearbook 2007.* New York: United Nations Statistical Office, 2008.

———. *Yearbook of International Trade Statistics.* New York: United Nations Statistical Office, various years.

United Nations Conference on Trade and Development. World Investment Report. Geneva: UNCTAD, various years.

United Nations Security Council, 6498th Meeting, *Resolution 1973 (2010) [Protection of Civilians in the Libyan Arab Jamahiriya],* March 17, 2011 (S/RES/1973).

Wiarda, Howard. *An Introduction to Latin American Politics and Development.* 7th ed. Boulder, CO: Westview, 2011.

Winham, Gilbert R. "The Evolution of the Global Trade Regime." In *Global Political Economy.* 3rd ed. John Ravenhill, ed.: 137–72. New York: Oxford University Press, 2011.

Yergin, Daniel. *The Prize: The Epic Quest for Oil, Money, and Power.* New York: Simon & Schuster, 1991.

PART VII: DIPLOMATIC DILEMMAS IN THE POST-9/11 WORLD

Almquist, Katherine J. "U.S. Foreign Assistance to Africa: Securing America's Investment for Lasting Development." In *Journal of International Affairs* 62, no. 2 (Spring/Summer 2009): 19–35.

The Amitage Report: The United States and Japan: Advancing toward a Mature Partnership. INSS (Institute for National Strategic Studies) Special Report, National Defense University (October 11, 2000).

Anaya, S. James. *Indigenous Peoples in International Law.* New York: Oxford University Press, 2004.

Anderson, Terry H. *Bush's Wars.* New York: Oxford University Press, 2011.

Armitage, Richard L., and Joseph S. Nye Jr. *A Smarter, More Secure America: Report of the CSIS Commission on Smart Power.* Washington, DC: Center for Strategic and International Studies, 2007.

Arms Control Association. http://www.armscontrol.org (accessed February 9, 2012).

Bacevich, Andrew J. *The Limits of Power.* New York: Metropolitan Books, 2008.

Ben-Zvi, Abraham. *United States and Israel: The Limits of the Special Relationship.* New York: Columbia University Press, 1993.

Bergen, Peter L. *Holy War Inc.: Inside the Secret World of Osama bin Laden.* New York: Free Press, 2001.

———. *The Longest War: The Enduring Conflict between America and Al Qaeda.* New York: Free Press, 2011.

Bergsten, C. Fred, Charles Freeman, Nicholas Lardy, and Derek Mitchell, eds. *China's Rise: Challenges and Opportunities.* Washington, DC: Institute for International Economics, 2008.

Bickerton, Ian, and Carla Klausner. *A Concise History of the Arab-Israeli Conflict.* Englewood Cliffs, NJ: Prentice Hall, 2002.

Bill and Melinda Gates Foundation. http://www.gatesfoundation.org (accessed May 5, 2011).

———. "Global Health Strategy Overview, September 2010." http://www.gatesfoundation.org/global-health/Documents/global-health-strategy_overview.pdf (accessed July 3, 2011).

Boy Scouts of America. Silver Buffalo Awards page. http://www.scouting.org/scoutsource/Awards/SilverBuffalo.aspx (accessed May 5, 2011).

Burgess, Stephen F. "In the National Interest? Authoritarian Decision-making and the Problematic Creation of US Africa Command." In *Contemporary Security Policy* 30, no. 1 (August 2007): 79–99.

Burns, Nicholas. "America's New Strategic Opportunity with India." In *Foreign Affairs* (November/December 2007).

Burns, William J. Under Secretary for Political Affairs. "India's Rise and the Promise of U.S.-Indian Partnership, June 1, 2010." http://www.state.gov/p/us/rm/2010/136718.htm.

Bush, George W. *Decision Points.* New York: Crown, 2010.

———. State of the Union Address, January 28, 2003. Transcript in *The Washington Post,* January 28, 2003. http://www.washingtonpost.com/wp-srv/onpolitics/transcripts/bushtext_012803.html (accessed July 3, 2011).

Chau, Donovan C. *Global Security Watch—Kenya.* Westport, CT: Praeger, 2010.

Chellaney, Brahma. *Asian Juggernaut: The Rise of China, India and Japan.* New York: Harper & Row, 2010.

Christensen, Thomas. "The Advantages of an Assertive China." In *Foreign Affairs* 90, no. 2 (March/April 2011): 54–67.

———. "Shaping the Choices of a Rising China: Recent Lessons for the Obama Administration." In *Washington Quarterly* 32, no. 3 (2009): 90–91.

———. *Worse Than a Monolith: Alliance Politics and Problems of Coercive Diplomacy in Asia.* Princeton, NJ: Princeton University Press, 2011.

Clarke, Richard A. *Against All Enemies: Inside America's War on Terror.* New York: Free Press, 2004.

Clinton, Hillary. "Comments by Secretary Clinton in Hanoi, July 23, 2010. http://www.america.gov/st/texttransenglish/2010/July/20100723164658su0.4912989.html.

———. "Inaugural Richard C. Holbrooke Lecture on a Broad Vision of U.S.-China Relations in the 21st Century." January 14, 2011. http://www.state.gov/secretary/rm/2011/01/154653.htm.

———. Interview with Michele Kelemen of NPR, Munich, Germany. February 6, 2011. http://www.state.gov/secretary/rm/2011/02/156050.htm (accessed July 12, 2011).

The Clinton/Gore Administration: A Record of Progress on HIV and AIDS. June 1999. http://clinton2.nara.gov/ONAP/pub/hivacc.pdf (accessed July 3, 2011).

Coll, Steve. *Ghost Wars: The Secret History of the CIA, Afghanistan, and Bin Laden from the Soviet Invasion to September 10, 2001.* New York: Penguin, 2004.

Cooke, Jennifer G., and J. Stephen Morrison, eds. *U.S. Africa Policy beyond the Bush Years.* Washington, DC: Center for Strategic and International Studies, 2009.

Daalder, Ivo. *America Unbound: The Bush Revolution in Foreign Policy.* Washington, DC: Brookings Institution, 2003.

Danner, Mark. *Torture and Truth: America, Abu Ghraib, and the War on Terror.* New York: New York Review of Books, 2004.

Davies, Wade, and Richmond L. Clow. *American Indian Sovereignty and Law: An Annotated Bibliography.* Lanham, MD: Scarecrow, 2009.

Defense Department. *Quadrennial Defense Review Report.* February 2, 2006. http://www.defense.gov/pubs/pdfs/QDR20060203.pdf.

Denmark, Abraham, and Nirav Patel, eds. *A Strategic Framework for a Global Relationship.* Washington, DC: Center for New America Security, 2009.

DeYoung, Karen. *Soldier: The Life of Colin Powell.* New York: Vintage Books, 2007.

Dietrich, John W. "The Politics of PEPFAR: The President's Emergency Plan for AIDS Relief." In *Ethics and International Affairs* 21, no. 3 (Fall 2007): 277–92. http://www.carnegiecouncil.org/resources/journal/21_3/essay/001.html (accessed July 11, 2011).

Drezner, Daniel. "Does Obama Have a Grand Strategy?" In *Foreign Affairs* (July 2011): 57–68.

Feigenbaum, Evan. "Obama's India Problem." Council on Foreign Relations Expert Brief, April 9, 2010.

"Foreign Policy" and "Speeches and Remarks" on The White House, President Barack Obama. http://www.whitehouse.gov.

Gardner, Lloyd C., and Marilyn B. Young. *Iraq and the Lessons of Vietnam.* New York: New Press, 2007.

Gellman, Barton. *Angler: The Cheney Vice Presidency.* New York: Penguin, 2008.

Gettleman, Jeffrey. "Congo Study Sets Estimate for Rapes Much Higher." In *The New York Times,* May 11, 2011. http://www.nytimes.com/2011/05/12/world/africa/12congo.html?ref=congothedemocraticrepublicof (accessed July 7, 2011).

Glaser, Bonnie. "First Contact: Qian Qichen Engages in Wide-ranging, Constructive Talks." In *Comparative Connections* (April 2001). http://www.csic.org/pacfor.

The Global Fund to Fight AIDS, Tuberculosis and Malaria. *Making a Difference: Global Fund Results Report 2011.* Geneva: Global Fund to Fight AIDS, Tuberculosis and Malaria, 2011. http://www.theglobalfund.org/en/library/publications/progressreports/ (accessed July 3, 2011).

Godement, Francois. "The United States and Asia in 2009." In *Asian Survey* 50, no. 1: 8–24.

———. "The United States and Asia in 2010." In *Asian Survey* 51, no. 1: 5–17.

Gordon, Michael R., and Bernard E. Trainor. *Cobra II: The Inside Story of the Invasion and Occupation of Iraq.* New York: Vintage Books, 2007.

Halabi, Yakub. *U.S. Foreign Policy in the Middle East: From Crisis to Change.* Surrey, England: Ashgate, 2009.

Hewko, John. *Millennium Challenge Corporation: Can the Experiment Survive?* Washington, DC: Carnegie Endowment for International Peace, 2010.

Hiebert, Murray. *The Bush Presidency: Implications for Asia.* New York: Asia Society, 2001.

Hillary Rodham Clinton's Senate Hearing Transcript. January 2009. http://www.foreignpolicy.com/files/KerryClintonQFRs.pdf.

Holm, A. L., and R. M. Davis. "Clearing the Airways: Advocacy and Regulation for Smoke-free Airlines." In *Tobacco Control* 13, Supplement I (2004): 30–36.

Ikenberry, G. John. *After Victory: Institutions, Strategic Restraint, and the Rebuilding of Order after Major Wars.* Princeton, NJ: Princeton University Press, 2001.

———, and Anne-Marie Slaughter. *Forging a World of Liberty under Law: U.S. National Security in the 21st Century, Final Report of the Princeton Project on National Security.* Washington, DC: Woodrow Wilson Center Press, 2006.

Kagan, Robert. *The Return of History and the End of Dreams.* New York: Alfred A. Knopf, 2008.

Keefe, John. *Anatomy of the EP-3 Incident, April 2001.* Alexandria, VA: Center for Naval Analysis, 2001.

Kennedy, Paul. *The Rise and Fall of the Great Powers: Economic Change and Military Conflict from 1500–2000.* New York: Vintage Books, 1989.

Kirk, Jason A. "India's Season of Discontent: U.S.-India Relations through the Prism of Obama's 'Af-Pak' Policy, Year One." In *Asian Affairs: An American Review* 37 (2010): 147–66.

Krauthammer, Charles. "The Unipolar Moment." In *Foreign Affairs* 70, no. 1 (1990/1991): 23–33.

Lizza, Ryan. "The Consequentialist: How the Arab Spring Remade Obama's Foreign Policy." In *The New Yorker* (May 2, 2011): 44–55.

Mann, James. *Rise of the Vulcans: The History of Bush's War Cabinet.* New York: Viking, 2004.

Mastny, Vojtech. "The Soviet Union's Partnership with India." In *Journal of Cold War Studies* 12, no. 3 (summer 2010): 50–90.

Mayer, Jane. *The Dark Side: The Inside Story of How the War on Terror Turned into a War on American Ideals.* New York: Anchor, 2009.

McAllister, William B. *Drug Diplomacy in the Twentieth Century: An International History.* New York: Routledge, 2000.

McNeill, John R. *Something New under the Sun: An Environmental History of the Twentieth-century World.* New York: Norton, 2001.

Meyerowitz, Joanne. *History and September 11th.* Philadelphia: Temple University Press, 2003.

Millennium Challenge Corporation. "A New Vision for Development: 2010 Annual Report." http://www.mcc.gov/documents/reports/report-2011001049801-2010annual.pdf (accessed July 12, 2011).

Millennium Challenge Corporation. "About MCC." http://www.mcc.gov/pages/about (accessed July 12, 2011).

Millennium Challenge Corporation. "Guide to the MCC Indicators and the Selection Process Fiscal Year 2011." http://www.mcc.gov/documents/reports/reference-2010001040503-fy11guidetotheindicators.pdf (accessed July 12, 2011).

"National Security Strategy, May 2010." http://www.whitehouse.gov/sites/default/files/rss_viewer/national_security_strategy.pdf.

The National Security Strategy of the United States of America. March 2006. http://www.comw.org/qdr/fulltext/nss2006.pdf.

The National Security Strategy of the United States of America. September 2002. http://www.comw.org/qdr/fulltext/nss2002.pdf.

The Nature Conservancy. http://www.nature.org (accessed May 5, 2011).

Ngolet, François. *Crisis in the Congo: The Rise and Fall of Laurent Kabila.* New York: Palgrave, 2011.

Nye, Joseph S., Jr. *The Future of Power.* New York: Public Affairs, 2011.

———. *Soft Power: The Means to Success in World Politics.* New York: Public Affairs, 2005.

Obama, Barack. "Statement of President Barack Obama, Recognition of the Republic of South Sudan." July 9, 2011. http://www.whitehouse.gov/the-press-office/2011/07/09/statement-president-barack-obama-recognition-republic-south-sudan (accessed July 10, 2011).

Organisation for Economic Co-operation and Development. 2009 Overseas Development Assistant page. http://webnet.oecd.org/oda2009 (accessed May 5, 2011).

Packer, George. *The Assassin's Gate: America in Iraq.* New York: Farrar, Strauss, and Giroux, 2005.

Parthasarathy, G. "Does Mr. Obama Care about India?" Op-ed in the *Wall Street Journal* (April 12, 2010).

"Person of the Year." In *Time Magazine* 166, no. 26 (December 26, 2005-January 2, 2006).

Pickering, Thomas R., and Chester A. Crocker. *America's Role in the World: Foreign Policy Choices for the Next President.* Washington, DC: Georgetown University Edmund A. Walsh Institute for the Study of Diplomacy, 2008.

Pomeranz, Kenneth. *The Great Divergence: China, Europe, and the Making of the Modern World Economy.* Princeton, NJ: Princeton University Press, 2001.

Pomfret, John. "China Lauds Bush for Comments on Taiwan." In *The Washington Post,* December 11, 2003.

Preble, Christopher A. *The Power Problem: How American Military Dominance Makes Us Less Safe, Less Prosperous, and Less Free.* Ithaca, NY: Cornell University Press, 2009.

President's Malaria Initiative. "Fast Facts: The President's Malaria Initiative," April 2011. http://www.fightingmalaria.gov/resources/reports/pmi_fastfacts.pdf (accessed July 11, 2011).

Przystup, James, and Phillip Saunders. "Visions of Order: Japan and China in U.S. Strategy." In *Strategic Forum* (Institute for National Strategic Studies, National Defense University) 220 (June 2006).

Public Broadcasting Service. "Libya, War Powers Start White House, Congress on Collision Course." *PBS Newshour.* June 15, 2011. http://www.pbs.org/newshour/bb/politics/jan-june11/warpowers2_06-15.html (accessed July 12, 2011).

Quandt, William B. *Peace Process: American Diplomacy and the Arab-Israeli Conflict since 1967.* Berkeley: University of California Press, 2001.

"Remarks of Secretary Clinton on June 3, 2010." http://www.state.gov/secretary/rm/2010/06/142642.htm.

Reydams, Luc, ed. *Global Activism Reader.* New York: Continuum, 2011.

Rice, Condoleezza. "Remarks with Indian External Affairs Minister Pranab Mukherjee, October 4, 2008." http://20012009.state.gov/secretary/rm/2008/10/110622.htm.

———. "Remarks at the U.S.-India Business Council 32nd Anniversary 'Global India' Summit, June 27, 2007." http://www.usindiafriendship.net/viewpoints1/rice-062707.htm.

Ricks, Thomas E. *Fiasco: The American Military Adventure in Iraq.* New York: Penguin, 2006.

Riedel, Bruce. *Deadly Embrace: Pakistan, America, and the Future of Global Jihad.* Washington, DC: Brookings Institution, 2011.

Ross, Dennis, and David Makovsky. *Myths, Illusions, and Peace: Finding a New Direction for America in the Middle East.* New York: Viking, 2009.

Rumsfeld, Donald. *Known and Unknown: A Memoir.* New York: Penguin, 2011.

Schaffer, Teresita C. *India and the United States in the 21st Century: Reinventing Partnership.* Washington, DC: Center for Strategic and International Studies, 2009.

Schoenbaum, David. *The United States and the State of Israel.* New York: Oxford University Press, 1993.

Secretariat of the Convention on Biological Diversity. *Convention on Biological Diversity.* http://www.cbd.int (accessed May 5, 2011).

Secretary Clinton's and Minister Krishna's June 3, 2010, Remarks to the Media. http://www.state.gov/secretary/rm/2010/06/142642.htm.

Shambaugh, David. "U.S.-Chinese Relations Take a New Direction, Part I." January 24, 2011. Yale Global Online. http://yaleglobal.yale.edu.

Sharp, Jeremy. "U.S. Foreign Assistance to the Middle East: Historical Background, Recent Trends, and the FY2011 Request." Prepared for the Congressional Research Service, June 15, 2010. http://www.fas.org/sgp/crs/mideast/RL32260.pdf (accessed July 12, 2011).

Sieff, Martin. *Shifting Superpowers: The New and Emerging Relationship between the United States, China and India.* Washington, DC: CATO Institute, 2009.

Slaughter, Anne-Marie. *The Idea That Is America: Keeping Faith with Our Values in a Dangerous World.* New York: Basic Books, 2008.

Smith, Kimberly. "Statistical Reporting by the Bill and Melinda Gates Foundation to the OECD DAC: Aid to Health Data Now Includes World's Largest Private Foundation." April 2011. http://www.oecd.org/dataoecd/5/60/47539494.pdf (accessed July 11, 2011).

Sokolski, Henry, ed. *Gauging U.S.-Indian Strategic Cooperation.* March 2007. http:www.StrategicStudiesInstitute.army.mil (accessed May 30, 2011).

"Somali Joy as Ethiopians Withdraw." BBC News. January 13, 2009. http://news.bbc.co.uk/2/hi/africa/7825626.stm (accessed July 12, 2011).

Stanger, Allison. *One Nation, Under Contract: The Outsourcing of American Power and the Future of Foreign Policy.* New Haven, CT: Yale University Press, 2009.

State of Arizona. *Arizona Support our Law Enforcement and Safe Neighborhoods Act of 2010.* 2010 Arizona Session Laws, Chapter 113, Forty-ninth Legislature, Second Regular Session, Senate Bill 1070, House Engrossed Senate Bill, Arizona State Legislature, and, 2010 Arizona Session Laws, Chapter 211, Forty-ninth Legislature, Second Regular Session, House Bill 2162, Conference Version, Arizona State Legislature.

State of California. *California Global Warming Solution Act of 2006.* California Assembly Bill 32, Chapter 488, Statutes of 2006.

———. *California Sustainable Communities and Climate Protection Act of 2008.* California Senate Bill 375, Statutes of 2008.

Statements of Assistant Secretary Robert Blake on November 16, 2009. http://www.state.gov/p/sca/rls/rmks/2009/132053.htm.

Steinberg, James B. "China's Arrival: The Long March to Global Power." Keynote address to the Center for a New American Security, Washington, DC, September 24, 2009. http://www.cnas.org/node/3415.

Studlar, Donley T. *Tobacco Control: Comparative Politics in the United States and Canada.* Peterborough, ON: Broadview Press, 2002.

Susskind, Ron. *The One Percent Doctrine: Deep Inside America's Pursuit of Its Enemies since 9/11.* New York: Simon & Schuster, 2006.

Sutter, Robert. "Dealing with a Rising China: U.S. Strategy and Policy." In *Making New Partnership: A Rising China and Its Neighbors,* Zhang Yunlin, ed. Beijing: Social Sciences Academic Press, 2008.

———. *U.S.-Chinese Relations: Perilous Past, Pragmatic Present.* New York: Rowman & Littlefield, 2010.

Tai Xie and Benjamin Page. "Americans and the Rise of China as a World Power." In *Journal of Contemporary China* 19:65 (2010 June).

"Telephonic Conversation between EAM and U.S. Secretary of State." January 23, 2009. http://www.indembassy.be/pr2009_jan_23.html.

Tellis, Ashley. "More Than Just Symbols." Op-ed in *Indian Express,* December 9, 2009.

"Timeline: Egypt's revolution. A chronicle of the revolution that ended the three-decade-long presidency of Hosni Mubarak." *Al Jazeera.* http://english.aljazeera.net/news/middleeast/2011/01/201112511533871490.html (accessed July 11, 2011).

United Nations. Department of Economic and Social Affairs, Division of Sustainable Development. *Agenda 21.* http://www.un.org/esa/dsd/agenda21 (accessed May 5, 2011).

———. *Framework Convention on Climate Change.* http://unfccc.int/2860.php (accessed May 5, 2011).

———. General Assembly. *Report of the United Nations Conference on Environment and Development, Annex I, Rio Declaration on Environment and Development.* U.N. Document A/Conf.151/26 (Vol. I). http://www.un.org/documents/ga/conf151/aconf15126-1annex1.htm (accessed May 5, 2011).

———. General Assembly. *Report of the United Nations Conference on Environment and Development, Annex III, Non-Legally Binding Authoritative Statement of Principles for a Global Consensus on the Management, Conservation, and Sustainable Development of All Types of Forests.* U.N. Document A/Conf.151/26 (Vol. III). http://www.un.org/documents/ga/conf151/aconf15126-3annex3.htm.(accessed May 5, 2011).

———. Joint United Nations Programme on HIV/AIDS (UNAIDS) and Economic Commission for Africa. *AIDS in Africa: Country by Country.* Geneva: Joint United Nations Programme on HIV/AIDS, 2000. http://data.unaids.org/publications/IRC-pub05/aidsafrica2000_en.pdf (accessed July 3, 2011).

———. Joint United Nations Programme on HIV/AIDS and the World Health Organization. *AIDS Epidemic Update: December 2000.* Geneva: UNAIDS/WHO, 2000, 5. http://www.aegis.com/files/unaids/waddecember2000_epidemic_report.pdf (accessed July 3, 2011).

———. Office of the United Nations High Commissioner for Refugees. "2011 UNHCR Country Operations Profile—Democratic Republic of the Congo." http://www.unhcr.org/cgi-bin/texis/vtx/page?page=49e45c366 (accessed July 12, 2011).

———. Permanent Observers Web page. http://www.un.org/en/members/intergovorg.shtml (accessed May 5, 2011).

———. Statistics Division. "Indicators on Income and Economic Activity." Updated December 2010. http://unstats.un.org/unsd/demographic/products/socind/inc-eco.htm#tech (accessed July 11, 2011).

———. United Nations Mission in the Sudan. Background. http://www.un.org/en/peacekeeping/missions/unmis/background.shtml (accessed July 1, 2011).

———. United Nations Mission in the Sudan. The Comprehensive Peace Agreement between the Government of the Republic of Sudan and the Sudan People's Liberation Movement/Sudan People's Liberation Army. http://unmis.unmissions.org/Portals/UNMIS/Documents/General/cpa-en.pdf (accessed July 3, 2011).

———. United Nations Resolution 1590 (2005). http://www.un.org/ga/search/view_doc.asp?symbol=S/RES/1590 (accessed July 3, 2011).

United Nations Security Council. Resolution 1851 (2008), December 16, 2008. http://daccess-dds-ny.un.org/doc/UNDOC/GEN/N08/655/01/PDF/N0865501.pdf (accessed July 12, 2011).

United Nations Security Council. Resolution 1973 (2011), March 17, 2011. http://daccess-dds-ny.un.org/doc/UNDOC/GEN/N11/268/39/PDF/N1126839.pdf (accessed July 12, 2011).

United States Africa Command Office of Public Affairs. *United States Africa Command: The First Three Years. . . .* Stuttgart: U.S. Africa Command Office of Public Affairs, 2011. http://www.africom.mil/research/USAfricaCommand-TheFirstThreeYears-March2011.pdf (accessed July 3, 2011).

U.S. Department of Commerce. "African Growth and Opportunity Act General Country Eligibility Provisions." Export.gov. http://www.agoa.gov/eligibility/country_eligibility.html (accessed July 3, 2011).

———. International Trade Administration, Current Retaliatory Actions, Mexico Trucking Retaliation page. http://www.trade.gov/mas/ian/tradedisputes-enforcement/retaliations/tg_ian_002094.asp (accessed May 5, 2011).

U.S. Department of Interior. http://www.doi.gov/index.cfm (accessed May 5, 2011).

U.S. Department of State. Bureau of African Affairs. "Background Note: Democratic Republic of the Congo," April 13, 2011. http://www.state.gov/r/pa/ei/bgn/2823.htm (accessed July 3, 2011).

———. Bureau of African Affairs. "The Recent Elections in Nigeria: Special Briefing by Johnnie Carson, Assistant Secretary, Bureau of African Affairs," April 28, 2011. http://www.state.gov/p/af/rls/spbr/2011/161931.htm (accessed July 12, 2011).

———. Bureau of African Affairs. Testimony by Johnnie Carson, Assistant Secretary of State for African Affairs before the Senate Foreign Relations Committee Subcommittee on African Affairs, April 14, 2011, on the FY2012 Budget Request for U.S. Policies on Africa. http://www.state.gov/p/af/rls/rm/2011/161202.htm (accessed July 9, 2011).

———. Bureau of Democracy, Human Rights, and Labor. "2010 Human Rights Report: Kenya." http://www.state.gov/documents/organization/160127.pdf (accessed July 12, 2011).

———. Bureau of Democracy, Human Rights, and Labor. "2010 Human Rights Report: Somalia," April 8, 2011. http://www.state.gov/documents/organization/160144.pdf (accessed July 12, 2011).

———. Bureau of Public Affairs. "Press Statement by Philip J. Crowley, Assistant Secretary, Bureau of Public Affairs, January 25, 2011." http://www.state.gov/r/pa/prs/ps/2011/01/155307.htm (accessed July 12, 2011).

———. Chiefs of Mission List. http://www.state.gov/m/dghr/cm (accessed May 5, 2011).

———. "International Response: Contact Group on Piracy off the Coast of Somalia." http://www.state.gov/t/pm/ppa/piracy/contactgroup/index.htm (accessed July 12, 2011).

———. Office of the Coordinator for Reconstruction and Stabilization. *2010 Year in Review: Conflict Prevention and Stabilization Operations.* http://www.state.gov/documents/organization/156036.pdf (accessed July 3, 2011).

———. Quadrennial Diplomacy and Development Review. http://www.state.gov/s/dmr/qddr (accessed May 5, 2011).

U.S. House of Representatives. Trade and Development Act of 2000, H.R. 434, 106th Congress, 2000. http://www.agoa.gov/agoa_legislation/agoatext.pdf (accessed July 3, 2011).

U.S. President's Emergency Plan for AIDS Relief. "Saving Lives through Smart Investments: Latest PEPFAR Results." http://www.pepfar.gov/documents/organization/153723.pdf (accessed July 5, 2011).

U.S. Trade Representative. "Fact Sheet on AGOA," September 2010. http://www.ustr.gov/sites/default/files/AGOA%20Fact%20Sheet%202010.pdf (accessed July 10, 2011).

U.S. White House. Office of the Press Secretary. "Remarks by the President at the U.S./China Strategic and Economic Dialogue," July 27, 2009. http://www.whitehouse.gov/the-press-office/remarks-president-uschina-strategic-andeconomic-dialogue.

———. Office of the Press Secretary. "Remarks by the President in Address to the Nation on Libya," March 28, 2011.

———. Office of the Press Secretary. "Statement by President Obama on the International Criminal Court Announcement, December 15, 2010." http://www.whitehouse.gov/the-press-office/2010/12/15/statement-president-obama-international-criminal-court-announcement (accessed July 12, 2011).

U.S.-India Strategic Dialogue Joint Statement, June 3, 2010. http://www.state.gov/r/pa/prs/ps/2010/06/142645.htm.

Vandiver, John. "AFRICOM Leaders to Mull Headquarters Location." In *Stars and Stripes* (January 6, 2011). http://www.stripes.com/news/africom-leaders-to-mull-headquarters-location-1.130831 (accessed July 12, 2011).

Weiner, Tim. *Legacy of Ashes: The History of the CIA.* New York: Anchor, 2008.

William J. Clinton Foundation. "Building a Better World: William J. Clinton Foundation Annual Report 2010 Financials." http://www.clintonfoundation.org/buildingabetterworld/financials_2010.php (accessed July 3, 2011).

William J. Clinton Foundation. "Building a Better World: William J. Clinton Foundation Annual Report 2010 Clinton Health Access Initiative." http://www.clintonfoundation.org/buildingabetterworld/projects.php?initiative=CHAI (accessed July 11, 2011).

Woodward, Bob. *Bush at War.* New York: Simon & Schuster, 2002.

———. *Obama's Wars.* New York: Simon & Schuster, 2010.

World Economic Forum. http://www.weforum.org (accessed May 5, 2011).

World Health Organization. *WHO Framework Convention on Tobacco Control.* Geneva: World Health Organization, 2003; updated reprint 2005.

Wright, Lawrence. *The Looming Tower: Al Qaeda and the Road to 9/11.* New York: Vintage Books, 2007.

Yearbook of International Organizations. 43rd ed. Vol. 5. Munich: K. G. Saur, 2006–2007.

Zakaria, Fareed. *The Post-American World.* New York: W. W. Norton, 2008.

Zoellick, Robert. "Whither China? From Membership to Responsibility?" National Committee for U.S.-China Relations, September 21, 2005. http://usinfo.state.gove/eap/Archive/2005/Sep/22-29048.html.

PRESIDENTS, SECRETARIES OF STATE, SECRETARIES OF WAR OR DEFENSE, AND NATIONAL SECURITY ADVISERS AND THEIR TERMS OF SERVICE

President	Term of Office	Secretary of State	Term of Office	Secretary of War/Defense	Term of Office	National Security Adviser	Term of Office
1. George Washington	1789–1797	Thomas Jefferson	1790–1793	Henry Knox	1789–1794		
		Edmund Jennings Randolph	1794–1795	Timothy Pickering	1795		
		Timothy Pickering	1795–1797	James McHenry	1796–1797		
2. John Adams	1797–1801	Timothy Pickering	1797–1800	James McHenry	1797–1800		
		John Marshall	1800–1801	Samuel Dexter	1800–1801		
3. Thomas Jefferson	1801–1809	James Madison	1801–1809	Henry Dearborn	1801–1809		
4. James Madison	1809–1817	Robert Smith	1809–1811	William Eustis	1809–1813		
		James Monroe	1811–1817	John Armstrong	1813–1814		
				James Monroe	1814–1815		
				William H. Crawford	1815–1816		
5. James Monroe	1817–1825	John Quincy Adams	1817–1825	John C. Calhoun	1817–1825		
6. John Quincy Adams	1825–1829	Henry Clay	1825–1829	James Barbour	1825–1828		
				Peter Buell Porter	1828–1829		
7. Andrew Jackson	1829–1837	Martin Van Buren	1829–1831	John Henry Eaton	1829–1831		
		Edward Livingston	1831–1833	Lewis Cass	1831–1836		
		Louis McLane	1833–1834				
		John Forsyth	1834–1837				
8. Martin Van Buren	1837–1841	John Forsyth	1837–1841	Joel Roberts Poinsett	1837–1841		
9. William Henry Harrison	1841	Daniel Webster	1841	John Bell	1841		
10. John Tyler	1841–1845	Daniel Webster	1841–1843	John Bell	1841		
		Abel Parker Upshur	1843–1844	John C. Spencer	1841–1843		
		John Caldwell Calhoun	1844–1845	James Madison Porter	1843–1844		
				William Wilkins	1844–1845		
11. James K. Polk	1845–1849	James Buchanan	1845–1849	William L. Marcy	1845–1849		
12. Zachary Taylor	1849–1850	John Middleton Clayton	1849–1850	George Walker Crawford	1849–1850		
13. Millard Fillmore	1850–1853	Daniel Webster	1850–1852	Charles Magill Conrad	1850–1853		
		Edward Everett	1852–1853				
14. Franklin Pierce	1853–1857	William L. Marcy	1853–1857	Jefferson Davis	1853–1857		

	President	Term of Office	Secretary of State	Term of Office	Secretary of War/Defense	Term of Office	National Security Adviser	Term of Office
15.	James Buchanan	1857–1861	Lewis Cass	1857–1860	John Buchanan Floyd	1857–1860		
			Jeremiah Sullivan Black	1860–1861	Joseph Holt	1861		
16.	Abraham Lincoln	1861–1865	William Henry Seward	1861–1865	Simon Cameron	1861–1862		
					Edwin M. Stanton	1862–1865		
17.	Andrew Johnson	1865–1869	William Henry Seward	1865–1869	Edwin M. Stanton	1865–1868		
					John McAlister Schofield	1868–1869		
18.	Ulysses S. Grant	1869–1877	Elihu Benjamin Washburne	1869–1869	John Aaron Rawlins	1869		
			Hamilton Fish	1869–1877	William T. Sherman	1869		
					William W. Belknap	1869–1876		
					Alphonso Taft	1876		
					J. Donald Cameron	1876–1877		
19.	Rutherford B. Hayes	1877–1881	William Maxwell Evarts	1877–1881	George Washington McCrary	1877–1879		
					Alexander Ramsey	1879–1881		
20.	James A. Garfield	1881	James Gillespie Blaine	1881	Robert Todd Lincoln	1881		
21.	Chester A. Arthur	1881–1885	Frederick Frelinghuysen	1881–1885	Robert Todd Lincoln	1881–1885		
22.	Grover Cleveland	1885–1889	Thomas Francis Bayard	1885–1889	William C. Endicott	1885–1889		
23.	Benjamin Harrison	1889–1893	James Gillespie Blaine	1889–1892	Redfield Proctor	1889–1891		
			John Watson Foster	1892–1893	Stephen B. Elkins	1891–1893		
24.	Grover Cleveland	1893–1897	Walter Quintin Gresham	1893–1895	Daniel Scott Lamont	1893–1897		
			Richard Olney	1895–1897				
25.	William McKinley	1897–1901	John Sherman	1897–1898	Russell A. Alger	1897–1899		
			William Rufus Day	1898	Elihu Root	1899–1901		
			John Milton Hay	1898–1901				
26.	Theodore Roosevelt	1901–1909	John Milton Hay	1901–1905	Elihu Root	1901–1904		
			Elihu Root	1905–1909	William H. Taft	1904–1908		
					Luke Edward Wright	1908–1909		

(Continued)

(Continued)

	President	Term of Office	Secretary of State	Term of Office	Secretary of War/Defense	Term of Office	National Security Adviser	Term of Office
27.	William H. Taft	1909–1913	Philander Chase Knox	1909–1913	Jacob M. Dickinson	1909–1911		
					Henry L. Stimson	1911–1913		
28.	Woodrow Wilson	1913–1921	William Jennings Bryan	1913–1915	Lindley M. Garrison	1913–1916		
			Robert Lansing	1915–1920	Newton D. Baker	1916–1921		
			Bainbridge Colby	1920–1921				
29.	Warren G. Harding	1921–1923	Charles Evans Hughes	1921–1923	John W. Weeks	1921–1923		
30.	Calvin Coolidge	1923–1929	Charles Evans Hughes	1923–1925	John W. Weeks	1923–1925		
			Frank Billings Kellogg	1925–1929	Dwight F. Davis	1925–1929		
31.	Herbert C. Hoover	1929–1933	Henry Lewis Stimson	1929–1933	James W. Good	1929		
					Patrick J. Hurley	1929–1933		
32.	Franklin D. Roosevelt	1933–1945	Cordell Hull	1933–1944	George H. Dern	1933–1936		
			Edward Reilly Stettinius	1944–1945	Harry H. Woodring	1936–1940		
					Henry L. Stimson	1940–1945		
33.	Harry S. Truman	1945–1953	James Francis Byrnes	1945–1947	Henry L. Stimson	1945		
			George Marshall	1947–1949	Robert P. Patterson	1945–1947		
			Dean Acheson	1949–1953	Kenneth C. Royall	1947		
					James V. Forrestal[1]	1947–1949		
					Louis A. Johnson	1949–1950		
					George C. Marshall	1950–1951		
					Robert A. Lovett	1951–1953		
34.	Dwight D. Eisenhower	1953–1961	John Foster Dulles	1953–1959	Charles E. Wilson	1953–1957	Robert Cutler	1953–1955
			Christian Archibald Herter	1959–1961	Neil H. McElroy	1957–1959	Dillon Anderson	1955–1956
					Thomas S. Gates	1959–1961	William H. Jackson	1956–1957
							Robert Cutler	1957–1958
							Gordon Gray	1958–1961
35.	John F. Kennedy	1961–1963	David Dean Rusk	1961–1963	Robert S. McNamara	1961–1963	McGeorge Bundy	1961–1963

President	Term of Office	Secretary of State	Term of Office	Secretary of War/Defense	Term of Office	National Security Adviser	Term of Office
36. Lyndon B. Johnson	1963–1969	David Dean Rusk	1963–1969	Robert S. McNamara	1963–1968	McGeorge Bundy	1963–1966
				Clark M. Clifford	1968–1969		
37. Richard M. Nixon	1969–1974	William Pierce Rogers	1969–1973	Melvin R. Laird	1969–1973	Henry Kissinger	1969–1974
		Henry A. Kissinger	1973–1974	Elliot L. Richardson	1973		
				James R. Schlesinger	1973–1974		
38. Gerald R. Ford	1974–1977	Henry A. Kissinger	1974–1977	James R. Schlesinger	1974–1975	Henry Kissinger	1974–1975
				Donald H. Rumsfeld	1975–1977	Lt. Gen. Brent Scowcroft	1975–1977
39. Jimmy (James Earl) Carter	1977–1981	Cyrus Roberts Vance	1977–1980	Harold Brown	1977–1981	Zbigniew Brzezinski	1977–1981
		Edmund Muskie	1980–1981				
40. Ronald W. Reagan	1981–1989	Alexander Haig	1981–1982	Caspar W. Weinberger	1981–1987	Richard V. Allen	1981–1982
		George Shultz	1982–1989	Frank C. Carlucci	1987–1989	Lt. Col. Robert C. McFarlane	1983–1985
						VADM John M. Poindexter	1985–1986
						Frank C. Carlucci	1986–1987
						Gen. Colin L. Powell	1987–1989
41. George H.W. Bush	1989–1993	James Baker	1989–1992	Richard B. Cheney	1989–1993	Lt. Gen. Brent Scowcroft	1989–1993
		Lawrence Eagleburger	1992–1992				
42. Bill (William) Clinton	1993–2001	Warren Christopher	1993–1997	Les Aspin	1993–1994	W. Anthony Lake	1993–1997
		Madeleine Albright	1997–2001	William J. Perry	1994–1997	Samuel R. Berger	1997–2001
				William S. Cohen	1997–2001		
43. George W. Bush	2001–2009	Colin Powell	2001–2005	Donald H. Rumsfeld	2001–2006	Condoleezza Rice	2001–2005
		Condoleezza Rice	2005–2009	Robert M. Gates	2006–2009	Stephen Hadley	2005–2009
44. Barack Obama	2009–	Hillary Rodham Clinton	2009–	Robert M. Gates	2009–	Gen. James L. Jones	2009–2010
				Leon Edward Panetta	2011–	Tom Donilon	2010–

[1]Forrestal was the first U.S. Secretary of Defense.

★ INDEX

Figures, tables, boxes, illustrations/images, maps, and notes are indicated by *f, t, b, i, m,* and *n,* respectively, following the page number.

A

Abbas, Mahmoud, 572–573
Able Archer war games (1983), 427
Abolitionists, 22
Abu Ghraib prison, 529, 598
Abu Nidal group, 403
Acheson, Dean
    Bretton Woods and, 233–234
    on Greece, 241, 253*b*
    Hiss case and, 258
    Korean War and, 281–282, 285, 288
    Marshall and, 236*b*
    nuclear weapons and, 296
    on Washington Conference, 163*b*
Acheson-Lilienthal Report, 296
Act of Bogotá (1960), 331
Adams, Charles Francis, 37, 40*b,* 41, 44, 95
Adams, John, 4–6, 4*b,* 9–11, 70, 71*i,* 72
Adams, John Quincy
    Canadian border and, 27
    contraband and, 4*b*
    expansion and, 23, 25*b*
    Monroe Doctrine and, 74–76
    Obama and, 601
    public portrait of, 16*b*
    as Secretary of State, 14–16
    slavery and, 76
    trade and, 33
    War of 1812 and, 13, 640
Adams-Onís Treaty (Transcontinental Treaty) (1819),
    14–15, 24, 32*t,* 74, 74*b,* 607
Addams, Jane, 123, 152
Afghan War, 599*m*
    al Qaeda in, 512
    Arab-Israeli conflict, impact on, 577–578
    Bush and, 523*b,* 595–596, 598, 599–600
    Gates on, 499*b*
    Holbrooke and, 531*b*
    NATO and, 494*b,* 495, 497, 499
    Obama and, 499, 576, 577, 602–603
    reconstruction, failure of, 598
    Soviet invasion and occupation of, 401, 429, 448–449, 564
    surge strategy, 602
    Taliban in, 522

    U.S. aid to, 524, 566
    Vietnam Syndrome and, 351
    War on Terrorism and, 522, 574
    See also Taliban
Afghanistan
    coup against Daoud, 319, 381
    instability of, 587
    Soviet invasion and occupation of, 381–382, 401, 429,
        448–449, 564
    Soviet withdrawal from, 432
    under Taliban rule, 635–636
    U.S. aid to, 432
AFL-CIO, 419*b*
Africa
    borders, reshaping of, 586
    Central Africa as region, 557
    Cold War and, 547
    East Africa as region, 559
    economic growth, 552–554
    future of U.S. policy on, 560
    GDP per capita, by country, 553*t*
    health security, 547, 550–551*b,* 551–552
    Horn of Africa as region, 559
    military support and peacekeeper training, 549–550
    newly independent states, U.S. policy on, 547–549
    North Africa as region, 554–557
    oil exporters, 554*t*
    security concept and, 547, 548*b*
    Southern Africa as region, 559–560
    West Africa as region, 558–559
    See also Non-Aligned Movement (NAM); *specific countries*
Africa Growth and Opportunity Act (2000), 548
African Americans, 90–91, 131, 144*b,* 153*b. See also* Race and
    racism; Slavery
African Crisis Response Initiative (ACRI), 550
African Growth and Opportunity Act (AGOA) (2000),
    552–553, 558–559
African Union (AU), 607
AFRICOM (United States Africa Command), 550
Afro-Asian (Bandung) Conference (1955), 271, 311–312, 312*b,*
    316, 359–360
Agenda 21, 480
Agricultural Adjustment Act (1933), 177
Agricultural Marketing Act (1929), 173